NINTH EDITION

LANGUAGE AWARENESS

Readings for College Writers

Writing to Discover

Each selection begins with a journal prompt designed to get students writing — before they start reading — about their own experiences with the language issues discussed in the selection. Students are then more likely to approach the selection with a critical eye. From time to time, class activities or writing assignments ask students to return to these journal writings and to reflect on them before proceeding with more formal writing tasks.

Informative Headnotes

Headnotes preceding each selection discuss the content of the essay and emphasize the key language principles involved. Pertinent information about the author and where and when the selection was first published is also included.

End-of-Selection Questions

The format for the questions at the end of each selection emphasizes content and writing issues. This format includes two types of questions:

- FOCUSING ON CONTENT.   These questions help students to understand the content of the selection (and thus to understand an aspect of language) and to connect the information and ideas in the selection to their own experiences.
- FOCUSING ON WRITING.   The questions in this section take a number of directions. They may, for example, take a language principle presented in the selection, ask students to explore it, directing students to comment on writing applications they can envision for that principle. Other Focusing on Writing questions may highlight such techniques as the use of strong verbs, the active voice, tone, punctuation, or sentence structure and ask students to discuss them.

Language-in-Action Activities

To bring the outside world into *Language Awareness* and to give students a chance to analyze real world examples of the language issues discussed by the essayists, exciting Language in Action activities accompany most selections in the text. These activities — designed to be completed in about twenty minutes — ask students to take a hands-on approach to what they are learning from the essays and to demonstrate their growing language aptitude. The activities include poems, cartoons, movie reviews, parodies, advertisements, photographs, essay excerpts, letters to the editor, syndicated columns, and more. We believe they will challenge students to apply what they have learned to the world around them.

PREFACE

Since the first edition of *Language Awareness* appeared in 1974, its purpose has been twofold: to foster an appreciation of the richness, flexibility, and vitality of the English language and to help students to use their language more responsibly and effectively in speech and particularly in writing. Because of these purposes, *Language Awareness* has been used successfully in a variety of courses over the years. Its primary use, however, has been and continues to be in college composition courses. Clearly, many instructors believe as we do — that the study of language and the study of writing go hand in hand.

Because the study of language is so multifaceted, we cover a broad spectrum of topics, including the history of English, the relationship between language and culture, the language of new technologies, and the power of language in influencing advertising, politics, the media, and gender roles. Opening students' eyes to the power of language — its ability to shape and manipulate perceptions and cultural attitudes — is, we believe, one of the worthiest goals a writing class can pursue.

RETAINED FROM THE EIGHTH EDITION

Tested Areas of Language Study

Although new essays have been added to each chapter, eight areas of language study are carryovers from the eighth edition. Instructors have told us that the chapters on "Coming to an Awareness of Language," "Writers on Writing," "Politics, Propaganda, and Doublespeak," "Prejudice, Discrimination, and Stereotypes," "The Power of the Media," "I Can Sell You Anything," "Cultural Diversity," and "Names and Identity," are indispensable in the courses they teach. Not only are these topics legitimate areas of language study, but they also teach students useful ways to look at and write about the world around them. Each of these chapters has been updated to reflect recent trends, but they still retain the spirit and purpose of their predecessors.

For Bedford/St. Martin's

DEVELOPMENTAL EDITOR: Amanda Bristow
PRODUCTION EDITOR: Kendra LeFleur
PRODUCTION SUPERVISOR: Chris Gross
SENIOR MARKETING MANAGER: Rachel Falk
EDITORIAL ASSISTANTS: Caryn O'Connell, Stefanie Wortman
PRODUCTION ASSISTANT: Kristen Merrill
COPYEDITOR: Jeannine Thibodeau
TEXT DESIGN: Anna Palchik
COVER DESIGN: Donna Lee Dennison
COVER ART: *Fanelli Cafe.* Painting by Gus Heinze, 2000. Courtesy of the Bernaducci Meise Gallery.
COMPOSITION: Macmillan India
PRINTING AND BINDING: Haddon Craftsman, Inc., an R. R. Donnelley & Sons Company

PRESIDENT: Joan E. Feinberg
EDITORIAL DIRECTOR: Denise B. Wydra
EDITOR IN CHIEF: Karen S. Henry
DIRECTOR OF MARKETING: Karen Melton Soeltz
DIRECTOR OF EDITING, DESIGN, AND PRODUCTION: Marcia Cohen
MANAGING EDITOR: Elizabeth M. Schaaf

Library of Congress Control Number: 2004102161

Manufactured in the United States of America.

9 8 7 6 5 4
f e d c b a

For information, write:
Bedford/St. Martin's, 75 Arlington Street, Boston, MA 02116
(617-399-4000)

ISBN: 0–312–40702–5
EAN: 978–0–312–40702–5

Acknowledgments

Marjorie Agosín, "Always Living in Spanish." From *Poets & Writers Magazine*, Volume 27, Issue 2, March/April 1999. Copyright © 1999 by Marjorie Agosín. Reprinted by permission of the author.

NINTH EDITION

LANGUAGE AWARENESS

Readings for College Writers

Paul Eschholz

Alfred Rosa

Virginia Clark

UNIVERSITY OF VERMONT

BEDFORD / ST. MARTIN'S   Boston • New York

End-of-Selection Writing Assignments

To give students more opportunities to practice thinking and writing, we provide several Writing Suggestions at the end of every selection, each of which is designed to elicit a three- to five-page paper. Some assignments ask students to use their journal entries as springboards for an extended essay; for others, students use their analytical skills to play one article against another; and occasionally an assignment asks students to do — and write about — some library or community-based research. Students may, for example, examine the language used in local public documents, the language used in law offices, or campus slang.

Glossary of Rhetorical and Linguistic Terms

The Glossary of Rhetorical and Linguistic Terms includes definitions of key language terms and concepts as well as the standard terminology of rhetoric. Having all of these definitions in the book makes it easy for students to look up unfamiliar terms as they read.

Rhetorical Contents

At the end of the text, an alternate table of contents classifies the selections in *Language Awareness* according to the rhetorical strategies they exemplify, making it easier for instructors to assign readings that parallel the types of writing their students are doing.

NEW TO THIS EDITION

As in previous editions, we have emphasized selections that are written in nontechnical language on topics of current interest. Our questions and introductory material help students to understand those topics, providing clearly defined opportunities for thoughtful writing. Guided by comments and advice from hundreds of colleagues and students across the country who have used the previous editions, we have made some dramatic improvements in this ninth edition.

New Selections

Almost two-thirds of the seventy-nine selections in *Language Awareness* are new to this edition. However, we have retained many of the accessible, informative, well-written, class-tested, and very often entertaining essays from earlier editions, such as Helen Keller's "The Day Language Came into My Life," William Lutz's "The World of Doublespeak," Gloria

Naylor's "The Meanings of a Word," and George Orwell's "Politics and the English Language."

The fifty new selections, chosen for their insight and clear, thought-provoking writing, also reflect the language issues of an increasingly multicultural America. Representing a wide variety of ethnic voices, the readings also address the language concerns of other minority groups, with readings on gay rights and deaf culture. Selections include Audre Lorde's "The Transformation of Silence into Language and Action," as she urges all women to use language as a catalyst for change; Marjorie Agosín's "Always Living in Spanish," as she writes about the transition from writing in Spanish to writing in English; Riki Wilchins's "Because That's What We Do to Faggots," as she analyzes the use of hate-language toward the gay community; and Harlan Lane's "Representations of Deaf People," as he argues the case for public recognition of deaf communication as a language and culture of its own. We believe that the new selections will spark student interest and bring currency to the otherwise class-proven essays retained from earlier editions.

New Introduction "From Reading to Writing"

To supplement the study of language with instruction in writing itself, we have added a new general introduction, "From Reading to Writing." Based on years of classroom experience, this new material provides students with the essentials of college reading and writing. The first part, "On Reading Well," provides students with guidelines for critical reading, demonstrates how they can get the most out of their reading by taking advantage of the apparatus accompanying each selection, and shows how they can generate their own writing from the reading they do. The second part, "On Writing Well," details each step in the writing process and illustrates these with a student essay in progress.

New Thematic Chapters

Students and teachers, pleased with the relevancy of the thematic chapters in past editions of *Language Awareness*, asked us to add more material on both political language and the language of advertising. These themes, treated in the same chapter in our last edition, now have chapters of their own, "Politics, Propaganda, and Doublespeak" and "I Can Sell You Anything," respectively. Since reviewers also requested new material on language and gender issues, as well as additional coverage of technology, we added a new chapter entitled "Men and Women Talking" — with essays that examine the important language differences in the ways men and women discuss language and sexual discrimination — as well as a brand-new chapter entitled "America Wired."

New Case Studies

We have added additional Case Studies on language issues of current interest that appear in six of our ten thematic chapters. The topic of each Case Study addresses issues that lie within the scope of each chapter's central theme, including "The English-Only Debate," "Political Correctness and Speech Codes," "The Language of Sexual Discrimination," "Violence and the Media," "Marketing Diet and Health," and "Understanding Affirmative Action." Providing three to five viewpoints each, the multiple perspectives help students develop and refine their own opinions. The case studies begin with an introduction that will help students make sense of the multiple perspectives. "Examining the Issue Critically" questions at the end of each selection test students on the basic content of each reading. At the end of each Case Study, "Making Connections" questions extend the analyses by asking students to focus on the similarities and differences among the various perspectives of the writers.

New Images

Responding to students' increasingly visual world, we have added ten "Picturing Language" activities that encourage students to become better readers of visual texts. Paired with one of the essay selections in each chapter, these images — which include photographs, cartoons, advertisements, and graphics — are accompanied by questions that ask students to reflect upon how text, image, and words come together to elucidate ideas about the language of visual communication.

New Chapter Introductions

In order to help students connect language study to reading and writing, new one-page chapter introductions show how the readings connect to each language issue, and how the Case Studies serve as real-life examples of those issues.

New "Writing a Research Paper" Appendix

This helpful appendix presents a thorough discussion of the research process. We offer guidance on choosing a research topic, posing a worthwhile research question, conducting research using print and online sources, developing a working bibliography, using subject directories and keyword searches on the Internet, taking notes, integrating borrowed material, and documenting sources using MLA in-text citation style. In addition, we provide a thorough discussion of plagiarism with specific steps students can take to avoid plagiarism in their papers. Finally, this chapter includes an annotated sample MLA-style student research paper.

Instructor's Manual

Packed with teaching tips and suggested answers to end-of-selection questions, the new Instructor's Manual reflects all the features in the apparatus that accompanies each selection within the core chapters and case studies. It also offers advice on how to approach each of the Language in Action activities.

ACKNOWLEDGMENTS

We are grateful to the following respondents to a user survey, whose comments helped us shape this edition: Thomas Allbaugh, Azusa Pacific University; Tiger Byrd, University of Nevada; Mary Ann Cama, Youngstown State University; Ralph S. Carlson, Azusa Pacific University; Carol Conder, University of Nevada; Helen O'Hara Connell, Barry University; Judith Crowe, Millikin University; Jan DeNoble, University of Minnesota; David D. Esselstrom, Azusa Pacific University; Heather Fenstermaker, Youngstown State University; Jim Flick, Youngstown State University; William E. Gilbert, California State University at Long Beach; Dori-Ann Granger, Youngstown State University; Kathryn M. Hamilton, Columbus State University; Andrea Ivanov-Craig, Azusa Pacific University; Lambert Kern, University of Nevada; Ken Kuhlken, Azusa Pacific University; Pam Kuhlken, Azusa Pacific University; Trish Milhan, Azusa Pacific University; Susan Jane Mitchell, University of Nevada; Julie Nichols, Okaloosa-Walton Community College; Marilyn Schultz, California State University at Fullerton; Anne H. Southard, Okaloosa-Walton Community College; Vicki Stieha, Northern Kentucky University; Lisa Stiller, University of Las Vegas; Michael T. Warren, Maple Woods Community College; Cornelia Wells, William Paterson University; Lynn Zvara, Youngstown State University.

We would like to express our appreciation to the staff at Bedford/St. Martin's, especially Amanda Bristow for supporting us in our efforts to design innovative and engaging case studies that provide strong links between language study and real world issues. Her assistant, Caryn O'Connell, handled a number of important tasks and facilitated manuscript flow. Thanks go to Kendra LeFleur, our production editor; to Jeannine Thibodeau, our superlative copyeditor; Sandy Schechter and Sue Brekka for clearing permissions, and Elizabeth Bristow for art research. Thanks also go to Valerie Duff and Alex Carey for writing the Instructor's Manual that accompanies this edition. Finally, we are grateful to all our students at the University of Vermont for their enthusiasm for language study and writing and their invaluable responses to the new materials included in this book. They teach us something new every day.

PAUL ESCHHOLZ
ALFRED ROSA
VIRGINIA CLARK

CONTENTS

NINTH EDITION

LANGUAGE AWARENESS

Readings for College Writers

From Reading
to Writing

ON READING WELL

The readings in *Language Awareness* emphasize the crucial role language plays in virtually every aspect of our lives and reveal the essential elements of the writer's craft. As you read and study the selections in this text, you will become more aware of your own language usage and how it affects others. In addition, you will become more sensitive to how the language of others affects you. You will also become more familiar with different types of writing and learn how good writers — depending upon their purpose in writing — make important decisions about strategies and techniques. All of the insights that you gain will help you become a better reader and, equally important, a better writer.

Reading Actively

Reading well means reading actively, in a thoughtful spirit and with an alert, inquiring mind. Reading actively also means learning how to analyze what you read. You must be able to discover what is happening in an essay, to figure out the writer's reasons for shaping the essay in a particular way, to decide whether the result works well or poorly — and the reasons why. At first such digging may seem odd, and for good reason. After all, we all know how to read. But do we know how to read actively?

Active reading is a skill that takes time to acquire. By becoming more familiar with different types of writing as you read, you will sharpen your critical thinking skills and learn how good writers make decisions in their writing. After reading an essay, most people feel more confident talking about the content of the piece than about the writer's style. Content is more tangible than style, which always seems elusive. In large part, this discrepancy results from our schooling. Most of us have been taught to read for ideas. Not many of us, however, have been trained to read actively, to engage a writer and his or her writing, to ask why we like one piece of writing and not another. Likewise, most of us do not ask ourselves why one piece is more believable or convincing than another.

When you learn to read actively, you begin to answer these important questions and come to appreciate the craftsmanship involved in writing.

Active reading, then, is a skill you need if you are truly to engage and understand the content of a piece of writing as well as the craft that shapes the writer's ideas into a presentable form. Active reading will repay your efforts by helping you read more effectively and write more persuasively.

Getting the Most Out of Your Reading

Active reading requires, first of all, that you commit time and effort. Second, try to take a positive interest in what you are reading, even if the subject matter does not immediately appeal to you. Remember, you are not reading for content alone but also to understand a writer's methods — to see firsthand the kinds of choices writers make while they write.

To help you get the most out of your reading, here are some guidelines for (1) preparing yourself to read a selection, (2) reading the selection the first time, (3) rereading the selection, (4) annotating the text with marginal notes, and (5) analyzing the text with questions.

1. Prereading: Preparing Yourself

Instead of diving into any given selection in *Language Awareness* or any other book, there are a few things that you can do that will prepare you to get the most out of what you will read. It's helpful, for example, to get a context for what you'll read. What's the essay about? What do you know about the writer's background and reputation? Where was the essay first published? Who was the intended audience for the essay? And, finally, how much do you already know about the subject of the reading selection? We encourage you to consider carefully the materials that precede each selection in this book. Each selection in this book begins with a title, headnote, and journal prompt. From the **title** you often discover the writer's position on an issue or attitude toward the topic. On occasion, the title can give clues about the intended audience and the writer's purpose in writing the piece. The **headnote** contains a biographical note about the author followed by publication information and rhetorical highlights about the selection. In addition to information on the person's life and work, you'll read about his or her reputation and authority to write on the subject of the piece. The **publication information** indicates when the essay was published and in what book or magazine it first appeared. This information, in turn, gives you insight about the intended audience. The **rhetorical highlights** direct your attention to one or more aspects of how the selection was written. Finally, the **journal prompt** encourages you to collect your thoughts and opinions about the topic or related issues before you commence reading. The journal prompt makes it easy to keep a record of your own knowledge or thinking on a topic before you see what the writer has to offer.

To demonstrate how these context-building materials can work for you, carefully review the following materials that accompany Henry Louis Gates Jr.'s essay "What's in a Name?" The essay itself appears later in this introduction.

What's in a Name?

Title

HENRY LOUIS GATES JR.

The preeminent African American scholar of our time,   Headnote
Henry Louis Gates Jr. is the W. E. B. Du Bois Professor of
Humanities, chair of Afro-American Studies, and director
of the W. E. B. Du Bois Institute of Afro-American Research
at Harvard University. Among his impressive list of publica-
tions are Figures in Black: Words, Signs and the "Racial"
Self *(1987),* The Signifying Monkey: A Theory of Afro-
American Literary Criticism *(1988),* Loose Canons:
Notes on Culture Wars *(1992),* The Future of the Race   Biographi-
(1997), and Thirteen Ways of Looking at a Black Man   cal note
(1999). His most recent book is Mr. Jefferson and Miss
Wheatley *(2003). His* Colored People: A Memoir *(1994)*
recollects in a wonderful prose style his youth growing up in
Piedmont, West Virginia, and his emerging sexual and
racial awareness. Gates graduated from Yale University and
earned his advanced degrees at Clare College at the Univer-
sity of Cambridge. He has been honored with a MacArthur
Foundation Fellowship, inclusion in Time *magazine's "25*
Most Influential Americans" list, a National Humanities
Medal, and election to the American Academy of Arts and
Letters. In "What's in a Name?", excerpted from a longer   Publication
article published in the fall 1989 issue of Dissent *magazine,*   information
Gates tells the story of an early encounter with the language
of prejudice. In learning how one of the "bynames" used by
white people to refer to African Americans robs them of   Rhetorical
their identity, he feels the sting of racism firsthand.   highlights

WRITING TO DISCOVER: *Reflect on racially charged*   Journal
language you have heard. For example, has anyone ever   prompt
used a racial epithet or name to refer to you? When did you
first become aware that such names existed? How do you
feel about being characterized or defined by your race? If
you have ever used such names, what was your intent in
using them? What response did you receive?

From reading these preliminary materials, what expectations do you have for the selection itself? How does this knowledge equip you to engage the selection before you read it? From the *title* you probably inferred that Gates will answer the question he poses and tell you something surprising about a name. His purpose clearly is to answer the question and to make a point about names in the process. The short biographical note reveals that Gates is an African American and that, as a teacher and a writer, he is recognized as a leader and a scholar. He has written a number of books about various aspects of the African American experience in America. The background material reveals that the subject of Gates's 1989 essay is autobiographical and likely to give us some insight into prejudice and racial tensions. This assumption is strengthened when you learn that the essay first appeared in the magazine *Dissent*. The rhetorical highlight advises that Gates is telling a story and will therefore use narration. Finally, the journal prompt asks you to look for and consider racial and/or ethnic language slurs in your everyday life. It's a good practice to reflect for several minutes on what you already know about a particular issue and where you stand on it. After reading Gates's essay, you can compare your own experiences with prejudicial language with those of Gates.

2. Reading: Getting an Overview of the Selection

Always read the selection at least twice, no matter how long it is. The first reading gives you a chance to get acquainted with the essay and to form your first impressions. With the first reading you want to get an overall sense of what the writer is saying, keeping in mind the essay's title and what you know about the writer. The essay will offer you information, ideas, and arguments — some you may have expected; some you may not have. As you read, you may find yourself modifying your sense of the writer's message and purpose. If there are any words that you do not recognize, circle them so that you can look them up in a dictionary. Put a "?" alongside any passages that are not immediately clear. You may, in fact, want to delay most of your annotating until a second reading so that your first reading can be fast and free, enabling you to concentrate on the larger issues.

3. Rereading: Coming to an Understanding of the Selection

Your second reading should be quite different from the first. You will know what the essay is about, where it is going, and how it gets there; now you can relate the parts of the essay more accurately to the whole. Use your second reading to test your first impressions against the words on the page, developing and deepening your sense of how the essay is written, and how well. Because you now have a general understanding of the essay, you can pay special attention to the author's purpose and means of achieving it. You can look for features of organization and style that you can learn from and adapt to your own work.

4. Responding to Your Reading: Making Marginal Notes

When you annotate a text, you should do more than simply under-line or highlight what you think are important points to remember. It is easy to underline so much that the notations become almost meaningless because you forget why you underlined passages in the first place. Instead, as you read, write down your thoughts in the margins or on a separate piece of paper. Mark the selection's main point when you find it stated directly. Look for the pattern or patterns of development the author uses to explore and support that point, and record the information. If you disagree with a statement or conclusion, object in the margin: "No!" If you feel skeptical, indicate that response: "Why?" or "Explain." If you are impressed by an argument or turn of phrase, compliment the writer: "Good point!" Place vertical lines or a star in the margin to indicate important points.

Jot down whatever marginal notes come naturally to you. Most readers combine brief responses written in the margins with underlining, circling, highlighting, stars, or question marks.

How to Annotate a Text

Here are some suggestions of elements you may want to mark to help you keep a record of your responses as you read:

- Memorable statements of important points
- Key terms or concepts
- Central issues or themes
- Examples that support a main point
- Unfamiliar words
- Questions you have about a point or passage
- Your responses to a specific point or passage

Remember that there are no hard-and-fast rules for which elements you annotate. Choose a method of annotation that works best for you and that will make sense to you when you go back to recollect your thoughts and responses to the essay. When annotating a text, don't be timid. Mark up your book as much as you like, or jot down as many responses in your notebook as you think will be helpful. Don't let annotating become burdensome. A word or phrase is usually as good as a sentence. One helpful way to focus your annotations is to ask yourself questions as you read the selection a second time.

5. Asking Yourself Questions as You Read

As you read the essay a second time, probing for a deeper under-standing of and appreciation for what the writer has done, focus your at-tention by asking yourself some basic questions about its content and its form.

Questions to Ask Yourself as You Read

1. What does the writer say about language? What is the writer's main point or thesis?
2. Why does the writer want to make this point? What is the writer's purpose?
3. How is the essay organized and developed? Does the writer use chronological order, go from the most important point to the least important, use spatial order, or follow some other logical pattern of organization? What strategies of development are used? Narration? Illustration? Comparison and Contrast? Definition? Process Analysis? Argument? Others?
4. How does the writer's strategy of development suit his or her subject and purpose?
5. What is the writer's attitude toward the subject of the essay — positive, critical, objective, ironic, hostile?
6. To whom is the essay addressed? To a general audience with little or no background knowledge of the subject? To a spe-cialized group familiar with the topic? To those who are likely to disagree with the argument?
7. Does the writer supply enough information to support the essay's main idea? Are there sufficient examples, descriptions, expert opinions, or other kinds of support?
8. How effective is the essay? Does the writer make his or her points clear?

Each essay in *Language Awareness* is followed by study questions similar to the ones suggested here but more specific to the essay. These questions help you analyze both the content of an essay and the writer's craft. As you read the essay a second time, look for details from the selec-tion that will support your answers to these questions, and then answer the questions as fully as you can.

An Example: Annotating Henry Louis Gates Jr.'s "What's in a Name?"

Notice how one of our students, guided by the eight questions above, recorded her responses to Gates's text with marginal annotations.

The question of color takes up so much space in these pages, but the question of color, especially in this country, operates to hide the graver questions of the self.

— JAMES BALDWIN, *1961*

Two epigraphs set forth the theme of Gates's essay.

. . . blood, darky, Tar Baby, Kaffir, shine . . . moor, blackamoor, Jim Crow, spook . . . quadroon, meriney, red bone, high yellow . . . Manny, porch monkey, home, homeboy, George . . . spearchucker, schwarze, Leroy, Smokey . . . mouli, buck, Ethiopian, brother, sistah. . . .

— TREY ELLIS, *1989*

I had forgotten the incident completely, until I read Trey Ellis's essay, "Remembering My Name" in a recent issue of the *Village Voice* (June 13, 1989). But there, in the middle of an extended italicized list of the bynames of "the race" ("The race" or "our people" being the terms my parents used in polite or reverential discourse, "jigaboo" or "nigger" more commonly used in anger, jest, or pure disgust) it was: "George." Now the events of that very brief exchange return to mind so vividly that I wonder why I had forgotten it.

Article Gates read triggers childhood memory.

My father and I were walking home at dusk from his second job. He "moonlighted" as a janitor in the evenings for the telephone company. Every day but Saturday, he would come home at 3:30 from his regular job at the paper mill, wash up, eat supper, then at 4:30 head downtown to his second job. He used to make jokes frequently about a union official who moonlighted. I never got the joke, but he and his friends thought it was hilarious. All I knew was that my family always ate well, that my brother and I had new clothes to wear, and that all of the white people in Piedmont, West Virginia, treated my parents with an odd mixture of resentment and respect that even we understood at the time had something directly to do with a small but certain measure of financial security.

Gates establishes context for his story — who, what, where, when, and why.

He had left a little early that evening because I was with him and I had to be in bed early. I could not have been more than five or six, and we had stopped off at the Cut-Rate Drug Store (where no black person in town but my father could sit down to eat, and eat off real plates with real silverware) so that I could buy some caramel ice cream, two scoops in a wafer cone, please, which I was busy licking when Mr. Wilson walked by.

Mr. Wilson was a very quiet man, whose stony, brooding, silent manner seemed designed to scare off any overtures of friendship, even from white people. He was Irish, as was one-third of our village (another third being Italian), the more affluent among who sent their children to "Catholic School" across the bridge in Maryland. He had white straight hair, like my Uncle Jo, who he uncannily resembled, and he carried a black worn metal lunch pail, the kind that Riley carried on the television show. My father always spoke to him, and for reasons that we never did understand, he always spoke to my father.

> Gates's description of Mr. Wilson provides telling details.

"Hello, Mr. Wilson," I heard my father say.

"Hello, George."

I stopped licking my ice cream cone, and asked my Dad in a loud voice why Mr. Wilson had called him "George."

"Doesn't he know your name, Daddy? Why don't you tell him your name? Your name isn't George."

> Gates use of dialogue captures the language of the encounter and gives it immediacy.

For a moment I tried to think of who Mr. Wilson was mixing Pop up with. But we didn't have any Georges among the colored people in Piedmont; nor were there colored Georges living in the neighboring towns and working at the mill.

"Tell him your name, Daddy."

"He knows my name, boy," my father said after a long pause. "He calls all colored people George."

A long silence ensued. It was "one of those things," as my Mom would put it. Even then, that early, I knew when I was in the presence of "one of those things," one of those things that provided a glimpse, through a rent curtain, at another world that we could not affect but that affected us. There would be a painful moment of silence, and you would wait for it to give way to a discussion of a black superstar such as Sugar Ray or Jackie Robinson.

> The pain of the father's words leads to Gates's conclusions about race in America.

"Nobody hits better in a clutch than Jackie Robinson."

"That's right. Nobody."

I never again looked Mr. Wilson in the eye.

Now that you have heard about the essentials of the reading process — what you can do to prepare yourself to read a selection, what you should look for during a first reading, what you should annotate, and some questions you might ask yourself as you reread a selection — you are ready to read an entire selection to practice what you have learned.

Practice: Reading and Annotating
Laurence Perrine's "Coming to Terms with Paradox"

Before you read the following essay, think about its title, the biographical and rhetorical information in the headnote, and the journal prompt. Make some marginal notes of your expectations for the essay, and write out a response to the journal prompt. Then, as you read the essay itself for the first time, try not to stop; take it all in as if in one breath. The second time, however, pause to annotate key points in the text, using the marginal rules we have provided alongside each para-graph. As you read, remember the eight basic questions we mentioned earlier:

1. What does Perrine say about language? What is his thesis?
2. Why does he want to make this point? What is his purpose?
3. How has Perrine organized and developed his essay?
4. How does Perrine's strategy of development suit his subject and purpose?
5. What is Perrine's attitude toward his subject?
6. To whom is Perrine addressing his essay?
7. Does Perrine supply enough information to support the main idea?
8. How effective is Perrine's essay? Why?

Coming to Terms with Paradox

LAURENCE PERRINE

An educator and poet, Laurence Perrine (1915–1995) was born in Toronto, Ontario, Canada. After graduating from Oberlin College with both a B.A. and an M.A. in 1939, he served in the U.S. Army from 1941 to 1945, attaining the rank of master sergeant. A prolific writer, Perrine made a name for himself as the author of texts on poetry. In fact, for many Americans his name is almost synonymous with poetry. His life-long love of literature and language found voice in his many books, which include Sound and Sense: An Introduction to Poetry *(1956) now in its eleventh edition,* Story and Structure *(1959),* Poetry: Theory and Practice *(1962),* 100 American Poems of the Twentieth Century *(1966) with James Reid, and* Literature: Structure, Sound, and Sense *(1970). The following brief selection is from Perrine's engaging text* Sound and Sense: An Introduction to

Title:

_____
_____

Biographical
note:

_____
_____
_____

Publication
information:

_____
_____
_____
_____

Poetry. *First published in 1956, this book has intro-*
duced generations of high school and college students
to the excitement and art of the language of poetry.
Notice how Perrine uses vivid examples to illustrate
the two types of paradox he defines.

Rhetorical
highlights:
_____
_____
_____

WRITING TO DISCOVER: *When people respond to*
words in unexpected ways, they are often greeted with
the response, "You're being too literal." What does
being "too literal" mean to you? How else can a per-
son understand what is being said if not literally?
Explain.

Journal prompt:
_____
_____
_____

Aesop tells the tale of a traveler who sought
refuge with a Satyr on a bitter night. On entering the
Satyr's lodging, he blew on his fingers, and was asked
by the Satyr what he did it for. "To warm them up,"
he explained. Later, on being served with a piping
hot bowl of porridge, he blew also on it, and again
was asked what he did it for. "To cool it off," he explained. The Satyr thereupon thrust him out of
doors, for he would have nothing to do with a man
who could blow hot and cold with the same breath.

1. _____
_____
_____
_____
_____

A *paradox* is an apparent contradiction that is
nevertheless somehow true. It may be either a situation or a statement. Aesop's tale of the traveler illustrates a paradoxical situation. As a figure of
speech, paradox is a statement. When Alexander
Pope wrote that a literary critic of his time would
"damn with faint praise," he was using a verbal paradox, for how can a man damn by praising?

2. _____
_____
_____
_____
_____

When we understand all the conditions and circumstances involved in a paradox, we find that what
at first seemed impossible is actually entirely plausible
and not strange at all. The paradox of the cold hands
and hot porridge is not strange to a man who knows
that a stream of air directed upon an object of different temperature will tend to bring that object closer
to its own temperature. And Pope's paradox is not
strange when we realize the *damn* is being used figuratively, and that Pope means only that a too reserved praise may damage an author with the public
almost as much as adverse criticism. In a paradoxical
statement the contradiction usually stems from one
of the words being used figuratively or in more than
one sense.

3. _____
_____
_____
_____
_____

The value of paradox is its shock value. Its   4. _____
seemingly impossibility startles the reader into at-   _____
tention and, thus, by the fact of its apparent absurd-   _____
ity, it underscores the truth of what is being said.

Once you have read and reread Perrine's essay and annotated the text,
write your own answers to the eight basic questions listed on page 9.
Then compare your answers with the set of student answers that follows.

1. *What does Perrine say about language? What is his main point or
thesis?*

Perrine wants to tell his readers what paradox is: "an apparent contradiction that is nevertheless somehow true." He also wants to show how
paradox works and how it can be useful for writers. His main point
seems to be that "the value of paradox is its shock value. Its seemingly
impossibility startles the reader into attention and, thus, by the fact of
its apparent absurdity, it underscores the truth of what is being said."

2. *Why does he want to make this point? What is his purpose?*

Perrine's purpose is to explain the meaning of the word *paradox* so
that his readers can better understand the concept and how it works
in practice. He would also like his readers to appreciate how valuable
and interesting examples of paradox can be to storytellers, poets, and
writers in general. So Perrine's purpose is to inform and to persuade.

3. *How has Perrine organized and developed his essay?*

Overall, Perrine uses the pattern of definition. He gives what reads
like a dictionary definition of *paradox* in the second paragraph ("A
paradox is an apparent contradiction that is nevertheless somehow
true"); but he elaborates on his formal definition in several ways,
mainly through illustration — that is, by giving examples. The first
paragraph is a narration that serves as an example of a paradoxical situation, while the quotation from Alexander Pope at the end of paragraph 2 provides an example of a paradoxical statement.

4. *How does Perrine's strategy of development suit his subject and purpose?*

Perrine selects definition as a strategy because his purpose is to explain the meaning of a term unfamiliar to his readers. And for a
complicated abstraction like *paradox*, the two specific examples he
uses are crucial to make his meaning clear. In this case the use of illustration works well with definition because it makes the definition
more vivid and interesting — in short, real. The concrete examples
Perrine includes serve to show rather than merely tell what a paradox is and how it works. By beginning his essay with a clever story
that provides a strong example of his subject, Perrine catches his
readers' attention immediately and prepares them for the formal
definition of paradox in paragraph 2. He also uses a combination of

strategies (definition along with illustration) to make this selection more compelling.

5. *What is Perrine's attitude toward his subject?*

Perrine is excited about the shock value of paradox. He presents both examples in an animated, fun way that clearly illustrates the seemingly contradictory nature of paradox. He wants his readers to share in his appreciation for and delight in the language of paradox.

6. *To whom is Perrine addressing his essay?*

The audience for this essay is a cross-section of high school and college students who are reading Perrine as an introduction to poetry. Therefore, he is careful to define his terms and clearly illustrate his points with examples.

7. *Does Perrine supply enough information to support the essay's main idea?*

It is often difficult to say when enough is enough. Because Perrine develops each of his examples in great detail and because each of his examples clearly illustrates his main idea as stated in the final paragraph, he has supplied enough information. To give more examples would be overkill.

8. *How effective is Perrine's essay? Why?*

Perrine's essay is effective because it serves his purpose very well. He helps his readers understand what paradox is and appreciate how it works. His definition is to the point and easy to follow, while his examples from Aesop and Pope effectively combine illustration with definition, show how interesting paradoxes can be, and clearly demonstrate why writers use paradox.

Using Your Reading in the Writing Process

Reading and writing are the two sides of the same coin. Many people view writing as the making of reading. But the connection does not end there. Active reading is a means to help you become a better writer. We know that one of the best ways to learn to write and to improve our writing is to read. By reading we can begin to see how other writers have communicated their experiences, ideas, thoughts, and feelings in their writing. We can study how they have effectively used the various elements of the essay — thesis, unity, organization, beginnings and endings, paragraphs, transitions, effective sentences, word choice, tone, and figurative language — to say what they wanted to say. By studying the style, technique, and rhetorical strategies of other writers we learn how we might effectively do the same. The more we read and write, the more we begin to read as writers and, in turn, to write knowing what readers expect.

Reading as a Writer

What does it mean to read as a writer? Most of us have not been taught to read with a writer's eye, to ask why we like one piece of writing and not another. Likewise, most of us do not ask ourselves why one piece of writing is more believable or convincing than another. When you learn to read with a writer's eye, you begin to answer these important questions and, in the process, you come to appreciate what is involved in selecting and focusing a subject as well as the craftsmanship involved in writing — how a writer selects descriptive details, uses an unobtrusive organizational pattern, opts for fresh and lively language, chooses representative and persuasive examples, and emphasizes important points with sentence variety.

On one level, reading stimulates your thinking by providing you with subjects to write about. After reading David Raymond's essay "On Being 17, Bright, and Unable to Read," Helen Keller's "The Day Language Came into My Life," Malcolm X's "Discovering the Power of Language," Edite Cunha's "Talking in the New Land," or Tom Rosenberg's "Changing My Name after Sixty Years," you might, for example, be inspired to write about a powerful language experience you have had and how that experience, in retrospect, was a "turning point" in your life.

On a second level, reading provides you with information, ideas, and perspectives for developing your own paper. In this way, you respond to what you read, using material from what you've read in an essay. For example, after reading Diane Ravitch's essay on the "language police," you might want to elaborate on what she has written, drawing on your own experiences and either agreeing with her examples or generating better ones of your own. You could also qualify her argument or take issue against it. The Case Studies in *Language Awareness* offer you the opportunity to read extensively on a focused topic — the English-only debate, political correctness and censorship, sexually biased language, violence and the media, marketing diet and health, and Affirmative Action — and to use the information and opinions expressed in these essays as invaluable resources for your own thesis-driven paper.

On a third level, active reading can increase your awareness of how others' writing affects you, thus making you more sensitive to how your own writing will affect your readers. For example, if you have been impressed by an author who uses convincing evidence to support each of her claims, you might be more likely to back up your own claims carefully. If you have been impressed by an apt turn of phrase or absorbed by a writer's new idea, you may be less inclined to feed your readers dull, worn out, and trite phrases. More to the point, however, the active reading that you will be encouraged to do in *Language Awareness* will help you to recognize and analyze the essential elements of the essay. When you see, for example, how a writer like Tom Shachtman uses a strong thesis statement about how television talk shows are "dumbing down" America to control the parts of his essay, you can better appreciate the importance of having a clear thesis statement in your writing. When you see the way Susanne K. Langer uses transitions to link key phrases with important ideas so that readers can recognize clearly how the parts of her essay are meant to flow together, you have a better idea of how to achieve such coherence in your own writing. And when you see the way Donna Woolfolk Cross uses a division and classification organizational plan to differentiate clearly the various categories of propaganda, you see a powerful way in which you too can organize an essay using this method of development.

Finally, another important reason to master the skills of active reading is that you will be your own first reader and critic for everything you write. How well you are able to scrutinize your own drafts will powerfully affect how well you revise them, and revising well is crucial to writing well. Reading others' writing with a critical eye is useful and important practice; the more you read, the more practice you will have in sharpening your skills.

Remember, writing is the making of reading. The more sensitive you become to the content and style decisions made by the writers in *Language Awareness*, the more skilled you will be at making similar decisions in your own writing.

ON WRITING WELL

The Writing Process

Have you ever thought about what you do when you write, the process that you follow in writing a composition? Do you try to write a finished essay in one draft, or do you revise a number of times? Do you start to write as soon as you have a general subject, or do you gather information and ideas first? Do you worry about grammar and punctuation at every stage of the writing, especially if you are writing for your English instructor? It is helpful to think about the way you write and learn how others go about it because you may find ways to refine or improve the steps in your own writing process. You may even learn a new approach to writing.

Although each writer approaches a writing task somewhat differently, most experienced writers follow similar steps. For example, they usually decide on a specific topic and collect information about it before proceeding with drafting, revising, and editing. This chapter describes the various activities in each step of the typical writing process. The following description briefly summarizes these steps and provides a general overview.

PREWRITING

Collecting Information: Information lies at the heart of good writing. Experienced writers realize that effective writing draws from an abundance of specific, accurate information. You can acquire information in a variety of ways: reading, interviewing people, doing on-line research, plumbing your memory, observing events and processes, and jotting down what your five senses tell you. The discovery techniques discussed later in this chapter, such as journal writing and brainstorming, will help you keep track of your information and ideas and begin to see the connections among them.

Connecting Information, Linking Ideas, and Planning: It is also important to connect or see relationships in the information and ideas that you gather. By studying what you have collected and by thinking about it, you will begin to see patterns of meaning, linkages on which to build your writing. With these connections in mind, you can begin to plan your first draft's thesis and organization.

WRITING

Drafting the Paper: A first draft, which is usually written fairly quickly, helps you discover what you know and what you still need to find out, what works and what doesn't. Discovering what works is especially important because you can best build your writing on a strong foundation.

REVISING

Developing the Draft: The next step is to analyze your draft to see if each point you make is thoroughly developed. You may need to add definitions, descriptions, stories, statistics, or other types of support to your draft to deepen and extend its meaning. You will also want to pay attention to how the draft holds together, making sure that all your ideas progress logically.

Clarifying Meaning: At this point, you should try to read your writing as your audience might, asking the questions that your readers might ask. Then try to answer those questions by building explanations into your draft. Your writing should answer most, if not all, of the questions that it raises.

EDITING AND PROOFREADING

Editing and Proofreading Your Draft: At this final stage, you need to make sure that your writing flows smoothly from sentence to sentence and from paragraph to paragraph. You also need to check your composition for accurate spelling, grammar, and punctuation. Reading aloud, line by line, is a good way to assess the smoothness of the writing and to test for appropriate word choice and correct grammar and punctuation.

Now that you have a general idea of the typical writing process, let's look at each step in that process in more detail.

Prewriting

Understand Your Writing Assignment

When you first receive an assignment, read it over several times and pay attention to the main verbs. For example, consider what you are being asked to do in each of the following assignments:

> Tell about an experience you have had that dramatically revealed to you the importance of being accurate and precise in your use of language.

> Many languages are lost over time because the speakers of those languages die. When a language is lost, the particular culture embodied in the language is also lost. Using an extinct culture and language as an example, explain how a language embodies a culture and exactly what is lost when a language becomes extinct.

> Advocates of the English-only movement want to see English adopted as our country's official language. Argue against the philosophy behind this movement.

The first assignment asks you to write about a personal experience that gave you some insight into the power of language in general and more specifically into the importance of using accurate and precise language. Have you ever been seriously inconvenienced or denied an opportunity because the directions or explanations you were following were unclear? Have you ever been unclear in your own statements to someone, causing that person to fail? The verb *tell* is important in this assignment because it alerts you to the fact that you must share the details of the experience so that your readers can appreciate it firsthand.

The verb *explain* is the key to the second assignment. The assignment asks for clearly illustrated insights into the subject of dying languages, a subject not understood by the general public. How many languages have become extinct? How many are threatened with extinction today? In what specific ways is culture carried within a language? Should the loss of languages concern us? Why?

The third assignment asks you to *argue* for a particular position — to persuade readers to see things your way. To do so you need to understand all sides in the English-only debate. Why do some people think our country needs an official language? What problems are created when a nation's people speak a wide variety of languages? What are the advantages of a multilingual people? What problems might result if English were declared the official language of the United States?

After reading an assignment several times, check with your instructor if you are still unsure about what is being asked of you. He or she will be glad to clear up any possible confusion before you start writing. Be sure, as well, that you understand any additional requirements of the assignment, such as length or format.

Determine Your Purpose

All effective writing is done with a purpose. While good writing may be written for many specific reasons, it generally has one of three purposes: to express thoughts and feelings and lessons learned from life experiences, to inform readers by explaining something about the world around them, or to persuade readers to accept some belief or take some action.

EXPRESSION. In *expressive writing*, most commonly written from experience, writers put their thoughts and feelings before all other concerns. You will encounter several examples of expressive writing in later chapters. In Chapter 9, for example, Edite Cunha shares with us her anxiety about having to translate her father's Portuguese into English, and Sojourner Truth, the great traveling preacher and abolitionist, tells us in a very personal way what a woman can do and what it means to be a woman. Each of these writers clarifies an important life experience and conveys what she has learned from it.

EXPLANATION. *Informative writing* provides information to the reader about the outside world. Informative writing reports, explains, analyzes, defines, classifies, compares, describes a process, or examines causes and effects. When Paul Roberts explains what language is in Chapter 1, when William Zinsser offers advice on how to write simply in Chapter 2, and when Diane Ravitch explains who the language police are and how their censorship manipulates reality in Chapter 4, each is writing to inform.

PERSUASION. *Persuasive writing*, or *argument*, seeks to influence readers' thinking and attitudes toward a subject or issue and, in some cases, to move them to a particular course of action. Persuasive writing often uses logical reasoning, authoritative evidence, and testimony, and it sometimes includes emotionally charged language and examples. S. I. Hayakawa in Chapter 3 argues for the English-only movement, George Orwell in

Chapter 2 argues against doublespeak and for truth in the language of politics, and Natalie Goldberg in Chapter 10 uses numerous examples to persuade us to be specific when we write.

Know Your Audience

The best writers keep their audience in mind as they write. They try to empathize with their readers, address their difficulties and concerns, and appeal to their rational and emotional faculties. To identify the specific audience for whom you are writing, ask yourself the following questions:

- Who are my readers? Are they a specialized or a general group?
- What do I know about my audience's age, gender, education, religious affiliation, economic status, and political attitudes?
- What does my audience know about my subject?
- What does my audience need to know from me?
- Do I need to explain or avoid any specialized language so that my audience can understand my subject?
- What do I want my audience to think as a result of reading my writing?

Find a Subject and Topic

Although your instructor will usually give you specific writing assignments, sometimes you may be asked to choose your own subject and topic. When this is the case, first select a broad subject within the area of language studies that you think you may enjoy writing about like professional jargon, dialects, political speeches, advertising language, or propaganda. A language issue that you have experienced firsthand or something you've read may bring particular subjects to mind. You might also consider a language-related issue that involves your career ambitions, such as the areas of business, law, nursing, or journalism. Another option is to list some subjects you enjoy discussing with friends and that you can approach from a language perspective: music, television, dating.

Next, try to narrow your general subject by coming up with topics or issues that are more specific. The process of narrowing your subject is an important one because it is too difficult to tackle an entire general subject in a brief essay. Finally, narrow your topic further until you arrive at one that will be interesting to your readers and appropriate for the length of your paper. The following chart shows how the general areas of jargon, journalism, and television commercials might be narrowed to a specific essay topic. Some of the discovery techniques discussed in the next section may help you think of general subjects and develop specific topics as well.

General Subject Area	Narrowed Topic	Specific Essay Topic
Jargon	Medical jargon	Medical jargon used between doctors and terminally ill patients
Journalism	Slanted language in newswriting	Slanted language in newspapers' coverage of international events
Television commercials	Hidden messages in television commercials	Hidden messages in television commercials on children's Saturday morning programs

Use Discovery Techniques

Most writers use one or more discovery techniques to help them gather information, zero-in on a specific topic, or find connections among ideas. Some of the most common techniques are explained below.

KEEPING A JOURNAL. Many writers use a journal to record thoughts and observations that might be mined for future writing projects. They have learned not to rely on their memories to retain ideas, facts, and statistics they have heard or read about. Writers also use journals to keep all kinds of lists: lists of questions they would like answers to; lists of issues that concern them; lists of topics they would like to write about someday.

To aid your journal writing as you use this text, each reading selection in *Language Awareness* begins with a journal prompt called "Writing to Discover." The purpose of each prompt is to get you thinking and writing about your own experiences with the language issues discussed in the selection before you start reading. You thus have the opportunity to discover what you already know about a particular topic and to explore your observations, feelings, and opinions about it. The writing you do at this point is something you can always return to after reading each piece.

FREEWRITING. Journals are also useful if you want to freewrite. *Freewriting* is simply writing for a brief uninterrupted period of time — say, ten or fifteen minutes — on anything that comes to your mind. It is a way to get your mind working and to ease into a writing task. Start with a blank sheet of paper or computer screen and write about the general subject you are considering. Write as quickly as you can, don't stop for any reason, and don't worry about punctuation, grammar, or spelling. Write as though you were talking to your best friend, and let your writing take you in any direction. If you run out of ideas, don't stop; just repeat the last few things you wrote over and over again, and you'll be surprised — more ideas will begin to emerge. Once you become comfortable with open-ended freewrite, you can move to more focused freewriting, in which you write about a specific aspect of your subject. For example, if your original freewriting was on the subject of occupational jargon, your more focused freewrite might be limited to the topic of lawyers' language. Just as regular exercise gets you in shape, regular freewriting will help you feel more natural and comfortable when writing.

BRAINSTORMING. Another good way to generate ideas and information about a topic is to *brainstorm* — to list everything you know about a topic, freely associating one idea with another. Don't worry about order or level of importance. Try to capture everything that comes to mind because you never know what might prove valuable later on. Write quickly, but if you get stalled, reread what you have written; doing so will help you move in new directions. Keep your list handy so that you can add to it over the course of several days. Here, for example, is a student's brainstorming list on why Martin Luther King Jr.'s speech, "I Have a Dream," has endured:

Why "I Have a Dream" Is Memorable

civil rights demonstration in Washington, D.C., delivered on steps of Lincoln Memorial

repetition of "I have a dream"

references to the Bible, spirituals

"bad check" metaphor

other memorable figures of speech

200,000 people

reminds me of other great American documents and speeches — Declaration of Independence and Gettysburg Address

refers to various parts of the country

embraces all races and religions

sermon format

displays energy and passion

ASKING QUESTIONS. *Asking questions* about a particular topic or experience may help you generate information before you start to write. If you are writing about a personal experience, for example, asking questions may refresh your memory about the details and circumstances of the incident or help you discover why the experience is still so memorable. The newspaper reporter's five Ws and an H — Who? What? Where? When? Why? and How? — are excellent questions to start with.

One student, for example, developed the following questions to help her explore an experience of verbal abuse:

1. Who was involved in the abusive situation?
2. What specific language was used?
3. Where did the abuse most often take place?
4. When did the verbal abuse first occur?
5. Why did the abusive situation get started? Why did it continue?
6. How did I feel about the abuse as it was happening? How do I feel about it now?

As the student jotted down answers to these questions, other questions came to mind, such as, What did I try to do after the verbal abuse occurred? Did I seek help from anyone else? How can I help others who are being verbally abused? Before long, the student had recalled enough information for a rough draft about her experience.

CLUSTERING.   Another strategy for generating ideas and gathering information is *clustering*. Put your topic, or a key word or phrase about your topic, in the center of a sheet of paper and draw a circle around it. (The student example on page 22 shows the topic "hospital jargon at summer job" in the center.) Draw three or more lines out from this circle, and jot down main ideas about your topic, drawing a circle around each one. Repeat the process by drawing lines from the main-idea circles and adding examples, details, or questions you have. You may wind up pursuing one line of thought through many add-on circles before beginning a new cluster.

One advantage of clustering is that it allows you to sort your ideas and information into meaningful groups right from the start. As you carefully sort your ideas and information, you may begin to see an organizational plan for your writing. In the following example, the student's clustering is based on the experiences he had while working one summer in a hospital emergency room. Does the clustering provide any clues to how he might organize his essay?

Formulate a Thesis Statement

Once you have chosen a subject and topic and generated sufficient ideas and information, you are ready to organize your material and write a thesis statement. The *thesis* of an essay is its main idea, the point the essay tries to make. The thesis is often expressed in one or two sentences called a *thesis statement*, such as the following example:

There is no better place to see language change take place than in the area of student slang.

The thesis statement should not be confused with a *purpose statement.* While a thesis statement makes an assertion about your topic, a purpose statement specifically addresses what you are trying to do in the paper. For example,

> I want to learn how much slang is used on campus and in what areas of student life slang is the most prevalent.

A thesis statement should be

a. the most important point you make about your topic;
b. more general than the ideas and facts used to support it;
c. focused enough to be covered in the space allotted.

A thesis statement should not be a question but an assertion. If you find yourself writing a question for a thesis statement, answer the question first and then write your statement.

An effective strategy for developing a thesis statement is to begin by writing *What I want to say is that . . .* , as in this example:

What I want to say is that unless language barriers between patients and health-care providers are bridged, many patients' lives will be endangered.

Later, you can delete the formulaic opening, and you will be left with the thesis statement.

Unless language barriers between patients and health-care providers are bridged, many patients' lives will be endangered.

The thesis statement is usually set forth near the beginning of an essay, after a writer offers several sentences that establish a context for the piece. One common strategy is to position the thesis statement as the final sentence of the first paragraph. Occasionally, the thesis is stated elsewhere in an essay, sometimes at the very end.

Is Your Thesis Solid?

Once you have a possible thesis statement in mind for an essay, ask yourself the following questions:

- Does my thesis statement take a clear stance on an issue? If so, what is that stance?
- Is my thesis too general?
- Is my thesis too specific?
- Does my thesis apply to a larger audience than myself? If so, what is the audience, and how does the thesis apply?

Use One or More Strategies of Development

After you have done enough discovery work and have a tentative thesis in mind, it is time to put your ideas and information together more carefully. Think again about your purpose and ask yourself, "What is the best way to guide readers through my essay so that they understand my main point?" Before writers begin writing, they have usually thought about one or more strategies that will help them develop their essay. These strategies, such as description, narration, or definition, are basic ways of thinking about a topic and aiding readers in understanding it.

As you plan your essay, you may decide to focus on one strategy of development throughout. For example, if you were writing an essay to inform readers about the differences between the writing of men and women, you might use the strategy of *comparison and contrast*, discussing the similarities and differences between genders.

Often, you will find yourself using one strategy in support of another within a single essay. At some point, for example, you may want to *describe* an object to your readers so that they get a clear sense of its character. Or you may want to *narrate* a story at the outset of your essay to get your readers' attention. With another strategy, *process analysis*, you explain to readers how a particular process works, sometimes even showing them how to do something themselves in step-by-step fashion. Often, *dividing* your subject into discrete categories and then using *classification* to group examples helps readers because you are simplifying your subject. And in almost every essay, you will want to *define* difficult words or concepts and provide *examples* to support your ideas.

Suppose, for instance, that you want to write an essay about the college slang you hear on campus. Depending on your purpose, you might find it helpful to use one or more of the following strategies:

Definition: to explain what slang is

Exemplification: to give examples of slang

Comparison and Contrast: to differentiate slang from other types of speech, such as Standard English

Division and Classification: to categorize different types of slang or different topics that slang terms are used for — courses, students, food, grades

As you become a more skillful writer you will try different strategies and combine them in different ways. You will learn how to use one strategy to support another, and you will come to know almost intuitively what strategy would be perfect for any given subject.

Determine Your Organization

Once you have thought about the strategies of development you will use, your next task is to determine an organizational pattern, or order, that seems both natural and logical to you. There are several organizational patterns you might follow. You are already familiar with the most common one — *chronological order*. In this pattern, which is often used when you narrate a story, explain a process, or relate a series of events, you start with the earliest occurrence and move forward in time.

In a comparison-and-contrast essay, you might follow a *block* pattern or a *point-by-point* organization. In a block pattern, a writer provides all the information about one subject, followed by a block of comparable information about the other subject. In a point-by-point comparison, on the other hand, the writer starts by comparing both subjects in terms of a particular point, then compares both on a second point, and so on. In an essay about two dialects of American English, you could follow the block pattern, covering all the characteristics of one dialect and then all the characteristics of the other. Or, you could cover several major characteristics of (points about) the two dialects, comparing both point by point.

Other patterns of organization include moving from *the general to the specific*, from *smallest to largest*, from *least important to most important*, or from *the usual to the unusual*. In an essay about medical jargon, for instance, you might cover its general characteristics first and then move to specifics, or you might begin with what is most usual about doctors' language and then discuss what is unusual about it. Whatever order you choose, keep in mind that what you present first and last will probably stay in the reader's mind the longest.

After you choose an organizational pattern, jot down the main ideas in your essay. In other words, make a scratch outline. As you add more information and ideas to your scratch outline, you may want to develop a formal and more detailed outline of your paper. In writing a formal outline, follow these rules:

`1. Include the title of your essay, a statement of purpose, and the thesis statement.
2. Write in complete sentences unless your meaning is immediately clear from a phrase.
3. If you divide any category, make sure there are at least two subcategories. The reason for this is simple: You cannot divide something into fewer than two parts.
4. Observe the traditional conventions of formal outlining. Notice how each new level of specificity is given a new letter or number designation.

Title:
Purpose:
Thesis:
I.
  A.
  B.
    1.
    2.
      a.
      b.
      c.
II.

Writing Your First Draft

Sometimes we are so eager to get on with the writing of a first draft that we begin before we are ready, and the results are disappointing.

Before beginning to write, therefore, ask yourself, "Have I done enough prewriting? Is there a point to what I want to say?" If you have done a thorough job of gathering ideas and information, if you think you can accomplish the purpose of your paper, and if you are comfortable with your organizational plan, your answers will be "yes."

If, however, you feel uneasy, review the various prewriting steps to try to resolve the problem. Do you need to gather more information? Sharpen your thesis? Rethink your purpose? Refine your organization? Now is the time to think about these issues, to evaluate and clarify your writing plan. Time spent at this juncture is time well spent because it will not only improve your paper but will save you time and effort later on.

As you write, don't be discouraged if you do not find the most appropriate language for your ideas or if your ideas do not flow easily. Push ahead with the writing, realizing that you will be able to revise the material later, adding information and clarifications wherever necessary. Be sure to keep your audience in mind as you write, so that your diction and coverage stay at the appropriate level. Remember also to bridge all the logical and emotional leaps for your audience. Rereading what you have already written as you go along will help you to further develop your ideas and tie them together. Once completed, a first draft will give you a sense of accomplishment. You will see that you have something to work with, something to build on and improve during the revision process.

Revising

After you complete your first draft, you will need to revise it. During the revision stage of the writing process, you will focus on the large issues of thesis, purpose, evidence, organization, and paragraph structure to make sure that your writing says what you want it to say. First, though, it is crucial that you set your draft aside for a while. Then you can come back to it with a fresh eye and some objectivity. When you do, resist the temptation to plunge immediately into a second draft: Scattered changes will not necessarily improve the piece. Instead, try to look at your writing as a whole and to tackle your writing problems systematically. Use the following guidelines:

- Make revisions on a hard copy of your paper. (Triple-space your draft so that you can make changes more easily.)
- Read your paper aloud, listening for parts that do not make sense.
- Ask a fellow student to read your essay and critique it.

One way to begin the revision process is to compare the earlier outline of your first draft to an outline of how it actually came out. This

---

A Brief Guide to Peer Critiquing

When critiquing someone else's paper:

- Read the essay carefully. Read it to yourself first, and then, if possible, have the writer read it to you at the beginning of the session. Some flaws become obvious when read aloud.
- Ask the writer to state his or her purpose for writing and to identify the thesis statement within the paper itself.
- Be positive, but be honest. Never denigrate the paper's content or the writer's effort, but do your best to identify how the writer can improve the paper through revision.
- Try to address the most important issues first. Think about the thesis and the organization of the paper before moving on to more specific topics like word choice.
- Do not be dismissive, and do not dictate changes. Ask questions that encourage the writer to reconsider parts of the paper that you find confusing or ineffective.

When someone critiques your work:

- Give your reviewer a copy of your paper before your meeting.
- Listen carefully to your reviewer, and try not to discuss or argue each issue. Record comments, and evaluate them later.
- Do not get defensive or explain what you wanted to say if the reviewer misunderstands what you meant. Try to understand the reviewer's point of view, and learn what you need to revise to clear up the misunderstanding.
- Consider every suggestion, but only use the ones that make sense to you in your revision.
- Be sure to thank your reviewer for his or her effort on your behalf.

---

will help you see, in abbreviated form, the organization and flow of the essential components of your essay and perhaps detect flaws in reasoning.

Another method you can use in revising is to start with large-scale issues, such as your overall structure, and then concentrate on finer and finer points. As you examine your essay, ask yourself about what you have written and address the large elements of your essay: thesis, purpose, organization, paragraphs, and evidence.

Revising the Large Elements of an Essay

- Is my topic specific enough?
- Does my thesis statement identify my topic and make an assertion about it?
- Is my essay organized the best way, given my purpose?
- Are my paragraphs adequately developed, and does each support my thesis?
- Have I accomplished my purpose?
- How effective is my beginning? My ending?
- Is my title effective?

Once you have addressed the major problems in your essay by writing a second draft, you should be ready to turn your attention to the finer elements of sentence structure, word choice, and usage.

Revising Sentence-Level Elements

- Do my sentences convey my thoughts clearly, and do they emphasize the most important parts of my thinking?
- Are my sentences stylistically varied?
- Is my choice of words fresh and forceful, or is my writing weighed down by clichés and unnecessary wordiness?
- Have I made any errors of usage?

Finally, if you find yourself dissatisfied with specific elements of your draft, look at several essays in *Language Awareness* to see how other writers have dealt with the particular situation you are confronting. For example, if you don't like the way the essay starts, find some beginnings you think are particularly effective; if your paragraphs don't seem to flow into one another, examine how various writers use transitions; if an example seems unconvincing, examine the way other writers include details, anecdotes, and facts and statistics to strengthen their illustrations. Remember that the readings in the text are there as a resource for you as you write.

Editing and Proofreading

Now that you have revised in order to make your essay "right," it is time to think about making it "correct." During the editing stage of the writing process, check your writing for errors in grammar, punctuation, capitalization, spelling, and manuscript format. Both your dictionary and your college handbook will help you answer specific editing questions about your paper.

Addressing Common Editing Problems and Errors

- Do my verbs agree in number with their subjects?
- Do my pronouns have clear antecedents — that is, do they clearly refer to specific nouns earlier in my sentences?
- Do I have any sentence fragments, comma splices, or run-on sentences?
- Have I made any unnecessary shifts in person, tense, or number?
- Have I used the comma properly in all instances?
- Have I checked for misspellings, mistakes in capitalization, and typos?
- Have I inadvertently confused words like *their*, *they're*, and *there* or *it's* and *its*?
- Have I followed the prescribed guidelines for formatting my manuscript?

Having revised and edited your essay, you are ready to print your final copy. Be sure to proofread your work before submitting it to your instructor. Even though you may have used your computer's spell checker, you might find that you have typed *worm* instead of *word*, or *form* instead of *from*. Also check to see that your essay is properly line-spaced and that the text is legible.

The following essay was written by Rebekah Sandlin while she was a student at Miami University in Oxford, Ohio. After Rebekah read the essays in the chapter on prejudice, stereotypes, and language, her instructor, Linda Parks, asked her to write about a personal experience with biased language and how that language affected her. Rebekah vividly remembered an experience she had in the third grade, when she used the phrase "just like a nigger" to mock a classmate. Using that experience as the starting point of her essay, she then traces a series of subsequent encounters she had with the word *nigger* and recounts her resulting personal growth. By the end of her essay, Rebekah makes it clear to her readers why she felt compelled to tell her story.

Rebekah Sandlin   Sandlin 1

English 111 sec. BD

October 23, 2003

Paper #3

                        The "Negro Revolt" in Me

     She said "seven" when the answer was clearly "ten." We were in the
third grade and had been studying multiplication for a few weeks. Our
teacher, Mrs. Jones, reminded Monica that, "we are multiplying now, not
adding. Five times two will always be ten." I laughed at Monica. How did she
not know the answer to five times two? We had been over it and practiced it
so many times. My laughter encouraged the other kids in the class to join in
with me. Within seconds the laughing had escalated into pointing fingers
and calling her stupid. That's when "it" happened. That's when I said what I
will always regret for the rest of my life. I said, "Just like a nigger." Playing
on her weaknesses in math, laughing at her, encouraging the rest of the
class to point at her, and calling her the most degrading word in history still
eats at my insides. The class stopped laughing. Monica cried. Mrs. Jones
gasped and yanked me into the hallway where she scolded me for a good
half an hour. That is how I learned that language could be used as a
dangerous tool. That's when I learned about prejudice and its effects on
people. That's how it happened. This is how it has affected my life.
     Mrs. Jones sent me home with a note explaining my "behavior" in
class. I remember being terribly afraid to give that note to my mom. I felt
guilty, confused, and embarrassed, but I wasn't sure why I felt that way. No
one had taken the time to explain to me why the word had such a negative
connotation. No one told me that blacks were once treated terribly wrong or
that they were used as slaves. No one told me about the interracial rapes
that occurred on plantations or about the children being taken and sold to
rich white landowners. No one told me about them being denied an education
and proper shelter. No one told me. I was just a small white girl living in a
predominately white city and going to a predominately white school. I knew
nothing about diversity and equal rights for everyone. I knew nothing.
     My mom sat me down at the kitchen table and asked me how I could
have said such a terrible thing. "Where did you learn that word?" she
asked. She sounded furious and embarrassed. She kept asking me where I
had heard the word and who taught it to me. Before I had a chance to
respond she knew the answer. My dad was on the phone in the next room
talking to his father. He was laughing and he said, "just like a nigger." My
mom lowered her head and whispered, "go to your room." I quietly got up
and obeyed her command. I'm not sure what she said to him, but I could
hear their mumbled fighting through the vents. I pressed my ear to the
vent on the floor to try and make sense of my mother's cries. It was no use.
Two hours later they came upstairs to give me one of their "you did

something wrong" speeches. Except this speech was different from most. It
began with an apology and an attempt to justify my father's words.

It started with a story. My dad grew up on a tobacco farm in southern
Georgia. His family hired blacks to work out in the fields. "No," he
reassured, "they weren't slaves. We paid them." His family was prejudiced
toward blacks. Their language and actions rubbed off onto my dad. The only
difference was that my dad learned that what he said and how he treated
blacks was wrong. Through growing up and living in integrated working
environments, he learned how "not to act" in the presence of a black
person. However, when he talked to his father he still acted and talked like
he was prejudiced. He said that he didn't understand why he did it other
than he desperately wanted to be accepted by his own father. He admitted
that he was wrong and told me that I was lucky because I was going to
learn the "real way" to treat people. He promised to never use the word
again as long as I promised to do the same thing. I agreed.

I was in the fifth grade the next time I heard the word used.
Ironically, I was in a math class again. Except this time I didn't say it,
someone else did. Unlike Monica, this girl didn't cry. Instead, she gave an
evil glare. I was the one that stood up to say something in her defense. I
yelled at Dan and told him that what he had said was rude and degrading.
"How would you like it if someone called you honky?" I screamed. He
hauled off and hit me right in the arm! He called me a "nigger-lover." The
teacher broke it up, and we were sent to the principal's office. I was
suspended for using vulgar language. I had used the word "honky." Dan was
given a warning and sent back to class. I had plenty of time to think about
what I had done wrong while I waited in the office for my mom to come and
pick me up. No matter how hard I tried, I couldn't see what I had done
wrong. That girl did not want to be called a nigger. I was just trying to show
him what it would feel like if someone had said something like that to him.
My mom did not agree with me. I learned an important lesson that day.
Using bad words to stop other bad words is like using violence to stop
violence — it doesn't work. My mom was supportive and said that she
respected what I was trying to do but next time I should use better sense. I
didn't want there to be a next time.

Unfortunately, there was a next time. I was in the seventh grade. It
was the week of April 26th, 1992. Riots based on the Rodney King verdict
"broke-out" through our public school system. Blacks attacked whites.
Whites attacked blacks. Racism. Hatred. Anger. Stupidity. I was confused
and feared for my personal safety within the hallways of my school. There
was a black eighth grader running down the hallways pushing and hitting
every white kid that he saw. He was screaming, "down with whitey." He was
approaching me fast. I'll never forget his anger or the sound of his voice. I
was terrified. As he ran past he slammed my locker door shut on my hand.

Frustration. Pain. We both felt it. I yelled directly at him. "Don't you understand that I'm on your side. I know," I said, "it's not fair. But, we aren't all the same. I'm on your side. I'm on your . . . " He hovered over the top of me. He had heard my words, and I was terrified that he was going to hurt me. That wasn't at all what he wanted to do. Instead, he just stared at me. His mouth was half open as if he was shocked by my comment. I wasn't sure if he was going to hurt me or hug me.

"How's your hand?" he asked.

"It will be okay, I guess."

"You have guts. Most people wouldn't have said what you said."

"Violence doesn't solve anything. I wish everyone could see that."

"You should put your ideas to use. Who knows, someone might actually like to hear what you have to say."

He shrugged his shoulders and walked away. Halfway down the hall he turned to look back at me and gave a subtle wink. Even though my hand "hurt like hell," I was a lucky girl. I could have been seriously hurt. That afternoon I went to my counselor's office and asked him what I could do to stop the riots in our school. He chuckled and said, "not much." He told me about a meeting that would be held in the auditorium the next morning. The principal was going to give a speech to the student body. It seemed to be the counselor's opinion that the principal was going to deal with the situation by telling us how stupid we were being. That wasn't the solution that I was hoping for.

So, I went to see the principal. I begged for his attention on this serious matter. I told him that none of us wanted to be put down and talked to like we were stupid. Abuse doesn't stop abuse. "Please," I begged, "talk to us like we are adults. Treat us like you would want to be treated. This is a touchy, painful subject for many people. Please don't make things worse than what they already are." I left his office feeling conquered and as though I was fighting for the equality that everyone wanted but no one expected to get. I prayed that night. I prayed that God would give our principal the strength, knowledge, and patience to deal with our problem. I'm not sure if God answered my prayer or if what I said triggered something in our principal, but his speech was incredible. It was the only time that I saw the entire seventh and eighth grade class sit quietly and respectfully during an auditorium gathering.

Throughout high school I joined many clubs and groups that promoted integration between blacks and whites. Sometimes I gained respect from my peers and other times I was called a "nigger-lover." These experiences were difficult and frustrating, but they turned out to be some of the best experiences that I ever had during high school. Now I am a freshman here at Miami University. Once again I am a small white girl in a predominately white town and in a predominately white school. The only difference

between this time and the time before is that I've learned from my
mistakes. I only hope that the same is true about the people that I sit next
to in my classes. I was never able to express how sorry I was for what I
said to Monica. I wonder how my comment has affected her life. Maybe she
is writing a similar paper right now. I learned a lesson on that cool autumn
day in the third grade that will stick with me for the rest of my life. My
fear is that Monica also learned something that will stick with her for the
rest of her life.

1

COMING TO AN AWARENESS OF LANGUAGE

Most of us accept language as we accept the air we breathe; we cannot get along without it, and we take it for granted almost all of the time. Many days we find ourselves on language overload, bombarded by a steady stream of verbal messages — some invited, others not — but how much do we really know about language? How well do we understand how language works? Few of us are aware of the extent to which language is used to mislead and manipulate. Still fewer of us are fully conscious of the ways, subtle and not, in which our use of language may affect others. And still fewer of us recognize that our very perceptions of the world are influenced, and our thoughts at least partially shaped, by language. However, we are also the beneficiaries of language far more than we are its victims. Language is one of humankind's greatest achievements and most important resources, and it is a subject endlessly fascinating in itself.

If it is true that we are all in some sense prisoners of language, it is equally true that liberation begins with an awareness of that fact. We begin Chapter 1 with three personal narratives in which individuals tell of their language struggles and how they came to discover the tremendous power of language. In "Discovering the Power of Language," Malcolm X relates how he came to understand the power of words while serving time in the Norfolk Prison Colony. He remembers his frustration and feelings of inadequacy when he recognized the limitations of his slang-filled street talk. Not one to sit around and drown in self-pity, Malcolm X charts a course that empowered and liberated his mind. Next, we read the inspiring story of Helen Keller, a woman who broke the chains of blindness and deafness and connected to the world around her. In "The Day Language Came into My Life," Keller recounts the day she, with the help of her teacher Anne Mansfield Sullivan, discovered "everything had a name, and each name gave birth to a new thought." In the third essay, "On Being 17, Bright, and Unable to Read," David Raymond describes what it is like to be a dyslexic high school student, and how he met his language challenge.

The writers of the final three selections in this chapter explore some language fundamentals that give us a greater appreciation for the miracle of language that we humans share. In "Language and Thought," philosopher Susanne K. Langer explains how language separates humans from the rest of the animal kingdom. She demonstrates the power of language and shows how "without it anything properly called 'thought' is impossible." In "A Brief History of English," Paul Roberts charts high spots in the long and complicated history of the English language from its beginnings around A.D. 600 to the present. He explains how a "minor language, spoken by a few people on a small island" in 1500 evolved into what "is perhaps the greatest language of the world." Finally, on a decidedly lighter note, Nedra Newkirk Lamar has fun with the incongruities that result when the "rules" of English are applied meticulously. In "Does a Finger Fing?" she lets us know that there is room for humor in language study.

Discovering the Power of Language

Malcolm X

On February 21, 1965, Malcolm X, the Black Muslim leader, was shot to death as he addressed an afternoon rally in Harlem. He was thirty-nine years old. In the course of his brief life, he had risen from a world of thieving, pimping, and drug pushing to become one of the most articulate and powerful African Americans in the United States during the early 1960s. In 1992 his life was reexamined in Spike Lee's film Malcolm X. *With the assistance of the late Alex Haley, the author of* Roots, *Malcolm X told his story in* The Autobiography of Malcolm X *(1964), a moving account of his search for fulfillment. This selection is taken from the* Autobiography.*

All of us have been in situations in which we have felt somehow betrayed by our language, unable to find just the right words to express ourselves. "Words," as lexicographer Bergen Evans has said, "are the tools for the job of saying what you want to say." As our repertoire of words expands so does our ability to express ourselves — to articulate clearly our thoughts, feelings, hopes, fears, likes, and dislikes. Frustration at not being able to express himself in the letters he wrote drove Malcolm X to the dictionary, where he discovered the power of words.

WRITING TO DISCOVER: *Write about a time when someone told you that it is important to have a good vocabulary. What did you think when you heard this advice? Why do you think people believe that vocabulary is important? How would you assess your own vocabulary?*

I've never been one for inaction. Everything I've ever felt strongly about, I've done something about. I guess that's why, unable to do anything else, I soon began writing to people I had known in the hustling world, such as Sammy the Pimp, John Hughes, the gambling house owner, the thief Jumpsteady, and several dope peddlers. I wrote them all about Allah and Islam and Mr. Elijah Muhammad. I had no idea where most of them lived. I addressed their letters in care of the Harlem or Roxbury bars and clubs where I'd known them.

I never got a single reply. The average hustler and criminal was too uneducated to write a letter. I have known many slick sharp-looking hustlers, who would have you think they had an interest in Wall Street; privately, they would get someone else to read a letter if they received one. Besides, neither would I have replied to anyone writing me something as wild as "the white man is the devil."

What certainly went on the Harlem and Roxbury wires was that Detroit Red was going crazy in stir,[1] or else he was trying some hype to shake up the warden's office.

During the years that I stayed in the Norfolk Prison Colony, never did any official directly say anything to me about those letters, although, of course, they all passed through the prison censorship. I'm sure, however, they monitored what I wrote to add to the files which every state and federal prison keeps on the conversion of Negro inmates by the teachings of Mr. Elijah Muhammad.

But at that time, I felt that the real reason was that the white man   5
knew that he was the devil.

Later on, I even wrote to the Mayor of Boston, to the Governor of Massachusetts, and to Harry S. Truman. They never answered; they probably never even saw my letters. I handscratched to them how the white man's society was responsible for the black man's condition in this wilderness of North America.

It was because of my letters that I happened to stumble upon starting to acquire some kind of homemade education.

I became increasingly frustrated at not being able to express what I wanted to convey in letters that I wrote, especially those to Mr. Elijah Muhammad. In the street, I had been the most articulate hustler out there — I had commanded attention when I said something. But now, trying to write simple English, I not only wasn't articulate, I wasn't even functional. How would I sound writing in slang, the way I would *say* it, something such as, "Look daddy, let me pull your coat about a cat. Elijah Muhammad — "

Many who today hear me somewhere in person, or on television, or those who read something I've said, will think I went to school far beyond the eighth grade. This impression is due entirely to my prison studies.

It had really begun back in the Charlestown Prison, when Bimbi first   10
made me feel envy of his stock of knowledge. Bimbi had always taken charge of any conversation he was in, and I had tried to emulate him. But every book I picked up had few sentences which didn't contain anywhere from one to nearly all of the words that might as well have been in Chinese. When I just skipped those words, of course, I really ended up with little idea of what the book said. So I had come to the Norfolk Prison Colony still going through only book-reading motions. Pretty soon, I would have quit even these motions, unless I had received the motivation that I did.

I saw that the best thing I could do was get hold of a dictionary — to study, to learn some words. I was lucky enough to reason also that I should try to improve my penmanship. It was sad. I couldn't even write in a straight line. It was both ideas together that moved me to request a dictionary along with some tablets and pencils from the Norfolk Prison Colony school.

---

1. Slang for being in jail.

I spent two days just riffling uncertainly through the dictionary's pages. I'd never realized so many words existed! I didn't know *which* words I needed to learn. Finally, just to start some kind of action, I began copying.

In my slow, painstaking, ragged handwriting, I copied into my tablet everything printed on that first page, down to the punctuation marks.

I believe it took me a day. Then, aloud, I read back, to myself, everything I'd written on the tablet. Over and over, aloud, to myself, I read my own handwriting.

I woke up the next morning, thinking about those words — immensely proud to realize that not only had I written so much at one time, but I'd written words that I never knew were in the world. Moreover, with a little effort, I also could remember what many of these words meant. I reviewed the words whose meanings I didn't remember. Funny thing, from the dictionary's first page right now, that "aardvark" springs to my mind. The dictionary had a picture of it, a long-tailed, long-eared, burrowing African mammal, which lives off termites caught by sticking out its tongue as an anteater does for ants. 15

I was so fascinated that I went on — I copied the dictionary's next page. And the same experience came when I studied that. With every succeeding page, I also learned of people and places and events from history. Actually the dictionary is like a miniature encyclopedia. Finally the dictionary's A section had filled a whole tablet — and I went on into the B's. That was the way I started copying what eventually became the entire dictionary. It went a lot faster after so much practice helped me pick up handwriting speed. Between what I wrote in my tablet, and writing letters, during the rest of my time in prison I would guess I wrote a million words.

I suppose it was inevitable that as my word-base broadened, I could for the first time pick up a book and read and now begin to understand what the book was saying. Anyone who has read a great deal can imagine the new world that opened. Let me tell you something: from then until I left that prison, in every free moment I had, if I was not reading in the library, I was reading on my bunk. You couldn't have gotten me out of books with a wedge. Between Mr. Muhammad's teachings, my correspondence, my visitors . . . and my reading of books, months passed without my even thinking about being imprisoned. In fact, up to then, I never had been so truly free in my life.

FOCUSING ON CONTENT

1. What motivated Malcolm X "to acquire some kind of homemade education" (7)?

2. For many, *vocabulary building* means learning strange, multisyllabic, difficult-to-spell words. But acquiring an effective vocabulary does not need to be any of these things. What, for you, constitutes an effective vocabulary? How would you characterize Malcolm X's vocabulary in this selection? Do you find his word choice appropriate for his purpose? (Glossary: *Purpose*) Explain.

3. What is the nature of the freedom that Malcolm X refers to in the final sentence? In what sense is language liberating? Is it possible for people to be "prisoners" of their own language? Explain.

FOCUSING ON WRITING

1. In paragraph 8, Malcolm X remembers thinking how he would "sound writing in slang" and feeling inadequate because he recognized how slang or street talk limited his options. (Glossary: *Slang*) In what kinds of situations is slang useful and appropriate? When is Standard English more appropriate? (Glossary: *Standard English*)

2. In paragraph 8, Malcolm X describes himself as having been "the most articulate hustler out there" but in writing he says he "wasn't even functional." What differences between speaking and writing could account for such a discrepancy? How does the tone of this essay help you understand Malcolm X's dilemma? (Glossary: *Tone*)

3. Malcolm X narrates his experience as a prisoner using the first-person pronoun *I*. Why is the first person particularly appropriate? What would be lost or gained had he told his story using the third-person pronoun *he*? (Glossary: *Point of View*)

LANGUAGE IN ACTION

Many newspapers carry regular vocabulary-building columns, and the *Reader's Digest* has for many years included a section called "It Pays to Enrich Your Word Power." You might enjoy taking the following quiz, which is excerpted from the April 1999 issue of *Reader's Digest*.

IT PAYS TO ENRICH YOUR
WORD POWER

Zeus and his thunderbolts, Thor and his hammer, Medusa and her power to turn flesh into stone: these are all fascinating figures in mythology and folklore. Associated with such legends are words we use today, including the 10 selected below.

1. **panic** *n.* — A: pain. B: relief. C: mess. D: fear.

2. **bacchanal** (*BAK ih NAL*) *n.* — A: drunken party. B: graduation ceremony. C: backache remedy. D: victory parade.

3. **puckish** *adj.* — A: wrinkly. B: quirky. C: quarrelsome. D: mischievous.

4. **cyclopean** (*SIGH klo PEA en*) *adj.* — A: wise. B: gigantic. C: wealthy. D: repetitious.

5. **hector** *v.* — A: to curse. B: bully. C: disown. D: injure.

6. **cupidity** (*kyoo PID ih tee*) *n.* — A: thankfulness. B: ignorance. C: abundance. D: desire.

7. **mnemonic** (*knee MON ik*) *adj.* — pertaining to A: memory. B: speech. C: hearing. D: sight.

8. **stygian** (*STIJ ee an*) *adj.* — A: stingy. B: hellish. C: uncompromising. D: dirty.

9. **narcissistic** *adj.* — A: indecisive. B: very sleepy. C: very vain. D: just.

10. **zephyr** (*ZEF er*) *n.* — A: breeze. B: dog. C: horse. D: tornado.

ANSWERS:

1. **panic** — *[D]* Fear; widespread terror; as, An outbreak of Ebola led to *panic* in the small village. *Pan*, frightening Greek god of nature.

2. **bacchanal** — *[A]* Drunken party; orgy; as, Complaints to the police broke up the *bacchanal. Bacchus*, Roman god of wine.

3. **puckish** — *[D]* Mischievous; prankish. *Puck*, a trick-loving sprite or fairy.

4. **cyclopean** — *[B]* Gigantic; huge; as, the *cyclopean* home runs of Mark McGwire. *Cyclopes*, a race of fierce, one-eyed giants.

5. **hector** — *[B]* To bully; threaten. *Hector*, Trojan leader slain by Achilles and portrayed as a bragging menace in some dramas.

6. **cupidity** — *[D]* Strong desire. *Cupid*, Roman god of love.

7. **mnemonic** — *[A]* Pertaining to memory; as, "Spring forward and fall back" is a *mnemonic* spur to change time twice a year. *Mnemosyne*, Greek goddess of memory.

8. **stygian** — *[B]* Hellish; dark and gloomy. *Styx*, a river in Hades.

9. **narcissistic** — *[C]* Very vain; self-loving; as, The *narcissistic* actress preened for the photographers. *Narcissus*, a youth who fell in love with his own reflection.

10. **zephyr** — *[A]* Soft breeze; as, The storm tapered off to a *zephyr*. *Zephyrus*, gentle Greek god of the west wind.

Are you familiar with most of the words on the quiz? Did some of the answers surprise you? In your opinion, is the level of difficulty appropriate for the *Reader's Digest* audience? What does the continuing popularity of vocabulary-building features suggest about the attitudes of many Americans toward language?

WRITING SUGGESTIONS

1. All of us have been in situations in which our ability to use language seemed inadequate — for example, when taking an exam; being interviewed for a job; giving directions; or expressing sympathy, anger, or grief. Write a brief essay in which you recount one such frustrating incident in your life. Before beginning to write, review your reactions to Malcolm X's frustrations with his limited vocabulary. Share your experiences with your classmates.

2. Malcolm X solved the problem of his own illiteracy by carefully studying the dictionary. Would this be a viable solution to the national problem of illiteracy? Are there more practical alternatives to Malcolm X's approach? What, for example, is being done in your community to combat illiteracy? What are some of the more successful approaches being used in other parts of the country? Write a brief essay about the problem of illiteracy. In addition to using your library for research, you may want to check out the Internet to see what it has to offer.

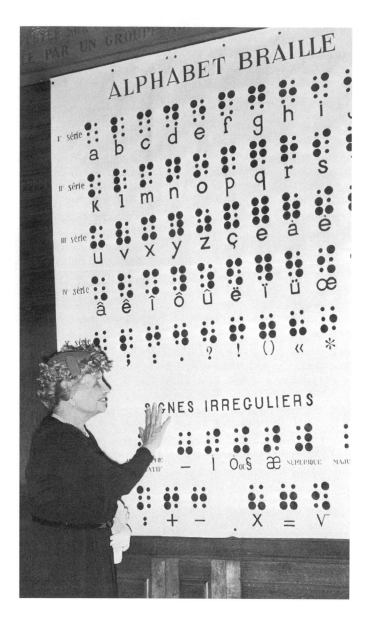

PICTURING LANGUAGE

Helen Keller was visually and hearing impaired from early childhood, unable to read or listen to people speak. With Braille, written and spoken language was transformed into a system of touchable symbols. Here Helen Keller reads a chart of Braille alphabet during her speech at the Sorbonne in Paris, France, on June 23, 1952, commemorating the hundredth anniversary of the death of Louis Braille. In what ways do you think "touchable language" liberated Helen Keller and others who share her impairment?

The Day Language Came into My Life

HELEN KELLER

Helen Keller (1880–1968) became blind and deaf at the age of eighteen months as a result of a disease. As a child, then, Keller became accustomed to her limited world for it was all that she knew. She experienced only certain fundamental sensations, such as the warmth of the sun on her face, and few emotions, such as anger and bitterness. It wasn't until she was almost seven years old that her family hired Anne Sullivan, a young woman who would turn out to be an extraordinary teacher, to help her. As Keller learned to communicate and think, the world opened up to her. She recorded her experiences in an autobiography, The Story of My Life *(1903), from which the following selection is taken.*

Helen Keller is in a unique position to remind us of what it is like to pass from the "fog" of prethought into the world where "everything had a name, and each name gave birth to a new thought." Her experiences as a deaf and blind child also raise a number of questions about the relationship between language and thought, emotions, ideas, and memory. Over time, Keller's acquisition of language allowed her to assume all the advantages of her birthright. Her rapid intellectual and emotional growth as a result of language suggests that we, too, have the potential to achieve a greater measure of our humanity by further refining our language abilities.

WRITING TO DISCOVER: *Consider what your life would be like today if you had been born without the ability to understand language or speak or if you had suddenly lost the ability to use language later in life. Write about those aspects of your life that you think would be affected most severely.*

The most important day I remember in all my life is the one on which my teacher, Anne Mansfield Sullivan, came to me. I am filled with wonder when I consider the immeasurable contrast between the two lives which it connects. It was the third of March 1887, three months before I was seven years old.

On the afternoon of that eventful day, I stood on the porch, dumb, expectant. I guessed vaguely from my mother's signs and from the hurrying to and fro in the house that something unusual was about to happen, so I went to the door and waited on the steps. The afternoon sun penetrated the mass of honeysuckle that covered the porch and fell on my upturned face. My fingers lingered almost unconsciously on the familiar leaves and blossoms which had just come forth to greet the sweet southern spring. I did not know what the future held of marvel or surprise for me. Anger and bitterness had preyed upon me continually for weeks and a deep languor had succeeded this passionate struggle.

Have you ever been at sea in a dense fog, when it seemed as if a tangible white darkness shut you in, and the great ship, tense and anxious, groped her way toward the shore with plummet and sounding-line, and you waited with beating heart for something to happen? I was like that ship before my education began, only I was without compass or sounding- line and had no way of knowing how near the harbor was. "Light! give me light!" was the wordless cry of my soul, and the light of love shone on me in that very hour.

I felt approaching footsteps. I stretched out my hand as I supposed to my mother. Someone took it, and I was caught up and held close in the arms of her who had come to reveal all things to me, and, more than all things else, to love me.

The morning after my teacher came she led me into her room and   5
gave me a doll. The little blind children at the Perkins Institution had sent it and Laura Bridgman had dressed it; but I did not know this until afterward. When I had played with it a little while, Miss Sullivan slowly spelled into my hand the word "d-o-l-l." I was at once interested in this finger play and tried to imitate it. When I finally succeeded in making the letters correctly I was flushed with childhood pleasure and pride. Running downstairs to my mother I held up my hand and made the letters for doll. I did not know that I was spelling a word or even that words existed; I was simply making my fingers go in monkeylike imitation. In the days that followed I learned to spell in this uncomprehending way a great many words, among them *pin, hat, cup* and a few verbs like *sit, stand* and *walk*. But my teacher had been with me several weeks before I understood that everything has a name.

One day, while I was playing with my new doll, Miss Sullivan put my big rag doll into my lap also, spelled "d-o-l-l" and tried to make me understand that "d-o-l-l" applied to both. Earlier in the day we had had a tussle over the words "m-u-g" and "w-a-t-e-r." Miss Sullivan had tried to impress it upon me that "m-u-g" is *mug* and that "w-a-t-e-r" is *water*, but I persisted in confounding the two. In despair she had dropped the subject for the time, only to renew it at the first opportunity. I became impatient at her repeated attempts and, seizing the new doll, I dashed it upon the floor. I was keenly delighted when I felt the fragments of the broken doll at my feet. Neither sorrow nor regret followed my passionate outburst. I had not loved the doll. In the still, dark world in which I lived there was no strong sentiment or tenderness. I felt my teacher sweep the fragments to one side of the hearth, and I had a sense of satisfaction that the cause of my discomfort was removed. She brought me my hat, and I knew I was going out into the warm sunshine. This thought, if a wordless sensation may be called a thought, made me hop and skip with pleasure.

We walked down the path to the well-house, attracted by the fragrance of the honeysuckle with which it was covered. Some one was drawing water and my teacher placed my hand under the spout. As the cool stream gushed over one hand she spelled into the other the word *water*, first slowly, then rapidly. I stood still, my whole attention fixed upon the motions of her fingers. Suddenly I felt a misty consciousness as of something forgotten — a thrill of returning thought; and somehow the mystery of language was revealed to me. I knew then that "w-a-t-e-r" meant the wonderful cool something that was flowing over my hand. The living word awakened my soul, gave it light, hope, joy, set it free! There were barriers still, it is true, but barriers that could in time be swept away.

I left the well-house eager to learn. Everything had a name, and each name gave birth to a new thought. As we returned to the house every object which I touched seemed to quiver with life. That was because I saw everything with the strange, new sight that had come to me. On entering the door I remembered the doll I had broken. I felt my way to the hearth and picked up the pieces. I tried vainly to put them together. Then my eyes filled with tears; for I realized what I had done, and for the first time I felt repentance and sorrow.

I learned a great many new words that day. I do not remember what they all were; but I do know that *mother, father, sister, teacher* were among them — words that were to make the world blossom for me, "like Aaron's rod, with flowers." It would have been difficult to find a happier child than I was as I lay in my crib at the close of that eventful day and lived over the joys it had brought me, and for the first time longed for a new day to come.

FOCUSING ON CONTENT

1. In paragraph 6, Keller writes, "One day, while I was playing with my new doll, Miss Sullivan put my big rag doll into my lap also, spelled 'd-o-l-l' and tried to make me understand that 'd-o-l-l' applied to both." Why do you think Miss Sullivan placed a different doll in her lap? What essential fact about language did the action demonstrate to Keller?

2. In paragraph 6, Keller also tells us that in trying to learn the difference between "m-u-g" and "w-a-t-e-r" she "persisted in confounding the two" terms. In a letter to her home institution, Sullivan elaborated on this confusion, revealing that it was caused by Keller thinking that both words meant "drink." How in paragraph 7 does Keller finally come to understand these words? What does she come to understand about the relationship between them?

3. In paragraph 8, after the experience at the well, Keller comes to believe that "everything had a name, and each name gave birth to a new thought." Reflect on that statement. Does she mean that the process of naming leads to thinking?

FOCUSING ON WRITING

1. Keller realized that over time words would make her world open up for her. Identify the parts of speech of her first words. In what ways do these parts of speech open up one's world? Explain how these words or parts of speech provide insights into the nature of writing. How does Keller's early language use compare to her use of English in her essay?

2. While it is fairly easy to see how Keller could learn the names of concrete items, it may be more difficult for us to understand how she learned about her emotions. What does her difficulty in coming to terms with abstractions — such as love, bitterness, frustration, repentance, sorrow — tell us as writers about the strategies we need to use to effectively convey emotions and feelings to our readers? In considering your answer, examine the diction Keller uses in her essay. (Glossary: *Diction*)

3. In paragraph 3, Keller uses the metaphor of being lost in a fog to explain her feeling of helplessness and her frustration at not being able to communicate. Perhaps you have had a similar feeling about an inability to communicate with parents or teachers or of not being able to realize some other longed-for goal. Try using a fresh metaphor to describe feelings you might have had that are similar to Keller's. (Glossary: *Figures of Speech*) Before beginning, however, think about why the fog metaphor works so well.

LANGUAGE IN ACTION

A recent series of books by Rich Hall "and friends" gives lists of so-called *sniglets*, words for things without names. Notice that *sniglet* is itself a made-up word. Do you know of a person, place, thought, or action that is without a word but needs one? What word would you give it? What does the experience of "naming the unnamed" reveal about the desirability of an extensive vocabulary? What does it reveal about the possibilities and limitations of language? What do the following sniglets reveal about the authors' understanding of the world?

---

elbonics (*el bon' iks*) n. The actions of two people maneuvering for one armrest in a movie theater.

glackett (*glak' it*) n. The noisy ball inside a spray-paint can.

gription (*grip' shun*) n. The sound of sneakers squeaking against the floor during basketball games.

hangle (*han' gul*) n. A cluster of coat hangers.

lactomangulation (*lak' to man gyu lay' shun*) n. Manhandling the "open here" spout on a milk carton so badly that one has to resort to using the "illegal" side.

motspur (*mot' sper*) n. The pesky fourth wheel on a shopping cart that refuses to cooperate with the other three.

napjerk (*nap' jurk*) n. The sudden convulsion of the body just as one is about to doze off.

optortionist (*op tor' shun ist*) n. The kid in school who can turn his eyelids inside
    out.

psychophobia (*sy ko fo' be uh*) n. The compulsion, when using a host's bathroom,
    to peer behind the shower curtain and make sure no one is waiting for you.

xiidigitation (*ksi dij I tay' shun*) n. The practice of trying to determine the
    year a movie was made by deciphering the roman numerals at the end of the
    credits.

WRITING SUGGESTIONS

1. It could be said that we process our world in terms of our language. Using a
   variety of examples from your own experience, write an essay illustrating the
   validity of this observation. For example, aside from the photographs you
   took on your last vacation, your trip exists only in the words you use to describe it, whether in conversations or in writing.

2. Helen Keller explains that she felt no remorse when she shattered her doll.
   "In the still, dark world in which I lived there was no strong sentiment or
   tenderness" (6) she recalls. However, once she understood that things had
   names, Keller was able to feel repentance and sorrow. In your own words, try
   to describe why you think her feelings changed. Before you begin to write,
   you may want to reread your Writing to Discover entry for the Keller article.
   You may also want to discuss this issue with classmates or your instructor and
   do some research of your own into the ways language alters perception
   among people who are blind or deaf.

On Being 17, Bright, and Unable to Read

DAVID RAYMOND

When the following article appeared in the New York Times *in 1976, David Raymond was a high school student in Connecticut. In 1981, Raymond graduated from Curry College in Milton, Massachusetts, one of the few colleges with learning-disability programs at the time. He and his family now live in Fairfield, Connecticut, where he works as a builder.*

In his essay, Raymond shares his story of being language challenged in a world of readers. Even though testing revealed that Raymond had above-average intelligence, he always felt "dumb" in school. In his plea for understanding for other dyslexic children, he poignantly discusses the emotionally charged difficulties his own dyslexia caused and the many problems he experienced in school as a result.

WRITING TO DISCOVER: *One of the fundamental language arts skills that we are supposed to learn in school is how to read. How do you rate yourself as a reader? How dependent are you on reading in your everyday life? How would your life change if you were unable to read?*

One day a substitute teacher picked me to read aloud from the textbook. When I told her "No, thank you," she came unhinged. She thought I was acting smart, and told me so. I kept calm, and that got her madder and madder. We must have spent 10 minutes trying to solve the problem, and finally she got so red in the face I thought she'd blow up. She told me she'd see me after class.

Maybe someone like me was a new thing for that teacher. But she wasn't new to me. I've been through scenes like that all my life. You see, even though I'm 17 and a junior in high school, I can't read because I have dyslexia. I'm told I read "at a fourth-grade level," but from where I sit, that's not reading. You can't know what that means unless you've been there. It's not easy to tell how it feels when you can't read your homework assignments or the newspaper or a menu in a restaurant or even notes from your own friends.

My family began to suspect I was having problems almost from the first day I started school. My father says my early years in school were the worst years of his life. They weren't so good for me, either. As I look back on it now, I can't find the words to express how bad it really was. I wanted to die. I'd come home from school screaming, "I'm dumb. I'm dumb — I wish I were dead!"

I guess I couldn't read anything at all then — not even my own name — and they tell me I didn't talk as good as other kids. But what I remember about those days is that I couldn't throw a ball where it was supposed to go, I couldn't learn to swim, and I wouldn't learn to ride a bike, because no matter what anyone told me, I knew I'd fail.

Sometimes my teachers would try to be encouraging. When I couldn't   5 read the words on the board they'd say, "Come on, David, you know that word." Only I didn't. And it was embarrassing. I just felt dumb. And dumb was how the kids treated me. They'd make fun of me every chance they got, asking me to spell "cat" or something like that. Even if I knew how to spell it, I wouldn't; they'd only give me another word. Anyway, it was awful, because more than anything I wanted friends. On my birthday when I blew out the candles I didn't wish I could learn to read; what I wished for was that the kids would like me.

With the bad reports coming from school, and with me moaning about wanting to die and how everybody hated me, my parents began looking for help. That's when the testing started. The school tested me, the child-guidance center tested me, private psychiatrists tested me. Everybody knew something was wrong — especially me.

It didn't help much when they stuck a fancy name onto it. I couldn't pronounce it then — I was only in second grade — and I was ashamed to talk about it. Now it rolls off my tongue, because I've been living with it for a lot of years — dyslexia.

All through elementary school it wasn't easy. I was always having to do things that were "different," things the other kids didn't have to do. I had to go to a child psychiatrist, for instance.

One summer my family forced me to go to a camp for children with reading problems. I hated the idea, but the camp turned out pretty good, and I had a good time. I met a lot of kids who couldn't read and somehow that helped. The director of the camp said I had a higher I.Q. than 90 percent of the population. I didn't believe him.

About the worst thing I had to do in fifth and sixth grade was go to a   10 special education class in another school in our town. A bus picked me up, and I didn't like that at all. The bus also picked up emotionally disturbed kids and retarded kids. It was like going to a school for the retarded. I always worried that someone I knew would see me on that bus. It was a relief to go to the regular junior high school.

Life began to change a little for me then, because I began to feel better about myself. I found the teachers cared; they had meetings about me and I worked harder for them for a while. I began to work on the potter's wheel, making vases and pots that the teachers said were pretty good. Also, I got a letter for being on the track team. I could always run pretty fast.

At high school the teachers are good, and everyone is trying to help me. I've gotten honors some marking periods, and I've won a letter on the cross-country team. Next quarter I think the school might hold a show of my pottery. I've got some friends. But there are still some embarrassing times. For instance, every time there is writing in the class, I get up and go to the special education room. Kids ask me where I go all the time. Sometimes I say, "to Mars."

Homework is a real problem. During free periods in school I go into the special ed room and staff members read assignments to me. When I get home my mother reads to me. Sometimes she reads an assignment into a tape recorder, and then I go into my room and listen to it. If we have a novel or something like that to read, she reads it out loud to me. Then I sit down with her and we do the assignment. She'll write, while I talk my answers to her. Lately I've taken to dictating into a tape recorder, and then someone — my father, a private tutor, or my mother — types up what I've dictated. Whatever homework I do takes someone else's time, too. That makes me feel bad.

We had a big meeting in school the other day — eight of us, four from the guidance department, my private tutor, my parents, and me. The subject was me. I said I wanted to go to college, and they told me about colleges that have facilities and staff to handle people like me. That's nice to hear.

As for what happens after college, I don't know and I'm worried   15
about that. How can I make a living if I can't read? Who will hire me? How will I fill out the application form? The only thing that gives me any courage is the fact that I've learned about well-known people who couldn't read or had other problems and still made it. Like Albert Einstein, who didn't talk until he was 4 and flunked math. Like Leonardo da Vinci, who everyone seems to think had dyslexia.

I've told this story because maybe some teacher will read it and go easy on a kid in the classroom who has what I've got. Or, maybe some parent will stop nagging his kid, and stop calling him lazy. Maybe he's not lazy or dumb. Maybe he just can't read and doesn't know what's wrong. Maybe he's scared, like I was.

FOCUSING ON CONTENT

1. What is dyslexia? Is it essential for an understanding of the essay that we know more about dyslexia than Raymond tells us? Explain.

2. Before being diagnosed dyslexic, Raymond remembers feeling "dumb" and the other kids treating him as though he were. How intelligent do you think Raymond is? What evidence did you use to arrive at your conclusion? Explain.

3. What does Raymond's story tell us about the importance of our early childhood experiences, especially within our educational system?

4. What hope did Raymond find in the stories of Albert Einstein and Leonardo da Vinci?

FOCUSING ON WRITING

1. Raymond reveals the purpose of his story in the final paragraph. Why do you suppose he did not announce his intention earlier in the essay? (Glossary: *Purpose*)

2. How has Raymond organized his story? (Glossary: *Organization*)

3. Raymond uses many colloquial and idiomatic expressions, such as "she came unhinged" and "she got so red in the face I thought she'd blow up" (1). (Glossary: *Colloquial Expression*) Identify other examples of such diction. How do they affect your reaction to the essay?

4. How would you describe Raymond's tone in this essay? (Glossary: *Tone*)

LANGUAGE IN ACTION

To help teachers recognize students who might be dyslexic, *Dyslexia Teacher* has posted the following list of dyslexia symptoms on its Web site, www.dyslexia-teacher.com:

- a noticeable difference between the pupil's ability and their actual achievement;
- a family history of learning difficulties;
- difficulties with spelling;
- confusion over left and right;
- writing letters or numbers backwards;
- difficulties with math/science;
- difficulties with organizing themselves;
- difficulty following 2- or 3-step instructions.

Spelling gets singled out as one area that is important to look at when diagnosing dyslexia. According to *Dyslexia Teacher*,

> Spelling is the activity which causes most difficulty for dyslexic children. The observation of spelling errors in short, simple words is the way in which most dyslexic children first come to our attention. Examples of words which cause particular difficulty are: *any, many, island, said, they, because, enough,* and *friend.* Other words will sometimes be spelt in the way that you would expect them to be spelt if our spelling system were rational, for example, *does/dus, please/pleeze, knock/nock, search/serch, journey/jerney,* etc.
>
> Dyslexic children also experience difficulties with "jumbled spellings." These are spelling attempts in which all the correct letters are present, but are written in the wrong order. Examples include *dose/does, freind/friend, siad/said, bule/blue, becuase/because,* and *wores/worse.* "Jumbled spellings" show that the child is experiencing difficulty with visual memory. Non-dyslexic children and adults often use their visual memory when trying to remember a difficult spelling: they write down two or three possible versions of the word on a spare piece of paper and see which spelling "looks

right." They are relying on their visual memory to help them, but the visual memory of a dyslexic child may not be adequate for this task.

After hearing of the difficulties that dyslexic children and adults experience, are you better able to empathize with David Raymond's experiences? Imagine you are dyslexic and discuss with your class what it would feel like for you to exhibit some or all of the symptoms described.

WRITING SUGGESTIONS

1. Using your response to the Writing to Discover prompt for the Raymond selection as a starting point, write an essay about the importance of reading and literacy in your life.

2. Imagine that you are away at school. Recently you were caught in a speed trap — you were going seventy miles per hour in a fifty-mile-per-hour zone — and have just lost your license; you will not be able to drive home this coming weekend, as you had planned. Write two letters in which you explain why you will not be able to go home, one to your parents and the other to your best friend. Your audience is different in each case, so be sure to choose your diction accordingly. Try to imitate Raymond's informal yet serious and sincere tone in one of your letters.

Language and Thought

Susanne K. Langer

Susanne K. Langer was born in New York City in 1895 and attended Radcliffe College. There she studied philosophy, an interest she maintained until her death in 1985. She stayed in Cambridge, Massachusetts, as a tutor at Harvard University from 1927 to 1942. Langer then taught at the University of Delaware, Columbia University, and Connecticut College, where she remained from 1954 until the end of her distinguished teaching career. Her books include Philosophy in a New Key: A Study of the Symbolism of Reason, Rite, and Art *(1942),* Feeling and Form *(1953), and* Mind: An Essay in Human Feeling *(1967).*

In the following essay, which originally appeared in Ms. *magazine, Langer explores how language separates humans from the rest of the animal kingdom. She contends that the use of symbols — in addition to the use of signs that animals also use — frees humans not only to react to their environment but also to think about it. Moreover, symbols allow us to create imagery and ideas not directly related to the real world, so that we can plan, imagine, and communicate abstractions — to do, in essence, the things that make us human.*

WRITING TO DISCOVER: *Young children must often communicate — and be communicated to — without the use of language. To a child, for example, a danger sticker on a bottle can mean "don't touch," and a green traffic light might mean "the car will start again." Think back to your own childhood experiences. Write about how communication took place without language. What associations were you able to make?*

A symbol is not the same thing as a sign; that is a fact that psychologists and philosophers often overlook. All intelligent animals use signs; so do we. To them as well as to us sounds and smells and motions are signs of food, danger, the presence of other beings, or of rain or storm. Furthermore, some animals not only attend to signs but produce them for the benefit of others. Dogs bark at the door to be let in; rabbits thump to call each other; the cooing of doves and the growl of a wolf defending his kill are unequivocal signs of feelings and intentions to be reckoned with by other creatures.

We use signs just as animals do, though with considerably more elaboration. We stop at red lights and go on green; we answer calls and bells, watch the sky for coming storms, read trouble or promise or anger in each other's eyes. That is animal intelligence raised to the human level. Those of us who are dog lovers can probably all tell wonderful stories of

how high our dogs have sometimes risen in the scale of clever sign interpretation and sign using.

A sign is anything that announces the existence or the imminence of
some event, the presence of a thing or a person, or a change in the state
of affairs. There are signs of the weather, signs of danger, signs of future
good or evil, signs of what the past has been. In every case a sign is
closely bound up with something to be noted or expected in experience.
It is always a part of the situation to which it refers, though the reference
may be remote in space and time. In so far as we are led to note or expect
the signified event we are making correct use of a sign. This is the essence
of rational behavior, which animals show in varying degrees. It is entirely
realistic, being closely bound up with the actual objective course of
history — learned by experience, and cashed in or voided by further experience.

If man had kept to the straight and narrow path of sign using, he
would be like the other animals, though perhaps a little brighter. He
would not talk, but grunt and gesticulate the point. He would make his
wishes known, give warnings, perhaps develop a social system like that of
bees and ants, with such a wonderful efficiency of communal enterprise
that all men would have plenty to eat, warm apartments — all exactly
alike and perfectly convenient — to live in, and everybody could and
would sit in the sun or by the fire, as the climate demanded, not talking
but just basking, with every want satisfied, most of his life. The young
would romp and make love, the old would sleep, the middle-aged would
do the routine work almost unconsciously and eat a great deal. But that
would be the life of a social, superintelligent, purely sign-using animal.

To us who are human, it does not sound very glorious. We want to   5
go places and do things, own all sorts of gadgets that we do not absolutely need, and when we sit down to take it easy we want to talk.
Rights and property, social position, special talents and virtues, and above
all our ideas, are what we live for. We have gone off on a tangent that
takes us far away from the mere biological cycle that animal generations
accomplish; and that is because we can use not only signs but symbols.

A symbol differs from a sign in that it does not announce the presence of the object, the being, condition, or whatnot, which is its meaning, but merely *brings this thing to mind*. It is not a mere "substitute
sign" to which we react as though it were the object itself. The fact is that
our reaction to hearing a person's name is quite different from our reaction to the person himself. There are certain rare cases where a symbol
stands directly for its meaning: in religious experience, for instance, the
Host is not only a symbol but a Presence. But symbols in the ordinary
sense are not mystic. They are the same sort of thing that ordinary signs
are; only they do not call our attention to something necessarily present
or to be physically dealt with — they call up merely a conception of the
thing they "mean."

The difference between a sign and a symbol is, in brief, that a sign causes us to think or act *in face* of the thing signified, whereas a symbol causes us to think *about* the thing symbolized. Therein lies the great importance of symbolism for human life, its power to make this life so different from any other animal biography that generations of men have found it incredible to suppose that they were of purely zoological origin. A sign is always embedded in reality, in a present that emerges from the actual past and stretches to the future; but a symbol may be divorced from reality altogether. It may refer to what is not the case, to a mere idea, a figment, a dream. It serves, therefore, to liberate thought from the immediate stimuli of a physically present world; and that liberation marks the essential difference between human and nonhuman mentality. Animals think, but they think *of* and *at* things; men think primarily *about* things. Words, pictures, and memory images are symbols that may be combined and varied in a thousand ways. The result is a symbolic structure whose meaning is a complex of all their respective meanings, and this kaleidoscope of *ideas* is the typical product of the human brain that we call the "stream of thought."

The process of transforming all direct experience into imagery or into that supreme mode of symbolic expression, language, has so completely taken possession of the human mind that it is not only a special talent but a dominant, organic need. All our sense impressions leave their traces in our memory not only as signs disposing our practical reactions in the future but also as symbols, images representing our *ideas* of things; and the tendency to manipulate ideas, to combine and abstract, mix and extend them by playing with symbols, is man's outstanding characteristic. It seems to be what his brain most naturally and spontaneously does. Therefore his primitive mental function is not judging reality, but *dreaming his desires.*

Dreaming is apparently a basic function of human brains, for it is free and unexhausting like our metabolism, heartbeat, and breath. It is easier to dream than not to dream, as it is easier to breathe than to refrain from breathing. The symbolic character of dreams is fairly well established. Symbol mongering, on this ineffectual, uncritical level, seems to be instinctive, the fulfillment of an elementary need rather than the purposeful exercise of a high and difficult talent.

The special power of man's mind rests on the evolution of this special   10
activity, not on any transcendently high development of animal intelligence. We are not immeasurably higher than other animals; we are different. We have a biological need and with it a biological gift that they do not share.

Because man has not only the ability but the constant need of *conceiving* what has happened to him, what surrounds him, what is demanded of him — in short, of symbolizing nature, himself, and his hopes and fears — he has a constant and crying need of *expression*. What he cannot express, he cannot conceive; what he cannot conceive is chaos, and fills him with terror.

If we bear in mind this all-important craving for expression we get a new picture of man's behavior; for from this trait spring his powers and his weaknesses. The process of symbolic transformation that all our experiences undergo is nothing more nor less than the process of *conception*, underlying the human faculties of abstraction and imagination.

When we are faced with a strange or difficult situation, we cannot react directly, as other creatures do, with flight, aggression, or any such simple instinctive pattern. Our whole reaction depends on how we manage to conceive the situation — whether we cast it in a definite dramatic form, whether we see it as a disaster, a challenge, a fulfillment of doom, or a fiat of the Divine Will. In words or dreamlike images, in artistic or religious or even in cynical form, we must *construe* the events of life. There is great virtue in the figure of speech, "I can *make* nothing of it," to express a failure to understand something. Thought and memory are processes of *making* the thought content and the memory image; the pattern of our ideas is given by the symbols through which we express them. And in the course of manipulating those symbols we inevitably distort the original experience, as we abstract certain features of it, embroider and reinforce those features with other ideas, until the conception we project on the screen of memory is quite different from anything in our real history.

Conception is a necessary and elementary process; what we do with our conceptions is another story. That is the entire history of human culture — of intelligence and morality, folly and superstition, ritual, language, and the arts — all the phenomena that set man apart from, and above, the rest of the animal kingdom. As the religious mind has to make all human history a drama of sin and salvation in order to define its own moral attitudes, so a scientist wrestles with the mere presentation of "the facts" before he can reason about them. The process of *envisaging* facts, values, hopes, and fears underlies our whole behavior pattern; and this process is reflected in the evolution of an extraordinary phenomenon found always, and only, in human societies — the phenomenon of language.

Language is the highest and most amazing achievement of the symbolistic human mind. The power it bestows is almost inestimable, for without it anything properly called "thought" is impossible. The birth of language is the dawn of humanity. The line between man and beast — between the highest ape and the lowest savage — is the language line. Whether the primitive Neanderthal man was anthropoid or human depends less on his cranial capacity, his upright posture, or even his use of tools and fire, than on one issue we shall probably never be able to settle — whether or not he spoke.

In all physical traits and practical responses, such as skills and visual judgments, we can find a certain continuity between animal and human

15

mentality. Sign using is an ever evolving, ever improving function throughout the whole animal kingdom, from the lowly worm that shrinks into his hole at the sound of an approaching foot, to the dog obeying his master's command, and even to the learned scientist who watches the movements of an index needle.

The continuity of the sign-using talent has led psychologists to the belief that language is evolved from the vocal expressions, grunts and coos and cries, whereby animals vent their feelings or signal their fellows; that man has elaborated this sort of communion to the point where it makes a perfect exchange of ideas possible.

I do not believe that this doctrine of the origin of language is correct. The essence of language is symbolic, not signific; we use it first and most vitally to formulate and hold ideas in our own minds. Conception, not social control, is its first and foremost benefit.

Watch a young child that is just learning to speak play with a toy; he says the name of the object, e.g.: "Horsey! horsey! horsey!" over and over again, looks at the object, moves it, always saying the name to himself or to the world at large. It's quite a time before he talks to anyone in particular; he talks first of all to himself. This is his way of forming and fixing the *conception* of the object in his mind, and around this conception all his knowledge of it grows. *Names* are the essence of language; for the *name* is what abstracts the conception of the horse from the horse itself, and lets the mere idea recur at the speaking of the name. This permits the conception gathered from one horse experience to be exemplified again by another instance of a horse, so that the notion embodied in the name is a general notion.

To this end, the baby uses a word long before he *asks* for the object; when he wants his horsey he is likely to cry and fret, because he is reacting to an actual environment, not forming ideas. He uses the animal language of *signs* for his wants; talking is still a purely symbolic process — its practical value has not really impressed him yet.

Language need not be vocal; it may be purely visual, like written language, or even tactual, like the deaf-mute system of speech; but it *must be denotative*. The sounds, intended or unintended, whereby animals communicate do not constitute a language because they are signs, not names. They never fall into an organic pattern, a meaningful syntax of even the most rudimentary sort, as all language seems to do with a sort of driving necessity. That is because signs refer to actual situations, in which things have obvious relations to each other that require only to be noted; but symbols refer to ideas, which are not physically there for inspection, so their connections and features have to be represented. This gives all true language a natural tendency toward growth and development, which seems almost like a life of its own. Languages are not invented; they grow with our need for expression.

In contrast, animal "speech" never has a structure. It is merely an emotional response. Apes may greet their ration of yams with a shout of "Nga!" But they do not say "Nga" between meals. If they could *talk about* their yams instead of just saluting them, they would be the most primitive men instead of the most anthropoid of beasts. They would have ideas, and tell each other things true and false, rational or irrational; they would make plans and invent laws and sing their own praises, as men do.

FOCUSING ON CONTENT

1. Define what Langer refers to as a sign. Define symbol. (Glossary: *Definition* and *Symbol*) Why is the distinction between the two so important?

2. What is the essential difference between the way animals "think" and the way humans think? How has that changed human mental function at an organic level? How has the biological change affected our development in relation to animals?

3. What does Langer mean when she says, "In words or dreamlike images . . . we must *construe* the events of life" (13)? How does this claim relate to the process of conception?

4. Comment on the statements Langer makes in paragraph 11. As she claims, do you feel the need to conceptualize and to express? Explain.

FOCUSING ON WRITING

1. What is Langer's thesis in this essay? Where does she state it? (Glossary: *Thesis*)

2. What examples of signs and symbols does Langer provide? (Glossary: *Examples*) How effective do you find her examples? What examples of signs and symbols can you provide?

3. In paragraph 11, Langer states: "What [man] cannot express, he cannot conceive; what he cannot conceive is chaos, and fills him with terror." Review the first ten paragraphs of the essay. How does Langer prepare the reader to accept this abstract and bold statement? (Glossary: *Concrete/Abstract* and *Organization*)

LANGUAGE IN ACTION

Review what Langer has to say about signs and symbols, particularly the differences she draws between them in paragraphs 6 and 7. Then examine the following graphics. What does each graphic mean? Which ones are signs, and which are symbols? Be prepared to defend your conclusions in a classroom discussion.

WRITING SUGGESTIONS

1. Using symbols for expression need not involve explicit use of language. Within the framework of a particular society, many methods of symbolic communication are possible. When you walk across campus, for example, what do you want to communicate to others even if you do not speak to anyone? How do you communicate this message? For instance, how does your facial expression, clothing, hairstyle, or jewelry serve as a symbol? Write an essay in which you describe and analyze the nonlanguage symbols you use to communicate.

2. It has often been said that language reveals the character of the person using it. Write an essay in which you analyze the character of a particular writer based on his or her use of language. You may want to comment on a writer in this text whose article you have read, such as Langer. Consider such areas as vocabulary range, sentence variety, slang, correct grammar, technical language, and tone. What do these elements tell you about the character of the person? (Glossary: *Slang, Technical Language,* and *Tone*)

3. Research recent experiments involving animal communication. Some experiments, for example, reveal the gorilla's use of sign language; others show that dolphins have complex communication systems that we are only beginning to understand. Write a paper in which you summarize the research and discuss how it relates to Langer's ideas about human and animal use of signs and symbols. Did you find any evidence that certain animals can use basic symbols? Is there a possibility that gorillas and dolphins can think *about* things rather than simply *of* and *at* them?

A Brief History of English

PAUL ROBERTS

Paul Roberts (1917–1967) was a linguist, teacher, and writer. Born in California, he received his B.A. from San Jose State University and his M.A. and Ph.D. from the University of California at Berkeley. After teaching at San Jose State and then Cornell University, Roberts became director of language at the Center of American Studies in Rome. His books include Understanding Grammar *(1954),* Patterns of English *(1956),* Understanding English *(1958),* English Sentences *(1962), and* English Syntax *(1964).*

In the following selection from Understanding English, *Roberts recounts the major events in the history of England and discusses their relationship to the development of the English language. He tells how the people who invaded England influenced the language and how, in recent times, the rapid spread of English has resulted in its becoming a major world language.*

WRITING TO DISCOVER: *Think about a work you have read that was written in nonmodern English, such as those by Shakespeare, Chaucer, Swift, or their contemporaries. How difficult was it for you to understand the work? Write about what it taught you about the evolution of the English language.*

HISTORICAL BACKGROUNDS

No understanding of the English language can be very satisfactory without a notion of the history of the language. But we shall have to make do with just a notion. The history of English is long and complicated, and we can only hit the high spots.

The history of our language begins a little after A.D. 600. Everything before that is pre-history, which means that we can guess at it but can't prove much. For a thousand years or so before the birth of Christ our linguistic ancestors were savages wandering through the forests of northern Europe. Their language was a part of the Germanic branch of the Indo-European Family.

At the time of the Roman Empire — say, from the beginning of the Christian Era to around A.D. 400 — the speakers of what was to become English were scattered along the northern coast of Europe. They spoke a dialect of Low German. More exactly, they spoke several different dialects, since they were several different tribes. The names given to the tribes who got to England are *Angles, Saxons,* and *Jutes.* For convenience, we can refer to them as Anglo-Saxons.

The first contact with civilization was a rather thin acquaintance with the Roman Empire on whose borders they lived. Probably some of the Anglo-Saxons wandered into the Empire occasionally, and certainly Roman merchants and traders traveled among the tribes. At any rate, this period was the first of our many borrowings from Latin. Such words as *kettle, wine, cheese, butter, cheap, plum, gem, bishop, church* were borrowed at this time. They show something of the relationship of the Anglo-Saxons with the Romans. The Anglo-Saxons were learning, getting their first taste of civilization.

They still had a long way to go, however, and their first step was to   5
help smash the civilization they were learning from. In the fourth century the Roman power weakened badly. While the Goths were pounding away at the Romans in the Mediterranean countries, their relatives, the Anglo-Saxons, began to attack Britain.

The Romans had been the ruling power in Britain since A.D. 43. They had subjugated the Celts whom they found living there and had succeeded in setting up a Roman administration. The Roman influence did not extend to the outlying parts of the British Isles. In Scotland, Wales, and Ireland the Celts remained free and wild, and they made periodic forays against the Romans in England. Among other defense measures, the Romans built the famous Roman Wall to ward off the tribes in the north.

Even in England the Roman power was thin. Latin did not become the language of the country as it did in Gaul and Spain. The mass of people continued to speak Celtic, with Latin and the Roman civilization it contained in use as a top dressing.

In the fourth century, troubles multiplied for the Romans in Britain. Not only did the untamed tribes of Scotland and Wales grow more and more restive, but the Anglo-Saxons began to make pirate raids on the eastern coast. Furthermore, there was growing difficulty everywhere in the Empire, and the legions in Britain were siphoned off to fight elsewhere. Finally, in A.D. 410, the last Roman ruler in England, bent on becoming emperor, left the islands and took the last of the legions with him. The Celts were left in possession of Britain but almost defenseless against the impending Anglo-Saxon attack.

Not much is surely known about the arrival of the Anglo-Saxons in England. According to the best early source, the eighth-century historian Bede, the Jutes came in 449 in response to a plea from the Celtic king, Vortigern, who wanted their help against the Picts attacking from the north. The Jutes subdued the Picts but then quarreled and fought with Vortigern, and, with reinforcements from the Continent, settled permanently in Kent. Somewhat later the Angles established themselves in eastern England and the Saxons in the south and west. Bede's account is plausible enough, and these were probably the main lines of the invasion.

We do know, however, that the Angles, Saxons, and Jutes were a   10
long time securing themselves in England. Fighting went on for as long as a hundred years before the Celts in England were all killed, driven into

Wales, or reduced to slavery. This is the period of King Arthur, who was not entirely mythological. He was a Romanized Celt, a general, though probably not a king. He had some success against the Anglo-Saxons, but it was only temporary. By 550 or so the Anglo-Saxons were firmly established. English was in England.

OLD ENGLISH

All this is pre-history, so far as the language is concerned. We have no record of the English language until after 600, when the Anglo-Saxons were converted to Christianity and learned the Latin alphabet. The conversion began, to be precise, in the year 597 and was accomplished within thirty or forty years. The conversion was a great advance for the Anglo-Saxons, not only because of the spiritual benefits but because it reestablished contact with what remained of Roman civilization. This civilization didn't amount to much in the year 600, but it was certainly superior to anything in England up to that time.

It is customary to divide the history of the English language into three periods: Old English, Middle English, and Modern English. Old English runs from the earliest records — i.e., seventh century — to about 1100; Middle English from 1100 to 1450 or 1500; Modern English from 1500 to the present day. Sometimes Modern English is further divided into Early Modern, 1500–1700, and Late Modern, 1700 to the present.

When England came into history, it was divided into several more or less autonomous kingdoms, some of which at times exercised a certain amount of control over the others. In the century after the conversion the most advanced kingdom was Northumbria, the area between the Humber River and the Scottish border. By A.D. 700 the Northumbrians had developed a respectable civilization, the finest in Europe. It is sometimes called the Northumbrian Renaissance, and it was the first of the several renaissances through which Europe struggled upward out of the ruins of the Roman Empire. It was in this period that the best of the Old English literature was written, including the epic poem *Beowulf.*

In the eighth century, Northumbrian power declined, and the center of influence moved southward to Mercia, the kingdom of the Midlands. A century later the center shifted again, and Wessex, the country of the West Saxons, became the leading power. The most famous king of the West Saxons was Alfred the Great, who reigned in the second half of the ninth century, dying in 901. He was famous not only as a military man and administrator but also as a champion of learning. He founded and supported schools and translated or caused to be translated many books from Latin into English. At this time also much of the Northumbrian literature of two centuries earlier was copied in West Saxon. Indeed, the great bulk of Old English writing which has come down to us is in the West Saxon dialect of 900 or later.

In the military sphere, Alfred's great accomplishment was his success-   15
ful opposition to the Viking invasions. In the ninth and tenth centuries,
the Norsemen emerged in their ships from their homelands in Denmark
and the Scandinavian peninsula. They traveled far and attacked and plun-
dered at will and almost with impunity. They ravaged Italy and Greece,
settled in France, Russia, and Ireland, colonized Iceland and Greenland,
and discovered America several centuries before Columbus. Nor did they
overlook England.

After many years of hit-and-run raids, the Norsemen landed an army
on the east coast of England in the year 866. There was nothing much to
oppose them except the Wessex power led by Alfred. The long struggle
ended in 877 with a treaty by which a line was drawn roughly from the
northwest of England to the southeast. On the eastern side of the line
Norse rule was to prevail. This was called the Danelaw. The western side was
to be governed by Wessex.

The linguistic result of all this was a considerable injection of Norse
into the English language. Norse was at this time not so different from
English as Norwegian or Danish is now. Probably speakers of English
could understand, more or less, the language of the newcomers who had
moved into eastern England. At any rate, there was considerable inter-
change and word borrowing. Examples of Norse words in the English
language are *sky, give, law, egg, outlaw, leg, ugly, scant, sly, crawl, scowl,
take, thrust*. There are hundreds more. We have even borrowed some
pronouns from Norse — *they, their*, and *them*. These words were borrowed first by the eastern and northern dialects and then in the course of
hundreds of years made their way into English generally.

It is supposed also — indeed, it must be true — that the Norsemen
influenced the sound structure and the grammar of English. But this is
hard to demonstrate in detail.

A SPECIMEN OF OLD ENGLISH

We may now have an example of Old English. The favorite illustration is the Lord's Prayer, since it needs no translation. This has come to
us in several different versions. Here is one:

Fæder ure,
þou þe eart on heofonum,
si þin nama gehalgod.
Tobecume þin rice.
Gewurþe ðin willa on eor ðan swa swa on heofenum.
Urne gedæghwamlican hlaf syle us to dæg.
And forgyf us ure gyltas, swa swa we forgyfa ðurum gyltendum.
And ne gelæd þu us on costnunge,
ac alys us of yfele. Soþlice.

Some of the differences between this and Modern English are merely   20
differences in orthography. For instance, the sign *æ* is what Old English
writers used for a vowel sound like that in modern *hat* or *and*. The *th*
sounds of modern *thin* or *then* are represented in Old English by *þ* or *ð*.
But of course there are many differences in sound too. *Ure* is the ancestor
of modern *our*, but the first vowel was like that in *too* or *ooze*. *Hlaf* is
modern *loaf*; we had dropped the *h* sound and changed the vowel, which
in *hlaf* was pronounced something like the vowel in *father*. Old English
had some sounds which we do not have. The sound represented by *y*
does not occur in Modern English. If you pronounce the vowel in *bit*
with your lips rounded, you may approach it.

In grammar, Old English was much more highly inflected than Modern English is. That is, there were more case endings for nouns, more
person and number endings for verbs, a more complicated pronoun system, various endings for adjectives, and so on. Old English nouns had
four cases — nominative, genitive, dative, accusative. Adjectives had five —
all these and an instrumental case besides. Present-day English has only
two cases for nouns — common case and possessive case. Adjectives now
have no case system at all. On the other hand, we now use a more rigid
word order and more structure words (prepositions, auxiliaries, and the
like) to express relationships than Old English did.

Some of this grammar we can see in the Lord's Prayer. *Heofonum*, for
instance, is a dative plural; the nominative singular was *heofon*. *Urne* is an
accusative singular; the nominative is *ure*. In *urum glytendum* both words
are dative plural. *Forgyfaþ* is the first person plural form of the verb. Word
order is different: "urne gedæghwamlican hlaf syle us" in place of "Give
us our daily bread." And so on.

In vocabulary Old English is quite different from Modern English.
Most of the Old English words are what we may call native English: that
is, words which have not been borrowed from other languages but which
have been a part of English ever since English was a part of Indo-European. Old English did certainly contain borrowed words. We have seen
that many borrowings were coming in from Norse. Rather large numbers
had been borrowed from Latin, too. Some of these were taken while the
Anglo-Saxons were still on the Continent (*cheese, butter, bishop, kettle,
etc.*); a large number came into English after the conversion (*angel, candle, priest, martyr, radish, oyster, purple, school, spend*, etc.). But the great
majority of Old English words were native English.

Now, on the contrary, the majority of words in English are borrowed,
taken mostly from Latin and French. Of the words in *The American College Dictionary* only about 14 percent are native. Most of these, to be
sure, are common, high-frequency words — *the, of, I, and, because, man,
mother, road*, etc.; of the thousand most common words in English, some
62 percent are native English. Even so, the modern vocabulary is very
much Latinized and Frenchified. The Old English vocabulary was not.

MIDDLE ENGLISH

Sometime between the years 1000 and 1200 various important   25
changes took place in the structure of English, and Old English became
Middle English. The political event which facilitated these changes was
the Norman Conquest. The Normans, as the name shows, came originally from Scandinavia. In the early tenth century they established themselves in northern France, adopted the French language, and developed a
vigorous kingdom and a very passable civilization. In the year 1066, led
by Duke William, they crossed the Channel and made themselves masters
of England. For the next several hundred years, England was ruled by
kings whose first language was French.

One might wonder why, after the Norman Conquest, French did not
become the national language, replacing English entirely. The reason is
that the Conquest was not a national migration, as the earlier Anglo-
Saxon invasion had been. Great numbers of Normans came to England,
but they came as rulers and landlords. French became the language of the
court, the language of the nobility, the language of polite society, the language of literature. But it did not replace English as the language of the
people. There must always have been hundreds of towns and villages in
which French was never heard except when visitors of high station passed
through.

But English, though it survived as the national language, was profoundly changed after the Norman Conquest. Some of the changes — in
sound structure and grammar — would no doubt have taken place
whether there had been a Conquest or not. Even before 1066 the case
system of English nouns and adjectives was becoming simplified; people
came to rely more on word order and prepositions than on inflectional
endings to communicate their meanings. The process was speeded up by
sound changes which caused many of the endings to sound alike. But no
doubt the Conquest facilitated the change. German, which didn't experience a Norman Conquest, is today rather highly inflected compared to its
cousin English.

But it is in vocabulary that the effects of the Conquest are most obvious. French ceased, after a hundred years or so, to be the native language
of very many people in England, but it continued — and continues still —
to be a zealously cultivated second language, the mirror of elegance and
civilization. When one spoke English, one introduced not only French
ideas and French things but also their French names. This was not only
easy but socially useful. To pepper one's conversation with French expressions was to show that one was well-bred, elegant, *au courant.* The
last sentence shows that the process is not yet dead. By using *au courant*
instead of, say, *abreast of things,* the writer indicates that he is no dull clod
who knows only English but an elegant person aware of how things are
done in *le haut monde.*

Thus French words came into English, all sorts of them. There were words to do with government: *parliament, majesty, treaty, alliance, tax, government;* church words: *parson, sermon, baptism, incense, crucifix, religion;* words for foods: *veal, beef, mutton, bacon, jelly, peach, lemon, cream, biscuit;* colors: *blue, scarlet, vermilion;* household words: *curtain, chair, lamp, towel, blanket, parlor;* play words: *dance, chess, music, leisure, conversation;* literary words: *story, romance, poet, literary;* learned words: *study, logic, grammar, noun, surgeon, anatomy, stomach;* just ordinary words of all sorts; *nice, second, very, age, bucket, gentle, final, fault, flower, cry, count, sure, move, surprise, plain.*

All these and thousands more poured into the English vocabulary   30
between 1100 and 1500 until, at the end of that time, many people must have had more French words than English at their command. This is not to say that English became French. English remained English in sound structure and in grammar, though these also felt the ripples of French influence. The very heart of the vocabulary, too, remained English. Most of the high-frequency words — the pronouns, the prepositions, the conjunctions, the auxiliaries, as well as a great many ordinary nouns and verbs and adjectives — were not replaced by borrowings.

Middle English, then, was still a Germanic language, but it differed from Old English in many ways. The sound system and the grammar changed a good deal. Speakers made less use of case systems and other inflectional devices and relied more on word order and structure words to express their meanings. This is often said to be a simplification, but it isn't really. Languages don't become simpler; they merely exchange one kind of complexity for another. Modern English is not a simple language, as any foreign speaker who tries to learn it will hasten to tell you.

For us Middle English is simpler than Old English just because it is closer to Modern English. It takes three or four months at least to learn to read Old English prose and more than that for poetry. But a week of good study should put one in touch with the Middle English poet Chaucer. Indeed, you may be able to make some sense of Chaucer straight off, though you would need instruction in pronunciation to make it sound like poetry. Here is a famous passage from the *General Prologue to the Canterbury Tales,* fourteenth century:

> Ther was also a nonne, a Prioresse,
> That of hir smyling was ful symple and coy,
> Hir gretteste oath was but by Seinte Loy,
> And she was cleped[1] Madame Eglentyne.
> Ful wel she song the service dyvync,
> Entuned in hir nose ful semely.

---

1. named.

And Frenshe she spak ful faire and fetisly,[2]
After the scole of Stratford-atte-Bowe,
For Frenshe of Parys was to hir unknowe.

EARLY MODERN ENGLISH

Sometime between 1400 and 1600 English underwent a couple of sound changes which made the language of Shakespeare quite different from that of Chaucer. Incidentally, these changes contributed much to the chaos in which English spelling now finds itself.

One change was the elimination of a vowel sound in certain unstressed positions at the end of words. For instance, the words *name, stone, wine, dance* were pronounced as two syllables by Chaucer but as just one by Shakespeare. The *e* in these words became, as we say, "silent." But it wasn't silent for Chaucer; it represented a vowel sound. So also the words *laughed, seemed, stored* would have been pronounced by Chaucer as two-syllable words. The change was an important one because it affected thousands of words and gave a different aspect to the whole language.

The other change is what is called the Great Vowel Shift. This was a   35
systematic shifting of half a dozen vowels and diphthongs in stressed syllables. For instance, the word *name* had in Middle English a vowel something like that in the modern word *father; wine* had the vowel of modern *mean; he* was pronounced something like modern *hey; mouse* sounded like *moose; moon* had the vowel of *moan.* Again the shift was thoroughgoing and affected all the words in which these vowel sounds occurred. Since we still keep the Middle English system of spelling these words, the differences between Modern English and Middle English are often more real than apparent.

The vowel shift has meant also that we have come to use an entirely different set of symbols for representing vowel sounds than is used by writers of such languages as French, Italian, or Spanish, in which no such vowel shift occurred. If you come across a strange word — say, *bine* — in an English book, you will pronounce it according to the English system, with the vowel of *wine* or *dine.* But if you read *bine* in a French, Italian, or Spanish book, you pronounce it with the vowel of *mean* or *seen.*

These two changes, then, produced the basic differences between Middle English and Modern English. But there were several other developments that had an effect upon the language. One was the invention of printing, an invention introduced into England by William

---

2. elegantly.

Caxton in the year 1475. Where before books had been rare and costly, they suddenly became cheap and common. More and more people learned to read and write. This was the first of many advances in communication which have worked to unify languages and to arrest the development of dialect differences, though of course printing affects writing principally rather than speech. Among other things it hastened the standardization of spelling.

The period of Early Modern English — that is, the sixteenth and seventeenth centuries — was also the period of the English Renaissance, when people developed, on the one hand, a keen interest in the past and, on the other, a more daring and imaginative view of the future. New ideas multiplied, and new ideas meant new language. Englishmen had grown accustomed to borrowing words from French as a result of the Norman Conquest; now they borrowed from Latin and Greek. As we have seen, English had been raiding Latin from Old English times and before, but now the floodgates really opened, and thousands of words from the classical languages poured in. *Pedestrian, bonus, anatomy, contradict, climax, dictionary, benefit, multiply, exist, paragraph, initiate, scene, inspire* are random examples. Probably the average educated American today has more words from French in his vocabulary than from native English sources, and more from Latin than from French.

The greatest writer of the Early Modern English period is of course Shakespeare, and the best-known book is the King James Version of the Bible, published in 1611. The Bible (if not Shakespeare) has made many features of Early Modern English perfectly familiar to many people down to the present time, even though we do not use these features in present-day speech and writing. For instance, the old pronouns *thou* and *thee* have dropped out of use now, together with their verb forms, but they are still familiar to us in prayer and in Biblical quotations: "Whither thou goest, I will go." Such forms as *hath* and *doth* have been replaced by *has* and *does;* "Goes he hence tonight?" would now be "Is he going away tonight?"; Shakespeare's "Fie, on't, sirrah" would be "Nuts to that, Mac." Still, all these expressions linger with us because of the power of the works in which they occur.

It is not always realized, however, that considerable sound changes 40 have taken place between Early Modern English and the English of the present day. Shakespearian actors putting on a play speak the words, properly enough, in their modern pronunciation. But it is very doubtful that this pronunciation would be understood at all by Shakespeare. In Shakespeare's time, the word *reason* was pronounced like modern *raisin;* *face* had the sound of modern *glass;* the *l* in *would, should, palm* was pronounced. In these points and a great many others the English language has moved a long way from what it was in 1600.

RECENT DEVELOPMENTS

The history of English since 1700 is filled with many movements and countermovements, of which we can notice only a couple. One of these is the vigorous attempt made in the eighteenth century, and the rather half-hearted attempts made since, to regulate and control the English language. Many people of the eighteenth century, not understanding very well the forces which govern language, proposed to polish and prune and restrict English, which they felt was proliferating too wildly. There was much talk of an academy which would rule on what people could and could not say and write. The academy never came into being, but the eighteenth century did succeed in establishing certain attitudes which, though they haven't had much effect on the development of the language itself, have certainly changed the native speaker's feeling about the language.

In part, a product of the wish to fix and establish the language was the development of the dictionary. The first English dictionary was published in 1603; it was a list of 2,500 words briefly defined. Many others were published with gradual improvements until Samuel Johnson published his *English Dictionary* in 1755. This, steadily revised, dominated the field in England for nearly a hundred years. Meanwhile in America, Noah Webster published his dictionary in 1828, and before long dictionary publishing was big business in this country. The last century has seen the publication of one great dictionary: the twelve-volume *Oxford English Dictionary,* compiled in the course of seventy-five years through the labors of many scholars. We have also, of course, numerous commercial dictionaries which are as good as the public wants them to be if not, indeed, rather better.

Another product of the eighteenth century was the invention of "English grammar." As English came to replace Latin as the language of scholarship, it was felt that one should also be able to control and dissect it, parse and analyze it, as one could Latin. What happened in practice was that the grammatical description that applied to Latin was removed and superimposed on English. This was silly, because English is an entirely different kind of language, with its own forms and signals and ways of producing meaning. Nevertheless, English grammars on the Latin model were worked out and taught in the schools. In many schools they are still being taught. This activity is not often popular with school children, but it is sometimes an interesting and instructive exercise in logic. The principal harm in it is that it has tended to keep people from being interested in English and has obscured the real features of English structure.

But probably the most important force on the development of English in the modern period has been the tremendous expansion of English-speaking peoples. In 1500 English was a minor language, spoken by a few people on a small island. Now it is perhaps the greatest language of the world, spoken natively by over a quarter of a billion people and as a second language by many millions more. When we speak of English now, we must specify whether we mean American English, British English, Australian English, Indian English, or what, since the differences are considerable. The American cannot go to England or the Englishman to America confident that he will always understand and be understood. The Alabaman in Iowa or the Iowan in Alabama shows himself a foreigner every time he speaks. It is only because communication has become fast and easy that English in this period of its expansion has not broken into a dozen mutually unintelligible languages.

FOCUSING ON CONTENT

1. Why is Roberts careful to describe the relationship between historical events in England and the development of the English language? In what ways did the historical events affect the English language?

2. How would you characterize in social terms the French words that were brought into English by the Norman Conquest? In what areas of life did the French have the greatest influence?

3. Explain what changes the English language underwent as a result of the Great Vowel Shift. What is the importance of this linguistic phenomenon for the history of English?

4. Having read Roberts's essay, do you think it is helpful to your education to know something about the history of English? Why or why not?

FOCUSING ON WRITING

1. What is Roberts's thesis in this essay? (Glossary: *Thesis*) Where does he state it? Does he convince you of his thesis? Why or why not?

2. Roberts makes extensive use of examples. (Glossary: *Examples*) Why is his use of examples particularly appropriate for his topic? What did you learn about writing from reading an essay that is so reliant on examples?

3. Roberts wrote this essay in the 1950s, when people were less sensitive to racial and ethnic slurs in writing than they are today. (Glossary: *Biased Language*) Reread the first ten paragraphs, paying particular attention to Roberts's use of such words as *savages, untamed tribes,* and *civilization.* Do you find any of his diction offensive or see how others might find it so? (Glossary: *Diction*) Suggest specific ways to change Roberts's diction in order to improve the impression his writing makes on contemporary readers. How do you as a writer guard against biased writing?

LANGUAGE IN ACTION

The following passage from Frances Mayes's best-seller *Under the Tuscan Sun: At Home in Italy* (1996) refers to the etymology, or history, of the interesting word *boustrophedon.*

A few summers ago, a friend and I hiked in Majorca above Soller. We climbed across and through miles of dramatic, enormous olives on broad terraces. Up high, we came upon stone huts where the grove tenders sheltered themselves. Although we got lost and encountered a pacing bull in a meadow, we felt this immense peace all day, walking among those trees that looked and may have been a thousand years old. Walking these few curving acres here gives me the same feeling. Unnatural as it is, terracing has a natural feel to it. Some of the earliest methods of writing, called boustrophedon, run from right to left, then from left to right. If we were trained that way, it probably is a more efficient way to read. The etymology of the word reveals Greek roots meaning "to turn like an ox plowing." And that writing is like the rising terraces: The U-turn space required by an ox with plow suddenly loops up a level and you're going in the other direction.

Using your college dictionary, identify the language from which each of the following words was borrowed:

barbecue
buffalo
casino
decoy
ditto
fruit
hustle
marmalade
orangutan
posse
raccoon
veranda

WRITING SUGGESTIONS

1. During its relatively brief four-hundred-year history, American English has consistently been characterized by change. How is American English still changing today? Write about the effects, if any, the war in Iraq, the war on terrorism, the NASA space program, the drug culture, computers and other new technology, the women's movement, the global economy and community, or recent waves of immigration have had on American English.

2. In paragraph 1 Roberts writes, "No understanding of the English language can be very satisfactory without a notion of the history of the language." What exactly does Roberts mean by *understanding*? Write an essay in which you dispute or substantiate his claim.

Does a Finger Fing?

Nedra Newkirk Lamar

Freelance writer Nedra Newkirk Lamar writes extensively on the English language and on effective communication. She has authored a number of books on writing and speaking, including How to Speak the Written Word, Pronunciation of Bible Names and Places, *and* 1000 Hard and Easy Words Frequently Mispronounced. *Lamar knows that we learn how to form new words in English in many different ways. We add* -ment *to some verbs, for example, to form nouns like* excitement *and* development. *Or we combine words like* snow *and* board *to create* snowboard, *or shorten words like* referee, laboratory, *and* mathematics *to* ref, lab, *and* math. *As you may have expected, the rules for word formation are not always consistent. In the following essay, which first appeared in the* Christian Science Monitor *in February 1970, Lamar takes a close look at what happens when we add the suffix* -er *to words. Experience tells us that when we add* -er *to a word like* teach *we create the new word* teacher, *meaning "one who teaches." But, as Lamar points out, this is not always the case. With a twinkle in her eye, she reveals the incongruities that result when "rules" are applied mechanically.*

WRITING TO DISCOVER: *Many of us grew up memorizing the following traditional rhyme for* ie *and* ei *spellings:*

Write i *before* e
Except after c
Or when sounded like ay
As in neighbor *or* weigh.

But do you remember the exceptions? Does this little rhyme remind you of other "rules" you learned in school? What do you remember about learning to speak and write in English?

Everybody knows that a tongue-twister is something that twists the tongue, and a skyscraper is something that scrapes the sky, but is an eavesdropper someone who drops eaves? A thinker is someone who thinks but is a tinker someone who tinks? Is a clabber something that goes around clabbing?

Somewhere along the way we all must have had an English teacher who gave us the fascinating information that words that end in *-er* mean something or somebody who *does* something, like trapper, designer, or stopper.

A stinger is something that stings, but is a finger something that fings? Fing fang fung. Today I fing. Yesterday I fang. Day before yesterday I had already fung.

You'd expect eyes, then, to be called seers and ears to be hearers. We'd wear our shoes on our walkers and our sleeves on our reachers. But we don't. The only parts of the body that sound as if they might indicate what they're supposed to do are our fingers, which we've already counted out, our livers, and our shoulders. And they don't do what they sound as if they might. At least, I've never seen anyone use his shoulders for shoulding. You shoulder your way through a crowd, but you don't should your way. It's only in slang that we follow the pattern, when we smell with our smellers and kiss with our kissers.

The animal pattern seems to have more of a feeling for this formation 5 than people do, because insects actually do feel with their feelers. But do cats use their whiskers for whisking?

I've seen people mend socks and knit socks, but I've never seen anyone dolage a sock. Yet there must be people who do, else how could we have sock-dolagers?

Is a humdinger one who dings hums? And what is a hum anyway, and how would one go about dinging it? Maybe Winnie the Pooh could have told us. He was always humming hums, but A. A. Milne never tells us whether he also was fond of dinging them. He sang them but do you suppose he ever dang them?

Sometimes occupational names do reveal what the worker does, though. Manufacturers manufacture, miners mine, adjusters adjust — or at least try to. But does a grocer groce? Does a fruiterer fruiter? Does a butler buttle?

No, you just can't trust the English language. You can love it because it's your mother tongue. You can take pride in it because it's the language Shakespeare was dramatic in. You can thrill to it because it's the language Browning and Tennyson were poetic in. You can have fun with it because it's the language Dickens and Mark Twain and Lewis Carroll were funny in. You can revere it because it's the language Milton was majestic in. You can be grateful to it because it's the language the Magna Carta and the Declaration of Independence were expressed in.

But you just can't trust it! 10

FOCUSING ON CONTENT

1. What is the main idea in Lamar's essay, and where does she state it? (Glossary: *Thesis*)

2. What do you think Lamar means when she says, "you just can't trust the English language"?

3. What did you learn about the English language from reading Lamar's essay?

FOCUSING ON WRITING

1. As a reader, do you think Lamar was trying to tell you something, describe something for you, explain something to you, or convince you of something? (Glossary: *Purpose*) Explain.

2. Lamar's tone in this essay can best be described as playful. In what ways is this tone appropriate for her subject and purpose?

3. Lamar's opening paragraph consists of three rhetorical questions that focus on words that end in the suffix -*er*. (Glossary: *Rhetorical Question*) Did these questions engage you and start you thinking about the incongruities of the English language? How effective did you find this strategy for beginning an essay? (Glossary: *Beginnings and Endings*) Where else does Lamar use rhetorical questions in her essay?

4. One of the real strengths of Lamar's essay is her examples. (Glossary: *Examples*) What specifically do these well-chosen examples add to her essay? Which examples worked best for you? Explain why.

5. In paragraph 9, Lamar uses a number of strong verbs (Glossary: *Verb*) to explain all that there is to like about the English language. Identify each of these strong verbs. Now substitute the verb *like* for each of the verbs you identified. What is lost when you make this substitution?

LANGUAGE IN ACTION

Read the following English folktale, which is taken from Joseph Jacob's 1890 book *English Fairy Tales*. What do you learn about the nature of words from this story? Explain.

FROM "MASTER OF ALL MASTERS"

A girl once went to a fair to be hired as a servant. At last a funny-looking old gentleman engaged her and took her home to his house. When she got there he told her he had something to teach her for in his house he had his own names for things.

He said to her: "What will you call me?"

"Master or Mister or whatever you please, sir."

"You must call me 'Master of Masters.' And what would you call this?" pointing to his bed.

"Bed or couch or whatever you please, sir."

"No, that's my 'barnacle'. And what do you call these?" said he, pointing to his pants.

"Breeches or trousers or whatever you please, sir."

"You must call them 'squibs and crackers'. And what do you call her?" pointing to the cat.

"Kit or cat or whatever you please, sir."

"You must call her 'white-faced simminy.' And this now," showing the fire, "what would you call this?"

"Fire or flame or whatever you please, sir."

"You must call it 'hot cockalorum,' and what this?" he went on, pointing to the water.

"Water or wet or whatever you please, sir."

"No, 'pandalorum' is its name. And what do you call this?" asked he, as he pointed to the house.

"House or cottage or whatever you please, sir."

"You must call it 'high topper mountain.'"

That very night the servant woke her master up in a fright and said: "Master of all masters, get out of your barnacle and put on your squibs and crackers. For white-face simminy has got a spark of hot cockalorum on its tail, and unless you get some pandalorum high topper mountain will be all on hot cockalorum." . . . That's all.

WRITING SUGGESTIONS

1. Using Lamar's statement "you just can't trust the English language" as a starting point, write an essay in which you recount one or more of your own frustrating experiences with the English language. In what ways did you believe that the language had let you down? You may find it helpful to read what you wrote in response to the journal prompt for this selection before starting to write your essay.

2. In paragraph 9, Lamar lists many of the reasons why we can love or take pride in the English language. Do you agree with the reasons she lists? Why or why not? What reasons of your own can you add to Lamar's list? What do all these reasons say about the power of language in our lives? Write an essay in which you discuss the importance of language in your own life.

2

WRITERS
ON WRITING

Learning to write well is a demanding and difficult pursuit, but the ability to express exactly what you mean can be one of the most enjoyable and rewarding skills you can possess. And, as with any sought-after goal, there is plenty of help available for the aspiring writer. We have gathered some of the best of that advice, written by professional writers and respected teachers of writing. All writing is based on the accurate and sensitive use of language, and in that sense, is the ultimate benefit of language awareness.

The essays included in Writers on Writing are based on the writing process and current research and thinking on how writers go about their work. So, it is fitting that we begin with Maxine Hairston's excellent essay, "What Happens When People Write?" wherein she provides an overview of the writing process and explains how professional writers compose. A number of factors affect the type of writing process one follows — the two most important being explanatory and exploratory writing. "To put it briefly, although much too simply, explanatory writing *tends* to be about information; exploratory writing *tends* to be about ideas," she explains before delineating their different approaches.

The rest of the essays in this chapter look more deeply into the writer's tool bag. Linda Flower analyzes what we mean by audience: "The goal of the writer is to create a momentary common ground between the reader and the writer." She explains that writers need to know as much about their readers as possible so as to lessen the differences between writer and reader and make it easier for the writer to communicate effectively to a given audience. She then looks closer at what the writer must understand about the reader's knowledge, attitudes, and needs. Popular novelist and teacher of writing Anne Lamott recognizes that even though writers may start out with a firm purpose and clear thinking, rough drafts are inevitably very messy and very confused affairs. William Zinsser, the author of "Simplicity," makes the case for reducing the clutter that overwhelms contemporary prose and for writing simply. His advice, helpful to the experienced writer as well as to the beginner, is that writers must know what they want to say and think clearly as they start to write. In "The Maker's Eye: Revising Your Own Manuscripts," Donald M. Murray recognizes the need to produce a first draft, however messy, so as to begin the real job of writing. In fact, for him, as for almost all practicing writers, writing is revising. Finally, Pico Iyer, the popular travel writer, focuses on perhaps the smallest of all the writer's tools, the "humble comma," from which he suggests writing takes its very breath. That an established writer of Iyer's stature is so enamored of the comma encourages us all to review the rules for using commas and to be careful, especially in the editing stage of the writing process, to make sure we use each comma with precision and purpose.

We end the chapter with an essay by Marjorie Agosín, a poet and essayist, on the relationship between writing and culture. She writes poignantly about her need to continue to express herself in Spanish as a way of returning to her childhood experiences in Chile and retaining her cultural identity.

What Happens When People Write?

MAXINE HAIRSTON

Maxine Hairston is Professor Emerita of Rhetoric and Composition at the University of Texas at Austin, where she served as coordinator of advanced expository writing courses, director of first-year English, and associate dean of humanities. She is a past chair of the Conference on College Composition and Communication and has written many articles on rhetoric and teaching writing. She has also authored and coauthored several textbooks, including The Scott, Foresman Handbook for Writers, *6th ed. (2001).*

In the following selection, taken from Hairston's textbook Successful Writing *(2003), now in its fifth edition, she takes the mystery out of writing by giving an overview of the writing process. By looking at the way professional writers work, she shows us how to establish realistic expectations of what should happen each time we sit down to write. Next, Hairston focuses on the differences between two major types of writing — explanatory and exploratory — that writers should master and value equally. She explains how a writer's writing process can change depending on the type of writing someone is doing.*

WRITING TO DISCOVER: *Think about what happens when you sit down to write. Do you have one particular pen that you like to use, or do you compose on a personal computer? Where do you like to write? Do you have any special rituals that you go through before settling into your task? Briefly describe the process you go through from the time you make the decision to put an idea in writing (or are given an assignment) to the time that you submit final copy. Is the process roughly the same for all the different types of writing that you do? Explain.*

Many people who have trouble writing believe that writing is a mysterious process that the average person cannot master. They assume that anyone who writes well does so because of a magic mixture of talent and inspiration, and that people who are not lucky enough to have those gifts can never become writers. Thus they take an "either you have it or you don't" attitude that discourages them before they even start to write.

Like most myths, this one has a grain of truth in it, but only a grain. Admittedly the best writers are people with talent just as the best musicians or athletes or chemists are people with talent. But that qualification does not mean that only talented people can write well any more than it means that only a few gifted people can become good tennis players. Tennis coaches know differently. From experience, they know any reasonably well-coordinated and healthy person can learn to play a fairly good game of tennis if he or she will learn the principles of the game and work at putting them into practice. They help people become tennis players by showing them the strategies that experts use and by giving them criticism and reinforcement as they practice those strategies. In recent years, as we have learned more about the processes of working writers, many teachers have begun to work with their writing students in the same way.

AN OVERVIEW OF THE WRITING PROCESS

How Professional Writers Work

- Most writers don't wait for inspiration. They write whether they feel like it or not. Usually they write on a schedule, putting in regular hours just as they would on a job.
- Professional writers consistently work in the same places with the same tools — pencil, typewriter, or word processor. The physical details of writing are important to them so they take trouble to create a good writing environment for themselves.
- Successful writers work constantly at observing what goes on around them and have a system for gathering and storing material. They collect clippings, keep notebooks, or write in journals.
- Even successful writers need deadlines to make them work, just like everyone else.
- Successful writers make plans before they start to write, but they keep their plans flexible, subject to revision.
- Successful writers usually have some audience in mind and stay aware of that audience as they write and revise.
- Most successful writers work rather slowly; four to six double-spaced pages is considered a good day's work.
- Even successful writers often have trouble getting started; they expect it and don't panic.
- Successful writers seldom know precisely what they are going to write before they start, and they plan on discovering at least part of their content as they work. (See section below on explanatory and exploratory writing.)
- Successful writers stop frequently to reread what they've written and consider such rereading an important part of the writing process.
- Successful writers revise as they write and expect to do two or more drafts of anything they write.
- Like ordinary mortals, successful writers often procrastinate and feel guilty about it; unlike less experienced writers, however, most of them have a good sense of how long they can procrastinate and still avoid disaster.

Explanatory and Exploratory Writing

Several variables affect the method and speed with which writers work — how much time they have, how important their task is, how skilled they are, and so on. The most important variable, however, is the kind of writing they are doing. I am going to focus on two major kinds here: *explanatory* and *exploratory*. To put it briefly, although much too simply, explanatory writing *tends* to be about information; exploratory writing *tends* to be about ideas.

Explanatory writing can take many forms: a movie review, an expla-   5
nation of new software, an analysis of historical causes, a report on a re-
cent political development, a biographical sketch. These are just a few possibilities. The distinguishing feature of all these examples and other kinds of explanatory writing is that the writer either knows most of what he or she is going to say before starting to write or knows where to find the material needed to get started. A typical explanatory essay might be on some aspect of global warming for an environmental studies course. The material for such a paper already exists — you're not going to create it or discover it within your subconscious. Your job as a writer is to dig out the material, organize it, and shape it into a clearly written, carefully supported essay. Usually you would know who your readers are for an explanatory essay and, from the beginning, shape it for that audience.

Writers usually make plans when they are doing explanatory writing, plans that can range from a page of notes to a full outline. Such plans help them to keep track of their material, put it in some kind of order, and find a pattern for presenting it. For explanatory writing, many writers find that the traditional methods work well; assertion/support, cause and effect, process, compare/contrast, and so on. Much of the writing that students do in college is explanatory, as is much business writing. Many magazine articles and nonfiction books are primarily explanatory writing. It's a crucially important kind of writing, one that we depend on for information and education, one that keeps the machinery of business and government going.

Explanatory writing is not necessarily easy to do nor is it usually formulaic. It takes skill and care to write an accurate, interesting story about the physician who won a Nobel Prize for initiating kidney transplants or an entertaining and informative report on how the movie *Dick Tracy* was made. But the process for explanatory writing is manageable. You identify the task, decide what the purpose and who the audience are, map out a plan for finding and organizing information, then divide the writing itself into doable chunks and start working. Progress may be painful, and you may have to draft and revise several times to clarify points or get the tone just right, but with persistence, you can do it.

Exploratory writing may also take many forms: a reflective personal essay, a profile of a homeless family, an argument in support of funding for multimillion dollar science projects, or a speculative essay about the future of the women's movement. These are only a few possibilities. What distinguishes these examples and exploratory writing in general is that the writer has only a partially formed idea of what he or she is going to write before starting. A typical piece of exploratory writing might be a speculative essay on why movies about the Mafia appeal so much to the American public. You might hit on the idea of writing such a piece after you have seen several mob movies — *Goodfellas, Miller's Crossing,* and *Godfather III* — but not really know what you would say or who your audience would be. The material for such a paper doesn't exist; you would have to begin by reading, talking to people, and by drawing on the ideas and insights you've gleaned from different sources to reach your own point of view. And you would certainly expect some of your most important ideas — your own conclusions — to come to you as you wrote.

Because you don't know ahead of time exactly what you're going to say in exploratory writing, it's hard to make a detailed plan or outline; however, you can and should take copious notes as you prepare to write. You might be able to put down a tentative thesis sentence, for example, "American moviegoers are drawn to movies about the Mafia and mob violence because they appeal to a streak of lawlessness that has always been strong in American character." Such a sentence could be an anchor to get you started writing, but as a main idea, it could change or even disappear as the paper developed.

Many papers you write in college will be exploratory papers, for example, an interpretive paper in a literature course, an essay on the future of an ethnic community for a cultural anthropology course, or an argumentative paper for a government course proposing changes in our election laws. Many magazine articles and books are also exploratory, for example, an article on the roots of violence in American cities or an autobiographical account of being tagged a "slow learner" early in one's school career. Both in and out of college, exploratory writing is as important as explanatory writing because it is the springboard and testing ground for new ideas. 10

Exploratory writing isn't necessarily harder to do than explanatory writing, but it is harder to plan because it resists any systematic approach. That makes it appeal to some writers, particularly those who have a reflective or speculative turn of mind. They like the freedom of being able just to write to see what is going to develop. But although exploratory writers start out with more freedom, eventually they too have to discipline themselves to organize their writing into clear, readable form. They also have to realize that exploratory writing usually takes longer and requires more drafts.

When you're doing exploratory writing, anticipate that your process will be messy. You have to tolerate uncertainty longer because ideas keep coming as you write and it's not always clear what you're going to do with them and how — or if — you can fit them into your paper. Exploratory writing is also hard to organize — sometimes you'll have to outline *after* you've written your first draft in order to get the paper under control. Finally, you also have to have confidence in your own instincts; now that you are focusing on ideas and reflections more than on facts, you have to believe that you have something worth writing about and that other people are interested in reading it.

Of course, not all writing can be easily classified as either explanatory or exploratory; sometimes you'll be working with information and ideas in the same paper and move from presenting facts to reflecting about their implications. For example, in an economics course you might report on how much Japan has invested in the United States economy over the last decade and where those investments have been made; then you could speculate about the long-range impact on American business. If you were writing a case study of a teenage mother for a social work class, you would use mostly explanatory writing to document the young woman's background, schooling, and important facts about her present situation; then you could go to exploratory writing to suggest how her options for the future can be improved.

In general, readers respond best to writing that thoughtfully connects facts to reflections, explanations to explorations. So don't hesitate to mix the two kinds of writing if it makes your paper stronger and more interesting. At this point, you might ask "Why do these distinctions matter to me?" I think there are several reasons.

First, it helps to realize that there isn't *a* writing process — there are   15
writing *processes*, and some work better than others in specific situations. Although by temperament and habit you may be the "just give me the facts, ma'am," kind of person who prefers to do explanatory writing, you also need to become proficient at exploratory writing in order to write the speculative, reflective papers that are necessary when you have to write about long-range goals or speculate about philosophical issues. If, on the other hand, by temperament you'd rather ignore outlines and prefer to spin theories instead of report on facts, you also need to become proficient at explanatory writing. In almost any profession, you're going to have to write reports, summarize data, or present results of research.

Second, you'll become a more proficient and relaxed writer if you develop the habit of analyzing before you start, whether you are going to be doing primarily explanatory or exploratory writing. Once you decide, you can consciously switch into certain writing patterns and write more efficiently. For instance, when you're writing reports, case studies, research papers, or analyses, take the time to rough out an outline and make a careful list of the main points you need to make. Schedule time for research and checking facts, details are going to be important. Review some of the routine but useful patterns you could use to develop your paper: cause and effect, definition, process, narration, and so forth. They can work well when you have a fairly clear idea of your purpose and what you're going to say.

If you're starting on a less clearly defined, more open-ended paper — for example, a reflective essay about Picasso's portrayal of women for an art history course — allow yourself to be less organized for a while. Be willing to start without knowing where you're going. Look at some paintings to get your ideas flowing, talk to some other students, and then just start writing, confident that you'll find your content and your direction. Don't worry if you can't get the first paragraph right — it will come later. Your first goal with exploratory writing should be to generate a fairly complete first draft in order to give yourself something to work with. Remember to give yourself plenty of time to revise. You'll need it.

Finally, resist the idea that one kind of writing is better than another. It's not. Sometimes there's a tendency, particularly in liberal arts classes, to believe that people who do theoretical or reflective writing are superior; that exploratory writing is loftier and more admirable than writing in which people present facts and argue for concrete causes. That's not really the case. Imaginative, thoughtful writing about theories and opinions is important and interesting, but informative, factual writing is also critically important, and people who can do it well are invaluable. Anyone who hopes to be an effective, confident writer should cultivate the habits that enable him or her to do both kinds of writing well.

FOCUSING ON CONTENT

1. According to Hairston, in what ways is a writing teacher like a tennis coach? Does this analogy help you to view your writing teacher differently? (Glossary: *Analogy*) Explain.

2. Review the list of items that Hairston provides to explain how professional writers work. How many points on the list are you already doing? What items, if any, surprised you?

3. What are the main differences between explanatory and exploratory writing? Which type do you usually find yourself doing? Is Hairston's essay explanatory, exploratory, or a combination of both types of writing?

FOCUSING ON WRITING

1. Carefully examine Hairston's diction or choice of words in this selection. (Glossary: *Diction*) Would you consider any of her words the technical language or jargon of writing teachers? (Glossary: *Technical Language*) Is her language appropriate for her intended audience? Explain.

2. Discuss how Hairston uses comparison and contrast to explain the differences between explanatory and exploratory writing. (Glossary: *Comparison and Contrast*) What examples does she use to illustrate her points? (Glossary: *Examples*)

3. What transitions does Hairston use to connect the ideas in paragraphs 15 and 16? (Glossary: *Transitions*) Briefly explain how her transitions work.

4. How would you describe Hairston's tone in this essay? (Glossary: *Tone*) Explain how her choice of words helps her create this tone. (Glossary: *Diction*) Use examples from the text to show what you mean. How important is tone to writers? To readers?

LANGUAGE IN ACTION

Consider the following cartoon from the *New Yorker*. What insights into the writing process does the cartoon give you? How does humor help people talk about situations that might otherwise be difficult to discuss? Explain.

"No wonder you can't write. You're not plugged in!"

WRITING SUGGESTIONS

1. How well do you know yourself as a writer? Drawing on what you wrote in your Writing to Discover entry for this selection, write an essay in which you describe the process you normally follow in writing a composition. Do you begin by brainstorming for ideas, thinking before you write, or do you simply start writing, hoping that ideas will come to you as you write? How many drafts does it usually take before you have a piece of writing that satisfies you? What part of the process is the most difficult for you? The easiest for you?

2. In list form, describe the processes for writing an explanatory and an exploratory essay. Discuss your lists with others in your class. What are the main differences between the two processes? Write an essay about these differences.

3. How useful do you find outlining? When in the writing process do you usually prepare an outline? Do your outlining practices vary according to the
   type of writing you are doing? What recommendations about outlining have
   your previous teachers made? Consult several texts in the library about outlining. Then, using the preceding questions as a starting point, compose a
   brief questionnaire about outlining practices and the benefits of outlining,
   and give the questionnaire to the other students in your writing class. What
   conclusions can you draw from your tabulated questionnaires? Based on your
   findings, write an essay arguing for or against the benefits of outlining.

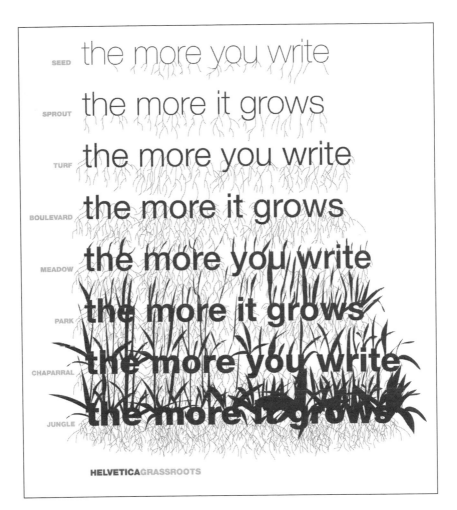

PICTURING LANGUAGE

How has the designer of HELVETICAGRASSROOTS, an invented type font, used style to illustrate both the meaning of the sentence "the more you write the more it grows" and the words running down the left-hand side of the illustration? The designer has graphically illustrated style; for you, what is style in the world of writing? What role does style play in helping a writer communicate to an audience?

Writing for an Audience

Linda Flower

Linda Flower is professor of English at Carnegie-Mellon University, where she directed the Business Communication program for a number of years. She has been a leading researcher on the composing process, and the results of her investigations have shaped and informed her influential writing text Problem-Solving Strategies for Writing *(1993).*

In this selection, which is taken from that text, Flower's focus is on audience — the people for whom we write. She believes that writers must establish a "common ground" between themselves and their readers, one that lessens their differences in knowledge, attitudes, and needs. Although we can never be certain who might read what we write, it is nevertheless important for us to have a target audience in mind. Many of the decisions that we make as writers are influenced by that real or imagined reader.

Writing to Discover: *Imagine for a moment that you just received a speeding ticket for going sixty-five miles per hour in a thirty-mile-per-hour zone. How would you describe the episode to your best friend? To your parents? To the judge in court? Sketch out the three versions, and then write about how the three versions of your story differ. How do you account for these differences?*

The goal of the writer is to create a momentary common ground between the reader and the writer. You want the reader to share your knowledge and your attitude toward that knowledge. Even if the reader eventually disagrees, you want him or her to be able for the moment to *see things as you see them.* A good piece of writing closes the gap between you and the reader.

ANALYZE YOUR AUDIENCE

The first step in closing that gap is to gauge the distance between the two of you. Imagine, for example, that you are a student writing your parents, who have always lived in New York City, about a wilderness survival expedition you want to go on over spring break. Sometimes obvious differences such as age or background will be important, but the critical differences for writers usually fall into three areas: the reader's *knowledge* about the topic, his or her *attitude* toward it, and his or her personal or professional *needs*. Because these differences often exist, good writers do more than simply express their meaning; they pinpoint the critical differences between themselves and their reader and design their writing to reduce those differences. Let us look at these areas in more detail.

KNOWLEDGE.   This is usually the easiest difference to handle. What does your reader need to know? What are the main ideas you hope to teach? Does your reader have enough background knowledge to really understand you? If not, what would he or she have to learn?

ATTITUDES.   When we say a person has knowledge, we usually refer to his conscious awareness of explicit facts and clearly defined concepts. This kind of knowledge can be easily written down or told to someone else. However, much of what we "know" is not held in this formal, explicit way. Instead it is held as an attitude or image — as a loose cluster of associations. For instance, my image of lakes includes associations many people would have, including fishing, water skiing, stalled outboards, and lots of kids catching night crawlers with flashlights. However, the most salient or powerful parts of my image, which strongly color my whole attitude toward lakes, are thoughts of cloudy skies, long rainy days, and feeling generally cold and damp. By contrast, one of my best friends has a very different cluster of associations: to him a lake means sun, swimming, sailing, and happily sitting on the end of a dock. Needless to say, our differing images cause us to react quite differently to a proposal that we visit a lake. Likewise, one reason people often find it difficult to discuss religion and politics is that terms such as "capitalism" conjure up radically different images.

As you can see, a reader's image of a subject is often the source of at-   5
titudes and feelings that are unexpected and, at times, impervious to mere facts. A simple statement that seems quite persuasive to you, such as "Lake Wampago would be a great place to locate the new music camp," could have little impact on your reader if he or she simply doesn't visualize a lake as a "great place." In fact, many people accept uncritically any statement that fits in with their own attitudes — and reject, just as uncritically, anything that does not.

Whether your purpose is to persuade or simply to present your perspective, it helps to know the image and attitudes that your reader already holds. The more these differ from your own, the more you will have to do to make him or her *see* what you mean.

NEEDS.   When writers discover a large gap between their own knowledge and attitudes and those of the reader, they usually try to change the reader in some way. Needs, however, are different. When you analyze a reader's needs, it is so that you, the writer, can adapt to him. If you ask a friend majoring in biology how to keep your fish tank from clouding, you don't want to hear a textbook recitation on the life processes of algae. You expect a friend to adapt his or her knowledge and tell you exactly how to solve your problem.

The ability to adapt your knowledge to the needs of the reader is often crucial to your success as a writer. This is especially true in writing done on a job. For example, as producer of a public affairs program for a television station, 80 percent of your time may be taken up planning the details of new shows, contacting guests, and scheduling the taping sessions. But when you write a program proposal to the station director, your job is to show how the program will fit into the cost guidelines, the FCC requirements for relevance, and the overall programming plan for the station. When you write that report your role in the organization changes from producer to proposal writer. Why? Because your reader needs that information in order to make a decision. He may be *interested* in your scheduling problems and the specific content of the shows, but he *reads* your report because of his own needs as station director of the organization. He has to act.

In college, where the reader is also a teacher, the reader's needs are a little less concrete but just as important. Most papers are assigned as a way to teach something. So the real purpose of a paper may be for you to make connections between two historical periods, to discover for yourself the principle behind a laboratory experiment, or to develop and support your own interpretation of a novel. A good college paper doesn't just rehash the facts; it demonstrates what your reader, as a teacher, needs to know — that you are learning the thinking skills his or her course is trying to teach.

Effective writers are not simply expressing what they know, like a stu-   10
dent madly filling up an examination bluebook. Instead they are *using* their knowledge: reorganizing, maybe even rethinking their ideas to meet the demands of an assignment or the needs of their reader.

FOCUSING ON CONTENT

1. How, according to Flower, does a competent writer achieve the goal of closing the gap between himself or herself and the reader? How does a writer determine what a reader's "personal or professional needs" (2) are?

2. What, for Flower, is the difference between knowledge and attitude? Why is it important for writers to understand this difference?

3. In paragraph 4, Flower discusses the fact that many words have both positive and negative associations. How do you think words come to have associations? (Glossary: *Connotation/Denotation*) Consider, for example, such words as *home, anger, royalty, welfare, politician,* and *strawberry shortcake.*

4. What does Flower believe constitutes a "good college paper" (9)? Do you agree with her assessment? Why or why not?

FOCUSING ON WRITING

1. Flower wrote this selection for college students. How well did she assess your knowledge, attitude, and needs about the subject of a writer's audience? Does Flower's use of language and examples show a sensitivity to her audience? Provide specific examples to support your view. (Glossary: *Examples*)

2. Flower notes in paragraph 4 that many words often have "a loose cluster of associations." Explain how you can use this fact to advantage when writing an argument. A personal essay. An informative piece.

3. When using technical language in a paper on a subject you have thoroughly researched or are already familiar with, why is it important for you to know

your audience? (Glossary: *Audience*) What language strategies might you use to adapt your knowledge to your audience? Explain. How could your classmates, friends, or parents help you?

LANGUAGE IN ACTION

Analyze the language of the advertisement below for a hard drive workstation from Corporate Systems Center. Based on your own familiarity with computer language, identify those words that you consider computer jargon. (Glossary: *Technical Language*) Which words are appropriate for a general audience? An expert audience? For what kind of audience do you think this ad was written? Explain.

CLONE, TEST OR REPAIR
ANY HARD DRIVE

"THE MOST COMPLETE HARD DRIVE WORKSTATION WE'VE SEEN!" BOB ROSENBLOOM, DIGITAL VIDEO, INC.

DRIVE SERVICE STATION

Copy entire hard drives with ease. Drive duplicators are essential tools for dealers and system builders. Don't spend hours installing and formatting drives. Do it instantly with the Pro. Set up any SCSI or IDE drive with your original software. Connect blank drives to the Pro and press start. You'll copy entire drives faster and more accurately than is possible on any PC. You can even copy data between IDE and SCSI interfaces. The Pro includes both 2.5" and 3.5" interface adapters. The Pro also supports SCA and Wide SCSI drives.

Choose the Pro, and you'll also have an entire factory drive test and repair system for under $1000.

BUY DIRECT: $995
408 330-5544

The Pro gives you the ability to copy, reformat, repair translate, and test any hard drive. Use the Pro to put any hard drive through its paces. A full factory final test and performance analysis is performed. Complete test and repair reports are sent to any standard printer.

The Pro will also reassign and eliminate drive defects. Here's how it works: First, a precise media analysis system scans the disk for errors. Defects are mapped out, and effectively "erased." The error correcting system then "trains" the drive to permanently avoid defective areas. Data is stored only on

the safe areas of the disk. Capacity is reduced by an insignificant amount, and the drive works flawlessly once again. Get the technology used by major repair shops and data recovery centers. The Pro repairs all disk defects caused by normal wear. Drives with mechanical damage may not be repairable.

CORPORATE SYSTEMS CENTER
3310 WOODWARD AVE., SANTA CLARA, CA 95054
WWW.DRIVEDUPLICATORS.COM

Winfo No. 463 at: www.winmag.com/winfo

Call today for high volume multi-drive copiers and CD Duplicators
Sold and intended for backup purposes only. Copyright laws must be observed.

WRITING SUGGESTIONS

1. Write an essay in which you discuss the proposition that honesty is a prerequisite of good writing. Ask yourself what it means to write honestly. What does dishonest writing look and sound like? Do you have a responsibility to be an honest writer? How is honesty in writing related to audience? Be sure to illustrate your essay with examples from your own experiences.

2. In order to write well, a writer has to identify his or her audience. Choose a topic that is important to you and, taking into account what Flower calls your audience's knowledge, attitude, and needs, write a letter about that topic to your best friend. Then write a letter on the same topic to your instructor. How does your message differ from letter to letter? How does your diction change? (Glossary: *Diction*) What conclusions about audience can you draw from your two letters? How successful do you think you were in closing "the gap between you and the reader" in each letter?

Shitty First Drafts

ANNE LAMOTT

Born in San Francisco in 1954, Anne Lamott is a graduate of Goucher College in Baltimore and is the author of six novels, including Rosie *(1983),* Crooked Little Heart *(1997),* All New People *(2000), and* Blue Shoes *(2002). She has also been the food reviewer for* California *magazine, a book reviewer for* Mademoiselle, *and a regular contributor to* Salon's *"Mothers Who Think." Her nonfiction books include* Operating Instructions: A Journal of My Son's First Year *(1993), in which she describes her adventures as a single parent, and* Tender Mercies: Some Thoughts on Faith *(1999), in which she charts her journey toward faith in God.*

In the following selection, taken from Lamott's popular book about writing, Bird by Bird *(1994), she argues for the need to let go and write those "shitty first drafts" that lead to clarity and sometimes brilliance in our second and third drafts.*

WRITING TO DISCOVER: *Many professional writers view first drafts as something they have to do before they can begin the real work of writing — revision. How do you view the writing of your first drafts? What patterns, if any, do you see in your writing behavior when working on first drafts? Is the work liberating? Restricting? Pleasant? Unpleasant?*

Now, practically even better news than that of short assignments is the idea of shitty first drafts. All good writers write them. This is how they end up with good second drafts and terrific third drafts. People tend to look at successful writers, writers who are getting their books published and maybe even doing well financially, and think that they sit down at their desks every morning feeling like a million dollars, feeling great about who they are and how much talent they have and what a great story they have to tell; that they take in a few deep breaths, push back their sleeves, roll their necks a few times to get all the cricks out, and dive in, typing fully formed passages as fast as a court reporter. But this is just the fantasy of the uninitiated. I know some very great writers, writers you love who write beautifully and have made a great deal of money, and not one of them sits down routinely feeling wildly enthusiastic and confident. Not one of them writes elegant first drafts. All right, one of them does, but we do not like her very much. We do not think that she has a rich inner life or that God likes her or can even stand her. (Although when I mentioned this to my priest friend Tom, he said you can safely assume you've created God in your own image when it turns out that God hates all the same people you do.)

Very few writers really know what they are doing until they've done it. Nor do they go about their business feeling dewy and thrilled. They do not type a few stiff warm-up sentences and then find themselves bounding along like huskies across the snow. One writer I know tells me that he sits down every morning and says to himself nicely, "It's not like you don't have a choice, because you do — you can either type or kill yourself." We all often feel like we are pulling teeth, even those writers whose prose ends up being the most natural and fluid. The right words and sentences just do not come pouring out like ticker tape most of the time. Now, Muriel Spark is said to have felt that she was taking dictation from God every morning — sitting there, one supposes, plugged into a Dictaphone, typing away, humming. But this is a very hostile and aggressive position. One might hope for bad things to rain down on a person like this.

For me and most of the other writers I know, writing is not rapturous. In fact, the only way I can get anything written at all is to write really, really shitty first drafts.

The first draft is the child's draft, where you let it all pour out and then let it romp all over the place, knowing that no one is going to see it and that you can shape it later. You just let this childlike part of you channel whatever voices and visions come through and onto the page. If one of the characters wants to say, "Well, so what, Mr. Poopy Pants?," you let her. No one is going to see it. If the kid wants to get into really sentimental, weepy, emotional territory, you let him. Just get it all down on paper, because there may be something great in those six crazy pages that you would never have gotten to by more rational, grown-up means. There may be something in the very last line of the very last paragraph on page six that you just love, that is so beautiful or wild that you now know what you're supposed to be writing about, more or less, or in what direction you might go — but there was no way to get to this without first getting through the first five and a half pages.

I used to write food reviews for *California* magazine before it folded. 5
(My writing food reviews had nothing to do with the magazine folding, although every single review did cause a couple of canceled subscriptions. Some readers took umbrage at my comparing mounds of vegetable puree with various ex-presidents' brains.) These reviews always took two days to write. First I'd go to a restaurant several times with a few opinionated, articulate friends in tow. I'd sit there writing down everything anyone said that was at all interesting or funny. Then on the following Monday I'd sit down at my desk with my notes, and try to write the review. Even after I'd been doing this for years, panic would set in. I'd try to write a lead, but instead I'd write a couple of dreadful sentences, xx them out, try again, xx everything out, and then feel despair and worry settle on my chest like an x-ray apron. It's over, I'd think, calmly. I'm not going to be able to get the magic to work this time. I'm ruined. I'm through. I'm toast. Maybe, I'd think, I can get my old job back as a clerk-typist. But probably not. I'd get up and study my teeth in the mirror for a while.

Then I'd stop, remember to breathe, make a few phone calls, hit the kitchen and chow down. Eventually I'd go back and sit down at my desk, and *sigh* for the next ten minutes. Finally I would pick up my one-inch picture frame, stare into it as if for the answer, and every time the answer would come: all I had to do was to write a really shitty first draft of, say, the opening paragraph. And no one was going to see it.

So I'd start writing without reining myself in. It was almost just typing, just making my fingers move. And the writing would be terrible. I'd write a lead paragraph that was a whole page, even though the entire review could only be three pages long, and then I'd start writing up descriptions of the food, one dish at a time, bird by bird, and the critics would be sitting on my shoulders, commenting like cartoon characters. They'd be pretending to snore, or rolling their eyes at my overwrought descriptions, no matter how hard I tried to tone those descriptions down, no matter how conscious I was of what a friend said to me gently in my early days of restaurant reviewing. "Annie," she said, "it is just a piece of *chicken*. It is just a bit of *cake*."

But because by then I had been writing for so long, I would eventually let myself trust the process — sort of, more or less. I'd write a first draft that was maybe twice as long as it should be, with a self-indulgent and boring beginning, stupefying descriptions of the meal, lots of quotes from my black-humored friends that made them sound more like the Manson girls than food lovers, and no ending to speak of. The whole thing would be so long and incoherent and hideous that for the rest of the day I'd obsess about getting creamed by a car before I could write a decent second draft. I'd worry that people would read what I'd written and believe that the accident had really been a suicide, that I had panicked because my talent was waning and my mind was shot.

The next day, though, I'd sit down, go through it all with a colored pen, take out everything I possibly could, find a new lead somewhere on the second page, figure out a kicky place to end it, and then write a second draft. It always turned out fine, sometimes even funny and weird and helpful. I'd go over it one more time and mail it in.

Then, a month later, when it was time for another review, the whole process would start again, complete with the fears that people would find my first draft before I could rewrite it.

FOCUSING ON CONTENT

1. Lamott says that the perceptions most people have of how writers work is different from the reality of the work itself. She refers to this in paragraph 1 as "the fantasy of the uninitiated." What does she mean?

2. In paragraph 7 Lamott refers to a time when, through experience, she "eventually let [herself] trust the process — sort of, more or less." She is referring to the writing process, of course, but why "more or less"? Do you think her wariness is personal, or is she speaking for all writers in this regard? Explain.

3. From what Lamott has to say, is writing a first draft more about content or psychology? Do you agree in regard to your own first drafts? Explain.

FOCUSING ON WRITING

1. What is Lamott's thesis, and where is her statement of the thesis? (Glossary: *Thesis*)

2. Lamott adds humor to her argument for "shitty first drafts." Give some examples. Do her attempts at humor add or detract from the points she makes? Explain.

3. In paragraph 5, Lamott offers a narrative of her experiences writing a food review in which she refers to an almost ritualistic set of behaviors. What is her purpose in telling her readers this story and the difficulties she has? (Glossary: *Narration*) Is it helpful for us to know this information? Explain.

4. Paragraphs 3 and 9 of Lamott's essay are shorter than the rest of her paragraphs. Why?

5. What do you think of Lamott's use of the word "shitty" in her title and in the essay itself? Is it in keeping with the tone of her essay? (Glossary: *Tone*) Are you offended by her use of the word? Why or why not? What would be lost or gained if she used a different word?

LANGUAGE IN ACTION

In his 1990 book *The Play of Words*, Richard Lederer presents the following activity called "Verbs with Verve." What do you learn about the power of verbs from this exercise? Explain.

Researchers showed groups of test subjects a picture of an automobile accident and then asked this question: "How fast were the cars going when they ———?" The blank was variously filled in with *bumped, contacted, hit, collided,* or *smashed*. Groups that were asked "How fast were the cars going when they smashed?" responded with the highest estimates of speed.

All of which proves that verbs create specific images in the mind's eye. Because verbs are the words in a sentence that express action and movement, they are the spark plugs of effective style. The more specific the verbs you choose in your speaking and writing, the more sparky will be the images you flash on the minds of your listeners and readers.

Suppose you write, "'No,' she said and left the room." Grammatically there is nothing wrong with this sentence. But because the verbs *say* and *leave* are among the most general and colorless in the English language, you have missed the chance to create a vivid word picture. Consider the alternatives:

SAID		LEFT	
apologized	jabbered	backed	sauntered
asserted	minced	bolted	skipped

blubbered	mumbled	bounced	staggered
blurted	murmured	crawled	stamped
boasted	shrieked	darted	stole
cackled	sighed	flew	strode
commanded	slurred	hobbled	strutted
drawled	snapped	lurched	stumbled
giggled	sobbed	marched	tiptoed
groaned	whispered	plodded	wandered
gurgled	whooped	pranced	whirled

If you had chosen from among these vivid verbs and had crafted the sentence "'No,' she sobbed, and stumbled out of the room," you would have created a powerful picture of someone quite distraught.

Here are brief descriptions of twenty different people. Choosing from the two lists of synonyms for *said* and *left*, fill in the blanks of the sentence "'No,' he/she _____, and _____ out of the room." Select the pair of verbs that best create the most vivid picture of each person described. Throughout your answers try to use as many different verbs as you can:

1. an angry person	11. an excited person
2. a baby	12. a frightened person
3. a braggart	13. a happy person
4. a child	14. someone in a hurry
5. a clown	15. an injured person
6. a confused person	16. a military officer
7. a cowboy/cowgirl	17. a sneaky person
8. someone crying	18. a timid person
9. a drunkard	19. a tired person
10. an embarrassed person	20. a witch

WRITING SUGGESTIONS

1. In order to become a better writer, it is essential to be conscious of what you do as a writer. In other words, you need to reflect on what you are thinking and feeling at each stage of the writing process. Lamott has done just this in writing her essay. Think about what you do at other stages of the writing process — prewriting (gathering information, selecting evidence, checking on the reliability of sources, separating facts from opinions), revising, editing, and proofreading, for example. Write an essay modeled on Lamott's in which you narrate an experience you have had with a particular type of writing or assignment.

2. Lamott's essay is about appearances versus reality. Write an essay in which you set the record straight by exposing the myths or misperceptions people have about a particular job, place, thing, or situation. Naturally, you need to ask yourself how much of an "inside story" you can reveal based upon actual experiences you have had. In other words, you know that being a lifeguard is not as romantic as most people think because you have been one. Try to create the same informative but lighthearted tone that Lamott does in her essay by paying particular attention to the language you use.

Simplicity

WILLIAM ZINSSER

*Born in New York City in 1922, William Zinsser was educated at
Princeton University. After serving in the army in World War II,
he worked at the* New York Herald Tribune *as an editor, writer,
and critic. During the 1970s he taught a popular course in nonfiction at Yale University, and from 1979 to 1987 he was general editor of the Book-of-the-Month Club. Zinsser has written more than a
dozen books, including* The City Dwellers *(1962),* Pop Goes
America *(1966),* Spring Training *(1989), and three widely used
books on writing:* On Writing Well *(2001),* Writing with a Word
Processor *(1983), and* Writing to Learn *(1993). Currently, he
teaches at the New School in New York City, and his freelance writing regularly appears in some of our leading magazines.*

The following selection is taken from On Writing Well. *This
book grew out of Zinsser's many years of experience as a professional
writer and teacher. In this essay, Zinsser exposes what he believes is
the writer's number one problem — "clutter." He sees Americans
"strangling in unnecessary words, circular constructions, pompous
frills, and meaningless jargon." His solution is simple: Writers must
know what they want to say and must be thinking clearly as they
start to compose. Then self-discipline and hard work are necessary to
achieve clear, simple prose. No matter what your experience as a
writer has been, you will find Zinsser's observations sound and his
advice practical.*

WRITING TO DISCOVER: *Some people view writing as "thinking
on paper." They believe that by seeing something written on a page
they are better able to "see what they think." Write about the relationship, for you, between writing and thinking. Are you one of
those people who likes to "see" ideas on paper while trying to work
things out? Or do you like to think through ideas before writing
about them?*

Clutter is the disease of American writing. We are a society strangling
in unnecessary words, circular constructions, pompous frills, and meaningless jargon.

Who can understand the viscous language of everyday American
commerce: the memo, the corporation report, the business letter, the notice from the bank explaining its latest "simplified" statement? What
member of an insurance or medical plan can decipher the brochure explaining his costs and benefits? What father or mother can put together a
child's toy from the instructions on the box? Our national tendency is to

inflate and thereby sound important. The airline pilot who announces that he is presently anticipating experiencing considerable precipitation wouldn't think of saying it may rain. The sentence is too simple — there must be something wrong with it.

But the secret of good writing is to strip every sentence to its cleanest components. Every word that serves no function, every long word that could be a short word, every adverb that carries the same meaning that's already in the verb, every passive construction that leaves the reader unsure of who is doing what — these are the thousand and one adulterants that weaken the strength of a sentence. And they usually occur in proportion to education and rank.

During the 1960s the president of my university wrote a letter to mollify the alumni after a spell of campus unrest. "You are probably aware," he began, "that we have been experiencing very considerable potentially explosive expressions of dissatisfaction on issues only partially related." He meant the students had been hassling them about different things. I was far more upset by the president's English than by the students' potentially explosive expressions of dissatisfaction. I would have preferred the presidential approach taken by Franklin D. Roosevelt when he tried to convert into English his own government's memos, such as this blackout order of 1942:

> Such preparations shall be made as will completely obscure all Federal buildings and non-Federal buildings occupied by the Federal government during an air raid for any period of time from visibility by reason of internal or external illumination.

"Tell them," Roosevelt said, "that in buildings where they have to keep the work going to put something across the windows."

Simplify, simplify. Thoreau said it, as we are so often reminded, and no American writer more consistently practiced what he preached. Open *Walden* to any page and you will find a man saying in a plain and orderly way what is on his mind:

> I went to the woods because I wished to live deliberately, to front only the essential facts of life, and see if I could not learn what it had to teach, and not, when I came to die, discover that I had not lived.

How can the rest of us achieve such enviable freedom from clutter? The answer is to clear our heads of clutter. Clear thinking becomes clear writing; one can't exist without the other. It's impossible for a muddy thinker to write good English. You may get away with it for a paragraph or two, but soon the reader will be lost, and there's no sin so grave, for the reader will not easily be lured back.

Who is this elusive creature, the reader? The reader is someone with an attention span of about 30 seconds — a person assailed by other forces competing for attention. At one time these forces weren't so numerous:

newspapers, radio, spouse, home, children. Today they also include a "home entertainment center" (TV, VCR, tapes, CDs), pets, a fitness program, a yard and all the gadgets that have been bought to keep it spruce, and that most potent of competitors, sleep. The person snoozing in a chair with a magazine or a book is a person who was being given too much unnecessary trouble by the writer.

It won't do to say that the reader is too dumb or too lazy to keep pace with the train of thought. If the reader is lost, it's usually because the writer hasn't been careful enough. The carelessness can take any number of forms. Perhaps a sentence is so excessively cluttered that the reader, hacking through the verbiage, simply doesn't know what it means. Perhaps a sentence has been so shoddily constructed that the reader could read it in several ways. Perhaps the writer has switched pronouns in mid-sentence, or has switched tenses, so the reader loses track of who is talking or when the action took place. Perhaps Sentence B is not a logical sequel to Sentence A — the writer, in whose head the connection is clear, hasn't bothered to provide the missing link. Perhaps the writer has used an important word incorrectly by not taking the trouble to look it up. The writer may think "sanguine" and "sanguinary" mean the same thing, but the difference is a bloody big one. The reader can only infer (speaking of big differences) what the writer is trying to imply.

Faced with such obstacles, readers are at first tenacious. They blame themselves — they obviously missed something, and they go back over the mystifying sentence, or over the whole paragraph, piecing it out like an ancient rune, making guesses and moving on. But they won't do this for long. The writer is making them work too hard, and they will look for one who is better at the craft.

Writers must therefore constantly ask: What am I trying to say? Surprisingly often they don't know. Then they must look at what they have written and ask: Have I said it? Is it clear to someone encountering the subject for the first time? If it's not, some fuzz has worked its way into the machinery. The clear writer is someone clearheaded enough to see this stuff for what it is: fuzz.

I don't mean that some people are born clearheaded and are therefore natural writers, whereas others are naturally fuzzy and will never write well. Thinking clearly is a conscious act that writers must force upon themselves, as if they were working on any other project that requires logic: adding up a laundry list or doing an algebra problem. Good writing doesn't come naturally, though most people obviously think it does. Professional writers are constantly being bearded by strangers who say they'd like to "try a little writing sometime" — meaning when they retire from their real profession, which is difficult, like insurance or real estate. Or they say, "I could write a book about that." I doubt it.

Writing is hard work. A clear sentence is not accident. Very few sentences come out right the first time, or even the third time. Remember this in moments of despair. If you find that writing is hard, it's because it *is* hard. It's one of the hardest things people do.

FOCUSING ON CONTENT

1. What exactly is clutter? When do words qualify as clutter, and when do they not?

2. In paragraph 2, Zinsser states that "Our national tendency is to inflate and thereby sound important." What do you think he means by inflate? Provide several examples to illustrate how people use language to inflate.

3. In paragraph 9, Zinsser lists some of the language-based obstacles that a reader may encounter in carelessly constructed prose. Which of these problems most tries your patience? Why?

4. One would hope that education would help in the battle against clutter, but, as Zinsser notes, wordiness "usually occur[s] in proportion to education and rank" (3). Do your own experiences or observations support Zinsser's claim? Discuss.

FOCUSING ON WRITING

1. What assumptions does Zinsser make about readers? According to Zinsser, what responsibilities do writers have to readers? How do these responsibilities manifest themselves in Zinsser's writing? How do you think Linda Flower (pp. 88–90) would respond to what Zinsser says about audience? (Glossary: *Audience*) Explain.

2. Zinsser believes that writers need to ask themselves two questions — "What am I trying to say?" and "Have I said it?" — constantly as they write (11). How would these questions help you eliminate clutter from your own writing? Give some examples from one of your essays.

3. In order "to strip every sentence to its cleanest components," we need to be sensitive to the words we use and know how they function within our sentences. For each of the "adulterants that weaken the strength of a sentence," which Zinsser identifies in paragraph 3, provide an example from your own writing.

4. Zinsser knows that sentence variety is an important feature of good writing. Locate several examples of the short sentences (seven or fewer words) he uses in this essay, and explain how each relates in length, meaning, and impact to the sentences around it.

LANGUAGE IN ACTION

The following two pages show a passage from Zinsser's final manuscript for this essay. Carefully study the manuscript, and discuss how Zinsser eliminated clutter in his own prose. Then, using Zinsser as a model, judiciously eliminate the clutter from several paragraphs in one of your papers.

5 --

is too dumb or too lazy to keep pace with the ~~writer's~~ train
of thought. My sympathics are ~~entirely~~ with him.) ~~He's not
so dumb.~~ (If the reader is lost, it is generally because the
writer ~~of the article~~ has not been careful enough to keep
him on the ~~proper~~ path.

This carelessness can take any number of ~~different~~ forms.
Perhaps a sentence is so excessively ~~long and~~ cluttered that
the reader, hacking his way through ~~all~~ the verbiage, simply
doesn't know what _it_ ~~the writer~~ means. Perhaps a sentence has
been so shoddily constructed that the reader could read it in
any of _several_ ~~two or three different~~ ways. ~~He thinks he knows what
the writer is trying to say, but he's not sure.~~ Perhaps the
writer has switched pronouns in mid-sentence, or ~~perhaps he~~
has switched tenses, so the reader loses track of who is
talking ~~to whom~~ or ~~exactly~~ when the action took place. Perhaps Sentence B is not a logical sequel to Sentence A -- the
writer, in whose head the connection is ~~perfectly~~ clear, has
not _bothered to provide_ ~~given enough thought to providing~~ the missing link. Perhaps the writer has used an important word incorrectly by not
taking the trouble to look it up ~~and make sure.~~ He may think
that "sanguine" and "sanguinary" mean the same thing, but)
~~I can assure you that~~ (the difference is a bloody big one ~~to the
reader.~~ _The reader_ ~~He~~ can only ~~try to~~ infer ~~what~~ (speaking of big differences) what the writer is trying to imply.

Faced with _these_ ~~such a variety of~~ obstacles, the reader
is at first a remarkably tenacious bird. He ~~tends to~~ blame _s_
himself. ~~He~~ obviously missed something, ~~he thinks,~~ and he goes
back over the mystifying sentence, or over the whole paragraph,
piecing it out like an ancient rune, making guesses and moving
on. But he won't do this for long. ~~He will soon run out of
patience.~~ (The writer is making him work too hard ~~-- harder
than he should have to work --~~ (and the reader will look for
one ~~a writer~~ who is better at his craft.

6 --

The writer must therefore constantly ask himself: What am I trying to say? ~~in this sentence?~~ (Surprisingly often, he doesn't know.) ~~And~~ Then he must look at what he has ~~just~~ written and ask: Have I said it? Is it clear to someone ~~who is coming upon~~ [encountering] the subject for the first time? If it's not~~,~~ ~~clear,~~ it is because some fuzz has worked its way into the machinery. The clear writer is a person ~~who is~~ clear-headed enough to see this stuff for what it is: fuzz.

I don't mean ~~to suggest~~ that some people are born clear-headed and are therefore natural writers, whereas ~~other people~~ [others] are naturally fuzzy and will ~~therefore~~ never write well. Thinking clearly is ~~an entirely~~ [a] conscious act that the writer must ~~keep forcing~~ [force] upon himself, just as if he were ~~starting~~ [embarking] out on any other ~~kind of~~ project that ~~calls for~~ [requires] logic: adding up a laundry list or doing an algebra problem ~~or playing chess.~~ Good writing doesn't ~~just~~ come naturally, though most people obviously think ~~it's as easy as walking.~~ [it does.] The professional

WRITING SUGGESTIONS

1. Each of the essays in Chapter 2, "Writers on Writing," is concerned with the importance of writing well, of using language effectively and responsibly. Write an essay in which you explore one of the common themes (audience, revision, diction, simplicity) that is emphasized in two or more of the selections.

2. Visit your library or local bookstore and examine the reference books offering advice on writing. What kinds of books did you find? What does the large number of such books say to you about Americans' attitudes toward writing? Compare and contrast the approaches several books take and the audiences at which each book is aimed. What conclusions can you draw from your comparisons?

The Maker's Eye: Revising Your Own Manuscripts

Donald M. Murray

Born in Boston, Massachusetts, in 1924, Donald M. Murray taught writing for many years at the University of New Hampshire, his alma mater. He has served as an editor at Time *magazine, and he won the Pulitzer Prize in 1954 for editorials that appeared in the* Boston Globe. *Murray's published works include novels, short stories, poetry, and sourcebooks for teachers of writing, like* A Writer Teaches Writing: A Complete Revision *(1985),* The Craft of Revision *(1991), and* Learning by Teaching *(1982), in which he explores aspects of the writing process.* Write to Learn *(7th ed., 2002), a textbook for college composition courses, is based on Murray's belief that writers learn to write by writing, by taking a piece of writing through the whole process, from invention to revision. In the past few years Murray has been producing a weekly column entitled "Now and Then" for the* Boston Globe.

In the following essay, first published in the Writer *in October 1973 and later revised for this text, Murray discusses the importance of revision to the work of the writer. Most professional writers live by the maxim that "writing is rewriting." And to rewrite or revise effectively, we need to become better readers of our own work, open to discovering new meanings, and sensitive to our use of language. Murray draws on the experiences of many writers to make a compelling argument for careful revising and editing.*

WRITING TO DISCOVER: *Thinking back on your education to date, what did you think you had to do when teachers asked you to revise a piece of your writing? How did the request to revise make you feel? Write about your earliest memories of revising some of your writing. What kinds of changes do you remember making?*

When students complete a first draft, they consider the job of writing done — and their teachers too often agree. When professional writers complete a first draft, they usually feel that they are at the start of the writing process. When a draft is completed, the job of writing can begin.

That difference in attitude is the difference between amateur and professional, inexperience and experience, journeyman and craftsman. Peter F. Drucker, the prolific business writer, calls his first draft "the zero draft" — after that he can start counting. Most writers share the feeling that the first draft, and all of those which follow, are opportunities to discover what they have to say and how best they can say it.

To produce a progression of drafts, each of which says more and says it more clearly, the writer has to develop a special kind of reading skill. In school we are taught to decode what appears on the page as finished writing. Writers, however, face a different category of possibility and responsibility when they read their own drafts. To them the words on the page are never finished. Each can be changed and rearranged, can set off a chain reaction of confusion or clarified meaning. This is a different kind of reading which is possibly more difficult and certainly more exciting.

Writers must learn to be their own best enemy. They must accept the criticism of others and be suspicious of it; they must accept the praise of others and be even more suspicious of it. Writers cannot depend on others. They must detach themselves from their own pages so that they can apply both their caring and their craft to their own work.

Such detachment is not easy. Science-fiction writer Ray Bradbury   5 supposedly puts each manuscript away for a year to the day and then rereads it as a stranger. Not many writers have the discipline or the time to do this. We must read when our judgment may be at its worst, when we are close to the euphoric moment of creation.

Then the writer, counsels novelist Nancy Hale, "should be critical of everything that seems to him most delightful in his style. He should excise what he most admires, because he wouldn't thus admire it if he weren't . . . in a sense protecting it from criticism." John Ciardi, the poet, adds, "The last act of the writing must be to become one's own reader. It is, I suppose, a schizophrenic process, to begin passionately and to end critically, to begin hot and to end cold; and, more important, to be passion-hot and critic-cold at the same time."

Most people think that the principal problem is that writers are too proud of what they have written. Actually, a greater problem for most professional writers is one shared by the majority of students. They are overly critical, think everything is dreadful, tear up page after page, never complete a draft, see the task as hopeless.

The writer must learn to read critically but constructively, to cut what is bad, to reveal what is good. Eleanor Estes, the children's book author, explains: "The writer must survey his work critically, coolly, as though he were a stranger to it. He must be willing to prune, expertly and hard-heartedly. At the end of each revision, a manuscript may look . . . worked over, torn apart, pinned together, added to, deleted from, words changed and words changed back. Yet the book must maintain its original freshness and spontaneity."

Most readers underestimate the amount of rewriting it usually takes to produce spontaneous reading. This is a great disadvantage to the student writer, who sees only a finished product and never watches the craftsman who takes the necessary step back, studies the work carefully, returns to the task, steps back, returns, steps back, again and again. Anthony

Burgess, one of the most prolific writers in the English-speaking world, admits, "I might revise a page twenty times." Roald Dahl, the popular children's writer, states, "By the time I'm nearing the end of a story, the first part will have been reread and altered and corrected at least 150 times. . . . Good writing is essentially rewriting. I am positive of this."

Rewriting isn't virtuous. It isn't something that ought to be done. It is simply something that most writers find they have to do to discover what they have to say and how to say it. It is a condition of the writer's life.

There are, however, a few writers who do little formal rewriting, primarily because they have the capacity and experience to create and review a large number of invisible drafts in their minds before they approach the page. And some writers slowly produce finished pages, performing all the tasks of revision simultaneously, page by page, rather than draft by draft. But it is still possible to see the sequence followed by most writers most of the time in rereading their own work.

Most writers scan their drafts first, reading as quickly as possible to catch the larger problems of subject and form, and then move in closer and closer as they read and write, reread and rewrite.

The first thing writers look for in their drafts is *information*. They know that a good piece of writing is built from specific, accurate, and interesting information. The writer must have an abundance of information from which to construct a readable piece of writing.

Next writers look for *meaning* in the information. The specifics must build to a pattern of significance. Each piece of specific information must carry the reader toward meaning.

Writers reading their own drafts are aware of *audience*. They put themselves in the reader's situation and make sure that they deliver information which a reader wants to know or needs to know in a manner which is easily digested. Writers try to be sure that they anticipate and answer the questions a critical reader will ask when reading the piece of writing.

Writers make sure that the *form* is appropriate to the subject and the audience. Form, or genre, is the vehicle which carries meaning to the reader, but form cannot be selected until the writer has adequate information to discover its significance and an audience which needs or wants that meaning.

Once writers are sure the form is appropriate, they must then look at the *structure*, the order of what they have written. Good writing is built on a solid framework of logic, argument, narrative, or motivation which runs through the entire piece of writing and holds it together. This is the time when many writers find it most effective to outline as a way of visualizing the hidden spine by which the piece of writing is supported.

The element on which writers may spend a majority of their time is *development*. Each section of a piece of writing must be adequately developed. It must give readers enough information so that they are satisfied.

How much information is enough? That's as difficult as asking how much garlic belongs in a salad. It must be done to taste, but most beginning writers underdevelop, underestimating the reader's hunger for information.

As writers solve development problems, they often have to consider questions of *dimension*. There must be a pleasing and effective proportion among all the parts of the piece of writing. There is a continual process of subtracting and adding to keep the piece of writing in balance.

Finally, writers have to listen to their own voices. *Voice* is the force   20
which drives a piece of writing forward. It is an expression of the writer's authority and concern. It is what is between the words on the page, what glues the piece of writing together. A good piece of writing is always marked by a consistent, individual voice.

As writers read and reread, write and rewrite, they move closer and closer to the page until they are doing line-by-line editing. Writers read their own pages with infinite care. Each sentence, each line, each clause, each phrase, each word, each mark of punctuation, each section of white space between the type has to contribute to the clarification of meaning.

Slowly the writer moves from word to word, looking through language to see the subject. As a word is changed, cut, or added, as a construction is rearranged, all the words used before that moment and all those that follow that moment must be considered and reconsidered.

Writers often read aloud at this stage of the editing process, muttering or whispering to themselves, calling on the ear's experience with language. Does this sound right — or that? Writers edit, shifting back and forth from eye to page to ear to page. I find I must do this careful editing in short runs, no more than fifteen or twenty minutes at a stretch, or I become too kind with myself. I begin to see what I hope is on the page, not what actually is on the page.

This sounds tedious if you haven't done it, but actually it is fun. Making something right is immensely satisfying, for writers begin to learn what they are writing about by writing. Language leads them to meaning, and there is the joy of discovery, of understanding, of making meaning clear as the writer employs the technical skills of language.

Words have double meanings, even triple and quadruple meanings.   25
Each word has its own potential of connotation and denotation. And when writers rub one word against the other, they are often rewarded with a sudden insight, an unexpected clarification.

The maker's eye moves back and forth from word to phrase to sentence to paragraph to sentence to phrase to word. The maker's eye sees the need for variety and balance, for a firmer structure, for a more appropriate form. It peers into the interior of the paragraph, looking for coherence, unity, and emphasis, which make meaning clear.

I learned something about this process when my first bifocals were prescribed. I had ordered a larger section of the reading portion of the glass because of my work, but even so, I could not contain my eyes within this new limit of vision. And I still find myself taking off my glasses and bending my nose toward the page, for my eyes unconsciously flick back and forth across the page, back to another page, forward to still another, as I try to see each evolving line in relation to every other line.

When does this process end? Most writers agree with the great Russian writer Tolstoy, who said, "I scarcely ever reread my published writings, if by chance I come across a page, it always strikes me: all this must be rewritten; this is how I should have written it."

The maker's eye is never satisfied, for each word has the potential to ignite new meaning. This article has been twice written all the way through the writing process . . . . Now it is to be republished in a book. The editors made a few small suggestions, and then I read it with my maker's eye. Now it has been re-edited, re-revised, re-read, and re-re-edited, for each piece of writing to the writer is full of potential and alternatives.

A piece of writing is never finished. It is delivered to a deadline, torn   30
out of the typewriter on demand, sent off with a sense of accomplishment and shame and pride and frustration. If only there were a couple more days, time for just another run at it, perhaps then . . . .

FOCUSING ON CONTENT

1. How does Murray define *information* and *meaning* (13–14)? Why is the distinction between the two terms important?

2. According to Murray, at what point(s) in the writing process do writers become concerned about the individual words they are using? What do you think Murray means when he says in paragraph 24 that "language leads [writers] to meaning"?

3. The phrase "the maker's eye" appears in Murray's title and in several places throughout the essay. What do you suppose he means by this? Consider how the maker's eye could be different from the reader's eye.

4. According to Murray, when is a piece of writing finished? What, for him, is the function of deadlines?

FOCUSING ON WRITING

1. What does Murray see as the connection between reading and writing? How does reading help the writer? What should writers be looking for in their reading? What kinds of writing techniques or strategies does Murray use in his essay? Why should we read a novel or magazine article differently than we would a draft of one of our own essays?

2. According to Murray, writers look for information, meaning, audience, form, structure, development, dimension, and voice in their drafts. What rationale

or logic do you see, if any, in the way Murray has ordered these items? Are these the kinds of concerns you have when reading your drafts? Explain.

3. What are the essential differences between revising and editing? What types of language concerns are dealt with at each stage? Why is it important to revise before editing?

4. Murray notes that writers often reach a stage in their editing where they read aloud, "muttering or whispering to themselves, calling on the ear's experience with language" (23). What exactly do you think writers are listening for when they read aloud? Try reading several paragraphs of Murray's essay aloud. Explain what you learned about his writing. Have you ever read your own writing aloud? If so, what did you discover?

5. Compared to the paragraphs of many other writers, Murray's paragraphs are short. Why do you suppose Murray chose to use short paragraphs? What, for example, would be lost if paragraphs 12–14 or 24–25 were joined together? Explain.

LANGUAGE IN ACTION

Carefully read the opening four paragraphs of Annie Dillard's "Living Like Weasels," which is taken from *Teaching a Stone to Talk* (1982). Using two different color pens, first circle the subject and underline the verb in each main clause in one color, and then circle the subject and underline the verb in each subordinate clause with the other. What does this exercise reveal about Dillard's diction (nouns and verbs) and sentence structure? (Glossary: *Diction*)

A weasel is wild. Who knows what he thinks? He sleeps in his underground den, his tail draped over his nose. Sometimes he lives in his den for two days without leaving. Outside, he stalks rabbits, mice, muskrats, and birds, killing more bodies than he can eat warm, and often dragging the carcasses home. Obedient to instinct, he bites his prey at the neck, either splitting the jugular vein at the throat or crunching the brain at the base of the skull, and he does not let go. One naturalist refused to kill a weasel who was socketed into his hand deeply as a rattlesnake. The man could in no way pry the tiny weasel off, and he had to walk half a mile to water, the weasel dangling from his palm, and soak him off like a stubborn label.

And once, says Ernest Thompson Seton — once, a man shot an eagle out of the sky. He examined the eagle and found the dry skull of a weasel fixed by the jaws to his throat. The supposition is that the eagle had pounced on the weasel and the weasel swiveled and bit as instinct taught him, tooth to neck, and nearly won. I would like to have seen that eagle from the air a few weeks or months before he was shot: was the whole weasel still attached to his feathered throat, a fur pendant? Or did the eagle eat what he could reach, gutting the living weasel with his talons before his breast, bending his beak, cleaning the beautiful airborne bones?

I have been reading about weasels because I saw one last week. I startled a weasel who startled me, and we exchanged a long glance.

Twenty minutes from my house, through the woods by the quarry and across the highway, is Hollins Pond, a remarkable piece of shallowness, where I like to go at sunset and sit on a tree trunk. Hollins Pond is also called Murray's Pond; it covers two acres of bottomland near Tinker Creek with six inches of water and six thousand lily pads. In winter, brown-and-white steers stand in the middle of it, merely dampening their hooves; from the distant shore they look like miracle itself, complete with miracle's nonchalance. Now, in summer, the steers are gone. The water lilies have blossomed and spread to a green horizontal plane that is terra firma to plodding blackbirds, and tremulous ceiling to black leeches, crayfish, and carp.

WRITING SUGGESTIONS

1. Why do you suppose teachers report that revision is the most difficult stage in the writing process for their students? What is it about revision that makes it difficult, or at least makes people perceive it as being difficult? Write an essay in which you explore your own experiences with revision. You may find it helpful to review what you wrote for the Writing to Discover prompt at the beginning of this essay.

2. Writing about pressing social issues usually requires a clear statement of a particular problem and the precise definition of critical terms. For example, if you were writing about the increasing number of people being kept alive by machines, you would need to examine the debate surrounding the legal and medical definitions of the word *death*. Debates continue about the meanings of other controversial terms, such as *morality, minority* (ethnic), *alcoholism, racism, sexual harassment, life* (as in the abortion issue), *pornography, liberal, gay, censorship, conservative, remedial, insanity, literacy, political correctness, assisted suicide, lying, high crimes and misdemeanors,* and *kidnapping* (as in custody disputes). Select one of these words or one of your own. After carefully researching some of the controversial people, situations, and events surrounding your word, write an essay in which you discuss the problems associated with the term and its definition.

In Praise of the Humble Comma

Pico Iyer

Pico Iyer is one of the most popular travel writers at work today. "Travel," writes Iyer, "is how we put a face on the Other and step a little beyond our secondhand images of the alien." Born in 1957 to Indian parents, Iyer graduated from Eton, England's most famous preparatory school, and Oxford University. What is particularly noteworthy about Iyer's travel writing is that he crosses ethnic and cultural barriers with an easy and natural style, taking note of both the borders and the essences of the countries he visits. His books include Video Night in Kathmandu and Other Reports from the Not-So-Distant Far East *(1988);* The Lady and the Monk: Four Seasons in Kyoto *(1991);* Falling Off the Map: Some Lonely Places of the World *(1993);* Cuba and the Night: A Novel *(1995);* Tropical Classical: Essays from Several Directions *(1998);* The Global Soul: Jet Lag, Shopping Malls, and the Search for Home *(2000); and the novel* Abandon *(2003). In the following essay, which first appeared in* Time *magazine on June 13, 1988, Iyer takes an apparent detour from his travel writing to offer his take on the nuances and importance of the lowly comma, a mark of punctuation we often take for granted. As you read, however, notice the way that he uses his vast cross-cultural travel experience to inform his analysis of the stylistic messages that the comma can convey. Pay particular attention to the way Iyer constructs his paragraphs and the manner in which he progresses from one to the next.*

WRITING TO DISCOVER: *In "Notes on Punctuation" the late Lewis Thomas had this to say about commas:*

The commas are the most useful and usable of all stops. It is highly important to put them in place as you go along. If you try to come back after doing a paragraph and stick them in the various spots that tempt you you will discover that they tend to swarm like minnows into all sorts of crevices whose existence you hadn't realized before and before you know it the whole long sentence becomes immobilized and lashed up squirming in commas. Better to use them sparingly, and with affection, precisely when the need for each arises, nicely, by itself.

What has been your experience in using commas? Do commas confuse you, or do you know the rules for their use?

The gods, they say, give breath, and they take it away. But the same could be said — could it not? — of the humble comma. Add it to the present clause, and, of a sudden, the mind is, quite literally, given pause

111

to think; take it out if you wish or forget it and the mind is deprived of a resting place. Yet still the comma gets no respect. It seems just a slip of a thing, a pedant's tick, a blip on the edge of our consciousness, a kind of printer's smudge almost. Small, we claim, is beautiful (especially in the age of the microchip). Yet what is so often used, and so rarely recalled, as the comma — unless it be breath itself?

Punctuation, one is taught, has a point: to keep up law and order. Punctuation marks are the road signs placed along the highway of our communications — to control speeds, provide directions, and prevent head-on collisions. A period has the unblinking finality of a red light; the comma is a flashing yellow light that asks us only to slow down; and the semicolon is a stop sign that tells us to ease gradually to a halt, before gradually starting up again. By establishing the relations between words, punctuation establishes the relations between people using words. That may be one reason why schoolteachers exalt it and lovers defy it ("We love each other and belong to each other let's don't ever hurt each other Nicole let's don't ever hurt each other," wrote Gary Gilmore to his girlfriend). A comma, he must have known, "separates inseparables," in the clinching words of H. W. Fowler, King of English Usage.

Punctuation, then, is a civic prop, a pillar that holds society upright. (A run-on sentence, its phrases piling up without division, is as unsightly as a sink piled high with dirty dishes.) Small wonder, then, that punctuation was one of the first proprieties of the Victorian age, the age of the corset, that the modernists threw off: the sexual revolution might be said to have begun when Joyce's Molly Bloom spilled out all her private thoughts in 36 pages of unbridled, almost unperioded, and officially censored prose; and another rebellion was surely marked when e. e. cummings first felt free to commit "God" to the lower case.

Punctuation thus becomes the signature of cultures. The hot-blooded Spaniard seems to be revealed in the passion and urgency of his doubled exclamation points and question marks *("¡Caramba!" "¿Quien sabe?")*, while the impassive Chinese traditionally added to his so-called inscrutability by omitting directions from his ideograms. The anarchy and commotion of the '60s were given voice in the exploding exclamation marks, riotous capital letters, and Day-Glo italics of Tom Wolfe's spray-paint prose; and in Communist societies, where the State is absolute, the dignity — and divinity — of capital letters is reserved for Ministries, Sub-Committees, and Secretariats.

Yet punctuation is something more than a culture's birthmark; it scores the music in our minds, gets our thoughts moving to the rhythm of our hearts. Punctuation is the notation in the sheet music of our words, telling us where to rest, or when to raise our voices; it acknowledges that the meaning of our discourse, as of any symphonic composition, lies not in the units but in the pauses, the pacing, and the phrasing.

Punctuation is the way one bats one's eyes, lowers one's voice, or blushes demurely. Punctuation adjusts the tone and color and volume till the feeling comes into perfect focus, not disgust exactly, but distaste; not lust, or like, but love.

Punctuation, in short, gives us the human voice, and all the meanings that lie between the words. "You aren't young, are you?" loses its innocence when it loses the question mark. Every child knows the menace of a dropped apostrophe (the parent's "Don't do that" shifting to the more enunciated "Do not do that"), and every believer, the ignominy of having his faith reduced to "faith." Add an exclamation point to "To be or not to be . . ." and the gloomy Dane has all the resolve he needs; add a comma, and the noble sobriety of "God save the Queen" becomes a cry of desperation bordering on double sacrilege.

Sometimes, of course, our markings may be simply a matter of aesthetics. Popping in a comma can be like slipping on the necklace that gives an outfit quiet elegance, or like catching the sound of running water that complements, as it completes, the silence of the Japanese landscape. When V. S. Naipaul, in his latest novel, writes, "He was a middle-aged man, with glasses," the first comma can seem a little precious. Yet it gives the description a spin, as well as a subtlety, that it otherwise lacks, and it shows that the glasses are not part of the middle-agedness, but something else.

Thus all these tiny scratches give us breadth and heft and depth. A world that only has periods is a world without inflections. It is a world without shade. It has a music without sharps and flats. It is a martial music. It has a jackboot rhythm. Words cannot bend and curve. A comma, by comparison, catches the gentle drift of the mind in thought, turning in on itself and back on itself, reversing, redoubling and returning along the course of its own sweet river music; while the semicolon brings clauses and thoughts together with all the silent discretion of a hostess arranging guests around her dinner table.

Punctuation, then, is a matter of care. Care for words, yes, but also, and more important, for what the words imply. Only a lover notices the small things: the way the afternoon light catches the nape of the neck, or how a strand of hair slips out from behind an ear, or the way a finger curls around a cup. And no one scans a letter so closely as a lover, searching for its small print, straining to hear its nuances, its gasps, its sighs and hesitation, poring over the secret messages that lie in every cadence. The difference between "Jane (whom I adore)" and "Jane, whom I adore," and the difference between them both and "Jane — whom I adore — " marks all the distance between ecstasy and heartache. "No iron can pierce the heart with such force as a period put at just the right place," in Isaac Babel's lovely words: a comma can let us hear a voice break, or a heart. Punctuation, in fact, is a labor of love. Which brings us back, in a way, to gods.

FOCUSING ON CONTENT

1. Iyer makes several statements that might be considered thesis statements. (Glossary: *Thesis*) What are they, and which one do you think is best qualified as an expression of what his essay is all about?

2. Iyer uses commas in his own sentences to demonstrate their conventional uses and also to show how they can be used to achieve stylistic effects. Point out several examples, and explain them.

3. In paragraph 4 Iyer writes, "Punctuation thus becomes the signature of cultures." What does he mean by this, and where does he offer evidence to support this idea?

4. Has Iyer made a good case for the importance of the "humble comma"? Why or why not? If the comma is as significant as he claims, why has it been so unused and misused?

FOCUSING ON WRITING

1. Choose any two of Iyer's paragraphs and examine them for paragraph unity. Consult the glossary for any terms with which you are unfamiliar. Ask yourself the following questions about each one:

   Does the paragraph have a clear topic sentence?

   Has the author developed the paragraph clearly and effectively?

   Is the paragraph unified?

   Is the paragraph coherent?

   Has the author used transitions (repeated key words, references to ideas that come before and after, and transitional expressions) to link the paragraph to those before and after it?

   Be prepared to discuss the two paragraphs you examined and to discuss their integrity.

2. How effective are the beginning and the ending of Iyer's essay? What is the relationship between them? How do the beginning and ending support Iyer's thesis? (Glossary: *Beginnings and Endings, Thesis*).

3. Iyer uses a number of figures of speech in his essay. (Glossary: *Figures of Speech*) Point out three or four examples, and explain how effective each is in furthering his observations about the role commas play in writing.

LANGUAGE IN ACTION

In an article in *Newsweek* entitled "Its Academic, or Is It?," Charles R. Larson, a professor of literature at American University in Washington, D.C., takes a stand for correct usage of the apostrophe. Here are the first three paragraphs of his article:

IT'S ACADEMIC, OR IS IT?

If you're 35 years or older, you probably identify a common grammatical error in the heading on this page. Younger than that and, well, you likely have another opinion: "Its all relative" — except, of course, for the apostrophe. Unfortunately, age appears to be the demarcation here. For those in the older group, youth has already won the battle. I've been keeping a list of places where *its* is misused: newspapers, magazines, op-eds in major publications and, more recently, wall texts in museums. A few weeks ago I encountered the error in a book title: *St. Simons: A Summary of It's History,* by R. Edwin and Mary A. Green. My list is getting longer and longer.

Does it even matter that the apostrophe is going the way of the stop sign and the directional signal in our society? Does punctuation count any longer? Are my complaints the ramblings of an old goat who's taught English for too many years?

What's the big deal, anyway? Who cares whether it's *its* or *it's*? Editors don't seem to know when the apostrophe's necessary. (One of them confessed to me that people have always been confused about the apostrophe — better just get rid of it.) My university undergraduates are clearly befuddled by the correct usage. Too many graduate applications — especially those of students aspiring to be creative writers — provide no clue that the writer understands when an apostrophe is required. Even some of my colleagues are confused by this ugglesome contraction.

What have been some of your own experiences in using the apostrophe? How valid are Larson's claims, in your opinion? Research in the library or on the Internet to learn about the apostrophe, its history, and its purpose.

WRITING SUGGESTIONS

1. Iyer has focused his essay on the "humble comma." Write an essay in which you explore some other mark of punctuation, such as the colon or semicolon. Following in Iyer's footsteps, try to use the mark of punctuation you discuss to demonstrate the points you make. Make sure that you carefully develop the content of each paragraph and its topic sentence. Check that you have used transitions within each paragraph and between paragraphs to enhance the flow of ideas throughout the essay.

2. Write an essay in which you explore what might be said about the importance of the paragraph as a compositional building block. To what extent can it be a mini-essay in itself? To what extent might it be some other structural device within an essay? What, for example, is a transitional paragraph or a paragraph block?

Always Living in Spanish

Marjorie Agosín

Defying all conventional impressions of South American writers, the poet, essayist, and international human rights activist Marjorie Agosín was born in 1955 in Bethesda, Maryland, and raised in Santiago de Chile. A descendent of Russian and Austrian Jews, Agosín left Chile and settled in Georgia with her family when rumors that a military coup to overthrow the Marxist government of Salvatore Allende was about to become a reality. The brutal dictatorship of Auguste Pinochet resulted in many atrocities and an untold number of disappearances, an estimated 10 percent of them Jews. In that history was born Agosín's literary and human rights concerns. After receiving her B.A. from the University of Georgia and her Ph.D. from the University of Indiana, she went on to become professor and chair of the Department of Spanish at Wellesley College in Massachusetts. The recipient of numerous awards, Agosín has also published many books, including Tapestries of Hope, Threads of Love *(1996), accounts of the lives of women under the Pinochet government;* A Cross and a Star: Memoirs of a Jewish Girl in Chile *(1997) about her mother;* Always from Somewhere Else *(1998) about her father; and* Dear Anne Frank *(1998), a collection of bilingual poems.*

In "Always Living in Spanish" (translated by Celeste Kostopulos-Cooperman), which first appeared in Poets & Writers *(March/April 1999), Agosín reflects on her dilemma of living, thinking, and writing in Spanish while residing in America and her need to always write in Spanish in order to recover her Chilean childhood and guard the memory of those lost. As she writes, "The new and learned English language did not fit with the visceral emotions and themes that my poetry contained, but by writing in Spanish I could recover fragrances, spoken rhythms, and the passion of my own identity."*

Writing to Discover: *Reread Agosín's statement above about her need to write in Spanish and reflect on the power of language as a way of returning to something or someone that you once knew. If you are bilingual or multilingual, comment on the accuracy of Agosín's observations about "recovering" through language based on your own experiences.*

In the evenings in the northern hemisphere, I repeat the ancient ritual that I observed as a child in the southern hemisphere: going out while the night is still warm and trying to recognize the stars as it begins to grow dark silently. In the sky of my country, Chile, that long and wide stretch of land that the poets blessed and dictators abused, I could easily name the stars: the three Marias, the Southern Cross, and the three Lilies, names of beloved and courageous women.

But here in the United States, where I have lived since I was a young girl, the solitude of exile makes me feel that so little is mine, that not even the sky has the same constellations, the trees and the fauna the same names or sounds, or the rubbish the same smell. How does one recover the familiar? How does one name the unfamiliar? How can one be another or live in a foreign language? These are the dilemmas of one who writes in Spanish and lives in translation.

Since my earliest childhood in Chile I lived with the tempos and the melodies of a multiplicity of tongues: German, Yiddish, Russian, Turkish, and many Latin songs. Because everyone was from somewhere else, my relatives laughed, sang, and fought in a Babylon of languages. Spanish was reserved for matters of extreme seriousness, for commercial transactions, or for illnesses, but everyone's mother tongue was always associated with the memory of spaces inhabited in the past: the shtetl, the flowering and vast Vienna avenues, the minarets of Turkey, and the Ladino whispers of Toledo. When my paternal grandmother sang old songs in Turkish, her voice and body assumed the passion of one who was there in the city of Istanbul, gazing by turns toward the west and the east.

Destiny and the always ambiguous nature of history continued my family's enforced migration, and because of it I, too, became one who had to live and speak in translation. The disappearances, torture, and clandestine deaths in my country in the early seventies drove us to the United States, that other America that looked with suspicion at those who did not speak English and especially those who came from the supposedly uncivilized regions of Latin America. I had left a dangerous place that was my home, only to arrive in a dangerous place that was not: a high school in the small town of Athens, Georgia, where my poor English and my accent were the cause of ridicule and insult. The only way I could recover my usurped country and my Chilean childhood was by continuing to write in Spanish, the same way my grandparents had sung in their own tongues in diasporic sites.

The new and learned English language did not fit with the visceral   5
emotions and themes that my poetry contained, but by writing in Spanish I could recover fragrances, spoken rhythms, and the passion of my own identity. Daily I felt the need to translate myself for the strangers living all around me, to tell them why we were in Georgia, why we ate differently, why we had fled, why my accent was so thick, and why I did not look Hispanic. Only at night, writing poems in Spanish, could I return to my senses, and soothe my own sorrow over what I had left behind.

This is how I became a Chilean poet who wrote in Spanish and lived in the southern United States. And then, one day, a poem of mine was translated and published in the English language. Finally, for the first time since I had left Chile, I felt I didn't have to explain myself. My poem, expressed in another language, spoke for itself . . . and for me.

Sometimes the austere sounds of English help me bear the solitude of knowing that I am foreign and so far away from those about whom I write. I must admit I would like more opportunities to read in Spanish to people whose language and culture is also mine, to join in our common heritage and in the feast of our sounds. I would also like readers of English to understand the beauty of the spoken word in Spanish, that constant flow of oxytonic and paraoxytonic syllables (*Verde que te quiero verdo*), the joy of writing — of dancing — in another language. I believe that many exiles share the unresolvable torment of not being able to live in the language of their childhood.

I miss that undulating and sensuous language of mine, those baroque descriptions, the sense of being and feeling that Spanish gives me. It is perhaps for this reason that I have chosen and will always choose to write in Spanish. Nothing else from my childhood world remains. My country seems to be frozen in gestures of silence and oblivion. My relatives have died, and I have grown up not knowing a young generation of cousins and nieces and nephews. Many of my friends disappeared, others were tortured, and the most fortunate, like me, became guardians of memory. For us, to write in Spanish is to always be in active pursuit of memory. I seek to recapture a world lost to me on that sorrowful afternoon when the blue electric sky and the Andean cordillera bade me farewell. On that, my last Chilean day, I carried under my arm my innocence recorded in a little blue notebook I kept even then. Gradually that diary filled with memoranda, poems written in free verse, descriptions of dreams and of the thresholds of my house surrounded by cherry trees and gardenias. To write in Spanish is for me a gesture of survival. And because of translation, my memory has now become a part of the memory of many others.

Translators are not traitors, as the proverb says, but rather splendid friends in this great human community of language.

FOCUSING ON CONTENT

1. Why does Agosín feel "so little is mine" (2) here in the United States?

2. Why does Agosín say that she "left a dangerous place that was my home, only to arrive in a dangerous place that was not" (4)?

3. Why does Agosín see her first poem that was translated into English as so important? Cite some of the comments Agosín makes about translation. In what ways is translation important for her?

4. Why does the author say she will never write in any language but Spanish?

FOCUSING ON WRITING

1. What is Agosín's thesis in this essay? (Glossary: *Thesis*) Where is the best statement of her thesis?

2. Agosín says that she would like her readers to experience Spanish, "that constant flow of oxytonic and paraoxytonic syllables" (7). What do these two terms mean, and what quality does she say they give Spanish?

3. How effective is the beginning of Agosín's essay? (Glossary: *Beginnings and Endings*)

4. Agosín's essay was first published in *Poets & Writers*, a journal for writers. In what ways do you think Agosín's essay might be helpful to the journal's readers? (Glossary: *Audience*)

LANGUAGE IN ACTION

Agosín's essay is about translation, and in her final paragraph she makes an oblique reference to the Italian proverb "Traduttore, traditore!" which roughly translates as "the translator is a traitor." Examine the following translations taken from "Archived Humorous Translations" at www.wordmill.com/archive2.html.

- These Japanese instructions were found on an air conditioner: *Cooles & heats. If you want just condition of warm in your room, please control yourself.*
- This copy was found in an advertisement for a Hong Kong dentist: *Teeth extracted by the latest Methodists.*
- A Swiss restaurant's menu boasts: *Our wines leave you nothing to hope for.*
- When the Parker Pen marketed a ballpoint pen in Mexico, its ads were supposed to say, "It won't leak in your pocket and embarrass you." However, a translator for the company mistakenly translated "embarrass" to the Spanish word "embarazar." Instead the ads said: *It won't leak in your pocket and make you pregnant.*
- The Coors beer slogan "Turn it loose" was mistranslated into Spanish as *Suffer from diarrhea.*
- A sign posted at a onetime German Café in Berkeley, California: *This rest room is for use of our only customer.* No wonder they went out of business.
- This detour sign was posted in Kyushi, Japan: *Stop! Drive sideways.*
- This notice was found on the back of a restroom door in Basra, Iraq: *Have you left your ring? Have you left your watch? Have you anything of value left?*

Why do you suppose it is so difficult to translate ideas from one language to another? If you, or any members of your class, speak one of the languages in the examples above, try to explain what went wrong with the translation. What insights into the nature of language do you get from this exercise? Do the problems with these translations help you to better understand Agosín's need to write in her native Spanish?

WRITING SUGGESTIONS

1. It is not always possible to go home. One way to do so, however, is to eat the food that those at home cooked and cherished. Another way is to speak the language of where you used to live. One need not be from a foreign culture to experience a different way of speaking. After all, there are regional and social differences in the ways people speak right here in the United States. Write a personal essay about food or language as a way of going home, of recapturing a time gone by, and of bringing to life the people you know and love.

2. Agosín's writing has been forged in the turmoil created by Chile's unstable political history in the later part of the twentieth century. The fact that she and the members of her family were historically forced to claim that they were from "somewhere else" not only forces her to remember those relatives and their circumstances but also causes her to see cultural differences that anyone who has lived in one country exclusively could not possibly see or understand. More importantly, the experiences she had with the members of her family and their many tongues made her a devoted lover of language in ways well beyond that usually seen in writers. Write an essay in which you discuss the importance of language for foreign writers who want and, indeed, need to see their work translated. Make use of Agosín's essay as well of the works of other world authors you have read.

3

POLITICS, PROPAGANDA, AND DOUBLESPEAK

Political language is powerful; it is persuasive. At its best political language inspires people and challenges them to make a difference, offering the hope that in working together, we can create a better world. Over forty years ago President John F. Kennedy energized a nation by exhorting its citizens to "ask not what your country can do for you — ask what you can do for your country." And we have heard stories of how, with powerful words, Franklin D. Roosevelt and Winston Churchill rallied their nations to defeat Nazi Germany during World War II and how Mahatma Gandhi, Martin Luther King Jr., and Nelson Mandela championed nonviolence in leading the fight against oppression and racism in India, America, and South Africa.

But political language can be abused. At its worst, political language can be deliberately manipulated to mislead, deceive, or cover up. In the wake of the war in Vietnam, the Watergate scandal and the subsequent resignation of President Nixon, the Iran-Contra affair, and the Clinton-Lewinsky scandal, Americans have grown cynical about their political leaders' promises and programs. As presidential campaigns seem to get started earlier and earlier, we are fed a daily diet of political language. Political speech saturates the American media. In daily newspapers and on the evening news we listen to fiery sound bites and seemingly spontaneous one-liners — presented as though they contained an entire argument or philosophy. Our politicians are savvy about the time constraints in news media, and their speechwriters make sure that long speeches have at least a few headline-grabbing quotes that might win them wide, albeit brief, coverage. But in the end, we are left wondering what we can believe and who we can trust.

We begin this chapter with three essays to help you think critically about the political language that you hear every day so that you can function as a responsible citizen. In the first essay, "Propaganda: How Not to Be Bamboozled," Donna Woolfolk Cross takes the mystery out of the oft-misunderstood word *propaganda* as she identifies and defines thirteen of the rhetorical devices the propagandist uses to manipulate language for political purposes. Her examples and advice, in turn, will help you to detect these nasty "tricks" and not to be mislead by the silver tongues of politicians. George Orwell, in his classic essay "Politics and the English Language," picks up where Cross leaves off. Orwell knows that language is power, and he argues for a clear, simplified English that everyone can understand. He takes politicians to task for language which he claims is "designed to make lies sound truthful and murder respectable, and to give an appearance of solidity to pure wind." In "The World of Double-speak," political watchdog William Lutz examines the language of government and corporate bureaucrats, "language which pretends to communicate but doesn't." His examples illustrate how language can be used to deliberately "mislead, distort, deceive, inflate, circumvent, obfuscate." The next two articles examine specific language phenomena in the political arena. First, Cullen Murphy takes a somewhat tongue-in-cheek look at America's love affair with euphemisms in "The E Word." Like the rest of us, he wants to know if euphemisms are really all that bad for us. On a more serious note, Walter Isaacson, in "How They Chose These Words," tells the story of how the Declaration of Independence was written and analyzes the powerful impact that Benjamin Franklin's seemingly insignificant editorial changes had on one of this country's most important political documents. His analysis provides insight into several of the rhetorical techniques and strategies that form the foundation of the American political tradition.

CASE STUDY: THE ENGLISH-ONLY DEBATE

For over two hundred years, English has been the unofficial language of the United States. So why now is there a push for legislation to make English America's "official" language? The articles in this Case Study give us many perspectives on the heated debate over making English the "official" language of the United States. We start with an essay that provides the historical context for a meaningful discussion of the relationship between language and government. Next we present the argument of U.S. English, an organization founded to promote English-only legislation. The third essay argues that bilingual education promoted in the name of "diversity" puts children whose first language is not standard English at a distinct disadvantage. Finally, we present two personal perspectives on the issue, one by an Hispanic American and the other by an African American.

Propaganda: How Not to Be Bamboozled

DONNA WOOLFOLK CROSS

Donna Woolfolk Cross graduated from the University of Pennsylvania in 1969 and went on to receive her M.A. from the University of California, Los Angeles. A professor of English at Onondaga Community College in Syracuse, New York, Cross has written extensively about language that manipulates, including the books Mediaspeak: How Television Makes Up Your Mind *(1981) and* Word Abuse: How the Words We Use Use Us *(1979), which won an award from the National Council of Teachers of English. Her early work as a writer of advertising copy influences her teaching and writing. In an interview she remarked, "I was horrified to discover that first-year college students were completely unaware of — and, therefore, unable to defend themselves against — the most obvious plays of admen and politicians. . . . We tend to think of language as something we use; we are much less often aware of the way we are used by language. The only defense is to become wise to the ways of words."*

Although most people are against propaganda in principle, few know exactly what it is and how it works. In the following essay, which first appeared in Speaking of Words: A Language Reader *(1977), Cross takes the mystery out of propaganda. She starts by providing a definition of it, and then she classifies the tricks of the propagandist into thirteen major categories. Cross's essay is chock-full of useful advice on how not to be manipulated by propaganda.*

WRITING TO DISCOVER: *What do you think of when you hear the word* propaganda? *What kinds of people, organizations, or issues do you associate with it? Write about why you think people use propaganda.*

Propaganda. If an opinion poll were taken tomorrow, we can be sure that nearly everyone would be against it because it *sounds* so bad. When we say, "Oh, that's just propaganda," it means, to most people, "That's a pack of lies." But really, propaganda is simply a means of persuasion and so it can be put to work for good causes as well as bad — to persuade people to give to charity, for example, or to love their neighbors, or to stop polluting the environment.

For good or evil, propaganda pervades our daily lives, helping to shape our attitudes on a thousand subjects. Propaganda probably determines the brand of toothpaste you use, the movies you see, the candidates you elect when you get to the polls. Propaganda works by tricking us, by momentarily distracting the eye while the rabbit pops out from beneath the cloth. Propaganda works best with an uncritical audience. Joseph

Goebbels, propaganda minister in Nazi Germany, once defined his work as "the conquest of the masses." The masses would not have been conquered, however, if they had known how to challenge and to question, how to make distinctions between propaganda and reasonable argument.

People are bamboozled mainly because they don't recognize propaganda when they see it. They need to be informed about the various devices that can be used to mislead and deceive — about the propagandist's overflowing bag of tricks. The following, then, are some common pitfalls for the unwary.

1. NAME-CALLING

As its title suggests, this device consists of labeling people or ideas with words of bad connotation, literally, "calling them names." Here the propagandist tries to arouse our contempt so we will dismiss the "bad name" person or idea without examining its merits.

Bad names have played a tremendously important role in the history   5
of the world. They have ruined reputations and ended lives, sent people to prison and to war, and just generally made us mad at each other for centuries.

Name-calling can be used against policies, practices, beliefs and ideals, as well as against individuals, groups, races, nations. Name-calling is at work when we hear a candidate for office described as a "foolish idealist" or a "two-faced liar" or when an incumbent's policies are denounced as "reckless," "reactionary," or just plain "stupid." Some of the most effective names a public figure can be called are ones that may not denote anything specific: "Congresswoman Jane Doe is a *bleeding heart!*" (Did she vote for funds to help paraplegics?) or "The senator is a *tool of Washington!*" (Did he happen to agree with the president?) Senator Yakalot uses name-calling when he denounces his opponent's "radical policies" and calls them (and him) "socialist," "pinko," and part of a "heartless plot." He also uses it when he calls cars "puddle-jumpers," "can openers," and "motorized baby buggies."

The point here is that when the propagandist uses name-calling, he doesn't want us to think — merely to react, blindly, unquestioningly. So the best defense against being taken in by name-calling is to stop and ask, "Forgetting the bad name attached to it, what are the merits of the idea itself? What does this name really mean, anyway?"

2. GLITTERING GENERALITIES

Glittering generalities are really name-calling in reverse. Name-calling uses words with bad connotations; glittering generalities are words with good connotations — "virtue words," as the Institute for Propaganda Analysis has called them. The Institute explains that while name-calling tries to get us to *reject* and *condemn* someone or something without examining the evidence, glittering generalities try to get us to *accept* and *agree* without examining the evidence.

We believe in, fight for, live by "virtue words" which we feel deeply about: "justice," "motherhood," "the American way," "our Constitutional rights," "our Christian heritage." These sound good, but when we examine them closely, they turn out to have no specific, definable meaning. They just make us feel good. Senator Yakalot uses glittering generalities when he says, "I stand for all that is good in America, for our American way and our American birthright." But what exactly *is* "good for America"? How can we define our "American birthright"? Just what parts of the American society and culture does "our American way" refer to?

We often make the mistake of assuming we are personally unaffected   10
by glittering generalities. The next time you find yourself assuming that, listen to a political candidate's speech on TV and see how often the use of glittering generalities elicits cheers and applause. That's the danger of propaganda; it *works*. Once again, our defense against it is to ask questions: Forgetting the virtue words attached to it, what are the merits of the idea itself? What does "Americanism" (or "freedom" or "truth") really *mean* here? . . .

Both name-calling and glittering generalities work by stirring our emotions in the hope that this will cloud our thinking. Another approach that propaganda uses is to create a distraction, a "red herring," that will make people forget or ignore the real issues. There are several different kinds of "red herrings" that can be used to distract attention.

3. PLAIN-FOLKS APPEAL

"Plain folks" is the device by which a speaker tries to win our confidence and support by appearing to be a person like ourselves — "just one of the plain folks." The plain-folks appeal is at work when candidates go around shaking hands with factory workers, kissing babies in supermarkets, and sampling pasta with Italians, fried chicken with Southerners, bagels and blintzes with Jews. "Now I'm a businessman like yourselves" is a plain-folks appeal, as is "I've been a farm boy all my life." Senator Yakalot tries the plain-folks appeal when he says, "I'm just a small-town boy like you fine people." The use of such expressions once prompted Lyndon Johnson to quip, "Whenever I hear someone say, 'I'm just an old country lawyer,' the first thing I reach for is my wallet to make sure it's still there."

The irrelevancy of the plain-folks appeal is obvious: even if the man *is* "one of us" (which may not be true at all), that doesn't mean that his ideas and programs are sound — or even that he honestly has our best interests at heart. As with glittering generalities, the danger here is that we may mistakenly assume we are immune to this appeal. But propagandists wouldn't use it unless it had been proved to work. You can protect yourself by asking, "Aside from his 'nice guy next door' image, what does this man stand for? Are his ideas and his past record really supportive of my best interests?"

4. ARGUMENTUM AD POPULUM (STROKING)

Argumentum ad populum means "argument to the people" or "telling the people what they want to hear." The colloquial term from the Watergate era is "stroking," which conjures up pictures of small animals or children being stroked or soothed with compliments until they come to like the person doing the complimenting — and, by extension, his or her ideas.

We all like to hear nice things about ourselves and the group we belong to — we like to be liked — so it stands to reason that we will respond warmly to a person who tells us we are "hard-working taxpayers" or "the most generous, free-spirited nation in the world." Politicians tell farmers they are the "backbone of the American economy" and college students that they are the "leaders and policy makers of tomorrow." Commercial advertisers use stroking more insidiously by asking a question which invites a flattering answer: "What kind of a man reads *Playboy?*" (Does he really drive a Porsche and own $10,000 worth of sound equipment?) Senator Yakalot is stroking his audience when he calls them the "decent law-abiding citizens that are the great pulsing heart and the life blood of this, our beloved country," and when he repeatedly refers to them as "you fine people," "you wonderful folks."

Obviously, the intent here is to sidetrack us from thinking critically about the man and his ideas. Our own good qualities have nothing to do with the issue at hand. Ask yourself, "Apart from the nice things he has to say about me (and my church, my nation, my ethnic group, my neighbors), what does the candidate stand for? Are his or her ideas in my best interests?"

5. ARGUMENTUM AD HOMINEM

Argumentum ad hominem means "argument to the man" and that's exactly what it is. When a propagandist uses *argumentum ad hominem*, he wants to distract our attention from the issue under consideration with personal attacks on the people involved. For example, when Lincoln issued the Emancipation Proclamation, some people responded by calling him the "baboon." But Lincoln's long arms and awkward carriage had nothing to do with the merits of the Proclamation or the question of whether or not slavery should be abolished.

Today *argumentum ad hominem* is still widely used and very effective. You may or may not support the Equal Rights Amendment, but you should be sure your judgment is based on the merits of the idea itself, and not the result of someone's denunciation of the people who support the ERA as "fanatics" or "lesbians" or "frustrated old maids." Senator Yakalot is using *argumentum ad hominem* when he dismisses the idea of using smaller automobiles with a reference to the personal appearance of one of its supporters, Congresswoman Doris Schlepp. Refuse to be waylaid by *argumentum ad hominem* and ask, "Do the personal qualities of the person being discussed have anything to do with the issue at hand? Leaving him or her aside, how good is the idea itself?"

6. TRANSFER (GUILT OR GLORY BY ASSOCIATION)

In *argumentum ad hominem*, an attempt is made to associate negative aspects of a person's character or personal appearance with an issue or idea he supports. The transfer device uses this same process of association to make us accept or condemn a given person or idea.

A better name for the transfer device is guilt (or glory) by association. In glory by association, the propagandist tries to transfer the positive feelings of something we love and respect to the group or idea he wants us to accept. "This bill for a new dam is in the best tradition of this country, the land of Lincoln, Jefferson, and Washington," is glory by association at work. Lincoln, Jefferson, and Washington were great leaders that most of us revere and respect, but they have no logical connection to the proposal under consideration — the bill to build a new dam. Senator Yakalot uses glory by association when he says full-sized cars "have always been as American as Mom's apple pie or a Sunday drive in the country."

The process works equally well in reverse, when guilt by association is used to transfer our dislike or disapproval of one idea or group to some other idea or group that the propagandist wants us to reject and condemn. "John Doe says we need to make some changes in the way our government operates; well, that's exactly what the Ku Klux Klan has said, so there's a meeting of great minds!" That's guilt by association for you; there's no logical connection between John Doe and the Ku Klux Klan apart from the one the propagandist is trying to create in our minds. He wants to distract our attention from John Doe and get us thinking (and worrying) about the Ku Klux Klan and its politics of violence. (Of course, there are sometimes legitimate associations between the two things; if John Doe had been a *member* of the Ku Klux Klan, it would be reasonable and fair to draw a connection between the man and his group.) Senator Yakalot tries to trick his audience with guilt by association when he remarks that "the words 'community' and 'communism' look an awful lot alike!" He does it again when he mentions that Mr. Stu Pott "sports a Fidel Castro beard."

20

How can we learn to spot the transfer device and distinguish between fair and unfair associations? We can teach ourselves to *suspend judgment* until we have answered these questions: "Is there any legitimate connection between the idea under discussion and the thing it is associated with? Leaving the transfer device out of the picture, what are the merits of the idea by itself?"

7. BANDWAGON

Ever hear of the small, ratlike animal called the lemming? Lemmings are arctic rodents with a very odd habit: periodically, for reasons no one entirely knows, they mass together in a large herd and commit suicide by rushing into deep water and drowning themselves. They all run in together, blindly, and not one of them ever seems to stop and ask, "*Why* am I doing this? Is this really what I want to do?" and thus save itself from destruction. Obviously, lemmings are driven to perform their strange mass suicide rites by common instinct. People choose to "follow the herd" for more complex reasons, yet we are still all too often the unwitting victims of the bandwagon appeal.

Essentially, the bandwagon urges us to support an action or an opinion because it is popular — because "everyone else is doing it." This call to "get on the bandwagon" appeals to the strong desire in most of us to be one of the crowd, not to be left out or alone. Advertising makes extensive use of the bandwagon appeal ("join the Pepsi people"), but so do politicians ("Let us join together in this great cause"). Senator Yakalot uses the bandwagon appeal when he says that "More and more citizens are rallying to my cause every day," and asks his audience to "join them — and me — in our fight for America."

One of the ways we can see the bandwagon appeal at work is in the   25
overwhelming success of various fashions and trends which capture the interest (and the money) of thousands of people for a short time, then disappear suddenly and completely. For a year or two in the fifties, every child in North America wanted a coonskin cap so they could be like Davy Crockett; no one wanted to be left out. After that there was the hula-hoop craze that helped to dislocate the hips of thousands of Americans. More recently, what made millions of people rush out to buy their very own "pet rocks"?

The problem here is obvious: just because everyone's doing it doesn't mean that *we* should too. Group approval does not prove that something is true or is worth doing. Large numbers of people have supported actions we now condemn. Just a generation ago, Hitler and Mussolini rose to absolute and catastrophically repressive rule in two of the most sophisticated and cultured countries of Europe. When they came into power they were welled up by massive popular support from millions of people who didn't want to be "left out" at a great historical moment.

Once the mass begins to move — on the bandwagon — it becomes harder and harder to perceive the leader *riding* the bandwagon. So don't be a lemming, rushing blindly on to destruction because "everyone else is doing it." Stop and ask, "Where is this bandwagon headed? Never mind about everybody else, is this what is best for *me*?" . . .

As we have seen, propaganda can appeal to us by arousing our emotions or distracting our attention from the real issues at hand. But there's a third way that propaganda can be put to work against us — by the use of faulty logic. This approach is really more insidious than the other two because it gives the appearance of reasonable, fair argument. It is only when we look more closely that the holes in the logical fiber show up. The following are some of the devices that make use of faulty logic to distort and mislead.

8. FAULTY CAUSE AND EFFECT

As the name suggests, this device sets up a cause-and-effect relationship that may not be true. The Latin name for this logical fallacy is *post hoc ergo propter hoc*, which means "after this, therefore because of this." But just because one thing happened after another doesn't mean that one *caused* the other.

An example of false cause-and-effect reasoning is offered by the story (probably invented) of the woman aboard the ship *Titanic*. She woke up from a nap and, feeling seasick, looked around for a call button to summon the steward to bring her some medication. She finally located a small button on one of the walls of her cabin and pushed it. A split second later, the *Titanic* grazed an iceberg in the terrible crash that was to send the entire ship to its destruction. The woman screamed and said, "Oh, God, what have I done? What have I done?" The humor of that anecdote comes from the absurdity of the woman's assumption that pushing the small red button resulted in the destruction of a ship weighing several hundred tons: "It happened after I pushed it, therefore it must be *because* I pushed it" — *post hoc ergo propter hoc* reasoning. There is, of course, no cause-and-effect relationship there.

The false cause-and-effect fallacy is used very often by political candidates. "After I came to office, the rate of inflation dropped to 6 percent." But did the person do anything to cause the lower rate of inflation or was it the result of other conditions? Would the rate of inflation have dropped anyway, even if he hadn't come to office? Senator Yakalot uses false cause and effect when he says "our forefathers who made this country great never had free hot meal handouts! And look what they did for our country!" He does it again when he concludes that "driving full-sized cars means a better car safety record on our American roads today."

False cause-and-effect reasoning is terribly persuasive because it seems so logical. Its appeal is apparently to experience. We swallowed X product — and the headache went away. We elected Y official and unemployment went down. Many people think, "There *must* be a connection." But causality is an immensely complex phenomenon; you need a

30

good deal of evidence to prove that an event that follows another in time was "therefore" caused by the first event.

Don't be taken in by false cause and effect; be sure to ask, "Is there enough evidence to prove that this cause led to that effect? Could there have been any *other* causes?"

9. FALSE ANALOGY

An analogy is a comparison between two ideas, events, or things. But comparisons can be fairly made only when the things being compared are alike in significant ways. When they are not, false analogy is the result.

A famous example of this is the old proverb "Don't change horses in   35 the middle of a stream," often used as an analogy to convince voters not to change administrations in the middle of a war or other crisis. But the analogy is misleading because there are so many differences between the things compared. In what ways is a war or political crisis like a stream? Is the president or head of state really very much like a horse? And is a nation of millions of people comparable to a man trying to get across a stream? Analogy is false and unfair when it compares two things that have little in common and assumes that they are identical. Senator Yakalot tries to hoodwink his listeners with false analogy when he says, "Trying to take Americans out of the kind of cars they love is as undemocratic as trying to deprive them of the right to vote."

Of course, analogies can be drawn that are reasonable and fair. It would be reasonable, for example, to compare the results of busing in one small Southern city with the possible results in another, *if* the towns have the same kind of history, population, and school policy. We can decide for ourselves whether an analogy is false or fair by asking, "Are the things being compared truly alike in significant ways? Do the differences between them affect the comparison?"

10. BEGGING THE QUESTION

Actually, the name of this device is rather misleading, because it does not appear in the form of a question. Begging the question occurs when, in discussing a questionable or debatable point, a person assumes as already established the very point that he is trying to prove. For example, "No thinking citizen could approve such a completely unacceptable policy as this one." But isn't the question of whether or not the policy *is* acceptable the very point to be established? Senator Yakalot begs the question when he announces that his opponent's plan won't work "because it is unworkable."

We can protect ourselves against this kind of faulty logic by asking, "What is assumed in this statement? Is the assumption reasonable, or does it need more proof?"

11. THE TWO-EXTREMES FALLACY (FALSE DILEMMA)

Linguists have long noted that the English language tends to view reality in sets of two extremes or polar opposites. In English, things are either black or white, tall or short, up or down, front or back, left or right, good or bad, guilty or not guilty. We can ask for a "straightforward yes-or-no answer" to a question, the understanding being that we will not accept or consider anything in between. In fact, reality cannot always be dissected along such strict lines. There may be (usually are) *more* than just two possibilities or extremes to consider. We are often told to "listen to both sides of the argument." But who's to say that every argument has only two sides? Can't there be a third — even a fourth or fifth — point of view?

The two-extremes fallacy is at work in this statement by Lenin, the great Marxist leader: "You cannot eliminate *one* basic assumption, one substantial part of this philosophy of Marxism (it is as if it were a block of steel), without abandoning truth, without falling into the arms of bourgeois-reactionary falsehood." In other words, if we don't agree 100 percent with every premise of Marxism, we must be placed at the opposite end of the political-economic spectrum — for Lenin, "bourgeois-reactionary falsehood." If we are not entirely *with* him, we must be against him; those are the only two possibilities open to us. Of course, this is a logical fallacy; in real life there are any number of political positions one can maintain *between* the two extremes of Marxism and capitalism. Senator Yakalot uses the two-extremes fallacy in the same way as Lenin when he tells his audience that "in this world a man's either for private enterprise or he's for socialism."

One of the most famous examples of the two-extremes fallacy in recent history is the slogan, "America: Love it or leave it," with its implicit suggestion that we either accept everything just as it is in America today without complaint — or get out. Again, it should be obvious that there is a whole range of action and belief between those two extremes.

Don't be duped; stop and ask, "Are those really the only two options I can choose from? Are there other alternatives not mentioned that deserve consideration?"

12. CARD STACKING

Some questions are so multifaceted and complex that no one can make an intelligent decision about them without considering a wide variety of evidence. One selection of facts could make us feel one way and another selection could make us feel just the opposite. Card stacking is a device of propaganda which selects only the facts that support the propagandist's point of view, and ignores all the others. For example, a candidate could be made to look like a legislative dynamo if you say, "Representative McNerd introduced more new bills than any other member of the Congress," and neglect to mention that most of them were so preposterous that they were laughed off the floor.

Senator Yakalot engages in card stacking when he talks about the proposal to use smaller cars. He talks only about jobs without mentioning the cost to the taxpayers or the very real — though still denied — threat of depletion of resources. He says he wants to help his countrymen keep their jobs, but doesn't mention that the corporations that offer the jobs will also make large profits. He praises the "American chrome industry," overlooking the fact that most chrome is imported. And so on.

The best protection against card stacking is to take the "Yes, but . . ." attitude. This device of propaganda is not untrue, but then again it is not the *whole* truth. So ask yourself, "Is this person leaving something out that I should know about? Is there some other information that should be brought to bear on this question?" . . . 45

So far, we have considered three approaches that the propagandist can use to influence our thinking: appealing to our emotions, distracting our attention, and misleading us with logic that may appear to be reasonable but is in fact faulty and deceiving. But there is a fourth approach that is probably the most common propaganda trick of them all.

13. TESTIMONIAL

The testimonial device consists in having some loved or respected person give a statement of support (testimonial) for a given product or idea. The problem is that the person being quoted may *not* be an expert in the field; in fact, he may know nothing at all about it. Using the name of a man who is skilled and famous in one field to give a testimonial for something in another field is unfair and unreasonable.

Senator Yakalot tries to mislead his audience with testimonial when he tells them that "full-sized cars have been praised by great Americans like John Wayne and Jack Jones, as well as by leading experts on car safety and comfort."

Testimonial is used extensively in TV ads, where it often appears in such bizarre forms as Joe Namath's endorsement of a pantyhose brand. Here, of course, the "authority" giving the testimonial not only is no expert about pantyhose, but obviously stands to gain something (money!) by making the testimonial.

When celebrities endorse a political candidate, they may not be making money by doing so, but we should still question whether they are in any better position to judge than we ourselves. Too often we are willing to let others we like or respect make our decisions *for us*, while we follow along acquiescently. And this is the purpose of testimonial — to get us to agree and accept *without* stopping to think. Be sure to ask, "Is there any reason to believe that this person (or organization or publication or whatever) has 50 any more knowledge or information than I do on this subject? What does the idea amount to on its own merits, without the benefit of testimonial?"

The cornerstone of democratic society is reliance upon an informed and educated electorate. To be fully effective citizens we need to be able to challenge and to question wisely. A dangerous feeling of indifference toward our political processes exists today. We often abandon our right, our duty, to criticize and evaluate by dismissing *all* politicians as "crooked," *all* new bills and proposals as "just more government bureaucracy." But there are important distinctions to be made, and this kind of apathy can be fatal to democracy.

If we are to be led, let us not be led blindly, but critically, intelligently, with our eyes open. If we are to continue to be a government "by the people," let us become informed about the methods and purposes of propaganda, so we can be the masters, not the slaves of our destiny.

FOCUSING ON CONTENT

1. According to Cross, what is propaganda? Who uses propaganda? Why is it used? (Glossary: *Propaganda*)

2. Why does Cross believe that it is necessary for people in a democratic society to become informed about the methods and practices of propaganda? What is her advice for dealing with propaganda?

3. What is a "red herring," and why do people use this technique?

4. What is "begging the question"? (Glossary: *Logical Fallacies*)

5. What, according to Cross, is the most common propaganda trick? Provide some examples of it from your own experience.

FOCUSING ON WRITING

1. What is Cross's purpose in this essay? (Glossary: *Purpose)*

2. Given her subject and purpose, why is classification an appropriate strategy of development for this essay? (Glossary: *Division and Classification*) With what other subjects might you use this strategy?

3. How does Cross organize the discussion of each propaganda device she includes in her essay? (Glossary: *Organization*)

4. How does Cross use examples in her essay? (Glossary: *Examples*) What do you think of the examples from Senator Yakalot? What, if anything, does this hypothetical senator add to the essay? Which other examples do you find most effective? Least effective? Explain why.

5. In her discussion of the bandwagon appeal (23–28), Cross uses the analogy of the lemmings. How does the analogy work? Why is it not a false analogy? (Glossary: *Analogy*) How do analogies help you, as a writer, explain your subject to readers?

LANGUAGE IN ACTION

At the beginning of her essay, Cross claims that propaganda "can be put to work for good causes as well as bad." Consider the advertisements below and on page 135 for the U.S. Postal Service's breast-cancer-stamp campaign and for the University of Vermont's Direct Service Programs. How would you characterize the appeal of each? What propaganda techniques does each use? Do you ever find appeals such as these objectionable? Why or why not? In what situations do you think it would be acceptable for you to use propaganda devices in your own writing?

Women Helping Battered Women

Summer or Fall Semester

Internships

Join the fight against domestic violence! You will work in a friendly, supportive environment. You will do challenging work for a worthwile cause. You will have lots of learning opportunities. We need reliable people who are committed to social justice. You will need good communication skills, an open mind, and the ability to work somewhat independently.

We are now accepting Applications.

Internships will be offered in the following programs:

Shelter Services
Hotline Program
Children's Shelter Services
Children's Playgroup Program
Development and Fundraising

Work Study Positions available in all the above programs as well as in the financial and administrative programs.

All interns in Direct Service Programs have to complete the full Volunteer Training. The next trainings will be in May and September 1999. Call now for more information: 658-3131.

WRITING SUGGESTIONS

1. Using several of the devices described by Cross, write a piece of propaganda. You may want to persuade your classmates to join a particular campus organization, support a controversial movement or issue, or vote for a particular candidate in an election.

2. Cross acknowledges in paragraph 1 that propaganda is "simply a means of persuasion," but she quickly cautions that people need to recognize propaganda and be alert to its potential to mislead or deceive. Write an essay for your campus newspaper arguing for a "short course" on propaganda recognition at your school. You might want to consider the following questions in your essay: How do propaganda and argumentation differ? Do both always

have the same intended effect? What could happen to people who don't recognize or understand propaganda when they encounter it?

3. Using Cross's list of propaganda devices, write an essay analyzing several newspaper editorials, political speeches, public-service advertising campaigns, or comparable examples of contemporary prose. What did you learn about the people or organizations as a result of your analysis? How were their positions on issues or their purposes expressed? Which propaganda devices did they use? After reading Cross's essay, did you find yourself "buying" the propaganda or recognizing and questioning it? Submit the original editorials, speeches, or advertisements with your essay.

PICTURING LANGUAGE

You may remember this image from news coverage of the fall of Saddam Hussein during the recent war in Iraq. When Baghdad was captured, what emotions did the picture elicit from you? What emotions does this picture elicit now? What accounts for the differences, if any, in your attitude toward the photograph? What, for you, is the political message conveyed by the placement of the flag over Saddam's face?

Politics and the English Language

GEORGE ORWELL

George Orwell (1903–1950), one of the most brilliant social critics of the twentieth century, grew up in England and received a traditional education at Eton. Instead of going on to a university, he joined the civil service and was sent to Burma at the age of nineteen as an assistant superintendent of police. Disillusioned with British imperialism, Orwell resigned in 1929 and began a decade of studying social and political issues firsthand and then writing about them in such works as Down and Out in Paris and London *(1933) and* The Road to Wigan Pier *(1937). His most famous books are* Animal Farm *(1945), a satire of the Russian Revolution, and* 1984 *(1949), a chilling novel set in an imagined totalitarian state of the future.*

In 1984, *the government has imposed on its subjects a simplified language, Newspeak, which is continually revised to give them fewer words with which to express themselves. Words like* terrible, abhorrent, *and* evil, *for example, have been replaced by the single expression* double-plus-ungood. *The way people use language, Orwell maintains, is a result of the way they think as well as an important influence on their thought. This is also the point of his classic essay "Politics and the English Language." Even though it was published in 1946, the essay is as accurate and relevant now as it was more than fifty years ago. Indeed, during the wars in Vietnam, Iraq, and Kosovo, various American officials were still using euphemisms such as* pacification, transfer of population, *and* ethnic cleansing — *words and phrases Orwell had exposed as doubletalk. Orwell, however, goes beyond exposé in this essay. He holds up to public view and ridicule some choice examples of political language at its worst, but he also offers a few short and effective rules for those who want to write more clearly.*

WRITING TO DISCOVER: *Have you ever stopped to think about what clichéd phrases like* toe the line, walk the straight and narrow, sharp as a tack, *and* fly off the handle *really mean? Jot down the clichés that you find yourself or hear others using. What images come to mind when you hear them? Are these words and phrases effective expressions, or are they a kind of verbal shorthand that we automatically depend on? Explain.*

Most people who bother with the matter at all would admit that the English language is in a bad way, but it is generally assumed that we cannot by conscious action do anything about it. Our civilization is decadent

138

and our language — so the argument runs — must inevitably share in the general collapse. It follows that any struggle against the abuse of language is a sentimental archaism, like preferring candles to electric light or hansom cabs to aeroplanes. Underneath this lies the half-conscious belief that language is a natural growth and not an instrument which we shape for our own purposes.

Now, it is clear that the decline of a language must ultimately have political and economic causes: it is not due simply to the bad influence of this or that individual writer. But an effect can become a cause, reinforcing the original cause and producing the same effect in an intensified form, and so on indefinitely. A man may take to drink because he feels himself to be a failure, and then fail all the more completely because he drinks. It is rather the same thing that is happening to the English language. It becomes ugly and inaccurate because our thoughts are foolish, but the slovenliness of our language makes it easier for us to have foolish thoughts. The point is that the process is reversible. Modern English, especially written English, is full of bad habits which spread by imitation and which can be avoided if one is willing to take the necessary trouble. If one gets rid of these habits one can think more clearly, and to think clearly is a necessary first step towards political regeneration: so that the fight against bad English is not frivolous and is not the exclusive concern of professional writers. I will come back to this presently, and I hope that by that time the meaning of what I have said here will have become clearer. Meanwhile here are five specimens of the English language as it is now habitually written.

These five passages have not been picked out because they are especially bad — I could have quoted far worse if I had chosen — but because they illustrate various of the mental vices from which we now suffer. They are a little below the average, but are fairly representative samples. I number them so that I can refer back to them when necessary:

> (1) I am not, indeed, sure whether it is not true to say that the Milton who once seemed not unlike a seventeenth-century Shelley had not become, out of an experience ever more bitter in each year, more alien [*sic*] to the founder of that Jesuit sect which nothing could induce him to tolerate.
> Professor Harold Laski (Essay in *Freedom of Expression*)

> (2) Above all, we cannot play ducks and drakes with a native battery of idioms which prescribes such egregious collocations of vocables as the Basic *put up with* for *tolerate* or *put at a loss* for *bewilder*.
> Professor Lancelot Hogben (*Interglossa*)

> (3) On the one side we have the free personality: by definition it is not neurotic, for it has neither conflict nor dream. Its desires, such as they are, are transparent, for they are just what institutional approval keeps in the forefront of consciousness; another institutional pattern would alter their number and intensity; there is little in them that is natural,

irreducible, or culturally dangerous. But *on the other side*, the social bond itself is nothing but the mutual reflection of these self-secure integrities. Recall the definition of love. Is not this the very picture of a small academic? Where is there a place in this hall of mirrors for either personality or fraternity?

Essay on psychology in Politics (New York)

(4) All the "best people" from the gentlemen's clubs, and all the frantic fascist captains, united in common hatred of Socialism and bestial horror of the rising tide of the mass revolutionary movement, have turned to acts of provocation, to foul incendiarism, to medieval legends of poisoned wells, to legalize their own destruction of proletarian organizations, and rouse the agitated petty-bourgeoisie to chauvinistic fervor on behalf of the fight against the revolutionary way out of the crisis.

Communist pamphlet

(5) If a new spirit *is* to be infused into this old country, there is one thorny and contentious reform which must be tackled, and that is the humanization and galvanization of the B.B.C. Timidity here will bespeak canker and atrophy of the soul. The heart of Britain may be sound and of strong beat, for instance, but the British lion's roar at present is like that of Bottom in Shakespeare's *Midsummer Night's Dream* — as gentle as any sucking dove. A virile new Britain cannot continue indefinitely to be traduced in the eyes or rather ears, of the world by the effete languors of Langham Place, brazenly masquerading as "standard English." When the voice of Britain is heard at nine o'clock, better far and infinitely less ludicrous to hear aitches honestly dropped than the present priggish, inflated, inhibited, school-ma'amish arch braying of blameless bashful mewing maidens!

Letter in Tribune

Each of these passages has faults of its own, but, quite apart from avoidable ugliness, two qualities are common to all of them. The first is staleness of imagery; the other is lack of precision. The writer either has a meaning and cannot express it, or he inadvertently says something else, or he is almost indifferent as to whether his words mean anything or not. This mixture of vagueness and sheer incompetence is the most marked characteristic of modern English prose, and especially of any kind of political writing. As soon as certain topics are raised, the concrete melts into the abstract and no one seems able to think of turns of speech that are not hackneyed: prose consists less and less of *words* chosen for the sake of their meaning, and more and more of *phrases* tacked together like the sections of a prefabricated henhouse. I list below, with notes and examples, various of the tricks by means of which the work of prose-construction is habitually dodged:

DYING METAPHORS. A newly invented metaphor assists thought by evoking a visual image, while on the other hand a metaphor which is technically "dead" (e.g., *iron resolution*) has in effect reverted to being an ordinary word and can generally be used without loss of vividness. But in between these two classes there is a huge dump of worn-out metaphors which have lost all evocative power and are merely used because they save people the trouble of inventing phrases for themselves. Examples are: *ring the changes on, take up the cudgels for, toe the line, ride roughshod over, stand shoulder to shoulder with, play into the hands of, no axe to grind, grist to the mill, fishing in troubled waters, on the order of the day, Achilles' heel, swan song, hotbed.* Many of these are used without knowledge of their meaning (what is a "rift," for instance?), and incompatible metaphors are frequently mixed, a sure sign that the writer is not interested in what he is saying. Some metaphors now current have been twisted out of their original meaning without those who use them even being aware of the fact. For example, *toe the line* is sometimes written *tow the line.* Another example is the *hammer and the anvil,* now always used with the implication that the anvil gets the worst of it. In real life it is always the anvil that breaks the hammer, never the other way about: a writer who stopped to think what he was saying would be aware of this, and would avoid perverting the original phrase.

OPERATORS OR VERBAL FALSE LIMBS. These save the trouble of picking out appropriate verbs and nouns, and at the same time pad each sentence with extra syllables which give it an appearance of symmetry. Characteristic phrases are *render inoperative, militate against, make contact with, be subjected to, give rise to, give grounds for, have the effect of, play a leading part (role) in, make itself felt, take effect, exhibit a tendency to, serve the purpose of,* etc., etc. The keynote is the elimination of simple verbs. Instead of being a single word, such as *break, stop, spoil, mend, kill,* a verb becomes a *phrase,* made up of a noun or adjective tacked on to some general-purpose verb such as *prove, serve, form, play, render.* In addition, the passive voice is wherever possible used in preference to the active, and noun constructions are used instead of gerunds (*by examination of* instead of *by examining*). The range of verbs is further cut down by means of the *-ize* and *de-* formations, and the banal statements are given an appearance of profundity by means of the *not un-* formation. Simple conjunctions and prepositions are replaced by such phrases as *with respect to, having regard to, the fact that, by dint of, in view of, in the interests of, on the hypothesis that;* and the ends of sentences are saved from anticlimax by such resounding common-places as *greatly to be desired, cannot be left out of account, a development to be expected in the near future, deserving of serious consideration, brought to a satisfactory conclusion,* and so on and so forth.

PRETENTIOUS DICTION. Words like *phenomenon, element, individual* (as noun), *objective, categorical, effective, virtual, basic, primary, promote, constitute, exhibit, exploit, utilize, eliminate, liquidate,* are used to dress up simple statements and give an air of scientific impartiality to biased judgments. Adjectives like *epoch-making, epic, historic, unforgettable, triumphant, age-old, inevitable, inexorable, veritable,* are used to dignify the sordid processes of international politics, while writing that aims at glorifying war usually takes on an archaic color, its characteristic words being: *realm, throne, chariot, mailed fist, trident, sword, shield, buckler, banner, jackboot, clarion.* Foreign words and expressions such as *cul de sac, ancien régime, deus ex machina, mutatis mutandis, status quo, gleichschaltung, weltanschauung,* are used to give an air of culture and elegance. Except for the useful abbreviations *i.e., e.g.,* and *etc.,* there is no real need for any of the hundreds of foreign phrases now current in English. Bad writers, and especially scientific, political, and sociological writers, are nearly always haunted by the notion that Latin or Greek words are grander than Saxon ones, and unnecessary words like *expedite, ameliorate, predict, extraneous, deracinated, clandestine, subaqueous* and hundreds of others constantly gain ground from their Anglo-Saxon opposite numbers.[1] The jargon peculiar to Marxist writing (*hyena, hangman, cannibal, petty bourgeois, these gentry, lacquey, flunkey, mad dog, White Guard,* etc.) consists largely of words and phrases translated from Russian, German, or French; but the normal way of coining a new word is to use a Latin or Greek root with the appropriate affix and, where necessary, the *-ize* formation. It is often easier to make up words of this kind (*deregionalize, impermissible, extramarital, non-fragmentary,* and so forth) than to think up the English words that will cover one's meaning. The result, in general, is an increase in slovenliness and vagueness.

MEANINGLESS WORDS.   In certain kinds of writing, particularly in art criticism and literary criticism, it is normal to come across long passages which are almost completely lacking in meaning.[2] Words like *romantic, plastic, values, human, dead, sentimental, natural, vitality,* as used in art criticism, are strictly meaningless, in the sense that they not only do not point to any discoverable object, but are hardly ever expected to do so by the reader. When one critic writes, "The outstanding feature of Mr. X's work is its living quality," while another writes, "The

---

1. An interesting illustration of this is the way in which the English flower names which were in use till very recently are being ousted by Greek ones, *snapdragon* becoming *antirrhinum, forget-me-not* becoming *myosotis,* etc. It is hard to see any practical reason for this change of fashion: it is probably due to an instinctive turning-away from the more homely word and a vague feeling that the Greek word is scientific.

2. Example: "Comfort's catholicity of perception and image, strangely Whitmanesque in range, almost the exact opposite in esthetic compulsion, continues to evoke that trembling atmospheric accumulative hinting at a cruel, an inexorably serene timelessness. . . . Wrey Gardiner scores by aiming at simple bull's-eyes with precision. Only they are not so simple, and through this contented sadness runs more than the surface bittersweet of resignation." (*Poetry Quarterly*)

immediately striking thing about Mr. X's work is its peculiar deadness," the reader accepts this as a simple difference of opinion. If words like *black* and *white* were involved, instead of the jargon words *dead* and *living*, he would see at once that language was being used in an improper way. Many political words arc similarly abused. The word *Fascism* has now no meaning except in so far as it signifies "something not desirable." The words *democracy, freedom, patriotic, realistic, justice,* have each of them several different meanings which cannot be reconciled with one another. In the case of a word like *democracy,* not only is there no agreed definition, but the attempt to make one is resisted from all sides. It is almost universally felt that when we call a country democratic we are praising it: consequently the defenders of every kind of regime claim that it is a democracy, and fear that they might have to stop using the word if it were tied down to any one meaning. Words of this kind are often used in a consciously dishonest way. That is, the person who uses them has his own private definition, but allows his hearer to think he means something quite different. Statements like, *Marshal Pétain was a true patriot, The Soviet Press is the freest in the world, the Catholic Church is opposed to persecution,* are almost always made with intent to deceive. Other words used in variable meanings, in most cases more or less dishonestly, are: *class, totalitarian, science, progressive, reactionary, bourgeois, equality.*

Now that I have made this catalogue of swindles and perversions, let me give another example of the kind of writing that they lead to. This time it must of its nature be an imaginary one. I am going to translate a passage of good English into modern English of the worst sort. Here is a well-known verse from *Ecclesiastes:*

> I returned and saw under the sun, that the race is not to the swift, nor the battle to the strong, neither yet bread to the wise, nor yet riches to men of understanding, nor yet favour to men of skill; but time and chance happeneth to them all.

Here it is in modern English: 10

> Objective consideration of contemporary phenomena compels the conclusion that success or failure in competitive activities exhibits no tendency to be commensurate with innate capacity, but that a considerable element of the unpredictable must invariably be taken into account.

This is a parody, but a very gross one. Exhibit (3), above, for instance, contains several patches of the same kind of English. It will be seen that I have not made a full translation. The beginning and ending of the sentence follow the original meaning fairly closely, but in the middle the concrete illustrations — race, battle, bread — dissolve into the vague phrase "success or failure in competitive activities." This had to be so, because no modern writer of the kind I am discussing — no one capable of using phrases like "objective consideration of contemporary phenomena" — would ever tabulate his thoughts in that precise and detailed way. The whole tendency of modern prose is away from concreteness. Now analyze these two sentences a little more closely. The first contains forty-nine words but only sixty syllables, and all its words are those of everyday life. The second contains thirty-eight words of ninety syllables: eighteen of its words are from Latin roots, and one from Greek. The first sentence contains six vivid images, and only one phrase ("time and chance") that could be called vague. The second contains not a single fresh, arresting phrase, and in spite of its ninety syllables it gives only a shortened version of the meaning contained in the first. Yet without a doubt it is the second kind of sentence that is gaining ground in modern English. I do not want to exaggerate. This kind of writing is not yet universal, and outcrops of simplicity will occur here and there in the worst-written page. Still, if you or I were told to write a few lines on the uncertainty of human fortunes, we should probably come much nearer to my imaginary sentence than to the one from *Ecclesiastes*.

As I have tried to show, modern writing at its worst does not consist in picking out words for the sake of their meaning and inventing images in order to make the meaning clearer. It consists in gumming together long strips of words which have already been set in order by someone else, and making the results presentable by sheer humbug. The attraction of this way of writing is that it is easy. It is easier — even quicker, once you have the habit — to say *In my opinion it is not an unjustifiable assumption that* than to say *I think*. If you use ready-made phrases, you not only don't have to hunt about for words; you also don't have to bother with the rhythms of your sentences, since these phrases are generally so arranged as to be more or less euphonious. When you are composing in a hurry — when you are dictating to a stenographer, for instance, or making a public speech — it is natural to fall into a pretentious, Latinized style. Tags like *a consideration which we should do well to bear in mind* or *a conclusion to which all of us would readily assent* will save many a sentence from coming down with a bump. By using stale metaphors, similes, and idioms, you save much mental effort, at the cost of leaving your meaning vague, not only for your reader but for yourself. This is the significance of mixed metaphors. The sole aim of a metaphor is to call up a visual image. When these images clash — as in *The Fascist octopus has sung its swan song, the jackboot is thrown into the melting pot* — it can be taken as certain that the writer is not seeing a mental image of the objects he is naming; in other words he is not really thinking. Look again at the examples I gave at the beginning of this essay. Professor Laski (1) uses five negatives in fifty-three words. One of these is superfluous, making nonsense of the whole passage, and in addition there is the slip *alien* for *akin*, making further nonsense, and several avoidable pieces of clumsiness which increase the general vagueness. Professor Hogben (2) plays ducks and drakes with a battery which is able to write prescriptions, and, while disapproving of the everyday phrase *put up with*, is unwilling to look *egregious* up in the dictionary and see what it means; (3), if one takes an uncharitable attitude towards it, is simply meaningless: probably one could work out its intended meaning by reading the whole of the article in which it occurs. In (4), the writer knows more or less what he wants to say, but an accumulation of stale phrases chokes him like tea leaves blocking a sink. In (5), words and meaning have almost parted company. People who write in this manner usually have a general emotional meaning — they dislike one thing and want to express solidarity with another — but they are not interested in the detail of what they are saying. A scrupulous writer, in every sentence that he writes, will ask himself at least four questions, thus: What am I trying to say? What words will express it? What image or idiom will make it clearer? Is this image fresh enough to have an effect? And he will probably ask himself two more: Could I put it more shortly? Have I said anything that is avoidably ugly? But you are not obliged to go to all this trouble. You can shirk it by simply throwing your mind open and letting the ready-made phrases come crowding in. They will construct your sentences for you — even think your thoughts for you, to a certain extent — and at need they will perform the important service of partially concealing your meaning even from yourself. It is at this point that the special connection between politics and the debasement of language becomes clear.

In our time it is broadly true that political writing is bad writing. Where it is not true, it will generally be found that the writer is some kind of rebel, expressing his private opinions and not a "party line." Orthodoxy, of whatever color, seems to demand a lifeless, imitative style. The political dialects to be found in pamphlets, leading articles, manifestos, White Papers, and the speeches of under-secretaries do, of course, vary from party to party, but they are all alike in that one almost never finds in them a fresh, vivid, homemade turn of speech. When one watches some tired hack on the platform mechanically repeating the familiar phrases — *bestial atrocities, iron heel, bloodstained tyranny, free peoples of the world, stand shoulder to shoulder* — one often has a curious feeling that one is not watching a live human being but some kind of dummy: a feeling which suddenly becomes stronger at moments when the light catches the speaker's spectacles and turns them into blank discs which seem to have no eyes behind them. And this is not altogether fanciful. A speaker who uses that kind of phraseology has gone some distance towards turning himself into a machine. The appropriate noises are coming out of his larynx, but his brain is not involved as it would be if he were choosing his words for himself. If the speech he is making is one that he is accustomed to make over and over again, he may be almost unconscious of what he is saying, as one is when one utters the responses in church. And this reduced state of consciousness, if not indispensable, is at any rate favorable to political conformity.

In our time, political speech and writing are largely the defense of the indefensible. Things like the continuance of British rule in India, the Russian purges and deportations, the dropping of the atom bombs on Japan, can indeed be defended, but only by arguments which are too brutal for most people to face, and which do not square with the professed aims of political parties. Thus political language has to consist largely of euphemism, question-begging, and sheer cloudy vagueness. Defenseless villages are bombarded from the air, the inhabitants driven out into the countryside, the cattle machine-gunned, the huts set on fire with incendiary bullets: this is called *pacification*. Millions of peasants are robbed of their farms and sent trudging along the roads with no more than they can carry: this is called *transfer of population* or *rectification of frontiers*. People are imprisoned for years without trial, or shot in the back of the neck or sent to die of scurvy in Arctic lumber camps: this is called *elimination of unreliable elements*. Such phraseology is needed if one wants to name things without calling up mental pictures of them. Consider for instance some comfortable English professor defending Russian totalitarianism. He cannot say outright, "I believe in killing off your opponents when you can get good results by doing so." Probably, therefore, he will say something like this:

> While freely conceding that the Soviet régime exhibits certain features which the humanitarian may be inclined to deplore, we must, I think, agree that a certain curtailment of the right to political opposition is an unavoidable concomitant of transitional periods, and that the rigors which the Russian people have been called upon to undergo have been amply justified in the sphere of concrete achievement.

The inflated style is itself a kind of euphemism. A mass of Latin words falls upon the facts like soft snow, blurring the outlines and covering up all the details. The great enemy of clear language is insincerity. When there is a gap between one's real and one's declared aims, one turns as it were instinctively to long words and exhausted idioms, like a cuttlefish squirting out ink. In our age there is no such thing as "keeping out of politics." All issues are political issues, and politics itself is a mass of lies, evasions, folly, hatred, and schizophrenia. When the general atmosphere is bad, language must suffer. I should expect to find — this is a guess which I have not sufficient knowledge to verify — that the German, Russian, and Italian languages have all deteriorated in the last ten or fifteen years, as a result of dictatorship.

But if thought corrupts language, language can also corrupt thought. A bad usage can spread by tradition and imitation, even among people who should and do know better. The debased language that I have been discussing is in some ways very convenient. Phrases like *a not unjustifiable assumption, leaves much to be desired, would serve no good purpose, a consideration which we should do well to bear in mind*, are a continuous temptation, a packet of aspirins always at one's elbow. Look back through this essay, and for certain you will find that I have again and again committed the very faults I am protesting against. By this morning's post I have received a pamphlet dealing with conditions in Germany. The author tells me that he "felt impelled" to write it. I open it at random, and here is almost the first sentence that I see: "[The Allies] have an opportunity not only of achieving a radical transformation of Germany's social and political structure in such a way as to avoid a nationalistic reaction in Germany itself, but at the same time of laying the foundations of a cooperative and unified Europe." You see, he "feels impelled" to write — feels, presumably, that he has something new to say — and yet his words, like cavalry horses answering the bugle, group themselves automatically into the familiar dreary pattern. The invasion of one's mind by ready-made phrases (*lay the foundations, achieve a radical transformation*) can only be prevented if one is constantly on guard against them, and every such phrase anesthetizes a portion of one's brain.

I said earlier that the decadence of our language is probably curable. Those who deny this would argue, if they produced an argument at all, that language merely reflects existing social conditions, and that we cannot influence its development by any direct tinkering with words and constructions. So far as the general tone or spirit of a language goes, this may be true, but it is not true in detail. Silly words and expressions have often disappeared, not through any evolutionary process but owing to the conscious action of a minority. Two recent examples were *explore every avenue* and *leave no stone unturned*, which were killed by the jeers of a few journalists. There is a long list of fly-blown metaphors which could similarly be got rid of if enough people would interest themselves in the job; and it should also be possible to laugh the *not un-* formation out of existence,[3] to reduce the amount of Latin and Greek in the average sentence, to drive out foreign phrases and strayed scientific words, and, in general, to make pretentiousness unfashionable. But all these are minor points. The defense of the English language implies more than this, and perhaps it is best to start by saying what it does *not* imply.

To begin with, it has nothing to do with archaism, with the salvaging of obsolete words and turns of speech, or with the setting up of a "standard English" which must never be departed from. On the contrary, it is especially concerned with the scrapping of every word or idiom which has outworn its usefulness. It has nothing to do with correct grammar and syntax, which are of no importance so long as one makes one's meaning clear, or with the avoidance of Americanisms, or with having what is called a "good prose style." On the other hand it is not concerned with

---

3. One can cure oneself of the *not un-* formation by memorizing this sentence. *A not unblack dog was chasing a not unsmall rabbit across a not ungreen field.*

fake simplicity and the attempt to make written English colloquial. Nor does it even imply in every case preferring the Saxon word to the Latin one, though it does imply using the fewest and shortest words that will cover one's meaning. What is above all needed is to let the meaning choose the word, and not the other way about. In prose, the worst thing one can do with words is to surrender to them. When you think of a concrete object, you think wordlessly, and then, if you want to describe the thing you have been visualizing you probably hunt about till you find the exact words that seem to fit it. When you think of something abstract you are more inclined to use words from the start, and unless you make a conscious effort to prevent it, the existing dialect will come rushing in and do the job for you, at the expense of blurring or even changing your meaning. Probably it is better to put off using words as long as possible and get one's meaning as clear as one can through pictures or sensations. Afterwards one can choose — not simply *accept* — the phrases that will best cover the meaning, and then switch round and decide what impression one's words are likely to make on another person. This last effort of the mind cuts out all stale or mixed images, all prefabricated phrases, needless repetitions, and humbug and vagueness generally. But one can often be in doubt about the effect of a word or a phrase, and one needs rules that one can rely on when instinct fails. I think the following rules will cover most cases:

1. Never use a metaphor, simile, or other figure of speech which you are used to seeing in print.
2. Never use a long word where a short one will do.
3. If it is possible to cut a word out, always cut it out.
4. Never use the passive where you can use the active.
5. Never use a foreign phrase, a scientific word, or a jargon word if you can think of an everyday English equivalent.
6. Break any of these rules sooner than say anything outright barbarous.

These rules sound elementary, and so they are, but they demand a deep change of attitude in anyone who has grown used to writing in the style now fashionable. One could keep all of them and still write bad English, but one could not write the kind of stuff that I quoted in those five specimens at the beginning of this article.

I have not here been considering the literary use of language, but merely language as an instrument for expressing and not for concealing or preventing thought. Stuart Chase and others have come near to claiming that all abstract words are meaningless, and have used this as a pretext for advocating a kind of political quietism. Since you don't know what Fascism is, how can you struggle against Fascism? One need not swallow such absurdities as this, but one ought to recognize that the present political chaos is connected with the decay of language, and that one can probably bring about some improvement by starting at the verbal end. If you simplify your English, you are freed from the worst follies of orthodoxy. You cannot speak any of the necessary dialects, and when you make a stupid remark its stupidity will be obvious, even to yourself. Political language — and with variations this is true of all political parties, from Conservatives to Anarchists — is designed to make lies sound truthful and murder respectable, and to give an appearance of solidity to pure wind. One cannot change this all in a moment, but one can at least change one's own habits, and from time to time one can even, if one jeers loudly enough, send some worn-out and useless phrase — some *jackboot, Achilles' heel, hotbed, melting pot, acid test, veritable inferno,* or other lump of verbal refuse — into the dustbin where it belongs.

FOCUSING ON CONTENT

1. In your own words, summarize Orwell's argument in this essay. (Glossary: *Argument*) Do you agree or disagree with him? Explain why.

2. Grammarians and usage experts have long objected to mixed metaphors (for example, "Politicians who have their heads in the sand are leading the country over the precipice") because they are inaccurate. For Orwell, a mixed metaphor is symptomatic of a greater problem (12). What is that problem?

3. What are dead and dying metaphors (5)? (Glossary: *Figures of Speech*) Why do dying metaphors disgust Orwell?

4. According to Orwell, what are four important prewriting questions scrupulous writers ask themselves (12)?

5. Orwell says that one of the evils of political language is question-begging (14). What does he mean? Why, according to Orwell, has political language deteriorated? Do you agree with him that "the decadence of our language is probably curable" (17)? Why or why not?

FOCUSING ON WRITING

1. What is Orwell's thesis, and where is it presented? (Glossary: *Thesis*)

2. How would you describe Orwell's purpose in this essay? (Glossary: *Purpose*) What in the essay leads you to this conclusion?

3. For what audience do you think Orwell wrote this essay? (Glossary: *Audience*) What in his diction leads you to this conclusion? (Glossary: *Diction*)

4. Following are some of the metaphors and similes that Orwell uses in his essay. (Glossary: *Figures of Speech*) Explain how each one works and comment on its effectiveness.

   a. "Prose consists less and less of *words* chosen for the sake of their meaning, and more and more of *phrases* tacked together like the sections of a pre-fabricated hen-house" (4).

b. "But in between these two classes there is a huge dump of worn-out metaphors which have lost all evocative power" (5).

c. "The writer knows more or less what he wants to say, but an accumulation of stale phrases chokes him like tea leaves blocking a sink" (12).

d. "A mass of Latin words falls upon the facts like soft snow, blurring the outlines and covering up all the details" (15).

e. "When there is a gap between one's real and one's declared aims, one turns . . . instinctively to long words and exhausted idioms, like a cuttlefish squirting out ink" (15).

f. "He . . . feels, presumably, that he has something new to say — and yet his words, like cavalry horses answering the bugle, group themselves automatically into the familiar dreary pattern" (16).

5. In this essay, Orwell moves from negative arguments (criticisms) to positive ones (proposals). Where does he make the transition from criticisms to proposals? (Glossary: *Transitions*) Do you find the organization of his argument effective? (Glossary: *Organization*) Explain.

LANGUAGE IN ACTION

Read Robert Yoakum's "Everyspeech," a parody that first appeared in the *New York Times* in November 1994. Yoakum was a speechwriter for John F. Kennedy's successful 1960 campaign. As you read, identify the features of political speech that are the butt of Yoakum's humor. Does he point out the same language abuses that Orwell criticizes in his essay? What propaganda devices does Yoakum use (see Cross's essay on pp. 123–33)?

EVERYSPEECH

Ladies and gentlemen. I am delighted to see so many friends from the Third Congressional District. And what better site for some straight talk than at this greatest of all state fairs, where ribbons reward American individual enterprise, whether for the biggest beets or the best bull?

Speaking of bull, my opponent has said some mighty dishonest things about me. But what can you expect from a typical politician? I want to address some fundamental issues that set me apart from my opponent and his failed party — the party of gutlessness and gridlock.

The American people are ready for straight talk, although don't count on the press to report it straight. The press, like my opponent, has no respect for the public.

This democracy must return to its roots or it will perish, and its roots are you — the honest, hard-working, God-fearing people who made this the greatest nation on earth. Yes, we have problems. But what problems would not be solved if the press and politicians had faith in the people?

Take crime, for example. Rampant, brutal crime. My rival in this race believes that redemption and rehabilitation are the answers to the lawlessness that is tearing our society apart.

Well, if R and R is what you want for those robbers and rapists, don't vote for me. If pampering the punks is what you want, vote for my opponent.

Do I believe in the death penalty? You bet! Do I believe in three strikes and you're out? No, I believe in *two* strikes and you're out! I believe in three strikes and you're *dead*!

You can count on me to crack down on crime, but I won't ignore the other big C word: character. Character made our nation great. Character, and respect for family values. A belief in children and parents. In brothers and sisters and grandparents.

Oh, sure, that sounds corny. Those cynical inside-the-Beltway journalists will ridicule me tomorrow, but I would rather be guilty of a corny defense of family values than of coddling criminals.

While I'm making myself unpopular with the press and a lot of politicians, I might as well alienate even more Washington wimps by telling you frankly how I feel about taxes. I'm against them! Not just in an election year, like my adversary, but every year!

I'm in favor of slashing wasteful welfare, which is where a lot of your hard-earned tax dollars go. The American people have said "enough!" to welfare, but inside the Beltway they don't give a hoot about the industrious folks I see before me today. They're too busy with their cocktail parties, diplomatic functions, and society balls.

My opponent loves those affairs, but I'd rather be with my good friends here than with those fork-tongued lawyers, cookie-pushing State Department fops, and high-priced lobbyists. I promise that when elected, my main office will be right here in the Third District. My branch office will be in D.C. And I promise you this: I shall serve only two terms and then return to live with the folks I love.

So on Nov. 8, if you want someone with an independent mind and the courage to change — *to change back to good old American values* — if you've had enough and want someone tough, vote for me. Thank you, and God bless America.

WRITING SUGGESTIONS

1. Orwell claims that political speech is filled with such words as *patriotism, democracy, freedom, realistic,* and *justice,* words that have "several different meanings which cannot be reconciled with one another" (8). Why is Orwell so uneasy about these words? What do these words mean to you? How do your meanings differ from those of others? For example, someone who has served in the armed forces, been a political prisoner, or served as a juror may attach distinct meanings to the words *patriotism, freedom,* or *justice.* In a brief essay, recount an experience that gave you real insight into the meaning of one of these words or a word similar to them.

2. Collect examples of bureaucratic writing on your campus. How would you characterize most of this writing? Who on your campus seems to be prone to manipulative language — college administrators, student leaders, or faculty? Use information from the Orwell and Cross articles in this chapter and from Birk and Birk's article "Selection, Slanting, and Charged Language" (pp. 351–59) to analyze the writing you collect. Then write an essay in which you assess the health of the English language at your school.

The World of Doublespeak

WILLIAM LUTZ

Originally from Racine, Wisconsin, William Lutz has been a pro-fessor of English at Rutgers University for the past fourteen years and was the editor the Quarterly Review of Doublespeak. *Through his book* Doublespeak: From Revenue Enhancement to Terminal Living *(1980), Lutz first awakened Americans to how people in important positions were manipulating language. As chair of the National Council of Teachers of English's Committee on Public Doublespeak, Lutz has been a watchdog of public officials who use language to "mislead, distort, deceive, inflate, circumvent, obfus-cate." Each year the committee presents the Orwell Awards, recog-nizing the most outrageous uses of public doublespeak in the worlds of government and business. Lutz's most recent books are* The New Doublespeak: Why No One Knows What Anyone's Saying Any-more *(1997) and* Doublespeak Defined: Cut through the Bull**** and Get to the Point *(1999).*

In the following essay, which first appeared in Christopher Ricks and Leonard Michaels's anthology State of the Language *(1990), Lutz examines doublespeak, "language which pretends to communicate but doesn't, language which makes the bad seem good, the negative appear positive, the unpleasant attractive, or at least tolerable." He identifies the various types of doublespeak and cautions us about the possible serious effects that doublespeak can have on our thinking.*

WRITING TO DISCOVER: *Have you ever heard or read language that you thought was deliberately evasive, language that manipu-lated your perception of reality, or, worse yet, language that com-municated nothing? Jot down your thoughts about such language. For example, what kinds of language do people use to talk about death, cancer, mental illness, firing a person, killing someone, or ending a relationship? Do you think evasive or manipulative lan-guage is ever justified? Explain.*

Farmers no longer have cows, pigs, chickens, or other animals on their farms; according to the U.S. Department of Agriculture, farmers have "grain-consuming animal units" (which, according to the Tax Re-form Act of 1986, are kept in "single-purpose agricultural structures," not pig pens and chicken coops). Attentive observers of the English lan-guage also learned recently that the multibillion dollar stock market crash of 1987 was simply a "fourth quarter equity retreat"; that airplanes don't crash, they just have "uncontrolled contact with the ground"; that janitors are really "environmental technicians"; that it was a "diagnostic misadventure of a high magnitude" which caused the death of a patient in a Philadelphia hospital, not medical malpractice; and that President Reagan wasn't really unconscious while he underwent minor surgery, he was just in a "non-decision-making form." In other words, doublespeak continues to spread as the official language of public discourse.

Doublespeak is a blanket term for language which pretends to communicate but doesn't, language which makes the bad seem good, the negative appear positive, the unpleasant attractive, or at least tolerable. It is language which avoids, shifts, or denies responsibility, language which is at variance with its real or its purported meaning. It is language which conceals or prevents thought. Basic to doublespeak is incongruity, the incongruity between what is said, or left unsaid, and what really is: between the word and the referent, between seem and be, between the essential function of language, communication, and what doublespeak does — mislead, distort, deceive, inflate, circumvent, obfuscate.

When shopping, we are asked to check our packages at the desk "for our convenience," when it's not for our convenience at all but for the store's "program to reduce inventory shrinkage." We see advertisements for "preowned," "experienced," or "previously distinguished" cars, for "genuine imitation leather," "virgin vinyl," or "real counterfeit diamonds." Television offers not reruns but "encore telecasts." There are no slums or ghettos, just the "inner city" or "substandard housing" where the "disadvantaged," "economically nonaffluent," or "fiscal underachievers" live. Nonprofit organizations don't make a profit, they have "negative deficits" or "revenue excesses." In the world of doublespeak dying is "terminal living."

We know that a toothbrush is still a toothbrush even if the advertisements on television call it a "home plaque removal instrument," and even that "nutritional avoidance therapy" means a diet. But who would guess that a "volume-related production schedule adjustment" means closing an entire factory in the doublespeak of General Motors, or that "advanced downward adjustments" means budget cuts in the doublespeak of Caspar Weinberger, or that "energetic disassembly" means an explosion in a nuclear power plant in the doublespeak of the nuclear power industry?

The euphemism, an inoffensive or positive word or phrase designed   5
to avoid a harsh, unpleasant, or distasteful reality, can at times be doublespeak. But the euphemism can also be a tactful word or phrase; for example, "passed away" functions not just to protect the feelings of another person but also to express our concern for another's grief. This use of the euphemism is not doublespeak but the language of courtesy. A euphemism used to mislead or deceive, however, becomes doublespeak. In 1984, the U.S. State Department announced that in its annual reports on the status of human rights in countries around the world it would no longer use the word "killing." Instead, it would use the

phrase "unlawful or arbitrary deprivation of life." Thus the State Department avoids discussing government-sanctioned killings in countries that the United States supports and has certified as respecting human rights.

The Pentagon also avoids unpleasant realities when it refers to bombs and artillery shells which fall on civilian targets as "incontinent ordnance" or killing the enemy as "servicing the target." In 1977 the Pentagon tried to slip funding for the neutron bomb unnoticed into an appropriations bill by calling it an "enhanced radiation device." And in 1971 the CIA gave us that most famous of examples of doublespeak when it used the phrase "eliminate with extreme prejudice" to refer to the execution of a suspected double agent in Vietnam.

Jargon, the specialized language of a trade or profession, allows colleagues to communicate with each other clearly, efficiently, and quickly. Indeed, it is a mark of membership to be able to use and understand the group's jargon. But it can also be doublespeak — pretentious, obscure, and esoteric terminology used to make the simple appear complex, and not to express but impress. In the doublespeak of jargon, smelling something becomes "organoleptic analysis," glass becomes "fused silicate," a crack in a metal support beam becomes a "discontinuity," conservative economic policies become "distributionally conservative notions."

Lawyers and tax accountants speak of an "involuntary conversion" of property when discussing the loss or destruction of property through theft, accident, or condemnation. So if your house burns down, or your car is stolen or destroyed in an accident, you have, in legal jargon, suffered an "involuntary conversion" of your property. This is a legal term with a specific meaning in law and all lawyers can be expected to understand it. But when it is used to communicate with a person outside the group who does not understand such language, it is doublespeak. In 1978 a National Airlines 727 airplane crashed while attempting to land at the Pensacola, Florida, airport, killing three passengers, injuring twenty-one others, and destroying the airplane. Since the insured value of the airplane was greater than its book value, National made an after-tax insurance benefit of $1.7 million on the destroyed airplane, or an extra eighteen cents a share. In its annual report, National reported that this $1.7 million was due to "the involuntary conversion of a 727," thus explaining the profit without even hinting at the crash and the deaths of three passengers.

Gobbledygook or bureaucratese is another kind of doublespeak. Such doublespeak is simply a matter of overwhelming the audience with technical, unfamiliar words. When asked why U.S. forces lacked intelligence information on Grenada before they invaded the island in 1983, Admiral Wesley L. McDonald told reporters that "We were not micromanaging Grenada intelligence-wise until about that time frame."

Some gobbledygook, however impressive it may sound, doesn't even   10
make sense. During the 1988 presidential campaign, vice presidential candidate Senator Dan Quayle explained the need for a strategic defense initiative by saying: "Why wouldn't an enhanced deterrent, a more stable
peace, a better prospect to denying the ones who enter conflict in the first
place to have a reduction of offensive systems and an introduction to defensive capability. I believe this is the route the country will eventually go."

In 1974, Alan Greenspan, then chairman of the President's Council
of Economic Advisors, was testifying before a Senate Committee and was
in the difficult position of trying to explain why President Nixon's economic policies weren't effective in fighting inflation: "It is a tricky problem to find the particular calibration in timing that would be appropriate
to stem the acceleration in risk premiums created by falling incomes without prematurely aborting the decline in the inflation-generated risk premiums." In 1988, when speaking to a meeting of the Economic Club of
New York, Mr. Greenspan, now Federal Reserve chairman, said, "I guess
I should warn you, if I turn out to be particularly clear, you've probably
misunderstood what I've said."

The investigation into the Challenger disaster in 1986 revealed the
gobbledygook and bureaucratese used by many involved in the shuttle
program. When Jesse Moore, NASA's associate administrator, was asked
if the performance of the shuttle program had improved with each launch
or if it had remained the same, he answered, "I think our performance in
terms of the liftoff performance and in terms of the orbital performance,
we knew more about the envelope we were operating under, and we have
been pretty accurately staying in that. And so I would say the performance has not by design drastically improved. I think we have been able to
characterize the performance more as a function of our launch experience
as opposed to it improving as a function of time."

A final kind of doublespeak is simply inflated language. Car mechan-
ics may be called "automotive internists," elevator operators "members
of the vertical transportation corps," and grocery store checkout clerks
"career associate scanning professionals," while television sets are proclaimed to have "nonmulticolor capability." When a company "initiates a
career alternative enhancement program" it is really laying off five thousand workers; "negative patient care outcome" means that the patient
died; and "rapid oxidation" means a fire in a nuclear power plant.

The doublespeak of inflated language can have serious consequences.
The U.S. Navy didn't pay $2,043 a piece for steel nuts; it paid all that
money for "hexiform rotatable surface compression units," which, by the
way, "underwent catastrophic stress related shaft detachment." Not to be
outdone, the U.S. Air Force paid $214 a piece for Emergency Exit
Lights, or flashlights. This doublespeak is in keeping with such military
doublespeak as "preemptive counterattack" for first strike, "engage the
enemy on all sides" for ambush, "tactical redeployment" for retreat, and

"air support" for bombing. In the doublespeak of the military, the 1983 invasion of Grenada was conducted not by the U.S. Army, Navy, Air Force, and Marines but by the "Caribbean Peace Keeping Forces." But then according to the Pentagon it wasn't an invasion, it was a "predawn vertical insertion."

These last examples of doublespeak should make it clear that double-speak is not the product of careless language or sloppy thinking. Indeed, serious doublespeak is the product of clear thinking and is carefully designed and constructed to appear to communicate but in fact to mislead. Thus, it's not a tax increase but "revenue enhancement," "tax base broadening," or "user fees," so how can you complain about higher taxes? It's not acid rain, it's just "poorly buffered precipitation," so don't worry about all those dead trees. That isn't the Mafia in Atlantic City, those are just "members of a career-offender cartel," so don't worry about the influence of organized crime in the city. The Supreme Court Justice wasn't addicted to the painkilling drug he was taking, it's just that the drug had simply "established an interrelationship with the body, such that if the drug is removed precipitously, there is a reaction," so don't worry that his decisions might have been influenced by his drug addition. It's not a Titan II nuclear-armed, intercontinental, ballistic missile 630 times more powerful than the atomic bomb dropped on Hiroshima, it's just a "very large, potentially disruptive reentry system," so don't worry about the threat of nuclear destruction. Serious doublespeak is highly strategic, and it breeds suspicion, cynicism, distrust, and, ultimately, hostility.

In his famous and now-classic essay "Politics and the English Language," which was published in 1946, George Orwell wrote that the "great enemy of clear language is insincerity. When there is a gap between one's real and one's declared aims, one turns as it were instinctively to long words and exhausted idioms, like a cuttlefish squirting out ink." For Orwell, language was an instrument for "expressing and not for concealing or preventing thought." In his most biting comment, Orwell observes that "in our time, political speech and writing are largely the defense of the indefensible. . . . Political language has to consist largely of euphemism, question-begging, and sheer cloudy vagueness. . . . Political language . . . is designed to make lies sound truthful and murder respectable, and to give an appearance of solidity to pure wind."

Orwell understood well the power of language as both a tool and a weapon. In the nightmare world of his novel *1984*, he depicted language as one of the most important tools of the totalitarian state. Newspeak, the official state language in *1984*, was designed not to extend but to *diminish* the range of human thought, to make only "correct" thought possible and all other modes of thought impossible. It was, in short, a language designed to create a reality which the state wanted.

Newspeak had another important function in Orwell's world of *1984*. It provided the means of expression for doublethink, which Orwell described in his novel as "the power of holding two contradictory beliefs in one's mind simultaneously, and accepting both of them." The classic example of doublethink in Orwell's novel is the slogan "War is Peace." And lest you think doublethink is confined only to Orwell's novel, you need only recall the words of Secretary of State Alexander Haig when he testified before a Congressional Committee in 1982 that a continued weapons build-up by the United States is "absolutely essential to our hopes for meaningful arms reduction." Or the words of Senator Orrin Hatch in 1988: "Capital punishment is our society's recognition of the sanctity of human life."

The more sophisticated and powerful uses of doublespeak can at times be difficult to identify. On 27 July 1981, President Ronald Reagan said in a television speech: "I will not stand by and see those of you who are dependent on Social Security deprived of the benefits you've worked so hard to earn. You will continue to receive your checks in the full amount due you." This speech had been billed as President Reagan's position on Social Security, a subject of much debate at the time. After the speech, public opinion polls recorded the great majority of the public as believing that President Reagan had affirmed his support for Social Security and that he would not support cuts in benefits. Five days after the speech, however, White House spokesperson David Gergen was quoted in the press as saying that President Reagan's words had been "carefully chosen." What President Reagan did mean, according to Gergen, was that he was reserving the right to decide who was "dependent" on those benefits, who had "earned" them, and who, therefore, was "due" them.

During the 1982 Congressional election campaign, the Republican National Committee sponsored a television advertisement which pictured an elderly, folksy postman delivering Social Security checks "with the 7.4 percent cost-of-living raise that President Reagan promised." Looking directly at his audience, the postman then adds that Reagan "promised that raise and he kept his promise, in spite of those sticks-in-the-mud who tried to keep him from doing what we elected him to do."

The commercial was deliberately misleading. The cost-of-living increases had been provided automatically by law since 1975, and President Reagan had tried three times to roll them back or delay them but was overruled by congressional opposition. When these discrepancies were pointed out to an official of the Republican National Committee, he called the commercial "inoffensive" and added, "Since when is a commercial supposed to be accurate? Do women really smile when they clean their ovens?"

In 1986, with the Challenger tragedy and subsequent investigation, we discovered that doublespeak seemed to be the official language of NASA, the National Aeronautics and Space Administration, and of the contractors engaged in the space shuttle program. The first thing we learned is that the Challenger tragedy wasn't an accident. As Kay Parker of NASA said, experts were "working in the anomaly investigation." The "anomaly" was the explosion of the Challenger.

When NASA reported that it was having difficulty determining how or exactly when the Challenger astronauts died, Rear Admiral Richard Truly reported that "whether or not a cabin rupture occurred prior to water impact has not yet been determined by a superficial examination of the recovered components." The "recovered components" were the bodies of the astronauts. Admiral Truly also said that "extremely large forces were imposed on the vehicle as evidenced by the immediate breakup into many pieces." He went on to say that "once these forces have been accurately determined, if in fact they can be, the structural analysts will attempt to estimate the effect on the structural and pressure integrity of the crew module." NASA referred to the coffins of the astronauts as "crew transfer containers."

Arnold Aldrich, manager of the national space transportation systems program at Johnson Space Center, said that "the normal process during the countdown is that the countdown proceeds, assuming we are in a go posture, and at various points during the countdown we tag up on the operational loops and face to face in the firing room to ascertain the facts that project elements that are monitoring the data and that are understanding the situation as we proceed are still in the go condition."

In testimony before the commission investigating the Challenger accident, Allen McDonald, an engineer for Morton Thiokol (the maker of the rocket), said he had expressed concern about the possible effect of cold weather on the booster rocker's O-ring seals the night before the launch: "I made the comment that lower temperatures are in the direction of badness for both O-rings, because it slows down the timing function."

Larry Mulloy, manager of the space shuttle solid rocket booster program at Marshall Space Flight Center, responded to a question assessing whether problems with the O-rings or with the insulation of the liner of the nozzle posed a greater threat to the shuttle by saying, "The criticality in answering your question, sir, it would be a real foot race as to which one would be considered more critical, depending on the particular time that you looked at your experience with that."

After several executives of Rockwell International, the main contractor to build the shuttle, had testified that Rockwell had been opposed to launching the shuttle because of the danger posed by ice formation on the launch platform, Martin Cioffoletti, vice president for space transportation at Rockwell, said: "I felt that by telling them we did not have a sufficient data base and could not analyze the trajectory of the ice, I felt he understood that Rockwell was not giving a positive indication that we were for the launch."

Officials at Morton Thiokol, when asked why they reversed earlier decisions not to launch the shuttle, said the reversal was "based on the reevaluation of those discussions." The Presidential commission investigating the accident suggested that this statement could be translated to mean there was pressure from NASA.

One of the most chilling uses of doublespeak occurred in 1981 when then Secretary of State Alexander Haig was testifying before congressional committees about the murder of three American nuns and a Catholic lay worker in El Salvador. The four women had been raped and then shot at close range, and there was clear evidence that the crime had been committed by soldiers of the Salvadoran government. Before the House Foreign Affairs Committee, Secretary Haig said, "I'd like to suggest to you that some of the investigations would lead one to believe that perhaps the vehicle the nuns were riding in may have tried to run a roadblock, or may accidentally have been perceived to have been doing so, and there'd been an exchange of fire and then perhaps those who inflicted the casualties sought to cover it up. And this could have been at a very low level of both competence and motivation in the context of the issue itself. But the facts on this are not clear enough for anyone to draw a definitive conclusion."

The next day, before the Senate Foreign Relations Committee, Secretary Haig claimed that press reports on his previous testimony were inaccurate. When Senator Claiborne Pell asked whether Secretary Haig was suggesting the possibility that "the nuns may have run through a roadblock," Secretary Haig replied, "You mean that they tried to violate . . . ? Not at all, no, not at all. My heavens! The dear nuns who raised me in my parochial schooling would forever isolate me from their affections and respect." When Senator Pell asked Secretary Haig, "Did you mean that the nuns were firing at the people, or what did 'an exchange of fire' mean?" Secretary Haig replied, "I haven't met any pistol-packing nuns in my day, Senator. What I meant was that if one fellow starts shooting, then the next thing you know they all panic." Thus did the Secretary of State of the United States explain official government policy on the murder of four American citizens in a foreign land.

The congressional hearings for the Irancontra affair produced more doublespeak. During his second day of testimony before the Select Committee on Secret Military Assistance to Iran and the Nicaraguan Opposition, Oliver North admitted that he had on different occasions lied to the Iranians, his colleague Maj. Gen. Richard Secord, congressional investigators, and the Congress, and that he had destroyed evidence and created false documents. North then asserted to the committee that everything he was about to say would be the truth.

North used the words "residuals" and "diversions" to refer to the millions of dollars which were raised for the contras by overcharging Iran for arms. North also said that he "cleaned" and "fixed" things up, that he was "cleaning up the historical record," and that he "took steps to ensure" that things never "came out" — meaning he lied, destroyed official government documents, and created false documents. Some documents weren't destroyed; they were "non-log [ged]" or kept "out of the system so that outside knowledge would not necessarily be derived from having the documents themselves."

North was also careful not to "infect other people with unnecessary knowledge." He explained that the Nicaraguan Humanitarian Assistance Office provided humanitarian aid in "mixed loads," which, according to North, "meant . . . beans and Band-Aids and boots and bullets." For North, people in other countries who helped him were "assets." "Project Democracy" was a "euphemism" he used at the time to refer to the organization that was building an airfield for the contras.

In speaking of a false chronology of events which he helped construct, North said that he "was provided with additional input that was radically different from the truth. I assisted in furthering that version." He mentions "a different version from the facts" and calls the chronology "inaccurate." North also testified that he and William Casey, then head of the C.I.A., together falsified the testimony that Casey was to give to Congress. "Director Casey and I fixed that testimony and removed the offensive portions. We fixed it by omission. We left out — it wasn't made accurate, it wasn't made fulsome, it was fixed by omission." Official lies were "plausible deniability."

While North admitted that he had shredded documents after being   35 informed that officials from the Attorney General's office wanted to inspect some of the documents in his office, he said, "I would prefer to say that I shredded documents that day like I did on all other days, but perhaps with increased intensity."

North also preferred to use the passive to avoid responsibility. When asked "Where are the non-logged documents?" he replied, "I think they were shredded." Again, when asked on what authority he agreed to allow Secord to make a personal profit off the arms sale to Iran, North replied with a long, wordy response filled with such passive constructions as "it was clearly indicated," "it was already known," and "it was recognized." But he never answered the question.

For North, the whole investigation by Congress was just an attempt "to criminalize policy differences between coequal branches of government and the Executive's conduct of foreign affairs." Lying to Congress, shredding official documents, violating laws, conducting unauthorized activities were all just "policy differences" to North. But North was generous with the committee: "I think there's fault to go on both sides. I've said that repeatedly throughout my testimony. And I have accepted the responsibility for my role in it." While North accepts responsibility, he does not accept accountability.

This final statement of North's bears close reading for it reveals the subtlety of his language. North states as fact that Congress was at fault, but at fault for what he doesn't specify. Furthermore, he does not accept responsibility for any specific action, only for his "role," whatever that may have been, in "it." In short, while he may be "responsible" (not guilty) for violating the law, Congress shares in that responsibility for having passed the law.

In Oliver North's doublespeak, then, defying a law is complying with it, noncompliance is compliance. North's doublespeak allowed him to help draft a letter to Congress saying that "we are complying with the letter and spirit" of the Boland Amendment, when what the letter really meant, North later admitted, was that "Boland doesn't apply to us and so we're complying with its letter and spirit."

Contrary to his claim that he was a "stand up guy" who would tell all 40 and take whatever was coming to him, North disclaimed all responsibility for his actions: "I was authorized to do everything that I did." Yet when he was asked who gave him authorization, North replied, "My superiors." When asked which superior, he replied: "Well, who — look who sign — I didn't sign those letters to the — to this body." And North's renowned steel-trap memory went vague or forgetful again.

After North had testified, Admiral John Poindexter, North's superior, testified before the committee. Once again, doublespeak flourished. In the world of Admiral John Poindexter, one does not lie but "misleads" or "withholds information." Likewise, one engages in "secret activities" which are not the same as covert actions. In Poindexter's world, one can "acquiesce" in a shipment of weapons while at the same time not authorize the shipment. One can transfer millions of dollars of government money as a "technical implementation" without making a "substantive decision." One can also send subordinates to lie to congressional committees if one does not "micromanage" them. In Poindexter's world, "outside interference" occurs when Congress attempts to fulfill its constitutional function of passing legislation.

For Poindexter, withholding information was not lying. When asked about Col. North's testimony that he had lied to a congressional committee and that Poindexter had known that North intended to lie, Poindexter replied, "there was a general understanding that he [North] was to withhold information. . . . I . . . did not expect him to lie to the committee. I expected him to be evasive. . . . I'm sure they [North's answers] were very carefully crafted, nuanced. The total impact, I am sure, was one of withholding information from the Congress, but I'm still not convinced . . . that he lied."

Yet Poindexter protested that it is not "fair to say that I have misinformed Congress or other Cabinet officers. I haven't testified to that. I've testified that I withheld information from Congress. And with regard to the Cabinet officers, I didn't withhold anything from them that they didn't want withheld from them." Poindexter did not explain how it is possible to withhold information that a person wants withheld.

The doublespeak of Alexander Haig, Oliver North, and John Poindexter occurred during their testimony before congressional committees.

Perhaps their doublespeak was not premeditated but just happened to be the way they spoke, and thought. President Jimmy Carter in 1980 could call the aborted raid to free the American hostages in Tehran an "incomplete success" and really believe that he had made a statement that clearly communicated with the American public. So too could President Ronald Reagan say in 1985 that "ultimately our security and our hopes for success at the arms reduction talks hinge on the determination that we show here to continue our program to rebuild and refortify our defenses" and really believe that greatly increasing the amount of money spent building new weapons will lead to a reduction in the number of weapons in the world. If we really believe that we understand such language and that such language communicates and promotes clear thought, then the world of *1984* with its control of reality through language is upon us.

FOCUSING ON CONTENT

1. What, according to Lutz, is doublespeak? What are its essential characteristics?

2. What is a euphemism? Are all euphemisms examples of doublespeak? Explain.

3. In his discussion of Oliver North's testimony during the Irancontra hearings, Lutz states, "While North accepts responsibility, he does not accept accountability" (37). Explain what Lutz means here. What differences do you draw between responsibility and accountability?

4. Why, according to Lutz, does "doublespeak continue to spread as the official language of public discourse" (1)? In your opinion, is doublespeak as widespread today as it was when Lutz wrote his article? What examples can you provide to back up your opinion?

5. Why does Lutz believe that we must recognize doublespeak for what it is and voice our dissatisfaction with those who use it?

FOCUSING ON WRITING

1. In paragraph 2, Lutz provides readers with a comprehensive definition of *doublespeak*. What does he achieve as a writer by clearly defining this term early in his essay? (Glossary: *Definition*)

2. What is Lutz's purpose in this essay — to inform, to express thoughts or feelings, to persuade? (Glossary: *Purpose*) What in his essay leads you to this conclusion?

3. Lutz discusses four basic types or categories of doublespeak — euphemism, jargon, gobbledygook, and inflated language. In what ways does this classification serve to clarify not only the concept of doublespeak but also its many uses? (Glossary: *Classification*)

4. Lutz is careful to illustrate each of the basic types of doublespeak with examples. Why is it important to use plenty of examples in an essay like this? (Glossary: *Examples*) What do his many examples reveal about Lutz's expertise on the subject?

5. How does paragraph 15 function in the context of the entire essay? How are paragraphs 16–44 related to Lutz's statement that "serious doublespeak is highly strategic, and it breeds suspicion, cynicism, distrust, and, ultimately, hostility" (15)?

LANGUAGE IN ACTION

In an article called "Public Doublespeak," Terence Moran presents the following list of recommended language, which school administrators in Brooklyn gave their elementary school teachers to use when discussing students with their parents.

FOR PARENT INTERVIEWS AND REPORT CARDS

Harsh Expression (Avoid)	Acceptable Expression (Use)
Does all right if pushed	Accomplishes tasks when interest is stimulated.
Too free with fists	Resorts to physical means of winning his point or attracting attention.
Lies (Dishonest)	Shows difficulty in distinguishing between imaginary and factual material.
Cheats	Needs help in learning to adhere to rules and standards of fair play.
Steals	Needs help in learning to respect the property rights of others.
Noisy	Needs to develop quieter habits of communication.
Lazy	Needs ample supervision in order to work well.
Is a bully	Has qualities of leadership but needs help in learning to use them democratically.
Associates with "gangs"	Seems to feel secure only in group situations; needs to develop sense of independence.
Disliked by other children	Needs help in learning to form lasting friendships.

What are your reactions to these recommendations? Why do you suppose the school administrators made up this list? What purpose does such language serve? Do you believe the "acceptable" language belongs in our nation's schools? Why or why not?

WRITING SUGGESTIONS

1. Think of the ways that you encounter doublespeak every day, whether in school or at work, or while reading a newspaper or watching television. How does it affect you? What do you suppose the speakers' or writers' motives are in using doublespeak? Using your own experiences and observations, write an essay in which you explore the reasons why people use doublespeak. Before starting to write, you may find it helpful to review your Writing to Discover response for the Lutz essay.

2. In his concluding paragraph Lutz states, "If we really believe that we understand [doublespeak] and that such language communicates and promotes clear thought, then the world of *1984* with its control of reality through language is upon us." In an essay, discuss whether or not Lutz is overstating the case and being too pessimistic and whether or not the American public is really unaware of — or apathetic about — how doublespeak manipulates and deceives. Consider also whether or not the American public has reacted to doublespeak with, as Lutz suggests, "suspicion, cynicism, distrust, and, ultimately, hostility."

3. Using resources in your library or on the Internet, write a paper about the language of funeral directors, stockbrokers, college professors, health-care professionals, or some other occupation of your choice. How pervasive is doublespeak in the occupation you selected? Based on the results of your research, why do you think people with this type of job use such language? Do you find this language troublesome? If so, what can be done to change the situation? If not, why not?

The E Word

CULLEN MURPHY

Cullen Murphy was born in New Rochelle, New York, and grew up in Greenwich, Connecticut. After graduating from Amherst College in 1974, Murphy went to work for both Change, *an education magazine, and the* Wilson Quarterly. *Later he joined the* Atlantic Monthly *and has been the managing editor there since 1985. His books include* Rubbish! *(1992), a study of landfill practices coauthored with William Rathje, and* Just Curious *(1995), a collection of his* Harper's *and* Atlantic Monthly *essays. His most recent book is* The Word According to Eve: Women and the Bible in Ancient Times and Our Own *(1998). For over twenty years Murphy has also written the text for the popular comic strip* Prince Valiant, *which his father draws.*

In the following essay, which first appeared in the Atlantic Monthly *in September 1996, Murphy examines Americans' love affair with the euphemism. In fact, euphemisms — pretty or important-sounding names for essentially harsh realities — have become so widespread that Murphy dubs them "the characteristic literary device of our time."*

WRITING TO DISCOVER: *Many Americans believe that nothing is taboo anymore — that anything that can be imagined can be said, filmed, printed, or sent into cyberspace on the World Wide Web. Write down your views on this kind of thinking. Do you think Americans really tell it like it is, or are there subjects that we talk about only in clothed language, if at all?*

"We are not at war with Egypt. We are in a state of armed conflict."
– ANTHONY EDEN, *during the Suez Crisis, 1956*

Driving along a highway in southern New Mexico not long ago, I came within the gravitational pull of a truck stop, and was ineluctably drawn in. This was not one of those mom-and-pop "truck stops," so prevalent in the East, where cars outnumber semis and the restaurant has a children's menu. This was the real thing, lit up in the desert darkness like an outpost in Mad Max, visible from six counties. Cars in the parking lot looked like Piper Cubs at O'Hare. It was the kind of place where tough men sit at the counter and call the waitress "doll," which she likes, and order flesh and starch while they smoke, leaning over the counter, a crescent of lower back visible between pants and shirt. Outside, their mounts hungrily lap up petrochemicals.

In a truck stop such as this the aesthetic pinnacle is typically reached in the design of the men's-room condom dispenser, and here I was not disappointed. Taking up nearly one full wall was a kind of Ghent Altar-piece of prophylaxis, each glass panel displaying its own delicately crafted vignette: a yellow sunset through palm trees, a couple strolling lazily along a beach, a herd of galloping white stallions, a flaxen-haired suc-cubus in gauzy silhouette — exquisite examples of late-*novecento* venereal iconography.

Above it hung a sign saying FAMILY PLANNING CENTER.

Robert Burchfield, for many years the editor of *The Oxford English Dictionary,* once observed that "a language without euphemisms would be a defective instrument of communication." By this criterion, at least, contemporary American English cannot be judged defective. All epochs, of course, have employed euphemisms both to downplay and to amplify: to camouflage the forbidden, to dress up the unseemly and the unpleas-ant, and, like Chaucer's Wife of Bath, to find genteel expression for some earthy fun. Some periods have specialized. The eighteenth century is fa-mous as a time of inventive sexual innuendo and political circumlocution (consult almost any passage in *Gulliver's Travels*). The Victorians were linguistically circumspect not only about sex and the human body but also about money and death. But in the late twentieth century euphe-mism has achieved what it never achieved before: it has become a fit medium for the expression of just about everything. Putty as it is in the hands of its employer, bereft (unlike irony) of any solid core, euphemism can take on almost any task at all. It is the characteristic literary device of our time — as much a hallmark of the era as were inflated honorifics in fifth-century Rome.

The one thing that all euphemisms have in common is their willing-ness to show themselves in public — sometimes with audacity. A press re-lease arrived recently from the Fur Information Council of America, and it contained this sentence: "Twice as many animals are killed each year in animal shelters and pounds as are used by the fur industry." The word "partition" was politically unacceptable in the Dayton Agreement, signed by the warring parties in the former Yugoslavia, and so the agreement does not employ it; but what might the term "inter-entity boundary" mean? A spokesperson for the United Nations, asked to explain the rou-tine disappearance of millions of dollars' worth of computers, vehicles, and cash whenever UN forces withdraw from a locale, blamed a phenom-enon she called "end-of-mission *tristesse*."

Most euphemisms, though, do not call such attention to themselves; we slide right over them. Some weeks ago I decided to spend a day with the euphemism detector set on high, just to see what kinds of things turned up in newspapers and magazines, on radio and television, and in ordinary conversation. Here is part of the harvest: "deer management" for the enlistment of paid sharpshooters; "remedial college skills" for reading; "traffic-calming measures" for speed bumps; "comparative ads" for attack ads; "legacy device" for an obsolete computer; "assistance devices" for hearing aids: "firm," in the parlance of produce merchants, for underripe; "hand-check," in the parlance of basketball players, for shove; "peace enforcement" for combat; "hard to place" for disturbed; "growth going backwards" for recession (itself a euphemism); "post-verdict response" for riot; "cult favorite" for low-rated; and "gated community" for affluent residential compound with private security. (Imagine a sign outside Windsor Castle 500 years ago: A GATED COMMUNITY.) This is but a modest sample, and I have not included any euphemism ending with "syndrome" or "challenged."

The newest category of euphemism — which takes the idea into unexplored metaphysical territory — is one in which a euphemistic term is invented for a word or idea that actually requires none, the euphemism thereby implicitly back-tainting the original word or idea itself. In its most widespread manifestation this kind of euphemizing takes its form from such locutions for unutterables as "the F word" and, in a racial context, "the N word." Thus, during his race for the presidency against Michael Dukakis, George Bush castigated his opponent for being a liberal by bringing up what he called "the L word." Since then we have had "the O word," referring to orphanages (or, at the other demographic extreme, to old age); "the T word," referring to taxes; "the U word" (unions); "the V word" (vouchers); and "the W word" (welfare). William Safire, who briefly took note of this phenomenon in its infancy, during the 1988 campaign, predicted that it would "probably peter out in a few years, after we go through the alphabet and begin to get confused about what a given letter is supposed to signify." In fact the euphemistic abecedarium is now both complete and several meanings deep, and seems to be evincing considerable staying power. The cheap mass production of E words has apparently proved irresistible.

On balance, are euphemisms bad for us? One school of thought holds that a truly healthy, stable, psychologically mature society would have no need for euphemisms. Those who subscribe to this school would hold further, with George Orwell, that political euphemism "is designed to make lies sound truthful and murder respectable, and to give an appearance of solidity to pure wind." They might add that the emergence of the new genre of faux euphemism is particularly insidious, in that it implies a kind of equivalence among the concepts or terminology represented by letters of the alphabet — as if "the L word" and "the T word" really did belong in the same category as "the N word." There is something to be said for all these points, the last one in particular. I'm surely not alone in observing that the phrase "the N word" has lately come into the mainstream, as the N word itself never could again.

A second school of thought about euphemisms might be called the white-blood-cell school; it holds that yes, an elevated count might well be a sign of mild or serious pathology — but it's also a sign that a natural defense mechanism has kicked in. By and large my sympathies lie with the white-blood-cell school. Although euphemism sets some to spluttering about its deceitfulness, I suspect that few people are really deceived — that, indeed, the transparent motives and awkward semantics only undermine the euphemist's intention. When a nuclear warhead is referred to as "the physics package," when genocide is referred to as "ethnic cleansing," when wife-beating is referred to as "getting physical" — in all these cases the terminology trains a spotlight on the truth.

Philosophers and linguists will argue the matter for years to come. In the meantime, though, it might be useful to begin acquiring a database of euphemisms by monitoring their prevalence in our national life. The model would be the Consumer Price Index.

The Consumer Price Index does not, of course, keep track of inflation by watching trends in the prices of everything. It focuses on a "basket" of major economic goods and services: food, clothing, rent, oil and gas, interest rates, and so on. With euphemisms, too, a handful of big items account for a disproportionate share of all euphemistic activity. Thus we might devise a preliminary formula with a basket of concepts including sex, God, money, politics, social pathology, bodily functions, disease, and death (along with, perhaps, a few minor bellwether indicators such as euphemisms for criminal behavior by juveniles and for lack of achievement in school). Logoplasticians, as those who study euphemisms might be called, would follow the emergence of promising synonyms in all these areas, producing at regular intervals a Semantic Engineering Index, or SEI.

Some might anticipate that in a society like ours the SEI would show gains quarter after quarter. I am not sure that this would happen in the aggregate: a macro-euphemistic view of history shows significant ups and downs over time. But in any event internal shifts would be abundant and revealing. Euphemisms are fragile organisms, surprisingly sensitive to the outside environment. Frequently they come to embody so fully the thing being euphemized that they themselves demand replacement. H. W. Fowler's *Modern English Usage* (Second Edition) shows how "toilet" is but the latest in a series of progressively superseded euphemisms — "water-closet," "latrine," "privy," "jakes" — going back many centuries. (Last year a Methodist singles group, recognizing the danger of euphemistic succession and hoping to stave it off, held a retreat with the theme "Intimacy Is Not a Euphemism for Sex." Good luck.) Some euphemisms eventually attract such knowing derision that their useful life is abbreviated. This was the case, for instance, with the term "revenue enhancement" as a stealthy substitute for "higher taxes." Other euphemisms, such as "custodial engineer" and "sandwich technician," pass from the moment of coinage into a state of ironic suspension without ever experiencing an intermediate condition of utility.

Given the avidity with which professional lexicographers today comb through books and periodicals for evidence of emerging and fading terminology, compiling a Semantic Engineering Index would no doubt be quite simple. And popular acceptance of the idea of "leading cuphemistic indicators" would come easily. "The SEI rose three tenths of a point this month, paced by a rise in the T word and public jitters about peace enforcement." I see a cult favorite already.

FOCUSING ON CONTENT

1. According to Murphy, "All epochs . . . have employed euphemisms both to downplay and to amplify: to camouflage the forbidden, to dress up the unseemly and unpleasant, and, like Chaucer's Wife of Bath, to find genteel expression for some earthy fun" (4). Using Murphy's many examples of euphemisms, illustrate each of the functions he mentions. Can you think of any functions that he doesn't mention? Explain.

2. What do you think Murphy means when he says in paragraph 4, "Putty as it is in the hands of its employers, bereft (unlike irony) of any solid core, euphemism can take on almost any task at all." What types of issues tend to attract the use of euphemisms? Why?

3. What is the euphemism in the Fur Information Council of America's statement, "Twice as many animals are killed each year in animal shelters and pounds as are used by the fur industry" (5)? Do you think most readers would detect this euphemism? Explain.

4. What, according to Murphy, is "the newest category of euphemism" (7)? How do the euphemisms in this category work? How does the title of Murphy's essay support what he says about such euphemisms?

5. In his discussion of euphemistic succession, Murphy mentions the Methodist singles group that organized a retreat around the theme "Intimacy Is Not a Euphemism for Sex." What are some of the popular euphemisms for *sex*? What do you think the singles group fears if *intimacy* becomes a euphemism for *sex*?

FOCUSING ON WRITING

1. Murphy illustrates his various points about euphemisms with numerous examples, and he takes these examples from a wide range of subject areas. (Glossary: *Examples*) Why do you suppose he uses as many examples as he does? Which ones do you find most effective? Least effective? Explain.

2. In paragraphs 8 and 9, Murphy compares and contrasts the two schools of thought on whether euphemisms are bad for us. What are the key differences between these two views? How does Murphy organize his comparison? (Glossary: *Comparison and Contrast*) What conclusion does he come to?

3. Murphy starts paragraph 8 with a rhetorical question. (Glossary: *Rhetorical Question*) How does this question function in the context of his essay?

4. Murphy introduces the concept of a Semantic Engineering Index in paragraphs 11–13. In your own words, what is the SEI? What is Murphy's tone
in these concluding paragraphs? (Glossary: *Tone*) What in his diction leads
you to this conclusion? (Glossary: *Diction*)

LANGUAGE IN ACTION

Real estate salespeople often use language that is designed to let potential
buyers' imaginations run wild. For example, one language analyst notes that
in her hometown "adorable" meant "small," "eat-in kitchen" meant "no
dining room," "handyman's special" meant "portion of building still standing," "by appointment only" meant "expensive," and "starter home" meant
"cheap." In this context, discuss the following cartoon by Jeff Danziger of
the *Los Angeles Times*.

*And here's that cozy eat-in kitchen, with that lovely
view of the water!*

WRITING SUGGESTIONS

1. In a September 19, 1969, article entitled "The Euphemism: Telling It Like
It Isn't" the editors of *Time* say that "despite its swaggering sexual candor,

much contemporary speech still hides behind that traditional enemy of plain talk, the euphemism." Do you think this statement is accurate today? Using examples from your own experiences or observations, write an essay in which you agree or disagree with the position taken by the editors of *Time*. Before you start writing, be sure to reread what you wrote in response to the Writing to Discover prompt for this selection.

2. Murphy claims in paragraph 9 that "although euphemism sets some to spluttering about its deceitfulness, I suspect that few people are really deceived — that, indeed, the transparent motives and awkward semantics only undermine the euphemist's intention." Where do you stand on this issue? Are you as optimistic about the minimal influence of euphemisms as Murphy seems to be? Do you and your peers readily pick up on euphemistic usage? If euphemisms haven't worked in the past — haven't changed people's perception of something simply by changing its name — why are they so widespread? Write an essay in which you answer Murphy's question, "On balance, are euphemisms bad for us?" Be sure to consider the following question as well: Do some euphemisms serve worthwhile social purposes?

3. Select a controversial policy or issue (such as abortion, school choice, welfare, social security, Affirmative Action, racism, alcohol consumption, fur products, cigarette smoking, war, gun control, school security, or nuclear energy) and study the language used by the various parties in the controversy. Consult resources in your library or on the Internet, and try to do some personal interviews if possible. How much euphemistic usage do you find, and what seems to be its intent? In his book *Crazy Talk, Stupid Talk* (1976), Neil Postman, a professor of media ecology at New York University, boldly says that "euphemizing is contemptible when a name makes us see something that is not true or diverts our attention from something that is." Is the euphemizing used to discuss the issue you selected contemptible, deceitful, somewhat annoying, or totally harmless? Write an essay in which you discuss and reach some conclusions about the language surrounding your issue.

How They Chose These Words

WALTER ISAACSON

Newspaper reporter, magazine editor, author, and television executive Walter Isaacson was born in 1952 in New Orleans, Louisiana. He graduated from Harvard University in 1974 with a degree in history and literature and as a Rhodes Scholar went on to Oxford University, where in 1976 he received an M.A. in philosophy and politics. Isaacson launched his career in journalism with the Sunday Times *of London and later returned to New Orleans, where he worked briefly with the* Times Picayune/States-Item *covering local politics before joining* Time *magazine. His career at* Time *spanned more than two decades, starting as a reporter covering Ronald Reagan's 1980 campaign and ending as managing editor. In 2001 he became chairman and CEO of CNN. Currently, he is president and CEO of the Aspen Institute, an international forum interested in environmental and economic issues. Isaacson is the author of* Kissinger: A Biography *(1992) and* Benjamin Franklin: An American Life *(2003), and is the coauthor of* The Wise Men: Six Friends and the World They Made *(1986), the story of American statesmen and the Cold War. In the following selection, first published in* Time *on July 7, 2003, Isaacson reveals how one small edit by Benjamin Franklin dramatically changed the impact of the Declaration of Independence, America's justification of its revolution to the world.*

WRITING TO DISCOVER: *Have you ever questioned a particular policy at your school, criticized a decision made by a public official, or had a difference of opinion with your parents? How did you handle the situation — did you engage the other party in discussion or did you express your concerns and feeling in writing? For you, what is the difference between talking about your views and putting them into writing? What does it take for you to put something into writing?*

As the Continental Congress prepared to vote on the question of American independence in 1776, it appointed a committee for what would turn out, in hindsight, to be a momentous task, but one that at the time did not seem so important: drafting a declaration that explained the decision. It included Franklin, of course, and Thomas Jefferson and John Adams as well as Connecticut merchant Roger Sherman and New York lawyer Robert Livingston.

How was it that Jefferson, at 33, got the honor of drafting the document? His name was listed first on the committee, signifying that he was the chairman, because he had gotten the most votes and because he was from Virginia, the colony that had proposed the resolution. His four colleagues had other committee assignments that they considered to be more important, and none of them realized that the document would eventually become viewed as a text akin to Scripture. As for Franklin, he was still laid up in bed with boils and gout when the committee first met. Besides, he later told Jefferson, "I have made it a rule, whenever in my power, to avoid becoming the draughtsman of papers to be reviewed by a public body."

And thus it was that Jefferson had the glorious honor of composing, on a little lap desk he had designed, some of the most famous phrases in history while sitting alone in a second-floor room of a home on Market Street in Philadelphia just a block from Franklin's house. "When in the course of human events . . ." he famously began. Significantly, what followed was an attack not on the British government (i.e., the ministers) but on the British state incarnate (i.e., the King). "To attack the King was," as historian Pauline Maier notes, "a constitutional form. It was the way Englishmen announced revolution."

The document Jefferson drafted was in some ways similar to what Franklin would have written. It contained a highly specific bill of particulars against the British, and it recounted, as Franklin had often done, the details of America's attempts to be conciliatory despite England's intransigence. Indeed, Jefferson's words echoed some of the language that Franklin had used, earlier that year, in a draft resolution that he never published: "Whereas, whenever kings, instead of protecting the lives and properties of their subjects, as is their bounden duty, do endeavor to perpetrate the destruction of either, they thereby cease to be kings, become tyrants, and dissolve all ties of allegiance between themselves and their people."

Jefferson's writing style, however, was different from Franklin's. It was graced with rolling cadences and mellifluous phrases, soaring in their poetry and powerful despite their polish. In addition, Jefferson drew on a depth of philosophy not found in Franklin. He echoed both the language and grand theories of English and Scottish Enlightenment thinkers, most notably the concept of natural rights propounded by John Locke, whose *Second Treatise on Government* he had read at least three times. And he built his case, in a manner more sophisticated than Franklin would have, on a contract between government and the governed that was founded on the consent of the people. Jefferson also, it should be noted, borrowed freely from the phrasings of others, including the resounding Declaration of Rights in the new Virginia constitution that had just been drafted by his fellow planter George Mason, in a manner that today might subject him to questions of plagiarism but back then was considered not only proper but learned.

When he had finished a draft and incorporated some changes from Adams, Jefferson sent it to Franklin on the morning of Friday, June 21. "Will Doctor Franklin be so good as to peruse it," he wrote in his cover note, "and suggest such alterations as his more enlarged view of the subject will dictate?" People were much more polite to editors back then.

Franklin made only a few changes, some of which can be viewed written in his hand on what Jefferson referred to as the "rough draft" of the Declaration. (This remarkable document is at the Library of Congress and on its Web site.) The most important of his edits was small but resounding. He crossed out, using the heavy backslashes that he often employed, the last three words of Jefferson's phrase "We hold these truths to be sacred and undeniable" and changed them to the words now enshrined in history: "We hold these truths to be self-evident."

The idea of "self-evident" truths was one that drew less on Locke, who was Jefferson's favored philosopher, than on the scientific determinism espoused by Isaac Newton and the analytic empiricism of Franklin's close friend David Hume. In what became known as "Hume's fork," the great Scottish philosopher had developed a theory that distinguished between "synthetic" truths that describe matters of fact (such as "London is bigger than Philadelphia") and "analytic" truths that are so by virtue of reason and definition ("the angles of a triangle total 180 degrees"; "all bachelors are unmarried"). Hume referred to the latter type of axioms as "self-evident" truths. By using the word "sacred," Jefferson had implied, intentionally or not, that the principle in question – the equality of men and their endowment by their creator with inalienable rights – was an assertion of religion. Franklin's edit turned it instead into an assertion of rationality.

Franklin's other edits were less felicitous. He changed Jefferson's "reduce them to arbitrary power" to "reduce them under absolute despotism," and he took out the literary flourish in Jefferson's "invade and deluge us in blood" to make it more sparse: "invade and destroy us." And a few of his changes seemed somewhat pedantic. "Amount of their salaries" became "amount and payment of their salaries."

On July 2, the Continental Congress finally took the momentous   10
step of voting for independence. Pennsylvania was one of the last states to hold out; until June, its legislature had instructed its delegates to "utterly reject" any actions "that may cause or lead to a separation from our Mother Country." But under pressure from a more radical rump legislature, the instructions were changed. Led by Franklin, Pennsylvania's delegation joined the rest of the colonies in voting for independence.

As soon as the vote was completed, the Congress formed itself into a committee of the whole to consider Jefferson's draft Declaration. They were not as light in their editing as Franklin had been. Large sections were eviscerated, most notably the one that criticized the King for perpetuating the slave trade. Congress also, to its credit, cut by more than half the draft's final five paragraphs, in which Jefferson had begun to ramble in a way that detracted from the document's power. Jefferson was distraught. "I was sitting by Dr. Franklin," he recalled, "who perceived that I was not insensible to these mutilations." Franklin did his best to console him.

At the official signing of the parchment copy on August 2, John Hancock, the president of the Congress, penned his name with his famous flourish. "There must be no pulling different ways," he declared. "We must all hang together." According to the early American historian Jared Sparks, Franklin replied, "Yes, we must, indeed, all hang together, or most assuredly we shall all hang separately." Their lives, as well as their sacred honor, had been put on the line.

FOCUSING ON CONTENT

1. Isaacson starts paragraph 2 with the question: "How was it that Jefferson, at 33, got the honor of drafting the document [the Declaration of Independence]?" How does he answer that question?

2. In what ways was the draft declaration written by Jefferson similar to what Franklin might have drafted? According to Isaacson, how does Jefferson's writing style differ from Franklin's?

3. What, according to Isaacson, was the most important of Franklin's edits on Jefferson's draft of the Declaration of Independence? Why was this change significant? What does this example show you about the power of words? Explain.

4. After describing the signing of the Declaration on August 2, 1776, Isaacson says, "their lives, as well as their sacred honor, had been put on the line." What do you think he means by this statement?

FOCUSING ON WRITING

1. How has Isaacson organized his essay? (Glossary: *Organization*) In what ways is this organization appropriate given his subject and purpose?

2. What does Isaacson gain by quoting historian Pauline Maier in paragraph 3? Why do you suppose Isaacson chose to quote Jefferson's cover note to Franklin in paragraph 6 instead of capturing the gist of the message in his own words? Explain.

3. Who is the intended audience of Isaacson's essay? (Glossary: *Audience*) How do you know? Who was the intended audience of the Declaration of Independence in 1776?

4. What transitional techniques does Isaacson use to move smoothly from one paragraph to the next? (Glossary: *Transition*)

LANGUAGE IN ACTION

On January 20, 1961, President John F. Kennedy electrified the American people with his "Inaugural Address." In the words of his daughter Caroline, "he addressed the challenging global politics of the Cold War era. His eloquent defense of freedom and his call to public service inspired a generation of Americans and offered hope to people around the world." Since his assassination on November 22, 1963, millions have viewed that historic speech on video, while thousands of others have quoted his memorable lines or imitated its rhetoric for their own purposes. Following are several passages from the text of Kennedy's speech.

Let every nation know, whether it wishes us well or ill, that we shall pay any price, bear any burden, meet any hardship, support any friend, oppose any foe to assure the survival and the success of liberty.

This much we pledge — and more. . . .

In your hands, my fellow citizens, more than mine, will rest the final success or failure of our course. Since this country was founded, each generation of Americans has been summoned to give testimony to its national loyalty. The graves of young Americans who answered the call to service surround the globe.

Now the trumpet summons us again — not as a call to bear arms, though arms we need — not as a call to battle, though embattled we are — but a call to bear the burden of a long twilight struggle, year in and year out, "rejoicing in hope, patient in tribulation" — a struggle against the common enemies of man: tyranny, poverty, disease, and war itself.

Can we forge against these enemies a grand and global alliance, North and South, East and West, that can assure a more fruitful life for all mankind? Will you join in that historic effort?

In the long history of the world, only a few generations have been granted the role of defending freedom in its hour of maximum danger. I do not shrink from this responsibility — I welcome it. I do not believe that any of us would exchange places with any other people or any other generation. The energy, the faith, the devotion which we bring to this endeavor will light our country and all who serve it — and the glow from that fire can truly light the world.

And so, my fellow Americans: ask not what your country can do for you — ask what you can do for your country.

My fellow citizens of the world: ask not what America will do for you, but what together we can do for the freedom of man.

Finally, whether you are citizens of America or citizens of the world, ask of us here the same high standards of strength and sacrifice which we ask of you. With a good conscience our only sure reward, with history the final judge of our deeds, let us go forth to lead the land we love, asking His blessing and His help, but knowing that here on ear th God's work must truly be our own.

Analyze Kennedy's style and diction in the "Inaugural Address." What in particular about his style and diction works to inspire Americans to become involved in the work of their country and to challenge the world community to join the fight against the spread of Communism?

WRITING SUGGESTIONS

1. Have you ever wondered why people value the written word, why receiving a handwritten letter is such a special occasion? When was the last time you wrote a letter by hand to a friend or other important person in your life? Or like so many others have you given in to the convenience of cell phones and computers to communicate? Has electronic communication and instant messaging given new meaning to the old adage "talk is cheap"? Write an essay in which you explore the value of the written word for yourself. You may find it helpful to review your response to the journal prompt for this selection before starting to write.

2. With the possible exception of the Declaration of Independence, no document of American history is as famous as Lincoln's speech dedicating the national cemetery at Gettysburg on November 19, 1863. Since that day, millions of Americans have memorized the speech and countless others have quoted it or imitated its rhetoric for their own purposes. The following is the text of Lincoln's speech.

    > Four score and seven years ago our fathers brought forth on this continent, a new nation, conceived in Liberty, and dedicated to the proposition that all men are created equal.

    > Now we are engaged in a great civil war, testing whether that nation or any nation so conceived and so dedicated, can long endure. We are met on a great battlefield of that war. We have come to dedicate a portion of that field, as a final resting place for those who here gave their lives that this nation might live. It is altogether fitting and proper that we should do this.

    > But, in a larger sense, we can not dedicate — we can not consecrate — we can not hallow — this ground. The brave men, living and dead, who struggled here, have consecrated it, far above our poor power to add or detract. The world will little note, nor long remember what we say here, but it can never forget what they did here. It is for us the living, rather, to be dedicated here to the unfinished work which they who fought here have thus far so nobly advanced. It is rather for us to be here dedicated to the great task remaining before us — that from these honored dead we take increased devotion to that cause for which they gave the last full measure of devotion — that we here highly resolve that these dead shall not have died in vain — that this nation, under God, shall have a new birth of freedom — and that government of the people, by the people, for the people, shall not perish from the earth.

    Write an essay analyzing Lincoln's diction in the "Gettysburg Address." Explore how his diction is calculated to achieve a tone appropriate for his subject and the occasion and to have a certain effect on listeners and readers. In what ways does your analysis explain why Lincoln's speech is such a memorable text?

CASE STUDY:
The English-Only Debate

Since Great Britain gained control over what is now the United States, English has been the dominant language in our country. Despite the multitude of cultures and ethnicities that comprise the United States, English has been a common thread linking them together. It may be somewhat surprising, then, that there is no official U.S. language. Now, even as English literacy becomes a necessity for people in many parts of the world, some people in the United States believe its primacy is being threatened right at home. Much of the current controversy focuses on Hispanic communities with large Spanish-speaking populations, who may feel little or no pressure to learn English. Yet in order for everyone to participate in our society, some way must be found to bridge the communication gap.

Recent government efforts in this regard have included bilingual programs in schools, on ballots, for providing emergency notices, and so on. The goal of the programs is to maintain a respect for the heritage and language of the non-English speakers while they learn the English language. The programs have come under fire, however, from those who believe that the U.S. government should conduct itself only in English. If people come here, the argument goes, they should take the responsibility to learn the native language as quickly as possible. And, English-only proponents reason, if immigrants do not or are not willing to learn English, the government should not accommodate them in another language. Moreover, there should be a mandate that the official language of the United States is English and that the government will conduct business in no other language. Many state governments have, in fact, already made such a declaration.

The other side of the argument has two components. One is the belief that it is discriminatory to mandate English because those who do not speak it are then denied basic rights until they learn the language. The second part of this argument is that the current situation is nothing new: There have always been groups of immigrants that were slow to assimilate into American culture, but they all eventually integrated, and the controversy will resolve itself. Furthermore, English is not threatened, and its use does not need to be legislated. Indeed, according to English-only critics, declaring English the official U.S. language could create far more problems than it solves.

The first three selections address the issue head on. Robert King asks "Should English Be the Law?" in the context of our history and that of countries around the world. He notes that compared to similar situations in other countries, including the French Canadian separatist crisis just to our north, the problems here seem almost trivial. If being American still means anything unique, he concludes, we should be able to enjoy our linguistic diversity rather than be threatened by it. S. I. Hayakawa's "Bilingualism in America: English Should Be the *Official* Language" obviously comes to the opposite conclusion. Hayakawa, a former U.S. Senator from California and cofounder of U.S. English, an organization formed to promote English-only legislation, finds the recent policies accommodating bilingualism in schools and government alarming and presents a forceful argument in favor of establishing English as the official language of the United States.

In "An Open Letter to Diversity's Victims," Greg Lewis takes on the advocates' bilingual education in the name of diversity or multiculturalism. He believes that when we don't help all children to become proficient speakers and writers of Standard English, we are in fact condemning them to a life of second-class citizenship.

The last two selections provide a rich personal context for the English-only debate. In "Why and When We Speak Spanish in Public," Myriam Marquez explains why she and her parents continue to speak Spanish when they are together, why they "haven't adopted English as our official family language." She knew that in order to get ahead in this country she had to learn English, but she also clearly understands that "being an American has very little to do with the language we use during our free time in a free country." In the essay "From Outside, In," Barbara Mellix shares her literacy journey. She tells of growing up in Greeleyville, South Carolina, a world that was predominantly black, and learning to speak both Black English and Standard or "proper" English. She remembers feeling more comfortable using the "ordinary everyday speech of 'country' coloreds." As an African American and a speaker of Black English vernacular, Mellix struggled for years with feelings of inferiority when confronted with the proper language of those she called the "others." She always thought of herself as a person "who stood outside Standard English, hugging to herself a disabling mistrust of a language she thought could not represent a person with her history and experience" — until she took a college writing course and discovered the liberating "generative power of language."

WRITING TO DISCOVER: *It is now possible to go many places in the world and get along pretty well in English, no matter what other languages are spoken in the host country. If you were to emigrate, how hard would you work to learn the predominant language of your chosen country? What advantages would there be in learning that language, even if you could get by in English? How would you feel if the country had a law that forced you to learn its language as quickly as possible? Write down your thoughts about these questions.*

Should English Be the Law?

ROBERT D. KING

Scholar and teacher Robert D. King was born in Mississippi in 1936. He graduated from the Georgia Institute of Technology in 1959 with a degree in mathematics, beginning a distinguished and diverse career in academe. After a brief stint at IBM, King went to the University of Wisconsin, receiving a Ph.D. in German linguistics in 1965. He was hired by the University of Texas at Austin to teach German that same year and has spent more than three decades there teaching linguistics and Asian studies in addition to German. He also served as the dean of the College of Liberal Arts from 1979 until 1989 and currently holds the Audre and Bernard Rapoport Regents Chair of Liberal Arts. Indian studies have captured his attention lately, and his most recent book is Nehru and the Language Politics of India, *published in 1996.*

The language politics of the United States has become a hot topic in recent years as well. In the following selection, first published in the April 1997 issue of the Atlantic, *King provides historical background and perspective on the English-only debate.*

We have known race riots, draft riots, labor violence, secession, antiwar protests, and a whiskey rebellion, but one kind of trouble we've never had: a language riot. Language riot? It sounds like a joke. The very idea of language as a political force — as something that might threaten to split a country wide apart — is alien to our way of thinking and to our cultural traditions.

This may be changing. On August 1 of last year [1996] the U.S. House of Representatives approved a bill that would make English the official language of the United States. The vote was 259 to 169, with 223 Republicans and thirty-six Democrats voting in favor and eight Republicans, 160 Democrats, and one independent voting against. The debate was intense, acrid, and partisan. On March 25 of last year the Supreme Court agreed to review a case involving an Arizona law that would require public employees to conduct government business only in English. Arizona is one of several states that have passed "Official English" or "English Only" laws. The appeal to the Supreme Court followed a 6-to-5 ruling, in October of 1995, by a federal appeals court striking down the Arizona law. These events suggest how divisive a public issue language could become in America — even if it has until now scarcely been taken seriously.

Traditionally, the American way has been to make English the national language — but to do so quietly, locally, without fuss. The Constitution is silent on language: the Founding Fathers had no need to legislate that English be the official language of the country. It has always been taken for granted that English *is* the national language, and that one must learn English in order to make it in America.

To say that language has never been a major force in American history of politics, however, is not to say that politicians have always resisted linguistic jingoism. In 1753 Benjamin Franklin voiced his concern that German immigrants were not learning English: "Those [Germans] who come hither are generally the most ignorant Stupid Sort of their own Nation. . . . they will soon so out number us, that all the advantages we have will not, in My Opinion, be able to preserve our language, and even our government will become precarious." Theodore Roosevelt articulated the unspoken American linguistic-melting-pot theory when he boomed, "We have room for but one language here, and that is the English language, for we intended to see that the crucible turns our people out as Americans, of American nationality, and not as dwellers in a polyglot boarding house." And: "We must have but one flag. We must also have but one language. That must be the language of the Declaration of Independence, of Washington's Farewell address, of Lincoln's Gettysburg speech and Second Inaugural."

OFFICIAL ENGLISH

TR's linguistic tub-thumping long typified the tradition of American   5
politics. That tradition began to change in the wake of the anything-goes attitudes and the celebration of cultural differences arising in the 1960s. A 1975 amendment to the Voting Rights Action of 1965 mandated the "bilingual ballot" under certain circumstances, notably when the voters of selected language groups reached five percent or more in a voting district. Bilingual education became a byword of educational thinking during the 1960s. By the 1970s linguists had demonstrated convincingly — at least to other academics — that black English (today called African-American vernacular English or Ebonics) was not "bad" English but a different kind of authentic English with its own rules. Predictably, there have been scattered demands that black English be included in bilingual-education programs.

It was against this background that the movement to make English the official language of the country arose. In 1981 Senator S. I. Hayakawa, long a leading critic of bilingual education and bilingual ballots, introduced in the U.S. Senate a constitutional amendment that not only would have made English the official language but would have prohibited federal and state laws and regulations requiring the use of other languages. His English Language Amendment died in the Ninety-seventh Congress.

In 1983 the organization called U.S. English was founded by Hayakawa and John Tanton, a Michigan ophthalmologist. The primary purpose of the organization was to promote English as the official language of the United States. (The best background readings on America's "neolinguisticism" are the books *Hold Your Tongue*, by James Crawford, and *Language Loyalties*, edited by Crawford, both published in 1992.) Official English initiatives were passed by California in 1986, by Arkansas, Mississippi, North Carolina, North Dakota, and South Carolina in 1987, by Colorado, Florida, and Arizona in 1988, and by Alabama in 1990. The majorities voting for these initiatives were generally not insubstantial: California's, for example, passed by 73 percent.

It was probably inevitable that the Official English (or English-only — the two names are used almost interchangeably) movement would acquire a conservative, almost reactionary undertone in the 1990s. Official English is politically very incorrect. But its cofounder John Tanton brought with him strong liberal credentials. He had been active in the Sierra Club and Planned Parenthood, and in the 1970s served as the national president of Zero Population Growth. Early advisers of U.S. English resist ideological pigeonholing: they included Walter Annenberg, Jacques Barzun, Bruno Bettelheim, Alistair Cooke, Denton Cooley, Walter Cronkite, Angier Biddle Duke, George Gilder, Sidney Hook, Norman Podhoretz, Arnold Schwarzenegger, and Karl Shapiro. In 1987 U.S. English installed as its president Linda Chávez, a Hispanic who had been prominent in the Reagan Administration. A year later she resigned her position, citing "repugnant" and "anti-Hispanic" overtones in an internal memorandum written by Tanton. Tanton, too, resigned, and Walter Cronkite, describing the affair as "embarrassing," left the advisory board. One board member, Norman Cousins, defected in 1986, alluding to the "negative symbolic significance" of California's Official English initiative, Proposition 63. The current chairman of the board and CEO of U.S. English is Mauro E. Mujica, who claims that the organization has 650,000 members.

The popular wisdom is that conservatives are pro and liberals con. True, conservatives such as George Will and William F. Buckley Jr. have written columns supporting Official English. But would anyone characterize as conservatives the present and past U.S. English board members Alistair Cooke, Walter Cronkite, and Norman Cousins? One of the strongest opponents of bilingual education is the Mexican American writer Richard Rodriguez, best known for his eloquent autobiography, *Hunger of Memory* (1982). There is a strain of American liberalism that defines itself in nostalgic devotion to the melting pot.

For several years relevant bills awaited consideration in the U.S. House of Representatives. The Emerson Bill (H.R. 123), passed by the House last August, specifies English as the official language of government, and requires that the government "preserve and enhance" the official status of English. Exceptions are made for the teaching of foreign languages; for actions necessary for public health, international relations,

10

foreign trade, and the protection of the rights of criminal defendants; and for the use of "terms of art" from languages other than English. It would, for example, stop the Internal Revenue Service from sending out income-tax forms and instructions in languages other than English, but it would not ban the use of foreign languages in census materials or documents dealing with national security. "*E Pluribus Unum*" can still appear on American money. U.S. English supports the bill.

What are the chances that some version of Official English will become federal law? Any language bill will face tough odds in the Senate, because some western senators have opposed English-only measures in the past for various reasons, among them a desire by Republicans not to alienate the growing number of Hispanic Republicans, most of whom are uncomfortable with mandated monolingualism. Texas Governor George W. Bush, too, has forthrightly said that he would oppose any English Only proposals in his state. Several of the Republican candidates for President in 1996 (an interesting exception is Phil Gramm) endorsed versions of Official English, as has Newt Gingrich. While governor of Arkansas, Bill Clinton signed into law an English-only bill. As President, he has described his earlier action as a mistake.

Many issues intersect in the controversy over Official English: immigration (above all), the rights of minorities (Spanish-speaking minorities in particular), the pros and cons of bilingual education, tolerance, how best to educate the children of immigrants, and the place of cultural diversity in school curricula and in American society in general. The question that lies at the root of most of the uneasiness is this: Is America threatened by the preservation of languages other than English? Will America, if it continues on its traditional path of benign linguistic neglect, go the way of Belgium, Canada, and Sri Lanka — three countries among many whose unity is gravely imperiled by language and ethnic conflicts?

LANGUAGE AND NATIONALITY

Language and nationalism were not always so intimately intertwined. Never in the heyday of rule by sovereign was it a condition of employment that the King be able to speak the language of his subjects. George I spoke no English and spent much of his time away from England, attempting to use the power of his kingship to shore up his German possessions. In the Middle Ages nationalism was not even part of the picture: one owed loyalty to a lord, a prince, a ruler, a family, a tribe, a church, a piece of land, but not to a nation and least of all to a nation as a language unit. The capital city of the Austrian Hapsburg empire was Vienna, its ruler a monarch with effective control of peoples of the most varied and incompatible ethnicities, and languages, throughout Central and Eastern

Europe. The official language, and the lingua franca as well, was German. While it stood — and it stood for hundreds of years — the empire was an anachronistic relic of what for most of human history had been the normal relationship between country and language: none.

The marriage of language and nationalism goes back at least to Romanticism and specifically to Rousseau, who argued in his *Essay on the Origin of Languages* that language must develop before politics is possible and that language originally distinguished nations from one another. A little-remembered aim of the French Revolution — itself the legacy of Rousseau — was to impose a national language on France, where regional languages such as Provençal, Breton, and Basque were still strong competitors against standard French, the French of the Ile de France. As late as 1789, when the Revolution began, half the population of the south of France, which spoke Provençal, did not understand French. A century earlier the playwright Racine said that he had had to resort to Spanish and Italian to make himself understood in the southern French town of Uzès. After the Revolution nationhood itself became aligned with language.

In 1846 Jacob Grimm, one of the Brothers Grimm of fairy-tale fame but better known in the linguistic establishment as a forerunner of modern comparative and historical linguists, said that "a nation is the totality of people who speak the same language." After midcentury, language was invoked more than any other single criterion to define nationality. Language as a political force helped to bring about the unification of Italy and of Germany and the secession of Norway from its union with Sweden in 1905. Arnold Toynbee observed — unhappily — soon after the First World War that "the growing consciousness of Nationality had attached itself neither to traditional frontiers nor to new geographical associations but almost exclusively to mother tongues." 15

The crowning triumph of the new desideratum was the Treaty of Versailles, in 1919, when the allied victors of the First World War began redrawing the map of Central and Eastern Europe according to nationality as best they could. The magic word was "self-determination," and none of Woodrow Wilson's Fourteen Points mentioned the word "language" at all. Self-determination was thought of as being related to "nationality," which today we would be more likely to call "ethnicity"; but language was simpler to identify than nationality or ethnicity. When it came to drawing the boundary lines of various countries — Czechoslovakia, Yugoslavia, Romania, Hungary, Albania, Bulgaria, Poland — it was principally language that guided the draftsman's hand. (The main exceptions were Alsace-Lorraine, South Tyrol, and the German-speaking parts of Bohemia and Moravia.) Almost by default language became the defining characteristic of nationality.

And so it remains today. In much of the world, ethnic unity and cultural identification are routinely defined by language. To be Arab is to speak Arabic. Bengali identity is based on language in spite of the division of Bengali-speakers between Hindu India and Muslim Bangladesh. When eastern Pakistan seceded from greater Pakistan in 1971, it named itself Bangladesh: *desa* means "country"; *bangla* means not the Bengali people or the Bengali territory but the Bengali language.

Scratch most nationalist movements and you find a linguistic grievance. The demands for independence of the Baltic states (Latvia, Lithuania, and Estonia) were intimately bound up with fears for the loss of their respective languages and cultures in a sea of Russianness. In Belgium the war between French and Flemish threatens an already weakly fused country. The present atmosphere of Belgium is dark and anxious, costive; the metaphor of divorce is a staple of private and public discourse. The lines of terrorism in Sri Lanka are drawn between Tamil Hindus and Sinhalese Buddhists — and also between the Tamil and Sinhalese languages. Worship of the French language fortifies the movement for an independent Quebec. Whether a united Canada will survive into the twenty-first century is a question too close to call. Much of the anxiety about language in the United States is probably fueled by the "Quebec problem": unlike Belgium, which is a small European country, or Sri Lanka, which is halfway around the world, Canada is our close neighbor.

Language is a convenient surrogate for nonlinguistic claims that are often awkward to articulate, for they amount to a demand for more political and economic power. Militant Sikhs in India call for a state of their own: Khalistan ("Land of the Pure" in Punjabi). They frequently couch this as a demand for a linguistic state, which has a certain simplicity about it, a clarity of motive — justice, even, because states in India are normally linguistic states. But the Sikh demands blend religion, economics, language, and retribution for sins both punished and unpunished in a country where old sins cast long shadows.

Language is an explosive issue in the countries of the former Soviet Union. The language conflict in Estonia has been especially bitter. Ethnic Russians make up almost a third of Estonia's population, and most of them do not speak or read Estonian, although Russians have lived in Estonia for more than a generation. Estonia has passed legislation requiring knowledge of the Estonian language as a condition of citizenship. Nationalist groups in independent Lithuania sought restrictions on the use of Polish — again, old sins, long shadows.

In 1995 protests erupted in Moldova, formerly the Moldavian Soviet Socialist Republic, over language and the teaching of Moldovan history. Was Moldovan history a part of Romanian history or of Soviet history? Was Moldova's language Romanian? Moldovan — earlier called Moldavian — *is* Romanian, just as American English and British English are both English. But in the days of the Moldavian SSR, Moscow insisted that the two languages were different, and in a piece of linguistic nonsense required Moldavian to be written in the Cyrillic alphabet to strengthen the case that it was not Romanian.

The official language of Yugoslavia was Serbo-Croatian, which was never so much a language as a political accommodation. The Serbian and Croatian languages are mutually intelligible. Serbian is written in the Cyrillic alphabet, is identified with the Eastern Orthodox branch of the Catholic Church, and borrows its high-culture words from the east — from Russian and Old Church Slavic. Croatian is written in the Roman alphabet, is identified with Roman Catholicism and borrows its high-culture words from the west — from German, for example, and Latin. One of the first things the newly autonomous Republic of Serbia did, in 1991, was to pass a law decreeing Serbian in the Cyrillic alphabet the official language of the country. With Croatia divorced from Serbia, the Croatian and Serbian languages are diverging more and more. Serbo-Croatian has now passed into history, a language-museum relic from the brief period when Serbs and Croats called themselves Yugoslavs and pretended to like each other.

Slovakia, relieved now of the need to accommodate to Czech cosmopolitan sensibilities, has passed a law making Slovak its official language. (Czech is to Slovak pretty much as Croatian is to Serbian.) Doctors in state hospitals must speak to patients in Slovak, even if another language would aid diagnosis and treatment. Some 600,000 Slovaks — more than 10 percent of the population — are ethnically Hungarian. Even staff meetings in Hungarian-language schools must be in Slovak. (The government dropped a stipulation that church weddings be conducted in Slovak after heavy opposition from the Roman Catholic Church.) Language inspectors are told to weed out "all sins perpetrated on the regular Slovak language." Tensions between Slovaks and Hungarians, who had been getting along, have begun to arise.

The twentieth century is ending as it began — with trouble in the Balkans and with nationalist tensions flaring up in other parts of the globe. (Toward the end of his life Bismarck predicted that "some damn fool thing in the Balkans" would ignite the next war.) Language isn't always part of the problem. But it usually is.

UNIQUE OTHERNESS

Is there no hope for language tolerance? Some countries manage to   25
maintain their unity in the face of multilingualism. Examples are Finland, with a Swedish minority, and a number of African and Southeast Asian countries. Two others could not be more unlike as countries go: Switzerland and India.

German, French, Italian, and Romansh are the languages of Switzerland. The first three can be and are used for official purposes; all four are designated "national" languages. Switzerland is politically almost hyperstable. It has language problems (Romansh is losing ground), but they are not major, and they are never allowed to threaten national unity.

Contrary to public perception, India gets along pretty well with a host of different languages. The Indian constitution officially recognizes nineteen languages, English among them. Hindi is specified in the constitution as the national language of India, but that is a pious postcolonial fiction: outside the Hindi-speaking northern heartland of India, people don't want to learn it. English functions more nearly than Hindi as India's lingua franca.

From 1947, when India obtained its independence from the British, until the 1960s blood ran in the streets and people died because of language. Hindi absolutists wanted to force Hindi on the entire country, which would have split India between north and south and opened up other fracture lines as well. For as long as possible Jawaharlal Nehru, independent India's first Prime Minister, resisted nationalist demands to redraw the capricious state boundaries of British India according to language. By the time he capitulated, the country had gained a precious decade to prove its viability as a union.

Why is it that India preserves its unity with not just two languages to contend with, as Belgium, Canada, and Sri Lanka have, but nineteen? The answer is that India, like Switzerland, has a strong national identity. The two countries share something big and almost mystical that holds each together in a union transcending language. That something I call "unique otherness."

The Swiss have what the political scientist Karl Deutsch called   30
"learned habits, preferences, symbols, memories, and patterns of land-holding": customs, cultural traditions, and political institutions that bind them closer to one another than to people of France, Germany, or Italy living just across the border and speaking the same language. There is Switzerland's traditional neutrality, its system of universal military training (the "citizen army"), its consensual allegiance to a strong Swiss franc — and fondue, yodeling, skiing, and mountains. Set against all this, the fact that Switzerland has four languages doesn't even approach the threshold of becoming a threat.

As for India, what Vincent Smith, in the *Oxford History of India*, calls its "deep underlying fundamental unity" resides in institutions and beliefs such as caste, cow worship, sacred places, and much more. Consider *dharma, karma,* and *maya,* the three root convictions of Hinduism; India's historical epics; Gandhi; *ahimsa* (nonviolence); vegetarianism; a distinctive cuisine and way of eating; marriage customs; a shared past; and what the Indologist Ainslic Embree calls "Brahmanical ideology." In other words, "We are Indian; we are different."

Belgium and Canada have never managed to forge a stable national identity; Czechoslovakia and Yugoslavia never did either. Unique otherness immunizes countries against linguistic destabilization. Even Switzerland and especially India have problems; in any country with as many different languages as India has, language will never *not* be a problem.

However, it is one thing to have a major illness with a bleak prognosis; it is another to have a condition that is irritating and occasionally painful but not life-threatening.

History teaches a plain lesson about language and governments: there is almost nothing the government of a free country can do to change language usage and practice significantly, to force its citizens to use certain languages in preference to others, and to discourage people from speaking a language they wish to continue to speak. (The rebirth of Hebrew in Palestine and Israel's successful mandate that Hebrew be spoken and written by Israelis is a unique event in the annals of language history.) Quebec has since the 1970s passed an array of laws giving French a virtual monopoly in the province. One consequence — unintended, one wishes to believe — of these laws is that last year kosher products imported for Passover were kept off the shelves, because the packages were not labeled in French. Wise governments keep their hands off language to the extent that it is politically possible to do so.

We like to believe that to pass a law is to change behavior; but passing laws about language, in a free society, almost never changes attitudes or behavior. Gaelic (Irish) is living out a slow, inexorable decline in Ireland despite enormous government support of every possible kind since Ireland gained its independence from Britain. The Welsh language, in contrast, is alive today in Wales in spite of heavy discrimination during its history. Three out of four people in the northern and western counties of Gwynedd and Dyfed speak Welsh.

I said earlier that language is a convenient surrogate for other national problems. Official English obviously has a lot to do with concern about immigration, perhaps especially Hispanic immigration. America may be threatened by immigration; I don't know. But America is not threatened by language.   35

The usual arguments made by academics against Official English are commonsensical. Who needs a law when, according to the 1990 census, 94 percent of American residents speak English anyway? (Mauro E. Mujica, the chairman of U.S. English, cites a higher figure: 97 percent.) Not many of today's immigrants will see their first language survive into the second generation. This is in fact the common lament of first-generation immigrants: their children are not learning their language and are losing the culture of their parents. Spanish is hardly a threat to English, in spite of isolated (and easily visible) cases such as Miami, New York City, and pockets of the Southwest and southern California. The everyday language of south Texas is Spanish, and yet south Texas is not about to secede from America.

But empirical, calm arguments don't engage the real issue: language is a symbol, an icon. Nobody who favors a constitutional ban against flag burning will ever be persuaded by the argument that the flag is, after all, just a "piece of cloth." A draft card in the 1960s was never merely a piece of paper. Neither is a marriage license.

Language, as one linguist has said, is "not primarily a means of communication but a means of communion." Romanticism exalted language, made it mystical, sublime — a bond of national identity. At the same time, Romanticism created a monster: it made of language a means for destroying a country.

America has that unique otherness of which I spoke. In spite of all our racial divisions and economic unfairness, we have the frontier tradition, respect for the individual, and opportunity; we have our love affair with the automobile; we have in our history a civil war that freed the slaves and was fought with valor; and we have sports, hot dogs, hamburgers, and milk shakes — things big and small, noble and petty, important and trifling. "We are Americans; we are different."

If I'm wrong, then the great American experiment will fail — not because of language but because it no longer means anything to be an American; because we have forfeited that "willingness of the heart" that F. Scott Fitzgerald wrote was America; because we are not long joined by Lincoln's "mystic chords of memory." 40

We are not even close to the danger point. I suggest that we relax and luxuriate in our linguistic richness and our traditional tolerance of language differences. Language does not threaten American unity. Benign neglect is a good policy for any country when it comes to language, and it's a good policy for America.

EXAMINING THE ISSUE CRITICALLY

1. According to King, "It has always been taken for granted that English *is* the national language, and that one must learn English in order to make it in America" (3). What has changed in recent years to make learning English a political issue?

2. What does King mean when he says, "Official English is politically very incorrect" (8)?

3. What, according to King, makes the English-only issue so controversial? What other issues complicate the decision to make English the nation's language?

4. Why do you think King takes time to explain the evolution of the relationship between language and nationality in Europe and the rest of the world? What insights into the English-only issue does this brief history of language and culture give you? Explain.

5. What does King mean by the term "unique otherness"? What do you see as America's "unique otherness"? Do you agree with King's assessment that America's "unique otherness" will help us transcend our language differences? Why or why not?

6. King concludes that "benign neglect is a good policy for any country when it comes to language, and it's a good policy for America" (41). Do you share King's optimistic view?

Bilingualism in America: English Should Be the Official Language

S. I. HAYAKAWA

Samuel Ichiye Hayakawa was born to Japanese parents in Vancouver, Canada, in 1906. Educated at the University of Manitoba, McGill University, and the University of Wisconsin at Madison, Hayakawa had a distinguished career as a professor of linguistics and pioneer in semantics. He authored several books on language theory, including Our Language and Our World *in 1959. During his last teaching position at San Francisco State University, he was introduced to the political arena when he was named interim president of the college to deal with student rioters in 1968. His strict suppression of the uprising endeared him to conservatives throughout the country, and he went on to serve as a U.S. senator from California for one term (1977–1983).*

After leaving the Senate, Hayakawa became a leading figure in the effort to install English as the official language of the United States. In the following selection, first published in USA Today *in July 1989, he presents a concise argument that summarizes his position on the issue. Hayakawa died on February 27, 1992.*

During the dark days of World War II, Chinese immigrants in California wore badges proclaiming their original nationality so they would not be mistaken for Japanese. In fact, these two immigrant groups long had been at odds with each other. However, as new English-speaking generations came along, the Chinese and Japanese began to communicate with one another. They found they had much in common and began to socialize. Today, they get together and form Asian-American societies.

Such are the amicable results of sharing the English language. English unites us as American-immigrants and native-born alike. Communicating with each other in a single, common tongue encourages trust, while reducing racial hostility and bigotry.

My appreciation of English has led me to devote my retirement years to championing it. Several years ago, I helped to establish U.S. English, a Washington, D.C.-based public interest group that seeks an amendment to the U.S. Constitution declaring English our official language, regardless of what other languages we may use unofficially.

As an immigrant to this nation, I am keenly aware of the things that bind us as Americans and unite us as a single people. Foremost among these unifying forces is the common language we share. While it is certainly true that our love of freedom and devotion to democratic principles help to unite and give us a mutual purpose, it is English, our common language, that enables us to discuss our views and allows us to maintain a well-informed electorate, the cornerstone of democratic government.

Because we are a nation of immigrants, we do not share the characteristics of race, religion, ethnicity, or native language which form the common bonds of society in other countries. However, by agreeing to learn and use a single, universally spoken language, we have been able to forge a unified people from an incredibly diverse population.

Although our 200-year history should be enough to convince any skeptic of the powerful unifying effects of a common language, some still advocate the official recognition of other languages. They argue that a knowledge of English is not part of the formula for responsible citizenship in this country.

Some contemporary political leaders, like the former mayor of Miami, Maurice Ferre, maintain that "Language is not necessary to the system. Nowhere does our Constitution say that English is our language." He also told the *Tampa Tribune* that, "Within ten years there will not be a single word of English spoken [in Miami] — English is not Miami's official language — [and] one day residents will have to learn Spanish or leave."

The U.S. Department of Education also reported that countless speakers at a conference on bilingual education "expounded at length on the need for and eventually of, a multilingual, multicultural United States of America with a national language policy citing English and Spanish as the two 'legal languages.'"

As a former resident of California, I am completely familiar with a system that uses two official languages, and I would not advise any nation to move in such a direction unless forced to do so. While it is true that India functions with ten official languages, I haven't heard anyone suggest that it functions particularly well because of its multilingualism. In fact, most Indians will concede that the situation is a chaotic mess which has led to countless problems in the government's efforts to manage the nation's business. Out of necessity, English still is used extensively in India as a common language.

Belgium is another clear example of the diverse effects of two officially recognized languages in the same nation. Linguistic differences between Dutch- and French-speaking citizens have resulted in chronic political instability. Consequently, in the aftermath of the most recent government collapse, legislators are working on a plan to turn over most of its powers and responsibilities to the various regions, a clear recognition of the diverse effects of linguistic separateness.

There are other problems. Bilingualism is a costly and confusing bureaucratic nightmare. The Canadian government has estimated its bilingual costs to be nearly $400,000,000 per year. It is almost certain that these expenses will increase as a result of a massive expansion of bilingual services approved by the Canadian Parliament in 1988. In the United States, which has ten times the population of Canada, the cost of similar bilingual services easily would be in the billions.

We first should consider how politically infeasible it is that our nation ever could recognize Spanish as a second official language without opening the floodgates for official recognition of the more than 100 languages spoken in this country. How long would it take, under such an arrangement, before the United States started to make India look like a model of efficiency?

Even if we can agree that multilingualism would be a mistake, some would suggest that official recognition of English is not needed. After all, our nation has existed for over 200 years without this, and English as our common language has continued to flourish.

I could agree with this sentiment had government continued to adhere to its time-honored practice of operating in English and encouraging newcomers to learn the language. However, this is not the case. Over the last few decades, government has been edging slowly towards policies that place other languages on a par with English.

In reaction to the cultural consciousness movement of the 1960s and 1970s, government has been increasingly reluctant to press immigrants to learn the English language, lest it be accused of "cultural imperialism." Rather than insisting that it is the immigrant's duty to learn the language of this country, the government has acted instead as if it has a duty to accommodate an immigrant in his native language.   15

A prime example of this can be found in the continuing debate over Federal and state policies relating to bilingual education. At times, these have come dangerously close to making the main goal of this program the maintenance of the immigrant child's native language, rather than the early acquisition of English.

As a former U.S. senator from California, where we spend more on bilingual education programs than any other state, I am very familiar with both the rhetoric and reality that lie behind the current debate on bilingual education. My experience has convinced me that many of these programs are shortchanging immigrant children in their quest to learn English.

To set the record straight from the start, I do not oppose bilingual education *if it is truly bilingual.* Employing a child's native language to teach him (or her) English is entirely appropriate. What is not appropriate is continuing to use the children of Hispanic and other immigrant groups as guinea pigs in an unproven program that fails to teach English efficiently and perpetuates their dependency on their native language.

Under the dominant method of bilingual education used throughout this country, non-English-speaking students are taught all academic subjects such as math, science, and history exclusively in their native language. English is taught as a separate subject. The problem with this method is that there is no objective way to measure whether a child has learned enough English to be placed in classes where academic instruction is entirely in English. As a result, some children have been kept in native language classes for six years.

Some bilingual education advocates, who are more concerned with maintaining the child's use of their native language, may not see any problem with such a situation. However, those who feel that the most important goal of this program is to get children functioning quickly in English appropriately are alarmed.

In the Newhall School District in California, some Hispanic parents are raising their voices in criticism of its bilingual education program, which relies on native language instruction. Their children complain of systematically being segregated from their English-speaking peers. Now in high school, these students cite the failure of the program to teach them English first as the reason for being years behind their classmates.

Even more alarming is the Berkeley (Calif.) Unified School District, where educators have recognized that all-native-language instruction would be an inadequate response to the needs of their non-English-speaking pupils. Challenged by a student body that spoke more than four different languages and by budgetary constraints, teachers and administrators responded with innovative language programs that utilized many methods of teaching English. That school district is now in court answering charges that the education they provided was inadequate because it did not provide transitional bilingual education for every non-English speaker. What was introduced twenty years ago as an experimental project has become — despite inconclusive research evidence — the only acceptable method of teaching for bilingual education advocates.

When one considers the nearly 50 percent dropout rate among Hispanic students (the largest group receiving this type of instruction), one wonders about their ability to function in the English-speaking mainstream of this country. The school system may have succeeded wonderfully in maintaining their native language, but if it failed to help them to master the English language fully, what is the benefit?

ALTERNATIVES

If this method of bilingual education is not the answer, are we forced to return to the old, discredited, sink-or-swim approach? No, we are not, since, as shown in Berkeley and other school districts, there are a number of alternative methods that have been proven effective, while avoiding the problems of all native-language instruction.

Sheltered English and English as a Second Language (ESL) are just two programs that have helped to get children quickly proficient in English. Yet, political recognition of the viability of alternate methods has been slow in coming. In 1988, we witnessed the first crack in the monolithic hold that native language instruction has had on bilingual education funds at the Federal level. In its reauthorization of Federal bilingual education, Congress voted to increase the percentage of funds available for alternate methods from 4 to 25 percent of the total. This is a great breakthrough, but we should not be satisfied until 100 percent of the funds are available for any program that effectively and quickly can get children functioning in English, regardless of the amount of native language instruction it uses.

My goal as a student of language and a former educator is to see all students succeed academically, no matter what language is spoken in their homes. I want to see immigrant students finish their high school education and be able to compete for college scholarships. To help achieve this goal, instruction in English should start as early as possible. Students should be moved into English mainstream classes in one or, at the very most, two years. They should not continue to be segregated year after year from their English-speaking peers.

Another highly visible shift in Federal policy that I feel demonstrates quite clearly the eroding support of government for our common language is the requirement for bilingual voting ballots. Little evidence ever has been presented to show the need for ballots in other languages. Even prominent Hispanic organizations acknowledge that more than 90 percent of native-born Hispanics currently are fluent in English and more than half of that population is English monolingual.

Furthermore, if the proponents of bilingual ballots are correct when they claim that the absence of native language ballots prevents non-English-speaking citizens from exercising their right to vote, then current requirements are clearly unfair because they provide assistance to certain groups of voters while ignoring others. Under current Federal law, native language ballots are required only for certain groups: those speaking Spanish, Asian, or Native American languages. European or African immigrants are not provided ballots in their native language, even in jurisdictions covered by the Voting Rights Act.

As sensitive as Americans have been to racism, especially since the days of the civil rights movement, no one seems to have noticed the profound racism expressed in the amendment that created the "bilingual ballot." Brown people, like Mexicans and Puerto Ricans; red people, like American Indians; and yellow people, like the Japanese and Chinese, are assumed not to be smart enough to learn English. No provision is made, however, for non-English-speaking French-Canadians in Maine or Vermont, or Yiddish-speaking Hasidic Jews in Brooklyn, who are white and thus presumed to be able to learn English without difficulty.

Voters in San Francisco encountered ballots in Spanish and Chinese 30 for the first time in the elections of 1980, much to their surprise, since authorizing legislation had been passed by Congress with almost no debate, roll-call vote, or public discussion. Naturalized Americans, who had taken the trouble to learn English to become citizens, were especially angry and remain so. While native language ballots may be a convenience to some voters, the use of English ballots does not deprive citizens of their right to vote. Under current voting law, non-English-speaking voters are permitted to bring a friend or family member to the polls to assist them in casting their ballots. Absentee ballots could provide another method that would allow a voter to receive this help at home.

Congress should be looking for other methods to create greater access to the ballot box for the currently small number of citizens who cannot understand an English ballot, without resorting to the expense of requiring ballots in foreign languages. We cannot continue to overlook the message we are sending to immigrants about the connection between English language ability and citizenship when we print ballots in other languages. The ballot is the primary symbol of civic duty. When we tell immigrants that they should learn English — yet offer them full voting participation in their native language — I fear our actions will speak louder than our words.

If we are to prevent the expansion of policies such as these, moving us further along the multilingual path, we need to make a strong statement that our political leaders will understand. We must let them know that we do not choose to reside in a "Tower of Babel." Making English our nation's official language *by law* will send the proper signal to newcomers about the importance of learning English and provide the necessary guidance to legislators to preserve our traditional policy of a common language.

EXAMINING THE ISSUE CRITICALLY

1. To what extent does speaking a single common language encourage "trust, while reducing racial hostility and bigotry"(2)? According to Hayakawa, "we are a nation of immigrants"(5). How does this fact make the United States different from other countries?

2. How does Hayakawa counter the argument that the United States should have two official languages — English and Spanish?

3. Even though the United States has existed for over two hundred years without giving official recognition to English as the nation's language, why does Hayakawa believe that such recognition is now necessary?

4. Hayakawa claims that he is not opposed to bilingual education. How does his idea of how bilingual education should operate differ from methods in common practice throughout the country? What does he find wrong with the "native language instruction" approach to bilingual education? What alternatives does Hayakawa offer?

5. Do you think that legislation making English America's official language is as necessary as Hayakawa thinks it is? Why or why not? What points do you agree with Hayakawa on? Where do you differ from his position?

An Open Letter to Diversity's Victims

Greg Lewis

Born in Akron, Ohio, in 1942, Greg Lewis grew up in Cuyahoga Falls, a suburb of Akron. After graduating from the University of Florida in 1965, he earned his Ph.D. from Kent State University in 1969. Lewis taught at Kent State and St. Bonaventure University for six years and wrote scripts in Hollywood before starting his own business in Rochester, New York, where he lives today. As one of the pioneers of computer-based training technology, he developed interactive video training programs for corporate clients like Eastman Kodak Company, Marriott Corporation, and Hilton Hotels Corporation. In the mid-90s he divested his business interests to concentrate full time on writing. Together with Charles Gant, he authored End Your Addiction Now *(2002) and is completing work on a book of political analysis entitled* The Politics of Anger: How Marxism's Heirs Are Defining Liberalism in America Today. *He is a regular contributor of political and cultural commentary to the* Washington Dispatch *(WashingtonDispatch.com).*

"An Open Letter to Diversity's Victims" first appeared in the Washington Dispatch *on August 12, 2003. Lewis speaks out against those who champion bilingual programs in the name of cultural "diversity." He tells America's young people in no uncertain terms that "to succeed in America . . . it's important to speak, read, and understand English as most Americans speak it," and that, for Lewis, means Standard English.*

Those who promote what they call "diversity" have insisted that American schools provide instruction in both English and Spanish so that Hispanic children will not have to learn English. As near as I can determine, the reasoning is that Hispanic people living in the United States are at risk for losing their cultural identity if they learn the language spoken by the overwhelming majority of their fellow citizens.

Until 1998, California's liberal educators and administrators managed to buck common sense and the wishes of 85 percent of the state's Hispanic population to perpetuate their "separate but equal" doctrine of bilingual education. Proposition 227, which passed with a landslide majority in that year, effectively put an end to the practice in California. By August of 2000, the average reading scores of the state's more than one million Hispanic elementary students had improved more than 20 points across the board, confounding liberal educational segregationists.

In fact, because children who don't learn to speak "Standard" English have a much more difficult time achieving job and career success, liberals who still blindly support bilingual education are condemning a significant portion of Spanish-speaking children to second-class economic citizenship. One can only hope that in the near future Hispanics taught in their native language will claim victim status and bring a class-action lawsuit against the arrogant, agenda-driven educators who still hold out for bilingual education for not giving them the linguistic tools they needed to take advantage of the wonderful economic opportunities that would have been available to them had they been "forced" to learn English. This is one of the few instances I can think of in which the American legal profession might actually distinguish itself through class-action litigation.

California, you will recall, was also the state which tried to railroad its citizens into recognizing Ebonics (that is, so-called African American English) as a language, and to give credit to (primarily) inner-city students for having been raised to speak a dialect which is inadequate to the demands of the world beyond the circumscribed confines of their neighborhoods. How much better off would everyone involved be if the same effort had been put into teaching African American children English as a second language?

Simply put, bilingual education doesn't provide students whose first   5
language is not Standard English with the single most important skill they need for making their way in the broader culture. The fact that that broader culture is what its adversaries denigrate as "white" culture begs the question. To succeed in America — with a number of relatively minor although often highly visible exceptions — it's important to speak, read, and understand English as most Americans speak it. There's nothing cruel or unfair in that; it's just the way it is. And when liberals try to downplay that fact in the name of diversity or multiculturalism (or whatever the liberal buzzword *du jour* happens to be at the time), they're cynically appealing to a kind of cultural vanity that almost every one of us possesses. People don't want to be told that the way they speak (or dress or behave) won't gain them credence with a majority of Americans.

In this case, however, the appeal to cultural vanity is destructive. It results in a kind of collective blind spot among the blacks and Hispanics who allow themselves to be hoodwinked into believing that when they walk into a job interview for a responsible position and say, "Yo, 's up?" the person sitting across the desk from them — whether black or white, male or female — is going to throw some internal Ebonics switch and reply, "You got it."

I'm not talking about a McJob. I'm talking about a position for which there might be some competition, one whose pay starts in the high twenties or low thirties. I'm talking about a job for which the company that hires you is going to invest as much as $5,000.00 or more in instructors' salaries and the infrastructure necessary to support a good corporate entry-level management training function and to compensate you for the weeks you spend in training; that is, in order to provide you with everything you'll need to take advantage of an opportunity they want to see you succeed in.

Because we need to get something straight. Companies want to see their employees succeed. They don't care what color your skin is. They don't care if your first name is Lakeesha or your surname is Gonzales. (Well, they wouldn't if there weren't Federal regulations telling them they had to.) They want to see you do well, no matter your ethnicity or skin color. Corporate success is a win-win proposition. If you do well, you help the company you work for do well. If the company you work for does well, then there are expanding opportunities for you to move up to positions of increasing responsibility for which you will be rewarded with higher salaries and greater benefits.

And I can tell you: By the time you get to be regional Vice President of Sales overseeing a 15-state territory, or are appointed Corporate Head of Creative Development, or are chosen as one of the four key team members charged with opening your company's new European head-quarters in London, England . . . you're going to be damn glad you listened to all those teachers who, while respecting who you were and your ethnicity and your cultural heritage, nonetheless insisted that you learn your way around the English language, that you learn to communicate not just with your homeboys and homegirls but with other English-speaking human beings in the broader culture.

And it doesn't really have anything to do with someone's respecting   10
or not respecting who you are or where you came from, anyway. It does have to do with something that has very deep roots in the American soul. It has to do with a set of fundamental human values that we Americans hold sacred. Among the most important of those values is that every young person be given the opportunity to prosper through the exercise of his or her talents and skills. You may have heard the words "life, liberty, and the pursuit of happiness."

If it seems as though you have to compromise your identity or your integrity to accomplish these things, let me say this: It is actually those who promote "diversity" who ask you to deny your individuality and your humanity by insisting that you assume a collective identity as a member of a racial or ethnic or cultural group. Membership in these groups is reductive; it restricts your horizons and diminishes the likelihood that you'll be successful even in articulating your own personal aspirations, let alone achieving them.

Make no mistake about it: The values on which this country was founded are universal values which transcend culture and history and race and nationality. And no concept as flimsy and restrictive and, ultimately, indefensible as diversity should be enough to sway you from your chance to use your talents in the service of truly positive and universal values. Don't let diversity destroy your soul and rob you of the chance to be who you truly are.

EXAMINING THE ISSUE CRITICALLY

1. Why does Lewis believe that all students "whose first language is not Standard English"(5) should be taught Standard English? What was the most convincing part of his argument?

2. How does Lewis counter the arguments of liberals who support bilingual educational programs in the name of diversity or multiculturalism? Are liberals asking you "to deny your individuality and your humanity by insisting that you assume a collective identity as a member of a racial or ethnic or cultural group," as Lewis claims (11)? Where do you stand on this issue?

3. Do you think it is possible for teachers to respect their students' ethnicity and cultural heritage while insisting that they learn Standard English? Explain. Does learning Standard English in school mean that these students have to give up their first languages?

4. In his final three paragraphs Lewis talks about "fundamental human values that we Americans hold sacred." By not teaching a young person to be proficient with Standard English, are we in fact denying that person "the opportunity to prosper through the exercise of his or her talents and skills"?

Why and When We Speak Spanish in Public

Myriam Marquez

An award-winning columnist for the Orlando Sentinel, *Myriam Marquez was born in Cuba in 1954 and grew up in South Florida. After graduating from the University of Maryland in 1983 with a degree in journalism and a minor in political science, she worked for United Press International in Washington, D.C., and in Maryland, covering the Maryland legislature as statehouse bureau chief. Marquez joined the editorial board of the* Sentinel *in 1987 and, since 1990, has been writing three weekly columns. Her commentaries focus on state and national politics, the human condition, civil liberties, and issues important to women and Hispanics. She is a founding board member of the YMCA Achievers program, which aims to help Hispanic students succeed in high school. Since 2000, Marquez has mentored public school children with reading. The Florida Society of Newspaper Editors awarded her its highest award for commentary in 2003.*

As an Hispanic, Marquez recognizes that English is the "common language" in America but knows that being American has little if anything to do with what language one speaks. In this article, which first appeared in the Orlando Sentinel *on July 5, 1999, she explains why she and her parents, all bilingual, continue to speak Spanish when they are together, even though they have lived in the United States for forty years.*

When I'm shopping with my mother or standing in line with my stepdad to order fast food or anywhere else we might be together, we're going to speak to one another in Spanish.

That may appear rude to those who don't understand Spanish and overhear us in public places.

Those around us may get the impression that we're talking about them. They may wonder why we would insist on speaking in a foreign tongue, especially if they knew that my family has lived in the United States for 40 years and that my parents do understand English and speak it, albeit with difficulty and a heavy accent.

Let me explain why we haven't adopted English as our official family language. For me and most of the bilingual people I know, it's a matter of respect for our parents and comfort in our cultural roots.

It's not meant to be rude to others. It's not meant to alienate anyone or to Balkanize America. 5

It's certainly not meant to be un-American — what constitutes an "American" being defined by English speakers from North America.

Being an American has very little to do with what language we use during our free time in a free country. From its inception, this country was careful not to promote a government-mandated official language.

We understand that English is the common language of this country and the one most often heard in international business circles from Peru to Norway. We know that, to get ahead here, one must learn English.

But that ought not mean that somehow we must stop speaking in our native tongue whenever we're in a public area, as if we were ashamed of who we are, where we're from. As if talking in Spanish — or any other language, for that matter — is some sort of litmus test used to gauge American patriotism.

Throughout this nation's history, most immigrants — whether from Poland or Finland or Italy or wherever else — kept their language through the first generation and, often, the second. I suspect that they spoke among themselves in their native tongue — in public. Pennsylvania even provided voting ballots written in German during much of the 1800s for those who weren't fluent in English.

In this century, Latin American immigrants and others have fought for this country in U.S.-led wars. They have participated fully in this nation's democracy by voting, holding political office, and paying taxes. And they have watched their children and grandchildren become so "American" that they resist speaking in Spanish.

You know what's rude?

When there are two or more people who are bilingual and another person who speaks only English and the bilingual folks all of a sudden start speaking Spanish, which effectively leaves out the English-only speaker. I don't tolerate that.

One thing's for sure. If I'm ever in a public place with my mom or dad and bump into an acquaintance who doesn't speak Spanish, I will switch to English and introduce that person to my parents. They will respond in English, and do so with respect.

EXAMINING THE ISSUE CRITICALLY

1. How does Marquez explain the fact that she and her parents "haven't adopted English as our official family language"(4)? If you were standing next to the three of them and they were speaking in Spanish, would you consider their behavior rude? Why or why not?

2. Marquez claims that "from its inception, this country was careful not to promote a government-mandated official language"(7). Why do you suppose the U.S. government has steered clear of legislating an official language? Is there a need for such legislation now?

3. For Marquez, "being an American has very little to do with what language we use during our free time in a free country"(7). Do you think that the English-only debate gets muddied when people see language as "some sort of litmus text used to gauge American patriotism"(9)? Explain.

4. Under what circumstances would Marquez stop speaking Spanish and use English? If you were or are bilingual, would you behave the same in similar situations? Explain.

From Outside, In

BARBARA MELLIX

A native of Greeleyville, South Carolina, Barbara Mellix gradu-
ated from the University of Pittsburgh in 1984. She received her
M.F.A. in creative writing from the same institution two years later.
After teaching for a year at Pittsburgh's Greensburg campus, she re-
turned to her alma mater as assistant to the dean of the College of
Arts and Sciences. She is currently executive assistant dean of the
College of Arts and Sciences, director of the college's advising center,
and a teacher of composition at the University of Pittsburgh.

In this article, which first appeared in the Georgia Review *in*
1988, Mellix explains how she grew up speaking what amounted to
two languages: "the ordinary everyday speech of 'country' coloreds
and 'proper' English." She understood when she could speak Black
English and when she should speak Standard English, but she al-
ways felt uncomfortable with the standard version. It was in a col-
lege writing class as an adult that Mellix took on the language of
the outside world and discovered its remarkable power.

Two years ago, when I started writing this paper, trying to bring
order out of chaos, my ten-year-old daughter was suffering from an acute
attack of boredom. She drifted in and out of the room complaining that
she had nothing to do, no one to "be with" because none of her friends
were at home. Patiently I explained that I was working on something
special and needed peace and quiet, and I suggested that she paint, read,
or work with her computer. None of these interested her. Finally, she
pulled up a chair to my desk and watched me, now and then heaving
long, loud sighs. After two or three minutes (nine or ten sighs), I lost my
patience. "Looka here, Allie," I said, "you are too old for this kinda car-
ryin' on. I done told you this is important. You wronger than dirt to be
in here haggin' me like this and you know it. Now git on outta here and
leave me off before I put my foot all the way down."

I was at home, alone with my family, and my daughter understood
that this way of speaking was appropriate in that context. She knew, as a
matter of fact, that it was almost inevitable; when I get angry at home, I
speak some of my finest, most cherished Black English. Had I been
speaking to my daughter in this manner in certain other environments,
she would have been shocked and probably worried that I had taken
leave of my sense of propriety.

Like my children, I grew up speaking what I considered two distinctly different languages — Black English and Standard English (or as I
thought of them then, the ordinary everyday speech of "country"

coloreds and "proper" English) — and in the process of acquiring these languages, I developed an understanding of when, where, and how to use them. But unlike my children, I grew up in a world that was primarily black. My friends, neighbors, minister, teachers — almost everybody I associated with every day — were black. And we spoke to one another in our own special language: *That sho is a pretty dress you got on. If she don' soon leave me off I'm gon tell her head a mess. I was so mad I could'a pissed a blue rod. He all the time trying to low-rate somebody. Ain't that just about the nastiest thing you ever set ears on?*

Then there were the "others," the "proper" blacks, transplanted relatives and one-time friends who came home from the city for weddings, funerals, and vacations. To these we spoke Standard English. "Ain't?" my mother would yell at me when I used the term in the presence of "others." "You *know* better than that." And I would hang my head in shame and say the "proper" word.

I remember one summer sitting in my grandmother's house in Greeleyville, South Carolina, when it was full of the chatter of city relatives who were home on vacation. My parents sat quietly, only now and then volunteering a comment or answering a question. My mother's face took on a strained expression when she spoke. I could see that she was being careful to say just the right words in just the right way. Her voice sounded thick, muffled. And when she finished speaking, she would lapse into silence, her proper smile on her face. My father was more articulate, more aggressive. He spoke quickly, his words sharp and clear. But he held his proud head higher, a signal that he, too, was uncomfortable. My sisters and brothers and I stared at our aunts, uncles, and cousins, speaking only when prompted. Even then, we hesitated, formed our sentences in our minds, then spoke softly, shyly.

My parents looked small and anxious during those occasions, and I waited impatiently for our leave-taking when we would mock our relatives the moment we were out of their hearing. "Reeely," we would say to one another, flexing our wrists and rolling our eyes, "how dooo you stan' this heat? Chile, it just too hyooo-mid for words." Our relatives had made us feel "country," and this was our way of regaining pride in ourselves while getting a little revenge in the bargain. The words bubbled in our throats and rolled across our tongues, a balming.

As a child I felt this same doubleness in uptown Greeleyville where the whites lived. "Ain't that a pretty dress you're wearing!" Toby, the town policeman, said to me one day when I was fifteen. "Thank you very much," I replied, my voice barely audible in my own ears. The words felt wrong in my mouth, rigid, foreign. It was not that I had never spoken that phrase before — it was common in Black English, too — but I was extremely conscious that this was an occasion for proper English. I had taken out my English and put it on as I did my church clothes, and I felt as if I were wearing my Sunday best in the middle of the week. It did not

5

matter that Toby had not spoken grammatically correct English. He was white and could speak as he wished. I had something to prove. Toby did not.

Speaking Standard English to whites was our way of demonstrating that we knew their language and could use it. Speaking it to Standard-English-speaking blacks was our way of showing them that we, as well as they, could "put on airs." But when we spoke Standard English, we acknowledged (to ourselves and to others — but primarily to ourselves) that our customary way of speaking was inferior. We felt foolish, embarrassed, somehow diminished because we were ashamed to be our real selves. We were reserved, shy in the presence of those who owned and/or spoke *the* language.

My parents never set aside time to drill us in Standard English. Their forms of instruction were less formal. When my father was feeling particularly expansive, he would regale us with tales of his exploits in the outside world. In almost fluent English, complete with dialogue and flavored with gestures and embellishment, he told us about his attempt to get a haircut at a white barbershop; his refusal to acknowledge one of the town merchants until the man addressed him as "Mister"; the time he refused to step off the sidewalk uptown to let some whites pass; his airplane trip to New York City (to visit a sick relative) during which the stewardess and porters — recognizing that he was a "gentleman" — addressed him as "Sir." I did not realize then — nor, I think, did my father — that he was teaching us, among other things, Standard English and the relationship between language and power.

My mother's approach was different. Often, when one of us said, "I'm gon wash off my feet," she would say, "And what will you walk on if you wash them off?" Everyone would laugh at the victim of my mother's "proper" mood. But it was different when one of us children was in a proper mood. "You think you are so superior," I said to my oldest sister one day when we were arguing and she was winning. "Superior!" my sister mocked. "You mean I am acting 'biggidy'?" My sisters and brothers sniggered, then joined in teasing me. Finally, my mother said, "Leave your sister alone. There's nothing wrong with using proper English." There was a half-smile on her face. I had gotten "uppity," had "put on airs" for no good reason. I was at home, alone with the family, and I hadn't been prompted by one of my mother's proper moods. But there was also a proud light in my mother's eyes; her children were learning English very well.

Not until years later, as a college student, did I begin to understand our ambivalence toward English, our scorn of it, our need to master it, to own and be owned by it — an ambivalence that extended to the public school classroom. In our school, where there were no whites, my teachers taught Standard English but used Black English to do it. When my grammar-school teachers wanted us to write, for example, they usually said something like, "I want y'all to write five sentences that make a

10

statement. Anybody get done before the rest can color." It was probably almost those exact words that led me to write these sentences in 1953 when I was in the second grade:

> The white clouds are pretty.
> There are only 15 people in our room.
> We will go to gym.
> We have a new poster.
> We may go out doors.

Second grade came after "Little First" and "Big First," so by then I knew the implied rules that accompanied all writing assignments. Writing was an occasion for proper English. I was not to write in the way we spoke to one another: The white clouds pretty; There ain't but 15 people in our room; We going to gym; We got a new poster; We can go out in the yard. Rather I was to use the language of "other": clouds *are*, there *are*, we *will*, we *may*.

My sentences were short, rigid, perfunctory, like the letters my mother wrote to relatives:

> Dear Papa,
> How are you? How is Mamie? Fine I hope. We are fine. We will come to see you Sunday. Cousin Ned will give us a ride.
>   Love,
>   Daughter

The language was not ours. It was something from outside us, something we used for special occasions.

But my coloring on the other side of that second-grade paper is different. I drew three hearts and a sun. The sun has a smiling face that radiates and envelops everything it touches. And although the sun and its world are enclosed in a circle, the colors I used — red, blue, green, purple, orange, yellow, black — indicates that I was less restricted with drawing and coloring than I was with writing Standard English. My valentines were not just red. My sun was not just a yellow ball in the sky.

By the time I reached the twelfth grade, speaking and writing Standard English had taken on new importance. Each year, about half of the newly graduated seniors of our school moved to large cities — particularly in the North — to live with relatives and find work. Our English teacher constantly corrected our grammar: "Not 'ain't,' but 'isn't.'" We seldom wrote papers, and even those few were usually plot summaries of short stories. When our teacher returned the papers, she usually lectured on the importance of using Standard English: "I *am*; you *are*; he, she, or it *is*," she would say, writing on the chalkboard as she spoke. "How you gon git a job talking about 'I is,' or 'I isn't' or 'I ain't'?"

In Pittsburgh, where I moved after graduation, I watched my   15
aunt and uncle — who had always spoken Standard English when in

Greeleyville — switch from Black English to Standard English to a mixture of the two, according to where they were or who they were with. At home and with certain close relatives, friends, and neighbors, they spoke Black English. With those less close, they spoke a mixture. In public and with strangers, they generally spoke Standard English.

In time, I learned to speak Standard English with ease and to switch smoothly from Black to Standard or a mixture, and back again. But no matter where I was, no matter what the situation or occasion, I continued to write as I had in school:

> Dear Mommie,
> How are you? How is everybody else? Fine I hope. I am fine. So are Aunt and Uncle. Tell everyone I said hello. I will write again soon.
>   Love,
>   Barbara

At work, at a health insurance company, I learned to write letters to customers. I studied form letters and letters written by co-workers, memorizing the phrases and the ways in which they were used. I dictated:

> Thank you for your letter of January 5. We have made the changes in your coverage you requested. Your new premium will be $150 every three months. We are pleased to have been of service to you.

In a sense, I was proud of the letters I wrote for the company: they were proof of my ability to survive in the city, the outside world — an indication of my growing mastery of English. But they also indicate that writing was still mechanical for me, something that didn't require much thought.

Reading also became a more significant part of my life during those early years in Pittsburgh. I had always liked reading, but now I devoted more and more of my spare time to it. I read romances, mysteries, popular novels. Looking back, I realized that the books I liked best were simple, unambiguous: good versus bad and right versus wrong with right rewarded and wrong punished, mysteries unraveled and all set right in the end. It was how I remembered life in Greeleyville.

Of course I was romanticizing. Life in Greeleyville had not been so very uncomplicated. Back there I had been — first as a child, then as a young woman with limited experience in the outside world — living in a relatively closed-in society. But there were implicit and explicit principles that guided our way of life and shaped our relationships with one another and the people outside — principles that a newcomer would find elusive and baffling. In Pittsburgh, I had matured, become more experienced: I had worked at three different jobs, associated with a wider range of people, married, had children. This new environment with different prescripts for living required that I speak Standard English much of the time, and slowly, imperceptibly, I had ceased seeing a sharp distinction between myself and "others." Reading romances and mysteries, characterized by dichotomy, was a way of shying away from change, from the person I was becoming.

But that other part of me — that part which took great pride in my ability to hold a job writing business letters — was increasingly drawn to the new developments in my life and the attending possibilities, opportunities for even greater change. If I could write letters for a nationally known business, could I not also do something better, more challenging, more important? Could I not, perhaps, go to college and become a school teacher? For years, afraid and a little embarrassed, I did no more than imagine this different me, this possible me. But sixteen years after coming north, when my younger daughter entered kindergarten, I found myself unable — or unwilling — to resist the lure of possibility. I enrolled in my first college course: Basic Writing, at the University of Pittsburgh.

For the first time in my life, I was required to write extensively about myself. Using the most formal English at my command, I wrote these sentences near the beginning of the term:

> One of my duties as a homemaker is simply picking up after others. A day seldom passes that I don't search for a mislaid toy, book, or gym shoe, etc. I change the Ty-D-Bol, fight "ring around the collar," and keep our laundry smelling "April fresh." Occasionally, I settle arguments between my children and suggest things to do when they're bored. Taking telephone messages for my oldest daughter is my newest (and sometimes most aggravating) chore. Hanging the toilet paper is my most insignificant.

My concern was to use "appropriate" language, to sound as if I belonged in a college classroom. But I felt separate from the language — as if it did not and could not belong to me. I couldn't think and feel genuinely in that language, couldn't make it express what I thought and felt about being a housewife. A part of me resented, among other things, being judged by such things as the appearance of my family's laundry and toilet bowl, but in that language I could only imagine and write about a conventional housewife.

For the most part, the remainder of the term was a period of adjustment, a time of trying to find my bearings as a student in a college composition class, to learn to shut out my Black English whenever I composed, and to prevent it from creeping into my formulations; a time for trying to grasp the language of the classroom and reproduce it in my prose; for trying to talk about myself in that language, reach others through it. Each experience of writing was like standing naked and revealing my imperfection, my "otherness." And each new assignment was another chance to make myself over in language, reshape myself, make myself "better" in my rapidly changing image of a student in a college composition class.

But writing became increasingly unmanageable as the term progressed, and by the end of the semester, my sentences sounded like this:

> My excitement was soon dampened, however, by what seemed like a small voice in the back of my head saying that I should be careful with my long awaited opportunity. I felt frustrated and this seemed to make it difficult to concentrate.

There is a poverty of language in these sentences. By this point, I knew that the clichéd language of my housewife essay was unacceptable, and I generally recognized trite expressions. At the same time, I hadn't yet mastered the language of the classroom, hadn't yet come to see it as belonging to me. Most notable is the lifelessness of the prose, the apparent absence of a person behind the words. I wanted those sentences — and the rest of the essay — to convey the anguish of yearning to, at once, become something more and yet remain the same. I had the sensation of being split in two, part of me going into a future the other part didn't believe possible. As that person, the student writer at that moment, I was essentially mute. I could not — in the process of composing — use the language of the old me, yet I couldn't imagine myself in the language of "others."

I found this particularly discouraging because at midsemester I had been writing in a much different way. Note the language of this introduction to an essay I had written then, near the middle of the term:

> Pain is a constant companion to the people in "Footwork." Their jobs are physically damaging. Employers are insensitive to their feelings and in many cases add to their problems. The general public wounds them further by treating them with disgrace because of what they do for a living. Although the workers are as diverse as they are similar, there is a definite link between them. They suffer a great deal of abuse.

The voice here is stronger, more confident, appropriating terms like "physically damaging," "wounds them further," "insensitive," "diverse" — terms I couldn't have imagined using when writing about my own experience — and shaping them into sentences like "Although the workers are as diverse as they are similar, there is a definite link between them." And there is the sense of a personality behind the prose, someone who sympathizes with the workers. "The general public wounds them further by treating them with disgrace because of what they do for a living."

What causes these differences? I was, I believed, explaining other 25 people's thoughts and feelings, and I was free to move about in the language of "others" so long as I was speaking *of* others. I was unaware that I was transforming into my best classroom language my own thoughts and feelings about people whose experiences and ways of speaking were in many ways similar to mine.

The following year, unable to turn back or to let go of what had become something of an obsession with language (and hoping to catch and hold the sense of control that had eluded me in Basic Writing), I enrolled in a research writing course. I spent most of the term learning how to prepare for and write a research paper. I chose sex education as my subject and spent hours in libraries, searching for information, reading, taking notes. Then (not without messiness and often demoralizing frustration) I organized my information into categories, wrote a thesis statement, and composed my paper — a series of paragraphs and quotations spaced between carefully constructed transitions. The process and results felt artificial, but as I would later come to realize I was passing through a necessary stage. My sentences sounded like this:

> This reserve becomes understandable with examination of who the abusers are. In an overwhelming number of cases, they are people the victims know and trust. Family members, relatives, neighbors, and close family friends commit seventy-five percent of all reported sex crimes against children, and parents, parent substitutes and relatives are the offenders in thirty to eighty percent of all reported cases. While assault by strangers does occur, it is less common, and is usually a single episode. But abuse by family members, relatives and acquaintances may continue for an extended period of time. In cases of incest, for example, children are abused repeatedly for an average of eight years. In such cases, "the use of physical force is rarely necessary because of the child's trusting, dependent relationship with the offender. The child's cooperation is often facilitated by the adult's position of dominance, an offer of material goods, a threat of physical violence, or a misrepresentation of moral standards."

The completed paper gave me a sense of profound satisfaction, and I read it often after my professor returned it. I know now that what I was pleased with was the language I used and the professional voice it helped me maintain. "Use better words," my teacher had snapped at me one day after reading the notes I'd begun accumulating from my research, and slowly I began taking on the language of my sources. In my next set of notes, I used the word "vacillating"; my professor applauded. And by the time I composed the final draft, I felt at ease with terms like "overwhelming number of cases," "single episode," and "reserve," and I shaped them into sentences similar to those of my "expert" sources.

If I were writing the paper today, I would of course do some things differently. Rather than open with an anecdote — as my teacher suggested — I would begin simply with a quotation that caught my interest as I was researching my paper (and which I scribbled, without its source, in the margin of my notebook): "Truth does not do so much good in the world as the semblance of truth does evil." The quotation felt right because it captured what was for me the central idea of my essay — an idea that emerged gradually during the making of my paper — and expressed it in a way I would like to have said it. The anecdote, a hypothetical situation I invented to conform to the information in the paper, felt forced and insincere because it represented — to a great degree — my teacher's understanding of the essay, *her* idea of what in it was most significant. Improving upon my previous experiences with writing, I was beginning to think and feel in the language I used, to find my own voices in it, to sense that how one speaks influences how one means. But I was not yet secure enough, comfortable enough with the language to trust my intuition.

Now that I know that to seek knowledge, freedom, and autonomy means always to be in the concentrated process of becoming — always to be venturing into new territory, feeling one's way at first, then getting one's balance, negotiating, accommodating, discovering one's self in ways that previously defined "others" — I sometimes get tired. And I ask myself why I keep on participating in this highbrow form of violence, this slamming against perplexity. But there is no real futility in the question, no hint of that part of the old me who stood outside Standard English, hugging to herself a disabling mistrust of a language she thought could not represent a person with her history and experience. Rather, the question represents a person who feels the consequences of her education, the weight of her possibilities as a teacher and writer and human being, a voice in society. And I would not change that person, would not give back the good burden that accompanies my growing expertise, my increasing power to shape myself in language and share that self with "others."

"To speak," says Frantz Fanon, "means to be in a position to use a certain syntax, to grasp the morphology of this or that language, but it means above all to assume a culture, to support the weight of civilization."[1] To write means to do the same, but in a more profound sense. However, Fanon also says that to achieve mastery means to "get" in a position of power, to "grasp," to "assume." This I have learned — both as a student and subsequently as a teacher — can involve tremendous emotional and psychological conflict for those attempting to master academic discourse. Although as a beginning student writer I had a fairly good grasp of ordinary spoken English and was proficient at what Labov calls "code-switching" (and what John Baugh in *Black Street Speech* terms "style shifting"), when I came face to face with the demands of academic writing, I grew increasingly self-conscious, constantly aware of my status as a black and a speaker of one of the many Black English vernaculars — a traditional outsider. For the first time, I experienced my sense of doubleness as something menacing, a built-in enemy. Whenever I turned inward for salvation, the balm so available during my childhood, I found instead this new fragmentation which spoke to me in many voices. It was the voice of my desire to prosper, but at the same time it spoke of what I had relinquished and could not regain: a safe way of being, a state of powerlessness which exempted me from responsibility for who I was and might

---

1. *Black Skin, White Masks* (1952; rpt. New York: Grove Press, 1967), pp. 17–18.

be. And it accused me of betrayal, of turning away from blackness. To recover balance, I had to take on the language of the academy, the language of "others." And to do that, I had to learn to imagine myself as a part of the culture of that language, and therefore someone free to manage that language, to take liberties with it. Writing and rewriting, practicing, experimenting, I came to comprehend more fully the generative power of language. I discovered — with the help of some especially sensitive teachers — that through writing one can continually bring new selves into being, each with new responsibilities and difficulties, but also with new possibilities. Remarkable power, indeed. I write and continually give birth to myself.

EXAMINING THE ISSUE CRITICALLY

1. Explain the meaning of Mellix's title. In what ways does it reflect the journey she describes in her personal narrative?

2. Mellix remembers growing up "speaking what I considered two distinctly different languages — Black English and Standard English" (3). Through experience she learned when, where, and how to use each language. In what kinds of situations did she use Black English? And in what situations, Standard English? How did she feel about this "doubleness"?

3. For Mellix as a young woman, what did it mean to speak Standard English to whites? To Standard-English-speaking blacks? What was the pain of having to use Standard English?

4. What strategies did Mellix's parents use to teach her Standard English and the relationship between language and power? What do you see as the "power" of language?

5. Describe the transformation that Mellix experienced in her college composition class. What exactly did she learn about herself and her use of language?

MAKING CONNECTIONS: THE ENGLISH-ONLY DEBATE

*The following questions are offered to help you start to make meaningful connec-
tions among the five articles in this Case Study. These questions can be used for
class discussion, or you can answer any one of the questions by writing an essay.
If you choose the essay option, be sure to make specific references to at least two of
the Case Study articles.*

1. While it's no secret that English is the common language of the United
   States, few of us know, as Myriam Marquez is quick to remind us, that our
   country has been "careful not to promote a government-mandated official
   language." Why do you suppose that our federal government has chosen to
   keep its hands off the language issue? If it has not been necessary to mandate
   English in the past, why do you think that people now feel a need to declare
   English the "official language" of the United States? Do you think that this
   need is real? Explain why or why not.

2. Robert D. King explains that "in much of the world, ethnic unity and cultural identification are routinely defined by language." To what extent is this
   true in the United States? Why is it sometimes difficult for nonnative speakers of English who immigrate to the United States to take ownership of
   Standard English? What does it mean to you to take ownership of language?
   Does one need this ownership to succeed?

3. Barbara Mellix tells us what it was like growing up torn between the worlds
   of Black English and Standard English, and Myriam Marquez explains the
   bilingual world she shares with her parents. What insights, if any, do their
   personal reflections give us into the English-only debate? Where do you
   think each of these writers stands on the issue of English-only?

4. Is the English-only debate a political issue, a social issue, an economic issue,
   or some combination of the three? In this context, what do you see as the relationship between language and power?

5. The selections from King and S. I. Hayakawa address immigrant assimilation
   from an academic viewpoint, but it is a highly personal subject for those who
   come here. After all, they must confront their English-language deficiencies
   right from the start. When American students study a foreign language at
   school, however, almost all of the speaking and instruction is in English until
   they progress far enough to understand instruction and detailed conversations in the other language. Think about your classroom experience in learning a foreign language. What are the most difficult challenges for you in
   language studies? Are you comfortable expressing yourself in the language?
   If you absolutely needed to communicate in that language, how well could
   you do it? How do you respond to people who are just learning English? Do
   you get impatient with them or assume that they are poorly educated? Write
   an essay about how well you think you would do if suddenly you had to
   function in another country with a different language. How would you deal
   with those who were impatient with your language skills or dismissive of
   you? How self-conscious do you think you would be?

4

PREJUDICE, DISCRIMINATION, AND STEREOTYPES

No single issue has absorbed our national consciousness more than prejudice and discrimination. That we are defined and define others is an inevitability of our human condition, but the manner in which we relate to each other is a measure of our progress as a multiracial, multiethnic, and multicultural society. In a larger sense, it is a measure of our growth as a civilization. Not even the most enlightened observers of our society believe that equality is within sight or even ultimately possible, but implicit in all views of the subject is the notion that we can and must improve our appreciation of each other if we are to better our lives.

Our purpose in this section of *Language Awareness* is to introduce you to the very significant role that language plays in the perpetuation of prejudice and discrimination. We begin with Gordon Allport's classic essay in which he offers a foundation for understanding the rest of the articles in this section. His concepts of "nouns that cut slices" and "verbal realism and symbol phobia" demonstrate not only how language reflects prejudice but also how we can use language to escape bias and bigotry.

Allport's essay is followed by S. I. Hayakawa and Alan R. Hayakawa's "Words with Built-in Judgments." Their work is in the field of semantics, commonly referred to as the study of meanings. They demonstrate the intricate relationship between words and reality and how perilous that relationship is when it comes to language concerning race, religion, and politics. In her essay illustrating her family and friends, appropriation of the racially biased term *nigger* by turning it into a term of endearment, Gloria Naylor points to how words themselves do not exist in isolation but are the product of the minds and hearts that use them. Martin Luther King Jr.'s "I Have a Dream" speech, perhaps the greatest speech of the last century, uses brilliant rhetoric to summon equality for all Americans. Writer Urvashi Vaid focuses on the labels that special interest groups use to build unity but also create the opposite: not community but "separate and unequal" groups. We move next to Brent Staples's essay entitled "Black Men and Public Spaces" in which he reveals the way his body language and presence as an African American male alters public spaces by affecting the attitudes and actions of those around him. His analysis reaches into the world of kinesics, of the messages that we send through our use of spatial relationships and further highlights the deeply rooted prejudices that exist in our society.

CASE STUDY: POLITICAL CORRECTNESS AND SPEECH CODES

The language focus narrows in our Case Study as we consider political correctness and speech codes, both of which began as a means of combating prejudice and creating more sensitivity to forms of otherness. Ethan Bronner's "Big Brother Is Listening" sets the groundwork for the explanation of political correctness and the ideas of its supporters and detractors. Balancing Bronner's essay is John Leo's "Who Said PC Is Passé?" which provides us with a catalog of the extremes to which political correctness has taken us in the name of increased sensitivity. Your responses to the events and situations he chronicles will be varied and will say much about where we stand currently on the political correctness movement. Next, Steven Doloff in "Racism and the Risks of Ethnic Humor" cautions that we need to be careful about what we're laughing at when it comes to racial and ethnic humor to make sure we are not reinforcing in ourselves and especially in our young people "ill-formed antagonistic feelings and fears of other races." Finally, in "The Language Police," Diane Ravitch gives us an account of textbook censorship from both the political left and political right perspectives.

The Language of Prejudice

GORDON ALLPORT

Gordon Allport was born in Montezuma, Indiana, in 1897. He attended Harvard College and graduated Phi Beta Kappa in 1919 with majors in philosophy and economics. During his under-graduate years, he also became interested in psychology, and a meeting with Sigmund Freud in Vienna in 1920 — during which the founder of psychoanalysis failed to impress him — had a profound influence on him. After studying and teaching abroad, Allport returned to Harvard to teach social ethics and to pursue his Ph.D., which he received in 1922. He went on to become a full professor at Harvard in 1942, served as chairman of the psychology department, and received the Gold Medal Award of the American Psychological Foundation in 1963. He died in 1967.

Allport became known for his outspoken stances regarding racial prejudice, and he was hopeful about efforts being made to eradicate it. His book The Nature of Prejudice *(1954) is still regarded as one of the most important and influential texts on the subject. The following excerpt from that book analyzes the connections between language and prejudice and explains some of the specific ways in which language can induce and shape prejudice.*

WRITING TO DISCOVER: *While in high school and college, many students are associated with groups that bring together people of dis-parate racial and religious backgrounds but whose labels still carry with them positive or negative associations. You may have made such associations yourself without thinking twice about it, as in "He's just a jock," or "She's with the popular crowd — she'll never go out with me." To what group, if any, did you belong in high school? Briefly write about the effects on you and your classmates of cliques in your school. How did the labels associated with the differ-ent groups influence how you thought about the individual mem-bers of each group?*

Without words we should scarcely be able to form categories at all. A dog perhaps forms rudimentary generalizations, such as small-boys-are-to-be avoided — but this concept runs its course on the con-ditioned reflex level, and does not become the object of thought as such. In order to hold a generalization in mind for reflection and re-call, for identification and for action, we need to fix it in words. With-out words our world would be, as William James said, an "empirical sand-heap."

NOUNS THAT CUT SLICES

In the empirical world of human beings there are some two and a half billion grains of sand corresponding to our category "the human race." We cannot possibly deal with so many separate entities in our thought, nor can we individualize even among the hundreds whom we encounter in our daily round. We must group them, form clusters. We welcome, therefore, the names that help us to perform the clustering.

The most important property of a noun is that it brings many grains of sand into a single pail, disregarding the fact that the same grains might have fitted just as appropriately into another pail. To state the matter technically, a noun *abstracts* from a concrete reality some one feature and assembles different concrete realities only with respect to this one feature. The very act of classifying forces us to overlook all other features, many of which might offer a sounder basis than the rubric we select. Irving Lee gives the following example:

> I knew a man who had lost the use of both eyes. He was called a "blind man." He could also be called an expert typist, a conscientious worker, a good student, a careful listener, a man who wanted a job. But he couldn't get a job in the department store order room where employees sat and typed orders which came over the telephone. The personnel man was impatient to get the interview over. "But you're a blind man," he kept saying, and one could almost feel his silent assumption that somehow the incapacity in one aspect made the man incapable in every other. So blinded by the label was the interviewer that he could not be persuaded to look beyond it.

Some labels, such as "blind man," are exceedingly salient and powerful. They tend to prevent alternative classification, or even cross-classification. Ethnic labels are often of this type, particularly if they refer to some highly visible feature, e.g., Negro, Oriental. They resemble the labels that point to some outstanding incapacity — *feeble-minded, cripple, blind man*. Let us call such symbols "labels of primary potency." These symbols act like shrieking sirens, deafening us to all finer discriminations that we might otherwise perceive. Even though the blindness of one man and the darkness of pigmentation of another may be defining attributes for some purposes, they are irrelevant and "noisy" for others.

Most people are unaware of this basic law of language — that every label applied to a given person refers properly only to one aspect of his nature. You may correctly say that a certain man is *human, a philanthropist, a Chinese, a physician, an athlete*. A given person may be all of these; but the chances are that Chinese stands out in your mind as the symbol of primary potency. Yet neither this nor any other classificatory label can refer to the whole of a man's nature. (Only his proper name can do so.)

5

Thus each label we use, especially those of primary potency, distracts our attention from concrete reality. The living, breathing, complex individual — the ultimate unit of human nature — is lost to sight. As in the figure, the label magnifies one attribute out of all proportion to its true significance, and masks other important attributes of the individual. . . .

A category, once formed with the aid of a symbol of primary potency, tends to attract more attributes than it should. The category labeled *Chinese* comes to signify not only ethnic membership but also reticence, impassivity, poverty, treachery. To be sure, . . . there may be genuine ethnic linked traits, making for a certain *probability* that the member of an ethnic stock may have these attributes. But our cognitive process is not cautious. The labeled category, as we have seen, includes indiscriminately the defining attribute, probable attributes, and wholly fanciful, nonexistent attributes.

Even proper names — which ought to invite us to look at the individual person — may act like symbols of primary potency, especially if they arouse ethnic associations. Mr. Greenberg is a person, but since his name is Jewish, it activates in the hearer his entire category of Jews-as-a-whole. An ingenious experiment performed by Razran shows this

LABELS OF PRIMARY POTENCY

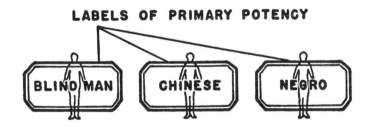

point clearly, and at the same time demonstrates how a proper name, acting like an ethnic symbol, may bring with it an avalanche of stereotypes.

> Thirty photographs of college girls were shown on a screen to 150 students. The subjects rated the girls on a scale from one to five for *beauty, intelligence, character, ambition, general likability*. Two months later the same subjects were asked to rate the same photographs (and fifteen additional ones introduced to complicate the memory factory). This time five of the original photographs were given Jewish surnames (Cohen, Kantor, etc.), five Italian (Valenti, etc.), and five Irish (O'Brien, etc.); and the remaining girls were given names chosen from the signers of the Declaration of Independence and from the Social Register (Davis, Adams, Clark, etc.).

When Jewish names were attached to photographs there occurred
the following changes in ratings:
    decrease in liking
    decrease in character
    decrease in beauty
    increase in intelligence
    increase in ambition
For those photographs given Italian names there occurred:
    decrease in liking
    decrease in character
    decrease in beauty
    decrease in intelligence

Thus a mere proper name leads to prejudgments of personal attributes.
The individual is fitted to the prejudice ethnic category, and not judged
in his own right.

While the Irish names also brought about depreciated judgment,
the depreciation was not as great as in the case of the Jews and Italians.
The falling of likability of the "Jewish girls" was twice as great as for
"Italians" and five times as great as for "Irish." We note, however, that
the "Jewish" photographs caused higher ratings in *intelligence* and in
ambition. Not all stereotypes of out-groups are unfavorable.

The anthropologist, Margaret Mead, has suggested that labels of primary potency lose some of their force when they are changed from nouns
into adjectives. To speak of a Negro soldier, a Catholic teacher, or a Jewish artist calls attention to the fact that some other group classifications
are just as legitimate as the racial or religious. If George Johnson is spoken of not only as a Negro but also as a *soldier*, we have at least two attributes to know him by, and two are more accurate than one. To depict
him truly as an individual, of course, we should have to name many more
attributes. It is a useful suggestion that we designate ethnic and religious
membership where possible with *adjectives* rather than *nouns*.

EMOTIONALLY TONED LABELS

Many categories have two kinds of labels — one less emotional and
one more emotional. Ask yourself how you feel, and what thoughts you
have, when you read the words *school teacher*, and then *school marm*. Certainly the second phrase calls up something more strict, more ridiculous,
more disagreeable than the former. Here are four innocent letters: m-a-r-m.
But they make us shudder a bit, laugh a bit, and scorn a bit. They call up
an image of a spare, humorless, irritable old maid. They do not tell us
that she is an individual human being with sorrows and troubles of her
own. They force her instantly into a rejective category.

In the ethnic sphere even plain labels such as Negro, Italian, Jew,
Catholic, Irish-American, French-Canadian may have emotional tone for

10

a reason that we shall soon explain. But they all have their higher key equivalents: nigger, wop, kike, papist, harp, canuck. When these labels are employed we can be almost certain that the speaker *intends* not only to characterize the person's membership, but also to disparage and reject him.

Quite apart from the insulting intent that lies behind the use of certain labels, there is also an inherent ("physiognomic") handicap in many terms designating ethnic membership. For example, the proper names characteristic of certain ethnic memberships strike us as absurd. (We compare them, of course, with what is familiar and therefore "right.") Chinese names are short and silly; Polish names intrinsically difficult and outlandish. Unfamiliar dialects strike us as ludicrous. Foreign dress (which, of course, is a visual ethnic symbol) seems unnecessarily queer.

But of all of these "physiognomic" handicaps the reference to color, clearly implied in certain symbols, is the greatest. The word Negro comes from the Latin *niger* meaning black. In point of fact, no Negro has a black complexion, but by comparison with other blonder stocks, he has come to be known as a "black man." Unfortunately *black* in the English language is a word having a preponderance of sinister connotations: the outlook is black, blackball, blackguard, black-hearted, black death, blacklist, blackmail, Black Hand. In his novel *Moby Dick*, Herman Melville considers at length the remarkably morbid connotations of black and the remarkably virtuous connotations of white.

Nor is the ominous flavor of black confined to the English language. A cross-cultural study reveals that the semantic significance of black is more or less universally the same. Among certain Siberian tribes, members of a privileged clan call themselves "white bones," and refer to all others as "black bones." Even among Uganda Negroes there is some evidence for a white god at the apex of the theocratic hierarchy; certain it is that a white cloth, signifying purity, is used to ward off evil spirits and disease.

There is thus an implied value-judgment in the very concept of *white race* and *black race*. One might also study the numerous unpleasant connotations of *yellow*, and their possible bearing on our conception of the people of the Orient.   15

Such reasoning should not be carried too far, since there are undoubtedly, in various contexts, pleasant associations with both black and yellow. Black velvet is agreeable, so too are chocolate and coffee. Yellow tulips are well liked; the sun and moon are radiantly yellow. Yet it is true that "color" words are used with chauvinistic overtones more than most people realize. There is certainly condescension indicated in many familiar phrases: dark as a nigger's pocket, darktown strutters, white hope (a term originated when a white contender was sought against the Negro heavyweight champion, Jack Johnson), the white man's burden, the yellow peril, black boy. Scores of everyday phrases are stamped with the flavor of prejudice, whether the user knows it or not.

We spoke of the fact that even the most proper and sedate labels for minority groups sometimes seem to exude a negative flavor. In many contexts and situations the very terms *French-Canadian, Mexican,* or *Jew,* correct and nonmalicious though they are, sound a bit opprobrious. The reason is that they are labels of social deviants. Especially in a culture where uniformity is prized, the name of *any* deviant carries with it *ipso facto* a negative value-judgment. Words like *insane, alcoholic, pervert* are presumably neutral designations of a human condition, but they are more: they are finger-pointing at a deviance. Minority groups are deviants, and for this reason, from the very outset, the most innocent labels in many situations imply a shading of disrepute. When we wish to highlight the deviance and denigrate it still further we use words of a higher emotional key: crackpot, soak, pansy, greaser, Okie, nigger, harp, kike.

Members of minority groups are often understandably sensitive to names given them. Not only do they object to deliberately insulting epithets, but sometimes see evil intent where none exists. Often the word Negro is spelled with a small *n*, occasionally as a studied insult, more often from ignorance. (The term is not cognate with white, which is not capitalized, but rather with Caucasian, which is.) Terms like "mulatto," or "octoroon" cause hard feeling because of the condescension with which they have often been used in the past. Sex differentiations are objectionable, since they seem doubly to emphasize ethnic difference: why speak of Jewess and not of Protestantess, or of Negress and not of whitess? Similar overemphasis is implied in the terms like Chinamen or Scotchman; why not American man? Grounds for misunderstanding lie in the fact that minority group members are sensitive to such shadings, while majority members may employ them unthinkingly.

THE COMMUNIST LABEL

Until we label an out-group it does not clearly exist in our minds. Take the curiously vague situation that we often meet when a person wishes to locate responsibility on the shoulders of some out-group whose nature he cannot specify. In such a case he usually employs the pronoun "they" without an antecedent. "Why don't they make these sidewalks wider?" "I hear they are going to build a factory in this town and hire a lot of foreigners." "I won't pay this tax bill; they can just whistle for their money." If asked "who?" the speaker is likely to grow confused and embarrassed. The common use of the orphaned pronoun *they* teaches us that people often want and need to designate out-groups (usually for the purpose of venting hostility) even when they have no clear conception of the out-group in question. And so long as the target of wrath remains vague and ill-defined specific prejudice cannot crystallize around it. To have enemies we need labels.

Until relatively recently [late 1940s] — strange as it may seem —   20
there was no agreed-upon symbol for *communist*. The word, of course,
existed but it had no special emotional connotation, and did not designate a public enemy. Even when, after World War I, there was a growing
feeling of economic and social menace in this country, there was no
agreement as to the actual source of the menace.

A content analysis of the Boston *Herald* for the year 1920 turned up
the following list of labels. Each was used in a context implying some
threat. Hysteria had overspread the country, as it did after World War II.
Someone must be responsible for the postwar malaise, rising prices, uncertainty. There must a villain. But in 1920 the villain was impartially designated by reporters and editorial writers with the following symbols:

> alien, agitator, anarchist, apostle of bomb and torch, Bolshevik, commu-
> nist, communist laborite, conspirator, emissary of false promise, extrem-
> ist, foreigner, hyphenated-American, incendiary, IWW, parlor anarchist,
> parlor pink, parlor socialist, plotter, radical, red, revolutionary, Russian
> agitator, socialist, Soviet, syndicalist, traitor, undesirable.

From this excited array we note that the *need* for an enemy (someone
to serve as a focus for discontent and jitters) was considerably more apparent than the precise *identity* of the enemy. At any rate, there was no
clearly agreed upon label. Perhaps partly for this reason the hysteria
abated. Since no clear category of "communism" existed there was no
true focus for the hostility.

But following World War II this collection of vaguely interchangeable labels became fewer in number and more commonly agreed upon.
The out-group menace came to be designated almost always as *communist* or *red*. In 1920 the threat, lacking a clear label, was vague; after 1945
both symbol and thing became more definite. Not that people knew precisely what they meant when they said "communist," but with the aid of
the term they were at least able to point consistently to *something* that inspired fear. The term developed the power of signifying menace and led
to various repressive measures against anyone to whom the label was
rightly or wrongly attached.

Logically, the label should apply to specifiable defining attributes,
such as members of the Communist Party, or people whose allegiance is
with the Russian system, or followers, historically, of Karl Marx. But the
label came in for far more extensive use.

What seems to have happened is approximately as follows. Having   25
suffered through a period of war and being acutely aware of devastating
revolutions abroad, it is natural that most people should be upset, dreading to lose their possessions, annoyed by high taxes, seeing customary
moral and religious values threatened, and dreading worse disasters to
come. Seeking an explanation for this unrest, a single identifiable enemy
is wanted. It is not enough to designate "Russia" or some other distant

land. Nor is it satisfactory to fix blame on "changing social conditions." What is needed is a human agent near at hand: someone in Washington, someone in our schools, in our factories, in our neighborhood. If we *feel* an immediate threat, we reason, there must be a near-lying danger. It is, we conclude, communism, not only in Russia but also in America, at our doorstep, in our government, in our churches, in our colleges, in our neighborhood.

Are we saying that hostility toward communism is prejudice? Not necessarily. There are certainly phases of the dispute wherein realistic social conflict is involved. American values (e.g., respect for the person) and totalitarian values as represented in Soviet practice are intrinsically at odds. A realistic opposition in some form will occur. Prejudice enters only when the defining attributes of *communist* grow imprecise, when anyone who favors any form of social change is called a communist. People who fear social change are the ones most likely to affix the label to any persons or practices that seem to them threatening.

For them the category is undifferentiated. It includes books, movies, preachers, teachers who utter what for them are uncongenial thoughts. If evil befalls — perhaps forest fires or a factory explosion — it is due to communist saboteurs. The category becomes monopolistic, covering almost anything that is uncongenial. On the floor of the House of Representatives in 1946, Representative Rankin called James Roosevelt a communist. Congressman Outland replied with psychological acumen, "Apparently everyone who disagrees with Mr. Rankin is a communist."

When differentiated thinking is at a low ebb — as it is in times of social crises — there is a magnification of two-valued logic. Things are perceived as either inside or outside a moral order. What is outside is likely to be called communist. Correspondingly — and here is where damage is done — whatever is called communist (however erroneously) is immediately cast outside the moral order.

This associative mechanism places enormous power in the hands of a demagogue. For several years Senator McCarthy managed to discredit many citizens who thought differently from himself by the simple device of calling them communist. Few people were able to see through this trick and many reputations were ruined. But the famous senator has no monopoly on the device. As reported in the Boston *Herald*: on November 1, 1946, Representative Joseph Martin, Republican leader in the House, ended his election campaign against his Democratic opponent by saying, "The people will vote tomorrow between chaos, confusion, bankruptcy, state socialism or communism, and the preservation of our American life, with all its freedom and its opportunities." Such an array of emotional labels placed his opponent outside the accepted moral order. Martin was re-elected. . . .

Not everyone, of course, is taken in. Demagogy, when it goes too far, 30 meets with ridicule. Elizabeth Dilling's book, *The Red Network*, was so exaggerated in its two-valued logic that it was shrugged off by many people with a smile. One reader remarked, "Apparently if you step off the sidewalk with your left foot you're a communist." But it is not easy in times of social strain and hysteria to keep one's balance, and to resist the tendency of a verbal symbol to manufacture large and fanciful categories of prejudiced thinking.

VERBAL REALISM AND SYMBOL PHOBIA

Most individuals rebel at being labeled, especially if the label is un-complimentary. Very few are willing to be called *fascistic*, *socialistic*, or *anti-Semitic*. Unsavory labels may apply to others; but not to us.

An illustration of the craving that people have to attach favorable symbols to themselves is seen in the community where white people banded together to force out a Negro family that had moved in. They called themselves "Neighborly Endeavor" and chose as their motto the Golden Rule. One of the first acts of this symbol-sanctified band was to sue the man who sold property to Negroes. They then flooded the house which another Negro couple planned to occupy. Such were the acts performed under the banner of the Golden Rule.

Studies made by Stagner and Hartmann show that a person's political attitudes may in fact entitle him to be called a fascist or a socialist, and yet he will emphatically repudiate the unsavory label, and fail to endorse any movement or candidate that overtly accepts them. In short, there is a *symbol phobia* that corresponds to *symbol realism*. We are more inclined to the former when we ourselves are concerned, though we are much less critical when epithets of "fascist," "communist," "blind man," "school marm" are applied to others.

When symbols provoke strong emotions they are sometimes regarded no longer as symbols, but as actual things. The expressions "son of a bitch" and "liar" are in our culture frequently regarded as "fighting words." Softer and more subtle expressions of contempt may be accepted. But in these particular cases, the epithet itself must be "taken back." We certainly do not change our opponent's attitude by making him take back a word, but it seems somehow important that the word itself be eradicated.

Such verbal realism may reach extreme length.   35

> The City Council of Cambridge, Massachusetts, unanimously passed a resolution (December, 1939) making it illegal "to possess, harbor, sequester, introduce or transport, within the city limits, any book, map, magazine, newspaper, pamphlet, handbill, or circular containing the words Lenin or Leningrad."

Such naiveté in confusing language with reality is hard to comprehend unless we recall that word-magic plays an appreciable part in human thinking. The following examples, like the one preceding, are taken from Hayakawa.

> The Malagasy soldier must eschew kidneys, because in the Malagasy language the word for kidney is the same as that for "shot"; so shot he would certainly be if he ate a kidney.

> In May, 1937, a state senator of New York bitterly opposed a bill for the control of syphilis because "the innocence of children might be corrupted by a widespread use of the term. . . . This particular word creates a shudder in every decent woman and decent man."

This tendency to reify words underscores the close cohesion that exists between category and symbol. Just the mention of "communist," "Negro," "Jew," "England," "Democrats," will send some people into a panic of fear or a frenzy of anger. Who can say whether it is the word or the thing that annoys them? The label is an intrinsic part of any monopolistic category. Hence to liberate a person from ethnic or political prejudice it is necessary at the same time to liberate him from *word fetishism*. This fact is well known to students of general semantics who tell us that prejudice is due in large part to verbal realism and to symbol phobia. Therefore any program for the reduction of prejudice must include a large measure of semantic therapy.

FOCUSING ON CONTENT

1. Nouns, or names, provide an essential service in making categorization possible. Yet according to Allport, nouns are also words that "cut slices." What does he mean by that term? What is inherently unfair about nouns?

2. What are "labels of primary potency" (4)? Why does Allport equate them with "shrieking sirens"? Why are such labels important to his essay?

3. What does the experiment with the nonlabeled and labeled photos demonstrate? How do labels affect the way the mind perceives reality?

4. What does Allport mean by the "orphaned pronoun *they*" (19)? Why is it used so often in conversation?

5. What does Allport mean by *symbol phobia* (33)? How does this concept illustrate the unfairness of labeling others?

FOCUSING ON WRITING

1. What is Allport's thesis, and where is it stated? (Glossary: *Thesis*)

2. In paragraph 2, why do you think Allport uses a metaphorical image — grains of sand — to represent people? (Glossary: *Figurative Language*) How does this metaphor help him present his point?

3. In paragraph 3, Allport uses Irving Lee's story of a blind man who was unable to get a job as an example of how powerful certain labels can be.

(Glossary: *Examples*) What other quotations does he use as examples? What is the purpose of each one? Do you think they are effective? Why or why not?

4. Allport wrote "The Language of Prejudice" in the early 1950s. Does this help explain why he devotes many paragraphs to the evolution of the label *communist?* What are the connotations of the word *communist* today? (Glossary: *Connotation/Denotation*)

LANGUAGE IN ACTION

Read the following brief article, which appeared in the *New York Times* on December 13, 1968. Then make a list of the arguments for and against the UN action. Do you think it's possible to legislate tolerance and tone down prejudice through the use — or nonuse — of language?

UN GROUP URGES DROPPING OF WORDS WITH RACIST TINGE

In an effort to combat racial prejudice, a group of United Nations experts is urging sweeping revision of the terminology used by teachers, mass media, and others dealing with race.

Words such as *Negro, primitive, savage, backward, colored, bushman,* and *uncivilized* would be banned as either "contemptuous, unjust, or inadequate." They were described as aftereffects of colonialism.

The report said that the terms were "so charged with emotive potential that their use, with or without conscious pejorative intent, to describe or characterize certain ethnic, social, or religious groups, generally provoked an adverse reaction on the part of these groups."

The report said further that even the term *race* should be used with particular care since its scientific validity was debatable and that it "often served to perpetuate prejudice." The experts suggested that the word *tribe* should be used as sparingly as possible, since most of the "population groups" referred to by this term have long since ceased to be tribes or are losing their tribal character. *A native* should be called *inhabitant,* the group advised, and instead of *paganism* the words *animists, Moslems, Brahmans,* and other precise words should be used. The word *savanna* is preferable to *jungle,* and the new countries should be described as *developing* rather than *underdeveloped,* the experts said.

WRITING SUGGESTIONS

1. Make an extensive list of the labels that have been or could be applied to you at this time. Write an essay in which you discuss the labels that you find "truly offensive," those you can "live with," and those that you "like to be associated with." Explain your reasons for putting particular labels in each of these categories.

2. Allport states, "Especially in a culture where uniformity is prized, the name of *any* deviant carries with it *ipso facto* a negative value-judgment" (17). This was written in the 1950s. Since then, the turbulent 1960s, the political correctness movement of the 1980s and 1990s and the years since the millennium, and the mainstreaming of "alternative" cultures have all attempted to persuade people to accept differences and be more tolerant. Write an essay in which you consider Allport's statement today. Which labels that identify someone as different still carry a negative association? Have the social movements of the past decades changed in a fundamental way how we think about others? Do you think there is more acceptance of nonconformity today, or is a nonconformist or member of a minority still subjected to negative, though perhaps more subtle, labeling? Support your conclusions with examples from your own experience and from the depiction of current events in the popular media.

3. Allport wrote *The Nature of Prejudice* before the civil rights movement began in earnest, though he did live to see it grow and reach its climax at the famous 1963 march on Washington. (See Martin Luther King Jr.'s celebrated "I Have a Dream" speech on p. 244) Obviously, part of the civil rights movement was in the arena of language, and its leaders often used impressive rhetoric to confront the language of prejudice. Write an essay in which you analyze how the kinds of labels and symbols identified by Allport were used in speeches and documents both to justify the continuation of segregation and prejudice and to decry it. How did the leaders of the civil rights movement use language to their advantage? To what emotions or ideas did the language of the opposition appeal? The Internet and your library have vast information about the movement's genesis and history, so it may be difficult at first to decide on a specific area of research. Start by looking at how language was used by both sides in the battle over civil rights.

Words with Built-in Judgments

S. I. HAYAKAWA AND ALAN R. HAYAKAWA

S. I. Hayakawa (1906–1992), a former senator from California and honorary chair of the English-only movement, wrote the influential semantics text Language in Thought and Action *in 1941. With the help of his son Alan, he brought out the fifth edition of the book in 1990. Born in Vancouver, Canada, to Japanese parents, Hayakawa attended the University of Manitoba, McGill University, and the University of Wisconsin before beginning a career as a professor of English. He later became president of San Francisco State University. Hayakawa's other language books include* Our Language and Our World *(1959) and* Symbol, Status, and Personality *(1963).*

Alan Hayakawa was born in Chicago in 1946 and received a B.A. in mathematics from Reed College in 1970. He began his writing career as a reporter for the Oregonian *in Portland, Oregon, in 1975, and he moved to Washington, D.C., in 1987 as the* Oregonian's *Washington correspondent. He is now the manager of the* InsideLine, *a telephone news and information service, at the* Patriot-News *in Harrisburg, Pennsylvania. In addition to coauthoring the fifth edition of* Language in Thought and Action, *Hayakawa has coauthored* The Blair Handbook *(4th ed., 2003), and the* College Writer's Reference *(2002), now in its third edition.*

In Language in Thought and Action, *from which the following selection is taken, the Hayakawas explore the complex relationships that exist between reality and the language we use to describe it. They demonstrate the power that some words — especially those associated with "race, religion, political heresy, and economic dissent" — have to evoke strong emotional responses. As Japanese Americans, they have felt this power firsthand. The Hayakawas explain how an awareness of the power of words can help writers and speakers avoid both stirring up traditional prejudices and unintentionally giving offense.*

WRITING TO DISCOVER: *People often use labels such as* teenager, Iraqi, blind, senior citizen, liberal, *and* Japanese *to describe other people quickly. Spend some time carefully listening to the labels you use, and make a list of them. Do these labels give an accurate picture of a whole person? Do they carry implied judgments? Explain.*

The fact that some words simultaneously arouse both informative and affective connotations gives a special complexity to discussions involving religious, racial, national, and political groups. To many people, the word "communist" has both the informative connotation of "one who believes in communism" and the affective connotation of "one whose ideals and purposes are altogether repellent." Words applying to occupations of which one disapproves ("pickpocket," racketeer," "prostitute") and those applying to believers in philosophies of which one disapproves ("atheist," "radical," "heretic," "materialist," "fundamentalist") likewise often communicate *simultaneously* a fact and a judgment on that fact. Such words may be called "loaded" — that is, their affective connotations may strongly shape people's thoughts.

In some parts of the United States, there is a strong prejudice against certain ethnic groups, such as Mexican Americans, whether immigrant or American-born. The strength of this prejudice is revealed by the fact that polite people and the press have stopped using the word "Mexican," using the term "Hispanic" instead to avoid any negative connotations. There are also terms such as "Chicano" and "Latino" that Mexican American and Spanish-speaking groups have chosen to describe themselves.

Names that are "loaded" tend to influence behavior toward those to whom they are applied. Currently, the shop doorways and freeway underpasses of American cities are sheltering tens of thousands of people who have no work and no homes. These people used to be referred to as "bums" — a word that suggests not only a lack of employment but a lack of desire to work, people who are lazy, satisfied with little, and who have no desire to enter the mainstream of the American middle class or subscribe to its values. Thus, to think of these people as "bums" is to think that they are only getting what they deserve. With the search for new names for such people — "street people," "homeless," "displaced persons" — we may find new ways of thinking about their situation that may in turn suggest new ways of helping deal with it. Similarly, "problem drinker" has replaced "drunkard" and "substance abuser" has replaced "junkie." "Developmentally disabled" has replaced "retarded," which in turn replaced "idiot."

The negative connotations of words sometimes change because of deliberate changes in the way they are used. Michael Harrington, the American socialist, has said that "socialist" became a political dirty word in the 1930s and 1940s in the United States when opposing politicians and editorialists repeatedly linked "socialism" and "communism," obscuring what adherents to the two philosophies saw as distinctions between them. In the 1964 presidential campaign, it was said by his opponents that Senator Barry Goldwater was "too conservative" to be made president. The negative connotations of "conservative" had receded by 1988; in that presidential campaign, then Vice President George Bush repeatedly amplified the negative connotations of the word "liberal" and then accused his opponent, Michael Dukakis, of being one.

The meaning of words also changes from speaker to speaker, from   5
hearer to hearer, and from decade to decade. An elderly Japanese woman
of my acquaintance used to squirm at the mention of the word "Jap."
"Whenever I hear that word," she used to say, "I feel dirty all over." She
was reacting to the negative connotations as it was used during the Second
World War and earlier. More recently, "JAP" is an acronym for "Jewish
American princess," heard as an insult by an entirely different ethnic group.

A black friend of mine recalls hitchhiking as a young man in the
1930s through an area of the country where very few blacks lived. He
was given a ride by a white couple, who fed him and gave him a place to
sleep in their home. However, they kept referring to him as "little nigger," which upset him profoundly. He finally asked them not to call him
by that "insulting term," a request they had difficulty understanding, as
they had not meant to offend him. One way my friend might have explained his point further would have been to say, "Excuse me, but in the
part of the country I come from, white people who wish to show contempt for my race call us 'niggers.' I assume this is not your intention."

In recent times, the negative connotations of the word "nigger" are
more widely understood. This is partly the result of efforts by black
Americans and others to educate the public. Early in 1942, when I was
living in Chicago and teaching at the Illinois Institute of Technology, I
was invited to become a columnist for the *Chicago Defender* — at that
time the most militant of Negro newspapers. I say "Negro" rather than
"black" because this was 1942 and it was the mission of that newspaper
to make people proud of being "Negro." The word "Negro" at that time
was used with dignity and pride. In its editorial policy, the *Defender* saw
to it that the word was used in that way. It was always capitalized. Later,
during the civil rights movement of the 1950s and 1960s, a wider effort
was made to make just this point in the mind of the American public as a
whole, first substituting "Negro" for "colored," "nigger," "nigrah," and,
later, substituting "black" for "Negro." "Black" is now the word most
frequently chosen by people of African origin in the United States to describe themselves, and the word "Negro" is considered by many to be
old-fashioned, and condescending. Most recently, it has been proposed
that "African American" be substituted for "black." *Those who believe that
the meaning of a word is innately part of the word risk offending or being
offended because of having ignored differences in context or current usage.*

The conflicts that erupt over words are invariably an index to social
concerns over the reality that the words refer to. Much debate has arisen
over the issue of sexual discrimination in language. Is it fair, many people
ask, that the word "man" should stand for all human beings, male and female? Should we say, "Everyone should cast his vote," when half the voters are women? Are there biases that are unfair to women — and to
men — built into the English language? If so, what can or should be
done about it?

The problem can be better understood if we look at the disputed words in the contexts in which they appear. In some contexts, the extensional meaning of "man" as a synonym for the species *Homo sapiens* covers both sexes, without any discrimination implied: men, women, and children; Englishmen, Chinese, Eskimos, Aborigines, next-door neighbors, and so forth. In other contexts, "man" refers only to the male: "There is a man at the door." The problems with connotation occur in a context such as: "The work team is short ten men." In such a case the employer may be inclined to look for ten more males to hire, even when the work can be done equally well by women.

The Chinese ideograph [人], also used in Japanese, stands for "man" 10 in the generic sense: "person," "human being." A different ideograph [男] is used for "man" in the sense of "male human being." Since women traditionally have been assigned subordinate roles in both Chinese and Japanese cultures, discrimination against women cannot be said to be due solely to the peculiarities of language.

For those who have no difficulty with the different meanings of "man," or who like the maleness they find in the generic term, the language needs no modification. But what about those who are dissatisfied with the masculine connotations of "man"? What about the woman on the softball team who insists on being called "first baseperson" or the committee leader who styles herself "chairperson"? What about the woman named "Cooperman" who wanted to change her name to "Cooperperson" and petitioned a court to legalize the change? (Her petition was denied.) Can the language accommodate them?

Fortunately, the language is flexible enough for people to make personal adjustments to meet their own standards. "Human beings" or "humans" or "people" are acceptable substitutes for the generic "man," though rhetorically they may not always sound as good. Instead of saying "Man is a tool-using animal," we can say, "Human beings are tool-using animals."

Once it becomes apparent that we can construct any sentence we please without incurring possible sexual stereotypes, a further question remains: Should we demand that all writers adopt a "nonsexist" vocabulary and always use it — for example, the neutral plural? On this point history offers some guidance.

Most of the attempts made to force living language into a doctrinaire program have failed resoundingly. Jonathan Swift once spoke out acidly against the use of the word "mob" as a corrupt shortening of the Latin term *mobile vulgus*. Dr. Samuel Johnson resisted, to no avail, the admission of the word "civilization" into his dictionary because it seemed to him a barbarism, despite its respectable Latin root. In this century, Mussolini tried to eliminate the informal *tu* in Italian (the second person singular pronoun, whose English counterpart, "thou," has disappeared in ordinary English usage). He covered Italy with posters commanding Italians to use the *voi* form instead. His campaign failed. The social forces that created the words in the first place could not be changed by logic, fiat, or program. Language has usually proven stronger than the individual.

It must not be forgotten that language, created over centuries and 15 inherited with our culture, does not exert its tyranny uniformly over all who use it. In the novel *Kingsblood Royal* by Sinclair Lewis, actually a tract against racial prejudice, the central character is a vicious racial bigot — but he is careful never to use the word "nigger."

Similarly, an individual who uses "sexist" terms uncritically may have all kinds of discriminatory attitudes towards women, or he — or she — may be entirely free of them. The presence or absence of such terms has no necessary connection with the presence or absence of the corresponding attitudes.

This does not mean that writers who are sensitive to sexual bias in language should resign themselves to what they consider a sorry state of affairs. They can carry out their own programs within their own speech and writing. These efforts are not without risk of accidentally engendering new, unintended meanings. For example, in revising the words of hymns, the Episcopal Church changed "Christian Men, Rejoice!" to "Christian Friends, Rejoice!" However, as Sara Mosle pointed out in *The New Republic*, the theological implications of extending joy only to friends — what about Christian enemies, or even strangers? — were entirely inappropriate to the message of the hymn. "How long would it be before Christmas cards read 'Peace on Earth, good will towards friends?' A different proposition altogether from the brotherly (or sisterly) benediction to all mankind."

The calling of attention to sex discrimination contained within language, a campaign conducted in a similar way to that by which "Negro" and then "black" were successfully substituted for "colored," has served to raise society's awareness of the problem of built-in bias in language, even though it has not yet transformed the language. Even if such efforts fail to dislodge all forms of gender bias in the language, the effort to correct the problem is, in itself, worthwhile. As the poet John Ciardi has observed:

> In the long run the usage of those who do not think about the language will prevail. Usages I resist will become acceptable. It will not do to resist uncompromisingly. Yet those who care have a duty to resist. Changes that occur against such resistance are tested changes. The language is better for them — and for the resistance.

One other curious fact needs to be recorded about the words we apply to such hotly debated issues as race, religion, political heresy, and economic dissent. Every reader is acquainted with people who, according to their own flattering descriptions of themselves, "believe in being frank" and like to "tell it like it is." By "telling it like it is," such people usually mean calling anything or anyone by the term which has the strongest and most disagreeable affective connotations. Why people should pin medals on themselves for "candor" for performing this nasty feat has often puzzled me. Sometimes it is necessary to violate verbal taboos as an aid to clearer thinking, but, more often, to insist upon "telling it like it is" is to provide our minds with a greased runway down which we may slide back into unexamined and reactive patterns of evaluation and behavior.

FOCUSING ON CONTENT

1. In the beginning of the essay, what do the Hayakawas mean by an informative connotation? An affective connotation? (Glossary: *Connotation/Denotation*) What do the Hayakawas mean when they characterize words that have both connotations as "loaded"(1)?

2. How can names "influence behavior toward those to whom they are applied" (3)? What is the difference in affective connotation between calling someone a "bum" and saying that a person is "homeless"?

3. What do the Hayakawas mean when they say, "*Those who believe that the meaning of a word is innately part of the word risk offending or being offended because of having ignored differences in context or current usage*" (7)?

4. What does history tell us about attempts to force changes on a living language?

5. Is a person who uses sexist terms necessarily sexist? (Glossary: *Sexist Language*) Explain.

FOCUSING ON WRITING

1. Trace one of the examples given by the Hayakawas in paragraph 3 regarding how potentially loaded words have evolved over the years, such as the evolution of the term *idiot*. How effective do you find their use of examples in general and this example in particular? (Glossary: *Examples*)

2. The Hayakawas structure paragraphs 11 and 12 as a question-and-answer segment. In paragraph 11, they ask if the language is able to accommodate those who seek to remove sexist or gender-specific references in everyday words. Paragraph 12 answers in the affirmative, concluding that gender-neutral substitutions are acceptable even though "they may not always sound as good." Why do you think the Hayakawas structure their discussion of gender-specific references in this way? What does it indicate about their intended audience? (Glossary: *Audience*)

3. In what is a rather academic and straightforward piece, the Hayakawas introduce the image of a "greased runway" at the very end of their discussion. To what does the greased runway refer? Do you find it an effective image? Do you think it's appropriate to introduce such a metaphor so late in the piece? (Glossary: *Figurative Language*) Why or why not?

LANGUAGE IN ACTION

Sometimes a word can become so loaded that it irrevocably affects other valid words. The following article by Steven Pinker, which first appeared in the *New York Times* on February 2, 1999, reveals how this can happen. Consider the plight of David Howard, whose correct, nonpejorative use of the word *niggardly* set off a firestorm of controversy and cost him his job. Jot down your reactions to the situation. Do you think Howard should have been fired? Do you agree that the word *niggardly* should be removed from the vocabulary of our society, regardless of its actual meaning and derivation? Explain your answers.

<hr />

RACIST LANGUAGE, REAL AND IMAGINED

Last week David Howard, an aide to the Mayor of Washington, resigned after a staff meeting in which he called his budget "niggardly." A colleague thought he had used a racial epithet, though in fact "niggard" is a Middle English word meaning "miser." It has nothing to do with the racial slur based on Spanish for "black," which came into English centuries later.

This is not the first time the inaccurate parsing of an innocent remark has led to confusion. Remember, in "Annie Hall," how Woody Allen thinks he has been the target of an anti-Semitic slur from two people on a New York street? One person had asked, "Dj'ou eat yet?" and his companion had replied, "No, dj'ou?"

Last week's misunderstanding was of a different sort. "Niggardly" may be unexceptional on etymological grounds, but given what we know about how the mind deals with language, the word was a disaster waiting to happen.

Most words and parts of words have many meanings, and when we listen to someone speak, our brains have to find the right ones. Some recent laboratory experiments indicate that this is a two-stage process.

First, all the meanings of a word, including inappropriate ones, light up willy-nilly in the brain. When we hear about "spiders, roaches, and bugs," the thought of surveillance devices flashes through our minds for a few hundredths of a second — until that misinterpretation is repressed by our analysis of the context.

Thus it is impossible for anyone to hear "niggardly" without thinking, if only for a moment, of the ethnic slur.

Worse, the context is of little help in squelching the wrong meaning. Everyone is an amateur linguist, and we all strive for a logical — though sometimes incorrect — parsing of what we hear. This is why folk etymologies are rampant in dialects, like "sparrowgrass" (asparagus) and "very-close" (varicose) veins.

Many phrases have become standard English, like chaise lounge (from the French chaise longue or "long chair"), cockroach (from the Spanish cucaracha) and bridegroom (originally bridgome, Middle English for "bride man").

"Niggardly" is easy to misparse. English grammar allows a "d" or "ed" to be stuck on a noun to form an adjective (as in "hook-nosed" and "left-handed"), and it allows "ly" to be put on an adjective to form an adverb.

Thus we get "absent-mindedly," "good-humoredly," "half-heartedly," "markedly," "otherworldly," "pointedly," "shame-facedly," and "single-handedly."

The "a" is not much help, because "ar" often substitutes for "er" — as in "beggar," "burglar," "hangar," and "scholar."

Worst of all, the deducible meaning makes all-too-good linguistic sense. Terms for stinginess and duplicitousness are among the most common examples of racist language: "to gyp" (probably from gypsy), "to welsh" (perhaps from Welsh), "Dutch treat," "Indian giver."

Does this mean a perfectly innocent word is doomed? It would not be the first time. Words are often sacrificed when they take on secondary, emotionally charged meanings. "Queer," for example, is now problematic, and many animals (like donkeys) are losing their fine old Anglo-Saxon names.

If you find yourself vaguely offended thinking of the other words I could have included here, you should have some sympathy for David Howard's audience.

Still, Mr. Howard should get his job back. Though "niggardly" begs to be misunderstood, the misunderstanding can be overruled. After the various associates of a word light up in the mental dictionary, the rest of the brain can squelch the unintended ones, thanks to the activity that psycholinguists call "post-lexical-access processing" and that other people call "common sense."

WRITING SUGGESTIONS

1. The Hayakawas' discussion of loaded words reflects a national movement and debate — termed *political correctness* — that, among other goals, seeks to aggressively remove loaded words from common use. Such terms as *chairperson, physically challenged,* and *sanitation technician* have become part of our everyday vocabulary. Still, many argue that political correctness has gone too far, and some even parody the movement: Should short people, for example, be termed *vertically challenged?* What do you think about political correctness? How has it changed the way you speak and the level of awareness — and respect — you have for others who are different from you? Write an essay in which you discuss your experiences with political correctness and how important you believe it is. Has it gone too far, making it too easy for some people to take offense at just about anything you say? Or is it helpful in eliminating loaded terms that imply disrespect?

2. Reread the quote from John Ciardi (18). He has a pessimistic view when he says, "In the long run the usage of those who do not think about the language will prevail." What does he mean by this statement? Write an essay in which you agree or disagree with his view. How does language change? How can those who do not care about it affect its change? What can those who do care about it do to fulfill what Ciardi calls their "duty to resist"?

The Meanings of a Word

GLORIA NAYLOR

*Novelist and essayist Gloria Naylor was born in New York City in
1950. She worked as a missionary for the Jehovah's Witnesses from
1967 to 1975 and then as a telephone operator until 1981, the year
she graduated from Brooklyn College. Naylor later started a graduate program in African American studies at Yale University. In
her fiction, she explores the lives of African American women,
drawing freely from her own experiences and those of her extended
family. As Naylor has stated, "I wanted to become a writer because
I felt that my presence as a black woman and my perspective as a
woman in general had been underrepresented in American literature." She received the American Book Award for First Fiction for*
The Women of Brewster Place *(1982), a novel that was later
adapted for television. This success was followed by* Linden Hills
(1985), Mama Day *(1988),* Bailey's Cafe *(1993), and* The Men
of Brewster Place *(1998). Naylor's short fiction and essays have appeared widely, and she has also edited* Children of the Night: Best
Short Stories by Black Writers, 1967–*(1995).*

*More than any other form of prejudiced language, racial slurs
are intended to wound and shame. In the following essay, which first
appeared in the* New York Times *in 1986, Naylor remembers a
time when a third-grade classmate called her a nigger. By examining the ways in which words can take on meaning depending on who
uses them and to what purpose, Naylor concludes that "words themselves are innocuous; it is the consensus that gives them true power."*

WRITING TO DISCOVER: *Have you or someone you know ever
been called a derogatory name? Write about how this made you feel.*

Language is the subject. It is the written form with which I've managed to keep the wolf away from the door and, in diaries, to keep my san-
ity. In spite of this, I consider the written word inferior to the spoken,
and much of the frustration experienced by novelists is the awareness that
whatever we manage to capture in even the most transcendent passages
falls far short of the richness of life. Dialogue achieves its power in the dynamics of a fleeting moment of sight, sound, smell, and touch.

I'm not going to enter the debate here about whether it is language
that shapes reality or vice versa. That battle is doomed to be waged
whenever we seek intermittent reprieve from the chicken and egg dispute. I will simply take the position that the spoken word, like the written
word, amounts to a nonsensical arrangement of sounds or letters without
a consensus that assigns "meaning." And building from the meanings of

what we hear, we order reality. Words themselves are innocuous; it is the consensus that gives them true power.

I remember the first time I heard the word *nigger*. In my third-grade class, our math tests were being passed down the rows, and as I handed the papers to a little boy in back of me, I remarked that once again he had received a much lower mark than I did. He snatched his test from me and spit out that word. Had he called me a nymphomaniac or a necrophiliac, I couldn't have been more puzzled. I didn't know what a nigger was, but I know that whatever it meant, it was something he shouldn't have called me. This was verified when I raised my hand, and in a loud voice repeated what he had said and watched the teacher scold him for using a "bad" word. I was later to go home and ask the inevitable question that every black parent must face — "Mommy, what does *nigger* mean?"

And what exactly did it mean? Thinking back, I realize that this could not have been the first time the word was used in my presence. I was part of a large extended family that had migrated from the rural South after World War II and formed a close-knit network that gravitated around my maternal grandparents. Their ground-floor apartment in one of the buildings they owned in Harlem was a weekend mecca for my immediate family, along with countless aunts, uncles, and cousins who brought along assorted friends. It was a bustling and open house with assorted neighbors and tenants popping in and out to exchange bits of gossip, pick up an old quarrel, or referee the ongoing checkers game in which my grandmother cheated shamelessly. They were all there to let down their hair and put up their feet after a week of labor in the factories, laundries, and shipyards of New York.

Amid the clamor, which could reach deafening proportions — two   5
or three conversations going on simultaneously, punctuated by the sound of a baby's crying somewhere in the back rooms or out on the street — there was still a rigid set of rules about what was said and how. Older children were sent out of the living room when it was time to get into the juicy details about "you-know-who" up on the third floor who had gone and gotten herself "p-r-e-g-n-a-n-t!" But my parents, knowing that I could spell well beyond my years, always demanded that I follow the others out to play. Beyond sexual misconduct and death, everything else was considered harmless for our young ears. And so among the anecdotes of the triumphs and disappointments in the various workings of their lives, the word *nigger* was used in my presence, but it was set within contexts and inflections that caused it to register in my mind as something else.

In the singular, the word was always applied to a man who had distinguished himself in some situation that brought their approval for his strength, intelligence, or drive:

"Did Johnny *really* do that?"

"I'm telling you, that nigger pulled in $6,000 of overtime last year. Said he got enough for a down payment on a house."

When used with a possessive adjective by a woman — "my nigger" — it became a term of endearment for her husband or boyfriend. But it could be more than just a term applied to a man. In their mouths it became the pure essence of manhood — a disembodied force that channeled their past history of struggle and present survival against the odds into a victorious statement of being: "Yeah, that old foreman found out quick enough — you don't mess with a nigger."

In the plural, it became a description of some group within the community that had overstepped the bounds of decency as my family defined it. Parents who neglected their children, a drunken couple who fought in public, people who simply refused to look for work, those with excessively dirty mouths or unkempt households were all "trifling niggers." This particular circle could forgive hard times, unemployment, the occasional bout of depression — they had gone through all of that themselves — but the unforgivable sin was a lack of self-respect.

A woman could never be a "nigger" in the singular, with its connotation of confirming worth. The noun *girl* was its closest equivalent in that sense, but only when used in direct address and regardless of the gender doing the addressing. *Girl* was a token of respect for a woman. The one-syllable word was drawn out to sound like three in recognition of the extra ounce of wit, nerve, or daring that the woman had shown in the situation under discussion.

"G-i-r-l, stop. You mean you said that to his face?"

But if the word was used in a third-person reference or shortened so that it almost snapped out of the mouth, it always involved some element of communal disapproval. And age became an important factor in these exchanges. It was only between individuals of the same generation, or from any older person to a younger (but never the other way around), that *girl* would be considered a compliment.

I don't agree with the argument that use of the word *nigger* at this social stratum of the black community was an internalization of racism. The dynamics were the exact opposite: the people in my grandmother's living room took a word that whites used to signify worthlessness or degradation and rendered it impotent. Gathering there together, they transformed *nigger* to signify the varied and complex human beings they knew themselves to be. If the word was to disappear totally from the mouths of even the most liberal of white society, no one in that room was naive enough to believe it would disappear from white minds. Meeting the word head-on, they proved it had absolutely nothing to do with the way they were determined to live their lives.

So there must have been dozens of times that *nigger* was spoken in front of me before I reached the third grade. But I didn't "hear" it until it was said by a small pair of lips that had already learned it could be a way to humiliate me. That was the word I went home and asked my mother about. And since she knew that I had to grow up in America, she took me in her lap and explained.

FOCUSING ON CONTENT

1. How, according to Naylor, do words get meanings?

2. Why does the boy sitting behind Naylor call her a nigger (3)? Why is she confused by this name-calling?

3. When Naylor was growing up, what two meanings did the word *girl* convey? How were those meanings defined by the speaker? In what way was age an important factor in the correct uses of *girl*?

4. Why does Naylor disagree with the notion that the use of the word *nigger* within her community was an internalization of racism?

FOCUSING ON WRITING

1. Naylor begins her essay with an abstract discussion about how words derive their meaning and power. How does this introduction tie in with her anecdote and discussion of the word *nigger*? (Glossary: *Abstract/Concrete*) Why is the introduction vital to the overall message of her essay?

2. Naylor says she must have heard the word *nigger* many times while she was growing up; yet she "heard" it for the first time when she was in the third grade (15). How does she explain this seeming contradiction? (Glossary: *Paradox*)

3. Define what *nigger* means to Naylor in the context of her family. (Glossary: *Definition*) Why do you suppose she offers so little in the way of definition of her classmate's use of the word?

4. How would you characterize Naylor's tone in her essay? (Glossary: *Tone*) Is she angry, objective, cynical, or something else? Cite examples of her diction to support your answer. (Glossary: *Diction*)

LANGUAGE IN ACTION

Naylor's essay discusses how those in her community used the word *nigger* for their own purposes and "rendered it impotent" (14). Nevertheless, the word still has a lot of negative power, as revealed in the following 1995 essay by Keith Woods, which was published by the Poynter Institute for Media Studies.

The consensus to which Naylor refers — here represented by Mark Fuhrman — gives the word that power, making news organizations report it in euphemisms or as a deleted expletive. You may remember that Mark Fuhrman was a Los Angeles homocide detective whose racial profiling and negative attitude toward African Americans made him one of the most controversial figures in the O. J. Simpson trial. In preparation for class discussion, think about your position on the following questions: What should be done about the word *nigger*? Should African Americans use it and try to "render it impotent" by creating their own prevailing context for it? Should the word be suppressed, forced into the fringes of racist thought, and represented in euphemisms? Or is there another way to address the word's negative power?

AN ESSAY ON A WICKEDLY
POWERFUL WORD

When I heard Mark Fuhrman's voice saying the word "nigger," I heard a lynch mob. I saw the grim and gleeful faces of murderous white men. I felt the coarse, hairy rope. I smelled the sap of the hangin' tree and saw Billie Holiday's "strange fruit" dangling from its strongest limb.

What a wickedly powerful word, nigger. So many other slurs could have slithered from Fuhrman's tongue and revealed his racism without provoking those images.

Jiggaboo.

Spade.

Coon.

I hear the hatred in those words, but I don't feel the fire's heat the way I do when this white former policeman says nigger. Somewhere in that visceral reflex is the reason news organizations had to use that word this time around.

Somewhere in the sting of seeing it, hearing it, feeling it is the reason they should think hard before using it the next time.

In context, there is no other way to report what Mark Furhman said. "Racial epithet" doesn't quite get it, does it? "Spearchucker" is a racial epithet, but it doesn't make you see burnt crosses and white sheets. Just rednecks.

The "n-word" sounds silly, childish, something you'd say when you don't want your 3-year-old to know what you're talking about. And "n----?" What does that accomplish other than to allow newspapers the dubious out of saying, "Well, it's actually the reader who's saying nigger, not us."

When Mark Fuhrman or any person armed with a club or a gun or a bat or a judicial robe or a teaching certificate or any measure of power says "nigger," it's more than an insult. It summons all the historic and modern-day violence that is packed into those six letters.

Nigger is "Know your place."

Nigger is, "I am better than you."

Nigger is, "I can frame you or flunk you or beat you or kill you because . . .".

Nigger is, "I own you."

You just can't convey that definition with n-dash-dash-dash-dash-dash. You can't communicate it with bleeps or blurbs or euphemisms. The problem is that sometimes the only way to do your job as a journalist is to say or write the word that furthers the mission of racists.

I'd like to believe that there's some lessening of harm every time the word sees the light of day. I once fantasized about a day when a group of black rappers or comedians would appropriate the white sheets and hoods of the KKK and go gallivanting across MTV or HBO and forever render that image so utterly ridiculous that no self-respecting racist would ever wear it again.

But then, Richard Pryor tried to appropriate nigger, didn't he? Took it right from the white folks and turned it into a career before he thought better of it. So did the rappers NWA ("Niggas With Attitudes"). So did my friends on the streets of New Orleans. So has a generation of young black people today.

Still, the definition didn't change.

Dick Gregory tried it. In the dedication of his autobiography, "Nigger," the comedian-turned-activist wrote: "Dear Momma — Wherever you are, if ever you hear the word "nigger" again, remember they are advertising my book."

He wrote that 31 years ago, but if Lucille Gregory were here to hear Mark Fuhrman, she'd surely know he wasn't talking about her son's novel. The definition doesn't change. It doesn't hurt any less after three decades. No less after three centuries.

It's the same word, spiked with the same poison, delivering the same message of inferiority, degradation, hatred, and shame. The same word whether it's Fuhrman saying it or Huck Finn or Def Comedy Jam or Snoop Doggy Dogg or my old friends from Touro Street (Because, they do call themselves nigger, you know).

It hurts every time it's in the paper or on the air or in the street. Every time. Sometimes there's no way around using it in the media, but only sometimes.

Could there come a day when you see it or read it or hear it from the homeboys so much that you hardly notice? When your eyebrow doesn't arch as often or your jaw suddenly drop when the six o'clock anchor plops the word onto your living room coffee table?

Maybe. And you might even say, that day, "Oh, they're just talking about niggers again."

Are we better off then?

WRITING SUGGESTIONS

1. Write an essay in which you describe the process through which you became aware of prejudice, either toward yourself or toward another person or group of people. Did a specific event spark your awareness, such as that detailed in your Writing to Discover entry? Or did you become aware of prejudice in a more gradual way? Did you learn about prejudice primarily from your peers, your parents, or someone else? How did your new awareness affect you? How have your experience(s) shaped the way you think and feel about prejudice today?

2. In addition to discussing the word *nigger*, Naylor talks about the use of *girl*, a word with far less negative baggage but one that can still be offensive when used in an inappropriate context. Write an essay in which you discuss your use of a contextually sensitive word. What is its strict definition? How do you use it? In what context(s) might its use be inappropriate? Why is the word used in different ways?

PICTURING LANGUAGE

"I Have a Dream," the keynote address for the March on Washington on June 23, 1963, is one of the most renowned and recognized speeches of the past century. Delivered from the steps of the Lincoln Memorial to commemorate the centennial of the Emancipation Proclamation, King's speech resonates with hope even as it condemns racial oppression. How do you read King's facial expression in this photograph? How do you read the facial expressions of those standing in support of him? What mood is conveyed by the scene depicted in this photograph?

I Have a Dream

Martin Luther King Jr.

Martin Luther King Jr., son of a Baptist minister, was born in 1929 and ordained at the age of eighteen. King went on to study at Morehouse College, Crozer Theological Seminary, Boston University, and Chicago Theological Seminary. He first came to prominence in 1955 when he led a successful boycott against the segregated bus system of Montgomery, Alabama. As the first president of the Southern Christian Leadership Conference, King promoted a policy of massive but nonviolent resistance to racial injustice. The leading spokesman for the civil rights movement during the 1950s and 1960s, he also championed women's rights and protested the Vietnam War. In 1964 his efforts won him the Nobel Peace Prize. King was assassinated in April 1968 after he spoke at a rally in Memphis, Tennessee.

King delivered "I Have a Dream" in 1963 from the steps of the Lincoln Memorial to more than two hundred thousand people who had come to Washington, D.C., to demonstrate for civil rights. In this mighty sermon — replete with allusions to the Bible, the Negro spiritual tradition, and great documents and speeches of the past — King presented his indictment of the present and his vision of the future.

WRITING TO DISCOVER: *Have you ever heard a speech that you found particularly inspiring or moving? Make some notes about why the speech or the speaker was so effective. How did the speech affect the way you now think about the speaker's subject?*

I am happy to join with you today in what will go down in history as the greatest demonstration for freedom in the history of our nation.

Five score years ago, a great American, in whose symbolic shadow we stand today, signed the Emancipation Proclamation. This momentous decree came as a great beacon light of hope to millions of Negro slaves who had been seared in the flames of withering injustice. It came as a joyous daybreak to end the long night of their captivity. But one hundred years later, the Negro still is not free. One hundred years later, the life of the Negro is still sadly crippled by the manacles of segregation and the chains of discrimination. One hundred years later, the Negro lives on a lonely island of poverty in the midst of a vast ocean of material prosperity. One hundred years later, the Negro is still anguished in the corners of American society and finds himself in exile in his own land. And so we have come here today to dramatize a shameful condition.

In a sense we have come to our nation's capital to cash a check. When the architects of our republic wrote the magnificent words of the Constitution and the Declaration of Independence, they were signing a promissory note to which every American was to fall heir. This note was the promise that all men — yes, Black men as well as white men — would be guaranteed the inalienable rights of life, liberty, and the pursuit of happiness.

It is obvious today that America has defaulted on this promissory note insofar as her citizens of color are concerned. Instead of honoring this sacred obligation, America has given the Negro people a bad check, a check which has come back marked "insufficient funds." But we refuse to believe that the bank of justice is bankrupt. We refuse to believe that there are insufficient funds in the great vaults of opportunity of this nation; and so we have come to cash this check, a check that will give us upon demand the riches of freedom and the security of justice.

We have also come to this hallowed spot to remind America of the   5
fierce urgency of *now*. This is no time to engage in the luxury of cooling off or to take the tranquilizing drug of gradualism. *Now* is the time to make real the promises of democracy. *Now* is the time to rise from the dark and desolate valley of segregation to the sunlit path of racial justice. Now is the time to lift our nation from the quicksands of racial injustice to the solid rock of brotherhood. *Now* is the time to make justice a reality for all of God's children.

It would be fatal for the nation to overlook the urgency of the moment. This sweltering summer of the Negro's legitimate discontent will not pass until there is an invigorating autumn of freedom and equality. Nineteen sixty-three is not an end, but a beginning. And those who hope that the Negro needed to blow off steam and will now be content will have a rude awakening if the nation returns to business as usual. There will be neither rest nor tranquility in America until the Negro is granted his citizenship rights. The whirlwinds of revolt will continue to shake the foundations of our nation until the bright day of justice emerges.

But there is something that I must say to my people who stand on the warm threshold which leads into the palace of justice. In the process of gaining our rightful place, we must not be guilty of wrongful deeds. Let us not seek to satisfy our thirst for freedom by drinking from the cup of bitterness and hatred. We must forever conduct our struggle on the high plane of dignity and discipline. We must not allow our creative protest to degenerate into physical violence. Again and again we must rise to the majestic heights of meeting physical force with soul force. And the marvelous new militancy which has engulfed the Negro community must not lead us to a distrust of all white people; for many of our white brothers, as evidenced by their presence here today, have come to realize that their destiny is tied up with our destiny, and they have come to realize that their freedom is inextricably bound to our freedom.

We cannot walk alone. And as we walk we must make the pledge that we shall always march ahead. We cannot turn back. There are those who are asking the devotees of civil rights, "When will you be satisfied?" We can never be satisfied as long as the Negro is the victim of the unspeakable horrors of police brutality. We can never be satisfied as long as our bodies, heavy with the fatigue of travel, cannot gain lodging in the motels of the highways and the hotels of the cities. We cannot be satisfied as long as the Negro's basic mobility is from a smaller ghetto to a larger one. We can never be satisfied as long as our children are stripped of their selfhood and robbed of their dignity by signs stating "For Whites Only." We cannot be satisfied as long as the Negro in Mississippi cannot vote and a Negro in New York believes he has nothing for which to vote. No, no, we are not satisfied, and we will not be satisfied until justice rolls down like waters and righteousness like a mighty stream.

I am not unmindful that some of you have come here out of great trials and tribulations. Some of you have come fresh from narrow jail cells. Some of you have come from areas where your quest for freedom left you battered by the storms of persecution and staggered by the winds of police brutality. You have been the veterans of creative suffering. Continue to work with the faith that unearned suffering is redemptive.

Go back to Mississippi, and go back to Alabama. Go back to South   10
Carolina. Go back to Georgia. Go back to Louisiana. Go back to the slums and ghettos of our Northern cities, knowing that somehow this situation can and will be changed. Let us not wallow in the valley of despair.

I say to you today, my friends, even though we face the difficulties of today and tomorrow, I still have a dream. It is a dream deeply rooted in the American dream. I have a dream that one day this nation will rise up and live out the true meaning of its creed: "We hold these truths to be self-evident, that all men are created equal." I have a dream that one day, on the red hills of Georgia, sons of former slaves and the sons of former slave owners will be able to sit down together at the table of brotherhood. I have a dream that one day even the state of Mississippi, a state sweltering with the heat of injustice, sweltering with the heat of oppression, will be transformed into an oasis of freedom and justice. I have a dream that my four little children will one day live in a nation where they will not be judged by the color of their skin, but by the content of their character.

I have a dream today. I have a dream that one day down in Alabama — with its vicious racists, with its governor's lips dripping with the words of interposition and nullification — one day right there in Alabama, little Black boys and Black girls will be able to join hands with little white boys and white girls as sisters and brothers.

I have a dream today. I have a dream that one day every valley shall be exalted and every hill and mountain shall be made low, the rough places will be made plain and the crooked places will be made straight, and the glory of the Lord shall be revealed, and all flesh shall see it together.

This is our hope. This is the faith that I go back to the South with. And with this faith we will be able to hew out of the mountain of despair a stone of hope. With this faith we will be able to transform the jangling discords of our nation into a beautiful symphony of brotherhood. With this faith we will be able to work together, to play together, to struggle together, to go to jail together, to stand up for freedom together, knowing that we will be free one day.

And this will be the day — this will be the day when all of God's chil-   15
dren will be able to sing with new meaning:

> My country, 'tis of thee,
> Sweet land of liberty,
>   Of thee I sing;
> Land where my fathers died,
> Land of the Pilgrims' pride,
> From every mountainside
>   Let freedom ring.

And if America is to be a great nation, this must become true.

And so let freedom ring from the prodigious hilltops of New Hampshire. Let freedom ring from the mighty mountains of New York. Let freedom ring from the heightening Alleghenies of Pennsylvania. Let freedom ring from the snow-capped Rockies of Colorado. Let freedom ring from the curvaceous slopes of California.

But not only that. Let freedom ring from Stone Mountain of Georgia. Let freedom ring from Lookout Mountain of Tennessee. Let freedom ring from every hill and molehill of Mississippi. "From every mountainside let freedom ring."

And when this happens — when we allow freedom to ring, when we let it ring from every village and every hamlet, from every state and every city — we will be able to speed up that day when all of God's children, Black men and white men, Jews and Gentiles, Protestants and Catholics, will be able to join hands and sing in the words of the old Negro spiritual: "Free at last! Free at last! Thank God Almighty. We are free at last!"

FOCUSING ON CONTENT

1. Why does King say that the Constitution and the Declaration of Independence act as a "promissory note" (3) to the American people? In what way has America "defaulted" (4) on its promise?

2. What does King mean when he says that in gaining a rightful place in society "we must not be guilty of wrongful deeds" (7)? Why is the issue so important to him?

3. When *will* King be satisfied in his quest for civil rights?

4. What, in a nutshell, is King's dream? What vision does he have for the future?

FOCUSING ON WRITING

1. King uses parallel constructions and repetition throughout his speech. Identify the phrases and words that he particularly emphasizes. Explain what these techniques add to the persuasiveness of his argument.

2. King makes liberal use of metaphor — and metaphorical imagery — in his speech. (Glossary: *Figures of Speech*) Choose a few examples, and examine what they add to the speech. How do they help King engage his listeners' feelings of injustice and give them hope for a better future?

3. King delivered his address to two audiences: the huge audience that listened to him in person, and another, even larger audience. (Glossary: *Audience*) What is that larger audience? What did King do in his speech to catch its attention and to deliver his point?

4. Explain King's choice of a title. (Glossary: *Title*) Why is the title particularly appropriate given the context in which the speech was delivered? What other titles might he have used?

5. Examine the speech, and determine how King organized his presentation. (Glossary: *Organization*) What are the main sections of the speech, and what is the purpose of each? How does the organization serve King's overall purpose? (Glossary: *Purpose*)

LANGUAGE IN ACTION

In using the photograph on the facing page of Martin Luther King Jr. in its "Think Different" advertising campaign, the Apple Computer company is relying on our cultural memory of King's "I Have a Dream" speech and of King as a person who was creative in his efforts to promote racial justice. To what extent does achieving racial equality depend on "thinking differently"?

WRITING SUGGESTIONS

1. King's language is powerful and his imagery is vivid, but the effectiveness of any speech depends partially upon its delivery. If read in monotone, King's use of repetition and parallel language would sound almost redundant rather than inspiring. Keeping presentation in mind, write a short speech that argues a point of view about which you feel strongly. Use King's speech as a model, and incorporate imagery, repetition, and metaphor to communicate your point. Read your speech aloud to a friend to see how it flows and how effective your use of language is. Refine your presentation — both your text and how you deliver it — and then present your speech to your class.

2. King uses a variety of metaphors in his speech, but a single encompassing metaphor can be useful to establish the tone and purpose of an essay. Write a description based on a metaphor that conveys an overall impression from the beginning. Try to avoid clichés ("My dorm is a beehive," "My life is an empty glass"), but make your metaphor readily understandable. For example, you could say, "A police siren is a lullaby in my neighborhood," or "My town is a car that has gone 15,000 miles since its last oil change." Carry the metaphor through the entire description.

Separate and Unequal

Urvashi Vaid

The Indian American lawyer and social activist, Urvashi Vaid, is a lesbian/gay community and grass-roots organizer who has been involved in the gay rights movement since the early 1980s. She was born in India in 1950 and moved to the United States with her family when she was eight years old. She told Vanity Fair, *"I was a very awkward young girl. I spoke with an Indian accent. I had these very thick glasses. I had long hair, very straight hair, Indian hair, down to my waist. I was such an intellectual. I read voraciously, and by the time I was 12, I was going through my parents' library. . . . I lived a lot in my head." After graduating from Vassar College in 1979 she entered Northeastern University Law School. In 1983 she founded the Boston Lesbian/Gay Political Alliance, a group that interviews and endorses candidates for political office and advocates for Boston's gay community. After graduating from law school in 1983, Vaid became involved with the National Gay Lesbian Task Force (NGLTF) and rose to become its director of public relations and in 1989 the executive director of its Policy Institute in Washington, D.C. In 1992, she resigned to write the book* Virtual Equality, *published in 1995.*

In the following "Last Word" column, taken from the October 29, 2002, issue of the Advocate, *a NGLTF publication, Vaid argues for more diversity within groups fighting for their freedom from oppression: "Mostly we live in parallel universes — gay men, African Americans, Latinos. We may find ourselves in the same rooms on occasion, but we do not mix culturally or very deeply. Our lives are barely more integrated than they were in the 1950s."*

WRITING TO DISCOVER: *We use language, particularly labels, to build identity and unity within groups of people — but can those labels work against such groups as the elderly, Native Americans, African Americans, and gays by isolating them from our larger society? Is it possible to build identity for special interest groups at the same time that we come together in common causes that cut across special interests?*

Recently I went to three activities that made me marvel at the intersections of age, class, and race embedded in the broad phrase *gay community.* First, I saw a triple-bill all-ages show by queer-friendly girl punks Le Tigre and Thalia Zedek, emceed by dyke poet Eileen Myles. The crowd was largely young, with a sizable minority of late-30- to 40-something lesbians. Like most punk audiences, it was fairly white, and though the dress code of the rock scene hides class, it was not the Prada set.

Next I attended a daylong seminar on race in America and how it affects the coalitions working for social justice. The seminar grew out of Lani Guinier and Gerald Torres's new book, *The Miner's Canary*, which argues that race should be understood as a political and not a biological category. Those who attended were a mix that defines the America you see in New York City every day — a variety of ages, sexual orientations, races, and classes. The day's highlight was a performance by Blackout, a poetry and hip-hop collective, which seemed, at least for an hour, to unify a room of white-haired law school deans, dreadlocked activists, middle-aged trade unionists, dykes with crew cuts, and people of all colors.

Later that same week I went to an extraordinary birthday party for a friend. It gathered his formidable political network — everyone from the president (Clinton, that is) to several senators, congresspeople, and GLBT activists. The evening was a lot of fun, but the crowd's vast privilege, and my own within it, made me take a critical look at myself.

There we were a crowd of comfortable, wealthy middle-aged and old mostly white people, enjoying the access that money buys, enjoying great food, having an experience that felt like utopia but had more in common with surrealism in the ways it ignored the presence of homophobia, racism, and economic inequality in the room with us. I feel the same uneasiness whenever I participate in a GLBT fund-raiser for a national organization — who is *not* in the room says as much as who is. And the people present in most of the rooms I am in is a homogenous group indeed.

Mostly we live in parallel universes — gay men, lesbians, African   5
Americans, Latinos. We may find ourselves in the same rooms on occasion, but we do not mix culturally or very deeply. Our lives are barely more integrated than they were in the 1950s.

The class divisions in the gay community are equally automatic because middle- and upper-middle-class people are the ones who compose the majority of GLBT organizations — and are the majority of its leaders. Poor GLBT people have few national advocates, little cultural visibility, and no political cache. Yet AIDS activists constantly remind us that more than 50 percent of people living with AIDS get their primary health care from Medicaid, a poverty program. And the statistics on income-distribution in GLBT communities suggest that there is a vast segment of our own who are part of the America still struggling to achieve a decent quality of life.

What's more, *intergenerationality* remains an awkward word and an even more elusive reality in GLBT communities: Age divides us as deeply as race and class. Ironically, age segregates us at the very instant that our movement is more of an "all-ages show" than ever — people of every generation are in our communities, organizing, building institutions, and living open lives.

These encounters reminded me of the urgency of conscious organizing to disrupt the momentum that leaves us separated by these deep divisions. I remain optimistic in my belief in multiracial spaces, in cross-generational interaction, in GLBT people supporting those who press for greater equity and fairness in our society. But creating inclusive communities is an aspiration our movement has long expressed — and its realization will require from many more of us a willingness to challenge our own separatism, to leave our parallel universes behind.

FOCUSING ON CONTENT

1. Vaid says in her opening sentence that the three events she attended made her marvel at the "intersections of age, class, and race embedded in the broad phrase *gay community*." She goes on to talk about the three events and, in so doing, ends up expressing her belief that something is not quite right among gays. What bothers her?

2. Vaid references situations in which people of differing ages, classes, and races have come together. She also speaks of a separatism in the gay community. How does she reconcile these apparently conflicting views? How do you? Does sharing space at social occasions necessarily constitute integration? Explain.

3. As Vaid says, "Our lives are barely more integrated than they were in the 1950s"(5). Why does she think separatism is not a good idea? Who is hurt by it?

4. Who is Vaid's audience for this article? (Glossary: *Audience*) What does she want her readers to consider doing?

5. Does the language used to describe and label the various GLBT (gay, lesbian, bisexual, transsexual) groups work to their benefit or their detriment, or both? Explain.

FOCUSING ON WRITING

1. What is Vaid's purpose in writing? (Glossary: *Purpose*) To argue, to explain, or to describe? Or does she do some of each? Explain.

2. What is Vaid's thesis? (Glossary: *Thesis*) Where is her thesis statement found? Does she support her thesis with evidence? (Glossary: *Evidence*)

3. How does Vaid link her paragraphs to build coherence? (Glossary: *Coherence* and *Transitions*)

4. What does Vaid mean by "parallel universes"(5)? (Glossary: *Diction*) Why is it a useful phrase for her?

LANGUAGE IN ACTION

Dominant groups within cultures have often used language to maintain their superior positions and to disempower others. For example, African Americans have been referred to by abusive terms such as *darky, nigger, spade,* and *blood*. Calling a woman *gal, little woman, the Mrs.,* or *honey* is patronizing and, in certain circumstances, insulting. Language that disempowers groups may be blatant or subtle. Not only can language deny equality, it can deny individuality as well. Assuming that all nurses are women and all pilots are men or that the president of a company is a man and the secretary to the president is a woman may lead you astray. To assume that all young people are immature or reckless is no better than assuming that all middle-aged people are out of touch or that all people in their later years are senile. Not all Latinos have dark complexions. Not all Southerners are Protestants. Not all East Asians are good at math and science. To believe so is to fall prey to stereotypes, to take from people their individuality and uniqueness, to deny reality.

In an effort to avoid language that promotes stereotypes, we should try to use bias-free words. For example, instead of *fireman,* use *fire fighter;* or, instead of *handicapped,* use *physically impaired.* Using these two examples as models, what bias-free alternatives can you suggest for each of the words in the left column?

USING BIAS-FREE LANGUAGE

Instead of	*Use*
blind	_____
mailman	_____
spic	_____
Indian	_____
faggot	_____
freshman	_____
deaf	_____
salesman	_____
stewardess	_____
newsman	_____
colored people	_____
landlady	_____

Discuss your alternative language with other members of your class.

WRITING SUGGESTIONS

1. Vaid's essay highlights a dilemma for those in society who are seeking equality. Even before we read her essay, we learn from her title that something is amiss. How can those in the gay community coalesce around similar beliefs while at the same time recognize the need for diversity and interaction among others who aspire to the same ideals of equality and fair treatment within society? Express your thoughts on this dilemma as you attempt to reconcile the differences that exist within the gay community. Can we belong to groups that are separate *and* equal at the same time?

2. Write an essay proposing a language solution to Vaid's dilemma of inequality in the gay community. Is there some language or labeling that might be used to encourage more inclusion and integration among gays and lesbians regardless of age, color, and class?

Black Men and Public Spaces

BRENT STAPLES

Brent Staples is an important voice in American culture. He was born in 1951 in Chester, Pennsylvania, an industrial city southwest of Philadelphia. He studied at Widener University in Chester and the University of Chicago, where he earned his Ph.D. in psychology. Formerly a teacher, Staples began his newspaper career as a reporter for the Chicago Sun-Times. *He later became an editor for the* New York Times Book Review *and now serves as assistant metropolitan editor for the* New York Times. *His memoir* Parallel Time: Growing Up in Black and White *(1994) won the 1995 Anisfield-Wolff Award, also given to such notable African American writers as James Baldwin, Ralph Ellison, and Zora Neale Hurston.*

In "Black Men and Public Spaces," which first appeared in Ms. *magazine in 1986, Staples recounts his experiences moving through public spaces at night. After innocently scaring a woman one night, Staples writes, "It was in the echo of that terrified woman's footfalls that I first began to know the unwieldy inheritance I'd come into — the ability to alter public space in ugly ways."*

WRITING TO DISCOVER: *Reflect on what you know about body language. Are you aware, for example, of the messages that might be conveyed by a person's physical features, gestures, and use of space? Try observing some people around you, in your dormitory, in the school cafeteria, or at work in order to gain some appreciation of the messages that they may be sending that either support or contradict their verbal messages.*

My first victim was a woman — white, well dressed, probably in her late twenties. I came upon her late one evening on a deserted street in Hyde Park, a relatively affluent neighborhood in an otherwise mean, impoverished section of Chicago. As I swung onto the avenue behind her, there seemed to be a discreet, uninflammatory distance between us. Not so. She cast back a worried glance. To her, the youngish black man — a broad six feet two inches with a beard and billowing hair, both hands shoved into the pockets of a bulky military jacket — seemed menacingly close. After a few more quick glimpses, she picked up her pace and was soon running in earnest. Within seconds, she disappeared into a cross street.

That was more than a decade ago. I was twenty-two years old, a graduate student newly arrived at the University of Chicago. It was in the echo of that terrified woman's footfalls that I first began to know the unwieldy inheritance I'd come into — the ability to alter public space in ugly ways. It was clear that she thought herself the quarry of a mugger, a rapist, or worse. Suffering a bout of insomnia, however, I was stalking sleep, not defenseless wayfarers. As a softy who is scarcely able to take a knife to a raw chicken — let alone hold one to a person's throat — I was surprised, embarrassed, and dismayed all at once. Her flight made me feel like an accomplice in tyranny. It also made it clear that I was indistinguishable from the muggers who occasionally seeped into the area from the surrounding ghetto. The first encounter, and those that followed, signified that a vast, unnerving gulf lay between nighttime pedestrians — particularly women — and me. And I soon gathered that being perceived as dangerous is a hazard in itself. I only needed to turn a corner into a dicey situation, or crowd some frightened, armed person in a foyer somewhere, or make an errant move after being pulled over by a policeman. Where fear and weapons meet — and they often do in urban America — there is always the possibility of death.

In that first year, my first away from my hometown, I was to become thoroughly familiar with the language of fear. At dark, shadowy intersections, I could cross in front of a car stopped at a traffic light and elicit the *thunk, thunk, thunk, thunk* of the driver — black, white, male, or female — hammering down the door locks. On less traveled streets after dark, I grew accustomed to but never comfortable with people crossing to the other side of the street rather than pass me. Then there were the standard unpleasantries with policemen, doormen, bouncers, cabdrivers, and others whose business it is to screen out troublesome individuals *before* there is any nastiness.

I moved to New York nearly two years ago and I have remained an avid night walker. In central Manhattan, the near-constant crowd cover minimizes tense one-on-one street encounters. Elsewhere — in SoHo, for example, where sidewalks are narrow and tightly spaced buildings shut out the sky — things can get very taut indeed.

After dark, on the warrenlike streets of Brooklyn where I live, I often   5
see women who fear the worst from me. They seem to have set their faces on neutral, and with their purse straps strung across their chests bandolier-style, they forge ahead as though bracing themselves against being tackled. I understand, of course, that the danger they perceive is not a hallucination. Women are particularly vulnerable to street violence, and young black males are drastically overrepresented among the perpetrators of that violence. Yet these truths are no solace against the kind of alienation that comes of being ever the suspect, a fearsome entity with whom pedestrians avoid making eye contact.

It is not altogether clear to me how I reached the ripe old age of twenty-two without being conscious of the lethality nighttime pedestrians attributed to me. Perhaps it was because in Chester, Pennsylvania, the small, angry industrial town where I came of age in the 1960s, I was scarcely noticeable against a backdrop of gang warfare, street knifings, and murders. I grew up one of the good boys, had perhaps a half-dozen fistfights. In retrospect, my shyness of combat has clear sources.

As a boy, I saw countless tough guys locked away; I have since buried several, too. They were babies, really — a teenage cousin, a brother of twenty-two, a childhood friend in his mid-twenties — all gone down in episodes of bravado played out in the streets. I came to doubt the virtues of intimidation early on. I chose, perhaps unconsciously, to remain a shadow — timid, but a survivor.

The fearsomeness mistakenly attributed to me in public places often has a perilous flavor. The most frightening of these confusions occurred in the late 1970s and early 1980s, when I worked as a journalist in Chicago. One day, rushing into the office of a magazine I was writing for with a deadline story in hand, I was mistaken for a burglar. The office manager called security and, with an ad hoc posse, pursued me through the labyrinthine halls, nearly to my editor's door. I had no way of proving who I was. I could only move briskly toward the company of someone who knew me.

Another time I was on assignment for a local paper and killing time before an interview. I entered a jewelry store on the city's affluent Near North Side. The proprietor excused himself and returned with an enormous red Doberman pinscher straining at the end of a leash. She stood, the dog extended toward me, silent to my questions, her eyes bulging nearly out of her head. I took a cursory look around, nodded, and bade her good night.

Relatively speaking, however, I never fared as badly as another black   10 male journalist. He went to nearby Waukegan, Illinois, a couple of summers ago to work on a story about a murderer who was born there. Mistaking the reporter for the killer, police officers hauled him from his car at gunpoint and but for his press credentials would probably have tried to book him. Such episodes are not uncommon. Black men trade tales like this all the time.

Over the years, I learned to smother the rage I felt at so often being taken for a criminal. Not to do so would surely have led to madness. I now take precautions to make myself less threatening. I move about with care, particularly late in the evening. I give a wide berth to nervous people on subway platforms during the wee hours, particularly when I have exchanged business clothes for jeans. If I happen to be entering a building behind some people who appear skittish, I may walk by, letting them clear the lobby before I return, so as not to seem to be following them. I have been calm and extremely congenial on those rare occasions when I've been pulled over by the police.

And on late-evening constitutionals I employ what has proved to be an excellent tension-reducing measure: I whistle melodies from Beethoven and Vivaldi and the more popular classical composers. Even steely New Yorkers hunching toward nighttime destinations seem to relax, and occasionally they even join in the tune. Virtually everybody seems to sense that a mugger wouldn't be warbling bright, sunny selections from Vivaldi's *Four Seasons*.

FOCUSING ON CONTENT

1. What is Staples's purpose in this essay? (Glossary: *Purpose*)

2. Staples's essay was first published in *Ms.* magazine, a publication that was very influential for young women, particularly in the beginning of the women's movement. Why is Staples's essay appropriate for that magazine? (Glossary: *Audience*)

3. Why is Staples's realization that he might cause fear in someone in a public space so surprising to him? What does he say about himself that explains the surprise he experienced?

4. Staples provides several examples to support his thesis that people have been conditioned to respond negatively to him in public spaces. (Glossary: *Evidence*) Recount several of those experiences. How effective were these examples in helping him make his case?

5. Staples never discusses his situation as an example of the racial prejudice that exists all around him. Would his essay be more or less effective if he made such statements? Explain.

FOCUSING ON WRITING

1. Staples begins his essay with the words: "My first victim was a woman — white, well dressed, probably in her late twenties." What effect did this beginning have on you? (Glossary: *Beginnings and Endings*)

2. What is one of the solutions that Staples has come up with to help him deal with strangers in public spaces? Are his solutions a concession to the fact that he sees no hope of changing attitudes around him, or are they an effort to change peoples' attitudes?

3. How effective is the analogy he uses in the final sentence of the essay? (Glossary: *Analogy*)

4. Discuss how Staples links his paragraphs. (Glossary: *Transitions*) Examine some of his transitions and explain how they work. Is his use of "And" to begin his final paragraph appropriate?

LANGUAGE IN ACTION

Brent Staples's essay is in part about the concept of "territoriality" and the nonverbal messages it sends. Most of our feelings of territoriality remain unconscious until "our territory" is violated. How would you react to each of the following situations?

a. after a class has been meeting for at least three weeks, someone deliberately sat in a seat that you have been regularly occupying

b. in your library or snack bar, if someone moved his or her books or food and sat down while you were temporarily away

c. in an uncrowded library or classroom, someone deliberately sat right next to you

d. in your dorm room or at home, someone deliberately sat (in a chair, at a desk, etc.) that "belongs" to you or another family member

You may wish to share your reactions with those of other members of your class. What conclusions can you draw about the way people regard invasions of their personal space?

WRITING SUGGESTIONS

1. Each of us makes an impression on those around us, either in public spaces or in more intimate surroundings. Each of us also has a more or less sensitive appreciation of the impressions we create on those around us. Describe the impression that you think you create in presenting yourself. Draw on examples of situations over time and in different settings that support the major ideas you are trying to present in your writing.

2. Write an essay that describes the various stereotypes that are created about students. What do you think of your fellow students? How do you think they regard you? How do students see themselves as a group? How does their body language reflect the way they see themselves? Do you think that most students see themselves as others do? Are the stereotypes that are applied to students fair in your judgment?

CASE STUDY:
Political Correctness and Speech Codes

The essays by Ethan Bronner, John Leo, Steven Doloff, and Diane Ravitch we have included in the following Case Study attempt to inform you about political correctness and speech codes issues that are swirling about you in your classrooms, in your dorm rooms, and in newspapers and newsmagazines you read while having your breakfast. We provide you with the resources necessary to understand what political correctness and speech codes are, the serious reasons for how and why they came about on our college campuses, the good that they have brought about, and the extremes to which their meanings have been stretched. We can neither unthinkingly embrace nor humorously dismiss movements that seek to increase sensitivity to the larger problems of prejudice and discrimination in our society. As critical-thinking citizens, we need to know as much as we can about these concerns and to be able to articulate in both speech and writing what we think so that we can be responsible in influencing the direction we take in the future.

> **WRITING TO DISCOVER:** *Reflect on what you know about political correctness and speech codes. Speculate on what might have given rise to them. Do you have any firsthand stories about attempts to censor speech or modify people's language and behavior? How effective have these attempts been? Have you changed the way you think and speak as a result of your growing awareness of the power of speech? How so?*

Big Brother Is Listening

ETHAN BRONNER

Ethan Bronner was born in New York City in 1954. A graduate of Wesleyan University and Columbia University's Graduate School of Journalism, he has been the national education correspondent for the New York Times *since the summer of 1997. He writes about trends in both higher education and grades K–12. Before joining the* Times, *Bronner wrote for the* Boston Globe *for twelve years. While serving as the* Globe's *legal affairs and Supreme Court correspondent in Washington D.C., he authored* Battle for Justice: How the Bork Nomination Shook America *(1989).*

In the following selection, which first appeared in the Education Life supplement to the New York Times *on April 4, 1999, Bronner revisits the speech codes that U.S. colleges and universities put into place more than a decade ago in an effort to create a more sensitive climate. Critics of such codes label them the worst form of political correctness, whereas supporters are fearful of a future without them.*

The issue that gray February day was one of delicate balance: how to assure the freedom to discourse on Hitler's *Mein Kampf,* as one participant put it, but not to use the word "Jew" as a verb, to lecture on sexuality but not to refer to female students as "babes."

The debate — over a faculty speech code — filled the pale blue faculty senate room in Bascom Hall with passion. It was the latest round in a dispute that began on the lakeside campus of the University of Wisconsin nearly two years ago but had been simmering, in some fashion, for generations. A plaque on the building's entrance celebrates freedom of inquiry — the "fearless sifting and winnowing by which alone the truth can be found" — installed after the 1894 exoneration of an economics professor accused of teaching socialism and other "dangerous ideas."

The question on the floor — and it is being mulled on hundreds of campuses across the country, from the University of California to Bowdoin College in Maine — was how to promote such "fearless sifting" while still creating a welcoming environment for groups that have historically felt slighted at American universities. For while robust intellectual inquiry is a self-stated goal of every university, so too is creating a diverse and tolerant nation.

Student and faculty codes punish, sometimes through suspension, expulsion, or firing, words or deeds that create an environment perceived as hostile. Backers say codes insure that minorities and other vulnerable groups will not be mistreated.

"There is a cost to freedom of speech and it is borne unfairly by certain members of the community," asserted Stanlie M. James, a professor of Afro-American and women's studies. "The harm is immeasurable."

Opponents see codes as the worst form of politically correct paternalism.

"We don't want Big Brother stepping in and telling us what to think," said Jason Shepard, a student member of the committee examining the Wisconsin faculty code. "They assume that all minority students, all members of the same group, have the same response to speech. That's ridiculous."

Alan Charles Kors, a professor at the University of Pennsylvania, and Harvey A. Silverglate, a Boston lawyer, sought to document the effect of the codes and similar programs in their 1998 book *The Shadow University.* The university today, they complained, "hands students a moral agenda upon arrival, subjects them to mandatory political re-education, sends them to sensitivity training, submerges their individuality in official group identity, intrudes upon private conscience, treats them with scandalous inequality and, when it chooses, suspends or expels them."

5

Between 1987 and 1992, about a third of the nation's colleges and universities enacted codes of conduct that covered offensive speech, said Jon Gould, a visiting scholar at the University of California, Berkeley, who wrote his doctoral dissertation on codes.

Typical was the code passed in 1987 at the University of Pennsylva-   10
nia that forbade "any behavior, verbal or physical, that stigmatizes or victimizes individuals on the basis of race, ethnic or national origin . . . and that has the purpose or effect of interfering with an individual's academic or work performance; and/or creates an intimidating or offensive academic, living, or work environment."

Most famously, the code was applied against a white Penn student named Eden Jacobowitz in 1993, when he called a group of noisy black sorority sisters outside his window "water buffalo." The university's judicial inquiry officer charged him with racial harassment. An Israeli-born Jew, Mr. Jacobowitz insisted the term — from the Hebrew *behema,* slang for a rude person but literally water buffalo — has no racial overtones. After a highly publicized hearing before an administrative board, charges were dropped. Later, the code was abandoned.

While some codes have been struck down by Federal courts as patently illegal or amended after coming under attack in the media or by students, many colleges and universities still have them, though they are rarely invoked.

That, in fact, was the situation with the faculty code at Wisconsin until last year, when First Amendment advocates decided it was time for it to be abolished. This was partly because the code, which had never led to a disciplinary act, had still been the basis of several investigations of faculty members. Its existence, opponents argued, chilled discourse. The Wisconsin student speech code had been struck down by a Federal court in 1991. Now it was the faculty's turn. But efforts to kill the code proved more complex than imagined.

The February debate began with the usual legal disquisitions from the podium — how to interpret the First Amendment in conjunction with Federal harassment regulations — but shifted course when Amelia Rideau from Montclair, New Jersey, rose to speak.

Ms. Rideau, a 20-year-old junior, recounted how in a recent Chaucer   15
class her professor described a character as "niggardly." Ms. Rideau, a vice president of the Wisconsin Black Student Union, did not know the word, which means stingy and has no racial origins. She was unaware of the controversy in Washington the previous week over the firing (and ultimate rehiring) of a white mayoral aide for using the same word. The only black in the class of fifty, Ms. Rideau said she approached the professor afterward and told him of her feelings.

Ms. Rideau thought the teacher had understood and agreed not to use the word again. But at the next class the professor brought in an article about the Washington flap and began a discussion about it.

"He used the word 'niggardly' over and over, five or six times," she said. "I ran out of the class in tears. It was as if he was saying to me, 'Your opinion has no value.'"

When her speech ended to vigorous applause from minority students in the Madison audience, most members of the faculty senate — historians, geneticists, and philosophers in worn sweaters and hiking shoes — sat in silence. There was no doubting the depth of Ms. Rideau's pain. But there was no way any code could be enacted that would bar a professor from using the word "niggardly." And that put the faculty in a quandary.

"Her talk created a sense that there are things here that students of color want that we can't deliver," David Ward, the university chancellor, asserted later.

Two percent of the student body at the University of Wisconsin, one   20
of the nation's premier research institutions, is black. How to increase that representation is very much a concern of administrators.

"In the early 70s, institutions like ours made promises to recruit minority groups, and by the late 1980s it was clear many had failed," said Roger W. Howard, the associate dean of students. "There built up a very significant level of frustration. We had said we wanted to be a different place, a more welcoming place. Yet we kept getting told that this was not a comfortable place for minorities. So we asked ourselves, 'What else can we do?' And that is partly where the speech codes came from."

After much debate in early March, the faculty senate decided, by a vote of 71 to 62, to narrow its speech code but not quite abolish it. Starting with the pledge that the university is "unswervingly committed to freedom of speech," the new language says that "all expression germane to the instructional setting — including but not limited to information, the presentation or advocacy of ideas, assignment of course materials, and teaching techniques — is protected from disciplinary action." This means that even if students are offended, professors cannot be punished if they prove the words were relevant to the lesson.

Wisconsin is not alone in its concerns or its solution. Attracting and retaining minority students is a top goal of every major university in the face of the growing legal and political threat to race-conscious admissions. In fact, the movement to end the codes is often allied with efforts to end those admissions policies. But just as often, the movement is spearheaded by people who believe universities have trampled on sacred free-speech grounds.

Mount Holyoke College in South Hadley, Massachusetts, is reviewing its student and faculty speech code to support free expression more vigorously. At Southern Utah University, a computer-use policy, which bars downloading material that is "racially offensive, threatening, harassing, or otherwise objectionable," has also come under attack and university review.

Yet, despite some people's belief that colleges today are Stalinist out-   25
posts where the slightest misstep into apparent intolerance is punished by
the political correctness police force (also known as deans of student affairs), campuses report few bias-related incidents. While there are occur-
rences involving hate e-mails or posters with racial slurs and intimidation
of homosexuals, university officials say campuses are not plagued with the
problems of a decade ago, when the codes were drafted.

For both faculty and students, it was a difficult time of transition
from a mostly homogeneous society to a more mixed culture. Before the
1980s, campuses were mostly white-guy clubs: homosexuality was less accepted, campus culture less accommodating of minority concerns, and far
fewer women were found on faculties and in professional schools.

As colleges diversified, speech codes for students and faculty were
seen as one buffer. Brown University ejected a student for yelling racial
and religious epithets outside the dormitories one night; Sarah Lawrence
College brought disciplinary action against a student using an antigay
slur and engaging in "inappropriate laughter" seen as mocking a gay
student.

The University of Connecticut banned "exhibiting, distributing, posting, or advertising publicly offensive, indecent, or abusive matter" after a
1987 incident in which eight Asian American students were spat on and
taunted by six white students. Paradoxically, it was another Asian American, Nina Wu, a junior, who challenged the protective policy by hanging a
poster listing groups she disliked, including "homos," on her dormitory
door. After throwing Ms. Wu out of university housing, the university re-
instated her under a judge's order and withdrew the restrictions.

In the mid-80s, when the Massachusetts Institute of Technology was
still heavily male (today it is nearly half female), a group of women students complained to the provost about sexual harassment on campus.
The provost, John Deutch, asked one of his deputies, Samuel Jay Keyser,
to devise a policy against sexual harassment.

Among the rules written by Mr. Keyser's committee was the banning   30
of any sexually explicit film on campus without a film board's approval.
The board, a mix of faculty, students, and administrative staff members,
was called the Ad Hoc Pornography Screening Committee, and it
adopted guidelines that included an insistence that the film "reflect believable reality or normalcy in the relationships and sexuality displayed"
and that the film "not unfairly reflect the viewpoint and sexual feelings of
men and/or women."

The code was challenged by Adam Dershowitz, a student (and
nephew of Alan Dershowitz, the Harvard law professor), who projected
the movie *Deep Throat* on the wall of an M.I.T. dormitory common
room on registration day, 1987. He was prosecuted by the university
under the code, but the charges were dismissed by a faculty-student
committee, which found that the film rules were "an excessive restraint

on freedom of expression at M.I.T." The code was quietly abandoned several years later.

Conservatives, horrified by what they saw as social engineering, soon joined forces with liberals who were worried about free speech to condemn all such codes. Critics said vigorous, sometimes hurtful debate was the point of a university. As Jonathan Rauch wrote in his 1993 book *Kindly Inquisitors*, "If you insist on an unhostile or nonoffensive environment, then you belong in a monastery, not a university."

Mr. Shepard, the University of Wisconsin student, said such codes do more harm than good by offering false comfort. The better way, he says, is for vulnerable groups to face the discomfort straight on: "Pursuit of knowledge requires us to ask the tough questions," Mr. Shepard, who is gay, said. "And when we do so, people feel uneasy. There is no way around that."

Today, Mr. Keyser, who is retired, agrees. "The codes were a mistake. They were a response to a significant group in our community that was unhappy. But you can't solve the problem with a code. It was an easy solution that didn't work."

That view is not universal. Apart from black, gay, and Hispanic stu-   35
dent groups who say that they suffer from humiliation, a number of women faculty members at Madison recalled the uneasy life before codes. Theresa Duello, a professor of obstetrics and gynecology at Wisconsin's medical school, said that when she joined her department in 1982, she was told by the chairman that he could not believe he had to introduce a woman who was taller than he and thought he would ask her to begin by discussing her first date.

Carin A. Clauss, a law professor who campaigned to keep the code, said she was especially sensitive to the need for regulations supporting minority groups and women because she went to law school when women made up fewer than one percent of the class.

Professor Clauss's main opponent in Madison was Donald Downs, a political scientist who has come full circle. His first foray into the free-expression issue was in 1978, when he wrote a book on American Nazis seeking to march in Skokie, Illinois, home to many Holocaust survivors.

"I really identified with how the survivors felt," Professor Downs recalled. "I argued that targeted racial vilification as a form of assaultive speech crosses the First Amendment line. I hadn't thought hard enough about the special place of free speech in a public forum."

Today, he says, he would favor permitting the Nazis to march in Skokie just as he favors doing away with all speech codes because they sacrifice something too significant. He draws parallels with Prohibition. He also sees an analogy with affirmative action, saying that, like codes, it gives rights to one group by taking rights away from another, something he opposes.

This is a central point made by Professor Kors and Mr. Silverglate in   40
their book *The Shadow University*.

They see the codes as part of a larger liberal orthodoxy imposed by the 60s generation that has taken over college faculties and administrations, especially the offices of student affairs, which promote sensitivity and diversity training during freshman orientation, for dormitory advisers and in classrooms.

They say the main victims of this orthodoxy are those who are not part of it, like Christians who consider homosexuality and abortion unacceptable and find themselves unable to express themselves on campuses.

There are others who say that while they oppose the codes now, they served a role when they were enacted. "There is no question that the codes did, to some unmeasurable extent, influence and help create more appropriate attitudes toward race and gender and sexual orientation," Professor Downs said. "But this was at the cost of instilling fear of intellectual honesty."

Richard Delgado, a law professor at the University of Colorado and an early advocate of codes, says that social scientists increasingly favor what is called the confrontation theory, which holds that the best way to dampen racism is through clear rules that punish offenders because the rules' very existence leads people to conform to their principles. He says this has largely replaced the social-contact theory, which asserts that racism is best overcome by placing people of different creeds in constant contact with one another, and that through such contact they will see the error of racist attitudes.

Despite the codes, despite the changes campuses have made in recent years, the vulnerability felt by minorities remains raw.   45

Michael S. McPherson, the president of Macalester College in St. Paul, says that in October 1997, a black student found racist slurs written on the note board she had hung outside her dormitory room. The culprit was never found but students held a vigil and public meetings. Even though there has been no similar event on the campus since, black students still tell Mr. McPherson how the incident upset them.

It is that gnawing sense of vulnerability that has made the idea of removing the codes unpalatable to the people they were set up to protect. They recognize the shaky legal ground on which they sit — no student speech code that has been challenged in court has survived — and worry that the codes will be abused if left on the books. But they fear the signal such a change would send to minority groups.

"As we have become more integrated, I have a sense that the sorts of incidents we had ten years ago we don't really have today," observed Professor Clauss of Wisconsin. "Now, women make up 47 percent of our law school and things are certainly easier. But we are getting Hmong and Muslim students. I am never sure that minority interests are adequately protected. There was a Muslim student in the health program here who raised religious objections to massage therapy and wanted accommodations to respect his belief. Whether we take those things seriously depends on sensitizing people. Who knows what minority will arrive tomorrow?"

EXAMINING THE ISSUE CRITICALLY

1. Did you ever attend a school or work for a company that had an official speech code, dress code, or some other code governing behavior? In your opinion, what is the purpose of such codes? Do you think they should be strictly enforced or eliminated? Does your opinion about them change depending on the code in question?

2. How do you feel about the use of the word *niggardly*? Is it a legitimate word that can be used in the classroom, or is it a word that can cause such emotional distress despite its actual meaning that it should be avoided altogether?

3. The major issue that Bronner discusses is how colleges and universities and indeed the population at large can chart a course between the protection of the First Amendment right to free speech and the protection of minorities from being mistreated and made to feel unwelcome on college and university campuses. Do you think that there are, or should be, some overriding principles that are applicable in this situation, or do you think that each case that arises will have to be decided on a case-by-case basis? If there are principles that we should not violate, what are they? If such principles are adhered to and people get hurt as a result, what responsibility do college administrators bear?

Who Said PC Is Passé?

John Leo

Dubbed the "cult columnist of the intelligentia" by Vanity Fair, *John Leo writes a weekly column on the state of our culture that appears in* U.S. News & World Report *and in over 140 newspapers across the country. He has been a reporter for the* New York Times, *covering intellectual trends and religion, and a senior writer for* Time *magazine, specializing in behavior and the social sciences. Leo has many books to his credit including* How the Russians Invented Baseball and Other Essays of Enlightenment *(1989), a book of humor;* Two Steps Ahead of the Thought Police *(1994), a collection of his* U.S. News & World Report *columns; and* Incorrect Thoughts: Notes on Our Wayward Culture *(2000).*

In the following essay, which first appeared in U.S. News & World Report *on May 12, 1997, Leo questions the usefulness of political correctness. Never one to duck an issue, Leo asks his readers to think about a series of humorous — if not always enlightened — examples.*

Like death and taxes, political correctness is always with us. But at least it's funnier than the other two permanent burdens. Some PC items in the news:

Thank God for magazines like this

Anyone who says, "God bless you," after you sneeze is trying to deprive you of your constitutional rights, according to *Free Inquiry,* a secular humanist magazine. Also on the magazine's list of "people or situations aimed at taking away your liberties and rights guaranteed by the U.S. Constitution" were such stark offenses as: (1) asking anyone, "Did you have a merry Christmas?" (2) inviting folks to a wedding that includes a religious ceremony, and (3) saying grace at a dinner party in your own home.

Mandatory sensitivity

The PC language rumor of the year is that the word "squaw" may come from a French corruption of the Iroquois slang word for "vagina." In Minnesota, students grew alarmed and complained to the Legislature. So the state passed a law ordering its counties to banish the word "squaw" from the names of all lakes, rivers, or other geographical features. One county responded to the order by officially changing the names of Squaw Creek and Squaw Bay to Politically Correct Creek and Politically Correct

Bay. No dice. The state overrode the new names as insensitive. Now it's time for Minnesota to finish the job by banning genital slurs from ice cream cartons — the word "vanilla" also comes from a word for vagina.

Comfortable with censorship

Fans of political correctness remember the fuss over *Naked Maja,* the classic Goya painting accused of harassing a sensitive college instructor at Penn State in 1991. The painting had been hanging there quietly in a classroom for ten years before it started harassing the teacher. Now *Gwen,* a painting hanging in a Tennessee city hall, has been accused of harassing a female municipal employee and creating a hostile environment.

The problem is that part of one nipple is visible in the painting, a   5
work by artist Maxine Henderson. The city attorney said he "felt more comfortable" siding with the Civil Rights Act's Title VII sexual harassment protections than with First Amendment protections, so the painting was removed. Henderson sued and won a judgment ($1), but the painting stayed down. Museums beware: The triumphant harassee explained that she finds Greek statues offensive and degrading too.

No white writers, please; we're students

California State University–Monterey Bay is the newest and most multicultural school in the California system. Nothing much is being taught there on America's cultural and historic roots, but faculty members say the students already know that stuff from high school. The college does, however, have a "vibrant" requirement, which means that students must "demonstrate knowledge of holistic health and wellness theory, concepts, and content."

Literature students must "compare and contrast the literatures of at least three different cultural groups, two of which are non-Eurocentric." The Eurocentric part might be a bit difficult since a recent visitor to the university bookstore found no literature by white authors. But Qun Wang, a literature instructor, hastened to note that one "Jewish American" writer was being read (Bernard Malamud) as well as Emily Dickinson, who, although white, presumably made the cut as a female. Wang noted in a letter that he supports the arguments of others that "we should not deify Shakespeare." The guiding spirit and paid adviser of the new college is Eurocentrically pigmented Leon Panetta, former White House chief of staff.

How about adding "vegetarians"?

Identity politics group of the year: At last, men who (1) live in Baltimore, (2) are gay, (3) are into S&M, and (4) suffer hearing loss have a group of their own: the Baltimore Leather Association of the Deaf.

Wimpy anti-president sought

Goddard College in Plainfield, Vermont, took out a newspaper ad in the *Chronicle of Higher Education* saying it needed a new college president "who is prepared to lead us through a process that questions the necessity of a president in the first place." Personally, we think it's a stupid, pointless job, so consider us hired.

So that's it!

Penn State art student Christine Enedy produced a campus sculpture   10
of the Virgin Mary emerging from a bloody vagina. Turmoil followed. Asked what she had in mind, exactly, she explained that the bloody Mary demonstrated her view of women's oppression in the church and elsewhere.

Yes, size matters

The Reverend John Papworth, Anglican priest in North London, England, said it is morally justifiable to steal from large supermarkets because these stores are putting smaller ones out of business.

Disney's pro-woman pirates

The pirates at the Pirates of the Caribbean ride in Disneyland are no longer chasing women around in wild abandon, as they have for thirty years. Instead, they are becoming sensitive New Age guys, showing the kind of respect for women that real pirates probably felt deep inside but were afraid to express. Columnist Clarence Page thinks Disney can go further. He thinks that David Crockett should no longer kill a bear at Disneyland — he should gently subdue the magnificent mammal and put it in a petting zoo.

Warning: This item may cause discomfort

Oberlin College's B&D/SM club, devoted to bondage, discipline, sadism, and masochism, generated quite a controversy on campus. Not the B&D/SM itself, of course, but the fact that the club held a campus "slave auction" that offended members of Abusua, the black student union. The S&Mers, in turn, were offended by criticism from people who don't know and respect their culture.

This comes from a year-in-retrospect article in the *Oberlin Review* exploring a year's worth of hurt feelings among campus race and sex groups. Four groups were offended by not being invited to a dinner at the college president's house. It was a mailing-list mistake, but the hurt feelings were all aired at the dinner, and all parties agreed that nobody should be marginalized.

A poster using the words "tribal sex" hurt the feelings of the Third   15
World Co-op, and talks were held "to discuss how to be more sensitive in
the future." Some women were "made to feel uncomfortable" by pictures in a campus art journal depicting women in submissive positions,
but as the *Review* summed up positively, "Efforts were made by residents
to rebuild the community through discussions and house meetings."

Heterophobia — a city's secret shame

A straight couple was thrown out of a gay bar in San Francisco for violating the bar's rules against heterosexual kissing. Morgan Gorrono,
manager of the bar, The Café, said he doesn't really mind heterosexual
behavior among his customers as long as they don't openly flaunt it. Besides, he said, the two straight kissers were drunk.

Why not just make the slaves white?

A six-part British miniseries due in 1998, *Sacred Hunger,* is based
on the prize-winning novel by Barry Unsworth about the African slave
trade, including the African slave barons who captured other blacks
and sold them to white merchants. An American company offered to
help finance the series and show it on U.S. television on one
condition — none of the slave traders could be black. No deal. The
British producer, Sir Peter Hall, declined to reveal the name of the
American company but complained about the "puritanical Stalinism" of
political correctness.

New war against Asian Americans

When the student senate at Tufts University cut $600 from the
budget of the Chinese Culture Club, a club spokesman said the cut
wasn't "face-to-face racism" but reflected "institutional bias." And
since some of the missing funds were intended to pay for containers
of Chinese food on Chinese New Year's, the spokesman said the budget
cut "questioned the authenticity of takeout food as part of our
culture."

Peter Leibert, an art professor at Connecticut College, creates works
that play on the word "wok," such as "Board Wok" and "Wok on the
Wild Side." But trouble arose when a New London museum displayed
Leibert's "Two Dogs on a Wok," which consisted of two tiny clay dogs
in a stoneware wok. An art critic suggested that the work was an ethnic
slur implying that Chinese Americans like to eat dogs. The secretary
of the state's Asian American League quickly agreed. Leibert calls the
league's interpretation "nutso."

Hiring the PC way

Alvaro Cardona applied for a $12.43-per-hour job at UCLA tutoring   20
needy students in English. He is a Latino honor student at the university
and an experienced tutor, but he didn't get the job. During his job interview, tutoring and English never came up. Instead, he was grilled on
whether he supports affirmative action (yes) and whether he sees lots of
"institutional racism" on campus (no).

Cardona says the interview was to test his ideological commitment to
politically correct race and gender "sensitivity." The supervisor said, no,
Cardona was rejected because he would have been the kind of person
who stressed learning, which is only 50 percent of the job. The missing
50 percent, she said, was validating the feelings of students.

EXAMINING THE ISSUE CRITICALLY

1. One response that a reader could have to Leo's list of political correctness
   excesses is that there are people who are unduly sensitive to certain events,
   words, works of art, and so forth, and that they ought to be more tolerant.
   The same could be said for those in positions of authority who respond positively to every charge from people who claim to have been offended or affronted in some way — that they, too, should be more tolerant. What should
   you do, however, if you feel affronted or if you are in a position of authority
   and someone comes to you with a problem? Is there some way to determine
   the line between frivolous issues and those of true significance that need
   remedying? Is there some set of procedures that you should follow in meas-
   uring the serious of problems?

2. What is the role of language in issues of political correctness? Is it always central to the political correctness issues that Leo reports? Is communication always central to the issues he raises?

3. Are reports of the excesses of those interested in promoting political correctness important for us to know? Do such reports of those excesses distort or
   give important insights into what's actually happening with respect to the
   rights of all individuals in our society?

4. If you have been involved in incidents of political correctness, either as someone who believes he or she has been victimized, or as someone who had to
   adjudicate a controversy, what have you learned? Has your involvement
   strengthened your commitment for or against political correctness?

Racism and the Risks of Ethnic Humor

STEVEN DOLOFF

Steven Doloff is a professor of English and humanities at Pratt Insti-
tute in New York City. He was born in New York City and received
his B.A. from the State University of New York at Stony Brook and
his Ph.D. from the City University of New York Graduate Center.
His academic work has been published in Shakespeare Quarterly,
James Joyce Quarterly, Keats-Shelley Review, Review of English
Studies, *and the* Huntington Library Quarterly. *His writing on*
culture and education has appeared in the New York Times, *the*
Washington Post, *the* Boston Globe, *and the* Philadelphia In-
quirer. *Doloff's cartoons have run in the* Chronicle of Higher Education *and* American Book Review. *He writes, "An essential*
mystery of language is its ability to convey and conceal meaning, si-
multaneously. That this can be true regardless of a speaker/writer's
intentions just adds to the puzzle. Humor, because it often relies on
language's ambivalent possibilities, may demonstrate better than
other forms of discourse this slippery function of semantics."

In the following selection, Doloff ponders what we are really
finding funny when we use ethnic humor or respond to it in a sup-
portive manner. This article first appeared in the Winter
1998–1999 issue of Free Inquiry.

Howard Stern, the wildly popular radio talk-show host, in commenting a while back on a local news story about a race-related murder of an
African American teenager, mentioned that a rumored motive for the
crime was that the victim had been suspected of dating an ex-girlfriend of
one of his white assailants. Stern turned this into a story about how the
girlfriend of a high school buddy of his was seduced by a black man with
gold teeth. He then called his friend on the air, and they both laughed
about his buddy's embarrassment at the time. No further mention was
made of the murdered teenager.

As an entertainer, Stern was of course in no way obliged to seriously
comment on the crime. He used it merely to introduce a comic anecdote
of teenage sexual insecurity. But a significant irony here, given the anti-
black crime as lead-in, was that Stern's anecdote ended with sympathetic
laughter commiserating with his white friend's romantic loss to a stereotyp-
ically oversexed black man. Indeed, Stern, and apparently other radio talk-
show personalities today, routinely make use of such exaggerated and
derisive stereotypes of African Americans, Hispanics, Asians, Arabs, homosexuals, and other minorities, all ostensibly for purposes of "harmless" fun.

It would seem that the times they are still a changin'. Not all that
long ago, when the civil rights movement was in early bloom, public

ethnic and racial humor in many places went through a period of heightened disapprobation. This attitude, whether affected or genuine, bespoke
the belief that verbal respect between races was a part of the solution to
the mass of problems the movement was confronting. It was not hip to
sound like a bigot, even in jest. I can remember a time when the telling
of a racial joke in a room of young people would make disapproving
heads turn either towards or away from the teller. This of course did not
mean that there were no prejudicial feelings. There always were, just as
there are now, plenty. But the times were such that open prejudice in the
form of satiric stereotyping was considered, hypocritically or not, socially
bad form. It was assumed by many, perhaps naively, that, if people got
into the habit of at least speaking civilly of other groups, their attitudes
and actions might eventually follow.

Unfortunately, the fundamental conditions conducive to racial and
ethnic friction have not even superficially changed. There still exists a
large, disadvantaged economic underclass of African Americans and
other minorities whom many middle- and lower-class whites perceive as
welfare freeloaders and criminals. And there still exists a predominantly
white middle and upper class whom minorities perceive as systematically excluding and oppressing them in a thousand both obvious and
subtle ways. These persistent perceptions seem to have eroded some of
that temporarily heightened resistance to public racial and minority
humor.

But if verbalized prejudice in the entertainment field is now some-   5
how more acceptable again, it has returned in a peculiarly tricky form. Its
rationale, offered only condescendingly and infrequently by its professional practitioners, is that we are all so socially evolved and sophisticated
these days that we can enjoy some laughs at one another's expense without meaning or taking offense. Moreover, it's argued, derisive racial and
ethnic stereotypes can also be used in self-referential and self-mocking
ways so as to actually ridicule and devitalize the misperceptions that have
created them. That sounds fine. But I don't think so.

The continuing incidence of prejudice-based violence around the
country indicates that we are simply not all that evolved and sophisticated. I suspect that there are a lot of people out there, many of them
young, who relate to racial and ethnic humor in the old-fashioned way —
as a method of indirectly venting hostility and encoding prejudices more
succinctly in their minds. When they laugh at a racial joke, they are not
laughing because a nasty old stereotype is being deconstructed, but because the stereotype involved affirms or coincidences with their own ill-
formed antagonistic feelings and fears of other races. Hearing such
stereotypes being legitimized by casual use in the media makes many
people simply more comfortable with them. What's more, there are kids
out there who are learning their initial racial attitudes and vocabularies
from such humor.

Satiric humor has always been and still is an artistic scalpel with which shrewd social critics have been able to skewer harmfully repressed and unhealthy beliefs. But ridicule and even laughter itself are not innately righteous or morally enlightening activities. We would do well to consider more seriously what it is that we find so funny.

EXAMINING THE ISSUE CRITICALLY

1. How do you respond when you hear a joke based on racial or ethnic stereotypes? Do you feel uncomfortable telling or hearing such jokes? Do you think some are too sensitive about such jokes? Are you afraid to speak out if you hear jokes and racially based stories? Should you remind the joke teller that what he or she is doing is not in anyone's best interest? Are you engaging in a politically correct activity if you make someone account for such joke telling?

2. Doloff writes that there is a difference between the satiric barb and prejudicial joke. What is satire? How does it work? Why does he say that satire is acceptable, but there is no place for ridicule or laughter, which themselves "are not innately righteous or morally enlightening activities"(7)?

3. It has been observed that all humor, with the exception of slapstick or physical humor, is essentially linguistic in nature. Reflecting on that statement, can you give some examples of jokes or anecdotes that rely on a sensitivity to language or subtle manipulations of language to create humor? What is the linguistic connection that makes the joke funny?

The Language Police

DIANE RAVITCH

Diane Ravitch is a distinguished educator who has been influential in both the private and public sectors. She is currently Research Professor of Education at New York University and holds the Brown Chair of Education at the Brookings Institution in Washington, D.C. Ravitch received her B.A. from Wellesley College and her Ph.D. in history from Columbia University. A prolific author, she has published, among others, the following books: The American Reader: Words That Moved a Nation *(1993);* New Schools for a New Century: The Redesign of Urban Education *(edited with Joseph Viteritti; 1997);* Left Back: A Century of Failed School Reforms *(2000);* Brookings Papers on Education Policy 2002 *(2002); and* The Language Police: How Pressure Groups Restrict What Students Learn *(2003).*

In the following article, taken from the Summer 2003 issue of the American Educator *and drawn from her book* The Language Police, *Ravitch describes the kinds of censorship, from both the political left and political right, that have had such a powerful impact on the education of young people in America.*

The word *censorship* refers to the deliberate removal of language, ideas, and books from the classroom or library because they are deemed offensive or controversial. The definition gets fuzzier, however, when making a distinction between censorship and selection. Selection is not censorship. Teachers have a responsibility to choose readings for their students based on their professional judgment of what students are likely to understand and what they need to learn. (It is also important to remember that people have a First Amendment right to complain about textbooks and library books they don't like.)

Censorship occurs when school officials or publishers (acting in anticipation of the legal requirements of certain states) delete words, ideas, and topics from textbooks and tests for no reason other than their fear of controversy. Censorship may take place before publication, as it does when publishers utilize guidelines that mandate the exclusion of certain language and topics, and it may happen after publication, as when parents and community members pressure school officials to remove certain books from school libraries or classrooms. Some people believe that censorship occurs only when government officials impose it, but publishers censor their products in order to secure government contracts. So the result is the same.

Censors on the political right aim to restore an idealized vision of the past, an Arcadia of happy family life, in which the family was intact, comprising a father, a mother, two or more children, and went to church every Sunday. Father was in charge, and Mother took care of the children. Father worked; Mother shopped and prepared the meals. Everyone sat around the dinner table at night. It was a happy, untroubled setting into which social problems seldom intruded. Pressure groups on the right believe that what children read in school should present this vision of the past to children and that showing it might make it so. They believe strongly in the power of the word, and they believe that children will model their behavior on whatever they read. If they read stories about disobedient children, they will be disobedient; if they read stories that conflict with their parents' religious values, they might abandon their religion. Critics on the right urge that whatever children read should model appropriate moral behavior.

Censors from the political left believe in an idealized vision of the future, a utopia in which egalitarianism prevails in all social relations. In this vision, there is no dominant group, no dominant father, no dominant race, and no dominant gender. In this world, youth is not an advantage, and disability is not a disadvantage. There is no hierarchy of better or worse; all nations and all cultures are of equal accomplishment and value. All individuals and groups share equally in the roles, rewards, and activities of society. In this world to be, everyone has high self-esteem, eats healthy foods, exercises, and enjoys being different. Pressure groups on the left feel as strongly about the power of the word as those on the right. They expect that children will be shaped by what they read and will model their behavior on what they read. They want children to read only descriptions of the world as they think it should be in order to help bring this new world into being.

For censors on both the right and the left, reading is a means of role   5 modeling and behavior modification. Neither wants children and adolescents to encounter books, textbooks, or videos that challenge their vision of what was or what might be, or that depict a reality contrary to that vision.

I. CENSORSHIP FROM THE RIGHT

In the 1980s, after a century of attacks on textbooks — animated by a search for anti-confederate or pro-communist sentiment, or any acknowledgement of evolution — right-wing censors launched an impassioned crusade against immoral books and textbooks and shifted their focus to religious and moral issues. Groups such as the Reverend Jerry Falwell's Moral Majority, Phyllis Schlafly's Eagle Forum, the Reverend Donald Wildmon's American Family Association, Dr. James Dobson's Focus on the Family, the Reverend Pat Robertson's National Legal Foundation, and Beverly La-Haye's Concerned Women for America, along with Mel and Norma Gabler's Educational Research Analysts in Texas, pressured local school districts and state boards of education to remove books that they considered objectionable.

The New Right attacked textbooks for teaching secular humanism, which they defined as a New Age religion that ignored biblical teachings and shunned moral absolutes. If it was right to exclude the Christian religion from the public schools, they argued, then secular humanism should be excluded too. If it was acceptable to teach secular humanism, they said, then Christian teaching should have equal time. The textbooks, said the critics, failed to distinguish between right and wrong, and thus taught the "situation ethics" of "secular humanism." They disapproved of portrayals of abortion, out-of-wedlock pregnancy, homosexuality, suicide, drug use, foul language, or other behavior that conflicted with their religious values. The right-wing critics also opposed stories that showed dissension within the family; such stories, they believed, would teach children to be disobedient and would damage families. They also insisted that textbooks must be patriotic and teach a positive view of the nation and its history.

The teaching of evolution was extensively litigated in the 1980s. The scientific community weighed in strongly on the side of evolution as the only scientifically grounded theory for teaching about biological origins. Fundamentalist Christians, however, insisted that public schools should give equal time to teaching the biblical version of creation. Several southern legislatures passed laws requiring "balanced treatment" of evolution and creationism, but such laws were consistently found to be unconstitutional by federal courts that held that evolution is science, and creationism is religion. In 1987, the United States Supreme Court ruled 7-2 against Louisiana's "balanced treatment" law. Yet fundamentalist insistence on "creation science" or "intelligent design" continued unabated. When states debated the adoption of science textbooks or science standards, critics demanded that competing theories should get equal time. In 2000, Republican primary voters in Kansas defeated two state school board members who had voted to remove evolution from the state's science standards.

The religious right mounted numerous challenges to textbooks in the 1980s. The most important was the case of *Mozert v. Hawkins County Board of Education* in Tennessee. In 1983, fundamentalist Christian parents in Hawkins County objected to the elementary school textbooks that were required reading in their schools. The readers were published by Holt, Rinehart, and Winston (now owned by Harcourt). The parents complained that the textbooks promoted secular humanism, satanism, witchcraft, fantasy, magic, the occult, disobedience, dishonesty, feminism, evolution, telepathy, one-world government, and New Age religion. They also asserted that some of the stories in the readers belittled the government, the military, free enterprise, and Christianity. At first, the parents wanted the textbooks removed from the local public schools. Eventually, however, they sought only that their own children be allowed to read alternate books that did not demean their religious views.

The parents received legal support from the Concerned Women for 10 America. The school board was backed by the liberal People for the American Way. The battle turned into an epic left-right political show-down: One side claimed that the case was about censorship, and the other side argued that it was about freedom of religion.

For five years the case garnered national headlines as it wound its way up and down the federal court system. In 1987, the parents lost in federal appeals court, and in 1988, the U.S. Supreme Court decided not to re-view the appellate court decision. The judges decided that "mere expo-sure" to ideas different from those of the parents' religious faith did not violate the First Amendment's guarantee of free exercise of religion.

Defenders of the Holt Basic Readers celebrated their legal victory, but it was a hollow one. In *Battleground*, a comprehensive account of the case, author Stephen Bates noted that the Holt readers were "once the most popular reading series in the nation," but were brought to "the verge of extinction" by the controversy associated with the court case. If publishers learned a lesson from the saga of the Holt reading series, it was the importance of avoiding controversy by censoring themselves in ad-vance and including nothing that might attract bad publicity or litigation. The 1986 revision of the series, designed to replace the 1983 edition that was on trial in Tennessee, omitted some of the passages that fundamen-talist parents objected to. The Holt readers won the legal battle but were commercially ruined. This was not a price that any textbook publisher would willingly pay.

A third major area for litigation in the 1980s involved efforts to ban books, both those that were assigned in class and those that were available in the school library. The first major test came not in the South, but in the Island Trees Union Free School District in New York. There, the local board directed school officials to remove ten books from their libraries because of their profanity and explicit sexual con-tent, including Bernard Malamud's *The Fixer*, Richard Wright's *Black Boy*, Kurt Vonnegut's *Slaughterhouse-Five*, and Eldridge Cleaver's *Soul on Ice*. The courts traditionally deferred to school officials when it came to curriculum and other policy-making, but in this instance the students who objected to the school officials' decision won by a narrow one-vote margin. In 1982, the U.S. Supreme Court ruled that the students had a "right to receive information." The decision was far from conclusive, however, as the justices wrote seven opinions, none of which had ma-jority support.

Many book-banning incidents were never challenged in the courts. In the 1970s and 1980s, school officials in different sections of the country removed certain books from school libraries or from classroom use, including J. D. Salinger's *The Catcher in the Rye*, John Steinbeck's *Grapes of Wrath*, Aldous Huxley's *Brave New World*, George Orwell's *1984*, MacKinley Kantor's *Andersonville*, and Gordon Parks's *Learning Tree*. In most cases, parents criticized the books' treatment of profanity, sex, religion, race, or violence.

The battle of the books shifted to Florida in the late 1980s. In Columbia County, a parent (who was a fundamentalist minister) complained to the local school board about a state-approved textbook used in an elective course for high school students. The parent objected to the book because it included Chaucer's "The Miller's Tale" and Aristophanes's *Lysistrata*. The school board banned the book and its decision was upheld in federal district court and in an appellate court. In Bay County, a parent complained about Robert Cormier's *I Am the Cheese*, a work of adolescent fiction that contains some mild profanity and not especially explicit sexual scenes. The school superintendent suppressed not only that book, but required teachers to write a rationale for every book they intended to assign unless it was on the state-approved list. The superintendent then proscribed a long list of literary classics that he deemed controversial, including several of Shakespeare's plays, Charles Dickens's *Great Expectations*, F. Scott Fitzgerald's *Great Gatsby*, and Ernest Hemingway's *A Farewell to Arms*. Parents, teachers, and students sued the local school board and the superintendent to prevent the book-banning, and a federal district judge ruled that it was acceptable to remove books because of vulgar language but not because of disagreement with the ideas in them. The litigation soon became moot, however, when the superintendent retired, and all of the books were restored in that particular district.

During the 1980s and 1990s, and after, there were numerous challenges to books by parents and organized groups. Many were directed against adolescent fiction, as authors of this genre became increasingly explicit about sexuality and more likely to utilize language and imagery that some adults considered inappropriate for children. The thirty "most frequently attacked" books from 1965 to the early 1980s included some that offended adults from different ends of the political spectrum. Some were assigned in class; others were in the school library. The list included such books as *The Adventures of Huckleberry Finn* by Mark Twain, *The Diary of a Young Girl* by Anne Frank, *Black Like Me* by John Howard Griffin, *The Scarlet Letter* by Nathaniel Hawthorne, *The Catcher in the Rye* by J. D. Salinger, and *Go Ask Alice* by anonymous.

By 2000, the American Library Association's list of the "most attacked" books had changed considerably. Most of the classics had fallen away. At the beginning of the new millennium, the most challenged books were of the Harry Potter series, assailed because of their references to the occult, satanism, violence, and religion, as well as Potter's dysfunctional family. Most of the other works that drew fire were written specifically

15

for adolescents. Some of these books were taught in classes; others were available in libraries.

The most heated controversy over textbooks in the early 1990s involved a K–6 reading series called Impressions, which was published by Holt, Rinehart, and Winston. The Impressions series consisted of grade-by-grade anthologies with a cumulative total of more than 800 reading selections from authors such as C. S. Lewis, Lewis Carroll, the Brothers Grimm, Rudyard Kipling, Martin Luther King Jr., and Laura Ingalls Wilder. Its purpose was to replace the old-fashioned "Dick and Jane"-style reader with literary anthologies of high interest for children.

The texts may have been altogether too interesting because they captured the avid attention of conservative family groups across the country. Before they became infamous among right-wing groups, the books were purchased by more than 1,500 elementary schools in 34 states. A small proportion of the series' literary selections, some of them drawn from classic fairy tales, described magic, fantasy, goblins, monsters, and witches.

Right-wing Christian groups, including Focus on the Family, Citizens for Excellence in Education, and the Traditional Values Coalition, organized against the Impressions series. The controversy became especially fierce in the early 1990s in California. The state-approved textbooks came under fire in half of California's school districts. Large numbers of parents turned out for school board meetings to demand the removal of the readers they claimed were terrifying their children. One district glued together some pages in the books to satisfy critics. Some districts dropped the series. Critics objected to stories about death, violence, and the supernatural. They charged that the series was promoting a New Age religion of paganism, the occult, and witchcraft. In one district, angry parents initiated a recall campaign against two local school board members who supported the books (the board members narrowly survived the recall vote). In another district, an evangelical Christian family filed a lawsuit charging that the district — by using the Impressions textbooks — violated the Constitution by promoting a religion of "neo-paganism" that relied on magic, trances, a veneration for nature and animal life, and a belief in the supernatural. In 1994, a federal appeals court ruled that the textbook series did not violate the Constitution.

Public ridicule helped to squelch some of the ardor of those who wanted to censor books. Editorial writers across California uniformly opposed efforts to remove the Impressions series from the public schools, providing important encouragement for public officials who were defending the books. The editorial writers read the books and saw that they contained good literature. Most reckoned that children do not live in a hermetically sealed environment. Children, they recognized, see plenty of conflict and violence on television and in real life as well. They confront,

20

sooner or later, the reality of death and loss. Most know the experience of losing a family member, a pet, a friend. Over the generations, fairy tales have served as a vehicle for children to deal with difficult situations and emotions. Even the Bible, the most revered of sacred documents in Western culture, is replete with stories of violence, betrayal, family dissension, and despicable behavior.

One cannot blame parents for wanting to protect their children's innocence from the excesses of popular culture. However, book censorship far exceeds reasonableness; usually, censors seek not just freedom from someone else's views, but the power to impose their views on others. Parents whose religious beliefs cause them to shun fantasy, magic, fairy tales, and ghost stories will have obvious difficulties adjusting to parts of the literature curriculum in public schools today. They would have had equal difficulty adjusting to the literary anthologies in American public schools 100 years ago, which customarily included myths and legends, stories about disobedient children, even tales of magical transformation. It may be impossible for a fundamentalist Christian (or Orthodox Jew or fundamentalist Muslim) to feel comfortable in a public institution that is committed to tolerance and respect among all creeds and promotion of none. This conflict cannot be avoided. Much of what is most imaginative in our culture draws upon themes that will prove objectionable to fundamentalist parents of every religion. Schools may offer alternative readings to children of fundamentalist parents, but they cannot provide readings of a sectarian nature, nor should the schools censor or ban books at the insistence of any religious or political group.

Even though the religious right has consistently lost court battles, its criticisms have not been wasted on educational publishers. The Impressions series, for all its literary excellence, was not republished and quietly vanished.

Fear of the pressures that sank the Impressions series has made publishers gun-shy about any stories that might anger fundamentalists. Textbook publishers are understandably wary about doing anything that would unleash hostile charges and countercharges and cause a public blow-up over their product.

Publishers of educational materials do not want controversy (general   25
publishers, of course, love controversy because it sells books in a competitive marketplace). Even if a publisher wins in court, its books are stigmatized as "controversial." Even if a textbook is adopted by a district or state over protests, it will lose in other districts that want to avoid similar battles. It is a far, far better thing to have no protests at all. Publishers know that a full-fledged attack, like the one waged against Impressions, means death to their product. And the best recipe for survival in a marketplace dominated by the political decisions of a handful of state boards is to delete whatever might offend anyone.

II. CENSORSHIP FROM THE LEFT

The left-wing groups that have been most active in campaigns to change textbooks are militantly feminist and militantly liberal. These groups hope to bring about an equitable society by purging certain language and images from textbooks.

Lee Burress, a leader of anticensorship activities for many years in the National Council of Teachers of English, describes in *The Battle of the Books* how feminists and liberals became censors as they sought to "raise consciousness" and to eliminate "offensive" stories and books. Joan DelFattore, in *What Johnny Shouldn't Read*, writes that political correctness, taken to its extreme, "denotes a form of intellectual terrorism in which people who express ideas that are offensive to any group other than white males of European heritage may be punished, *regardless of the accuracy or relevance of what they say*" (italics in the original). The censors from the left and right, she says, compel writers, editors, and public officials to suppress honest questions and to alter facts "solely to shape opinion." Once a society begins limiting freedom of expression to some points of view, then "all that remains is a trial of strength" to see whose sensibilities will prevail.

While the censors on the right have concentrated most of their ire on general books, the censors on the left have been most successful in criticizing textbooks. Although left-wing censors have occasionally targeted books too, they have achieved their greatest influence by shaping the bias guidelines of the educational publishing industry. Educational publishers have willingly acquiesced even to the most farfetched demands for language censorship, so long as the campaign's stated goal is "fairness." Only a George Orwell could fully appreciate how honorable words like *fairness* and *diversity* have been deployed to impose censorship and uniformity on everyday language.

The organization that led the left-wing censorship campaign was the Council on Interracial Books for Children (CIBC). Founded in 1966 in New York City, CIBC was active over the next quarter-century as the best-known critic of racism and sexism in children's books and textbooks. Directing its critiques not as much to the general public as to the publishing industry and educators, CIBC issued publications and conducted seminars for librarians and teachers to raise their consciousness about racism and sexism.

CIBC ceased its organizational life in 1990; its most enduring legacy proved to be its guidelines, which explained how to identify racism, sexism, and ageism, as well as a variety of other isms. They were the original template for the detailed bias guidelines that are now pervasive in the education publishing industry and that ban specific words, phrases, roles, activities, and images in textbooks and on tests. The CIBC guidelines are still cited; they circulate on many Web sites, and they continue to serve as training materials for bias and sensitivity reviewers.

CIBC's initial goal was to encourage publishers to include more realistic stories and more accurate historical treatments about blacks, Hispanics, Native Americans, and women. It awarded annual prizes for the best new children's books by minority writers. However, soon after it was founded in the mid-1960s, the nation's political and cultural climate changed dramatically. In the wake of riots and civil disorders in major American cities, including New York, the racial integration movement was swept away by movements for racial separatism and black power. CIBC was caught up in the radicalism of the times. Its goals shifted from inclusion to racial assertiveness, from the pursuit of racial harmony to angry rhetoric about colonialism and the "educational slaughter" of minority children. As its militancy grew, CIBC insisted that only those who were themselves members of a minority group were qualified to write about their own group's experience. It demanded that publishers subsidize minority-owned bookstores, printers, and publishers. It urged teachers and librarians to watch for and exclude those books that violated its bias guidelines.

CIBC's critiques of racial and gender stereotyping undoubtedly raised the consciousness of textbook publishers about the white-only world of their products and prompted necessary revisions. However, in the early 1970s, CIBC demanded elimination of books that it deemed "anti-human," racist, and sexist.

CIBC attacked numerous literary classics as racist, including Hugh Lofting's Dr. Dolittle books, Pamela Travers's *Mary Poppins*, Harriet Beecher Stowe's *Uncle Tom's Cabin*, Theodore Taylor's *The Cay*, Ezra Jack Keats's books (*Snowy Day* and *Whistle for Willie*), Roald Dahl's *Charlie and the Chocolate Factory*, and William H. Armstrong's *Sounder*. The American publisher of Dr. Dolittle, agreeing that the series contained stereotypical images of Africans, expurgated the books to remove offensive illustrations and text. The original version of the books has now disappeared from library shelves and bookstores.

CIBC attacked fairy tales as sexist, asserting that they promote "stereotypes, distortions, and anti-humanism." It charged that such traditional tales as "Little Red Riding Hood," "Cinderella," "Jack and the Beanstalk," "Snow-White," "Beauty and the Beast," "The Princess and the Pea," "Rumpelstiltskin," and "Hansel and Gretel" were irredeemably sexist because they portrayed females as "princesses or poor girls on their way to becoming princesses, fairy godmothers or good fairies, wicked and evil witches, jealous and spiteful sisters, proud, vain, and hateful stepmothers, or shrewish wives." The "good" females were depicted as beautiful, the "bad" ones as evil witches. The males were powerful and courageous, while the females were assigned to "traditional" roles as helpers. Typically, the characters in fairy tales rose from poverty to great wealth, CIBC complained, but no one ever asked about the "socioeconomic causes of their condition"; no one ever talked about the need for "collective action" to overcome injustice. In the eyes of CIBC, fairy tales were not only rife with sexist stereotypes, but with materialism, elitism, ethnocentrism, and racism too.

CIBC's *Human (and Anti-Human) Values in Children's Books* listed 235 children's books published in 1975. Each was evaluated against a checklist that measured whether it was racist, sexist, elitist, materialist, ageist, conformist, escapist, or individualist; or whether it was opposed to those values or indifferent to them; whether it "builds a positive image of females/minorities" or "builds a negative image of females/minorities"; whether it "inspires action versus oppression"; and whether it is "culturally authentic." Only members of a specific group reviewed books about their own group: Blacks reviewed books about blacks, Chicanos reviewed books about Chicanos, and so on. Few of the books reviewed had any lasting significance, and few of them are still in print a quarter-century later. One that is still read is John D. Fitzgerald's *The Great Brain Does It Again*, which CIBC rated as racist, sexist, materialist, individualist, conformist, and escapist.

The author Nat Hentoff reacted angrily to what he called CIBC's "righteous vigilanteism." Although he agreed with the council's egalitarian goals, he warned that its bias checklists and its demands for political correctness would stifle free expression. He interviewed other writers who complained about the CIBC checklist but were fearful of being identified. CIBC's efforts to eliminate offensive books and to rate books for their political content, he argued, were creating a climate in which "creative imagination, the writer's and the child's, must hide to survive." Its drive against "individualism," he said, was antithetical to literature and the literary imagination: "Collectivism is for politics," he said, not for writers.

In retrospect, CIBC appears to have had minimal impact on general books. Despite having been denounced as racist, *The Cay* and *Sounder* remain commercially successful. Fairy tales continue to enchant children (although they are seldom found in textbooks and are usually bowdlerized). The public was only dimly aware, if at all, of CIBC's lists of stereotypes, its reviews, and its ratings. Publishers kept printing and selling children's books that defied CIBC's strictures.

Where CIBC did make a difference, however, was with publishers of K–12 textbooks. Textbook houses could not risk ignoring CIBC or its labeling system. No publisher could afford to enter a statewide adoption process with a textbook whose contents had been branded racist or sexist or ageist or handicapist or biased against any other group. The publishers' fear of stigma gave CIBC enormous leverage. When publishers began writing their own bias guidelines in the late 1960s and early 1970s, they consulted with CIBC or hired members of its editorial advisory board to counsel them about identifying bias. James Banks, a member of the

CIBC advisory board, wrote the bias guidelines for McGraw-Hill; his wife, Cherry A. McGee Banks, was one of the main writers of the Scott Foresman–Addison Wesley guidelines.

CIBC multiplied its effectiveness when it worked in tandem with the National Organization for Women (NOW), which was also founded in 1966. Unlike CIBC, which operated from New York City, NOW had chapters in every state. CIBC and NOW frequently collaborated to fight sexism and to promote language censorship in the publishing industry and in textbooks. Feminist groups, some associated with NOW, others operating independently, testified at state hearings against unacceptable textbooks, pressured state and local school boards to exclude such books, and lobbied publishers to expunge sexist language from their books. Feminists demanded a 50-50 ratio of girls and boys, women and men, in every book. They counted illustrations to see how many female characters were represented. They noted whether girls and women were in passive or active roles as compared to boys and men. They made lists of the occupations represented, insisted that women have equal representation in professional roles, and objected if illustrations showed women as housewives, baking cookies, or sewing. They hectored publishers, textbook committees, and school boards with their complaints. And they made a difference.

In 1972, a group called Women on Words and Images published a pamphlet titled *Dick and Jane as Victims: Sex Stereotyping in Children's Readers* that documented the imbalanced representation of boys and girls in reading textbooks. In the most widely used readers of the mid-1960s, boys were more likely to be lead characters and to play an active role as compared to girls, who were portrayed as dependent, passive, and interested only in shopping and dressing up. At textbook hearings around the country, feminist groups brandished the book and demanded changes. Within a year of the pamphlet's appearance, the authors reported that they had drawn national attention to the problem. Publishers consulted with them for advice about how to revise their materials. By the mid-1970s, every major publishing company had adopted guidelines that banned sexist language and stereotypes from their textbooks.

By adopting bias guidelines, the publishers agreed to police their products and perform the censorship demanded by the politically correct left and the religious right. Publishers found it easier to exclude anything that offended anybody, be they feminists, religious groups, racial and ethnic groups, the disabled, or the elderly, rather than to get into a public controversy and see their product stigmatized. It was not all that difficult to delete a story or a paragraph or a test item, and most of the time no one noticed anyway.

The publishers reacted differently to pressure groups from the left and right. Companies did not share the Christian fundamentalist values of right-wing groups; they sometimes fought them in court, as Holt did in the *Mozert v. Hawkins* case described earlier. By contrast, editors at the big publishing companies often agreed quietly with the feminists and civil rights groups that attacked their textbooks; by and large, the editors and the left-wing critics came from the same cosmopolitan worlds and held similar political views. The publishers and editors did not mind if anyone thought them unsympathetic to the religious right, but they did not want to be considered racist by their friends, family, and professional peers. Nor did they oppose feminist demands for textbook changes, which had the tacit or open support of their own female editors. In retrospect, this dynamic helps to explain why the major publishing companies swiftly accepted the sweeping linguistic claims of feminist critics and willingly yielded to a code of censorship.

By the end of the 1980s, every publisher had complied with the demands of the critics, both from left and right. Publishers had established bias guidelines with which they could impose self-censorship and head off the outside censors, as well as satisfy state adoption reviews. Achieving demographic balance and excluding sensitive topics had become more important to their success than teaching children to read or to appreciate good literature. Stories written before 1970 had to be carefully screened for compliance with the bias guidelines; those written after 1970 were unlikely to be in compliance unless written for a textbook publisher. So long as books and stories continue to be strained through a sieve of political correctness, fashioned by partisans of both left and right, all that is left for students to read will be thin gruel.

EXAMINING THE ISSUE CRITICALLY

1. Controversies over political correctness often take the form of isolated incidents or situations, many of them based on college campuses and in college classrooms: for example, an instructor or student says something that offends administrators, other instructors, or students. The participants in such cases are often strident about their concerns and authorities rush in to put pressure on the parties to resolve their differences. Often it is difficult, therefore, to discern lessons or develop a guiding philosophy with regard to the validity of political correctness arguments. What makes Ravitch's analysis of political correctness in the world of textbook publishing different from those isolated but hot issues that arise from time on our campuses? Is the analysis of the publishing industry's censorship, from both the right and the left on the political spectrum, more or less abstract, more or less important than those incidents that so often make the news? What's at stake from Ravitch's perspective, and from your own, when it comes to the way information is imparted by college textbooks?

2. Have you found fault with any of your textbooks that seem to contain further examples of the kinds of censorship on the part of authors and college textbook publishers that Ravitch discusses? Do you have trouble knowing whether or not your texts have undergone censorship? Does the fact that it is difficult to know if censorship has taken place make the issue more or less important for you? Why?

3. To what extent is the publishing industry's "bottom line" the real problem with respect to the work of the language police? Is the public concerned about censorship in textbooks, or is this an "invisible issue" for most people? Does the public want unbiased textbooks? Who, or what group, could be put in charge of guaranteeing bias-free textbooks? Is a watch-dog oversight group a viable possibility? What solutions for this problem would you like to see put into effect?

MAKING CONNECTIONS: POLITICAL CORRECTNESS
AND SPEECH CODES

The following questions are offered to help you start to make meaningful connections among the four articles in this Case Study. These questions can be used for class discussion, or you can answer any one of the questions by writing an essay. If you choose the essay option, be sure to make specific references to at least two of the Case Study articles.

1. After reading the articles by Bronner, Leo, Doloff, and Ravitch, write an essay in which you argue one of the following positions: that the political correctness movement has taken a good idea and pushed it too far or that there is an ongoing need to monitor our language. Use examples from the articles in this Case Study, and your own experiences, to support your views.

2. What is the history of the term *politically correct*? When was it first used, by whom, and with what meaning? Has the meaning of the term changed over time? What is the status of the term today? Review the articles in this Case Study, particularly the one by Ravitch, for a summary of censorship from the right and the left, and find research materials in your library or on the Internet in order to write a report on the term *politically correct*.

3. After reading the articles by Bronner, Leo, Doloff, and Ravitch, where do you stand on the issue of speech codes? What are the historical reasons given for the need for speech codes? Do you think speech codes have, in fact, served a worthwhile purpose? Or, as their detractors claim, have speech codes silenced a segment of American society? Do you believe there is still a need to maintain speech codes? Write an essay explaining your position on campus speech codes.

4. Comment on the 1999 cartoon by Stuart Carlson on page 290, which appeared in the *Milwaukee Journal Sentinel*. What, for you, are the connotations of the term *language police*? What is Carlson's attitude toward political correctness? How do you suppose Leo would respond to this cartoon?

5

MEN AND WOMEN TALKING

During the thirty years since the first edition of *Language Awareness* was published, the women's movement has given rise to a tremendous interest in the roles that men and women play in our society and especially the way those roles are both reflected and reinforced in our language usage. Women have claimed that men have been oppressors in relegating women to subservient roles, arguing that the way to achieve equality is to speak out, to break the silences that so often have made such oppression seem normal. The women's movement has also worked to expose the manner in which male linguistic domination has institutionalized women's diminished status. At base, this approach rests on the notion that language reveals thoughts and attitudes and that the way to remedy inequality is first to sensitize ourselves to the language we use with each other, and then to encourage more thoughtful and appropriate language to correct our problems. Sociology aside, language may be responsible for inequality but it can also be used to rescue us from ourselves. Men, on the other hand, have been used to the assumption that they are merely inheritors of linguistic tradition, and are not purely responsible for sexist language — and they may be correct. Consequently, a good deal of commentary rejecting anti-male bashing has also been voiced and seen in print.

The articles we have gathered here attempt to show men and women talking both among themselves and to each other. We begin with Audre Lorde's powerful speech to women about the need to break silences, to speak out, and to realize themselves through action growing out of an awareness of language. We turn next to Nathan Cobb's "Gender Wars in Cyberspace" and a discussion of the promise of equality the Internet held for women and why equality in that arena still seems elusive. Our next author, using the pseudonym of Juliet Gabriel, points out that the language men and women use to write personal ads may not get the desired results because the writers don't recognize "the things that make them shine," nor how to find appropriate language to convey them. Deborah Tannen gives an analysis of the way men and women give and interpret orders in the workplace and how the examination of other cultures may give us some insight into ways we might improve our workplace communications. Finally, Clive Thompson reports on a newly developed computer program that can reliably determine by analysis of the words used in a text whether the author is male or female. The development of the program naturally gives rise to a whole new set of fascinating questions regarding what constitutes gender and language usage.

CASE STUDY: THE LANGUAGE OF SEXUAL DISCRIMINATION

The techniques and strategies used to cope with linguistic oppression over the past three decades have more recently focused on groups of people with complex sexual physiology and life styles. The major groups for which there are now advocacy organizations (in addition to gays, lesbians, and bisexuals), are transgenders, transsexuals, queers, twin-spariteds, and those who are intersexed and questioning. While their numbers may not be very large, they are speaking about their experiences with increasing frequency. It is worth remembering that their makeup includes women and other minorities — there are black transsexuals, for example — their suffering is real, and their victimization frightening. We begin the Case Study with an article by Martha Irvine in which she traces the history of the word *queer* from being synonymous for "odd" or "unusual," to its use as an anti-gay insult, to its being reclaimed, redefined, and embraced by the gay community. Next, the popular campus speaker and activist Riki Wilchins discusses recent attacks against two men — one gay and one straight — and argues that the attacks were not motivated by sexual prejudices but were directed against those who transgressed gender norms. Finally, in "Real Men Don't: Anti-Male Bias in English," Eugene R. August catalogs many examples of reverse sexism and worries that college campuses may be encouraging so much discrimination. These articles give further testimony to an undeniable truth — when it comes to understanding the relationship between men and women, sex and gender, and self-identification and well-being, an awareness of language can never be far from the center of our concerns as both the vehicle of oppression and the path to understanding.

The Transformation of Silence into Language and Action

AUDRE LORDE

Audre Lorde (1934–1992) was a professor of English at Hunter College in New York City. Born in New York, she studied at Hunter and at Columbia University. Her published works include several volumes of poetry, such as Undersong: Chosen Poems Old and New *(1982), which was revised in 1992; essay collections like* Sister Outsider *(1984) and* Burst of Light *(1988); and an autobiography,* Zami: A New Spelling of My Name *(1982). Her book of poems* The Arithmetics of Distance *appeared posthumously in 1993.*

The following speech was originally presented at a panel at the 1977 Modern Language Association Convention and later collected in her book Sister Outsider. *Notice that in this highly personal speech she refers specifically to herself and to those in her audience and yet also manages to make her message a universal one.*

WRITING TO DISCOVER: *Think about how important it is for you to voice your thoughts and beliefs. Do you sometimes feel frustrated by events taking place around you, by what seems to be your powerlessness to have an influence on your circumstances, particularly as a young person and a student? Comment on what roles speaking out and writing may play in helping you take control of your world.*

I have come to believe over and over again that what is most important to me must be spoken, made verbal and shared, even at the risk of having it bruised or misunderstood. That the speaking profits me, beyond any other effect. I am standing here as a black lesbian poet, and the meaning of all that waits upon the fact that I am still alive, and might not have been. Less than two months ago I was told by two doctors, one female and one male, that I would have to have breast surgery, and that there was a 60 to 80 percent chance that the tumor was malignant. Between that telling and the actual surgery, there was a three-week period of the agony of an involuntary reorganization of my entire life. The surgery was completed, and the growth was benign.

But within those three weeks, I was forced to look upon myself and my living with a harsh and urgent clarity that has left me still shaken but much stronger. This is a situation faced by many women, by some of you here today. Some of what I experienced during that time has helped elucidate for me much of what I feel concerning the transformation of silence into language and action.

In becoming forcibly and essentially aware of my mortality, and of what I wished and wanted for my life, however short it might be, priorities and omissions became strongly etched in a merciless light, and what I most regretted were my silences. Of what had I *ever* been afraid? To question or to speak as I believed could have meant pain, or death. But we all hurt in so many different ways, all the time, and pain will either change or end. Death, on the other hand, is the final silence. And that might be coming quickly, now, without regard for whether I had ever spoken what needed to be said, or had only betrayed myself into small silences, while I planned someday to speak, or waited for someone else's words. And I began to recognize a source of power within myself that comes from the knowledge that while it is most desirable not to be afraid, learning to put fear into a perspective gave me great strength.

I was going to die, if not sooner then later, whether or not I had ever spoken myself. My silences had not protected me. Your silence will not protect you. But for every real word spoken, for every attempt I had ever made to speak those truths for which I am still seeking, I had made contact with other women while we examined the words to fit a world in which we all believed, bridging our differences. And it was the concern and caring of all those women which gave me strength and enabled me to scrutinize the essentials of my living.

The women who sustained me through that period were black and white, old and young, lesbian, bisexual, and heterosexual, and we all shared a war against the tyrannies of silence. They all gave me a strength and concern without which I could not have survived intact. Within those weeks of acute fear came the knowledge — within the war we are all waging with the forces of death, subtle and otherwise, conscious or not — I am not only a casualty, I am also a warrior.   5

What are the words you do not yet have? What do you need to say? What are the tyrannies you swallow day by day and attempt to make your own, until you will sicken and die of them, still in silence? Perhaps for some of you here today, I am the face of one of your fears. Because I am woman, because I am black, because I am lesbian, because I am myself — a black woman warrior poet doing my work — come to ask you, are you doing yours?

And of course I am afraid, because the transformation of silence into language and action is an act of self-revelation, and that always seems fraught with danger. But my daughter, when I told her of our topic and my difficulty with it, said, "Tell them about how you're never really a whole person if you remain silent, because there's always that one little piece inside you that wants to be spoken out, and if you keep ignoring it, it gets madder and madder and hotter and hotter, and if you don't speak it out one day it will just up and punch you in the mouth from the inside."

In the cause of silence, each of us draws the face of her own fear — fear of contempt, of censure, or some judgment, or recognition, of challenge, of annihilation. But most of all, I think, we fear the visibility without which we cannot truly live. Within this country where racial difference creates a constant, if unspoken, distortion of vision, black women have on one hand always been highly visible, and so, on the other hand, have been rendered invisible through the depersonalization of racism. Even within the women's movement, we have had to fight, and still do, for that very visibility which also renders us most vulnerable, our blackness. For to survive in the mouth of this dragon we call america, we have had to learn this first and most vital lesson — that we were never meant to survive. Not as human beings. And neither were most of you here today, black or not. And that visibility which makes us most vulnerable is that which also is the source of our greatest strength. Because the machine will try to grind you into dust anyway, whether or not we speak. We can sit in our corners mute forever while our sisters and our selves are wasted, while our children are distorted and destroyed, while our earth is poisoned; we can sit in our safe corners mute as bottles, and we will still be no less afraid.

In my house this year we are celebrating the feast of Kwanza, the African-american festival of harvest which begins the day after Christmas and lasts for seven days. There are seven principles of Kwanza, one for each day. The first principle is Umoja, which means unity, the decision to strive for and maintain unity in self and community. The principle for yesterday, the second day, was Kujichagulia — self-determination — the decision to define ourselves, name ourselves, and speak for ourselves, instead of being defined and spoken for by others. Today is the third day of Kwanza, and the principle for today is Ujima — collective work and responsibility — the decision to build and maintain ourselves and our communities together and to recognize and solve our problems together.

Each of us is here now because in one way or another we share a   10
commitment to language and to the power of language, and to the reclaiming of that language which has been made to work against us. In the transformation of silence into language and action, it is vitally necessary for each one of us to establish or examine her function in that transformation and to recognize her role as vital within that transformation.

For those of us who write, it is necessary to scrutinize not only the truth of what we speak, but the truth of that language by which we speak it. For others, it is to share and spread also those words that are meaningful to us. But primarily for us all, it is necessary to teach by living and speaking those truths which we believe and know beyond understanding. Because in this way alone we can survive, by taking part in a process of life that is creative and continuing, that is growth.

And it is never without fear — of visibility, of the harsh light of scrutiny and perhaps judgment, of pain, of death. But we have lived through all of those already, in silence, except death. And I remind myself all the time now that if I were to have been born mute, or had maintained an oath of silence my whole life long for safety, I would still have suffered, and I would still die. It is very good for establishing perspective.

And where the words of women are crying to be heard, we must each of us recognize our responsibility to seek those words out, to read them and share them and examine them in their pertinence to our lives. That we not hide behind the mockeries of separations that have been imposed upon us and which so often we accept as our own. For instance, "I can't possibly teach black women's writing — their experience is so different from mine." Yet how many years have you spent teaching Plato and Shakespeare and Proust? Or another, "She's a white woman and what could she possibly have to say to me?" Or, "She's a lesbian, what would my husband say, or my chairman?" Or again, "This woman writes of her sons and I have no children." And all the other endless ways in which we rob ourselves of ourselves and each other.

We can learn to work and speak when we are afraid in the same way we have learned to work and speak when we are tired. For we have been socialized to respect fear more than our own needs for language and definition, and while we wait in silence for that final luxury of fearlessness, the weight of that silence will choke us.

The fact that we are here and that I speak these words is an attempt   15
to break that silence and bridge some of those differences between us, for it is not difference which immobilizes us, but silence. And there are so many silences to be broken.

FOCUSING ON CONTENT

1. What did the trauma of Lorde's breast surgery make apparent to her?

2. What exactly are the silences to which Lorde refers? Why does she think it's necessary for women to break those silences?

3. Lorde refers to fear a number of times. Is the fear of death the only thing she worries about? Explain.

4. What does Lorde say about the differences between herself and the members of her audience? What is it that overrides any differences among the people in the audience? What commonality do they share, and why does Lorde see it as so important?

FOCUSING ON WRITING

1. What is Lorde's thesis in this speech? (Glossary: *Thesis*) Where does she present her thesis?

2. What is Lorde's purpose? (Glossary: *Purpose*) What does she want her audience to do as a result of her speech?

3. Who is Lorde's audience? (Glossary: *Audience*) Where and how does she address those in her audience? What effect do her direct addresses have on you as a reader of the text? Are they distracting or helpful in appreciating what she has to say? Explain.

4. In paragraph 9, Lorde talks about the feast of Kwanza, "the African-american festival of harvest which begins the day after Christmas and lasts for seven days." What is her point in discussing Kwanza in terms of her overall purpose? Why do you think she chooses not to capitalize the word *American*?

LANGUAGE IN ACTION

Audre Lorde talks about the need for women to speak out. In the short essay presented here, Elizabeth Lyon, a writer, tells of her experience on September 11 and why it gave her a new reason to write. When you have finished reading the essay contemplate what other reasons both men and women may have for breaking silences.

HONORING THE LOST WRITERS OF SEPTEMBER 11

On Tuesday, September 11, 2001, my flight departed New York's La Guardia Airport at 8:20 A.M. The trip had been my seventeen-year-old daughter's first time in New York. Elaine and I craned our necks to peer out the tiny airplane portal for one last longing glance at a city that embodies the American dream. As I settled back, I felt a sense of accomplishment. I had given my literary agent a new book proposal. With my prior two books out of print, I could only hope I would continue my publishing career, but doubts swarmed like wasps.

Less than an hour into the flight, our United pilot broke my reverie. "Due to national security, all aircraft have been ordered to land immediately." Elaine and I stared at each other, not comprehending. *National security? All aircraft? Our plane?* I wondered if there had been a nuclear attack. I sat listening to the hum of the engines, my mind stuck on pause. Other passengers grabbed air phones. The news darted through the cabin: one tower, the second tower, Pennsylvania, the Pentagon, a rumor of more hijacked planes still on their way to destinations unknown. Tears trailed down Elaine's soft cheeks. We clasped hands. I used the airplane phone for the first time ever, dialing repeatedly until I got past busy signals and reached family, feeling insanely as if doing so would guarantee our safety.

Our flight was diverted to Chicago's O'Hare, where we landed on a tarmac eerily devoid of human life and entered a terminal that had been evacuated. When I saw a lone vendor with a sandwich cart, not knowing when or where we'd see our next meal, I bought more food than usual, only to put half back when the vendor couldn't take plastic and I didn't have enough cash. I sent Elaine to find an ATM. I joined other passengers, all of us in shock. We shuffled like zombies into a line to talk with a United airlines representative, only to learn we'd have to call their 800 line. Someone told me hotel rooms were all but filled. I grabbed Elaine and we headed downstairs into the baggage claim area.

Wall-to-wall confused people searched one conveyor after another, searching for luggage from the unscheduled landings. Finally, we heard an announcement that the baggage had been impounded. By sheer luck, I found us a room at a Radisson hotel.

We spent much of that first day staring at the images on TV, holding one another, and calling family. I left Elaine once to go to the gift shop to buy us Chicago t-shirts to sleep in, and I could not restrain from buying my daughter a stuffed angel bear. Emotionally strong throughout the ordeal, she clutched that bear. My emotions were a briar patch of intensity that blocked me from any expression, until a Shriner entered the hotel on our third day, set up a table, and passed out Snickers bars. This first act of human kindness nearly brought me to my knees.

Our days fell into a ritual of seeking a way home to Eugene, Oregon. I spent hours in repeated calls to United Airlines — making, breaking, and remaking reservations. I called rental car agencies. They had no cars to lease. On the afternoon of day three, Mayor Daly announced more delays at O'Hare, and United made a mistake that bumped us out of the displaced-passenger priority. My parents had made deposits to my checking, so we had cash, but my available credit was dwindling fast.

Over lunch, Elaine helped me brainstorm options; she excels at pointing out pros and cons. I considered buying a used car to resell later. Too risky. Too expensive. Thinking out loud, I said, "Is there any way I can use my skill as a writer?" I remembered the recall of Firestone tires; at home, I used their shop for repairs. I called the local Firestone and offered to write great public relations pieces if they'd loan us a vehicle to drive home. They called me back with a no, but gave me a name and number at U-Haul, where I was referred to publicity headquarters in Phoenix, where they, too, declined. Several calls later, I learned that Amtrak or the bus would get us home, but a week hence. I asked Elaine for her vote — stay and endure more waiting, knowing we'd probably get a flight out in three or four more days, or recheck rental cars and take five days of steady driving across country. "Drive," she said. "I agree," I said. During my next round of calls, I found a one-way rental car from Avis, and at 3:30 P.M. on Thursday, September 13, we began our 2,200-mile return to Eugene.

On the road, we followed the endless umbilical of American flags from Wisconsin to Minnesota to North Dakota, from North Dakota to Montana to Wyoming, from Wyoming to Idaho to Oregon. During the unbroken miles across the grassy plains, a realization startled me out of my numbness. On September 11, in Pennsylvania, New York, and Washington D.C., *writers died*. How many hoped to be novelists? Planned to write a family history, a memoir, a letter asking forgiveness? How many of the victims dreamed of getting published, of quitting a day job, of becoming best-selling authors? How many doubted their abilities and let doubt and distraction stop them from trying, and now it was too late? One hundred? Ten? How many? I felt the loss anew, not only for lives cut short but for dreams cut short. I thought about how close we had come to being on a different flight that would have ended my dreams of writing and Elaine's dreams of being an artist with her work displayed at New York's Metropolitan.

As we crossed the state line into the "Big Sky" country of Montana, I asked myself: What if I refuse to let myself say or even think "I can't"? What if I squelch the excuse, "I'm too busy"? I thought of the personal stories of the dead that had already reached the newspapers. I gazed at their happy faces, people in the prime of life a few days before September 11. Could I leave behind my habit of being too busy or my secret doubts about my writing ability?

A month after September 11, my agent called with the news I wanted to hear — and then some. An editor offered to re-release my prior books *and* publish the first two books of my proposed Writer's Compass series. A four-book contract! Not in my wildest dreams!

It may seem like a small, perhaps insignificant change to others, but September 11 awakened me to write as if I have no tomorrow — for myself and in honor of those writers who lost their chance.

The dedication of Elizabeth Lyon's first book in her new series, A Writer's Guide to Nonfiction, *reads: Dedicated to the memory of the writers throughout the world who lost their lives on September 11, 2001, or during the aftermath, and with that ending, lost the chance to share their dreams.*

WRITING SUGGESTIONS

1. Audre Lorde's speech is significant because it recognizes the need that we have to express ourselves and the importance of doing so. She speaks of the forces that work against our desire to voice our thoughts and feelings, the forces that work to maintain our silence. Write an essay about the issue of silence and the need to express yourself. Have you felt the need to speak or write? Have you been intimidated into silence? What were the circumstances of your remaining silent? What were the circumstances of your speaking out or writing what was on your mind? What advice can you give to those who remain silent? How might they eventually experience the self-affirming privilege of hearing their own voices?

2. It is a time-honored practice of writers to share with their readers their reasons for writing in essays often titled "Why I Write." If you are fond of writing, if you feel that you *must* write, share your reasons for writing in an essay entitled "Why I Write." To analyze your motivations and to trigger your imagination, think of writing as a way of clarifying your ideas, of gaining control of your world, or of powerfully imagining a world of your own creation.

Gender Wars in Cyberspace

NATHAN COBB

Born in Newton, Massachusetts, in 1943, journalist Nathan Cobb began his writing career after graduating from Pennsylvania State University in 1965 with a B.A. in English. He joined the staff of the Boston Globe *in 1969 and has remained there as a feature writer for the Living and Sunday magazine sections. He is the coauthor of two books:* Love and Hate on the Tennis Court *(1977) and* Cityside/Countryside *(1980), a collection of his columns from the* Boston Globe.

Although recent studies have identified significant differences in the way men and women communicate, the advent of the Internet seemed to signal a change — an anonymous, gender-neutral forum in which men and women could express themselves without traditional forms of gender association. In the following selection, originally published in the Boston Globe *in March 1995, Cobb discusses how and why the gender-neutral ideal of Internet communication remains elusive.*

WRITING TO DISCOVER: *How do you communicate? Would you characterize yourself as confrontational or as conciliatory when you enter into a potential conflict? To what extent do your online communications — e-mails, chat-room dialogues, and so on — reflect your face-to-face communication style? Write about an instance or two of conflict, and relate your reactions, classifying them as best you can.*

Consider the Yo alert.

Yo?

Yo. Subscribers to ECHO, a small online service based in Manhattan, use the greeting to signify important messages when they converse with one another via computer. But there's a difference between those who Yo and those who don't.

"What we've found is that men tend to 'Yo' a lot more than women," says Stacy Horn, who founded ECHO five years ago. "And they're much more likely to 'Yo' strangers. Women simply do not 'Yo' strangers."

But wait. Isn't cyberspace supposed to be gender neutral, a place 5 where women can feel empowered and men don't think they have to flex their pecs? Aren't the Internet and its commercial online siblings supposed to go beyond the notion that men are men and women are women, washing away this pre-Infobahn concept with rivers of sexless text? "Online, we don't know gender," declares Newton-based Internet analyst Daniel Dern.

A growing group of people beg to differ, no small number of them women. They contend not only that there are differences between male and female Netiquette — a.k.a. online manners — but also differences in the overall conversational styles used by men and women who "talk" via computer.

"Although a lot of people have said that online communication removes cues about gender, age, and background, that's not true," argues Laurel Sutton, a graduate student in linguistics at the University of California at Berkeley who has studied online discourse. "Everything that you communicate about yourself when you communicate face-to-face comes through when you communicate online. So men talk like men and women talk like women."

STILL A MAN'S CYBERWORLD

Statistically speaking, of course, it's still a man's cyberworld out there. Among the major online services, CompuServe estimates that 83 percent of its users are men, while America Online pegs its male subscribers at 84 percent. Prodigy claims a 60/40 male/female ratio among users. Nobody keeps figures for the Internet, the vast web of interconnected computer networks that is owned and operated by no single entity, but estimates of female participation run from 10 to 35 percent. Indeed, most of the computer culture is male-dominated.

If you don't think there's a shortage of women online, listen to the dialogue one recent evening inside an America Online "chat" room known as the Romance Connection, a kind of digital dating bar. When the lone female in the room departed — assuming she really was female — after entertaining the other 22 members of the group with a bit of softcore titillation, there was an awkward pause.

"What are we going to do now?" one participant typed.   10

"Who wants to play the naked female?" someone else asked.

"Not me," came a response.

"Not me, either," came another.

"Well, if you can't fake it, don't volunteer," offered the first.

Most women who go online quickly learn that many such chat areas   15
and certain Internet newsgroups — places where cyberians sharing similar interests can post messages to one another — are spots where testosterone-based life-forms are likely to harass them, inquiring about their measurements and sexual preferences as if they've phoned 1-900-DIAL-SEX. "It's like walking into a real bad '70s disco," says David Fox, the author of *Love Bytes,* a new book about online dating. "The fact that people can be anonymous is a major factor. I mean, a thirteen-year-old can go around living his teen-age fantasy of picking up women."

As a result, many women adopt gender-neutral screen names, switching from, say, Victoria to VBG, Nova to Vanity, and Marcia to Just Being

Me. "This way, if some jerk comes along you can always say you're a man," says Pleiades (real name: Phyllis), whose screen handle refers to the seven daughters of Atlas and Pleione but is apparently enough to throw off pursuers.

Almost everyone also agrees that men "flame" more than women, meaning they are more prone to firing off missives that are intended as insults or provocations. "For men, the ideal of the Internet is that it should be this exchange of conflicting views," says Susan Herring, a linguistics professor at University of Texas at Arlington who has written extensively about women's participation on computer networks. "But women are made uncomfortable by flaming. As little girls, women are taught to be nice. Little boys are taught to disagree and argue and even fight."

A recent case in point: Entering a debate on smoking in restaurants that was taking place in a newsgroup on the Internet, a user named Colleen politely staked out her position as a question. "Why is it necessary to smoke inside a restaurant?" she asked. In reply, a user named Peter instantly flamed. He announced he would not pay good money to eat if he couldn't smoke at the same time. "You people are complete and utter morons!" he declared.

"Women come online more to build relationships, to talk about issues," contends Susan William DeFife, the founding partner of Women's Leadership Connection (WLC), an online service linked to Prodigy.

Ask Rebecca Shnur of Easton, Pa., a WLC subscriber who effusively   20
likens being online to an "all-night college bull session. It's been a long time since I've talked like this with women," she says.

Men tend to be less concerned about making permanent connections. "I think they're much more willing to just jump online and see where it goes," says DeFife. "And, of course, to flame."

If men tend to be flamers, do women tend to be flamees? Nancy Tamosaitis, a New York author who has written several books about the online world, thinks they do. "By expressing any kind of strong opinion, women tend to get flamed a lot more than men do," Tamosaitis says. "There's a real strong culture on the Internet. Men feel they own it. It's like an old boys' club. They don't want women or newcomers, especially female newcomers."

When Tamosaitis is flamed, she points out, it's almost always by a man. "I can count the flames I've gotten from women on the fingers of both hands," she says. "And men seem to bring it to a personal level. A woman will say, 'You're out of place!' A man will say, 'You're ugly!'"

CONFRONTATION WORKS

But women who seek a softer, gentler information superhighway may find themselves sending messages into the wind. Says Sherry Terkle, an

MIT professor and an authoritative voice on the subject of sociology and technology: "If you send out an online message that's inclusive, that includes many points of view, or that's conciliatory, you may get no response. And women are more likely to make that kind of communication, whereupon no message comes back.

"But if you make a controversial statement, maybe even an exaggeration, you're more likely to get responses. So the medium pushes people toward a controversial style. It rewards the quick jab. It encourages a kind of confrontational style, which men are more comfortable with."

When Susan Herring, the University of Texas linguist, disseminated an electronic questionnaire on Netiquette, even some of the online comments about the survey itself took on male/female styles. "I hope this doesn't sound terribly rude, but a survey is one of the last things I want to see in my mailbox," apologized one woman in declining to respond. A man who also had better things to do was less polite. "What bothers me most," he declared, "are abuses of networking such as yours: unsolicited, lengthy, and intrusive postings designed to further others' research by wasting my time."

WOMEN ARE "LURKERS"

Meanwhile, research shows that women who go online tend to send fewer messages per capita than do men and that their messages are shorter. There is also a widespread belief that more women than men are "lurkers": people who go online to read other people's messages rather than to participate. "It's the same way you find many women sitting in physics class and acting like wallpaper," Terkle says, referring to male-dominated science classrooms. "They're just not comfortable because it matters who's in charge. It matters who seems to be in a position of power."

Even Michael O'Brien, an Internet magazine columnist who is by no means convinced that there is much difference between the online sexes ("I see fewer differences on the Internet than in everyday life"), allows that women "usually come across as the voice of reason. You almost never see a female counterflame. Men flame back and forth. Usually women just shut up and go away."

In her best-selling 1990 book, *You Just Don't Understand: Women & Men in Conversation*, Georgetown University linguist Deborah Tannen described men as being comfortable with the language of confrontation and women comfortable with consensus. A self-described e-mail junkie, Tannen sees much of the same behavior online. "Actually, I would say that the differences that typify men's and women's [offline] style actually get *exaggerated* online," she says. "I subscribe to very few universals, but one I believe in is that men are more likely to use opposition, or fighting, or even warlike images. Women are not as likely to do that. They're more likely to take things as a nasty attack."

Tannen recalls coming across a seemingly angry online message writ-   30
ten by a male graduate student that concluded with the command to
"get your hands off my Cyberspace!"

"I had an exchange with the fellow about it because it struck me, a
woman, as being fairly hostile and inappropriate," Tannen recalls. "But
then I realized I was overinterpreting the hostility of what to him was a
fairly ritualized and almost playful statement."

Nancy Rhine wishes more women would adopt this type of playful-
ness in cyberspace. Slightly more than a year ago, Rhine founded
Women's Wire, a minuscule online service (1,500 subscribers compared
to, say, American Online's 2 million), because she believed women
weren't participating enough online. Between 90 and 95 percent of her
subscribers are female, she says, and she contends that Women's Wire is a
more polite and less flame-filled place than other services.

"But there's a pro and con to that," she concedes. "On the one
hand, this is a very comfortable environment. On the other hand, I
sometimes wish there were more characters posting things that were
thought-provoking and stimulating.

"Women are conditioned to be nice, to be the caretakers, and that's
the way it feels online here," Rhine says. "But I'd like to see us take more
risks. I'd like to see women be more outrageous online."

FOCUSING ON CONTENT

1. What is the "Yo alert" (1–4)? Why is it particularly relevant to Cobb's essay?

2. In what ways are chat areas and newsgroups like "a real bad '70s disco"
   (15)? How does harassment influence how people communicate on the
   Internet?

3. According to the experts quoted by Cobb, why are men far more likely than
   women to flame? How does this tendency reflect the different goals men and
   women have when they communicate over the Internet?

4. What is a "lurker" (27)? Why do many women choose to lurk?

5. What can result when the members of a group of Internet subscribers are
   almost entirely female? What are the advantages of all-female communication? What are the disadvantages?

FOCUSING ON WRITING

1. Cobb begins his essay with an unusual three-sentence sequence. "Consider
   the Yo alert. Yo? Yo." Why is "Yo" an effective subject with which to open
   his essay? Do you find the beginning of the essay effective in capturing your
   attention? (Glossary: *Beginnings and Endings*) Why or why not?

2. Look at the essay again, paying close attention to the credentials of the experts Cobb quotes to support his arguments. (Glossary: *Evidence*) What do they have in common? Why do you think Cobb chooses them for his essay?

3. Cobb's essay has a light tone, despite the fact that it addresses two potentially controversial subjects. First, as he acknowledges, the assumption that the Internet is gender blind is still prevalent, so his argument may not be well received by some people. Second, gender differences are always a volatile topic. How does Cobb attempt to present his material in a non-threatening fashion? Identify several passages in which Cobb establishes his tone. (Glossary: *Tone*)

4. There has been much investigation of the new vocabulary spawned by the growth of the Internet. Even terms such as *e-mail* and *cyberspace*, which seem so ordinary now, were specialized terms in the early 1990s. Identify the Internet-specific vocabulary that Cobb uses in his piece. (Glossary: *Technical Language*) What does the use of such language indicate about Cobb's audience? (Glossary: *Audience*)

LANGUAGE IN ACTION

Several studies have explored how the different genders participate in various online discussions. The results of these studies agree with Cobb's anecdotal data — that men tend to post more, and longer, messages and that they tend to be more aggressive about promoting their views. Read the following excerpt from a 1993 study by S. C. Herring. Then jot down your thoughts about each posting. How did each make you react? Would you be more likely to respond to one or the other? Why? Discuss your reactions with your class. Why do you think gender is still so important in academic Internet discussion groups? How might women overcome the supposed "handicaps" of their communication style when participating in online discourse?

TABLE 1   Features of Women's and Men's Language

Women's Language	Men's Language
Attenuated assertions	Strong assertions
Apologies	Self-promotion
Explicit justifications	Presuppositions
Questions	Rhetorical questions
Personal orientation	Authoritative orientation
Supports others	Challenges others
	Humor/sarcasm

The following examples, taken from messages posted during the LINGUIST "issues" discussion, illustrate some of the features of each style.

Female Contributor: I am intrigued by your comment that work such as that represented in WFDT may not be as widely represented in LSA as other work because its argumentation style doesn't lend itself to falsification à la Popper. Could you say a bit more about what you mean here? I am interested because I think similar mismatches in argumentation are at stake in other areas of cognitive science, as well as because I study argumentation as a key (social and cognitive) tool for human knowledge construction.

[personal orientation, attenuation, questions, justification]

Male Contributor: It is obvious that there are two (and only two) paradigms for the conduct of scientific inquiry into an issue on which there is no consensus. One is [. . .]. But, deplorable as that may be, note that either paradigm (if pursued honestly) will lead to truth anyway. That is, whichever side is wrong will sooner or later discover that fact on its own. If, God forbid, autonomy and/or modularity should turn out to be His truth, then those who have other ideas will sooner or later find this out.

[authoritative orientation, strong assertions, sarcasm]

WRITING SUGGESTIONS

1. One of the important aspects of Internet communications — and a reason many assume the Internet is gender neutral — is anonymity. Participants in online discourse are judged by their words alone and may reveal only as much about themselves as they wish. Think about your own Internet correspondence, whether via e-mail, chat rooms, newsgroups, or other online forums. Write an essay in which you explore how the anonymity of Internet correspondence affects you. Are you more willing to be confrontational or provocative in online communication? Have you developed an online persona that differs from your typical personality? Or does your online voice closely resemble your actual personality and face-to-face communication style? Do you think your gender influences how you use the Internet? Explain your reasoning.

2. Consider the following quote from Nancy Tamosaitis: "There's a real strong culture on the Internet. Men feel they own it. It's like an old boys' club. They don't want women or newcomers, especially female newcomers" (22). Since 1995, when Cobb wrote his article, the Internet has become much less the domain of technology experts and far more a part of everyday life. Do you think Tamosaitis's quote is still valid? Write an essay in which you assess the current state of Internet communications and predict where they will go. Is there a chance that these communications can become the gender-neutral, inclusive forum so eagerly promoted by online service providers? Use Cobb's essay and your own observations to support your position.

Make Me Sound Like I Don't Suck

JULIET GABRIEL

*Juliet Gabriel is a pseudonym for a magazine editor and writer liv-
ing in New York. Along with the title of the article, the editor offered the following about the piece: "When my friends ask me for
help with their personal ads, I edit them the way I do writers at my
magazine, with a firm but gentle hand." This article appeared in
August 2003 in Salon.com as a response to the growing popularity
of online personal ads. Gabriel offers her perspective as editor in
order to humorously reveal how accurately, or inaccurately, men
and women represent themselves to each other in print.*

WRITING TO DISCOVER: *Have you ever written an online personal ad in which you attempted to describe yourself in a manner
appealing to the woman or man you hoped to communicate with
and eventually meet? What did you write about yourself? If you
haven't written such an advertisement, what do you think you
might want others to know about yourself in a personal ad? Would
you be honest?*

As an editor by trade, I get the odd request to look over a fellowship
application, a vituperative letter to AOL Time Warner cable customer
service, a story pitch/TV proposal/film treatment. But lately, friends
have also been asking me to edit their online personal profiles. It can't be
my own dating résumé that qualifies me for such a job, but the directives
are fairly straightforward: Don't tell anyone I'm doing this, and *do* make
me sound like I don't suck.

My ambivalence toward Internet-abetted dating turned to opposition when a friend wanted to set me up with a co-worker, who had his
own profile posted on Nerve.com. I qualified for a mortgage more easily
than satisfying the preferences of this fellow, who listed an atheistic/ag-
nostic/Buddhist, Caucasian/Latina/Middle Easterner, with a graduate
degree, at least 5-foot-2, as his ideal (me: none of the above). Who wants
to go on a date already handicapped? Still, I understand the limitations of
a screen's worth of one's wants and desires. In the spirit of "those who
can, do; those who can't, teach," I do my best to help my friends, though
perhaps they should know that my favorite personal ad, from a local Seattle newspaper, described what a date could come to expect as "stony
stares, long silences, and blunt objects."

As with all writers, my friends want me to help them present their
best selves. As with any editor, I try to do so without leaving footprints. I
don't always succeed. Sometimes I make them sound like someone I'd
want to date. (Or try editing the profile of someone you have a crush

on — I almost want to make them sound bad. On the other hand, I now have good intel.) But a career editing fussy writers serves me well with this job. The general rule I use as a magazine editor — be firm, but gentle — applies to personal-ad editing as well. As with some writers, my friends get defensive ("You're basically saying it sucks") or lazy ("Fine. You write it"). When one friend described her favorite on-screen sex scene as "the one with Jude Law as a Russian officer," I told her to do some reporting and sent her to IMDB.com to get the title (*Enemy at the Gates*). As with magazine editing, you part cheerlead, part ask for more, part ignore their protests and insist they trust you. And, of course, always let them think they've come up with the final product themselves.

Editing is subjective. One editor's treasure is another's trash. Under the "Five things I can't live without" section I can't delete intangibles like "laughter" and "the ability to dream" fast enough. Or, under "Things you'll find in my bedroom," "bare walls," "piles of paper," and "free stuff I get from work" says little. "Less Ikea furniture than before," tells me more (you're creative and upwardly mobile). I encourage them to be inventive (without inventing), as every answer might be the difference between someone hitting "reply to profile" and logging off.

Sometimes they're their own best editors: Wanting someone "who 5 can use the word 'eschew'" or "name the members of the Supreme Court" are details I couldn't come up with for them. Though I wish all profiles would banish the section, "Blank is sexy, Blank is sexier." For that one, my friends and I usually come to an agreement after a debate as confrontational and exhausting as a Thai massage. One male friend wrote, "Intelligence is sexy, sincerity is sexier," which I thought I had read before in the *New York* magazine personals. Instead, I suggested changing "sincerity" to "curiosity" — he wouldn't really want to go out with someone who was too sincere, anyway. He hated that as well as "Watching sports with me is sexy, discussing sports with me is sexier." (He didn't want to come off as the ESPN *SportsCenter* freak that he is.) After too many more potential scenarios, he finally agreed to the Nigella Lawson-inspired "cooking for someone is sexy, feeding someone is sexier."

Now that I've been doing this for a while, I've started to feel responsible for the outcomes: It will be my fault if a profile doesn't thwart a Friday night flipping between the History Channel and the Food Network. But the pleasant byproduct is learning more about my friends and how they view themselves. What surprises me is that, perhaps in some exercise in modesty, they don't write about the things that make them shine, at least to me. I ended up telling one friend in an IM exchange all the traits I found appealing, ones I thought he ought to consider mentioning.

"You are equally as comfortable at the theater as in a pool hall, as happy dining on foie gras as scarfing In-N-Out burgers."

"I am?"

"You can talk to anyone in a room, whether they're a film director, sports barfly, or wanderlust-bitten nomad."

"I can?"   10

And you're such a nice guy. Why aren't *we* dating? He didn't use any of my lines (I checked), but we understand each other a little better. I've also learned about my friends in regard to what they're looking for, what's important to them, what floats their boat. I thought I knew. Or assumed. Or never bothered to ask. One friend won't date a vegetarian (points for him). Another friend is willing to wait if his partner doesn't want to have sex until marriage. Who knew? I am impressed by their candor, their openness to risk, their willingness to be vulnerable. After all, my name or photo appears nowhere; editors work behind the scenes.

Whether or not the steak dinners they've scored are in some way attributable to my edits, in the end I think they just want to be told it's OK, it's great, you're OK, you're great. Don't change a thing. I love your profile. Don't change. You will be loved.

FOCUSING ON CONTENT

1. What does the author mean when she says that she attempts to help her friends with their online profiles but "to do so without leaving footprints"(3)?

2. What does Gabriel mean when she says that she encourages her writers "to be inventive (without inventing)"(4)?

3. In paragraph 5, Gabriel says she hates the "Blank is sexy, Blank is sexier" section of some online ads. She offers "Intelligence is sexy, curiosity is sexier" as being preferential to a friend's "Intelligence is sexy, sincerity is sexier." Why do you suppose she sees the former as preferable to the later? Do you agree?

4. Do Gabriel's friends really want to have their personal ads edited? If not, what are they seeking from her?

5. What impresses Gabriel most about the friends whose ads she edits?

FOCUSING ON WRITING

1. What is Gabriel's purpose in this article? (Glossary: *Purpose*) Is the article more about editing for print or online? Explain.

2. What is Gabriel's thesis? Is it stated or implied? Explain. (Glossary: *Thesis*)

3. The author gives herself a feminine pseudonym. Is there any indication that the author is, in fact, female?

4. How effective is Gabriel's conclusion in light of her thesis? (Glossary: *Beginnings and Endings*) Is the ending, in fact, her thesis? Explain.

LANGUAGE IN ACTION

Since the idea of matchmaking began there have been countless success stories of people being happily brought together to share their lives. Taking into account the nature of our contemporary society where time is short and romance might be aided by the latest technology, we can see the matchmaking business thriving in print media and online. Still, there has always been cynicism about the idea: If two people are attractive enough in looks and personality, genuine in their motives, and sincere in their interests, they would otherwise find mates and would not have to resort to something as mechanical as an arrangement contrived by a third party. Examine the following cartoon about personal ads, or as some now call them "Personal Profiles," and discuss the implications of cynicism about matchmaking.

"Here's one. Few-bricks-short-of-a-load
seeks One-oar-out-of-the-water."

WRITING SUGGESTIONS

1. Examine several Web sites that offer online personal profiles and study their formats. Chose one of the formats that appeals to you and craft a personal profile for yourself. Examine the profile and try to assess if you have been honest with yourself and with those who will read your profile. If you would like, extend this assignment and construct an essay about the writing of your profile, explaining your thoughts and feelings during the process of creating your profile.

2. Having read Gabriel's article and having engaged in attempts to help friends and classmates in both formal and informal settings to improve their writing, write an essay about what you have learned about the role of an editor. Among other bits of advice, Gabriel writes about being supportive but firm, not leaving any footprints, asking for more information, and the need to be imaginative without telling untruths. How might you elaborate on this advice and extend it to other issues?

PICTURING LANGUAGE

This photograph was taken in 1976. What, if anything, has changed since the time of the photograph with regard to the struggle for equality within the institution of marriage? How do you respond to this man's "demonstration"? What are the issues that he is addressing with his signs? What is his overall message? Are the demonstrator's issues legitimate for you, or do they simply represent a breakdown in communication between men and women? What issues or feelings about marriage or long-term relationships does this photograph raise for you?

How to Give Orders Like a Man

Deborah Tannen

Deborah Tannen, professor of linguistics at Georgetown University, was born in 1945 in Brooklyn, New York. Tannen received her B.A. in English from the State University of New York at Binghamton in 1966 and taught English in Greece until 1968. She then earned an M.A. in English literature from Wayne State University in 1970. While pursuing her Ph.D. in linguistics at the University of California, Berkeley, she received several prizes for her poetry and short fiction. Her work has appeared in New York, Vogue, *and the* New York Times Magazine. *In addition, she has authored four best-selling books on how people communicate:* That's Not What I Meant! *(1986),* You Just Don't Understand *(1990),* Talking from 9 to 5 *(1994), and* The Argument Culture: Stopping America's War of Words *(1998). The success of these books attests to the public's interest in language, especially when it pertains to gender differences. Tannen's most recent book is entitled* I only say this because I love you *(2001).*

In this essay, first published in the New York Times Magazine *in August 1994, Tannen looks at the variety of ways in which orders are given and received. Interestingly, she concludes that contrary to popular belief, directness is not necessarily logical or effective, and indirectness is not necessarily manipulative or insecure.*

WRITING TO DISCOVER: *Write about a time in your life when you were ordered to do something. Who gave you the order — a friend, a parent, maybe a teacher? Did the person's relationship to you affect how you carried out the order? Did it make a difference to you whether the order giver was male or female? Why?*

A university president was expecting a visit from a member of the board of trustees. When her secretary buzzed to tell her that the board member had arrived, she left her office and entered the reception area to greet him. Before ushering him into her office, she handed her secretary a sheet of paper and said: "I've just finished drafting this letter. Do you think you could type it right away? I'd like to get it out before lunch. And would you please do me a favor and hold all calls while I'm meeting with Mr. Smith?"

When they sat down behind the closed door of her office, Mr. Smith began by telling her that he thought she had spoken inappropriately to her secretary. "Don't forget," he said. "*You're* the president!"

Putting aside the question of the appropriateness of his admonishing the president on her way of speaking, it is revealing — and representative of many Americans' assumptions — that the indirect way in which the university president told her secretary what to do struck him as self-deprecating. He took it as evidence that she didn't think she had the right to make demands of her secretary. He probably thought he was giving her a needed pep talk, bolstering her self-confidence.

I challenge the assumption that talking in an indirect way necessarily reveals powerlessness, lack of self-confidence, or anything else about the character of the speaker. Indirectness is a fundamental element in human communication. It is also one of the elements that varies most from one culture to another, and one that can cause confusion and misunderstanding when speakers have different habits with regard to using it. I also want to dispel the assumption that American women tend to be more indirect than American men. Women and men are both indirect, but in addition to differences associated with their backgrounds — regional, ethnic, and class — they tend to be indirect in different situations and in different ways.

At work, we need to get others to do things, and we all have different   5
ways of accomplishing this. Any individual's ways will vary depending on who is being addressed — a boss, a peer, or a subordinate. At one extreme are bald commands. At the other are requests so indirect that they don't sound like requests at all, but are just a statement of need or a description of a situation. People with direct styles of asking others to do things perceive indirect requests — if they perceive them as requests at all — as manipulative. But this is often just a way of blaming others for our discomfort with their styles.

The indirect style is no more manipulative than making a telephone call, asking "Is Rachel there?" and expecting whoever answers the phone to put Rachel on. Only a child is likely to answer "Yes" and continue holding the phone — not out of orneriness but because of inexperience with the conventional meaning of the question. (A mischievous adult might do it to tease.) Those who feel that indirect orders are illogical or manipulative do not recognize the conventional nature of indirect requests.

Issuing orders indirectly can be the prerogative of those in power. Imagine, for example, a master who says "It's cold in here" and expects a servant to make a move to close a window, while a servant who says the same thing is not likely to see his employer rise to correct the situation and make him more comfortable. Indeed, a Frenchman raised in Brittany tells me that his family never gave bald commands to their servants but always communicated orders in indirect and highly polite ways. This pattern renders less surprising the finding of David Bellinger and Jean Berko Gleason that fathers' speech to their young children had a higher incidence than mothers' of both direct imperatives like "Turn the bolt with the wrench" *and* indirect orders like "The wheel is going to fall off."

The use of indirectness can hardly be understood without the cross-cultural perspective. Many Americans find it self-evident that directness is logical and aligned with power while indirectness is akin to dishonesty and reflects subservience. But for speakers raised in most of the world's cultures, varieties of indirectness are the norm in communication. This is the pattern found by a Japanese sociolinguist, Kunihiko Harada, in his analysis of a conversation he recorded between a Japanese boss and a subordinate.

The markers of superior status were clear. One speaker was a Japanese man in his late forties who managed the local branch of a Japanese private school in the United States. His conversational partner was a Japanese American woman in her early twenties who worked at the school. By virtue of his job, his age, and his native fluency in the language being taught, the man was in the superior position. Yet when he addressed the woman, he frequently used polite language and almost always used indirectness. For example, he had tried and failed to find a photography store that would make a black-and-white print from a color negative for a brochure they were producing. He let her know that he wanted her to take over the task by stating the situation and allowed her to volunteer to do it: (This is a translation of the Japanese conversation.)

> On this matter, that, that, on the leaflet? This photo, I'm thinking of changing it to black-and-white and making it clearer. . . . I went to a photo shop and asked them. They said they didn't do black-and-white. I asked if they knew any place that did. They said they didn't know. They weren't very helpful, but anyway, a place must be found, the negative brought to it, the picture developed.

Harada observes, "Given the fact that there are some duties to be   10
performed and that there are two parties present, the subordinate is supposed to assume that those are his or her obligation." It was precisely because of his higher status that the boss was free to choose whether to speak formally or informally, to assert his power or to play it down and build rapport — an option not available to the subordinate, who would have seemed cheeky if she had chosen a style that enhanced friendliness and closeness.

The same pattern was found by a Chinese sociolinguist, Yuling Pan, in a meeting of officials involved in a neighborhood youth program. All spoke in ways that reflected their place in the hierarchy. A subordinate addressing a superior always spoke in a deferential way, but a superior addressing a subordinate could either be authoritarian, demonstrating his power, or friendly, establishing rapport. The ones in power had the option of choosing which style to use. In this spirit, I have been told by people who prefer their bosses to give orders indirectly that those who issue bald commands must be pretty insecure; otherwise why would they have to bolster their egos by throwing their weight around?

I am not inclined to accept that those who give orders directly are really insecure and powerless, any more than I want to accept that judgment of those who give indirect orders. The conclusion to be drawn is that ways of talking should not be taken as obvious evidence of inner psychological states like insecurity or lack of confidence. Considering the many influences on conversational style, individuals have a wide range of ways of getting things done and expressing their emotional states. Person ality characteristics like insecurity cannot be linked to ways of speaking in an automatic, self-evident way.

Those who expect orders to be given indirectly are offended when they come unadorned. One woman said that when her boss gives her instructions, she feels she should click her heels, salute, and say "Yes, boss!" His directions strike her as so imperious as to border on the militaristic. Yet I received a letter from a man telling me that indirect orders were a fundamental part of his military training. He wrote:

> Many years ago, when I was in the Navy, I was training to be a radio technician. One class I was in was taught by a chief radioman, a regular Navy man who had been to sea, and who was then in his third hitch. The students, about 20 of us, were fresh out of boot camp, with no sea duty and little knowledge of real Navy life. One day in class the chief said it was hot in the room. The students didn't react, except perhaps to nod in agreement. The chief repeated himself: "It's hot in this room." Again there was no reaction from the students.
>
> Then the chief explained. He wasn't looking for agreement or discussion from us. When he said that the room was hot, he expected us to do something about it — like opening the window. He tried it one more time, and this time all of us left our workbenches and headed for the windows. We had learned. And we had many opportunities to apply what we had learned.

This letter especially intrigued me because "It's cold in here" is the standard sentence used by linguists to illustrate an indirect way of getting someone to do something — as I used it earlier. In this example, it is the very obviousness and rigidity of the military hierarchy that makes the statement of a problem sufficient to trigger corrective action on the part of subordinates.

A man who had worked at the Pentagon reinforced the view that the   15 burden of interpretation is on subordinates in the military — and he noticed the difference when he moved to a position in the private sector. He was frustrated when he'd say to his new secretary, for example, "Do we have a list of invitees?" and be told, "I don't know; we probably do" rather than "I'll get it for you." Indeed, he explained, at the Pentagon, such a question would likely be heard as a reproach that the list was not already on his desk.

The suggestion that indirectness is associated with the military must come as a surprise to many. But everyone is indirect, meaning more than is put into words and deriving meaning from words that are never actually said. It's a matter of where, when, and how we each tend to be

indirect and look for hidden meanings. But indirectness has a built-in liability. There is a risk that the other will either miss or choose to ignore
your meaning.

On January 13, 1982, a freezing cold, snowy day in Washington, Air
Florida Flight 90 took off from National Airport, but could not get the lift
it needed to keep climbing. It crashed into a bridge linking Washington to
the state of Virginia and plunged into the Potomac. Of the 79 people on
board, all but 5 perished, many floundering and drowning in the icy water
while horror-stricken bystanders watched helplessly from the river's edge
and millions more watched, aghast, on their television screens. Experts
later concluded that the plane had waited too long after deicing to take off.
Fresh buildup of ice on the wings and engine brought the plane down.
How could the pilot and co-pilot have made such a blunder? Didn't at least
one of them realize it was dangerous to take off under these conditions?

Charlotte Linde, a linguist at the Institute for Research on Learning
in Palo Alto, Calif., has studied the "black box" recordings of cockpit
conversations that preceded crashes as well as tape recordings of conversations that took place among crews during flight simulations in which
problems were presented. Among the black box conversations she studied was the one between the pilot and co-pilot just before the Air Florida
crash. The pilot, it turned out, had little experience flying in icy weather.
The co-pilot had a bit more, and it became heartbreakingly clear on
analysis that he had tried to warn the pilot, but he did so indirectly.

The co-pilot repeatedly called attention to the bad weather and to ice
building up on other planes:

> Co-pilot: Look how the ice is just hanging on his, ah, back, back there,
> see that?
> . . .
> Co-pilot: See all those icicles on the back there and everything?
> Captain: Yeah.

He expressed concern early on about the long waiting time between   20
deicing:

> Co-pilot: Boy, this is a, this is a losing battle here on trying to de-ice
> those things, it [gives] you a false feeling of security, that's all that does.

Shortly after they were given clearance to take off, he again expressed
concern:

> Co-pilot: Let's check these tops again since we been setting here awhile.
> Captain: I think we get to go here in a minute.

When they were about to take off, the co-pilot called attention to the
engine instrument readings, which were not normal:

> Co-pilot: That don't seem right, does it? [three-second pause] Ah,
> that's not right. . . .
> Captain: Yes, it is, there's 80.
> Co-pilot: Naw, I don't think that's right. [seven-second pause] Ah,
> maybe it is.
> Captain: Hundred and twenty.
> Co-pilot: I don't know.

The takeoff proceeded, and 37 seconds later the pilot and co-pilot exchanged their last words.

The co-pilot had repeatedly called the pilot's attention to dangerous conditions but did not directly suggest they abort the takeoff. In Linde's judgment, he was expressing his concern indirectly, and the captain didn't pick up on it — with tragic results.

That the co-pilot was trying to warn the captain indirectly is sup-   25
ported by evidence from another airline accident — a relatively minor one — investigated by Linde that also involved the unsuccessful use of indirectness.

On July 9, 1978, Allegheny Airlines Flight 453 was landing at Monroe County Airport in Rochester, when it overran the runway by 728 feet. Everyone survived. This meant that the captain and co-pilot could be interviewed. It turned out that the plane had been flying too fast for a safe landing. The captain should have realized this and flown around a second time, decreasing his speed before trying to land. The captain said he simply had not been aware that he was going too fast. But the co-pilot told interviewers that he "tried to warn the captain in subtle ways, like mentioning the possibility of a tail wind and the slowness of flap extension." His exact words were recorded in the black box. The crosshatches indicate words deleted by the National Transportation Safety Board and were probably expletives:

> Co-pilot: Yeah, it looks like you got a tail wind here.
> Captain: Yeah.
> [?]: Yeah [it] moves awfully # slow.
> Co-pilot: Yeah the # flaps are slower than a #.
> Captain: We'll make it, gonna have to add power.
> Co-pilot: I know.

The co-pilot thought the captain would understand that if there was a tail wind, it would result in the plane going too fast, and if the flaps were slow, they would be inadequate to break the speed sufficiently for a safe landing. He thought the captain would then correct for the error by not trying to land. But the captain said he didn't interpret the co-pilot's remarks to mean they were going too fast.

Linde believes it is not a coincidence that the people being indirect in these conversations were the co-pilots. In her analyses of flight crew conversations she found it was typical for the speech of subordinates to be more mitigated — polite, tentative, or indirect. She also found that topics broached in a mitigated way were more likely to fail, and that captains were more likely to ignore hints from their crew members than the other way around. These findings are evidence that not only can indirectness and other forms of mitigation be misunderstood, but they are also easier to ignore.

In the Air Florida case, it is doubtful that the captain did not realize what the co-pilot was suggesting when he said, "Let's check these tops again since we been setting here awhile" (though it seems safe to assume he did not realize the gravity of the co-pilot's concern). But the indirectness of the co-pilot's phrasing certainly made it easier for the pilot to ignore it. In this sense, the captain's response, "I think we get to go here in a minute," was an indirect way of saying, "I'd rather not." In view of these patterns, the flight crews of some airlines are now given training to express their concerns, even to superiors, in more direct ways.

The conclusion that people should learn to express themselves more   30
directly has a ring of truth to it — especially for Americans. But direct communication is not necessarily always preferable. If more direct expression is better communication, then the most direct-speaking crews should be the best ones. Linde was surprised to find in her research that crews that used the most mitigated speech were often judged the best crews. As part of the study of talk among cockpit crews in flight simulations, the trainers observed and rated the performances of the simulation crews. The crews they rated top in performance had a higher rate of mitigation than crews they judged to be poor.

This finding seems at odds with the role played by indirectness in the examples of crashes that we just saw. Linde concluded that since every utterance functions on two levels — the referential (what it says) and the relational (what it implies about the speaker's relationships), crews that attend to the relational level will be better crews. A similar explanation was suggested by Kunihiko Harada. He believes that the secret of successful communication lies not in teaching subordinates to be more direct, but in teaching higher-ups to be more sensitive to indirect meaning. In other words, the crashes resulted not only because the co-pilots tried to alert the captains to danger indirectly but also because the captains were not attuned to the co-pilots' hints. What made for successful performance among the best crews might have been the ability — or willingness — of listeners to pick up on hints, just as members of families or longstanding couples come to understand each other's meaning without anyone being particularly explicit.

It is not surprising that a Japanese sociolinguist came up with this explanation; what he described is the Japanese system, by which good communication is believed to take place when meaning is gleaned without being stated directly — or at all.

While Americans believe that "the squeaky wheel gets the grease" (so it's best to speak up), the Japanese say, "The nail that sticks out gets hammered back in" (so it's best to remain silent if you don't want to be hit on the head). Many Japanese scholars writing in English have tried to explain to bewildered Americans the ethics of a culture in which silence is often given greater value than speech, and ideas are believed to be best communicated without being explicitly stated. Key concepts in Japanese give a flavor of the attitudes toward language that they reveal — and set in relief the strategies that Americans encounter at work when talking to other Americans.

Takie Sugiyama Lebra, a Japanese-born anthropologist, explains that one of the most basic values in Japanese culture is *omoiyari*, which she translates as "empathy." Because of *omoiyari*, it should not be necessary to state one's meaning explicitly; people should be able to sense each other's meaning intuitively. Lebra explains that it is typical for a Japanese speaker to let sentences trail off rather than complete them because expressing ideas before knowing how they will be received seems intrusive. "Only an insensitive, uncouth person needs a direct, verbal, complete message," Lebra says.

Sasshi, the anticipation of another's message through insightful   35
guesswork, is considered an indication of maturity.

Considering the value placed on direct communication by Americans in general, and especially by American business people, it is easy to imagine that many American readers may scoff at such conversational habits. But the success of Japanese businesses makes it impossible to continue to maintain that there is anything inherently inefficient about such conversational conventions. With indirectness, as with all aspects of conversational style, our own habitual style seems to make sense — seems polite, right, and good. The light cast by the habits and assumptions of another culture can help us see our way to the flexibility and respect for other styles that is the only best way of speaking.

FOCUSING ON CONTENT

1. How does Tannen define indirect speech? What does she see as the built-in liability of indirect speech? Do you see comparable liability inherent in direct speech?

2. Tannen doesn't contest a finding that fathers had a higher incidence of both direct imperatives and indirect orders than mothers. How does she interpret the meaning of these results?

3. Why doesn't Tannen tell her audience how to deal with an insecure boss?

4. Why is it typical for Japanese speakers to let their sentences trail off?

FOCUSING ON WRITING

1. What is Tannen's thesis, and where does she present it? (Glossary: *Thesis*)

2. For what audience has Tannen written this essay? Does this help to explain why she focuses primarily on indirect communication? Why or why not? (Glossary: *Audience*)

3. Tannen gives two examples of flight accidents that resulted from indirect speech, and yet she then explains that top-performing flight teams used indirect speech more often than poorly performing teams. How do these seemingly contradictory examples support the author's argument?

4. Tannen uses several examples from other cultures. What do these examples help to show us about Americans?

LANGUAGE IN ACTION

Tannen's book *Talking from 9 to 5* (1994) deals with how to handle the different ways men and women communicate in a business setting. Problems at work that are created through gender-based misunderstandings can be significant, as indicated in the following excerpt from a communication seminar run by P. J. Poole, a company that specializes in such seminars. Using information in Tannen's essay, make a list of the specific problems gender-communication awareness can solve in work situations. What kinds of miscommunications might occur between men and women in the workplace? How might such communication create "systemic barriers — barriers that negatively impact individual productivity, morale, and job satisfaction"?

GENDER COMMUNICATION AWARENESS

Communication is a key issue facing today's organizations. Differences in gender communication styles can affect what gets done, how it gets done, who gets heard, who gets acknowledged, and who gets credit.

Consider that:

• Men and women communicate, approach work place challenges, solve problems, and provide leadership in remarkably different ways. What is interpreted as assertive in a man can be viewed as aggressive in a woman.

• Not understanding these differences creates systemic barriers — barriers that negatively impact individual productivity, morale, and job satisfaction. Not to mention that inhibiting employee contribution has a negative impact on your organization's bottom line.

Misunderstandings and miscommunications between men and women happen every day for two reasons. First, we have different communication styles. Second, and more importantly, we do not know it — we think that everyone communicates in the same way.

Awareness, understanding, and valuing our different communication styles removes barriers created by misunderstandings. It ensures that men and women are flexible and able to adapt to different situations. It impacts their ability to work together, as well as their ability to get ahead in the organization. In other words, it affects their productivity.

Understanding and valuing our different communication styles will result in:

- successful communications,
- the reduction of gender conflicts,
- the improvement of working relationships, and
- increased productivity.

WRITING SUGGESTIONS

1. Tannen concludes that "the light cast by the habits and assumptions of another culture can help us see our way to the flexibility and respect for other styles that is the only best way of speaking" (36). Write an essay in which you use concrete examples from your own experience, observation, or readings to agree or disagree with her conclusion.

2. Write an essay comparing the command styles of two people — either people you know or fictional characters. You might consider your parents, teachers, professors, coaches, television characters like President Bartlett (*The West Wing*) or Jack Briston (*Alias*) or characters from movies or novels. What conclusions can you draw from your analysis?

He and She: What's the Real Difference?

CLIVE THOMPSON

Clive Thompson was born in 1968 in Toronto, Canada, and received a B.A. in political science and English from the University of Toronto in 1987. He began his career writing about politics, but due to his lifelong interest in computers, switched to writing primarily about science technology. When asked to submit his biography for this book, Thompson wrote the following of this piece: "What interested me about this story was how the scientists used artificial intelligence to examine questions about male and female identity that are as old as the hills. Human philosophy and linguistics has for millennia been limited by the fact that human brains are only good at observing small collections of text at a time; when we try to think about the way language works, we rely on our knowledge of the thousands of books and articles we've read in our lifetime. But computers are able to scan millions and billions of pieces of human writing — allowing them to observe patterns that we ourselves would never be able to spot."

In 2002, Thompson was a Knight Science Journalism Fellow at M.I.T. His writing and research is archived online at www.collisiondetection.net. Thompson writes regularly for the New York Times Magazine, Discover, Wired, Details, *and the* Boston Globe, *where this article originally appeared on July 6, 2003. He currently lives in New York.*

WRITING TO DISCOVER: *Think about what we can learn about the author of a piece of writing aside from what the author tells us directly. Can you tell what a writer is like as a person, a writer's age, or if the writer is a male or female from the style of the writing? Explain how you came to your conclusions.*

Imagine, for a second, that no [author's name] is attached to this article. Judging by the words alone, can you figure out if I am a man or a woman?

Moshe Koppel can. This summer, a group of computer scientists — including Koppel, a professor at Israeli's Bar-Ilan University — are publishing two papers in which they describe the successful results of a gender-detection experiment. The scholars have developed a computer algorithm that can examine an anonymous text and determine, with accuracy rates of better than 80 percent, whether the author is male or female. For centuries, linguists and cultural pundits have argued heatedly about whether men and women communicate differently. But Koppel's group is the first to create an actual prediction machine.

A rather controversial one, too. When the group submitted its first paper to the prestigious journal *Proceedings of the National Academy of Sciences*, the referees rejected it "on ideological grounds," Koppel maintains. "They said, 'Hey, what do you mean? You're trying to make some claim about men and women being different, and we don't know if that's true. That's just the kind of thing that people are saying in order to oppress women!' And I said, 'Hey — I'm just reporting the numbers.'"

When they submitted their papers to other journals, the group made a significant tweak. One of the co-authors, Anat Shimoni, added her middle name "Rachel" to her byline, to make sure reviewers knew one member of the group was female. (The third scientist is a man, Shlomo Argamon.) The papers were accepted by the journals *Literary* and *Linguistic Computing and Text*, and are appearing over the next few months. Koppel says they haven't faced any further accusations of antifeminism.

The odd thing is that the language differences the researchers discovered would seem, at first blush, to be rather benign. They pertain not to complex, "important" words, but to the seemingly quotidian parts of speech: the ifs, ands, and buts. 5

For example, Koppel's group found that the single biggest difference is that women are far more likely than men to use personal pronouns — "I," "you," "she," "myself," or "yourself" and the like. Men, in contrast, are more likely to use determiners — "a," "the," "that," and "these" — as well as cardinal numbers and quantifiers like "more" or "some." As one of the papers published by Koppel's group notes, men are also more likely to use "post-head noun modification with an *of* phrase" — phrases like "garden of roses."

It seems surreal, even spooky, that such seemingly throwaway words would be so revealing of our identity. But text-analysis experts have long relied on these little parts of speech. When you or I write a text, we pay close attention to how we use the main topic-specific words — such as, in this article, the words "computer" and "program" and "gender." But we don't pay much attention to how we employ basic parts of speech, which means we're far more likely to use them in unconscious but revealing patterns. Years ago, Donald Foster, a professor of English at Vassar College, unmasked Joe Klein as the author of the anonymous book *Primary Colors*, partly by paying attention to words like "the" and "and," and to quirks in the use of punctuation. "They're like fingerprints," says Foster.

To divine these subtle patterns, Koppel's team crunched 604 texts taken from the British National Corpus, a collection of 4,124 documents assembled by academics to help study modern language use. Half of the chosen texts were written by men and half by women; they ranged from novels such as Julian Barnes's *Talking It Over* to works of nonfiction (including even some pop ephemera, such as an instant-biography of the singer Kylie Minogue). The scientists removed all the topic-specific words, leaving the non-topic-specific ones behind.

Then they fed the remaining text into an artificial-intelligence sorting algorithm and programmed it to look for elements that were relatively unique to the women's set and the men's set. "The more frequently a word got used in one set, the more weight it got. If the word 'you' got used in the female set very often and not in the male set, you give it a stronger female weighting," Koppel explains.

When the dust settled, the researchers wound up zeroing in on barely   10
50 features that had the most "weight," either male or female. Not a big group, but one with ferocious predictive power: When the scientists ran their test on new documents culled from the British National Corpus, they could predict the gender of the author with over 80 percent accuracy.

It may be unnerving to think that your gender is so obvious, and so dominates your behavior, that others can discover it by doing a simple word-count. But Koppel says the results actually make a sort of intuitive sense. As he points out, if women use personal pronouns more than men, it may be because of the old sociological saw: Women talk about people, men talk about things. Many scholars of gender and language have argued this for years.

"It's not too surprising," agrees Deborah Tannen, a linguist and author of best-sellers such as *You Just Don't Understand: Women and Men in Conversation*. "Because what are [personal] pronouns? They're talking about people. And we know that women write more about people." Also, she notes, women typically write in an "involved" style, trying to forge a more intimate connection with the reader, which leads to even heavier pronoun use. Meanwhile, if men are writing more frequently about things, that would explain why they're prone to using quantity words like "some" or "many." These differences are significant enough that even when Koppel's team analyzed scientific papers — which would seem to be as content-neutral as you can get — they could still spot male and female authors. "It blew my mind," he says.

But this gender-spotting eventually runs into a $64,000 conceptual question: What the heck is gender, anyway? At a basic level, Koppel's group assumes that there are only two different states — you're either male or female. ("Computer scientists love a binary problem," as Koppel jokes.) But some theorists of gender, such as Berkeley's Judith Butler, have argued that this is a false duality. Gender isn't simply innate or biological, the argument goes; it's as much about how you act as what you are.

Tannen once had a group of students analyze articles from men's and women's magazines, trying to see if they could guess which articles had appeared in which class of publication. It wasn't hard. In men's magazines, the sentences were always shorter, and the sentences in women's magazines had more "feeling verbs," which would seem to bolster Koppel's findings. But here's the catch: The actual identity of the author didn't matter. When women wrote for men's magazines, they wrote in the "male" style. "It clearly was performance," Tannen notes. "It didn't matter whether the author was male or female. What mattered was whether the intended audience was male or female."

Critics charge that experiments in gender-prediction don't discover in-　15 alienable male/female differences; rather, they help to create and exaggerate such differences. "You find what you're looking for. And that leads to this sneaking suspicion that it's all hardwired, instead of cultural," argues Janet Bing, a linguist at Old Dominion University in Norfolk, Virginia. She adds: "This whole rush to categorization usually works against women." Bing further notes that gays, lesbians, or transgendered people don't fit neatly into simple social definitions of male or female gender. Would Koppel's algorithm work as well if it analyzed a collection of books written mainly by them?

Koppel enthusiastically agrees it's an interesting question — but "we haven't run that experiment, so we don't know." In the end, he's hoping his group's data will keep critics at bay. "I'm just reporting the numbers," he adds, "but you can't be careful enough."

FOCUSING ON CONTENT

1. Describe the gender-detection experiment performed by computer scientists at Israel's Bar-Ilan University. How was the experiment set up and carried out?

2. What were the results of the experiment?

3. What were the original concerns of the editors of *Proceedings of the National Academy of Sciences* when the researchers submitted the results of their experiment? How did the researchers respond to the concerns other editors had?

4. Why doesn't Deborah Tannen find the results of the research that Koppel and his associates did surprising?

5. What question(s) are not answered by Koppel's research, according to linguist Janet Bing?

FOCUSING ON WRITING

1. What words are women far more likely to use? What words are men more likely to use? Why are the words in both cases rather surprising?

2. What is a "post-head noun modification with an *of* phrase"(6)? What is the example that Thompson gives? Are men or women more likely to use the construction?

3. Review paragraph 14 and explain how the research that Tannen did with her students extends the findings of the research that Koppel and his associates did. What role does audience play in the kinds of language that writers use? (Glossary: *Audience*)

4. Why do you suppose Thompson ends his article with a reiteration of the "I'm just reporting the numbers" quotation that he used earlier in his article? To what does Koppel refer when he's quoted at the end of the article by saying, "but you can't be careful enough"?

LANGUAGE IN ACTION

Using the tips that Clive Thompson says are at the heart of the new program developed to detect whether an author is likely male or female as well as the indicators provided in Nathan Cobb's article (pp. 300–04), examine the following passages to see if you can make a calculated guess as to the sex of their authors. Make sure you are able to explain to your instructor or the members of your class why you could or could not make a judgment in each case. (The authors' names are found on p. 348)

WRITER 1

I was saved from sin when I was going on thirteen. But not really saved. It happened like this. There was a big revival at my Auntie Reed's church. Every night for weeks there had been much preaching, singing, praying, and shouting, and some very hardened sinners had been brought to Christ, and the membership of the church had grown by leaps and bounds. Then just before the revival ended, they held a special meeting for children, "to bring the young lambs to the fold." My aunt spoke of it for days ahead. That night I was escorted to the front row and placed on the mourners' bench with all the other young sinners, who had not yet been brought to Jesus.

My aunt told me that when you were saved you saw a light, and something happened to you inside! And Jesus came into your life! And God was with you from then on! She said you could see and hear and feel Jesus in your soul. I believed her.

WRITER 2

The stealth of autumn catches one unaware. Was that a goldfinch perching in the early September woods, or just the first turning leaf? A red-winged blackbird or a sugar maple closing up shop for the winter? Keen-eyed as leopards, we stand still and squint hard, looking for signs of movement. Early-morning frost sits heavily on the grass, and turns barbed wire into a string of stars. On a distant hill, a small square of yellow appears to be a lighted stage. At last the truth dawns on us: Fall is staggering in, right on schedule, with its baggage of chilly nights, macabre holidays, and spectacular, heart-stoppingly beautiful leaves. Soon the leaves will start cringing on the trees, and roll up in clenched fists before they actually fall off. Dry seedpods will rattle like tiny gourds. But first there will be weeks of gushing color so bright, so pastel, so confettilike, that people will travel up and down the East Coast just to stare at it — a whole season of leaves.

WRITING SUGGESTIONS

1. In paragraph 13, Clive Thompson writes of the research that Koppel's group has done: "But this gender-spotting eventually runs into a $64,000 conceptual question: What the heck is gender, anyway? At a basic level, Koppel's group assumes that there are only two different states — you're either male or female. ('Computer scientists love a binary problem,' as Koppel jokes.)

But some theorists of gender, such as Berkeley's Judith Butler, have argued that this is a false duality. Gender isn't simply innate or biological, the argument goes; it's as much how you act as what you are." Write an essay in which you attempt to define the term *gender* using Thompson's essay as well as other sources that you find in your library or on the Internet.

2. If Deborah Tannen is correct, that the most important issue in word choice is the writer's intended audience, then it would seem that audience as a writer's concern is perhaps even more important than we have assumed. We are never sure who will read what we write, but we need an audience in mind as we write. Or do we? Is it possible to write for ourselves or for an audience so general that we don't have it clearly in mind? Write an essay in which you examine the concept of audience as it pertains to the writer's craft. Is it as important as writing teachers and theorists think? If so, why? What have writing experts said about audience that is important for us to know?

CASE STUDY:
The Language of Sexual Discrimination

Our purpose in this Case Study, unlike others in *Language Awareness*, is neither focused on a single issue such as the debate on Affirmative Action in college admissions nor on the principles and resources necessary to understand what political correctness or speech codes are and how they operate through our language. Rather, this Case Study gives examples of how different members of society have been affected by the language of sexual discrimination. By collecting the articles by Martha Irvine, Riki Wilchins, and Eugene R. August and making them easily available, we can better understand how language prejudices men and women of different sexual and gender orientations and how these writers are exercising Audre Lorde's imperative to speak out. These articles serve to illustrate the important role that language plays in categorizing people, whether they are heterosexual men and women, gays, lesbians, bisexuals, transsexuals, transgenders, or other. These essays explore how language has served to ridicule, harass, or further stereotype different genders, and how pointing out these debasing language practices is a means to better understanding.

WRITING TO DISCOVER: *How much do you know about people whose sexual and gender orientations are different from your own? If you consider yourself heterosexual, what do you know about the opposite sex, about gays, lesbians, and bisexuals? If you are homosexual or other, what do you know about heterosexuals? What do you know about transsexuals and transgenders? Do you have working definitions of the labels used to describe these various groups of people? How did you come upon these definitions? What role does language play when discussing sexual and gender orientations different from your own? Why might it be important for you to be informed about such matters?*

"Queer" Evolution: Word Goes Mainstream

MARTHA IRVINE

Martha Irvine is a graduate of the University of Michigan and the Columbia Graduate School of Journalism and began her journalism career in 1986. She has worked for publications in Australia, New Zealand, Michigan, Minnesota, and New York. She is now a national writer for the Associated Press and writes stories about issues and trends in popular culture for juveniles and young adults.

"Queer Evolution," an Associated Press article, was first published in a number of newspapers across the country on November 27, 2003. Irvine said the following about how she got the idea for the article: "The 'Queer Evolution' idea came to me after hearing more friends using the word in casual conversation — some of it tied to the television shows 'Queer as Folk' and 'Queer Eye for the Straight Guy,' though not exclusively so. I was aware that the word is — especially to older generations — difficult to hear, and often considered offensive. But this didn't seem to be the case with younger people, gay or straight. I wanted to see if there was a story there — and indeed, there was."

Something queer is happening to the word "queer."

Originally a synonym for "odd" or "unusual," the word evolved into an anti-gay insult in the last century, only to be reclaimed by defiant gay and lesbian activists who chanted: "We're here, we're queer, get used to it."

Now "queer" is sneaking into the mainstream — and taking on a hipster edge as a way to describe any sexual orientation beyond straight.

Jay Edwards, a 28-year-old gay man from Houston, has noticed it.

"Hey Jay," a straight co-worker recently said. "Have you met the new guy? He's really cute and queer, too. Just your type!" 5

It's the kind of exchange that still makes many — gay or straight — wince. That's because, in the 1920s and '30s the word "queer" became synonymous with "pansy," "sissy," and even "pervert," says Gregory Ward, a Northwestern University linguist who teaches a course on language and sexuality.

Now, Ward says, the increasing use of "queer" — as in the prime-time TV show titles *Queer Eye for the Straight Guy* and *Queer as Folk* — is changing the word's image.

"It's really losing the hurtful and quasi-violent nature it had," Ward says.

Trish McDermott, vice president of "romance" at the Match.com online dating service, says she's seeing the word appear more often in personal ads.

The title of one current ad: "Nice Guy for the Queer Guy." 10

Meanwhile, a recent review in the *Chicago Tribune*'s Metromix entertainment guide defined the crowd in a new upscale bar as "model-types and young clubbers amid dressy Trixies, middle-aged Gold Coast cigar chompers, and queer-eyed straight guys" (the latter term referring to straight men who've spiffed themselves up).

And while some in the gay community began using the word in the last decade or two as an umbrella term for "gay, lesbian, bisexual, and transgendered," today's young people say that "queer" encompasses even more.

"I love it because, in one word, you can refer to the alphabet soup of gay, lesbian, bisexual, questioning, 'heteroflexible,' 'omnisexual,' 'pansexual,' and all of the other shades of difference in that fluid, changing arena of human sexuality," says 27-year-old Stacy Harbaugh. She's the program coordinator for the Indiana Youth Group, a drop-in center in Indianapolis for youth who may place themselves into any of those categories.

"I find myself attracted to boy-like girls and girl-like boys," Harbaugh adds. "If 'lesbian' or 'bi' doesn't seem to fit, 'queer' certainly does."

Heteroflexible? Pansexual? The growing list of terms can be downright boggling.   15

James Cross, a 26-year-old Chicagoan, personally likes the term "metrosexual," meant to describe straight men like him who are into designer clothes, love art and fashion, and even enjoy shopping (much like "queer-eyed straight guys").

He's also noticed the word "queer" being bandied about more often, especially at the public relations firm where he works. But he says women are "definitely more comfortable" with it.

"I hate to admit it, but I certainly wear masks with the term. When I'm at work and talking with women, I'm down with it," he says. "But when I'm out on the rugby pitch or drinking beer with my 'bros,' I'm just one of the guys."

Indeed, use of a word that carries so much baggage can cause confusion.

Andy Rohr, a 26-year-old gay man living in Boston, noted that when   20
a straight co-worker told him she liked the show *Queer Eye for the Straight Guy*, she whispered the word 'queer,'" he says.

Dan Cordella says he, too, is perplexed about what he "can and can't say."

"An entire generation of suburban youth was taught to practically walk on eggshells with their wording around those that, one, chose an alternative lifestyle and, two, were of a different ethnic background," says Cordella, a 26-year-old straight man who lives in New York and grew up outside Boston.

Ward, the Northwestern linguist, says that people are wise to use "queer" carefully because it is still "very context-sensitive."

"It really matters who says it and why they're saying it," he says.

Edwards, from Houston, says he likes when straight people are comfortable using it.   25

"If they can say the word with as much casualness and confidence as my gay friends, it lets me know that they are comfortable with who I am," he says.

Rohr, from Boston, is less sure about its use in everyday conversation but says it works with the *Queer Eye* title because its use is "archaic and unexpected."

"The bottom line is, I think the term has lost its political potency, if it ever had any, and has just become campy," he says.

Others, especially those with strong memories of the word as an insult, still find its use hurtful. "I believe this word continues to marginalize us," says Robin Tyler, a California-based activist and lesbian who's in her sixties.

EXAMINING THE ISSUE CRITICALLY

1. What does the evolution of the word *queer* suggest about the flexibility of the English language? Do other words go through similar evolutions in meaning? Can you think of some examples of such words?

2. Why might the word *queer* show a greater speed of evolution than other words in our vocabulary? Is the word of greater service today than it used to be? If so, why?

3. How are people who live alternative lifestyles reclaiming the word *queer*? What have they done to its earlier meanings?

4. Why does Gregory Ward, the Northwestern University linguist, think that people should still be careful how they use the word *queer*?

5. What does Irvine mean by claiming that *queer* has taken on a "hipster edge" today(3)?

6. Irvine uses a number of sources in reporting on the evolution of *queer*. Why doesn't she just report on what she *thinks* the word means and how she *thinks* it has changed over the years?

Because That's What We Do to Faggots

RIKI WILCHINS

Riki Wilchins is the founder and executive director of Gender Public Advocacy Coalition (Gender PAC), a transgender organization based in Washington, D.C., which, according to its mission statement, "works to end discrimination and violence caused by gender stereotypes by changing public attitudes, educating elected officials, and expanding legal rights. GenderPAC also promotes an understanding of the connection between discrimination based on gender stereotypes and sex, sexual orientation, age, race, and class." Wilchins has been chosen by Time *in 2001 as one of six community activists from among their "100 Civic Innovators for the Twenty-first Century." A transgender herself, Wilchins has written numerous articles and columns on transgender issues. She is the author of* Sexual Subversion and the End of Gender *(1997),* GenderQueer: Voices from Beyond the Sexual Binary *(2002), and* Queer Theory/Gender Theory: An Instant Primer *(2004).*

In "Because That's What We Do to Faggots," first published in 2003 on Advocate.com, the National Gay and Lesbian Newsmagazine Web site, Wilchins reviews the recent cases of transgender victims of violence and asks, "When will we acknowledge that the hatred directed at 'faggots' is usually less about sexuality and more about transgressing gender norms?"

If two men — one gay and one straight — are both attacked, hundreds of miles apart, for the same reason, it certainly isn't because of whom they sleep with. When will we acknowledge that the hatred directed at "faggots" is usually less about sexuality and more about transgressing gender norms?

This is a story about an assault on America that wasn't the result of foreign terrorists or fundamentalist intolerance. It's just about our familiar, homegrown intolerance that still quietly claims childhoods, jobs, and lives even while our attention turns to faraway places and more exotic kinds of violence.

This is a story about three assaults on the person of Alexander Gray, a resident of Washington, D.C., who could have lived in almost any major American city. It's a tale of what still happens today to gay men — particularly black gay men — in a city where police still regularly respond with throw-down weapons and excessive force, and a society still marinated in fear and loathing of anything considered unmanly.

The first assault on Alexander Gray was on June 9, when three or four men jumped him and then beat him with a shovel and tire iron while shouting anti-gay epithets. When D.C. police arrived, Gray declined medical treatment, and they drove him home to his nearby apartment, where he was soon spitting up blood.

An ambulance was called, but Gray once again declined medical treatment. Two policemen who'd arrived with the ambulance complained that Gray, on the street outside his apartment, was indecently dressed — his pants were torn and part of his buttocks exposed. According to a friend, Gray was still in pain, upset over his assault, and walking toward his apartment. Even though witnesses testified that Gray's hands were empty and that he was not threatening anyone, D.C. police later testified that Gray was swinging a knife and menacing nearby bystanders and that he refused to drop his weapon when ordered to do so.

Seventh District police officer John Bevilacqua shot Gray in the   5
chest, killing him. That was the second assault.

Gray's funeral was held June 22 at the nearby Holy Christian Missionary Baptist Church. The Reverend Stephen Young stood over Gray's open coffin and told Gray's family and the 200 assembled mourners who were seeking consolation, "I don't agree with the gay lifestyle. It's a practice. I have to help you get out of that practice. . . . I hear people called Alex a faggot. . . . I don't like that lifestyle."

That was the third assault.

When asked why he attacked Gray, one of his assailants explained, "Because that's what we do to faggots."

It's 2001, and still gayness itself — whether strutting muscle-bound in South Beach or preening while "walking the balls" in New York City — remains in many minds synonymous with unmanliness.

This is especially true among youth. As Jim Anderson of the Gay,   10
Lesbian, and Straight Education Network recently told the *Bay Area Reporter,* "In five of the eight major school shootings, the word *faggot* or *gay* has been present," adding that the terms are used interchangeably to demasculinize males. Bullies who use anti gay taunts, Anderson noted, do not necessarily associate the words with homosexuality but rather with behavior incompatible with manliness.

This kind of animosity is not helped by the ongoing effort to distance gayness from issues of gender — the new *G* word is not welcome in most gay contexts. It's as if all of us have morphed from Jack on *Will & Grace* into Arnold Schwarzenegger — or at least that's how we want other people to think of us.

Today gay men sport muscles and butch attitudes with the same flamboyance that '70s gay men did the latest pastels. We're all tops (*never* bottoms) or at worst "versatile." We don't camp it up, and we all have wrists so rigid they may as well be reinforced with concrete. As one national gay leader told me, "The moms I work with are finally accepting that their little boys are gay; they just don't want them to be sissies."

"Gender" has become the new "gay": the thing we no longer talk about in polite society. It's the new thing we're closeted about.

If we're assaulted, it must be because of our sexual orientation, because of what we do in the privacy of our own bedrooms. But in public? We're all "just like straight people."

That won't wash anymore.   15

Take, for example, the sad case of Willie Houston, 46, another black man who was killed just two weeks after Gray. Houston, a Nashville Metro Transit driver who frequently drove vans for the elderly and disabled, became engaged to his girlfriend, Nedra Jones, on June 29.

They celebrated their engagement with friends on a midnight cruise and stopped afterward to use the dockside bathrooms. Jones asked Houston to hold her purse while she went into the women's room, and while doing so Houston helped their friend, who was blind, into the men's room: a purse on one arm, his male friend on the other.

He was spotted there by Lewis Davidson III, a man with a long and violent criminal record. Davidson harassed Houston, who left the rest room to avoid a confrontation. But Davidson retrieved a gun from his car, and again confronted Houston, who put his hands in the air and said he just wanted to go home. Davidson shot Houston in the chest. As he lay dying, he told Jones, "Just remember — I will always love you." They were to have been married two weeks later.

As with Alexander, the crime didn't get the mainstream coverage it deserved. Inexplicably, feminist groups appeared not to have covered the crime at all. And as with so many assaults, despite the fact that Mr. Houston was a heterosexual man killed for carrying a purse, gay media and groups were quick to term the murder simply "gay-related" and let it go at that.

Would that things were that simple. Unfortunately, behavior that   20
crosses gender lines, that smacks of anything that might threaten masculinity, still brings out the very worst in society, in particular its most violent bigots.

Arguing that gay men aren't necessarily unmasculine or need not be effeminate misses the point. As long as the defining characteristic of masculinity is sex with women — and its pinnacle impregnating one — *faggot* will continue to be a term of derision and male homosexuality intertwined with a certain kind of unmanliness. Because a man having sex with another man is in itself the most profound gender transgression possible.

The answer isn't to hide the problem and hope it goes away. Nor is it to avoid mentioning it, even when the circumstances cry out for it. The answer is to start speaking out — loudly, pointedly, and as frequently as possible — about how narrow, outdated gender roles hurt us all, gay and straight. In fact, they're killing us.

EXAMINING THE ISSUE CRITICALLY

1. What is the confusion over sex and gender that is inherent in our society, according to Wilchins? Why is that confusion so potentially dangerous?

2. What does Wilchins mean when she refers to "gender norms" at the beginning of the essay? Were the men Wilchins writes about victimized because of their sexual activities or their violation of gender norms?

3. Wilchins concludes with the following plea: "The answer is to start speaking out — loudly, pointedly, and as frequently as possible — about how narrow, outdated gender roles hurt us all, gay and straight. In fact, they're killing us"(22). Assuming you agree with her assessment and suggestion for alleviating the situation, what can actually be done to change gender roles and how we regard them? What role does our use of labels play in remedying the present situation?

Real Men Don't: Anti-Male Bias in English

EUGENE R. AUGUST

Eugene R. August is professor emeritus of English at the University of Dayton. A specialist in Victorian literature, he is best known as the first chair of the humanities at the university and the author of The New Men's Studies: A Selected and Annotated Interdisciplinary Bibliography *(1994), originally published in 1985. August is a scholar who has been instrumental in bringing into view and promoting men's studies as a legitimate area of research and study, and the second edition of his bibliography shows how much that area of investigation has grown over the last twenty years.*

In this recently revised and updated version of "Real Men Don't: Anti-Male Bias in English," first published in the University of Dayton Review 18 *(Winter/Spring, 1986–87), August examines the anti-male bias that is reflected in our language and, in turn, encourages yet more such bias. He claims, "Wholesale denunciations of males as oppressors, exploiters, rapists, Nazis, and slave-drivers have become all too familiar during the past three decades. Too often the academic community, rather than opposing this sexism, has been encouraging it."*

Despite numerous studies of sex bias in language during the past three decades, only rarely has anti-male bias been examined. In part, this neglect occurs because many of these studies have been based upon assumptions that, at best, are questionable and, at worst, exhibit their own sex bias. Whether explicitly or implicitly, many of these studies reduce human history to a tale of male oppressors and female victims or rebels. In this view of things, all societies become *patriarchal societies*, a familiar term used to suggest that for centuries males have conspired to exploit and demean females. Accordingly, it is alleged in many of these studies that men control language and that they use it to define women and women's roles as inferior.

Despite the popularity of such a view, it has received scant support from leading social scientists, including one of the giants of modern anthropology, Margaret Mead. Anticipating current ideology, Mead in *Male and Female* firmly rejected the notion of a "male conspiracy to keep women in their place," arguing instead that

> the historical trend that listed women among the abused minorities . . . lingers on to obscure the issue and gives apparent point to the contention that this is a man-made world in which women have always been abused and must always fight for their rights.

> It takes considerable effort on the part of both men and women to reorient ourselves to thinking — when we think basically — that this is a world not made by men alone, in which women are unwilling and helpless dupes and fools or else powerful schemers hiding their power under their ruffled petticoats, but a world made by mankind for human beings of both sexes. (298, 299–300)

The model described by Mead and other social scientists shows a world in which women and men have lived together throughout history in a symbiotic relationship, often mutually agreeing upon the definition of gender roles and the distribution of various powers and duties.

More importantly for the subject of bias in speech and writing, women — as well as men — have shaped language. As Walter J. Ong reminds us,

> Women talk and think as much as men do, and with few exceptions we all . . . learn to talk and think in the first instance largely from women, usually and predominantly our mothers. Our first tongue is called our "mother tongue" in English and in many other languages. . . . There are no father tongues. . . . (36)

Feminists such as Dorothy Dinnerstein agree: "There seems no reason to doubt that the baby-tending sex contributed at least equally with the history-making one to the most fundamental of all human inventions: language" (22). The idea that language is "man made," as Dale Spender and others argue, fits ideology better than the evidence.

During the past thirty years, anti-male bias in English has been greatly fostered by *misandry*, hatred of men, that is the acceptable sexism of the media, the educational world, and the entertainment industry. A related term is *androphobia*, an irrational fear and loathing of males. "There has been a veritable blitzkrieg on the male gender," note Robert Moore and Douglas Gillette, "what amounts to an outright demonization of men and a slander against masculinity" (156). This misandry has given rise to a language of anti-male hatred that excludes, restricts, and denigrates men and masculinity.

Much of this misandry is the work of what Christina Hoff Sommers   5
calls *gender feminists* (19–25). Distinguished from *equity feminists*, who seek legal and social equality between the sexes, gender feminists see themselves engaged in a crusade against a sex and gender system constructed by powerful males. This system, which they label *patriarchy*, allegedly oppresses females and privileges males. Gender feminism owes much to Marxist theory of class warfare and is often fueled by a lesbian separatist agenda (Spender ch. 4). It caricatures males as inherently evil, a class of privileged oppressors who hate and fear women. Among the tools of patriarchy's oppression are fatherhood, the two-parent family, and language. In Adrienne Rich's oft-quoted remark: "*This is the oppressors' language*" (qtd. in Spender, 178).

Gender feminist misandry, distortions of patriarchy, and views of language have all been challenged, mostly by equity feminists and men's rights advocates. Still, gender feminism remains perhaps the most influential ideology of our time. Its impact on nearly all aspects of life, including language, continues to be immense.

In modern English, three kinds of anti-male language are evident: first, gender-exclusive usage that omits males from certain kinds of consideration; second, gender-restrictive language that attempts to restrict males to an accepted gender role, some aspects of which may be outmoded, burdensome, or destructive; and third, negative stereotypes of males.

Gender feminists insist upon gender-inclusive language and seek to eradicate terms such as *man* and *he* used generically for humans of both sexes. Yet gender feminism fosters its own forms of gender-exclusive usage for political purposes. The Ms. Foundation, for example, resolutely refuses to alter its *Take Our Daughters to Work Day* to *Take Our Children to Work Day*, lest boys be invited. Gender feminist groups lobbied successfully in Congress for a *Violence Against Women Act*, even though American males are almost twice as likely as females to be victims of violent crimes (even when rape is included in the tally) and three times more likely to be victims of murder (Farrell *Myth*, 32). A woman who kills her male partner can plead the *Battered Woman's Syndrome*; a man who kills (or even defends himself against) a violent female partner cannot plead the *Battered Man's Syndrome*.

In the U.S. media, which is heavily influenced by gender feminism, language routinely excludes males as victims. Male victims are simply not news; women (and children) victims are. If men suffer harm, media language is gender-neutral: "Fifteen miners were killed in a West Virginia mine explosion today." If women are victims, the language becomes gender-specific: "Two women were among the fifteen miners killed in a West Virginia mine explosion today."

In academia and the media, there is an almost complete ban on discussing the victims of domestic violence, sexual harassment, and rape in gender-inclusive terms.

10

Every responsible study of domestic violence from the 1970s to the present has reported significant numbers of violent women and battered men (see, e.g., Straus, 40–41), but gender feminists steadfastly deny the existence of abusive women and abused men. The slogan for a national campaign against domestic violence reads: "Domestic violence is the one thing that hurts women and their children the most. . . ." Not only does the slogan erase all hint of battered men, but it also proclaims that children belong exclusively to mothers ("women and *their* children"). Similarly, the term *wife and child abuse* conceals the existence of an estimated 282,000 husbands who are battered annually (O'Reilly, 23).

Although males have already won court cases of sexual harassment against female bosses, *sexual harassment* is still widely defined as "harassment of women by men."

The term *rape* is a favorite with misandrists, who insist that rape is a crime committed *only* by males in which *only* females are victims. "Crime knows no gender," writes a reporter: "Yet, there is one crime that only women are prey to: rape" (Mougey). A college brochure defines *rape* as "*the* universal crime against women." Such statements ignore entirely the millions of boys and men who are raped each year, many of them (but by no means all) in so-called "correctional facilities." The belief that a male cannot be raped by a female is still widespread, despite evidence to the contrary (e.g., Sarrel, Struckman-Johnson).

The word *rape* is often used as a brush to tar all males. In *Against Our Will* Susan Brownmiller writes: "From prehistoric times to the present, I believe, rape . . . is nothing more or less than a conscious process of intimidation by which *all men* keep *all women* in a state of fear" (15; italics in original). Making the point explicitly, Marilyn French states, "All men are rapists and that's all they are" (Jennes 33). Given this kind of smear tactic, *rape* is often stretched into a vague "accordion term" or used metaphorically. To provide "evidence" of an epidemic of rape on college campuses, Mary Koss expanded the term *rape* so broadly that 73 percent of the women whom Koss defined as rape victims did not agree that they had been raped (Sommers, 213–14). Used metaphorically, *rape* means anything that one wishes to blame on males alone. Ecofeminist Andreé Collard's *Rape of the Wild: Man's Violence Against Animals and the Earth* suggests that only males do harm to the environment. Such usage trivializes the word *rape* and the suffering of genuine rape victims.

Unlike gender-exclusive language, gender-restrictive language is usu-   15
ally applied to males only, often to keep them within the confines of a socially prescribed gender role. When considering gender-restrictive language, one must keep in mind that — as Ruth E. Hartley has pointed out — the masculine gender role is enforced earlier and more harshly than the feminine role is (235). In addition, because the boy is often raised primarily by females in the virtual absence of close adult males, his grasp of what is required of him to be a man is often unsure. Likewise, prescriptions for male behavior are usually given in the negative, leading to the "Real Men Don't" syndrome, a process that further confuses the boy. Such circumstances leave many males extremely vulnerable to language that questions their masculinity.

Furthermore, during the past twenty years an increasing number of men and women have been arguing that aspects of our society's masculine gender role are emotionally constrictive, unnecessarily stressful, and potentially lethal. Rejecting "the myth of masculine privilege," psychologist Herb Goldberg reports in *The Hazards of Being Male* that "every critical statistic in the area of longevity [early death], disease, suicide, crime, accidents, childhood emotional disorders, alcoholism, and drug addiction shows a disproportionately higher male rate" (5). But changes in the masculine role are so disturbing to so many people that the male who attempts to break out of familiar gender patterns often finds himself facing hostile opposition which can be readily and powerfully expressed in a formidable array of sex-biased terms.

To see how the process works, let us begin early in the male life cycle. A boy quickly learns that, while it is usually acceptable for girls to be *tomboys*, God forbid that he should be a *sissy*. In *Sexual Signatures: On Being a Man or a Woman*, John Money and Patricia Tucker note:

> The current feminine stereotype in our culture is flexible enough to let a girl behave "boyishly" if she wants to without bringing her femininity into question, but any boy who exhibits "girlish" behavior is promptly suspected of being queer. There isn't even a word corresponding to "tomboy" to describe such a boy. "Sissy" perhaps comes closest, or "artistic" and "sensitive," but unlike "tomboy," such terms are burdened with unfavorable connotations. (72)

Lacking a favorable or even neutral term to describe the boy who is quiet, gentle, and emotional, the English language has long had a rich vocabulary to insult and ridicule such boys — *mama's boy, mollycoddle, milksop, muff, lightweight, twit, softy, creampuff, pantywaist, weakling, weenie, Miss Nancy,* and so on. The current popular *wimp* and *wuss* can be used to insult males from childhood right into adulthood.

Discussion of words such as *sissy* as insults have been often one-sided: most commentators are content to argue that the female, not the male, is being insulted by such usage. "The implicit sexism" in such terms, writes one commentator, "disparages the woman, not the man" (Sorrels, 87). Such arguments are typical of gender feminist special pleading. A boy who has been called a *sissy* knows that *he* has been insulted, not his sister. The object of ridicule in such expressions is not the feminine but the male who cannot differentiate himself from the feminine. Ong argues in *Fighting for Life* that most societies place heavy pressure on males to differentiate themselves from females because the prevailing environment of human society is feminine (70–71). In English-speaking societies, terms such as *sissy* and *weak sister*, which have been used by both females and males, are not insults to females but ridicule of males who have allegedly failed to differentiate themselves from feminine.

Being *all boy* carries penalties, however: for one thing, it means being less lovable. As the nursery rhyme tells children, little girls are made of "sugar and spice and all that's nice," while little boys are made of "frogs and snails and puppy-dogs' tails." Or, as an American version of the rhyme puts it:

> Girls are dandy,
> Made of candy —

> That's what little girls are made of.
> Boys are rotten,
> Made of cotton —
> That's what little boys are made of.
> (Baring-Gould, 176)

When not enjoined to *be all boy*, our young lad will be urged to *be a big boy*, *be a brave soldier*, and (the ultimate appeal) *be a man*. These expressions almost invariably mean that the boy is about to suffer some thing painful or humiliating. The variant — *take it like a man* — provides the clue. As Paul Theroux defines it, *be a man* means: "Be stupid, be un-feeling, obedient and soldierly, and stop thinking."

Following our boy further into the life cycle, we discover that in school he will find himself in a cruel bind: girls his age will be biologically and socially more mature than he is, at least until around age eighteen. Until then, any ineptness in his social role will be castigated by a host of terms that are reserved almost entirely for males. "For all practical purposes," John Gordon remarks, "the word 'turkey' (or whatever the equivalent is now) can be translated as 'a boy spurned by influential girls'" (141). The equivalents of *turkey* are many: *jerk, nerd, clod, klutz, schmuck, dummy, goon, dork, reject, retard, square, dweeb, jackass, meathead, geek, zero, goofball, drip*, and numerous others, including many obscene terms. A Michigan high school decided to do away with a scheduled "Nerd Day" after a fourteen-year-old male student, who apparently had been so harassed as a nerd by other students, committed suicide ("'Nerd' day"). In this case, the ability of language to devastate the emotionally vulnerable young male is powerfully and pathetically dramatized.

As our boy grows, he faces threats and taunts if he does not take risks or endure pain to prove his manhood. *Coward*, for example, is a word ap plied almost exclusively to males in our society, as are its numerous variants — *chicken, chicken-shit, yellow, yellow-bellied, lily-livered, weak-kneed, spineless, squirrelly, 'fraidy cat, gutless wonder, weakling, butterfly, jellyfish*, and so on. If our young man walks away from a stupid quarrel or prefers to settle differences more rationally than with a swift jab to the jaw, the English language is richly supplied with these and other expressions to call his masculinity into question.

Chief among the other expressions that question masculinity is a lengthy list of homophobic terms such as *queer, pansy, fag, faggot, queen, queeny, pervert, bugger, deviant, fairy, tinkerbell, puss, priss, flamer, feller, sweet, precious, fruit, twinkie, sodomite*, and numerous others, many obscene. For many people, *gay* is an all-purpose word of ridicule and condemnation. Although homosexuals are being insulted by these terms, the target is often the heterosexual male who fails or refuses to live up to someone else's idea of masculinity. In "Homophobia Among Men" Gregory K. Lehne explains, "Homophobia is used as a technique of social control by homosexist individuals to enforce the norms of male sex-role behavior. . . . [H]omosexuality is not the real threat, the real threat is change in the male sex-role" (77).

Nowhere is this threat more apparent than in challenges to our society's male-only military obligation. When a young man and a young woman reach the age of eighteen, both may register to vote; only the young man is required by law to register for military service. For the next decade at least, he must stand ready to be called into military service and even into combat duty in wars, "police actions," "peace-keeping missions," and "rescue missions," often initiated by legally dubious means. Should he resist this obligation, he may be called a *draft dodger, deserter, peace-nik, traitor, shirker, slacker, malingerer,* and similar terms. Should he declare himself a conscientious objector, he may be labeled a *conchy* or any of the variants of *coward*.

In his relationships with women, he will find that the age of equality has not yet arrived. Usually, he will be expected to take the initiative, do the driving, pick up the tab, and in general show a deferential respect for women that is a left-over from the chivalric code. Should he behave in an *ungentlemanly* fashion, a host of words — which are applied almost always to males alone — can be used to tell him so: *louse, rat, creep, sleaze, scum, stain, worm, fink, heel, beast, fascist, stinker, animal, savage, bounder, cad, wolf, gigolo, womanizer, Don Juan, pig, rotter, boor,* and so on.

In sexual matters he will usually be expected to take the initiative and 25 to *perform*. If he does not, he will be labeled *impotent*. While it is sexist to call a woman *frigid*, it is acceptable to call a man *impotent*. Metaphorically, *impotent* can be used to demean any male whose efforts in any area are deemed inadequate. Even if our young man succeeds at his sexual performance, the sex manuals are ready to warn him that if he reaches orgasm before a specified time, he is guilty of *premature ejaculation*.

When our young man marries, he will be required by law and social custom to support his wife and children. Should he not succeed as breadwinner or should he relax in his efforts, the language offers numerous terms to revile him: *loser, dead beat, bum, freeloader, leech, parasite, goldbrick, sponge, mooch, scrounger, ne'er-do-well, good for nothing,* and so on. If he does not meet child support payments, he will be labeled a *deadbeat dad* — even if he is disabled, unemployed, or broke. If women in our society hate being regarded as sex objects, men have been regarded as success objects, that is, judged by their ability to provide a standard of living. The title of a recent book — *How to Marry a Winner* — reveals immediately that the intended audience is female (Collier).

When he becomes a father, our young man will discover that he is a second-class parent, as the traditional interchangeability of *mother* and *parent* indicates. The law has been particularly obtuse in recognizing fathers as parents, as evidenced by the awarding of child custody to mothers in 90 percent of divorce cases. In one case a father's petition for custody of his four-year-old son was denied because, as the family court judge said, "Fathers don't make good mothers" (qtd. in Levine, 21). The judge apparently never considered whether *fathers* make good *parents*.

And so it goes throughout our young man's life: if he deviates from society's gender role norm, he will be penalized and he will hear about it.

The final form of anti-male bias to be considered here is negative stereotyping. Sometimes this stereotyping is indirectly embedded in the language, sometimes it resides in misandric assumptions about males that shape responses to seemingly neutral words, and sometimes it is overtly created for political reasons. It is one thing to say that some aspects of the traditional masculine gender role are limiting and hurtful; it is quite another to denounce males in general as evil or to portray them in wholesale fashion as oppressors and exploiters. In *The New Male* Goldberg writes, "Men may very well be the last remaining subgroup in our society that can be blatantly, negatively, and vilely stereotyped with little objection or resistance" (103). With the ascendancy of gender feminism, such sexist stereotyping is not only familiar but fashionable.

In English, crime and evil are usually attributed to the male. Nearly all the words for law-breakers suggest males rather than females. These words include *murderer, swindler, crook, criminal, burglar, thief, gangster, mobster, hood, hitman, killer, pickpocket, mugger,* and *terrorist*. For whatever reasons, English usage conveys a subtle suggestion that males are to be regarded as guilty in matters of law-breaking.

This hint of male guilt extends to a term like *suspect*. When the suspect is unknown, he or she is usually presumed to be a he. For example, even before a definite suspect had been identified, the perpetrator of a series of Atlanta child murders was popularly known as *The Man*. When a male and female are suspected of a crime, the male is usually presumed the guilty party. In a notorious murder case, when two suspects — Debra Brown and Alton Coleman — were apprehended, police discovered *Brown's* fingerprint in a victim's car and interpreted this as evidence of *Coleman's* guilt. As the Associated Press reported:

> Authorities say for the first time they have evidence linking Alton Coleman with the death of an Indianapolis man. A fingerprint found in the car of Eugene Scott has been identified as that of Debra Brown, Coleman's companion. . . . ("Police")

Nowhere does the article suggest that Brown's fingerprint found in the victim's car linked Brown with the death: the male suspect was presumed the guilty party, while the female was only a "traveling companion." Even after Brown had been convicted of two murders, the Associated Press was still describing her as "the accused accomplice of convicted killer Alton Coleman" ("Indiana").

In some cases, this presumption of male guilt extends to crimes in which males are not the principal offenders. As noted earlier, a term such as *wife and child abuse* ignores battered husbands, but it does more: it

30

suggests that males alone abuse children. In reality most child abuse is committed by mothers (Straus, 71). Despite this fact, a study of child abuse bears the title *Sins of the Fathers* (Inglis).

Not only crimes but vices of all sorts have been typically attributed to males. As Muriel R. Schulz points out, "The synonyms for inebriate . . . seem to be coded primarily 'male': for example, *boozer, drunkard, tippler, toper, swiller, tosspot, guzzler, barfly, drunk, lush, boozehound, souse, tank, stew, rummy,* and *bum*" (126). Likewise, someone may be *drunk as a lord* but never *drunk as a lady.*

Sex bias or sexism itself is widely held to be a male-only fault. When sexism is defined as "contempt for women" — as if there were no such thing as contempt for men — the definition of sexism is itself sexist (Bardwick, 34).

Part of the reason for this masculinization of evil may be that in the Western world the source of evil has long been depicted in male terms. In the Bible, the Evil One is consistently referred to as *he*, whether the reference is to the serpent in the Garden of Eden, Satan as Adversary in Job, Lucifer and Beelzebub in the gospels, Jesus' tempter in the desert, or the dragon in Revelations. Beelzebub, incidentally, is often translated as *lord of the flies*, a term designating the demon as masculine. So masculine is the word *devil* that the female prefix is needed, as in *she-devil*, to make a feminine noun of it. The masculinization of evil is so unconsciously accepted that writers often attest to it even while attempting to deny it, as in this passage:

> From the very beginning, the Judeo-Christian tradition has linked women and evil. When second-century theologians struggled to explain the Devil's origins, they surmised that Satan and his various devils had once been angels. (Gerzon, 224)

If the Judeo-Christian tradition has linked women and evil so closely, why is the writer using the masculine pronoun *his* to refer to Satan, the source of evil according to that tradition? Critics of sex-bias in religious language seldom notice or mention its masculinization of evil: of those objecting to God the Father as sexist, no one — to my knowledge — has suggested that designating Satan as the Father of Lies is equally sexist. Few theologians talk about Satan and her legions.

The tendency to blame nearly everything on men has climaxed in recent times with the popularity of such terms as *patriarchy, patriarchal society,* and *male-dominated society.* More political than descriptive, these terms are rapidly becoming meaningless, used as all-purpose smear words to conjure up images of male oppressors and female victims. They are a linguistic sleight of hand which obscures the point that, as Mead has observed (299–300), societies are largely created by both sexes for both sexes. By using a swift reference to *patriarchal structures* or *patriarchal attitudes,* a writer can absolve females of all blame for society's flaws while fixing the onus solely on males. The give-away of this ploy can be detected when *patriarchy* and its related terms are never used in a positive or neutral context, but are always used to assign blame to males alone.

Wholesale denunciations of males as oppressors, exploiters, rapists, Nazis, and slave-drivers have become all too familiar during the past three decades. Too often the academic community, rather than opposing this sexism, has been encouraging it. All too many scholars and teachers have hopped on the male-bashing bandwagon to disseminate what John Gordon calls "the myth of the monstrous male." With increasing frequency, this academically fashionable misandry can also be heard echoing from our students. "A white upper-middle-class straight male should seriously consider another college," declares a midwestern college student in the *New York Times Selective Guide to Colleges.* "You [the white male] are the bane of the world. . . . Ten generations of social ills can and will be strapped upon your shoulders" (qtd. in Fiske, 12). It would be comforting to dismiss this student's compound of misinformation, misandry, sexism, racism, and self-righteousness as an extreme example, but similar yahooisms go unchallenged almost everywhere in modern academia.

Surely it is time for men and women of good will to confront the misandry that prevails on most campuses. For teachers and writers, the first task is to recognize and condemn forms of anti-male bias in language, whether they are used to exclude males from equal consideration with females, to reinforce restrictive aspects of the masculine gender role, or to stereotype males callously. For whether males are told that fathers don't make good mothers, that real men don't cry, or that all men are rapists, the results are potentially dangerous: like any other group, males can be subtly shaped into what society keeps telling them they are. In *Why Men Are the Way They Are* Warren Farrell puts the matter succinctly: "The more we make men the enemy, the more they will have to behave like the enemy" (357).

Works Cited

Bardwick, Judith. *In Transition: How Feminism, Sexual Liberation, and the Search for Self-Fulfillment Have Altered Our Lives.* New York: Holt, 1979.

Baring-Gould, William S., and Ceil Baring-Gould. *The Annotated Mother Goose: Nursery Rhymes Old and New, Arranged and Explained.* New York: Clarkson N. Potter, 1962.

Brownmiller, Susan. *Against Our Will: Men, Women and Rape.* New York: Simon, 1975

Collier, Phyllis K. *How to Marry a Winner.* Upper Saddle River, NJ: Prentice Hall, 1982.

Dinnerstein, Dorothy. *The Mermaid and the Minotaur: Sexual Arrangements and Human Malaise.* New York: Harper, 1976.

Farrell, Warren. *The Myth of Male Power: Why Men Are the Disposable Sex.* New York: Simon, 1993.

_____. *Why Men Are the Way They Are: The Male-Female Dynamic.* New York: McGraw-Hill, 1986.

Fiske, Edward B. *The New York Times Selective Guide to Colleges.* New York: New York Times Books, 1982.

Gerzon, Mark. *A Choice of Heroes: The Changing Faces of American Manhood.* Boston: Houghton, 1982.

Goldberg, Herb. *The Hazards of Being Male: Surviving the Myth of Masculine Privilege.* Rev. ed. New York: NAL, 1987.

—————. *The New Male: From Self-Destruction to Self-Care.* New York: NAL, 1980.

Gordon, John. *The Myth of the Monstrous Male, and Other Feminist Fables.* New York: Playboy P, 1982.

Hartley, Ruth E. "Sex-Role Pressures and the Socialization of the Male Child." *The Forty-Nine Percent Majority: The Male Sex Role.* Eds. Deborah S. David and Robert Brannon. Reading, MA: Addison-Wesley, 1976. 235–44.

"Indiana jury finds Brown guilty of murder, molesting." *Dayton Daily News* 18 May 1986: 7A.

Inglis, Ruth. *Sins of the Fathers: A Study of the Physical and Emotional Abuse of Children.* New York: St. Martin's, 1978.

Jennes, Gail. "All Men Are Rapists." *People* 20 Feb. 1978: 33–34.

Lehne, Gregory K. "Homophobia Among Men." *The Forty-Nine Percent Majority: The Male Sex Role.* Eds. Deborah S. David and Robert Brannon. Reading, MA: Addison-Wesley, 1976. 66–88.

Levine, James A. *Who Will Raise the Children? New Options for Fathers (and Mothers).* Philadelphia: Lippincott, 1976.

Mead, Margaret. *Male and Female: A Study of the Sexes in a Changing World.* New York: Morrow, 1949, 1967.

Money, John, and Patricia Tucker. *Sexual Signatures: On Being a Man or a Woman.* Boston: Little, 1975.

Moore, Robert, and Douglas Gillette. *King Warrior Magician Lover: Rediscovering the Archetypes of the Mature Masculine.* New York: HarperCollins, 1990.

Mougey, Kate. "Rape: An act of confiscation." *Kettering-Oakwood* [OH] *Times* 4 Feb. 1981: 1b.

"'Nerd' day gets a boot after suicide." *Dayton Daily News* 24 Jan. 1986: 38.

Ong, Walter J. *Fighting for Life: Contest, Sexuality, and Consciousness.* Ithaca, NY: Cornell UP, 1981.

O'Reilly, Jane, et al. "Wife-Beating: The Silent Crime." *Time* 5 Sept. 1983: 23–24, 26.

"Police: Print links Coleman, death." *Dayton Daily News* 31 Aug. 1984: 26.

Sarrel, Philip M., and William H. Masters. "Sexual Molestation of Men by Women." *Archives of Sexual Behavior* 11 (1982): 117–31.

Schulz, Muriel R. "Is the English Language Anybody's Enemy?" *Speaking of Words: A Language Reader.* Eds. James MacKillop and Donna Woolfolk Cross. 3rd ed. New York: Holt, 1986. 125–27.

Sommers, Christina Hoff. *Who Stole Feminism? How Women Have Betrayed Women.* New York: Simon, 1994.

Sorrels, Bobbye D. *The Nonsexist Communicator: Solving the Problems of Gender and Awkwardness in Modern English.* Upper Saddle River, NJ: Prentice Hall, 1983.

Spender, Dale. *Man Made Language.* London: Routledge, 1980.

Straus, Murray A., Richard J. Gelles, and Suzanne K. Steinmetz. *Behind Closed Doors: Violence in the American Family.* Garden City, NY: Doubleday, 1981.

Struckman-Johnson, Cindy. "Forced Sex on Dates: It Happens to Men, Too." *Journal of Sex Research* 24 (1988): 234–41.

Theroux, Paul. "The Male Myth." *New York Times Magazine* 27 Nov. 1983: 116.

EXAMINING THE ISSUE CRITICALLY

1. Is August simply whining about prejudice directed toward men, or do you find some truth in his argument? Does his argument fall apart anywhere? Explain.

2. Using Judith Bardwick as a source, August says the following in paragraph 34: "Sex bias or sexism itself is widely held to be a male-only fault. When sexism is defined as 'contempt for women' — as if there were no such thing as contempt for men — the definition of scxism is itself sexist."

3. One of the more disturbing statements that August makes is the following: "Too often the academic community, rather than opposing this sexism, has been encouraging it"(37). Has that been true in your experience? If so, does it mean that we need to be less vigilant about prejudice directed against women? What is the answer to the problem, if you believe there is one?

MAKING CONNECTIONS: THE LANGUAGE OF
SEXUAL DISCRIMINATION

The following questions are offered to help you start to make meaningful connections among the three articles in this Case Study. These questions can be used for class discussion, or you can answer any one of the questions by writing an essay. If you choose the essay option, be sure to make specific references to at least two of the Case Study articles.

1. If it is true that many people are silenced by the people and events around them, why do they remain so for most or all of their lives? Are they educated into or out of their silence? Write an essay in which you attempt to explain the silence as a result of alienation, desperation, frustration, or futility, using examples from Irvine and Wilchins. Has the "silenced person" always been with us? What are the dangers of our being silenced, both for ourselves and for society? How is silence from homosexuals different from that of heterosexuals?

2. Write an essay in which you discuss the problem of anti-male bashing. Is it a real problem or a backlash, the work of threatened males? How would Wilchins respond to August's claims? Have you experienced this kind of prejudice or know anyone who has? What have you read about the problem? Whether you agree or are opposed to the idea that there is anti-male bashing, you may wish to consult *The New Men's Studies: A Selected and Annotated Interdisciplinary Bibliography* (1994), edited by August, for further reading on the subject.

3. What role does language play in the bonding that takes place in fraternities and sororities? For example, is slang, abusive language directed at fraternity brothers, or sexually-oriented speech about fraternity brothers' girlfriends a linguistic necessity for bonding within the group? Write an essay about such language and its possible counterpart within sororities. What kind of slang is necessary in gay culture? How do shows like '*Queer Eye for the Straight Guy*' perpetuate homosocial slang?

4. Write an essay in which you argue for or against the notion that abusive language is often a necessary prerequisite to acts of violence, especially in the case of hate crimes directed against gays, lesbians, and transgenders. Do some research in your library or on the Internet and interview faculty in the sociology of crime and sociolinguistics before coming to any firm conclusions. It may also be helpful to locate newspaper or magazine articles that deal with hate crimes (such as the killing of Matthew Shepard) for any possible linkage between abusive language and subsequent acts of aggression.

Authors on page 322:

Writer 1: Langston Hughes, "Salvation"
Writer 2: Diane Ackerman, "Why Leaves Turn Color in the Fall"

6

THE POWER
OF THE MEDIA

The media have become so commonplace in our day-to-day lives that we take their pervasiveness at face value. Little do we realize what a powerful, constant presence the media are in our lives. Think about how television, radio, newspapers, magazines, movies, and even commercials and billboards impact you from the time you get up in the morning to the time you fall asleep at night. If you are like most Americans, much of what you know about our world is dictated by what you see, hear, and read in the media. To understand the tremendous power that the media industry wields in our lives, we need to understand the world of mass media and the ways in which their writers use and abuse both language and visuals.

The way in which each of us perceives the world around us is largely determined by the language used to present it. In "Selection, Slanting, and Charged Language," Newman and Genevieve Birk give us a crash course on how the language people use subtly shapes perceptions. They introduce us to three simple but powerful concepts — selecting, slanting, and charging — that when understood, will change forever the way we read, watch, or listen to the media. For years, critics have described television programming as a vast wasteland which offers little or nothing in the way of value to viewers. Nowhere is this criticism more evident than on talk shows that air at almost any hour of the day. In "Talk Shows and the Dumbing of America," author and media critic Tom Shachtman exposes the barely literate though highly charged language modeled for viewers on eight mainstream syndicated talk shows. Critics and viewers alike have complained about the foul language used in movies and on television. In "You Can't Say That: The Networks Play Word Games," Tad Friend, a staff writer for *The New Yorker*, takes an historical look at how network internal censors have addressed these questions over the years. Officially known as the staff of the Standards and Practices department, these censors carefully weigh the interests of viewers and advertisers in determining just how many obscenities writers can incorporate into any given episode of a show. Often they battle with writers who want to use more foul language in the name of realism or titillation. The next two articles examine the world of television news. Neil Postman and Steve Powers argue in "Television News: The Language of Pictures," that television news programs can't compare to the coverage in newspapers. Even with the ability to present stories in moving pictures, television news, they believe, is at best closer to good entertainment than good journalism. Finally, in "Exposing Media Myths: TV Doesn't Affect You as Much as You Think," Joanmarie Kalter explores four long-held misconceptions about the powerful influence of television news on our lives.

CASE STUDY: VIOLENCE AND THE MEDIA

Americans seem to be of two minds about violence in our culture. On the one hand, we are deeply disturbed whenever we read about another school shooting or children resorting to violence in order to settle a disagreement, while on the other hand, we wage a war on terrorism, line up to attend violence-filled action movies, buy hip-hop CDs with destructive lyrics, and play video games that cheapen the value of human life. What does this all say about our culture and its love-hate affair with violence in the media? We have selected four writers to give various perspectives on this troubling issue in hopes of provoking serious discussion and debate on a part of our culture that affects us all.

Selection, Slanting, and Charged Language

NEWMAN P. BIRK AND GENEVIEVE B. BIRK

The more we learn about language and how it works, the more abundantly clear it becomes that our language shapes our perceptions of the world. Because most people have eyes to see, ears to hear, noses to smell, tongues to taste, and skins to feel, it seems as though our perceptions of reality should be pretty similar. We know, however, that this is not the case, and language, it seems, makes a big difference in how we perceive our world. In effect, language acts as a filter, heightening certain perceptions, dimming others, and totally voiding still others.

In the following selection from their book Understanding and Using Language *(1972), Newman and Genevieve Birk discuss how we use words, especially the tremendous powers that slanted and charged language wields. As a writer, you will be particularly interested to learn just how important your choice of words is. After reading what the Birks have to say, you'll never read another editorial, watch another commercial, or listen to another politician in quite the same way.*

WRITING TO DISCOVER: *Choose three different people and write a description of a person, an object, or an event from each of their perspectives. Consider how each would relate to the subject you chose, what details each would focus on, and the attitude each would have toward that subject.*

A. THE PRINCIPLE OF SELECTION

Before it is expressed in words, our knowledge, both inside and outside, is influenced by the principle of selection. What we know or observe depends on what we notice; that is, what we select, consciously or unconsciously, as worthy of notice or attention. As we observe, the principle of selection determines which facts we take in.

Suppose, for example, that three people, a lumberjack, an artist, and a tree surgeon, are examining a large tree in the forest. Since the tree itself is a complicated object, the number of particulars or facts about it that one could observe would be very great indeed. Which of these facts a particular observer will notice will be a matter of selection, a selection that is determined by his interests and purposes. A lumberjack might be interested in the best way to cut the tree down, cut it up and transport it to the lumber mill. His interest would then determine his principle of selection in observing and thinking about the tree. The artist might consider painting a picture of the tree, and his purpose would furnish his principle of selection. The tree surgeon's professional interest in the physical health of the tree might establish a principle of selection for him. If each man were now required to write an exhaustive, detailed report on every thing he observed about the tree, the facts supplied by each would differ, for each would report those facts that his particular principle of selection led him to notice.[1]

The principle of selection holds not only for the specific facts that people observe but also for the facts they remember. A student suddenly embarrassed may remember nothing of the next ten minutes of class discussion but may have a vivid recollection of the sensation of the blood mounting, as he blushed, up his face and into his ears. In both noticing and remembering, the principle of selection applies, and it is influenced not only by our special interest and point of view but by our whole mental state of the moment.

The principle of selection then serves as a kind of sieve or screen through which our knowledge passes before it becomes our knowledge. Since we can't notice everything about a complicated object or situation or action or state of our own consciousness, what we do notice is determined by whatever principle of selection is operating for us at the time we gain the knowledge.

It is important to remember that what is true of the way the principle   5
of selection works for us is true also for the way it works for others. Even before we or other people put knowledge into words to express meaning, that knowledge has been screened or selected. Before an historian or an economist writes a book, or before a reporter writes a news article, the facts that each is to present have been sifted through the screen of a principle of selection. Before one person passes on knowledge to another, that knowledge has already been selected and shaped, intentionally or unintentionally, by the mind of the communicator.

B. THE PRINCIPLE OF SLANTING

When we put our knowledge into words, a second process of selection, the process of slanting, takes place. Just as there is something, a rather mysterious principle of selection, which chooses for us what we will notice, and what will then become our knowledge, there is also a principle which operates, with or without our awareness, to select certain facts and feelings from our store of knowledge, and to choose the words and emphasis that we shall use to communicate our

---

1. Of course, all three observers would probably report a good many facts in common — the height of the tree, for example, and the size of the trunk. The point we wish to make is that each observer would give us a different impression of the tree because of the different principle of selection that guided his observation.

meaning.[2] Slanting may be defined as the process of selecting (1) knowledge — factual and attitudinal; (2) words; and (3) emphasis, to achieve the intention of the communicator. Slanting is present in some degree in all communication: one may *slant for* (favorable slanting), *slant against* (unfavorable slanting), or *slant both ways* (balanced slanting). . . .

C. SLANTING BY USE OF EMPHASIS

Slanting by use of the devices of emphasis is unavoidable,[3] for emphasis is simply the giving of stress to subject matter, and so indicating what is important and what is less important. In speech, for example, if we say that Socrates was *a wise old man*, we can give several slightly different meanings, one by stressing *wise*, another by stressing *old*, another by giving equal stress to *wise* and *old*, and still another by giving chief stress to *man*. Each different stress gives a different slant (favorable or unfavorable or balanced) to the statement because it conveys a different attitude toward Socrates or a different judgment of him. Connectives and word order also slant by the emphasis they give: consider the difference in slanting or emphasis produced by *old but wise, old and wise, wise but old*. In writing, we cannot indicate subtle stresses on words as clearly as in speech, but we can achieve our emphasis and so can slant by the use of more complex patterns of word order, by choice of connectives, by underlining heavily stressed words, and by marks of punctuation that indicate short or long pauses and so give light or heavy emphasis. Question marks, quotation marks, and exclamation points can also contribute to slanting.[4] It is impossible either in speech or in writing to put two facts together without giving some slight emphasis or slant. For example, if we have in mind only two facts about a man, his awkwardness and his strength, we subtly slant those facts favorably or unfavorably in whatever way we may choose to join them.

More Favorable Slanting	*Less Favorable Slanting*
He is awkward and strong.	He is strong and awkward.
He is awkward but strong.	He is strong but awkward.
Although he is somewhat awkward, he is very strong.	He may be strong, but he's very awkward.

2. Notice that the "principle of selection" is at work as *we take in* knowledge, and that slanting occurs *as we express* our knowledge in words.

3. When emphasis is present — and we can think of no instance in the use of language in which it is not — it necessarily influences the meaning by playing a part in the favorable, unfavorable, or balanced slant of the communicator. We are likely to emphasize by voice stress, even when we answer *yes* or *no* to simple questions.

4. Consider the slanting achieved by punctuation in the following sentences: He called the Senator an honest man? *He* called the Senator an honest man? He called the Senator an honest man! He said one more such "honest" senator would corrupt the state.

With more facts and in longer passages it is possible to maintain a delicate
balance by alternating favorable emphasis and so producing a balanced effect.

All communication, then, is in some degree slanted by the *emphasis*
of the communicator.

D. SLANTING BY SELECTION OF FACTS

To illustrate the technique of slanting by selection of facts, we shall examine three passages of informative writing which achieve different effects
simply by the selection and emphasis of material. Each passage is made up of
true statements or facts about a dog, yet the reader is given three different
impressions. The first passage is an example of objective writing or balanced
slanting, the second is slanted unfavorably, and the third is slanted favorably.

1. Balanced Presentation

Our dog, Toddy, sold to us as a cocker, produces various reactions
in various people. Those who come to the back door she usually growls
and barks at (a milkman has said that he is afraid of her); those who
come to the front door, she whines at and paws; also she tries to lick
people's faces unless we have forestalled her by putting a newspaper in
her mouth. (Some of our friends encourage these actions; others discourage them. Mrs. Firmly, one friend, slaps the dog with a newspaper
and says, "I know how hard dogs are to train.") Toddy knows and re-
sponds to a number of words and phrases, and guests sometimes remark
that she is a "very intelligent dog." She has fleas in the summer, and she
sheds, at times copiously, the year round. Her blonde hairs are conspicuous when they are on people's clothing or on rugs or furniture. Her
color and her large brown eyes frequently produce favorable comment.
An expert on cockers would say that her ears are too short and set too
high and that she is at least six pounds too heavy.

The passage above is made up of facts, verifiable facts,[5] deliberately se-   10
lected and emphasized to produce a *balanced* impression. Of course not
all the facts about the dog have been given — to supply *all* the facts on
any subject, even such a comparatively simple one, would be an almost
impossible task. Both favorable and unfavorable facts are used, however,
and an effort has been made to alternate favorable and unfavorable details

---

5. *Verifiable facts* are facts that can be checked and agreed upon and proved to be true
by people who wish to verify them. That a particular theme received a failing grade is a verifiable fact; one needs merely to see the theme with the grade on it. That the instructor
should have failed the theme is not, strictly speaking, a verifiable fact, but a matter of
opinion. That women on the average live longer than men is a verifiable fact; that they live
better is a matter of opinion, *a value judgment.*

so that neither will receive greater emphasis by position, proportion, or grammatical structure.

2. Facts Slanted Against

That dog put her paws on my white dress as soon as I came in the door, and she made so much noise that it was two minutes before she had quieted down enough for us to talk and hear each other. Then the gas man came and she did a great deal of barking. And her hairs are on the rug and on the furniture. If you wear a dark dress they stick to it like lint. When Mrs. Firmly came in, she actually hit the dog with a newspaper to make it stay down, and she made some remark about training dogs. I wish the Birks would take the hint or get rid of that noisy, short-eared, overweight "cocker" of theirs.

This unfavorably slanted version is based on the same facts, but now these facts have been selected and given a new emphasis. The speaker, using her selected facts to give her impression of the dog, is quite possibly unaware of her negative slanting.

Now for a favorably slanted version:

3. Facts Slanted For

What a lively and responsible dog! When I walked in the door, there she was with a newspaper in her mouth, whining and standing on her hind legs and wagging her tail all at the same time. And what an intelligent dog. If you suggest going for a walk, she will get her collar from the kitchen and hand it to you, and she brings Mrs. Birk's slippers whenever Mrs. Birk says she is "tired" or mentions slippers. At a command she catches balls, rolls over, "speaks," or stands on her hind feet and twirls around. She sits up and balances a piece of bread on her nose until she is told to take it; then she tosses it up and catches it. If you are eating something, she sits up in front of you and "begs" with those big dark brown eyes set in that light, buff-colored face of hers. When I got up to go and told her I was leaving, she rolled her eyes at me and sat up like a squirrel. She certainly is a lively and intelligent dog.

Speaker 3, like Speaker 2, is selecting from the "facts" summarized in balanced version 1, and is emphasizing his facts to communicate his impression.

All three passages are examples of *reporting* (i.e., consist only of verifiable facts), yet they give three very different impressions of the same dog because of the different ways the speakers slanted the facts. Some people say that figures don't lie, and many people believe that if they have the "facts," they have the "truth." Yet if we carefully examine the ways of thought and language, we see that any knowledge that comes to us through words has been subjected to the double screening of the principle of selection and the slanting of language. . . .

Wise listeners and readers realize that the double screening that is   15
produced by the principle of selection and by slanting takes place even
when people honestly try to report the facts as they know them. (Speakers 2 and 3, for instance, probably thought of themselves as simply giving
information about a dog and were not deliberately trying to mislead.)
Wise listeners and readers know too that deliberate manipulators of language, by mere selection and emphasis, can make their slanted facts appear to support almost any cause.

In arriving at opinions and values we cannot always be sure that the
facts that sift into our minds through language are representative and
relevant and true. We need to remember that much of our information
about politics, governmental activities, business conditions, and foreign
affairs comes to us selected and slanted. More than we realize, our opinions on these matters may depend on what newspaper we read or what
news commentator we listen to. Worthwhile opinions call for knowledge
of reliable facts and reasonable arguments for and against — and such
opinions include beliefs about morality and truth and religion as well as
about public affairs. Because complex subjects involve knowing and
dealing with many facts on both sides, reliable judgments are at best difficult to arrive at. If we want to be fairminded, we must be willing to
subject our opinions to continual testing by new knowledge, and must
realize that after all they *are* opinions, more or less trustworthy. Their
trustworthiness will depend on the representativeness of our facts, on
the quality of our reasoning, and on the standard of values that we
choose to apply.

We shall not give here a passage illustrating the unscrupulous slanting of facts. Such a passage would also include irrelevant facts and false
statements presented as facts, along with various subtle distortions of
fact. Yet to the uninformed reader the passage would be indistinguishable
from a passage intended to give a fair account. If two passages (2 and 3)
of casual and unintentional slanting of facts about a dog can give such
contradictory impressions of a simple subject, the reader can imagine
what a skilled and designing manipulation of facts and statistics could do
to mislead an uninformed reader about a really complex subject. An example of such manipulation might be the account of the United States
that Soviet propaganda has supplied to the average Russian. Such propaganda, however, would go beyond the mere slanting of the facts: it would
clothe the selected facts in charged words and would make use of the
many other devices of slanting that appear in charged language.

E. SLANTING BY USE OF CHARGED WORDS

In the passages describing the dog Toddy, we were illustrating the
technique of slanting by the selection and emphasis of facts. Though the

facts selected had to be expressed in words, the words chosen were as factual as possible, and it was the selection and emphasis of facts and not of words that was mainly responsible for the two distinctly different impressions of the dog. In the passages below we are demonstrating another way of slanting — by the use of charged words. This time the accounts are very similar in the facts they contain; the different impressions of the subject, Corlyn, are produced not by different facts but by the subtle selection of charged words.

The passages were written by a clever student who was told to choose as his subject a person in action, and to write two descriptions, each using the "same facts." The instructions required that one description be slanted positively and the other negatively, so that the first would make the reader favorably inclined toward the person and the action, and the second would make him unfavorably inclined.

Here is the favorably charged description. Read it carefully and form   20
your opinion of the person before you go on to read the second description.

Corlyn

Corlyn paused at the entrance to the room and glanced about. A well-cut black dress draped subtly about her slender form. Her long blonde hair gave her chiseled features the simple frame they required. She smiled an engaging smile as she accepted a cigarette from her escort. As he lit it for her she looked over the flame and into his eyes. Corlyn had that rare talent of making every male feel that he was the only man in the world.

She took his arm and they descended the steps into the room. She walked with an effortless grace and spoke with equal ease. They each took a cup of coffee and joined a group of friends near the fire. The flickering light danced across her face and lent an ethereal quality to her beauty. The good conversation, the crackling logs, and the stimulating coffee gave her a feeling of internal warmth. Her eyes danced with each leap of the flames.

Taken by itself this passage might seem just a description of an attractive girl. The favorable slanting by use of charged words has been done so skillfully that it is inconspicuous. Now we turn to the unfavorable slanted description of the "same" girl in the "same" actions:

Corlyn

Corlyn halted at the entrance to the room and looked around. A plain black dress hung on her thin frame. Her stringy bleached hair accentuated her harsh features. She smiled an inane smile as she took a cigarette from her escort. As he lit it for her she stared over the lighter and into his eyes. Corlyn had a habit of making every male feel that he was the last man on earth.

She grasped his arm and they walked down the steps and into the room. Her pace was fast and ungainly, as was her speed. They each reached for some coffee and broke into a group of acquaintances near the fire. The flickering light played across her face and revealed every flaw. The loud talk, the fire, and the coffee she had gulped down made her feel hot. Her eyes grew more red with each leap of the flames.

When the reader compares these two descriptions, he can see how charged words influence the reader's attitude. One needs to read the two descriptions several times to appreciate all the subtle differences between them. Words, some rather heavily charged, others innocent-looking but lightly charged, work together to carry to the reader a judgment of a person and a situation. If the reader had seen only the first description of Corlyn, he might well have thought that he had formed his "own judgment on the basis of the facts." And the examples just given only begin to suggest the techniques that may be used in heavily charged language. For one thing, the two descriptions of Corlyn contain no really good example of the use of charged abstractions; for another, the writer was obliged by the assignment to use the same set of facts and so could not slant by selecting his material.

F. SLANTING AND CHARGED LANGUAGE

. . . When slanting of facts, or words, or emphasis, or any combination of the three *significantly influences* feelings toward, or judgments about, a subject, the language used is charged language. . . .

Of course communications vary in the amount of charge they carry and in their effect on different people; what is very favorably charged for one person may have little or no charge, or may even be adversely charged, for others. It is sometimes hard to distinguish between charged and uncharged expression. But it is safe to say that whenever we wish to convey any kind of inner knowledge — feelings, attitudes, judgments, values — we are obliged to convey that attitudinal meaning through the medium of charged language; and when we wish to understand the inside knowledge of others, we have to interpret the charged language that they choose, or are obliged to use. Charged language, then, is the natural and necessary medium for the communication of charged or attitudinal meaning. At times we have difficulty in living with it, but we should have even greater difficulty in living without it.

Some of the difficulties in living with charged language are caused by its use in dishonest propaganda, in some editorials, in many political speeches, in most advertising, in certain kinds of effusive salesmanship, and in blatantly insincere, or exaggerated, or sentimental expressions of emotion. Other difficulties are caused by the misunderstandings and

25

misinterpretations that charged language produces. A charged phrase mis-interpreted in a love letter; a charged word spoken in haste or in anger; an acrimonious argument about religion or politics or athletics or fraterni-ties; the frustrating uncertainty produced by the effort to understand the complex attitudinal meaning in a poem or play or a short story — these troubles, all growing out of the use of charged language, may give us the feeling that Robert Louis Stevenson expressed when he said, "The battle goes sore against us to the going down of the sun."

But however charged language is abused and whatever misunder-standings it may cause, we still have to live with it — and even by it. It shapes our attitudes and values even without our conscious knowledge; it gives purpose to, and guides, our actions; through it we establish and maintain relations with other people and by means of it we exert our greatest influence on them. Without charged language, life would be but half life. The relatively uncharged language of bare factual statement, though it serves its informative purpose well and is much less open to abuse and to misunderstanding, can describe only the bare land of factual knowledge; to communicate knowledge of the turbulencies and the calms and the deep currents of the sea of inner experience we must use charged language.

FOCUSING ON CONTENT

1. What is the principle of selection, and how does it work?

2. According to the Birks, how is slanting different from the principle of selec-tion? What devices can a speaker or writer use to slant knowledge? When is it appropriate, if at all, to slant language?

3. What exactly are charged words? Demonstrate your understanding of charged language by picking some examples from the two descriptions of Corlyn.

4. Why is it important for writers and others to be aware of charged words? What can happen if you use charged language unknowingly? What are some of the difficulties in living in a world with charged language?

FOCUSING ON WRITING

1. What is the Birks's purpose in this essay? (Glossary: *Purpose*) Do they seem more intent on explaining or on arguing their position? Point to specific language that they use that led you to your conclusion. (Glossary: *Diction*)

2. Do you find the examples about Toddy the dog and Corlyn particularly helpful? (Glossary: *Examples*) Why or why not? What would have been lost, if anything, had the examples not been included?

3. How do the Birks organize their essay? (Glossary: *Organization*) Do you think the organizational pattern is appropriate given their subject matter and purpose? Explain.

4. How do the authors use transitional words and expressions to guide readers through the essay? (Glossary: *Transitions*) Mention some specific transitions.

5. The Birks wrote this essay in 1972, when people were not as sensitive to sexist language as they are today. (Glossary: *Sexist Language*) Reread several pages of their essay, paying particular attention to the Birks's use of pronouns and to the gender of the people in their examples. Suggest ways in which the Birks's diction could be changed so as to eliminate any sexist language.

LANGUAGE IN ACTION

According to the editors of *Newsweek*, the March 8, 1999, "Voices of the Century: Americans at War" issue "generated more than two hundred passionate responses from civilians and veterans." The following five letters are representative of those the editors received and published in the issue of March 29, 1999. Carefully read each letter, looking for slanting and charged language. Point out the verifiable facts you find. How do you know these facts are verifiable?

Kudos for your March 8 issue, "Voices of the Century: Americans at War." This issue surely ranks among the best magazines ever published. As a military historian, I gained a better perspective of this turbulent century from this single issue than from many other sources combined. The first person accounts are the genius of the issue. And your selection of storytellers was truly inspired. The "Voices of the Century" is so powerful that I will urge all of my friends to read it, buying copies for those who are not subscribers. Many persons today, especially those born after WWII, do not comprehend or appreciate the defining events of this century. How can we be more confident that they will be aware of our vital past when making important social and political decisions during the next century? I have great confidence in the American spirit and will, but this missing perspective is my principal concern as I leave this nation to the ministry of my daughters, my grandchildren, and their generation. Why not publish "Voices of the Century" as a booklet and make it readily available to all young people? Why not urge every school system to make it required reading prior to graduation from high school?

– ALAN R. McKIE, Springfield, VA

Your March 8 war issue was a powerfully illustrated essay of the men and women who have served our country and the people of other lands in so many capacities. But it was the photos that touched my soul and made me cry all over again for the human loss, *my* loss. As I stared at the pictures of the injured, dead, dying, and crying, I felt as though I were intruding on their private hell. God bless all of them, and my sincere thanks for a free America.

– DEBORAH AMES, Sparks, NV

I arrived in this country at 15 as a Jewish refugee from Nazism. I became an American soldier at 19 and a U.S. Foreign Service officer at 29. As a witness to much of the history covered in your special issue, I wanted to congratulate *Newsweek* on a superb job. In your excellent introduction, I found only one word with which I take issue: that "after the war Rosie and her cohort *happily* went back to the joys of motherhood and built the baby boom." Rosie and her cohort were forced back into their traditional gender roles, and it took the women's movement another generation or two to win back the gains achieved during the war.

– LUCIAN HEICHLER, Frederick, MD

Editor's note: The word "happily" was carefully chosen. Contemporary surveys indicated that most of the American women who joined the work force because of World War II were glad to get back to family life when it was over.

On the cover of your "Americans at War" issue, you have the accompanying text "From WWI to Vietnam: The Grunts and the Great Men — In Their Own Words." In each of these wars, the grunts *were* the great men.

– PAULA S. MCGUIRE, Charlotte, NC

Your March 8 issue was painful for me and other members of my family as a result of the photograph you included on page 62 showing a wounded soldier being dragged from the line of fire during the Tet Offensive. My family had previously confirmed with the photographer that the soldier was my youngest brother, Marine Cpl. Robert Mack Harrelson. His bullet-riddled body fought hard to survive and, with the assistance of many excellent, caring members of our U.S. Military Medical Staff, he was able to regain some degree of normalcy after his return. But the injuries he received were too great to overcome, resulting in the military funeral he had requested. The rekindled grief brought on by your photo is keenly felt throughout our large family, and especially so by our dear 85-year-old mother, who still speaks of Bob as though he might reappear at any time. In spite of the photo, I sincerely congratulate your fine publication for reminding the world of the tragedy of war.

– LOWELL L. HARRELSON, Bay Minette, AL

WRITING SUGGESTIONS

1. Describe a day at your school or university. Begin with details that help you create a single dominant impression. Be careful to select only details that support the attitude and meaning you wish to convey. Once you've finished, compare your essay to those of your peers. In what ways do the essays differ? How are they the same? How does this writing exercise reinforce the Birks's discussion of the principle of selection?

2. When used only positively or only negatively, charged words can alienate the reader and bring the author's reliability into question. Consider the Birks's two examples of Corlyn. In the first example Corlyn can do no wrong, and in the second she can do nothing right. Using these two examples as a guide, write your own multiparagraph description of a person you know well. Decide on the overall impression you want to convey to your

readers, and use charged words — both positive and negative — to create that impression.

3. Find a newspaper or magazine editorial on a subject that you have strong opinions about. Analyze the writer's selection of facts and use of charged language. How well does the writer present different viewpoints? Is the editorial convincing? Why or why not? After researching the topic further in your library or on the Internet, write a letter to the editor in response to the editorial. In your letter, use information from your research to make a point about the subject. Also comment on any charged or slanted language the editor used. Mail your letter to the editor.

Talk Shows and the Dumbing of America

Tom Shachtman

Award-winning documentarian and author, Tom Shachtman was born in 1942 in New York City. After graduating with a B.A. from Tufts University in 1963 and an M.A. from Carnegie-Mellon University in 1966, he pursued a career as a freelance writer, producer, and director for television, writing the widely acclaimed trilogy "Children of Poverty," "Children of Trouble," and "Children of Violence" in the 1970s. Shachtman has taught writing at Harvard's Extension School and at New York University. He is the author of both fiction and nonfiction works, including Video Power *(1988),* Skyscraper Dreams: The Great Real Estate Dynasties of New York *(1991),* Around the Block: The Business of a Neighborhood *(1997), and* Absolute Zero *(1999).*

The following selection is taken from his book The Inarticulate Society: Eloquence and Culture in America *(1995). In this excerpt, Shachtman examines eight popular syndicated television talk shows to discover the impact these shows are having on the language and minds of viewers. He provides convincing evidence that talk shows are dumbing down or debasing the English language rather than helping American society deal with its increasing inarticulateness.*

WRITING TO DISCOVER: *Whether or not you watch television talk shows, you have heard of some popular hosts and their shows — Oprah Winfrey, Jenny Jones, Jerry Springer, Ricki Lake, Regis Philbin and Kelly Ripa, Dr. Phil, and Montel Williams, to name just a few. Jot down your thoughts or observations about these hosts and their shows. Is your impression of talk shows generally positive? Negative? Indifferent? Explain.*

On an Oprah Winfrey broadcast, when a young doctor confessed that he was something of a romantic, he reportedly received 40,000 letters from women wishing to share his life. While not every talk program can generate that amount of attention, collectively talk shows have an enormous audience, as many as 80 million viewers daily, and as the doctor's story makes clear, it is an audience that pays close attention to what is being said on the programs. To learn more about how language is being modeled for us on talk shows, on November 9, 1993, I spent the day watching and listening to snippets of eight mainstream syndicated talk shows.

At nine in the morning in New York, while NBC and some other channels carry game shows and cartoons, and while Mr. Rogers holds forth on public television, there are three talk shows in head-to-head competition: Jane Whitney on CBS, Montel Williams on the Fox network, and Regis Philbin and Kathie Lee Gifford on ABC.

Jane Whitney features a man whose problem is that he has two girlfriends. Tina and Jim are the guests in the first segment. She is angry about the situation, while he seems as contented as the cat who swallowed the cream. We later learn that Jim called the program and offered to appear with his two girlfriends, ostensibly to resolve their predicament. Jane Whitney's questioning demonstrates that she knows the terms "psychobabble," "avoiding commitment," "relationship," and "monogamous," but most of her queries are monosyllabic: "Some people, like, sleep with only one person at a time."

Jim's two lovers have never met. Now, to applause, the second young woman emerges from behind a curtain, and then, under Jane's questioning, the two comment on how they are and are not alike.

JANE   Do you feel you have anything in common with her?

SECOND   Him.

TINA   How do you know he loves you? He loves me!

JANE   You're playing, like, seniority here. Like, bookends.

Montel Williams's guests are six couples made up of older women and younger men. Each woman introduces her young man, using such terms as "hunk," "sex appeal," and "perfect specimen of humanity," and making sure to announce his birth date, for the men are a decade or two younger than the women. The couples behave as though they are in the first flushes of affairs. We learn that the Montel Williams show arranged and taped a party at which these people were first introduced to one another, in exchange for promises to appear on the program. The basic subject of the program is sex. Queried by the host, one young man speaks of "not having to work for it" and another confides about older women, "they tell you what they want," which prompts an admission from one that "we want a little pleasure for ourselves." Titles over the screen inform us that "JOHN/Likes women of all ages" and "NICK/Loves older women." The snickering quotient of the program is high. At the transition to commercials, footage of the mixer party is followed by a snippet from tomorrow's show, "Two sisters, one man. . . . You'd be surprised at how often this happens." At least one set of sisters are twins. During a later segment of the broadcast, a ponytailed male therapist comments on the couples, using such phrases as "comfort . . . not expected to last . . . emotional ties are suspended." The therapist is then questioned by the panel, which induces Montel to tell about his own experiences with older women. A billboard asks us at home, "Are You a Mom Who Wishes Her Son Would Stop Dating Tramps?" Those who can answer "yes" are to call the show.

"Born to Be Unfaithful," Jane Whitney's next program, will feature people who have been unfaithful and are the offspring of unfaithful parents. The subject after that is "Mothers who allow their teenage daughters to have sex in the house"; on videotape, one such mother says she prefers her daughter and the daughter's boyfriend to have sex at home "where I know that they're safe."

Barbara Walters visits Regis and Kathie Lee to impart backstage chatter about the celebrities she has interviewed for her latest special, to be broadcast that evening. In a clip, Barbara tries to learn from Julia Roberts whether the movie star thinks her husband of a few months is ugly or just differently handsome. Julia opts for handsome. In the studio Barbara and Kathie Lee brush cheeks and make hand motions to convey that they must phone one another for a lunch date very soon.

Fred Rogers visits a pretzel bakery. In an apron and baker's hat, he observes the various processes of the assembly line and kneads some dough with his own hands. His conversation with the bakers, aimed at an audience of preschool children, employs almost as large a vocabulary as that of the nine o'clock talk shows.

Not yet ready to make conclusions from such a small sample, later that day I watch segments of five more talk shows: Joan Rivers on CBS and, on NBC, Jerry Springer, Maury Povich, Sally Jessy Raphael, and Phil Donahue.

"How going back to the trauma of birth will help you clear up present problems" is the way Joan Rivers touts the subject of her program, but before discussing that she chats with a gossip columnist about the recent birth of Marla Maples's child, in which "aroma therapy" was used, and welcomes a pair of married guests to talk about "past-life therapy." The couple maintains that they were actually married in a previous life. The wife says that through reliving and understanding an incident in Roman times, she has been cured: 10

> GUEST All that anger drained away. . . . My heart got tender. I got compassionate.
>
> JOAN All this in one session?

. . . Then we are finally introduced to a female "prenatal psychologist." To investigate "early traumas . . . impressed on the psyche," this woman helps patients to go back to the moment of birth, even to the moment of conception. She has brought along some patients, whom Joan Rivers introduces: "My next guests have all been reborn, not through religion." These guests include another ponytailed male psychologist, who has been rescued by regression therapy from suicidal impulses, and a mother-and-daughter pair, similarly rescued from allergies. We shortly see a videotape of a volunteer who has gone through the therapy backstage. After the tape is shown, the volunteer comes onto the set and comments on reliving the attempt to get out of the birth canal: "I was engaged in some sort of battle."

From Boston, Jerry Springer features several trios, each consisting of a grandmother, her teenage daughter, and the daughter's infant. The infants have been born out of wedlock, one to a girl who became pregnant at twelve, the others to girls who were thirteen and fourteen. The teenagers had all considered abortion but had decided against it. Jerry asks about birth control. . . . A new grandmother allows that in retrospect she does "feel guilty" at not having given her daughter birth control instruction. "At thirteen, I didn't think she was going to be — you know — actively having sex with her boyfriend," who was nineteen; "I was in denial." Jerry Springer nods, and in general his treatment of an important subject, the epidemic of teenage pregnancies, is evenhanded. He questions the women sympathetically and with dignity, although he never refers to them by their names but says "Mom" and "Grandmom." He asks a woman in the latter category if the sensation of becoming a grandmother could have been a proud one, given the circumstances. She says, "I don't know; it's like, I was in the delivery with her, and it's like — 'Memories.'" Audience members express their belief that the fathers should be arraigned on charges of statutory rape, but the new mothers and grandmothers all agree that would not help anyone. . . .

Maury Povich has gone to Texas for "Return to Waco: Answers in the Ashes." In front of an audience of former cult members and Waco residents, Povich questions Mark Breault, who left the Branch Davidians in 1989; Breault's complaints to the authorities have been blamed by some survivors for instigating the raids. . . .

The government's lead pathologist then summarizes his team's findings about the thirty-two people who died in the bunker. In the most literate language I have heard all day, language that is compassionate, direct, and precise, he details the manner and cause of death: So many had gunshot wounds, so many died of asphyxiation; a gunshot wound in the mouth may have been self-inflicted, but a wound in the back of the head almost certainly was not. His findings, being made public for the first time, devastate the people in the audience and on the set whose relatives died in that bunker — as we at home are forced to learn because the cameras focus on their faces so that we become privy to their emotions. While the pathologist tells the story, Maury Povich approaches one panel member whose face fills the screen and asks, "Is this what you think, Stan, happened to your family?"

"Could your sex life use a pick-me-up?" asks the announcer of the   15
Phil Donahue show. Then voice and tape display aphrodisiacs, love potions, and an acupuncturist at work, and a panelist comments that "I'm getting turned on just by watching."

That, of course, is just what was intended.

Sally Jessy Raphael's program on November 9, 1993, deals with two 1986 cyanide poisoning deaths in the Seattle area, for which the wife of one of the victims was convicted and imprisoned. Of all the programs of this day, it is the worst exemplar in terms of use of language. First, Sally encapsulates the story for us in emotional kindergarten language: "Some family members say Stella was railroaded. 'She's innocent. Poor Stella.' Some say her daughter Cynthia was really the mastermind behind the deaths." A journalist has written a book about the case. He has corralled the guest panelists, but during the course of the program he must frequently interpret and augment what these guests say, for the guests prove remarkably unable to present their thoughts coherently or even clothed in words that aptly convey their meaning.

> STELLA'S NIECE   I didn't think that — there wasn't enough problems that would institute her to kill my uncle . . .

> STELLA'S FRIEND   She was somebody that would've taken a gun and shot him point-blank, instead of being sneaky and committed murder in the way that she was convicted.

When one guest is entirely unable to convey her meaning, Sally is forced to correct her in order that the audience can understand the story:

> FORMER HOUSEMATE   She used me as a scapegoat.

> SALLY   As a screen.

> AUDIENCE MEMBER   Maybe Cynthia was child-abused.

As with my student's use of "emitted" for "admitted," these poor grammatical, vocabulary, and word usages are evidence of the sort of misperception of language that can only come from learning language in a secondarily oral way. Pop psychology terms aside, the discourse of the moderators, the guests, the experts, and most of the studio audience members of all these programs mixes grade-school vocabulary and grammar with a leavening of naughty language. Granted, there is no pretense of trying to be articulate, but neither are there many accidental instances of felicitous phrasing. Vocabulary levels are depressingly low, more in line with the spoken-word corpus than might be presumed, since parts of the programs are scripted, and since the guests and stars of these programs are not speaking in private but in rather public circumstances, in front of viewing audiences numbered in the tens of millions.

Talk-show language has become almost completely detached from the literate base of English. It is as though the program-makers have concluded that literate English has nothing to do with the emotive, real-life concerns of human beings, and therefore cannot be used to describe or analyze them. As a result, talk shows exist in the realm of vocabularies limited to the few hundred most commonly used words in the spoken language, augmented by a few terms pirated from the sublanguage of therapy. To talk of "Mothers who allow their teenage daughters to have sex in the house," or to inquire "Are You a Mom Who Wishes Her Son Would Stop Dating Tramps?" is to speak down to the audience, not even

20

to address the audience on its own level. These lines employ a vocabulary not much beyond that of a nine- or ten-year-old; the facts show that the daytime viewing audience is chronologically older and better educated than that. . . . But the programming elites seem to have nothing but contempt for their audiences composed of average Americans — for "the people we fly over," as one executive called them. Rather, the programmers embrace the fuzzy McLuhanesque belief that a world dominated by new electronic media will wholeheartedly share tribal emotions.

Walter Ong asserts [in *Rhetoric, Romance and Technology*, 1971] that the culture of secondary orality may mean a return to the primacy of the unconscious for those within it. That culture's gestation period is being shortened by the practices of today's news programs and talk shows, which encourage the audience to acquire information principally through images, and through a lexicon that mimics the oral rather than the literate language. The limited vocabulary, constrained syntax, unknowing or deliberate misuses of language, affectation of minor wit, constant reference to base emotions, and chronic citation of pop cultural icons in attempts to bond with the audience — these characteristic elements of news and talk programs constitute an enfeebled discourse.

The antidote is well known, since most of the people who create news programs and talk shows are themselves literate and fully capable of using the literate-based language. That antidote is to use the power of words to haul these programs back up to a literate level they once attained. Purveyors of talk shows currently reject such a goal as not commensurate with their objective of gaining the largest audience. However, there is no evidence of which I am aware that demonstrates any inverse relationship between the shows' popularity and the vocabulary and articulateness levels of talk show hosts and hostesses (and that of their carefully screened guests). Precisely the opposite may be true: Articulate behavior is part of the hosts' and hostesses' attractiveness. Phil Donahue and Oprah Winfrey are articulate as well as charismatic people. Rush Limbaugh's ability to deflate liberal icons and to create telling puns — "femi-nazis" for strident feminists — have attracted him a wide following. All three, and many others among the talk-show stars, possess good vocabularies, but they have yet to employ them to best use. All too often, they reach for the simple instead of using their tremendous abilities to make complicated matters exciting and understandable. Given these stars' large talents and capacities to enthrall, audiences would undoubtedly follow them up the scale of literacy as gladly (and in just as large numbers) as they have followed them down the scale.

As for news broadcasts, the transformation could be even simpler. News broadcasts need to take a pledge to not only convey information but to set aside time in the broadcast to have that information illuminated by the minds and vocabularies of the reporters. Permit reporters once again to do the tasks of synthesis and analysis of information, as well as the job of being on the spot to collect it. Utilize television's fabulous educative ability. Employ vocabularies that may once in a while send an audience member scurrying to a dictionary — or, better yet, set a goal of encouraging the audience to incorporate interesting words into their own vocabularies. During the Gulf War, millions of Americans learned a new word when Peter Jennings of ABC News spoke of oil as a "fungible" commodity, which he explained meant that a unit of it from one source was essentially the same as a unit of it from another source. Network news divisions could improve the articulateness levels of their viewers by raising the vocabulary and sentence-structure levels of their own broadcasts and by taking the pledge to use "fungible" and other such marvelous if unfamiliar words when they are clearly appropriate. How about one new word a day? Such a practice would be unlikely to provoke viewers to turn away from their favorite newscasters and to the competition.

We need for our broadcasters once again to champion and employ the power of words as well as the power of images. This is not only in the public interest, but in their own. Informative broadcasting relies, in the end, on an audience that places some premium on the value of ideas. If its discourse is increasingly impoverished, then the audience will retreat from information-based programs into the wholly pictorial realm of video games and interactive fictional programming, where the audience has the illusion of deciding what happens. Then there will be no more market for television news or talk shows. What the informative shows are doing by embracing images and diminished language is the equivalent of a restaurant slowly poisoning all of its customers.

FOCUSING ON CONTENT

1. How would you characterize the subjects of the talk-show programs that Shachtman watched? Do there seem to be any differences between the morning and afternoon talk shows? Why do you think so many people find such topics worth watching?

2. In what ways does the Maury Povich show about the Branch Davidians contrast with the other shows? What does it have in common with them?

3. In paragraph 19, what does Shachtman mean when he hypothesizes that many of the talk-show guests' "poor grammatical, vocabulary, and word usages . . . can only come from learning language in a secondarily oral way"? How does Walter Ong's description of the culture of secondary orality (21) support Shachtman's claim?

4. What is Shachtman's solution for what he considers the deplorable state of language on television talk shows? Do you think his solution is realistic? He praises newscaster Peter Jennings for introducing viewers to the word *fungible* (23). What does *fungible* mean? How does Jennings's action support Shachtman's views?

5. Why does Shachtman believe that today's broadcasters need "to champion and employ the power of words as well as the power of images" (24)? What does he fear will happen if our discourse becomes increasingly impoverished?

FOCUSING ON WRITING

1. In paragraph 1, what is the point of Shachtman's example of the young doctor on Oprah Winfrey's show? How effective is this story as an opening? (Glossary: *Beginnings and Endings*) Explain.

2. In paragraph 8, Shachtman discusses the content of *Mr. Rogers*. Explain the purpose this paragraph serves in the context of the essay.

3. How does Shachtman organize his essay? (Glossary: *Organization*) Explain how paragraphs 1–18 are related to paragraphs 19–24.

4. How would you characterize Shachtman's style — his vocabulary, sentence structure, paragraph length — in paragraphs 19–24? (Glossary: *Style*) What stylistic differences do you see between this group of paragraphs and the first 18 paragraphs? Discuss how the two styles reflect both the content and the purpose of each section of the essay.

5. What is Shachtman's attitude toward each of the talk-show topics he uses in his examples? How does his word choice help him to convey this attitude? (Glossary: *Attitude* and *Diction*)

LANGUAGE IN ACTION

In a chapter on the importance of words in his popular book *The Word-a-Day Vocabulary Builder* (1963), Bergen Evans gives the following account of two events in history that turned on the choice of a particular word. Discuss the ways in which these examples support Shachtman's call for broadcasters and talk-show hosts to model literate-based language for viewers.

Some of history's great disasters have been caused by misunderstood directions. The heroic but futile charge of the Light Brigade at Balaclava in the Crimean War is a striking example. "Someone had blundered," Tennyson wrote. That was true, and the blunder consisted of the confusion over one word, which meant one thing to the person speaking but another to the persons spoken to.

The brigade was ordered to charge "the guns." The man who gave the order was on a hilltop and had in mind a small battery which was very plain to him but was concealed from the soldiers in the valley by a slight rise. The only guns *they* could see were the main Russian batteries at the far end of the valley. Therefore they assumed that "the guns" referred to the batteries *they* saw. The command seemed utter madness, but it was a command and the leader of the Brigade, after filing a protest, carried it out. . . .

. . . When . . . America and Russia confronted each other during the Cuban crisis in 1962, and the world hovered for a few days on the brink of disaster, the use of the word *quarantine* instead of *blockade* was extremely important. A *blockade* is an act of war. No one knew quite what a *quarantine* meant, under the circumstances. But the very use of the word indicated that, while we were determined to protect ourselves, we wanted to avoid war. It was all a part of giving Russia some possibility of saving face. We wanted her missiles and planes out of Cuba and were prepared to fight even a nuclear war to get them out. But we certainly preferred to have them removed peacefully. We did not want to back Russia into a corner from which there could have been no escape except by violence.

Thus the use of *quarantine*, a purposefully vague word, was part of our strategy. Furthermore, it had other advantages over *blockade*. It is commonly associated with a restriction imposed by all civilized nations on people with certain communicable diseases to prevent them from spreading their disease throughout the community. It is a public health measure which, for all the inconvenience that it may impose on the afflicted individual, serves the public welfare. Thus, whereas a blockade would have been an announcement that we were proceeding aggressively to further our own interests, regardless of the rights of others, quarantine suggested a concern for the general welfare. In addition, it suggested that what was going on in Cuba was a dangerous disease which might spread.

WRITING SUGGESTIONS

1. How would you characterize your own vocabulary? Have you ever felt limited or restricted by your command of the English language when speaking in class or addressing some other audience? Using examples from your own experience or observations, write an essay in which you show how your vocabulary has helped you or restricted you.

2. The lexicographer Bergen Evans once wrote, "A vocabulary is a tool which one uses in formulating the important questions of life, the questions which must be asked before they can be answered. To a large extent, vocabulary shapes all the decisions we make. . . . Words are one of our chief means of adjusting to all the situations of life. The better control we have over words, the more successful our adjustment is likely to be." In short, Evans, like Shachtman, believes that if our vocabulary is impoverished our lives will be as well. Write a letter to a television network executive in which you support Shachtman's call for broadcasters "to champion and employ the power of words as well as the power of images" (24) Within your letter, you may want to quote or refer to the comments of other writers in this book, such as Malcolm X (pp. 37–39).

3. In an effort to see whether or not talk shows have changed since Shachtman watched and listened to eight shows on November 9, 1993, watch or videotape all of the mainstream syndicated shows for a single day or a week's worth of a single talk show. Analyze the shows in terms of the subjects presented, the guests who appear, and the level of language used by hosts and guests alike. Then write an essay based on your research. According to your analysis, is the language used on the shows better, worse, or about the same as the language Shachtman describes hearing in 1993? Has the subject matter changed or improved? After analyzing current talk shows, what advice do you have for their producers and hosts?

You Can't Say That:
The Networks Play Word Games

TAD FRIEND

A staff writer for The New Yorker, *Tad Friend has had his work published in* The Best American Sports Writing *and* The Utne Reader's *"Good Life." He is the author of* Lost in Mongolia *(2001), a collection of his essays from* The New Yorker, Esquire, *and* Outside. *He currently lives in New York City. In "You Can't Say That: The Networks Play Word Games," first published in the November 19, 2001, issue of* The New Yorker, *Tad Friend takes a close look at how network Standards and Practices departments function as internal self-censors of TV content — off-color language, touchy situations, and controversial topics. Friend explains that although their decisions seem rather tame in light of what we hear and see every day, these network censors must walk the fine line between what's realistic and what will offend viewers and advertisers. He reviews the history of what can and can't be said or seen on television, highlighting our changing attitudes toward propriety.*

WRITING TO DISCOVER: *In what situations have you encountered foul, obscene, or vulgar language? How do you react when you hear such language? How does it make you feel? Are you bothered when you hear such language on television or in the movies? Explain.*

As a cocreator of the television series *NYPD Blue*, the writer-producer Steven Bochco has done more than his share to broaden the vocabulary promulgated over America's favorite living-room appliance. This season, Bochco has a new legal drama, *Philly*, on ABC, and he decided to use its premiere episode as the occasion for another breakthrough. For the first time, the barnyard epithet of Nixon White House fame would be heard on a network show. In the *Philly* episode, a scrappy defense attorney who has been put in jail for a few hours is told by a fellow-prisoner that one of her clients killed a man. "Bullshit!" she says. "Bullshit?" the prisoner replies. "I saw it happen." Whereupon the network would cut to a commercial and boils would break out on man and beast; and, after the boils, there would be thunder and hail, and, after the hail, swarms of locusts.

That was the plan, anyway. But when I spoke with Bochco shortly before the episode aired, in late September, he'd just got off the phone with Alan Braverman, ABC's head of legal affairs, who told him that the network's Standards and Practices department considered the word "unacceptably coarse."

Bochco persisted. "I told Alan, 'The audience that watches my *NYPD Blue* and hears "scumbag," "douche bag," and "prick" isn't going to reach for the remote if it hears "bullshit." When you're surrounded by junkies and whores in a jailhouse bullpen, the word just goes by naturally. Furthermore, it's not about this one word; it's about trying to entertain adults at 10 P.M., when they can easily flip to *The Sopranos*.'" According to Bochco, Braverman replied, "We do live in the age of *The Sopranos*, but we also live in the world of restrictions placed by our advertisers and by the government. These are gut calls, but this word crosses a line."

ABC employs twenty-seven Standards and Practices censors, or "editors," and the other broadcast networks have similar staffs. Most Standards editors have experience as lawyers, teachers, and members of the clergy. They scrutinize every show and commercial for vulgarity, sexuality, violence, and subject matter that could violate FCC standards of obscenity, community standards of indecency, and, particularly, corporate standards of comfort. (They also insure that dramas present both sides of controversial subjects like gun control, that game shows are not rigged, and that "reality" shows are more or less unstaged.) A Standards department reports not to the entertainment division but to the corporate executives; it is the superego that shushes the programmers' noisy id. Bryce Zabel, who produced *MANTIS*, a 1995 Fox show about a black superhero, says, "The creative executives would ask me to up the 'action' quotient" — car chases, "run and jumps" (to a helicopter's dangling rope ladder, say), and "sneak and creeps" (gunfights in parking garages) — "and then Standards would question those very things."

Without the approval of the Standards people, nothing goes on the   5
air. They are the ones who insist that onscreen lesbian kisses be "romantic" but not "passionate" (i.e., no tongue); that nasty words be presented in an "empowering" context ("Who you callin' a bitch?"); that guns be aimed at people's heads only in hostage or war situations; that role models do not smoke; that we never see "instructional activities" like rolling a joint or cutting a line of cocaine; and that if someone does take drugs he faces "consequences" — if not arrest, rehab, AIDS, or death, then at least a weepy speech from a concerned friend. Standards departments limit the range of the characters we see — there are few jolly adulterers or lovable anarchists in prime time — and they try to keep stories uplifting. David Chase, the creator of *The Sopranos*, recalls that when he produced a made-for-television movie called *Off the Minnesota Strip* for ABC, in 1980, Standards wanted him to insert a soupy version of Beethoven's *Ode to Joy* over his ending, in which a fifteen-year-old girl heads off down the Sunset Strip, evidently to become a hooker. "This is a pro social job," Olivia Cohen-Cutler, the head of ABC's Standards department, told me. "We don't want evil to triumph."

The constantly shifting standards of Hollywood's Standards departments provide a sharper picture of mainstream American mores than any Gallup poll, presidential campaign, or John Irving novel. After the terrorist attacks of September 11th, Standards departments examined every show and commercial for material that could now seem raw or insensitive. Among many other redactions, NBC cancelled a *Law & Order* miniseries about a terrorist attack on New York City; the premiere of *Third Watch*, which dealt with a blackout and subsequent unrest in New York; and a repeat episode of *Will & Grace* which contained a few jokes about airport security. CBS pulled an episode of *The Agency* in which the CIA fights an anthrax threat, and cut an exchange from *The Ellen Show* in which Ellen DeGeneres's character says, "My business collapsed" and her mother replies, "Well, thank your lucky stars you weren't there at the time." Fox snipped a bin Laden joke from a *Family Guy* rerun and cut scenes of a terrorist blowing up a plane from the premiere of a new drama, *24*. Fox's head of Standards, Roland McFarland, told me, "The President has an approval rating of 90 percent. So we won't be taking any more satirical cheap shots at him at this time."

In the last decade, Standards departments have become more tolerant of sex and foul language, but they have cracked down on violence and become more insistent about the politically correct presentation of minorities. Lately, however, they seem to be swinging wildly back and forth between allowing everything and allowing nothing. As recently as 1990, television critics and watch-dog groups were outraged when CBS permitted a six-year-old girl on the sitcom *Uncle Buck* to say, "You suck!" Since then, "suck," "fart," "crap" and "friggin'" have all made their way into the network venacular, and on the pilot episodes of this fall's new shows you could see a man and a wolf-woman engage in topless quasi bestiality (the CBS drama *Wolf Lake*), hear a five-year-old girl announce, "I have a vagina" (the ABC sitcom *According to Jim*; a network spokesman insists that she actually says "bagina"), and even be inadvertently exposed to the NBC comedy *Emeril*.

Yet producers of situation comedies that air at eight o'clock — a time formerly known as "the family hour" — still routinely receive memos from Standards decreeing that "the number of 'hells' and 'damns' must be cut by one-half." Even if only three percent of a show's audience gets upset by a particular word or image, that's still a population the size of Salt Lake City that's up in arms. (In fact, it usually is Salt Lake City.) The goal of Standards is to make sure nobody's mad, ever.

This confused state of affairs was exemplified on CBS's *The Late Show with David Letterman* in May, when Letterman repeatedly showed a clip from CBS's live broadcast of *On Golden Pond* which featured the word "bullshit." When Letterman used the word nine times himself — to describe his feelings about not being able to use the word — network censors bleeped the second syllable every time. Martin D. Franks, the executive vice-president to whom CBS Program Practices reports, explained to me that "*On Golden Pond* has some classic status, so the term wasn't lazy or exploitative, as it might be if used simply to titillate on one of our eight-o'clock sitcoms." Why, then, couldn't Letterman use the term later at night? "I would say to David, 'Not to use the word in *Golden Pond* would be a compromise of creative freedom, but you haven't convinced me that the word is vital to your creative freedom.'"

As it happens, the tussle between Bochco and ABC over the word "bullshit" was satirized in advance in June, on a *South Park* episode that used the word "shit" for the first time on Comedy Central — and used it a hundred and sixty-two times. Comedy Central's advertisers weren't bothered by the episode, and programmers at other networks became more eager than ever to do away with Standards departments. The six-year-old UPN is the first modern network not to have such a department, and Dean Valentine, its president and CEO, dismisses his competitors' Standards and Practices guidelines as "the accumulated stupidities of the years."

"There's a huge struggle going on," Jeff Zucker, the president of NBC Entertainment, told me. "I'm not saying we should use 'fuck' and show frontal nudity, but standards shouldn't even be where they were a few years ago. I have weekly discussions with Alan Wurtzel" — the network's head of Standards and Practices — "in which I try to loosen the floodgates and he tries to dam them up. We're now arguing over the word 'asshole' in a pilot. I'm not winning."

"It's a tonnage issue," Wurtzel told me. "Last year, HBO became the creative gold standard, so all our drama guys are saying, 'Why can't we be like *The Sopranos*?' and all our sitcom guys are saying, 'Why can't we be like *Sex and the City*?' One 'asshole' is not going to cause the fall of the republic, but do we want to become known as the 'asshole' network?" On the other hand, Wurtzel acknowledged, Standards has to evolve: "If we're too far behind the culture, viewers will feel *ER* and *Friends* are getting stodgy, and they'll leave. But if we're too far ahead advertisers will get nervous, and they'll leave. Either way, we lose."

In 1953, Rod Serling, who later created *The Twilight Zone*, wrote, "Because TV is a mass medium, you have to be governed by mass medium taboos. Easy on sex. Easy on violence. Nix on religion. Gently does it on controversial themes." Television is to the culture as the seventies was to the sixties — not the locomotive of change but the caboose.

This timidity has its roots in the way television entertainment began. In the early 1950s, most shows, such as *Texaco Star Theatre*, were sponsored by a single advertiser who had enormous power over the program. The Mars Company, which sponsored *Circus Boy*, frowned on references to competing snacks such as cookies and ice cream. When the American Gas Association presented *Judgment at Nuremberg* live on CBS's *Playhouse 90*, in 1959, it insisted that the word "gas" be cut from the script, leading to the suggestion that millions of Jews died in " . . . chambers."

More recently, Standards departments have been affected by a different sort of economic imperative. The most startling show in the past decade has been *NYPD Blue*, which débuted on ABC in 1993, at a time when the network was flailing. After a year of negotiations, Steven Bochco persuaded ABC to let him use vulgarities thirty-seven times in each episode, as long as he confined himself to an agreed-upon glossary of such words as "balls," "bastard," "dickhead," "fat ass," "johnson," "prick," "screwing," "scumbag," and "tits." He could show breasts from the side (Standards combed the show's footage frame by frame, looking for a forbidden peep of nipple), and dorsal but not frontal nudity, and he could suggest, but never show, intercourse.

Fifty-seven affiliates refused to air the first episode, and ABC couldn't charge its full ad rate on the show for years. "The networks wouldn't let anyone follow my lead, out of fear." Bochco said. "But fear is also why ABC agreed to make the show — they allowed us latitude because they were getting killed in the ratings. It wasn't an artistic decision; it was an economic decision. It's never an artistic decision."

By watching television carefully, you can almost hear what Standards has taken out of a show, or see why risqué material was left in. A few basic rules clarify how a show's content reveals its place in the network's estimation.

1. The more times you hear "ass," the more successful the show is. "Ass" is the most common vulgarity on network television: According to the Parents Television Council, it can be heard 1.04 times per hour on eight-o'clock shows. When *Martin* first aired, on Fox, in 1992, the sitcom's producers were permitted one "ass" per half-hour episode. As *Martin* became successful, the show's producers were allowed two, then three, then unlimited "ass"es. (On a drama pilot at another network this year, producers were permitted three "ass"es, or 1.5 "ass"es per half hour, which indicates some mild "ass" inflation.)

2. If a show invites you to picture a character's genitalia, it's a proven hit. In the second season of *Friends*, Standards vetoed a story line about the girls fashioning an artificial foreskin for Joey, who was up for an acting role that, for reasons it would be tedious to describe, required an uncircumcised male. This spring, in its seventh season, *Friends* did the foreskin plot. And the "master of your domain" episode on *Seinfeld*, about masturbation, ran in the show's sixth season.

3. A program that shows large expanses of skin makes a lot of money 20 for the network. "When Standards raised a number of wardrobe issues on *Charlie's Angels* in the seventies," Fred Silverman, who was then the president of ABC Entertainment, says, "I'd take them up with my boss, Fred Pierce, and remind him that the show was doing a fifty share. And he'd say, 'Let 'em jiggle!'"

4. If a drama has commercials for Jhirmack shampoo and the Thighmaster, that's a sure indication that its subject was so controversial that the regular advertisers pulled out. A few weeks ago, Sears and

Federal Express withdrew their ads from ABC's *Politically Incorrect* after Bill Maher, the host, suggested that America's long-distance missile attacks were "cowardly." Recent shows ran ads for Trojan condoms and Craftmatic Adjustable Beds.

5. When a long-running drama is short on off-color language or risky topics, you can assume that the Standards people think it's no good. "Last year, we let Aaron Sorkin use the word 'prick' on *The West Wing*," Alan Wurtzel, at NBC, told me, "but only because it is clearly a quality show, and because the characters had been established for two years." A former NBC executive told me, "The producers of *Pretender* and *Profiler*, two extremely pedestrian shows, would always say, 'They used "ballbuster" on *Homicide* — can't we do it?' We'd say politely, 'Your show ain't *Homicide*.'"

Standards departments typically have vague written guidelines but no lists of forbidden words or proscribed scenarios. Theirs is an oral culture, one whose strictures are handed down like Inuit tribal lore. The fiats that emerge from the Standards editors' deliberations are scrupulous, nuanced, and often hilarious. The producers of the CBS drama *Delvecchio* were once told to amend the term "rat doo-doo" to "rat doo"; when a hunchback got knifed on *Get Smart*, the censors decreed that "it would be better if the knife were to go into the part of his back which isn't hunched."

Writers see Standards editors as Emily Posts who cling to archaic rules; the editors see themselves as Emily Dickinsons who strive to preserve a cultural standard. "We're accused of limiting creativity," a Standards editor told me. "But I feel we're challenging creativity. Instead of using 'damn' eleven times, can't you come up with some other word?" Censor-writer colloquies would delight William Safire: does "scumbag" connote a repellent individual, or will older viewers recall that it originally meant a condom? "Schmuck" means a jerk in Los Angeles, but is it still a synonym for "penis" in New York? "Dick" and "pussy" are now sometimes allowed, but only as insults (it may thus be permissible to say "You're a dick," but never "Your dick . . . ").

A few years ago, on a *Mad About You* episode in which Paul filmed   25
a documentary about horses, viewers saw a stallion and a mare coupling. "One horse had a huge erection, and if you're eight years old it's scary to see that," an NBC Standards executive says. "We got a lot of flak, and we deserved it. We'd broken the covenant not to surprise the audience."

That covenant is the one great unspoken standard. In 1997, when Ellen Morgan kissed another woman on *Ellen*, ABC put an "adult content" warning on the episode. An ABC Standards editor maintains, "We put the warning on because Ellen was making a big change. She had been asexual, the crazy single girl, and all of a sudden she became sexual." Yet ABC was clearly skittish about this particular change. The executive producer of *Ellen*, Tim Doyle, says, "I framed the Standards note saying, 'It is unacceptable for Laurie to kiss Ellen here. Please substitute another way for her to express her feeling of togetherness.'"

A forthcoming episode of Fox's *24* also features a gay interlude, and Standards responded with a memo: "The businessman could be startled with his shirt halfway off, or something similar . . . but we cannot accept any inference that Rogow is/was going down on the guy." Pivoting, with somewhat less concern, to deal with violence, the memo went on to say, "Please use good taste when depicting Bridgit getting hit by the 'long-distance, silenced shot to the head.'"

Standards departments pay particular attention to impiety. Aaron Sorkin, the creator of *The West Wing*, said. "What has surprised me most about television is that Standards and Practices made it very clear that I will be able to say 'mother-fucker' on the air before I can take the Lord's name in vain. They fear that religious groups will aggressively boycott our show." In one episode last year, President Bartlet exploded about being bested by a "damn street gang." "It didn't ring true," Sorkin said. "I originally wrote 'goddamn street gang.' In the movies, it would have been 'fucking street gang.' I'm fighting to get NBC to loosen the reins, and I feel 'bullshit' should be allowed, occasionally — 'That's crap' doesn't play."

The rules of engagement in this routine warfare are understood by everyone involved. Standards editors often tell one another, "Give them seven notes so you can negotiate." The writers, in turn, put "asshole" in the script a few times as "censor bait," knowing they'll have to cut it but hoping to keep two "bitch"es and a "balls" in exchange.

The latest injunction at the networks has been to present minorities as [30] role models. This effort has been so successful that the black boss and the black judge are now clichés. Unfortunately, this "advance" is largely a retreat into safety. In 1994, the producers of the Fox sitcom *Monty* were told that a character in the pilot could not get food poisoning from a Chinese restaurant. He also could not get it from an Italian restaurant. He could, however, get it from a restaurant.

This January, NBC apologized to the National Puerto Rican Coalition for a *Law & Order* episode based on an incident of mayhem during New York City's Puerto Rican Day parade, and said it would not rerun the episode. Six months later, NBC apologized to the Media Action Network for Asian Americans after Sarah Silverman made a joke about "Chinks" on *Late Night with Conan O'Brien*, and said it would cut the word from reruns. Alan Wurtzel, of NBC, says, "We understand that this joke was designed to be a satirical comment on racism. But, to the Asian

American community, 'Chinks' is equivalent to 'niggers' or 'kikes.' Our most difficult Standards issue is racial stereotyping — comedy producers say, 'Don't you have a sense of humor?' and drama producers say. 'But this situation exists in real life!'" Many producers believe that a show like *All in the Family*, in which Archie Bunker inveighed against "spics, spades, Chinks, [and] Hebes" in the first episode, would never make it on the air today.

Television's fundamental internal conflict is played out through the triumphs and defeats of the Standards and Practices departments. That conflict is not between art and commerce but between commerce and commerce. Standards' mandate is to help the network gain viewers (and thus advertisers) without going so far that it loses viewers (and thus advertisers). Fred Silverman, who in his long career helped lead the entertainment division of each of the three major networks, predicts, "If UPN has real success, and it needs to protect what it has, it'll get a Standards department." And yet Standards and Practices' insistence on presenting "commonly accepted values" also helps explain why the networks have lost half of their audience in the last fifteen years. Standards departments throw the baby out with the bathwater. Then the networks wonder why it's so quiet in the tub.

And so Steven Bochco's first episode of *Philly* did not contain the word "bullshit" after all. Instead, the defense attorney said, "No way!" "I'll revisit the matter if the show's a hit," Bochco told me. "Because then the network will be terrified to piss me off. And I guarantee you Aaron Sorkin would win his struggles with NBC if he got a really, really bad case of writer's block. We're going to win the 'bullshit' battle before long, because either I, or Aaron, or someone will be willing to be a real" — he paused, seeking the mot juste — "asshole."

FOCUSING ON CONTENT

1. What purpose do the Standards and Practices guidelines serve? What or whom are they intended to protect? How do you react to Dean Valentine's remark that network guidelines are "'the accumulated stupidities of the years'" (10)?

2. What topics are most likely to be given the most scrutiny by network censors? Why are network writers and producers envious of such shows as *The Sopranos*, *Sex and the City*, and *South Park*? Why aren't these programs held up to the same scrutiny as programs on the major networks?

3. Is the issue of censoring "coarse language" on television an artistic, a social, or an economic issue, or some combination of the three? Explain. According to Friend, what is the relationship between a show's content and its value to a network?

4. According to Friend, how have network Standards and Practices departments handled issues of race and race relationships?

5. There seems to be a double standard between what is allowed on television and what is allowed in the movies. How do you account for this
difference?

FOCUSING ON WRITING

1. Friend opens his essay with the story of writer-producer Steven Bochco's attempts to use the word *bullshit* in the premiere episode of the legal drama
Philly. How well do these first three paragraphs function as an introduction
to the essay? (Glossary: *Beginnings and Endings*) Were you bothered by the
fact that Friend leaves the debate between Bochco and his network Standards and Practices department unresolved at the end of paragraph 3 and
makes you wait until the end to find out what happened? Explain.

2. In paragraph 4, Friend provides a job description for network Standards and
Practices censors or editors. Why is it important for us to have this information before we hear about specific issues that network censors have and continue to struggle with?

3. Locate several quotations that Friend uses in his essay, and explain why you
think Friend elected to quote the speaker verbatim instead of paraphrasing.
(Glossary: *Paraphrase*) Which quotations did you find most effective? Explain why.

4. Friend starts paragraph 7 with the general statement: "In the last decade,
Standards departments have become more tolerant of sex and foul language,
but they have cracked down on violence and become more insistent about
the politically correct presentation of minorities." What examples does he
use to support the claims in this sentence? (Glossary: *Examples*) Where else
does Friend use examples effectively?

LANGUAGE IN ACTION

In the context of Friend's essay, comment on the following cartoon
by Nick Baker. What is Baker's attitude toward "coarse language" on
television? Is foul language "cute," as this cartoon suggests, or are parents
facing a real problem with television's influence? Do you see the cartoon
as a plea for or against network Standards and Practices departments?
Explain.

"Darling, he said his first F-word."

WRITING SUGGESTIONS

1. As Hollywood has allowed more foul language in movies and on television in the last decade or two, Americans have had to make some serious choices. Some have stopped going to theaters, and others have boycotted certain television programs that contain offensive language. Where do you stand on the issue of coarse or foul language in our culture? Do you think it is acceptable in everyday conversations? Appropriate for television programming? Necessary in mass-market films? For you, when does language violate "community standards of indecency, and . . . corporate standards of comfort" (4)? Are Americans still sensitive to the inappropriate use of crude language, or have we become numb to its widespread use? Write an essay in which you defend your position on this issue and the related questions that it raises.

2. Imagine that you are part of a public Standards and Practices team assigned to evaluate the appropriateness of language used in today's popular television series. Watch several episodes of one or more of the following shows: *Law & Order, NYPD Blue, The Sopranos, Sex in the City,* or a series of your choosing. Take accurate notes about the language the characters use. How much of the foul language do you think is used for creative artistic purposes, how much to titillate or excite the audience? Write an essay in which you report your conclusions about the language used on the show.

PICTURING LANGUAGE

This advertisement was featured on the back of a recent issue of a popular magazine. How do you react to this ad? What is the tone of the language used? What does the phrase "real journalism" mean to you? Does the use of upper- and lower-case letters give you any hint of an underlying message in this ad? What does it say about American society when networks have to advertise objectivity and fairness in the reporting of the news? In what ways, if at all, do the graphics complement the text of the ad?

Television News: The Language of Pictures

NEIL POSTMAN AND STEVE POWERS

A native of Brooklyn, New York, Neil Postman is a graduate of the State University of New York at Fredonia and Columbia University. He has authored eighteen books on language, education, the media, and communication theory. His books Discovering Your Language *(1996) and* Exploring Your Language *(1996) helped usher in an era of linguistic inquiry. He displays his skills as a media critic and cultural commentator in* The Disappearance of Childhood *(1982),* Amusing Ourselves to Death *(1985),* Conscientious Objections *(1988), and* Building a Bridge to the 18th Century *(1999). Postman's articles appear in the* New York Times Magazine, *the* Atlantic Monthly, *and the* Harvard Education Review, *and he is contributing editor to the* Nation. *Currently, he is University Professor and Paulette Goddard Chair of Media Ecology at New York University.*

Steve Powers was born in New York City in 1934. A graduate of Bernard M. Baruch College of the City University of New York, Powers has had a dual career as a professional musician and as a news correspondent for Fox Television News and the ABC Information Radio Network. Returning to New York University for a graduate degree in the 1980s, Powers started teaching at St. John's University in 1993. His interest in media literacy led him to team up with Postman to write the insightful and provocative book How to Watch a Television News Show *(1992).*

In the following selection, taken from that book, Postman and Powers look closely at what we as viewers are getting when we watch the news on television. They conclude that unless we come to television news with a "prepared mind . . . a news program is only a kind of rousing light show."

WRITING TO DISCOVER: *Where or how do you get news of what is happening in the world? Do you read a newspaper or watch network news programs on a regular basis? Do you read a weekly news magazine like* Time *or* Newsweek? *Write about which news sources you prefer and why.*

When a television news show distorts the truth by altering or manufacturing facts (through re-creations), a television viewer is defenseless even if a re-creation is properly labeled. Viewers are still vulnerable to misinformation since they will not know (at least in the case of docudramas) what parts are fiction and what parts are not. But the problems of verisimilitude posed by re-creations pale to insignificance when compared to the problems viewers face when encountering a straight (no-monkey-business) show. All news shows, in a sense, are re-creations in that what we hear and see on them are attempts to represent actual events, and are not the events themselves. Perhaps, to avoid ambiguity, we might call all news shows "re-presentations" instead of "re-creations." These re-presentations come to us in two forms: language and pictures.

. . . It is often said that a picture is worth a thousand words. Maybe so. But it is probably equally true that one word is worth a thousand pictures, at least sometimes — for example, when it comes to understanding the world we live in. Indeed, the whole problem with news on television comes down to this: all the words uttered in an hour of news coverage could be printed on one page of a newspaper. And the world cannot be understood in one page. Of course, there is a compensation: television offers pictures, and the pictures move. Moving pictures are a kind of language in themselves, but the language of pictures differs radically from oral and written language, and the differences are crucial for understanding television news.

To begin with, pictures, especially single pictures, speak only in particularities. Their vocabulary is limited to concrete representation. Unlike words and sentences, a picture does not present to us an idea or concept about the world, except as we use language itself to convert the image to idea. By itself, a picture cannot deal with the unseen, the remote, the internal, the abstract. It does not speak of "man," only of *a* man; not of "tree," only of *a* tree. You cannot produce an image of "nature," any more than an image of "the sea." You can only show a particular fragment of the here-and-now — a cliff of a certain terrain, in a certain condition of light; a wave at a moment in time, from a particular point of view. And just as "nature" and "the sea" cannot be photographed, such larger abstractions as truth, honor, love, and falsehood cannot be talked about in the lexicon of individual pictures. For "showing of" and "talking about" are two very different kinds of processes: individual pictures give us the world as object; language, the world as idea. There is no such thing in nature as "man" or "tree." The universe offers no such categories or simplifications; only flux and infinite variety. The picture documents and celebrates the particularities of the universe's infinite variety. Language makes them comprehensible.

Of course, moving pictures, video with sound, may bridge the gap by juxtaposing images, symbols, sound, and music. Such images can present emotions and rudimentary ideas. They can suggest the panorama of nature and the joys and miseries of humankind.

Picture — smoke pouring from the window, cut to people coughing, an ambulance racing to a hospital, a tombstone in a cemetery.   5

Picture — jet planes firing rockets, explosions, lines of foreign soldiers surrendering, the American flag waving in the wind.

Nonetheless, keep in mind that when terrorists want to prove to the world that their kidnap victims are still alive, they photograph them holding a copy of a recent newspaper. The dateline on the newspaper provides the proof that the photograph was taken on or after that date. Without the help of the written word, film and videotape cannot portray temporal dimensions with any precision. Consider a film clip showing an aircraft carrier at sea. One might be able to identify the ship as Soviet or American, but there would be no way of telling where in the world the carrier was, where it was headed, or when the pictures were taken. It is only through language — words spoken over the pictures or reproduced in them — that the image of the aircraft carrier takes on specific meaning.

Still, it is possible to enjoy the image of the carrier for its own sake. One might find the hugeness of the vessel interesting; it signifies military power on the move. There is a certain drama in watching the planes come in at high speeds and skid to a stop on the deck. Suppose the ship were burning: that would be even more interesting. This leads to an important point about the language of pictures. Moving pictures favor images that change. That is why violence and dynamic destruction find their way onto television so often. When something is destroyed violently it is altered in a highly visible way; hence the entrancing power of fire. Fire gives visual form to the ideas of consumption, disappearance, death — the thing that burned is actually taken away by fire. It is at this very basic level that fires make a good subject for television news. Something was here, now it's gone, and the change is recorded on film.

Earthquakes and typhoons have the same power. Before the viewer's eyes the world is taken apart. If a television viewer has relatives in Mexico City and an earthquake occurs there, then he or she may take a special interest in the images of destruction as a report from a specific place and time; that is, one may look at television pictures for information about an important event. But film of an earthquake can be interesting even if the viewer cares nothing about the event itself. Which is only to say, as we noted earlier, that there is another way of participating in the news — as a spectator who desires to be entertained. Actually to see buildings topple is exciting, no matter where the buildings are. The world turns to dust before our eyes.

Those who produce television news in America know that their 10 medium favors images that move. That is why they are wary of "talking heads," people who simply appear in front of a camera and speak. When talking heads appear on television, there is nothing to record or document, no change in process. In the cinema the situation is somewhat different. On a movie screen, close-ups of a good actor speaking dramatically can sometimes be interesting to watch. When Clint Eastwood narrows his eyes and challenges his rival to shoot first, the spectator sees the cool rage of the Eastwood character take visual form, and the narrowing of the eyes is dramatic. But much of the effect of this small movement depends on the size of the movie screen and the darkness of the theater, which make Eastwood and his every action "larger than life."

The television screen is smaller than life. It occupies about 15 percent of the viewer's visual field (compared to about 70 percent for the movie screen). It is not set in a darkened theater closed off from the world but in the viewer's ordinary living space. This means that visual changes must be more extreme and more dramatic to be interesting on television. A narrowing of the eyes will not do. A car crash, an earthquake, a burning factory are much better.

With these principles in mind, let us examine more closely the structure of a typical newscast, and here we will include in the discussion not only the pictures but all the nonlinguistic symbols that make up a television news show. For example, in America, almost all news shows begin with music, the tone of which suggests important events about to unfold. The music is very important, for it equates the news with various forms of drama and ritual — the opera, for example, or a wedding procession — in which musical themes underscore the meaning of the event. Music takes us immediately into the realm of the symbolic, a world that is not to be taken literally. After all, when events unfold in the real world, they do so without musical accompaniment. More symbolism follows. The sound of teletype machines can be heard in the studio, not because it is impossible to screen this noise out, but because the sound is a kind of music in itself. It tells us that data are pouring in from all corners of the globe, a sensation reinforced by the world map in the background (or clocks noting the time on different continents). The fact is that teletype machines are rarely used in TV news rooms, having been replaced by silent computer terminals. When seen, they have only a symbolic function.

Already, then, before a single news item is introduced, a great deal has been communicated. We know that we are in the presence of a symbolic event, a form of theater in which the day's events are to be dramatized. This theater takes the entire globe as its subject, although it may look at the world from the perspective of a single nation. A certain tension is present, like the atmosphere in a theater just before the curtain goes up. The tension is represented by the music, the staccato beat of the teletype machines, and often the sight of news workers scurrying around typing reports and answering phones. As a technical matter, it would be no problem to build a set in which the newsroom staff remained off camera, invisible to the viewer, but an important theatrical effect would be lost. By being busy on camera, the workers help communicate urgency about the events at hand, which suggests that situations are changing so rapidly that constant revision of the news is necessary.

The staff in the background also helps signal the importance of the person in the center, the anchor, "in command" of both the staff and the news. The anchor plays the role of host. He or she welcomes us to the newscast and welcomes us back from the different locations we visit during the filmed reports.

Many features of the newscast help the anchor to establish the impression of control. These are usually equated with production values in broadcasting. They include such things as graphics that tell the viewer   15 what is being shown, or maps and charts that suddenly appear on the screen and disappear on cue, or the orderly progression from story to story. They also include the absence of gaps, or "dead time," during the broadcast, even the simple fact that the news starts and ends at a certain hour. These common features are thought of as purely technical matters, which a professional crew handles as a matter of course. But they are also symbols of a dominant theme of television news: the imposition of an orderly world — called "the news" — upon the disorderly flow of events.

While the form of a news broadcast emphasizes tidiness and control, its content can best be described as fragmented. Because time is so precious on television, because the nature of the medium favors dynamic visual images, and because the pressures of a commercial structure require the news to hold its audience above all else, there is rarely any attempt to explain issues in depth or place events in their proper context. The news moves nervously from a warehouse fire to a court decision, from a guerrilla war to a World Cup match, the quality of the film most often determining the length of the story. Certain stories show up only because they offer dramatic pictures. Bleachers collapse in South America: hundreds of people are crushed — a perfect television news story, for the cameras can record the face of disaster in all its anguish. Back in Washington, a new budget is approved by Congress. Here there is nothing to photograph because a budget is not a physical event; it is a document full of language and numbers. So the producers of the news will show a photo of the document itself, focusing on the cover where it says "Budget of the United States of America." Or sometimes they will send a camera crew to the government printing plant where copies of the budget are produced. That evening, while the contents of the budget are summarized by a voice-over, the viewer sees stacks of documents being loaded into boxes at the government printing plant. Then a few of the budget's more important provisions will be flashed on the screen in written form, but this is such a time-consuming process — using television as a printed page — that the producers keep it to a minimum. In short, the budget is not televisable, and for that reason its time on the news must be brief. The bleacher collapse will get more time that evening.

While appearing somewhat chaotic, these disparate stories are not just dropped in the news program helter-skelter. The appearance of a scattershot story order is really orchestrated to draw the audience from one story to the next — from one section to the next — through the commercial breaks to the end of the show. The story order is constructed to hold and build the viewership rather than place events in context or explain issues in depth.

Of course, it is a tendency of journalism in general to concentrate on the surface of events rather than underlying conditions; this is as true for the newspaper as it is for the newscast. But several features of television undermine whatever efforts journalists may make to give sense to the world. One is that a television broadcast is a series of events that occur in sequence, and the sequence is the same for all viewers. This is not true for a newspaper page, which displays many items simultaneously, allowing readers to choose the order in which they read them. If newspaper readers want only a summary of the latest tax bill, they can read the headline and the first paragraph of an article, and if they want more, they can keep reading. In a sense, then, everyone reads a different newspaper, for no two readers will read (or ignore) the same items.

But all television viewers see the same broadcast. They have no choices. A report is either in the broadcast or out, which means that anything which is of narrow interest is unlikely to be included. As NBC News executive Reuven Frank once explained:

> A newspaper, for example, can easily afford to print an item of conceivable interest to only a fraction of its readers. A television news program must be put together with the assumption that each item will be of some interest to everyone that watches. Every time a newspaper includes a feature which will attract a specialized group it can assume it is adding at least a little bit to its circulation. To the degree a television news program includes an item of this sort . . . it must assume that its audience will diminish.

The need to "include everyone," an identifying feature of commercial television in all its forms, prevents journalists from offering lengthy or complex explanations, or from tracing the sequence of events leading up to today's headlines. One of the ironies of political life in modern democracies is that many problems which concern the "general welfare" are of interest only to specialized groups. Arms control, for example, is an issue that literally concerns everyone in the world, and yet the language of arms control and the complexity of the subject are so daunting that only a minority of people can actually follow the issue from week to week and month to month. If it wants to act responsibly, a newspaper can at least make available more information about arms control than most people want. Commercial television cannot afford to do so.

But even if commercial television could afford to do so, it wouldn't. The fact that television news is principally made up of moving pictures prevents it from offering lengthy, coherent explanations of events. A television news show reveals the world as a series of unrelated, fragmentary moments. It does not — and cannot be expected to — offer a sense of coherence or meaning. What does this suggest to a TV viewer? That the viewer must come with a prepared mind — information, opinions, a sense of proportion, an articulate value system. To the TV viewer lacking such mental equipment, a news program is only a kind of rousing light show. Here a falling building, there a five-alarm fire, everywhere the world as an object, much without meaning, connections, or continuity.

FOCUSING ON CONTENT

1. Why do Postman and Powers consider all news shows "re-creations" (1)?

2. In what ways does the language of pictures differ from spoken and written language? Why, according to Postman and Powers, are these differences important for understanding television news?

3. Why do scenes of violence and dynamic destruction have such appeal to viewers? Why do television producers avoid "talking heads"? In comparison to the movies, why must visual changes "be more extreme and more dramatic . . . on television" (11)?

4. In what ways can television news be considered a form of theater? According to Postman and Powers, how are news telecasts staged? What is the one dominant theme of television news, and how is this theme orchestrated?

5. What features of television news tend to undermine journalists' efforts to give context, depth, or sense to the world? What advantages do newspaper readers have over television viewers? Explain.

FOCUSING ON WRITING

1. What is Postman and Powers's main point about television news? (Glossary: *Thesis*) Where do they state their position? What changes, if any, do they want to see readers and viewers make as a result of reading this article?

2. What kinds of evidence do Postman and Powers provide to support their position? (Glossary: *Evidence*) Which evidence do you find most persuasive? Least persuasive? Explain.

3. How do Postman and Powers organize their argument? (Glossary: *Organization*)

4. Examine the writers' diction in the opening paragraph. (Glossary: *Diction*) What is their attitude toward television news? (Glossary: *Attitude*) What about their language led you to this conclusion? Does their diction throughout the essay support the impression created in the opening paragraph?

LANGUAGE IN ACTION

Postman and Powers suggest that moving pictures of destruction are entertaining because they show rapid and large-scale change. This, in turn, implies that pictures are chosen for the emotional effect they may have. Discuss your response to the following photograph in terms of its emotional effect. Keep in mind both the feeling the scene itself creates and that created by the destruction that is the implied aftermath of the soldiers' action. Postman and Powers also say that images can be converted to ideas. What ideas does this photograph convey about war? Explain how language could translate this image into different ideas about war or the military. How do such "translations" illustrate Postman and Powers's main point about language and pictures?

WRITING SUGGESTIONS

1. Select several pictures from a photo album — of a wedding, or graduation, or pictures from a recent trip you took with friends. Do the pictures capture or tell the story of the event, or did you really have to be there to get the whole story? If a video of the event is available, watch it for the sake of comparison. Write an essay in which you discuss the limitations of still photographs in capturing an event.

2. Watch (and videotape, if possible) at least two networks' versions of the same day's evening news. How are the news shows the same? Different? To what extent do the news telecasts support the analysis of news programs presented by Postman and Powers? Report your findings in an essay.

3. What was the impact of television news reporting on such memorable events as the Gulf War, the O. J. Simpson trial, the death and funeral of Princess Diana, President Clinton's impeachment trial, the death of John F. Kennedy Jr., September 11th the war in Iraq, or another newsworthy event? Research the event you chose in your library or on the Internet. Be sure to read accounts of your event in newspapers and magazines at the time it was happening. As you write an essay about the event, consider the following questions: To what extent can it be said that television news actually creates rather than reports the news? What impact do you think live coverage of events has on our perceptions of them? In what ways is live coverage different from an anchor's retelling of the news?

Exposing Media Myths:
TV Doesn't Affect You as Much as You Think

JOANMARIE KALTER

Joanmarie Kalter has written extensively about television news and about the press in the Third World. After graduating from Cornell University in 1972 and working as a freelance writer for a number of years, Kalter received her master's degree from the Columbia Graduate School of Journalism in 1981. She joined TV Guide *as a staff writer in 1984, but returned to freelancing in 1989. Her articles have appeared in numerous and diverse periodicals, including the* New York Times, *the* Christian Science Monitor, *the* Bulletin of Atomic Scientists, *and* Africa Report. *In the following selection, which first appeared in* TV Guide, *note how Kalter uses her evidence to chip away at some "false truths" about television news. She is careful to reveal the serious implications of the myths she exposes.*

WRITING TO DISCOVER: *Reflect on how important television news is to your life. Do you watch a news program regularly? Do you find it valuable to be apprised of the latest world events? How much of what you see and hear do you remember, and for how long?*

Once upon a time, there was a new invention — television. It became so popular, so quickly, that more American homes now have a TV set (98 percent) than an indoor toilet (97 percent). Around this new invention, then, an industry rapidly grew, and around this industry, a whole mythology. It has become a virtual truism, often heard and often repeated, that TV — and TV news, in particular — has an unparalleled influence on our lives.

Over the past twenty years, however, communications scholars have been quietly examining such truisms and have discovered, sometimes to their surprise, that many are not so true at all. *TV Guide* asked more than a dozen leading researchers for their findings and found an eye-opening collection of mythbusters. Indeed, they suggest that an entire body of political strategy and debate has been built upon false premises. . . .

MYTH NO. 1 Two-thirds of the American people receive most of their news from TV. This little canard is at the heart of our story. It can be traced to the now-famous Roper polls, in which Americans are queried: "I'd like to ask you where you usually get most of your news about what's going on in the world today. . . ." In 1959, when the poll was first conducted, 51 percent answered "television," with a steady increase ever since. The latest results show that 66 percent say they get most of their news from TV; only about a third credit newspapers.

Trouble is, that innocent poll question is downright impossible to answer. Just consider: it asks you to sort through the issues in your mind, pinpoint what and where you learned about each, tag it, and come up with a final score. Not too many of us can do it, especially since we get our news from a variety of sources. Even pollster Burns Roper concedes, "Memories do get fuzzy."

Scholars have found, however, that when they ask a less general,   5
more specific question — Did you read a newspaper yesterday? Did you watch a TV news show yesterday? — the results are quite different. Dr. John Robinson, professor of sociology at the University of Maryland, found that on a typical day 67 percent read a newspaper, while 52 percent see a local or national TV newscast. Dr. Robert Stevenson, professor of journalism at the University of North Carolina, analyzed detailed diaries of TV use, and further found that only 18 percent watch network news on an average day, and only 13 percent pay full attention to it. Says Robinson, "TV is part of our overall mix, but in no way is it our number one source of news."

Yet it's a myth with disturbing consequences. Indeed, it is so widespread, says Dr. Mark Levy, associate professor of journalism at the University of Maryland, that it shapes — or misshapes — our political process. In the words of Michael Deaver, White House deputy chief of staff during President Reagan's first term, "The majority of the people get their news from television, so . . . we construct events and craft photos that are designed for thirty seconds to a minute so that it can fit into that 'bite' on the evening news." And thus the myth, says Levy, "distorts the very dialogue of democracy, which cannot be responsibly conducted in thirty-second bites."

MYTH NO. 2   TV news sets the public agenda. It was first said succinctly in 1963, and has long been accepted: while the mass media may not tell us what to think, they definitely tell us what to think about. And on some issues, the impact of TV is indisputable: the Ethiopian famine, the Challenger explosion. Yet for the more routine story, new research has challenged that myth, suggesting TV's influence may be surprisingly more limited.

For one thing, TV news most often reacts to newspapers in framing issues of public concern. Dr. David Weaver, professor of journalism at Indiana University, found that newspapers led TV through the 1976 campaign. Given the brevity of broadcasts, of course, that's understandable. "TV has no page thirty-six," explains Dr. Maxwell McCombs, professor of communications at the University of Texas. "So TV journalists have to wait until an issue has already achieved substantial public interest." TV, then, does not so much set the public agenda as spotlight it.

Even among those issues spotlighted, viewers do make independent judgments. It seems the old "hypodermic" notions no longer hold, says Dr. Doris Graber, political science professor at the University of Illinois.

"We're not sponges for this stuff, and while TV may provide the raw material, people do select."

Indeed, even TV entertainment is less influential than once was 10 thought. According to Robinson, studies found no difference in racial attitudes among those who saw *Roots* and those who didn't. Ditto "The Day After" on nuclear war, and *Amerika* on the Soviets. As for news, Graber notes that the public took a long time to share the media's concern about Watergate, and even now are lagging the media on Iran-Contragate. And finally, there are many issues on which the press must belatedly catch up with the public. Which brings us to . . .

MYTH NO. 3　TV news changed public opinion about the war in Vietnam. Contrary to this most common of beliefs, research shows just the opposite. Lawrence Lichty, professor of radio/television/film at Northwestern University, analyzed network war coverage and found that it did not become relatively critical until 1967. By then, however, a majority of Americans already thought U.S. involvement in Vietnam was a mistake. And they thought so not because of TV coverage, but because of the number of young Americans dying.

Yet this fable about the "living-room war" is so accepted it has become "fact": that gory TV pictures of bloody battles undermined public support for the war; that, in a 1968 TV-news special, Walter Cronkite mistakenly presented the Tet offensive as a defeat for the U.S.; and that, because President Johnson so believed in the power of TV, he concluded then that his war effort was lost.

In fact, Lichty found few "gory" pictures. "TV presented a distant view," he says, with less than 5 percent of TV's war reports showing heavy combat. Nor, as we now know, was a rapt audience watching at home in their living rooms. As for Cronkite's report on the Tet offensive, the CBS anchor said on the evening news, "First and simplest, the Vietcong suffered a military defeat." And, in his now-famous TV special, Cronkite concluded, "we are mired in a stalemate," and should "negotiate." By that time, Lichty says, "public opinion had been on a downward trend for a year and a half. A majority of Americans agreed." And so Johnson's concern, it seems, was not that Cronkite would influence public opinion, but rather that he reflected it.

Indeed, Professor John Mueller of the University of Rochester has compared the curve of public opinion on the war in Vietnam, covered by TV, with that of the war in Korea, hardly covered. He found the two curves strikingly similar: in both cases, public support dropped as the number of American deaths rose.

Disturbingly, the misconception about TV's influence in Vietnam has 15 had broad consequences, for it has framed an important debate ever since. Can a democratic society, with a free flow of dramatic TV footage, retain the public will to fight a war? Many argue no. And this has been the rationale more recently for censoring the Western press in the Falklands and Grenada. Yet it is, says Lichty, a policy based on a myth.

MYTH NO. 4 TV today is the most effective medium in communicating news. Most of us think of TV fare as simple, direct, easy to understand — with the combination of words and pictures making it all the more powerful. But recent research shows that TV news, as distinct from entertainment, is often very confusing. In study after study, Robinson and Levy have found that viewers understand only about a third of network news stories.

Why is TV news so tough to understand? Dr. Dan Drew, professor of journalism at Indiana University, suggests that the verbal and visual often conflict. Unlike TV entertainment, in which the two are composed together, TV-news footage is gathered first, and the story it illustrates often diverges. We may see fighting across the Green Line in Beirut — for a story about peace talks. We may see "file footage" of Anglican envoy Terry Waite walking down the street — for a story on his disappearance. As viewers try to make sense of the visual, they lose the gist of the verbal. "The myth," says Levy, "is that since we are a visual medium, we must always have pictures. . . . But that's a disaster, a recipe for poor communication."

Journalists also are much more familiar with the world of public affairs, says Levy, and rely on its technical jargon: from "leading economic indicators" to "the Druse militia." Their stories, say researchers, are over-illustrated, with most pictures on the screen for less than twenty seconds. They assume, mistakenly, that viewers pay complete attention, and so they often do not repeat the main theme. Yet while understanding TV news takes concentration, watching TV is full of distractions. In one study, researchers mounted cameras on top of sets and recorded the amount of time viewers also read, talked, walked in and out of the room. They concluded that viewers actually watch only 55 percent of what's on.

The audience does recall the extraordinary, such as a man on the moon, and better comprehends human-interest stories. But since most news is not covered night after night, tomorrow's broadcast tends to wash away today's. "People don't remember much from TV news," says Graber. "It's like the ocean washing over traces that have been very faintly formed."

Today's TV news is carefully watched by politicians, who keep a   20
sharp eye on how they're covered. But while it may provide theater for a handful, this research increasingly shows it's lost on the American public. And sadly, then, hard-working TV journalists may be missing an opportunity to inform.

Yet TV remains a medium with great potential. And studies show that it does extend the awareness of the poor and ill-educated, who cannot afford additional sources. What's more, research suggests that the clarity of TV news can be improved — without compromising journalistic standards. "We have been glitzed by the glamour of TV, all these gee-whiz gimmicks," says Robinson. "And we have lost sight of one of the oldest and most durable findings of communications research. . . . The most important element is the writer, who sits at a typewriter and tries to tell the story in a simple and organized way. That's the crucial link."

Research also shows that viewers want a broadcast they can understand. The success of *60 Minutes* proves there's an audience still hungry for sophisticated factual information. "When someone does this for news, they'll grab the ratings," says Levy. "Nobody loses!" Ironically, no corporation would launch an ad campaign without extensive testing on how best to reach its audience. But many broadcast journalists, working under intense pressure, remain unaware of the problems. "There's a lot we have to learn about how people comprehend," says William Rubens, NBC research vice-president. "But no, it hasn't been the thrust of our research." According to Robinson and Levy, this requires the attention of those in charge, a collective corporate will. With the networks under a financial squeeze, their news audiences having recently declined some 15 percent, "This may be the time for them to rethink their broadcasts," says Levy.

And if they do, they may just live. . . happily ever after.

FOCUSING ON CONTENT

1. What are the four myths about television news that Kalter exposes? Do any of these myths surprise you? Explain.

2. Kalter uses the term *myth* to describe assumptions about TV news. Look up the definition of *myth* in your dictionary and explain how Kalter's use of this term helps her to influence her audience.

3. What, according to Kalter, is usually wrong with general survey questions sometimes asked on polls? How have the Roper polls contributed to the myths about television news?

4. How does Kalter explain the finding that TV news is often difficult to understand?

5. In what ways does television remain a "medium with great potential" (21)?

FOCUSING ON WRITING

1. Kalter begins by discussing television — and her title implies that the article is about television in general — but the focus of her article is television news. (Glossary: *Focus*) In what ways does narrowing the focus help Kalter argue her point? Explain.

2. How does Kalter organize her essay? (Glossary: *Organization*) How does she organize her argument in paragraphs 16–20? What does each paragraph in this sequence accomplish?

3. In the spirit of traditional storytelling, Kalter begins her essay with the opening line, "Once upon a time, there was a new invention — television." In what ways is such a beginning appropriate for an essay that will expose four myths about television? (Glossary: *Beginnings and Endings*) Does it work for you?

4. What kinds of evidence does Kalter present to substantiate each of the myths she exposes? (Glossary: *Evidence*) Which pieces of evidence did you find most effective or convincing? Explain why.

LANGUAGE IN ACTION

Consider the following cartoon by Jonny Hawkins on the subject of television news.

"...That was tonight's good news. Parental guidance is recommended for tonight's bad news."

What subjects would you consider "bad news"? What insights into the public's attitude toward current television news reporting does this cartoon give you? In your opinion, are there aspects of current television news programming that need "parental guidance"?

WRITING SUGGESTIONS

1. How much do you think television — and television news in particular — has affected you? Write an argumentative essay in which you either agree or disagree with Kalter's position, based on personal experience.

2. How would you change television news to make it more effective? Write a letter to the head of a network news program in which you argue for your proposed changes in the format of the newscast.

3. During the most recent war in Iraq, reporters were "embedded" among the coalition troops and delivered firsthand reports of the combat to the American public. Do some research on the Internet or in the library on network reporting of operations in Iraq, and the effect of war coverage on the war itself. What effects do you think this type of media reporting had on the public's perception of this war? In what ways has the media's influence on public opinion been different from its influence on the wars in Vietnam and Korea? In what ways similar? Explain your thinking in an essay. Use your research to back up your claims.

CASE STUDY:
Violence and the Media

From the Revolutionary War with England to the conquest of native peoples in our country's westward expansion, from the oppression of African slaves to the Civil War, from organized crime wars in the 1930s and '40s to the gang and drug killings of our own time, from the war in Vietnam to the war on terrorism, violence has been a dominant theme in American culture. For many around the world, violence is almost synonymous with American culture. Today, violence saturates the media. We are bombarded with stories of war and violent crime on television news, and in our newspapers and magazines. For entertainment, the fare is no different: We watch violent crime dramas on television, attend violent action movies that pit the "good guys" against the "bad guys," play violent and gory video games, and listen to song lyrics that glorify violence and denigrate women. For years sociologists and media critics have engaged in the "chicken and egg" debate about the impact of media violence on our nation's young people. Are the media to blame? Or are the media simply holding up a mirror to American culture? Should violence be marketed as entertainment? How much violence is too much? What can parents do to protect their children? In this case study we have assembled four writers with varying perspectives on the multifaceted issue of children, the media, violence, and public policy to provoke discussion and debate.

In "Indictment and Trial of Media's Crime Coverage," journalist Ted Gest takes on media critics who believe crime reporters encourage new crime, cause policymakers to overreact, and instill fear in the public by distorting the picture of crime, especially violent crime, in the United States. Farah Stockman warns that blockbuster action movies are not just entertainment filled with spectacular "special effects." In "Picturing America's Enemies," she claims that movies like *The Siege* and television series like *24* have the power to create disturbing new racial and ethnic stereotypes that can miseducate our nation's children. It took a trip to Senegal, Africa, for Aisha Finch to see clearly the violence and anger of African Americans that is exported around the globe via hip-hop lyrics and videos. In "If Hip-Hop Ruled the World" she sees an opportunity for hip-hop groups to create music and lyrics that could "inspire a new wave of Pan-African thinking," that would unite and empower black people around the world. Finally, in "Life Is Precious, or It's Not," Barbara Kingsolver confesses how unsettled she felt by the shootings at Colorado's Columbine High School and the public's inability to understand and to assume some responsibility for such happenings. She seizes the opportunity to show us how our culture embraces violence, teaches young people that killing is a way to solve problems, and in conclusion, offers her readers a challenge to solve our problem.

WRITING TO DISCOVER: *Consider the following cartoon by Baloo-Rex-May:*

"The following program includes violence, offensive language, adult content and oodles of left wing propaganda"

What are your impressions and reactions to violence, offensive language, and adult content on television? What meaning does Baloo's cartoon have for you? From your own experience and observations, do you think Americans want more or less violent action and language on television? Do you think that cartoons like this one trivialize the issue of violence in the media? Explain.

Indictment and Trial of Media's Crime Coverage

TED GEST

A graduate of Oberlin College and the Graduate School of Journalism at Columbia University, Ted Gest started his career in journalism in 1969 at the St. Louis Post-Dispatch, *where he was a writer and editor. From 1977 to 2000, he worked at U.S. News & World Report, a weekly newsmagazine. After covering the Carter White House, he became the magazine's chief legal affairs writer, focusing on the Supreme Court, the Justice Department, and crime and justice issues nationally. Later, he served as national news editor and wrote extensively about law schools and other education issues. In 1998 he became president of Criminal Justice Journalists, a national organization of criminal justice reporters, writers, and broadcasters. Gest is the author of* Crime and Politics *(2003), a book which analyzes America's anticrime policies since the late 1960s. Currently Gest directs the Program on Crime and the News Media at the Jerry Lee Center of Criminology at the University of Pennsylvania. In the following essay, first presented at the "Crime, Media, and Public Policy Symposium" at Central Missouri State University in November 2002 and later published in the* Journal of the Institute of Justice and International Studies *(2003), Gest addresses four key charges leveled against the media by its harshest critics. In keeping with his subject, he uses an "indictment and trial" format to organize his discussion.*

Crime totals have declined in recent years, but a long-term perspective is helpful to understand the trends. In 1969, when I began as a daily newspaper reporter at the *St. Louis Post-Dispatch*, 662,000 violent crimes were reported across the country, about 330 per 100,000 residents. In 2001, according to the FBI's Uniform Crime Reports, there were 1,437,000 violent crimes, more than 500 per 100,000 residents. Despite the welcome news about crime going down in the 1990s, more than twice as many violent incidents were reported 32 years after I started. The crime rate, taking the population into account, also went up dramatically. If crime totals include the unreported incidents, as the Justice Department's victimization survey estimates, the overall total is higher but it has declined since the early 1970s.

Whatever the actual figure, there is little doubt that the crime problem in this country has become more serious in the last half century, and that it deserves serious news coverage. In fact, the news media stand accused of covering sensational crimes to the point that public fears are exaggerated. A recent example is the sniper case in the Washington, D.C., area in the fall of 2002. While undeniably fascinating and scary, it dominated the airwaves for three weeks while most less-dramatic cases, including homicides, got little or no attention.

The news media and crime are locked in a symbiotic relationship. We can't seem to have one without the other. One threshold question for many of our inquiries — one that has spawned as much heat as light over the years — is the actual influence of the news media, whether it's over individual wrongdoers, government policy making, or fear of crime.

Critics argue that the media do exert an influence, and its results usually are bad. In the spirit of criminal-justice reporting, I will outline a four-count indictment against those of us in the media. We will examine each of the charges and decide whether the media are guilty.

- We violate privacy of victims and defendants alike to titillate our readers and viewers.
- We encourage people to commit new crimes by publicizing current and past ones.

- We promote overreactions by policymakers by creating an atmosphere that demands instant, often oversimplistic, reform.
- We give the public a misleading picture of crime in America.

Before we put the media on trial, let's define terms. I am referring to the news media, an increasingly unruly lot that started with newspapers and magazines, expanded to television and radio, and now includes any number of cable television and online news outlets. The media are not a monolithic force but instead a very fragmented institution that change format and content daily. That's one of the challenges to responsible criticism of the media: they are a moving target.

I do not take responsibility here for the many police, court, and crime drama programs on television, as well as for the video game industry. One could argue that they are media in the broad sense of the term, but we should separate them in our analysis. Some people do not. They argue, for example, that the 1999 massacre at Columbine High School was encouraged both by video games and the news media.

The first count of my indictment of the media was that they violate people's privacy to titillate the audience. We do violate privacy, but I maintain that we generally do it in the public interest. Some crime victim advocates contend that victims should be able to opt out of news stories about their cases. Generally, we in the media reject that idea. APBnews.com, an online news service covering crime that operated between 1998 and 2000, used the slogan "You have the right to know." We crime reporters say that the public does have the right to know about crimes committed against our fellow citizens, with the possible exception of offenses like incest and child abuse that occur within families and the details of sexual assaults. Some news organizations are re-examining their longstanding practices of shielding rape victims, if they choose to come forward and tell their stories.

We don't report on individual crimes to titillate but to inform. To be sure, some stories are told mostly for their shock value, and one can debate how much detail about a case is appropriate to include. My general practice is to include more detail than less. We should be able to find out about what crimes are occurring in our community, in part so that we can take action to protect ourselves. We also should know how our tax supported agencies are responding to crimes.

To be sure, most of the news media are profit-making enterprises, so we plan our news coverage in some measure to earn income. In large part, we view it also as a public service.

Different media do use varying standards on what is appropriate to report. In general, there is increasing sensitivity to victims, partly as a result of lobbying by victim advocacy groups. We don't always include addresses or personal details that would not help solve the crime or help the public protect itself. Some critics wonder about incidents like the photos of NASCAR driver Dale Earnhardt's autopsy. Mainstream media organizations did not plan to publish them but rather hoped to obtain them to do better reporting on the safety issues involved. (An Internet entrepreneur may indeed have planned to publish them.)

So on count number one, I conclude that some media are guilty of misdemeanors, and occasional felonies, if you count everything that may appear on the Web. Overall, most media are trying to inform their viewers and readers about a significant public problem.

Count number two is that we encourage people to commit crimes by publicizing them. This is a trickier one, because motivation can be very difficult to discern. Cases can be found in which criminals say they perpetrated certain acts because of something they saw on television or read in the newspaper. But these are anecdotal, and even if we could compile a fairly long list, I doubt that they would amount to a very large proportion of serious crimes overall.

And what's the alternative? If we were to report no crime, or cut down twenty percent on coverage, would crime disappear? Obviously not.

I will declare the news media, as distinct from video games and the entertainment media, not guilty here, but not before saying that this is a serious issue that deserves more discussion and research. It is particularly important during these days of concern over terrorism.

After September 11, 2001, government agencies took down Web sites   15
that they believed might provide critical information to terrorists, such as vulnerabilities in local utility systems. Open-government advocates asserted that terrorists could obtain such information readily without checking Web sites. Some continue that argument by maintaining that private citizens should know about any vulnerabilities so that they can be corrected. If discharges from a local chemical plant can leak to places near where my children go to school, shouldn't I have the right to know about it?

Let's consider the third count in the indictment of the media: that we promote overreaction among politicians. I would convict the media of at worst a misdemeanor here. Yes, we do report a lot about crime, but as I've said, crime is a major problem in this country, high on the list along with education, health care, the economy, and a few other issues.

Making crime a major subject of news reports does not in and of itself dictate poor public policy. Let's take one issue in which the news media might be implicated to some degree:

In the late 1980s, serious juvenile crime in America increased sharply. There were reports of more and more teenagers, seemingly without a conscience, robbing, maiming, and sometimes killing innocent citizens. Critics seized on the perception that the juvenile justice system was too lenient, allowing many delinquents to be released too quickly after their first few arrests.

These critics argued that what was needed was to send more of these so-called super-predators to the adult court system, where supposedly they would be treated more harshly. It sounded logical, but it proved not to be true. Academic research showed that those sent to the adult system often committed new crimes at a higher rate than those who were retained in juvenile court. Why was this?

One reason is that juveniles, not surprisingly, tend to enter the adult   20 system when they are somewhat less violent than their older counterparts. They may end up at the lower end of the penalty range. In other words, it's no certainty that the juveniles who are sent to the adult system get tougher penalties.

Yet the news media typically published politicians' assertions that it would be a good idea to require more juveniles to be tried as adults. For several years, Congress debated whether to require states to try more juveniles as adults automatically as a condition to receive federal aid to fight juvenile crime. The law never was enacted, although for several years the federal funding law encouraged programs that promote "accountability" of offenders.

Eventually, some in the media reported on the studies doubting the efficacy of trying large numbers of juveniles as adults. These included *U.S. News & World Report* and the *New York Times.*

But many references to trying juveniles as adults were uncritical. Some would argue that the news media were complicit in this and other arguably wrong-headed policies. I conclude that the media were culpable of inadequate reporting but that it amounted to a minor offense. The real failure is at the political level. I do not believe that the media must take the rap for not keeping politicians in check. Yes, we try to function as watchdogs, but we ultimately cannot be held responsible for the failures of government to pursue rational policies that are supported by good research.

Another fairly recent example often cited is the "three strikes and you're out" sentencing schemes that were popular in the late 1980s and 1990s. The news media did widely publicize the murders of youngster Polly Klaas in California and others who were victimized by repeat criminals. In 1994, the crucial year when crime rates were at their highest in modern times and legislation proceeded at both the federal and state levels to embody "three strikes" in the statute books, we dutifully reported endorsements of the idea by Democrat and Republicans alike. Some observers say that in California, the public and politicians received most of their information and commentary on the issue not from news reports but rather talk radio programs that discussed "three strikes" incessantly and provided large blocks of air time to three strikes proponents.

The news media also reported the concerns of opponents, who com-   25 plained that the state would end up incarcerating people for many years at great public expense for some offenses that were not very serious.

Now three strikes is under attack, in the U.S. Supreme Court and elsewhere, for having gone too far. Should we in the media have done a better job of explaining how three strikes would work, particularly in the harsh form that California adopted? Yes. But does our failure to do so make us responsible for enacting the measures? No. True, we are influential because we are the conduit through which the public gets much of its information about criminal justice issues as well as many others. We should do a more responsible job, but to declare us the guilty party responsible for flawed anticrime ideas — especially ones that we did not advocate — is unfair.

Let's consider the fourth and last count in my indictment of the news media: that we too often fail to give the public a true picture of crime in the United States. Here is where the media have been guilty of several felonies.

One way in which we do this is with our seeming obsession with the ups and downs of yearly crime rates, which resembles the way we report on the stock market or aggregate student test scores. In doing this, the media may get the annual numbers right but miss the big picture, which is that crime in America is a serious problem that has worsened in recent decades. One can debate whether the problem in certain years is more or less serious than the preceding year, depending on whether one relies on the FBI's compilation of reported crimes or the U.S. Bureau of Justice Statistics' victimization estimates that included unreported crimes.

The crime issue should not fall off the radar screens of either policy-makers or the news media just because crime rates went down in the late 1990s. If the result of that is to reduce government support for worthwhile anticrime programs, we are not doing ourselves much good to prepare for the future, when it's almost inevitable that crime will rise again; in fact, it may be happening now.

The news media's coverage of crime should be improved. More attention should be paid to the quality rather than merely to the quantity. Critics are prone to cite studies showing that during the 1990s, the national television networks increased the number of minutes devoted to homicides when the actual number of homicides was going down. This critique holds little merit for me. TV networks cover such a tiny proportion of murders — and they include the O.J. Simpson and Chandra Levy cases — that there is no logical relationship between quantity of coverage and the overall number of murders across the nation.

News organizations often do move from supposed crisis to crisis in focusing on one crime or type of crime. This is primarily true of the 24-hour cable networks, whose influence on more mainstream print and broadcast media may be growing. The phenomenon didn't start with O.J. Simpson — there were plenty of sensational crimes before that — but that is as good a place as any to start in the modern era, given its coincidence with the 1994 crime-wave peak.

Since then, there has been one sensational case after another — Jon-Benet Ramsey, Chandra Levy, the kidnappings of several young girls, and the Washington, D.C., sniper case of fall 2002. (It's not all violent crime;

in November 2002 it was the Winona Ryder shoplifting trial that got an inordinate amount of TV play.)

The saturation reporting of each of these episodes certainly has given rise to the idea that no one is safe and that we all should be fearful. One point in the media's defense is that it does seem that the amount of what crime analysts call "stranger to stranger" violence — crimes perpetrated by people unknown to the victims — has increased in recent decades.

But we are not even close to the point that most of us need to be fearful every time we go outside.

I lived through the Washington sniper case, which perhaps came closer to promoting this phenomenon than did any other recent incident. It was unnerving to know that someone was aiming a rifle at innocent citizens all over the metropolitan area.   35

The local media generally did a good job in keeping people up to date on hour-to-hour developments. Much of the national media overdid the coverage in a way that may have dissuaded outsiders from visiting the Washington area.

While certainly a fascinating story, did it deserve being the lead story on national nightly news programs every day for weeks? I doubt it.

One night, ABC and others led with news of Baltimore police checking out an ex-Marine with a rifle who had been involved in a shooting episode with his wife and drove a white van, supposedly the kind of vehicle used in the killings. It turned out that this lead was just one of hundreds or thousands of dead ends, but that didn't stop networks from reporting it — even after local authorities had dismissed it as almost certainly meaningless.

Then there was the succession of profilers speculating on characteristics of the sniper. Most of the speculation turned out to be wrong, including that the shooter never was in the military, probably lived in Montgomery County, Md., was a delivery truck driver, etc. A prominent criminologist defended his speculation, noting that he did end up getting a few things right, such as that two people were involved. Does that mean that we should measure media reporting like baseball averages — that if we get 3 out of 10 items right, we're batting .300, an all-star average? It was appropriate for us to consult experts and to report the thankfully limited history of so-called spree killers, but we should have used this material with a greater deal of caution.

Overall, much coverage of the sniper case was justified because it was so unusual and scary. It was a story that had to be reported. Even if there had been twenty percent less coverage, many youngsters still would have been afraid, even if their actual odds of being victimized were minuscule.   40

Just before the sniper case captured public attention, the news media suffered another black eye in a less sensational but also significant case.

It started for me on September 9, when I woke up to see in the *Washington Post* and *New York Times* an Associated Press story on the latest so-called victimization survey issued by the Bureau of Justice Statistics and based on a survey of Americans to determine how many had been victimized the previous year. I was surprised to see this report, because journalists normally get a heads up on this annual survey so that we can prepare reports during the few days before the release date. I had not heard about this one, and assumed that there had been some miscommunication between the Justice Department and the media.

It turned out to be worse. When I looked up the entire story online, I realized that the survey had been leaked. The full version was not available on the Justice Department Web site, which made it impossible for anyone else to do a story on it because the full data were not available. Even stranger to me was that the only two people quoted in the story were experts I had never heard of, and both said roughly the same thing, that the reported decline in crime in 2001 compared with 2000 was due in large part to the incarceration of more criminals. This didn't make much sense, because I didn't believe that incarceration had increased in that year, certainly not enough to affect the national crime rate.

I asked the AP reporter about all this, as did Fox Butterfield of the *New York Times*. It turned out that the reporter couldn't locate the quoted sources. When his bosses confronted him and then started checking his previous stories, it turned out that unidentifiable sources, mostly from special interest groups or from academia, were found in forty stories over the past few years. The reporter was fired, and AP recently published one of the longest corrections in history, listing the mysterious sources in all of the stories. Ironically, the identifying slug on one of them, quoting three untraceable people, was CATCHING LIARS.

Now this alone would qualify as being one of the worst scandals in modern media history, but that's not the entire story.   45

It turns out that the Associated Press made several errors in the statistical part of the victimization story, errors that have mostly remained uncorrected. These began with the very first words of the story, which said that "the number of Americans who were victims of violent crimes except for murder fell by 9 percent in 2001. . . . " In truth, it was not the number of Americans that dropped but the number of victimizations, and that went down by 10 percent, not 9. Remember that one person can be victimized several times in a given year.

There were several other mistakes, some of them major, like reporting that guns were used in 26 percent of violent crime, when in reality that applied to any weapon; firearms were only 9 percent of the total. And so on.

The Associated Press is considered to be the premier news agency for factual reporting of hard news in this country. Its reports are used by thousands of newspapers, radio and television stations, and Web sites all over, potentially more than 15,000 outlets by one count. Once the AP reported this story exclusively on a Sunday, it was unlikely that many other news organizations would do their own versions, with the primary source material unavailable, and few did. This means that this erroneous story remains in databases all over. (AP did run a short correction on some of the statistical points.)

It's easy to blame all of this on one bad apple, and thankfully there are few of them in our ranks. One disturbing question is, as media critic Jack Shafer put it on the Web site Slate.com, "What does it say about Associated Press methods and practices that nobody caught [reporter Newton] over the course of 32 months?" AP has said in March 2003 that it still was studying ways both to shore up its fact-checking procedures and to better train reporters in coverage of issues involving crime statistics.

In late 1997, a group of journalists began a national organization called Criminal Justice Journalists, with the aim of improving media coverage in this area. It's a tall order for a profession that largely has viewed police and crime reporting as an entry-level job that journalists can do with little or no preparation. In 2001, the Jerry Lee Center of Criminology at the University of Pennsylvania provided support so that I could devote most of my time to the effort.

We now have a Ford Foundation grant to begin a comprehensive guide for journalists on covering crime and justice issues, and we run a 500-member online discussion list that is based at the Poynter Institute (a journalism think tank in Florida) on which journalists can exchange information and helpful hints on stories and sources. We also run a Web site (www.reporters.net/cjj) and several conferences or seminars each year. We get some support from the National Center on Courts and Media of the National Judicial College in Nevada for programs on better court coverage. We are starting a daily headline service on important crime and justice issues that will help fill those gaps between the saturation coverage stories.

This must be a campaign for the long haul. Only a minority of journalists covering these issues belong to the group, and their ranks are changing constantly.

It must be understood that no professional organization like this tells journalists what stories they must cover. Rather, we can suggest important trends and sources, but let them fill in the details to their audiences as they see fit.

We also represent the interests of journalists who are denied access to crime scenes and court records, among other places. In October 2002, we held panels for journalists at the International Association of Chiefs of Police convention in Minneapolis. Before that meeting, we were required to fill out an application for a media pass that included a background check that asked us if we had ever been arrested, been a suspect, a victim, a witness to a crime, received any citations — traffic, criminal, or petty misdemeanor, made a police report in regards to ourselves or someone else, or been questioned by police for any reason at any time.

It may be appropriate to do a basic security check, but it is unneces-   55
sary to ask a person who covers law enforcement as a profession whether
a police officer ever has asked them a question.

In summary, the news media are not so bad about reporting on
crime and anticrime policies as some of the critics say, but we could stand
much improvement. If this were a criminal proceeding, we should plead
guilty to several offenses and agree to mend our ways.

EXAMINING THE ISSUE CRITICALLY

1. Media critics argue that the media have a negative influence on individual
   wrongdoers, government policymakers, and the public's fear of crime. Gest
   clearly articulates this criticism in the form of a "four-count indictment." In
   your own words, what are the four charges leveled against the media?

2. How does Gest define the term *news media*? Why is it important for him to
   make himself clear on this point before putting the media on trial?

3. How does Gest answer the charge that the media "promote overreaction
   among politicians" (16)? What do the critics see as the connection between
   news reporting and poor public policy? Who does Gest think should take the
   responsibility for public policy? Do you agree with his assessment? Explain
   why or why not.

4. According to Gest, in what ways has the media failed to give the American
   public a fair and accurate picture of crime in the United States? In recent
   years, how have you been affected by the extensive coverage given to America's "sensational" and/or celebrity crimes? Has this reporting affected your
   sense of personal safety? Explain.

5. Gest concludes his remarks by saying that "the news media are not so bad
   about reporting on crime and anticrime policies as some of the critics say,
   but we could stand much improvement. . . . We should plead guilty to several offenses and agree to mend our ways" (56). Do you find Gest's verdict
   fair given the evidence he cites as well as your personal experience and reading? Explain. In your view, what are the key problems still facing crime reporters in America? What can be done to improve the situation?

Picturing America's Enemies

FARAH STOCKMAN

Born in 1974, Farah Stockman was raised in East Lansing, Michigan. After graduating from Harvard University in 1996, she lived for four years in Kenya and Tanzania working as a teacher and a freelance journalist. While in Africa, she covered the investigations into the 1998 bombings of the American Embassies in Dar es Salaam and Nairobi, the search for justice after the Rwandan genocide, and the Burundi peace talks. She returned to the Boston area in 2000 to work for the Boston Globe, *where she has covered a range of issues from foster care to prisons to the fall of the Taliban. Stockman's articles have appeared in the* Boston Globe, *the* New York Times, *the* Christian Science Monitor, *and* Transition Magazine. *In "Picturing America's Enemies," an essay that first appeared in the* Boston Globe Magazine *on June 29, 2003, Stockman warns of the power of television and film to quietly create disturbing stereotypes while reassuring audiences of America's moral superiority.*

In other times, during other wars, other generations went to the movies to escape into the spectacle of a suave James Bond. For my parents' generation, that was Sean Connery, who kept the world safe during the turmoil of the 1960s. But to me, Bond was Timothy Dalton in *The Living Daylights.* As a kid, I sat mesmerized as he hunted down — and later won over — a gorgeous, duplicitous sniper. Without knowing that I knew it, her nationality made perfect sense to me then: She was Russian.

Remember when all of the bad guys were Russian? When no action film was complete without a crew of stiff, chisel-faced Soviets muttering merciless threats in bad accents?

Back then, growing up during the Cold War, I was too young to understand capitalism or Communism. My only awareness of Ronald Reagan, elected president when I was 6, revolved around the fact that he took the White House from that nice man who liked peanuts.

But I understood the movies, and I watched them with all the secret zealousness of a child who is discouraged from watching TV. I remember the deep impression that *Rocky IV* made on me, the dread that consumed me when Drago, a seemingly indestructible Soviet boxer, trained for a match against Rocky in a high-tech Soviet laboratory. Would Rocky win? I felt goose bumps when he stood victorious in the ring, bloody after a near-life-and-death struggle, wearing the American flag. I was only eleven then, just learning what it meant to be an American, but the movie's message was clear: Drago was cold, calculating, artificial, and ultimately even his own people would turn against him and cheer for Rocky, who was scrappy, independent, full of heart. That movie taught me that America is like Rocky, and America's scrappiness, independence, and heart will always kick butt.

By the time *Rambo III* came out, I was a little older, more aware of the very real threat of nuclear war. I had begun to suspect that the Russians did indeed love their children, too, and that American policy might not always be right. But still, like old nicknames we can't get rid of or locker combinations we can't forget, those movies were branded on my brain: How Rambo — a lone man with lots of cool weapons — faced incredible odds in his fight against dozens of Russian killer-helicopters in Afghanistan. 5

How Rambo — who didn't really even want to go to war, anyway — fought alongside mujahideen against the overwhelming Soviet army. I was relieved, in the end, to realize that *of course* they would win, because the Russians were totally bad guys and Rambo and his friends were totally good.

I don't watch many movies or much TV anymore. Yet, I can't help but notice that the bad guys are no longer Russian. The terrorists who attacked New York in *The Siege* were Arab. Recently, I watched *24*, a television series that featured a terrorist plot to set off a nuclear bomb in Los Angeles. I was stunned by its realism. Like me, the characters had grown up, become more sophisticated, less certain of their own immortality. The bad-guy Arab terrorists had children who made them cry. The good-guy American intelligence agents had faults and employed torture tactics. But the impression the show will make on this new generation is the same. Like a storyteller giving the oral history of a tribe, the television said: This, children, is what America is. This is the face of our enemy. And this is our life-and-death struggle.

These days, television carries a similar message to America's kids: the continuing coverage of the Iraq War aftermath, the barrage of expert opinion on terrorism, the conflict in the Middle East. But I bet it will be the movies — not the news — that American children will remember when they grow up. The unequivocal plot lines, the charming, likable heroes, the merciless enemies are far easier to follow than the mess of real killing. Even a war named Operation Iraqi Freedom or War on Terror (how much simpler could they sound?) can't tell us who we are with the certainty that we long for.

So we go to the movies, where we never have to wonder if James Bond and Rambo are truly good or if the people they are killing are truly bad. We flock to the theaters, where we never have to doubt that, before the credits roll, the heroes will have achieved their mission. And although we might wince at all those close calls, we know before the movie even begins who will make it out alive, that Rambo will never run out of ammunition and that Bond will always escape that last explosion just in the nick of time.

EXAMINING THE ISSUE CRITICALLY

1. What lessons does Stockman remember learning as a child from movies like *The Living Daylights* and *Rocky IV*? What stereotypes of Americans and Russians did these movies leave with her?

2. What, according to Stockman, is the message that American children are getting from television and the movies today? How does this message differ from the message that she received as a child? How is this message the same?

3. Stockman believes that "it will be the movies — not the news — that American children will remember when they grow up" (8). Do you agree with her assessment? What do you think accounts for the staying power of the movies? Explain.

4. Why do you think people seem to be more tolerant of violence in the movies or on television than they are of "the mess of real killing" (8)? If we truly abhor war and violence in our streets, why do we crave violence on the big screen or on television?

If Hip-Hop Ruled the World

AISHA K. FINCH

Aisha K. Finch wrote this essay during her senior year at Brown University in Rhode Island and had it published in Essence *magazine in March 1998. In it Finch tells about a trip she took to Senegal, "to the Motherland in search of ancestral roots and cultural understanding." To her surprise, she ran into the music of home — the music of America's hip-hop giants — on the streets of Dakar. This cultural disjuncture jolted her into rethinking and questioning the violent and angry images of African Americans that are exported around the globe through the music and lyrics of hip-hop.*

You know them well. You can pick them out anywhere. They are the homeboys. The B-boys. The hip-hop kids. We see them slouched against walls, hats pulled low, hands shoved into pockets. They nod a silent greeting to a member of the crew who passes, mumble a crude appreciation for the "honeys." Searching for the elusive facade of perfect cool while gingerly holding up the walls on street corners everywhere. Atlanta. New York. Los Angeles. Even Dakar, Senegal.

I spent my first few days in Senegal trying to adjust to many things: the sometimes-on-but-never-warm tap water, strangers who greeted me as if I were family, women who created five-course meals out of fish and rice. In the midst of all this "Africanness" and cultural immersion, I was hardly prepared for a chance run-in with the former president of Death Row Records: Dr. Dre himself was blasting from the speakers of a neighborhood hangout. He was followed in turn by Warren G, Snoop Doggy Dogg, and Tupac Shakur. I had come to the Motherland in search of ancestral roots and cultural understanding, and here I was, in the French-speaking nation of Senegal, face-to-face with a spread from Rap Pages.

My first reaction was to smile and shake my head. I was in a foreign land with so little familiar to me, so the rhythms of black America fell on my ears like the voice of an old friend. It is no secret that hip-hop as both a musical genre and a defined lifestyle has gained recognition and popularity around the globe. Acknowledging this on a cerebral level, however, and confronting it in person are two entirely different things.

Just as in the United States, the hardcore players of hip-hop seem to have the most influence with the young people of Dakar. But what kind of message is being sent out to black people around the world when the main ambassadors of hip-hop are people like the Notorious B.I.G. and Lil' Kim? Yes, it's true that many of hip-hop's most devoted followers in Dakar don't understand standard English, much less the intricacies of black American slang. But just because they cannot dissect the individual words doesn't mean they don't grasp the message. Besides, the videos that follow closely behind leave little room for confusion as to underlying meanings.

We as African Americans seriously need to stop and think about what 5 our music, and our popular culture in general, is saying about us. Certainly we have all heard songs whose lyrics we neither endorse nor act upon. Yet the extensive airtime allotted to songs with destructive lyrics, coupled with the visual counterpart, does take its toll. The repeated exposure to these sounds and images slowly desensitizes us to the violence, anger, and exploitative sexual images that have become staples in much of hip-hop music. Even if we don't condone these things, our initial indignation eventually subsides and then disappears altogether as we slide into the familiar seduction of pop-culture marketing at its best. I may realize that the by-now-trite image of the gun-toting gangbanger is hardly representative of black youth culture in the United States. But we would do well to remember that foreign listeners who have had little or no interaction with African Americans have no reason not to take the face on the screen or behind the album as a representative of contemporary black American morals, values, and lifestyles.

Say what you like in defense of gangsta lyrics, but there is no way to rewrite the following party scene to make it any less disturbing: A group of teenage party goers keeps right on groovin' as the sound of recorded gunshots rips through a heavy bass line. This is something I've witnessed a number of times on the home turf, and yet I had to travel four thousand miles to feel the full impact of those bullets. Maybe we've all become a little too indifferent to that sound. Or maybe those Senegalese teenagers in their baggy clothes don't quite understand that if you listen long enough, that hollow pelting can start to sound like the 3,862 black American males who were murdered in 1995 before the age of twenty-five.

The fact is, from Senegal to South Africa, from England to Japan, the export of hip-hop around the globe is more than just a pop phenomenon. So consider this: If young black America is going to be a cultural trendsetter on a global scale, why not use this to our advantage? Can you imagine what our influence could be if more groups like The Fugees or Tribe Called Quest created music and lyrics to inspire a new wave in Pan-African thinking? If hip-hop is destined to rule youth culture around the world, wouldn't you rather it be a reign that will unite and empower black people everywhere?

EXAMINING THE ISSUE CRITICALLY

1. What worries Finch about the message the hardcore hip-hop players send out to blacks around the world? Are the messages about African Americans that the lyrics and videos of hip-hop personalities like Notorious B.I.G., Lil'

Kim, Snoop Doggy Dogg, and Tupac Shakur send out representative of current morals, values, and lifestyles in the black community? Explain.

2. According to Finch, African Americans have been desensitized to the destructive lyrics and visual images that bombard them every day. If they don't
agree with what they hear and see, why don't more blacks speak out against
the "violence, anger, and exploitative sexual images" (5)?

3. What does Finch find so disturbing about gangsta lyrics? How did the statistic that concludes paragraph 6 strike you?

4. What opportunity for hope does Finch offer young black America? Is she
being realistic, in your view? Explain.

Life Is Precious, or It's Not

Barbara Kingsolver

The popular and prolific author Barbara Kingsolver was born in 1955 in eastern Kentucky. Although she has kept a journal since she was a child, she never dreamed that she would become a published writer. After graduating from DePauw University with a major in biology, Kingsolver traveled in Greece and France, taking a variety of jobs to support herself. After returning to the United States, she earned a master's degree in biology and ecology at the University of Arizona. It was here that she took a writing course from Francine Prose. First she worked as a science writer and later as a features writer for journals and newspapers. Kingsolver has published poetry, essays, and an oral history along with her novels, which include The Bean Trees *(1988),* Animal Dreams *(1990),* Pigs in Heaven *(1993), and* Prodigal Summer *(2002). In "Life Is Precious, or It's Not," taken from her collection of essays* Small Wonder *(2002), Kingsolver uses the tragedy at Columbine High School in Littleton, Colorado, as her starting point to argue for changes in our national attitude — an attitude she believes is strongly influenced by the media — that promotes violence and killing as quick and easy solutions to our problems.*

"Columbine used to be one of my favorite flowers," my friend told me, and we both fell silent. We'd been talking about what she might plant on the steep bank at the foot of the woods above her house, but a single word cut us suddenly adrift from our focus on the uncomplicated life in which flowers could matter. I understood why she no longer had the heart to plant columbines. I feel that way, too, and at the same time I feel we ought to plant them everywhere, to make sure we remember. In our backyards, on the graves of the children lost, even on the graves of the children who murdered, whose parents must surely live with the deepest emotional pain it is possible to bear.

In the aftermath of the Columbine High School shootings in Colorado, the whole country experienced grief and shock and — very noticeably — the spectacle of a nation acting bewildered. Even the op-ed commentators who usually tell us just what to think were asking, instead, what we should think. How could this happen in an ordinary school, an ordinary neighborhood? Why would any student, however frustrated with meanspirited tormentors, believe that guns and bombs were the answer?

I'm inclined to think all of us who are really interested in these questions might have started asking them a long while ago. Why does any person or nation, including ours, persist in celebrating violence as an

honorable expression of disapproval? In, let's say, Iraq, the Sudan, Waco —
anywhere we get fed up with meanspirited tormentors — why are we so
quick to assume that guns and bombs are the answer?

Some accidents and tragedies and bizarre twists of fate are truly senseless, as random as lightning bolts out of the blue. But this one at
Columbine High was not, and to say it was is irresponsible. "Senseless"
sounds like "without cause," and it requires no action, so that after an appropriate interval of dismayed hand-wringing, we can go back to business
as usual. What takes guts is to own up: This event made sense. Children
model the behavior of adults, on whatever scale is available to them. Ours
are growing up in a nation whose most important, influential men —
from presidents to the coolest film characters — solve problems by killing
people. Killing is quick and sure and altogether manly.

It is utterly predictable that some boys who are desperate for admira-   5
tion and influence will reach for guns and bombs. And it's not surprising
that this happened in a middle-class neighborhood; institutional violence
is right at home in the suburbs. Don't let's point too hard at the gangsta
rap in our brother's house until we've examined the video games, movies,
and political choices we support in our own. The tragedy in Littleton
grew out of a culture that is loudly and proudly rooting for the global
shootout. That culture is us.

Conventional wisdom tells us that Nazis, the U.S. Marines, the Ter-
minator, and the NYPD all kill for different reasons. But as every parent
knows, children are good at ignoring or seeing straight through the subtleties we spin. Here's what they must surely see: Killing is an exalted tool
for punishment and control. Americans who won't support it are
ridiculed, shamed, or even threatened. The Vietnam War was a morally
equivocal conflict by any historical measure, and yet to this day, candidates for public office who avoided being drafted into that war are widely
held to be unfit for leadership.

Most Americans believe bloodshed is necessary for preserving our
way of life, even though it means risking the occasional misfire — the
civilians strafed because they happened to live too close to the terrorist,
maybe, or the factory that actually made medicines but *might* have been
making weapons. We're willing to sacrifice the innocent man condemned
to death row because every crime must be paid for, and no jury is perfect.
The majority position in our country seems to be that violence is an appropriate means to power, and that the loss of certain innocents along
the way is the sad but inevitable cost.

I'd like to ask those who favor this position if they would be willing
to go to Littleton and explain to some mothers what constitutes an acceptable risk. Really. Because in a society that embraces violence, this is
what "our way of life" has come to mean. The question can't be *why* but
only "Why yours and not mine?" We have taught our children in a thousand ways, sometimes with flag-waving and sometimes with a laugh

track, that the bad guy deserves to die. But we easily forget a crucial component of this formula: "Bad" is defined by the aggressor. Any of our children may someday be, in one someone's mind, the bad guy.

For all of us who are clamoring for meaning, aching for the loss of these precious young lives in Littleton to mean something, my strongest instinct is to use the event to nail a permanent benchmark into our hearts: Life is that precious, period. It is possible to establish zero tolerance for murder as a solution to anything. Those of us who agree to this contract can start by removing from our households and lives every television program, video game, film, book, toy, and CD that presents the killing of humans (however symbolic) as an entertainment option, rather than the appalling loss it really is. Then we can move on to harder choices, such as discussing the moral lessons of capital punishment. Demanding from our elected officials the subtleties and intelligence of diplomacy instead of an endless war budget. Looking into what we did (and are still doing) to the living souls of Iraq, if we can bear it. And — this is important — telling our kids we aren't necessarily proud of the parts of our history that involved bombing people in countries whose policies we didn't agree with.

Sounds extreme? Let's be honest. *Death* is extreme, and the children   10
are paying attention.

EXAMINING THE ISSUE CRITICALLY

1. In paragraph 3, Kingsolver asks two fundamental questions: "Why does any person or nation, including ours, persist in celebrating violence as an honorable expression of disapproval?" and "Why are we so quick to assume that guns and bombs are the answer?" How does she answer these questions? Do you agree with her? Why or why not?

2. In paragraph 4, Kingsolver argues against the widely held view that the killings at Columbine High School were "senseless." Why does she say that they made sense?

3. Kingsolver claims that we live in a "culture that is loudly and proudly rooting for the global shootout" (5). In what ways do our "video games, movies, and political choices" support her claim?

4. Kingsolver believes that "it is possible to establish zero tolerance for murder as a solution to anything" (9). Is zero tolerance for murder a realistic position to take? Explain.

5. In paragraphs 9 and 10, Kingsolver challenges the American public to act. Do you think Americans will accept her challenge? Why or why not?

MAKING CONNECTIONS: VIOLENCE AND THE MEDIA

The following questions are offered to help you start to make meaningful connections among the four articles in this Case Study. These questions can be used for class discussion, or you can answer any one of the questions by writing an essay. If you choose the essay option, be sure to make specific references to at least two of the Case Study articles.

1. It's no secret that violence sells in America, and consequently violence is everywhere in the media. There's violence in our movies, violence in our music, violence in our news, violence in our video games, and violence in our television programs. Where do you stand on the issue of violence in the media? Is there a place for violence in the media? Does violence have any "entertainment" value for you? Or do the negative effects of violence outweigh any entertainment value it might have?

2. In writing about the destructive lyrics and videos of hip-hop music, Aisha K. Finch says that "the repeated exposure to these sounds and images slowly desensitizes us to the violence, anger, and exploitative sexual images that have become staples in much of hip-hop music. Even if we don't condone these things, our initial indignation eventually subsides and then disappears altogether as we slide into the familiar seduction of pop-culture marketing at its best" (5). Has American society been desensitized to the dangers of such media violence? Under the guise of seemingly innocent pop-culture marketing, have American parents been sold a bill of goods? Consider the Columbine killings and the role violent video games played in the blame assessment of that crime. Have children been left "unprotected" from the negative influences of violence? Using the thoughts and ideas of at least three writers in this Case Study, write an essay in which you address these key questions.

3. Some critics believe that television does not make children violent. On the contrary, they state that television violence makes children passive. How do you think Gest, Stockman, Finch, and Kingsolver would respond to an argument like this? What specifically in each of their essays led you to your conclusions?

4. Like many other writers and media critics, Barbara Kingsolver is concerned that media violence sends the wrong message to our nation's children. She believes that our children "are growing up in a nation whose most important, influential men — from presidents to the coolest film characters — solve problems by killing people" (4). She argues that to combat this message we must give human life meaning once again, we must "establish zero tolerance for murder as a solution to anything" (9). Kingsolver's solution sounds so sensible and humane at first glance. Yet even she admits that it's extreme and that there are people for whom acceptance of her contract would not be easy. How do you respond to Kingsolver's challenge? How do you think the other three writers in this Case Study would respond? What would be Aisha Finch's solution for the rap industry? How would Farah Stockman implement change in the film industry? Write an essay in which you present a plan for the implementation of Kingsolver's zero tolerance challenge for music,

television, film, and news coverage, thus reestablishing the basic human value that "life is that precious, period" (9).

5. Ted Gest believes that America's "crime problem . . . deserves serious news coverage" (2). Where do you stand on this issue? What are your reasons for taking this position? What does the phrase "serious news coverage" mean to you? Do you read any newspapers or magazines or watch any television newscasts where you think the crime reporters are doing a satisfactory job? Do reporters tend to sensationalize crime stories, especially when violence is present? Is there such a thing as too much coverage of a crime story? Write an essay in which you argue for what you think the public deserves from the news media on crime coverage.

6. In the wake of the terrorist attacks on September 11, 2001, the United States Congress passed the Patriot Act, a law that gave the federal government new powers to fight the war on terrorism. In retrospect, many political commentators and some legislators think that the Patriot Act may have gone too far, and that the law was passed out of fear, not sound judgment. Research the news media's coverage of the 9/11 attacks and the passage of the Patriot Act. Are there any connections between the coverage of the attacks and the swift passage of the legislation? Write an essay in which you report your findings.

7

I CAN SELL
YOU ANYTHING

Advertising is big business and a real part of our daily lives. We hear a steady stream of ads on the radio, see them on television, read them in newspapers and magazines, and even wear them on clothing. Today American businesses spend an estimated $225 billion a year on print ads and television commercials. Appealing to our fantasies of wealth, good looks, power, social acceptance, and happiness, advertising tries to persuade us to purchase particular products and services, many of which we don't need. Advertising is so pervasive that we tend to take it for granted — just how much do we really hear and see? Though every business hopes that its ads will be memorable and work effectively, we know that many of them fail. What makes one advertisement more persuasive than another? What goes into developing and producing an ad campaign? How do ads work on the minds of consumers? To answer these questions, we need to become more sensitive to advertising language and the ways advertisers combine verbal strategies with visual images.

In the opening selection, "The Hard Sell: Advertising in America," Bill Bryson provides a historical perspective and context for our exploration of the world of advertising — an industry that has come to dominate the American media in the twenty-first century. His historical sketch reads like a "Who's Who" of American business from Eastman Kodak to Perdue Chickens. We learn that many long popular slogans — Ivory Soap's "99 44/100 percent pure," Morton Salt's "When it rains, it pours," American Florist Association's "Say it with flowers," and Coca-Cola's "the pause that refreshes" — had their origin in the late nineteenth and early twentieth centuries. William Lutz challenges advertisers and their manipulative language in "Weasel Words" and exposes some of the secrets of successful advertising language. He shows us that when advertisers can't say something, they usually end up "weaseling" it, that is, they make you, the consumer, hear things that are not being said. In the third selection, "How to Advertise a Dangerous Product," advertising historian James B. Twitchell traces the origins of the now-famous Miss Clairol "Does she . . . or doesn't she?" campaign. Imagine — in the 1950s, hair coloring was a controversial and "dangerous" product.

Twitchell takes us behind the scenes to witness the development of the artfully ambiguous verbal and visual strategy that would make this ad campaign one of the most successful in the twentieth century.

CASE STUDY: MARKETING DIET AND HEALTH

What happens when health, diet, and advertising collide? Some people argue that advertising gives the American public a new awareness of healthy options in their diet. Others argue that current advertising has created a free-for-all bonanza for junk food manufacturers, resulting in this country's obesity epidemic. The articles in this Case Study explore how food is marketed in this county. What claims can manufacturers legally make about their products? How do advertisers manipulate language so that they appear to be saying what they can't legally say? And who are the victims of this onslaught of advertisements that encourage us to "supersize," to eat — and then eat some more? Finally, a portfolio of advertisements offers the opportunity to test your "ad literacy," to see if you can understand what is really being said when words and images are strategically combined.

The Hard Sell: Advertising in America

BILL BRYSON

Journalist Bill Bryson was born in Des Moines, Iowa, in 1951. He writes for National Geographic, *and his work regularly appears in the* New York Times, *the* Washington Post, Esquire, Granta, *and* GQ. *Bryson's interest in language is reflected in his books* A Dictionary of Troublesome Words *(1987)*, The Mother Tongue *(1990), and* Neither Here Nor There *(1992). His other books include* A Walk in the Woods: Rediscovering America on the Appalachian Trail *(1998) and* A Short History of Nearly Everything *(2003). After living in England for almost twenty years, Bryson now lives in Hanover, New Hampshire.*

The following essay is a chapter in Bryson's Made in America: An Informal History of the English Language in the United States *(1994). In it, he provides a historical perspective on advertising and explores some of the trends that have appeared over the years. It may surprise many people to learn that advertising as we know it is a modern invention, spanning only about a century. During that time, however, the influence of advertisements has grown so much that they now shape the way we see the world.*

WRITING TO DISCOVER: *Reactions to advertising vary, but most people would say that ads are a necessary evil and that they ignore them whenever possible. Yet advertising is a multibillion-dollar industry, which is financed by what we buy and sell. Think about some recent TV shows you've watched or newspapers you've read. Jot down the names of the products you saw advertised. Do you buy any of these products? Write about the influences, if any, advertising seems to have on the way you spend your money.*

In 1885, a young man named George Eastman formed the Eastman Dry Plate and Film Company in Rochester, New York. It was rather a bold thing to do. Aged just thirty-one, Eastman was a junior clerk in a bank on a comfortable but modest salary of $15 a week. He had no background in business. But he was passionately devoted to photography and had become increasingly gripped with the conviction that anyone who could develop a simple, untechnical camera, as opposed to the cumbersome, outsized, fussily complex contrivances then on the market, stood to make a fortune.

Eastman worked tirelessly for three years to perfect his invention, supporting himself in the meantime by making dry plates for commercial photographers, and in June 1888 produced a camera that was positively dazzling in its simplicity: a plain black box just six and a half inches long by three and a quarter inches wide, with a button on the side and a key for advancing the film. Eastman called his device the *Detective Camera*. Detectives were all the thing — Sherlock Holmes was just taking off with American readers — and the name implied that it was so small and simple that it could be used unnoticed, as a detective might.

The camera had no viewfinder and no way of focusing. The *photographer* or *photographist* (it took a while for the first word to become the established one) simply held the camera in front of him, pressed a button on the side, and hoped for the best. Each roll took a hundred pictures. When the roll was fully exposed, the anxious owner sent the entire camera to Rochester for developing. Eventually he received the camera back, freshly loaded with film, and — assuming all had gone well — one hundred small circular pictures, two and a half inches in diameter.

Often all didn't go well. The film Eastman used at first was made of paper, which tore easily and had to be carefully stripped of its emulsion before the exposures could be developed. It wasn't until the invention of celluloid roll film by a sixty-five-year-old Episcopal minister named Hannibal Goodwin in Newark, New Jersey — this truly was the age of the amateur inventor — that amateur photography became a reliable undertaking. Goodwin didn't call his invention *film* but *photographic pellicule*, and, as was usual, spent years fighting costly legal battles with Eastman without ever securing the recognition or financial payoff he deserved — though eventually, years after Goodwin's death, Eastman was ordered to pay $5 million to the company that inherited the patent.

In September 1888, Eastman changed the name of the camera to 5 *Kodak* — an odd choice, since it was meaningless, and in 1888 no one gave meaningless names to products, especially successful products. Since British patent applications at the time demanded a full explanation of trade and brand names, we know how Eastman arrived at his inspired name. He crisply summarized his reasoning in his patent application: "First. It is short. Second. It is not capable of mispronunciation. Third. It does not resemble anything in the art and cannot be associated with anything in the art except the Kodak." Four years later the whole enterprise was renamed the Eastman Kodak Company.

Despite the considerable expense involved — a Kodak camera sold for $25, and each roll of film cost $10, including developing — by 1895, over 100,000 Kodaks had been sold and Eastman was a seriously wealthy man. A lifelong bachelor, he lived with his mother in a thirty-seven-room mansion with twelve bathrooms. Soon people everywhere were talking about snapshots, originally a British shooting term for a hastily executed shot. Its photographic sense was coined by the English astronomer Sir John Herschel, who also gave the world the terms *positive* and *negative* in their photographic senses.

From the outset, Eastman developed three crucial strategies that have been the hallmarks of virtually every successful consumer goods company since. First, he went for the mass market, reasoning that it was better to make a little money each from a lot of people rather than a lot of money from a few. He also showed a tireless, obsessive dedication to making his products better and cheaper. In the 1890s, such an approach was widely perceived as insane. If you had a successful product you milked it for all it was worth. If competitors came along with something better, you bought them out or tried to squash them with lengthy patent fights or other bullying tactics. What you certainly did not do was create new products that made your existing lines obsolescent. Eastman did. Throughout the late 1890s, Kodak introduced a series of increasingly cheaper, niftier cameras — the Bull's Eye model of 1896, which cost just $12, and the famous slimline Folding Pocket Kodak of 1898, before finally in 1900 producing his eureka model: the little box Brownie, priced at just $1 and with film at 15 cents a reel (though with only six exposures per reel).

Above all, what set Eastman apart was the breathtaking lavishness of his advertising. In 1899 alone, he spent $750,000, an unheard-of sum, on advertising. Moreover, it was *good* advertising: crisp, catchy, reassuringly trustworthy. "You press the button — we do the rest" ran the company's first slogan, thus making a virtue of its shortcomings. Never mind that you couldn't load or unload the film yourself. Kodak would do it for you. In 1905, it followed with another classic slogan: "If It Isn't an Eastman, It Isn't a Kodak."

Kodak's success did not escape other businessmen, who also began to see virtue in the idea of steady product refinement and improvement. AT&T and Westinghouse, among others, set up research laboratories with the idea of creating a stream of new products, even at the risk of displacing old ones. Above all, everyone everywhere began to advertise.

Advertising was already a well-established phenomenon by the turn of the twentieth century. Newspapers had begun carrying ads as far back as the early 1700s, and magazines soon followed. (Benjamin Franklin has the distinction of having run the first magazine ad, seeking the whereabouts of a runaway slave, in 1741.) By 1850, the country had its first *advertising agency*, the American Newspaper Advertising Agency, though its function was to buy advertising space rather than come up with creative campaigns. The first advertising agency in the modern sense was N. W. Ayer & Sons of Philadelphia, established in 1869. *To advertise* originally carried the sense of to broadcast or disseminate news. Thus a nineteenth-century newspaper that called itself the *Advertiser* meant that it had lots of news, not lots of ads. By the early 1800s the term had been stretched to accommodate the idea of spreading the news of the availability of certain goods or services. A newspaper notice that read "Jos. Parker, Hatter" was essentially announcing that if anyone was in the market for hats, Jos. Parker had them. In the sense of persuading members of the public to acquire items they might not otherwise think of buying — items they didn't know they needed — advertising is a phenomenon of the modern age.

By the 1890s, advertising was appearing everywhere — in newspapers and magazines, on *billboards* (an Americanism dating from 1850), on the sides of buildings, on passing streetcars, on paper bags, even on matchbooks, which were invented in 1892 and were being extensively used as an advertising medium within three years.

Very early on, advertisers discovered the importance of a good slogan. Many of our more venerable slogans are older than you might think. Ivory Soap's "99 44/100 percent pure" dates from 1879. Schlitz has been calling itself "the beer that made Milwaukee famous" since 1895, and Heinz's "57 varieties" followed a year later. Morton Salt's "When it rains, it pours" dates from 1911, the American Florist Association's "Say it with flowers" was first used in 1912, and the "good to the last drop" of Maxwell House coffee, named for the Maxwell House Hotel in Nashville, where it was first served, has been with us since 1907. (The slogan is said to have originated with Teddy Roosevelt, who pronounced the coffee "good to the last drop," prompting one wit to ask, "So what's wrong with the last drop?")

Sometimes slogans took a little working on. Coca-Cola described itself as "the drink that makes a pause refreshing" before realizing, in 1929, that "the pause that refreshes" was rather more succinct and memorable. A slogan could make all the difference to a product's success. After advertising its soap as an efficacious way of dealing with "conspicuous nose pores," Woodbury's Facial Soap came up with the slogan "The skin you love to touch" and won the hearts of millions. The great thing about a slogan was that it didn't have to be accurate to be effective. Heinz never actually had exactly "57 varieties" of anything. The catchphrase arose simply because H. J. Heinz, the company's founder, decided he liked the sound of the number. Undeterred by considerations of verity, he had the slogan slapped on every one of the products he produced, already in 1896 far more than fifty-seven. For a time the company tried to arrange its products into fifty-seven arbitrary clusters, but in 1969 it gave up the ruse altogether and abandoned the slogan.

Early in the 1900s, advertisers discovered another perennial feature of marketing — the *giveaway*, as it was called almost from the start. Consumers soon became acquainted with the irresistibly tempting notion that if they bought a particular product they could expect a reward — the chance to receive a prize, a free book (almost always ostensibly dedicated to the general improvement of one's well-being but invariably a thinly disguised plug for the manufacturer's range of products), a free sample, or a rebate in the form of a shiny dime, or be otherwise endowed with some gratifying bagatelle. Typical of the genre was a turn-of-the-century tome called *The Vital Question Cook Book*, which was promoted as an aid to livelier meals, but which proved upon receipt to contain 112 pages of recipes all involving the use of Shredded Wheat. Many of these had a certain air of desperation about them, notably the "Shredded Wheat Biscuit

Jellied Apple Sandwich" and the "Creamed Spinach on Shredded Wheat Biscuit Toast." Almost all involved nothing more than spooning some everyday food on a piece of shredded wheat and giving it an inflated name. Nonetheless the company distributed no fewer than four million copies of *The Vital Question Cook Book* to eager consumers.

The great breakthrough in twentieth-century advertising, however, came with the identification and exploitation of the American consumer's Achilles' heel: anxiety. One of the first to master the form was King Gillette, inventor of the first safety razor and one of the most relentless advertisers of the early 1900s. Most of the early ads featured Gillette himself, who with his fussy toothbrush mustache and well-oiled hair looked more like a caricature of a Parisian waiter than a captain of industry. After starting with a few jaunty words about the ease and convenience of the safety razor — "Compact? Rather!" — he plunged the reader into the heart of the matter: "When you use my razor you are exempt from the dangers that men often encounter who allow their faces to come in contact with brush, soap, and barbershop accessories used on other people."

Here was an entirely new approach to selling goods. Gillette's ads were in effect telling you that not only did there exist a product that you never previously suspected you needed, but if you *didn't* use it you would very possibly attract a crop of facial diseases you never knew existed. The combination proved irresistible. Though the Gillette razor retailed for a hefty $5 — half the average workingman's weekly pay — it sold by the millions, and King Gillette became a very wealthy man. (Though only for a time, alas. Like many others of his era, he grew obsessed with the idea of the perfectibility of mankind and expended so much of his energies writing books of convoluted philosophy with titles like *The Human Drift* that he eventually lost control of his company and most of his fortune.)

By the 1920s, advertisers had so refined the art that a consumer could scarcely pick up a magazine without being bombarded with unsettling questions: "Do You Make These Mistakes in English?"; "Will Your Hair Stand Close Inspection?"; "When Your Guests Are Gone — Are You Sorry You Ever Invited Them?" (because, that is, you lack social polish); "Did Nature fail to put roses in your cheeks?"; "Will There be a Victrola in Your Home This Christmas?"[1] The 1920s truly were the Age of Anxiety. One ad pictured a former golf champion, "now only a wistful onlooker," whose career had gone sour because he had neglected his teeth. Scott Tissues mounted a campaign showing a forlorn-looking businessman sitting on a park bench beneath the bold caption "A Serious Business Handicap — These Troubles That Come from Harsh Toilet Tissue." Below the picture the text explained "65 percent of all men and

15

---

1. The most famous 1920s ad of them all didn't pose a question, but it did play on the readers's anxiety: "They Laughed When I Sat Down, but When I Started to Play . . ." It was originated by the U.S. School of Music in 1925.

women over 40 are suffering from some form of rectal trouble, estimates a prominent specialist connected with one of New York's largest hospitals. 'And one of the contributing causes,' he states, 'is inferior toilet tissue.'" There was almost nothing that one couldn't become uneasy about. One ad even asked: "Can You Buy a Radio Safely?" Distressed bowels were the most frequent target. The makers of Sal Hepatica warned: "We rush to meetings, we dash to parties. We are on the go all day long. We exercise too little, and we eat too much. And, in consequence, we impair our bodily functions — often we retain food within us too long. And when that occurs, poisons are set up — *Auto-Intoxication begins.*"

In addition to the dread of auto-intoxication, the American consumer faced a gauntlet of other newly minted maladies — *pyorrhea, halitosis* (coined as a medical term in 1874, but popularized by Listerine beginning in 1922 with the slogan "Even your best friend won't tell you"), *athlete's foot* (a term invented by the makers of Absorbine Jr. in 1928), *dead cuticles, scabby toes, iron-poor blood, vitamin deficiency (vitamins* had been coined in 1912, but the word didn't enter the general vocabulary until the 1920s, when advertisers realized it sounded worryingly scientific), *fallen stomach, tobacco breath,* and *psoriasis,* though Americans would have to wait until the next decade for the scientific identification of the gravest of personal disorders — *body odor,* a term invented in 1933 by the makers of Lifebuoy soap and so terrifying in its social consequences that it was soon abbreviated to a whispered *B.O.*

The white-coated technicians of American laboratories had not only identified these new conditions, but — miraculously, it seemed — simultaneously come up with cures for them. Among the products that were invented or rose to greatness in this busy, neurotic decade were *Cutex* (for those deceased cuticles), *Vick's VapoRub, Geritol, Serutan* ("Natures spelled backwards," as the voiceover always said with somewhat bewildering reassurance, as if spelling a product's name backward conferred some medicinal benefit), *Noxema* (for which read: "knocks eczema"), *Preparation H, Murine* eyedrops, and *Dr. Scholl's Foot Aids.*[2] It truly was an age of miracles — one in which you could even cure a smoker's cough by smoking, so long as it was Old Golds you smoked, because, as the slogan proudly if somewhat untruthfully boasted, they contained "Not a cough in a carload." (As late as 1953, L&M cigarettes were advertised as "just what the doctor ordered!")

By 1927, advertising was a $1.5-billion-a-year industry in the United States, and advertising people were held in such awe that they were asked not only to mastermind campaigns but even to name the products. An ad man named Henry N. McKinney, for instance, named *Keds* shoes, *Karo* syrup, *Meadow Gold* butter, and *Uneeda Biscuits.*

20

---

2. And yes, there really was a Dr. Scholl. His name was William Scholl; he was a real doctor, genuinely dedicated to the well-being of feet, and they are still very proud of him in his hometown of La Porter, Indiana.

Product names tended to cluster around certain sounds. Breakfast cereals often ended in *-ies (Wheaties, Rice Krispies, Frosties);* washing powders and detergents tended to be gravely monosyllabic (*Lux, Fab, Tide, Duz*). It is often possible to tell the era of a product's development by its termination. Thus products dating from the 1920s and early 1930s often ended in *-ex* (*Pyrex, Cutex, Kleenex, Windex*), while those ending in *-master (Mixmaster, Toastmaster)* generally betray a late 1930s or early-1940s genesis. The development of *Glo-Coat* floor wax in 1932 also heralded the beginning of American business's strange and long-standing infatuation with illiterate spellings, a trend that continued with *ReaLemon* juice in 1935, *Reddi-Wip* whipped cream in 1947, and many hundreds of others since, from *Tastee-Freez* drive-ins to *Toys 'Я' Us,* along with countless others with a *Kwik, E-Z,* or *U* (as in *While-U-Wait*) embedded in their titles. The late 1940s saw the birth of a brief vogue for endings in *-matic,* so that car manufacturers offered vehicles with *Seat-O-Matic* levers and *Cruise-O-Matic* transmissions, and even fitted sheets came with *Ezy-Matic* corners. Some companies became associated with certain types of names. Du Pont, for instance, had a special fondness for words ending in *-on.* The practice began with *nylon* — a name that was concocted out of thin air and owes nothing to its chemical properties — and was followed with *Rayon, Dacron, Orlon,* and *Teflon,* among many others. In recent years the company has moved on to what might be called its *Star Trek* phase with such compounds as *Tyvek, Kevlar, Sontara, Condura, Nomex,* and *Zemorain.*

Such names have more than passing importance to their owners. If American business has given us a large dose of anxiety in its ceaseless quest for a healthier *bottom line* (a term dating from the 1930s, though not part of mainstream English until the 1970s), we may draw some comfort from the thought that business has suffered a great deal of collective anxiety over protecting the names of its products.

A certain cruel paradox prevails in the matter of preserving brand names. Every business naturally wants to create a product that will dominate its market. But if that product so dominates the market that the brand name becomes indistinguishable in the public mind from the product itself — when people begin to ask for a *thermos* rather than a "Thermos brand vacuum flask" — then the term has become generic and the owner faces the loss of its trademark protection. That is why advertisements and labels so often carry faintly paranoid-sounding lines like "Tabasco is the registered trademark for the brand of pepper sauce made by McIlhenny Co." and why companies like Coca-Cola suffer palpitations when they see a passage like this (from John Steinbeck's *The Wayward Bus*):

> "Got any coke?" another character asked.
> "No," said the proprietor. "Few bottles of Pepsi-Cola. Haven't had any coke for a month. . . . It's the same stuff. You can't tell them apart."

An understandable measure of confusion exists concerning the distinction between patents and trademarks and between trademarks and trade names. A *patent* protects the name of the product and its method of manufacture for seventeen years. Thus from 1895 to 1912, no one but the Shredded Wheat Company could make shredded wheat. But because patents require manufacturers to divulge the secrets of their products — and thus make them available to rivals to copy when the patent runs out — companies sometimes choose not to seek their protection. *Coca-Cola,* for one, has never been patented. A *trademark* is effectively the name of a product, its *brand name.* A *trade name* is the name of the manufacturer. So *Ford* is a trade name, *Taurus* a trademark. Trademarks apply not just to names, but also to logos, drawings, and other symbols and depictions. The MGM lion, for instance, is a trademark. Unlike patents, trademark protection goes on forever, or at least as long as the manufacturer can protect it.

For a long time, it was felt that this permanence gave the holder an   25
unfair advantage. In consequence, America did not enact its first trademark law until 1870, almost a century after Britain, and then it was declared unconstitutional by the Supreme Court. Lasting trademark protection did not begin for American companies until 1881. Today, more than a million trademarks have been issued in the United States and the number is rising by about thirty thousand a year.

A good trademark is almost incalculably valuable. Invincible-seeming brand names do occasionally falter and fade. *Pepsodent, Rinso, Chase & Sanborn, Sal Hepatica, Vitalis, Brylcreem,* and *Burma-Shave* all once stood on the commanding heights of consumer recognition but are now defunct or have sunk to the status of what the trade calls "ghost brands" — products that are still produced but little promoted and largely forgotten. For the most part, however, once a product establishes a dominant position in a market, it is exceedingly difficult to depose it. In nineteen of twenty-two categories, the company that owned the leading American brand in 1925 still has it today — *Nabisco* in cookies, *Kellogg's* in breakfast cereals, *Kodak* in film, *Sherwin Williams* in paint, *Del Monte* in canned fruit, *Wrigleys* in chewing gum, *Singer* in sewing machines, *Ivory* in soap, *Campbell's* in soup, *Gillette* in razors. Few really successful brand names of today were not just as familiar to your grandparents or even great-grandparents, and a well-established brand name has a sort of self-perpetuating power. As *The Economist* has noted: "In the category of food blenders, consumers were still ranking General Electric second twenty years after the company had stopped making them."

An established brand name is so valuable that only about 5 percent of the sixteen thousand or so new products introduced in America each year bear all-new brand names. The others are variants on an existing product — *Tide with Bleach, Tropicana Twister Light Fruit Juices,* and so on. Among some types of product a certain glut is evident. At last count there were 220 types of branded breakfast cereal in America. In 1993, according to an international business survey, the world's most valuable brand was *Marlboro*, with a value estimated at $40 billion, slightly ahead of *Coca-Cola*. Among the other ten brands were *Intel, Kellogg's, Budweiser, Pepsi, Gillette*, and *Pampers. Nescafé* and *Bacardi* were the only foreign brands to make the top ten, underlining American dominance.

Huge amounts of effort go into choosing brand names. General Foods reviewed 2,800 names before deciding on *Dreamwhip*. (To put this in proportion, try to think of just ten names for an artificial whipped cream.) Ford considered more than twenty thousand possible car names before finally settling on *Edsel* (which proves that such care doesn't always pay), and Standard Oil a similar number of names before it opted for *Exxon*. Sometimes, however, the most successful names are the result of a moment's whimsy. *Betty Crocker* came in a flash to an executive of the Washburn Crosby Company (later absorbed by General Mills), who chose *Betty* because he thought it sounded wholesome and sincere and *Crocker* in memory of a beloved fellow executive who had recently died. At first the name was used only to sign letters responding to customers' requests for advice or information, but by the 1950s, Betty Crocker's smiling, confident face was appearing on more than fifty types of food product, and her loyal followers could buy her recipe books and even visit her "kitchen" at the General Foods headquarters.

Great efforts also go into finding out why people buy the brands they do. Advertisers and market researchers bandy about terms like *conjoint analysis technique, personal drive patterns, Gaussian distributions, fractals*, and other such arcana in their quest to winnow out every subliminal quirk in our buying habits. They know, for instance, that 40 percent of all people who move to a new address will also change their brand of toothpaste, that the average supermarket shopper makes fourteen impulse decisions in each visit, that 62 percent of shoppers will pay a premium for mayonnaise even when they think a cheaper brand is just as good, but that only 24 percent will show the same largely irrational loyalty to frozen vegetables.

To preserve a brand name involves a certain fussy attention to linguistic and orthographic details. To begin with, the name is normally expected to be treated not as a noun but as a proper adjective — that is, the name should be followed by an explanation of what it does: *Kleenex facial tissues, Q-Tip cotton swabs, Jell-O brand gelatin dessert, Sanka brand decaffeinated coffee*. Some types of products — notably cars — are granted an exemption, which explains why General Motors does not have to advertise *Cadillac self-propelled automobiles* or the like. In all cases, the name may not explicitly describe the product's function, though it may hint at what it does. Thus *Coppertone* is acceptable; *Coppertan* would not be.

The situation is more than a little bizarre. Having done all they can to make their products household words, manufacturers must then in their advertisements do all in their power to imply that they aren't. Before trademark law was clarified, advertisers positively encouraged the public to treat their products as generics. Kodak invited consumers to "Kodak as you go," turning the brand name into a dangerously ambiguous verb. It would never do that now. The American Thermos Product Company went so far as to boast, "Thermos is a household word," to its considerable cost. Donald F. Duncan, Inc., the original manufacturer of the *Yo-Yo*, lost its trademark protection partly because it was amazingly casual about capitalization in its own promotional literature. "In case you don't know what a yo-yo is . . ." one of its advertisements went, suggesting that in commercial terms Duncan didn't. Duncan also made the elemental error of declaring, "If It Isn't a Duncan, It Isn't a Yo-Yo," which on the face of it would seem a reasonable claim, but was in fact held by the courts to be inviting the reader to consider the product generic. Kodak had long since stopped saying "If it isn't an Eastman, it isn't a Kodak."

Because of the confusion, and occasional lack of fastidiousness on the part of their owners, many dozens of products have lost their trademark protection, among them *aspirin, linoleum, yo-yo, thermos, cellophane, milk of magnesia, mimeograph, lanolin, celluloid, dry ice, escalator, shredded wheat, kerosene,* and *zipper.* All were once proudly capitalized and worth a fortune.

On July 1, 1941, the New York television station WNBT-TV interrupted its normal viewing to show, without comment, a Bulova watch ticking. For sixty seconds the watch ticked away mysteriously, then the picture faded and normal programming resumed. It wasn't much, but it was the first television *commercial.*

Both the word and the idea were already well established. The first commercial — the term was used from the very beginning — had been broadcast by radio station WEAF in New York on August 28, 1922. It lasted for either ten or fifteen minutes, depending on which source you credit. Commercial radio was not an immediate hit. In its first two months, WEAF sold only $550 worth of airtime. But by the mid-1920s, sponsors were not only flocking to buy airtime but naming their programs after their products — *The Lucky Strike Hour, The A&P Gypsies, The Lux Radio Theater,* and so on. Such was the obsequiousness of the radio networks that by the early 1930s, many were allowing the sponsors to take complete artistic and production control of the programs. Many of the most popular shows were actually written by the advertising agencies, and the agencies naturally seldom missed an opportunity to work a favorable mention of the sponsor's products into the scripts.

With the rise of television in the 1950s, the practices of the radio era were effortlessly transferred to the new medium. Advertisers inserted their names into the program title — *Texaco Star Theater, Gillette Cavalcade of Sports, Chesterfield Sound-Off Time, The U.S. Steel Hour, Kraft Television Theater, The Chevy Show, The Alcoa Hour, The Ford Star Revue, Dick Clark's Beechnut Show,* and the arresting hybrid *The Lux-Schlitz Playhouse,* which seemed to suggest a cozy symbiosis between soapflakes and beer.

The commercial dominance of program titles reached a kind of hysterical peak with a program officially called *Your Kaiser Dealer Presents Kaiser-Frazer "Adventures in Mystery" Starring Betty Furness in "Byline."* Sponsors didn't write the programs any longer, but they did impose a firm control on the contents, most notoriously during a 1959 *Playhouse 90* broadcast of *Judgment at Nuremberg,* when the sponsor, the American Gas Association, managed to have all references to gas ovens and the gassing of Jews removed from the script.

Where commercial products of the late 1940s had scientific-sounding names, those of the 1950s relied increasingly on secret ingredients. Gleem toothpaste contained a mysterious piece of alchemy called *GL-70.*[3] There was never the slightest hint of what GL-70 was, but it would, according to the advertising, not only rout odor-causing bacteria but "wipe out their enzymes!"

A kind of creeping illiteracy invaded advertising, too, to the dismay of many. When Winston began advertising its cigarettes with the slogan "Winston tastes good like a cigarette should," nationally syndicated columnists like Sydney J. Harris wrote anguished essays on what the world was coming to — every educated person knew it should be "as a cigarette should" — but the die was cast. By 1958, Ford was advertising that you could "travel smooth" in a Thunderbird Sunliner and the maker of Ace Combs was urging buyers to "comb it handsome" — a trend that continues today with "pantihose that fits you real comfortable" and other grammatical manglings too numerous and dispiriting to dwell on.

We may smile at the advertising ruses of the 1920s — frightening people with the threat of "fallen stomach" and "scabby toes" — but in fact such creative manipulation still goes on, albeit at a slightly more sophisticated level. The *New York Times Magazine* reported in 1990 how an advertising copywriter had been told to come up with some impressive labels for a putative hand cream. She invented the arresting and healthful-sounding term *oxygenating moisturizers* and wrote accompanying copy with references to "tiny bubbles of oxygen that release moisture into your skin." This done, the advertising was turned over to the company's research and development department, which was instructed to come up with a product that matched the copy.

If we fall for such commercial manipulation, we have no one to blame but ourselves. When Kentucky Fried Chicken introduced "Extra Crispy" chicken to sell alongside its "Original" chicken, and sold it at the same price, sales were disappointing. But when its advertising agency persuaded it to promote "Extra Crispy" as a premium brand and to put the price up, sales soared. Much the same sort of verbal hypnosis was put

---

3. For purposes of research, I wrote to Procter & Gamble, Gleem's manufacturer, asking what GL-70 was, but the public relations department evidently thought it eccentric of me to wonder what I had been putting in my mouth all through childhood and declined to reply.

to work for the benefit of the fur industry. Dyed muskrat makes a perfectly good fur, for those who enjoy cladding themselves in dead animals,
but the name clearly lacks stylishness. The solution was to change the
name to *Hudson seal*. Never mind that the material contained not a
strand of seal fur. It sounded good, and sales skyrocketed.

Truth has seldom been a particularly visible feature of American ad-   40
vertising. In the early 1970s, Chevrolet ran a series of ads for the Chev-
elle boasting that the car had "109 advantages to keep it from becoming
old before its time." When looked into, it turned out that these 109
vaunted features included such items as rearview mirrors, backup lights,
balanced wheels, and many other components that were considered
pretty well basic to any car. Never mind; sales soared. At about the same
time, Ford, not to be outdone, introduced a "limited edition" Mercury
Monarch at $250 below the normal list price. It achieved this, it turned
out, by taking $250 worth of equipment off the standard Monarch.

And has all this deviousness led to a tightening of the rules concerning what is allowable in advertising? Hardly. In 1986, as William Lutz relates in *Doublespeak*, the insurance company John Hancock launched an
ad campaign in which "real people in real situations" discussed their financial predicaments with remarkable candor. When a journalist asked to
speak to these real people, a company spokesman conceded that they
were actors and "in that sense they are not real people."

During the 1982 presidential campaign, the Republican National
Committee ran a television advertisement praising President Reagan for
providing cost-of-living pay increases to federal workers "in spite of those
sticks-in-the-mud who tried to keep him from doing what we elected him
to do." When it was pointed out that the increases had in fact been mandated by law since 1975 and that Reagan had in any case three times tried
to block them, a Republican official responded: "Since when is a commercial supposed to be accurate?" Quite.

In linguistic terms, perhaps the most interesting challenge facing advertisers today is that of selling products in an increasingly multicultural society.
Spanish is a particular problem, not just because it is spoken over such a
widely scattered area but also because it is spoken in so many different
forms. Brown sugar is *azucar negra* in New York, *azucar prieta* in Miami,
azucar morena in much of Texas, and *azucar pardo* pretty much everywhere
else — and that's just one word. Much the same bewildering multiplicity applies to many others. In consequence, embarrassments are all but inevitable.

In mainstream Spanish, *bichos* means *insects*, but in Puerto Rico it
means *testicles*, so when a pesticide maker promised to bring death to the
bichos, Puerto Rican consumers were at least bemused, if not alarmed.
Much the same happened when a maker of bread referred to its product
as *un bollo de pan* and discovered that to Spanish-speaking Miamians of
Cuban extraction that means a woman's private parts. And when Perdue

Chickens translated its slogan "It takes a tough man to make a tender chicken" into Spanish, it came out as the slightly less macho "It takes a sexually excited man to make a chick sensual."

Never mind. Sales soared.   45

FOCUSING ON CONTENT

1. How did George Eastman use language to promote his products? Why do many consider Eastman an innovator in the business world? In what ways was he the founder of modern advertising practices?

2. It is important for companies to prevent their trademarks from becoming household words because they could lose their trademark protection. For example, advertisements for Kleenex and Xerox urge people to ask for a *tissue* or say they're going to *copy* a paper. Identify two or three current trademarks that you think could lose their trademark protection in the future, and explain your reasoning for choosing each trademark.

3. Bryson discusses what he calls a "creeping illiteracy" (37) that has invaded advertising. What form does this illiteracy take? In what ways might using poor English benefit advertisers?

4. In talking about the powers of advertising to persuade, Bryson discusses *commercial manipulation* and *verbal hypnosis* (39). What exactly does he mean by each term? How have advertisers used these techniques to sell their products? How do you think you as a consumer can guard against such advertising practices?

5. According to Bryson, what is one of the more interesting linguistic challenges facing today's advertisers?

FOCUSING ON WRITING

1. Why do you think Bryson begins his essay with an extensive passage on George Eastman before even mentioning advertising, the focus of his essay? Why is this background information important to the rest of the essay? (Glossary: *Beginnings and Endings*) What do you need to consider when writing an introduction to an essay?

2. What is Bryson's purpose in this essay — to express personal thoughts and feelings, to inform his audience, or to argue a particular position? (Glossary: *Purpose*) What in his essay leads you to this conclusion?

3. How does Bryson organize his essay? (Glossary: *Organization*) Is this organization appropriate for his subject matter and purpose? Explain.

4. Bryson peppers his essay with examples from the world of business and advertising. (Glossary: *Examples*) These examples serve not only to illustrate the points he makes but also to help establish his authority on the subject. Which examples do you find most effective? Least effective? Explain why.

LANGUAGE IN ACTION

In 1976, the Committee on Public Doublespeak (a committee of the National Council of Teachers of English) gave Professor Hugh Rank of Governors State University its Orwell Award for the Intensify/Downplay schema he developed to help people analyze public persuasion. As Rank explains, "All people *intensify* (commonly by *repetition, association, composition*) and *downplay* (commonly by *omission, diversion, confusion*) as they communicate in words, gestures, numbers, etc. But, 'professional persuaders' have more training, technology, money, and media access than the average citizen. Individuals can better cope with organized persuasion by recognizing the common ways that communication is intensified or downplayed, and by considering who is saying what to whom, with what intent and what result." Look closely at Rank's schema on pages 437 and 438, at the questions you can ask yourself about any type of advertisement.

Use Rank's schema to analyze the drinking-and-driving advertisements on pages 439–40. Find examples of intensifying and downplaying in each.

WRITING SUGGESTIONS

1. Think of a product that you have used and been disappointed by, one that has failed to live up to its advertising claims. Write a letter to the manufacturer in which you describe your experience with the product and explain why you believe the company's advertisements have been misleading. Send your letter to the president of the company or to the director of marketing.

2. Many product names are chosen because of their connotative or suggestive values. (Glossary: *Connotation/Denotation*) For example, the name *Tide* for a detergent suggests the power of the ocean tides and the rhythmic surge of cleansing waters; the name *Pride* for the wax suggests how the user will feel after using the product; the name *100% Natural* for the cereal suggests that the consumer is getting nothing less than nature's best; and the name *Taurus* for the Ford car suggests the strength and durability of a bull. Test what Bryson has said about brand names by exploring the connotations of the brand names in one of the following categories: cosmetics, deodorants, candy, paint, car batteries, fast-food sandwiches, pain relievers, disposable diapers, or cat food. You may find it helpful to read the article by J. C. Herz (pp. 638–40) in this connection. Report your findings in an essay.

3. In paragraph 12, Bryson reminds us that successful advertisers have always known the importance of good slogans. Some early slogans, such as the American Florist Association's "Say it with flowers," are still in use today even though they were coined years ago. Research five or six current product slogans that Bryson doesn't mention — like Microsoft's "Where do you want to go?" or Just for Men's "So natural no one can tell" — and write an essay in which you discuss the importance of slogans to advertising campaigns. How, for example, do slogans serve to focus, direct, and galvanize advertising campaigns? What do you think makes some slogans work and others fail? What makes a slogan memorable? As you start this project, you may find it helpful to search out materials in your library or on the Internet relating to slogans in general and how they engage people.

INTENSIFY

Repetition

How often have you seen the ad? On TV? In print? Do you recognize the **brand name? trademark? logo? company? package?** What key words or images repeated within ad? Any repetition patterns *(alliteration, anaphora, rhyme)* used? Any **slogan?** Can you hum or sing the **musical theme** or **jingle?** How long has this ad been running? How old were you when you first heard it? (For information on frequency, duration, and costs of ad campaigns, see *Advertising Age.)*

Association

What **"good things"** · already loved or desired by the intended audience · are associated with the product? Any links with basic needs *(food, activity, sex, security)?* With an appeal to save or gain money? With desire for certitude or outside approval (from *religion, science,* or the *"best," "most,"* or *"average" people)?* With desire for a sense of space *(neighborhood, nation, nature)?* With desire for love and belonging *(intimacy, family, groups)?* With other human desires *(esteem, play, generosity, curiosity, creativity, completion)?* Are **"bad things"** · things already hated or feared · stressed, as in a **"scare-and-sell"** ad? Are *problems* presented, with products as *solutions?* Are the speakers (models, endorsers) **authority figures:** people you respect, admire? Or **friend figures:** people you'd like as friends, identify with, or would like to be?

Composition

Look for the basic strategy of "the pitch": Hi . . . TRUST ME . . . YOU NEED . . . HURRY . . . BUY. What are the **attention-getting (HI)** words, images, devices? What are the **confidence-building (TRUST ME)** techniques: words, images, smiles, endorsers, brand names? Is the main **desire-stimulation (YOU NEED)** appeal focused on our benefit-seeking *to get* or *to keep* a "good," or *to avoid* or *to get rid of* a "bad"? Are you the **"target audience"?** If not, who is? Are you part of an unintended audience ? When and where did the ads appear? Are **product claims** made for: *superiority, quantity, beauty, efficiency, scarcity, novelty, stability, reliability, simplicity, utility, rapidity,* or *safety?* Are any **"added values"** suggested or implied by using any of the association techniques (see above)? Is there any **urgency-stressing (HURRY)** by words, movement, pace? Or is a "soft sell" conditioning for *later* purchase? Are there specific **response-triggering** words **(BUY):** to buy, to do, to call? Or is it conditioning (image building or public relations) to make us *"feel good"* about the company, to get favorable public opinion on *its* side *(against government regulations, laws, taxes)?* **Persuaders seek some kind of response!**

Omission

What "bad" aspects, disadvantages, drawbacks, hazards, have been **omitted** from the ad? Are there some unspoken assumptions? An unsaid story? Are some things implied or suggested, but not explicitly stated? Are there concealed problems concerning the **maker,** the **materials,** the **design,** the **use,** or the **purpose of the product? Are there any unwanted or harmful side effects:** *unsafe, unhealthy, uneconomical, inefficient, unneeded?* Does any **"disclosure law"** exist (or is needed) requiring public warning about a concealed hazard? In the ad, what gets less time, less attention, smaller print? *(Most ads are true, but incomplete.)*

Diversion

What benefits (low cost, high speed, etc.) get high priority in the ad's claim and promises? Are these **your** priorities? Significant, important to you? Is there any **"bait-and-switch"**? *(Ad stresses* low cost, *but the actual seller switches buyer's priority to* high quality.) Does ad divert focus from **key issues,** important things *(e.g., nutrition, health, safety)*? Does ad focus on **side-issues,** unmeaningful trivia *(common in parity products)*? Does ad divert attention from your other choices, other options: buy something else, use less, use less often, rent, borrow, share, do without? *(Ads need not show other choices, but* you *should know them.)*

Confusion

Are the words clear or ambiguous? Specific or vague? Are claims and promises absolute, or are there qualifying words *("may help," "some")*? Is the claim measurable? Or is it **"puffery"**? *(Laws permit most "sellers's talk"   of such general praise and subjective opinions.)* Are the words common, understandable, familiar? Uncommon? Jargon? Any parts difficult to "translate" or explain to others? Are analogies clear? Are comparisons within the same kind? Are examples related? Typical? Adequate? Enough examples? Any contradictions? Inconsistencies? Errors? Are there frequent changes, variations, revisions *(in size, price, options, extras, contents, packaging)*? Is it too complex: too much, too many? Disorganized? Incoherent? Unsorted? Any confusing statistics? Numbers? Do you know exact costs? Benefits? Risks? Are **your own goals,** priorities, and desires clear or vague? Fixed or shifting? Simple or complex? *(Confusion can also exist within us as well as within an ad. If any confusion exists: slow down, take care.)*

DOWNPLAY

Drive drunk and you could have a date with death. Get caught, and all your dates will be with Mom. Don't drink and drive or ride with a drunk driver.

PICTURING LANGUAGE

What statement is the cartoon "Sign Language" making about the influence of advertising and commercialism on our beliefs and behavior? Does the cartoon exaggerate the power of advertising in our lives? Explain. Why does the female protogonist in the cartoon find it necessary to use the billboard to "advertise" her own message? Why is a cartoon a good vehicle for conveying this message about the power of advertising?

Weasel Words: The Art of Saying Nothing at All

WILLIAM LUTZ

William Lutz, professor of English at Rutgers University, edits the Quarterly Review of Doublespeak. *Originally from Racine, Wisconsin, Lutz is best known for his important works* Doublespeak: From "Revenue Enhancement" to "Terminal Living" *(1990) and* The New Doublespeak: Why No One Knows What Anyone's Saying Anymore *(1996). His most recent book,* Doublespeak Defined: Cut through the Bull**** and Get to the Point, *was published in 1999. The term* doublespeak *comes from the Newspeak vocabulary of George Orwell's novel* Nineteen Eighty-Four. *It refers to speech or writing that presents two or more contradictory ideas in such a way that an unsuspecting audience is not consciously aware of the contradiction and is likely to be deceived. As chair of the National Council of Teachers of English's Committee on Public Doublespeak, Lutz has been a watchdog of public officials and business leaders who use language to "mislead, distort, deceive, inflate, circumvent, and obfuscate." Each year the committee presents the Orwell Awards, recognizing the most outrageous uses of public doublespeak in government and business.*

In the following excerpt from his book Doublespeak, *Lutz reveals some of the ways that advertisers use language to imply great things about products and services without promising anything at all. With considerable skill, advertisers can produce ads that make us believe a certain product is better than it is without actually lying about it. Lutz's word-by-word analysis of advertising claims reveals how misleading — and ridiculous — these slogans and claims can be.*

WRITING TO DISCOVER: *Imagine what it would be like if you were suddenly transported to a world in which there were no advertisements and no one trying to sell you a product. Write about how you would decide what to buy. How would you learn about new products? Would you prefer to live in such a world? Why or why not?*

WEASEL WORDS

One problem advertisers have when they try to convince you that the product they are pushing is really different from other, similar products is that their claims are subject to some laws. Not a lot of laws, but there are some designed to prevent fraudulent or untruthful claims in advertising. Even during the happy years of nonregulation under President Ronald Reagan, the FTC did crack down on the more blatant abuses in advertising

442

claims. Generally speaking, advertisers have to be careful in what they say in their ads, in the claims they make for the products they advertise. Parity claims are safe because they are legal and supported by a number of court decisions. But beyond parity claims there are weasel words.

Advertisers use weasel words to appear to be making a claim for a product when in fact they are making no claim at all. Weasel words get their name from the way weasels eat the eggs they find in the nests of other animals. A weasel will make a small hole in the egg, suck out the insides, then place the egg back in the nest. Only when the egg is examined closely is it found to be hollow. That's the way it is with weasel words in advertising: Examine weasel words closely and you'll find that they're as hollow as any egg sucked by a weasel. Weasel words appear to say one thing when in fact they say the opposite, or nothing at all.

"Help" — The Number One Weasel Word

The biggest weasel word used in advertising doublespeak is "help." Now "help" only means to aid or assist, nothing more. It does not mean to conquer, stop, eliminate, end, solve, heal, cure, or anything else. But once the ad says "help," it can say just about anything after that because "help" qualifies everything coming after it. The trick is that the claim that comes after the weasel word is usually so strong and so dramatic that you forget the word "help" and concentrate only on the dramatic claim. You read into the ad a message that the ad does not contain. More importantly, the advertiser is not responsible for the claim that you read into the ad, even though the advertiser wrote the ad so you would read that claim into it.

The next time you see an ad for a cold medicine that promises that it "helps relieve cold symptoms fast," don't rush out to buy it. Ask yourself what this claim is really saying. Remember, "help" means only that the medicine will aid or assist. What will it aid or assist in doing? Why, "relieve" your cold "symptoms." "Relieve" only means to ease, alleviate, or mitigate, not to stop, end, or cure. Nor does the claim say how much relieving this medicine will do. Nowhere does this ad claim it will cure anything. In fact, the ad doesn't even claim it will *do* anything at all. The ad only claims that it will aid in relieving (not curing) your cold symptoms, which are probably a runny nose, watery eyes, and a headache. In other words, this medicine probably contains a standard decongestant and some aspirin. By the way, what does "fast" mean? Ten minutes, one hour, one day? What is fast to one person can be very slow to another. Fast is another weasel word.

Ad claims using "help" are among the most popular ads. One says, 5 "Helps keep you young looking," but then a lot of things will help keep you young looking, including exercise, rest, good nutrition, and a facelift. More importantly, this ad doesn't say the product will keep you young, only "young *looking.*" Someone may look young to one person and old to another.

A toothpaste ad says, "Helps prevent cavities," but it doesn't say it will actually prevent cavities. Brushing your teeth regularly, avoiding sugars in food, and flossing daily will also help prevent cavities. A liquid cleaner ad says, "Helps keep your home germ free," but it doesn't say it actually kills germs, nor does it even specify which germs it might kill.

"Help" is such a useful weasel word that it is often combined with other action-verb weasel words such as "fight" and "control." Consider the claim, "Helps control dandruff symptoms with regular use." What does it really say? It will assist in controlling (not eliminating, stopping, ending, or curing) the *symptoms* of dandruff, not the cause of dandruff nor the dandruff itself. What are the symptoms of dandruff? The ad deliberately leaves that undefined, but assume that the symptoms referred to in the ad are the flaking and itching commonly associated with dandruff. But just shampooing with *any* shampoo will temporarily eliminate these symptoms, so this shampoo isn't any different from any other. Finally, in order to benefit from this product, you must use it regularly. What is "regular use" — daily, weekly, hourly? Using another shampoo "regularly" will have the same effect. Nowhere does this advertising claim say this particular shampoo stops, eliminates, or cures dandruff. In fact, this claim says nothing at all, thanks to all the weasel words.

Look at ads in magazines and newspapers, listen to ads on radio and television, and you'll find the word "help" in ads for all kinds of products. How often do you read or hear such phrases as "helps stop . . . ," "helps overcome . . . ," "helps eliminate . . . ," "helps you feel . . . ," or "helps you look . . ."? If you start looking for this weasel word in advertising, you'll be amazed at how often it occurs. Analyze the claims in the ads using "help," and you will discover that these ads are really saying nothing.

There are plenty of other weasel words used in advertising. In fact, there are so many that to list them all would fill the rest of this book. But, in order to identify the doublespeak of advertising and understand the real meaning of an ad, you have to be aware of the most popular weasel words in advertising today.

Virtually Spotless

One of the most powerful weasel words is "virtually," a word so in- 10
nocent that most people don't pay any attention to it when it is used in an advertising claim. But watch out. "Virtually" is used in advertising claims that appear to make specific, definite promises when there is no promise. After all, what does "virtually" mean? It means "in essence or effect, although not in fact." Look at that definition again. "Virtually" means *not in fact.* It does *not* mean "almost" or "just about the same as," or anything else. And before you dismiss all this concern over such a small word, remember that small words can have big consequences.

In 1971 a federal court rendered its decision on a case brought by a woman who became pregnant while taking birth control pills. She sued the manufacturer, Eli Lilly and Company, for breach of warranty. The woman lost her case. Basing its ruling on a statement in the pamphlet accompanying the pills, which stated that, "When taken as directed, the tablets offer virtually 100 percent protection," the court ruled that there was no warranty, expressed or implied, that the pills were absolutely effective. In its ruling, the court pointed out that, according to *Webster's Third New International Dictionary,* "virtually" means "almost entirely" and clearly does not mean "absolute" (*Whittington* v. *Eli Lilly and Company,* 333 F. Supp. 98). In other words, the Eli Lilly company was really saying that its birth control pill, even when taken as directed, *did not in fact* provide 100 percent protection against pregnancy. But Eli Lilly didn't want to put it that way because then many women might not have bought Lilly's birth control pills.

The next time you see the ad that says that this dishwasher detergent "leaves dishes virtually spotless," just remember how advertisers twist the meaning of the weasel word "virtually." You can have lots of spots on your dishes after using this detergent and the ad claim will still be true, because what this claim really means is that this detergent does not *in fact* leave your dishes spotless. Whenever you see or hear an ad claim that uses the word "virtually," just translate that claim into its real meaning. So the television set that is "virtually trouble free" becomes the television set that is not in fact trouble free, the "virtually foolproof operation" of any appliance becomes an operation that is in fact not foolproof, and the product that "virtually never needs service" becomes the product that is not in fact service free.

New and Improved

If "new" is the most frequently used word on a product package, "improved" is the second most frequent. In fact, the two words are almost always used together. It seems just about everything sold these days is "new and improved." The next time you're in the supermarket, try counting the number of times you see these words on products. But you'd better do it while you're walking down just one aisle, otherwise you'll need a calculator to keep track of your counting.

Just what do these words mean? The use of the word "new" is restricted by regulations, so an advertiser can't just use the word on a product or in an ad without meeting certain requirements. For example, a product is considered new for about six months during a national advertising campaign. If the product is being advertised only in a limited test market area, the word can be used longer, and in some instances has been used for as long as two years.

What makes a product "new"? Some products have been around for a long time, yet every once in a while you discover that they are being   15 advertised as "new." Well, an advertiser can call a product new if there has been "a material functional change" in the product. What is "a material functional change," you ask? Good question. In fact it's such a good question it's being asked all the time. It's up to the manufacturer to prove that the product has undergone such a change. And if the manufacturer isn't challenged on the claim, then there's no one to stop it. Moreover, the change does not have to be an improvement in the product. One manufacturer added an artificial lemon scent to a cleaning product and called it "new and improved," even though the product did not clean any better than without the lemon scent. The manufacturer defended the use of the word "new" on the grounds that the artificial scent changed the chemical formula of the product and therefore constituted "a material functional change."

Which brings up the word "improved." When used in advertising, "improved" does not mean "made better." It only means "changed" or "different from before." So, if the detergent maker puts a plastic pour spout on the box of detergent, the product has been "improved," and away we go with a whole new advertising campaign. Or, if the cereal maker adds more fruit or a different kind of fruit to the cereal, there's an improved product. Now you know why manufacturers are constantly making little changes in their products. Whole new advertising campaigns, designed to convince you that the product has been changed for the better, are based on small changes in superficial aspects of a product. The next time you see an ad for an "improved" product, ask yourself what was wrong with the old one. Ask yourself just how "improved" the product is. Finally, you might check to see whether the "improved" version costs more than the unimproved one. After all, someone has to pay for the millions of dollars spent advertising the improved product.

Of course, advertisers really like to run ads that claim a product is "new and improved." While what constitutes a "new" product may be subject to some regulation, "improved" is a subjective judgment. A manufacturer changes the shape of its stick deodorant, but the shape doesn't improve the function of the deodorant. That is, changing the shape doesn't affect the deodorizing ability of the deodorant, so the manufacturer calls it "improved." Another manufacturer adds ammonia to its liquid cleaner and calls it "new and improved." Since adding ammonia does affect the cleaning ability of the product, there has been a "material functional change" in the product, and the manufacturer can now call its cleaner "new," and "improved" as well. Now the weasel words "new and improved" are plastered all over the package and are the basis for a multimillion-dollar ad campaign. But after six months the word "new" will have to go, until someone can dream up another change in the product. Perhaps it will be adding color to the liquid, or changing the shape of the package, or maybe adding a new dripless pour spout, or perhaps a ___.

The "improvements" are endless, and so are the new advertising claims and campaigns.

"New" is just too useful and powerful a word in advertising for advertisers to pass it up easily. So they use weasel words that say "new" without really saying it. One of their favorites is "introducing," as in, "Introducing improved Tide," or "Introducing the stain remover." The first is simply saying, here's our improved soap; the second, here's our new advertising campaign for our detergent. Another favorite is "now," as in, "Now there's Sinex," which simply means that Sinex is available. Then there are phrases like "Today's Chevrolet," "Presenting Dristan," and "A fresh way to start the day." The list is really endless because advertisers are always finding new ways to say "new" without really saying it. If there is a second edition of [my] book, I'll just call it the "new and improved" edition. Wouldn't you really rather have a "new and improved" edition of [my] book rather than a "second" edition?

Acts Fast

"Acts" and "works" are two popular weasel words in advertising because they bring action to the product and to the advertising claim. When you see the ad for the cough syrup that "Acts on the cough control center," ask yourself what this cough syrup is claiming to do. Well, it's just claiming to "act," to do something, to perform an action. What is it that the cough syrup does? The ad doesn't say. It only claims to perform an action or do something on your "cough control center." By the way, what and where is your "cough control center"? I don't remember learning about that part of the body in human biology class.

Ads that use such phrases as "acts fast," "acts against," "acts to pre-   20
vent," and the like are saying essentially nothing, because "act" is a word empty of any specific meaning. The ads are always careful not to specify exactly what "act" the product performs. Just because a brand of aspirin claims to "act fast" for headache relief doesn't mean this aspirin is any better than any other aspirin. What is the "act" that this aspirin performs? You're never told. Maybe it just dissolves quickly. Since aspirin is a parity product, all aspirin is the same and therefore functions the same.

Works Like Anything Else

If you don't find the word "acts" in an ad, you will probably find the weasel word "works." In fact, the two words are almost interchangeable in advertising. Watch out for ads that say a product "works against," "works like," "works for," or "works longer." As with "acts," "works" is the same meaningless verb used to make you think that this product really does something, and maybe even something special or unique. But "works," like "acts," is basically a word empty of any specific meaning.

Like Magic

Whenever advertisers want you to stop thinking about the product and to start thinking about something bigger, better, or more attractive than the product, they use that very popular weasel word "like." The word "like" is the advertiser's equivalent of a magician's use of misdirection. "Like" gets you to ignore the product and concentrate on the claim the advertiser is making about it. "For skin like peaches and cream" claims the ad for a skin cream. What is this ad really claiming? It doesn't say this cream will give you peaches-and-cream skin. There is no verb in this claim, so it doesn't even mention using the product. How is skin ever like "peaches and cream"? Remember, ads must be read literally and exactly, according to the dictionary definition of words. (Remember "virtually" in the Eli Lilly case.) The ad is making absolutely no promise or claim whatsoever for this skin cream. If you think this cream will give you soft, smooth, youthful-looking skin, you are the one who has read that meaning into the ad.

The wine that claims "It's like taking a trip to France" wants you to think about a romantic evening in Paris as you walk along the boulevard after a wonderful meal in an intimate little bistro. Of course, you don't really believe that a wine can take you to France, but the goal of the ad is to get you to think pleasant, romantic thoughts about France and not about how the wine tastes or how expensive it may be. That little word "like" has taken you away from crushed grapes into a world of your own imaginative making. Who knows, maybe the next time you buy wine, you'll think those pleasant thoughts when you see this brand of wine, and you'll buy it. Or, maybe you weren't even thinking about buying wine at all, but now you just might pick up a bottle the next time you're shopping. Ah, the power of "like" in advertising.

How about the most famous "like" claim of all, "Winston tastes good like a cigarette should"? Ignoring the grammatical error here, you might want to know what this claim is saying. Whether a cigarette tastes good or bad is a subjective judgment because what tastes good to one person may well taste horrible to another. Not everyone likes fried snails, even if they are called escargot. (*De gustibus non est disputandum*, which was probably the Roman rule for advertising as well as for defending the games in the Colosseum.) There are many people who say all cigarettes taste terrible, other people who say only some cigarettes taste all right, and still others who say all cigarettes taste good. Who's right? Everyone, because taste is a matter of personal judgment.

Moreover, note the use of the conditional, "should." The complete claim is, "Winston tastes good like a cigarette should taste." But should cigarettes taste good? Again, this is a matter of personal judgment and probably depends most on one's experiences with smoking. So, the Winston ad is simply saying that Winston cigarettes are just like any other

25

cigarette: Some people like them and some people don't. On that statement R. J. Reynolds conducted a very successful multimillion-dollar advertising campaign that helped keep Winston the number-two-selling cigarette in the United States, close behind number one, Marlboro.

CAN IT BE UP TO THE CLAIM?

Analyzing ads for doublespeak requires that you pay attention to every word in the ad and determine what each word really means. Advertisers try to wrap their claims in language that sounds concrete, specific, and objective, when in fact the language of advertising is anything but. Your job is to read carefully and listen critically so that when the announcer says that "Crest can be of significant value . . ." you know immediately that this claim says absolutely nothing. Where is the doublespeak in this ad? Start with the second word.

Once again, you have to look at what words really mean, not what you think they mean or what the advertiser wants you to think they mean. The ad for Crest only says that using Crest "can be" of "significant value." What really throws you off in this ad is the brilliant use of "significant." It draws your attention to the word "value" and makes you forget that the ad only claims that Crest "can be." The ad doesn't say that Crest *is* of value, only that it is "able" or "possible" to be of value, because that's all that "can" means.

It's so easy to miss the importance of those little words, "can be." Almost as easy as missing the importance of the words "up to" in an ad. These words are very popular in sale ads. You know, the ones that say, "Up to 50% Off!" Now, what does that claim mean? Not much, because the store or manufacturer has to reduce the price of only a few items by 50 percent. Everything else can be reduced a lot less, or not even reduced. Moreover, don't you want to know 50 pecent off of what? Is it 50 percent off the "manufacturer's suggested list price," which is the highest possible price? Was the price artificially inflated and then reduced? In other ads, "up to" expresses an ideal situation. The medicine that works "up to ten times faster," the battery that lasts "up to twice as long," and the soap that gets you "up to twice as clean" all are based on ideal situations for using those products, situations in which you can be sure you will never find yourself.

UNFINISHED WORDS

Unfinished words are a kind of "up to" claim in advertising. The claim that a battery lasts "up to twice as long" usually doesn't finish the comparison — twice as long as what? A birthday candle? A tank of gas? A cheap battery made in a country not noted for its technological achievements? The implication is that the battery lasts twice as long as batteries made by other battery makers, or twice as long as earlier model batteries made by the advertiser, but the ad doesn't really make these claims. You read these claims into the ad, aided by the visual images the advertiser so carefully provides.

Unfinished words depend on you to finish them, to provide the   30
words the advertisers so thoughtfully left out of the ad. Pall Mall cigarettes were once advertised as "A longer finer and milder smoke." The question is, longer, finer, and milder than what? The aspirin that claims it contains "Twice as much of the pain reliever doctors recommend most" doesn't tell you what pain reliever it contains twice as much of. (By the way, it's aspirin. That's right; it just contains twice the amount of aspirin. And how much is twice the amount? Twice of what amount?) Panadol boasts that "nobody reduces fever faster," but, since Panadol is a parity product, this claim simply means that Panadol isn't any better than any other product in its parity class. "You can be sure if it's Westinghouse," you're told, but just exactly what it is you can be sure of is never mentioned. "Magnavox gives you more" doesn't tell you what you get more of. More value? More television? More than they gave you before? It sounds nice, but it means nothing, until you fill in the claim with your own words, the words the advertiser didn't use. Since each of us fills in the claim differently, the ad and the product can become all things to all people, and not promise a single thing.

Unfinished words abound in advertising because they appear to promise so much. More importantly, they can be joined with powerful visual images on television to appear to be making significant promises about a product's effectiveness without really making any promises. In a television ad, the aspirin product that claims fast relief can show a person with a headache taking the product and then, in what appears to be a matter of minutes, claiming complete relief. This visual image is far more powerful than any claim made in unfinished words. Indeed, the visual image completes the unfinished words for you, filling in with pictures what the words leave out. And you thought that ads didn't affect you. What brand of aspirin do you use?

Some years ago, Ford's advertisements proclaimed "Ford LTD — 700 percent quieter." Now, what do you think Ford was claiming with these unfinished words? What was the Ford LTD quieter than? A Cadillac? A Mercedes Benz? A BMW? Well, when the FTC asked Ford to substantiate this unfinished claim, Ford replied that it meant that the inside of the LTD was 700 percent quieter than the outside. How did you finish those unfinished words when you first read them? Did you even come close to Ford's meaning?

COMBINING WEASEL WORDS

A lot of ads don't fall neatly into one category or another because they use a variety of different devices and words. Different weasel words are often combined to make an ad claim. The claim, "Coffee-Mate gives coffee more body, more flavor," uses unfinished words ("more" than what?) and also uses words that have no specific meaning ("body" and "flavor"). Along with "taste" (remember the Winston ad and its claim to taste good), "body" and "flavor" mean nothing because their meaning is entirely subjective. To you, "body" in coffee might mean thick, black, almost bitter coffee, while I might take it to mean a light brown, delicate coffee. Now, if you think you understood that last sentence, read it again, because it said nothing of objective value; it was filled with weasel words of no specific meaning: "thick," "black," "bitter," "light brown," and "delicate." Each of those words has no specific, objective meaning, because each of us can interpret them differently.

Try this slogan: "Looks, smells, tastes like ground-roast coffee." So, are you now going to buy Taster's Choice instant coffee because of this ad? "Looks," "smells," and "tastes" are all words with no specific meaning and depend on your interpretation of them for any meaning. Then there's that great weasel word "like," which simply suggests a comparison but does not make the actual connection between the product and the quality. Besides, do you know what "ground-roast" coffee is? I don't, but it sure sounds good. So, out of seven words in this ad, four are definite weasel words, two are quite meaningless, and only one has clear meaning.

Remember the Anacin ad — "Twice as much of the pain reliever doctors recommend most"? There's a whole lot of weaseling going on in this ad. First, what's the pain reliever they're talking about in this ad? Aspirin, of course. In fact, any time you see or hear an ad using those words "pain reliever," you can automatically substitute the word "aspirin" for them. (Makers of acetaminophen and ibuprofen pain relievers are careful in their advertising to identify their products as nonaspirin products.) So, now we know that Anacin has aspirin in it. Moreover, we know that Anacin has twice as much aspirin in it, but we don't know twice as much as what. Does it have twice as much aspirin as an ordinary aspirin tablet? If so, what is a ordinary aspirin tablet, and how much aspirin does it contain? Twice as much as Excedrin or Bufferin? Twice as much as a chocolate chip cookie? Remember those unfinished words and how they lead you on without saying anything.

Finally, what about those doctors who are doing all that recommending? Who are they? How many of them are there? What kind of doctors are they? What are their qualifications? Who asked them about recommending pain relievers? What other pain relievers did they recommend? And there are a whole lot more questions about this "poll" of doctors to which I'd like to know the answers, but you get the point. Sometimes, when I call my doctor, she tells me to take two aspirin and call her office in the morning. Is that where Anacin got this ad?

FOCUSING ON CONTENT

1. What are weasel words? How, according to Lutz, did they get their name?

2. According to Lutz, why is *help* the biggest weasel word used by advertisers (3–8)? In what ways does it help them present their products without having to make promises about actual performance?

3. Why is *virtually* a particularly effective weasel word (10–12)? Why can advertisers get away with using words that literally mean the opposite of what they want to convey?

4. When advertisers use the word *like*, they often create a simile — "Ajax cleans *like* a white tornado." What, according to Lutz, is the power of similes in advertising (22–24)? Explain by citing several examples of your own.

5. What kinds of claims fit into Lutz's "unfinished words" category (29–32)? Why are they weasels? What makes them so difficult to detect?

6. Which of the various types of weasel words do you find most insidious? Why?

FOCUSING ON WRITING

1. What is Lutz's purpose in writing this essay? (Glossary: *Purpose*)

2. Lutz is careful to illustrate each of the various kinds of weasel words with examples of actual usage. (Glossary: *Examples*) What do these examples add to his essay? Which ones do you find most effective? Explain.

3. For what audience do you think Lutz wrote this essay? (Glossary: *Audience*) Do you consider yourself part of this audience? Do you find Lutz's diction and tone appropriate for his audience? (Glossary: *Diction* and *Tone*) Explain.

4. Lutz uses the strategy of division and classification to develop this essay. (Glossary: *Division and Classification*) Explain how he uses this strategy. Why do you suppose Lutz felt the need to create the "Combining Weasel Words" category? Did the headings in the essay help you follow his discussion? What would be lost had he not included them?

LANGUAGE IN ACTION

Carefully read the text in the advertisement on the opposite page. Jot down any words that Lutz would describe as weasels. How does recognizing such language affect your impression of the product being advertised? What would happen to the text of the ad if the weasels were eliminated?

WRITING SUGGESTIONS

1. Choose something that you own and like — a mountain bike, a CD or video collection, luggage, a comfortable sofa, a boombox, or anything else that you are glad you bought. Imagine that you need to sell it to raise some money for a special weekend, and to do so you need to advertise on radio. Write copy for a 30-second advertising spot in which you try to sell your item. Include a slogan or make up a product name and use it in the ad. Then write a short essay about your ad in which you discuss the features of your item you chose to highlight, the language you used to make it sound as appealing as possible, and how your slogan or name makes the advertisement more memorable.

2. Pay attention to the ads for companies that offer rival products or services (for example, Apple and IBM, Coca-Cola and Pepsi-Cola, Burger King and McDonald's, Charles Schwab and Smith Barney, and AT&T and MCI). Focusing on a single pair of ads, analyze the different appeals that companies make when comparing their products or services to those of the competition. To what audience does each ad appeal? How many weasel words can you detect? How does each ad use Intensify/Downplay (pp. 437–38) techniques to its product's advantage? Based on your analysis, write an essay about the advertising strategies companies use when in head-to-head competition with the products of other companies.

3. Look at several issues of one popular women's or men's magazine (such as *Cosmopolitan, Vogue, Elle, Glamour, Sports Illustrated, GQ, Playboy, Car and Driver, Field and Stream*), and analyze the advertisements they contain. What types of products or services are advertised? Which ads caught your eye? Why? Are the ads made up primarily of pictures, or do some have a lot of text? Do you detect any relationship beween the ads and the editorial content of the magazine? Write an essay in which you present the findings of your analysis.

How to Advertise a Dangerous Product

James B. Twitchell

Cultural critic and advertising historian James B. Twitchell was born in Burlington, Vermont, in 1943. After graduating from the University of Vermont in 1962, he attended the University of North Carolina at Chapel Hill where he earned his Ph.D. in 1969. Later he embarked on a career in education, teaching first at Duke University and then at the California State College at Bakersfield. Currently he is the Alumni Professor of English at the University of Florida where he teaches courses in writing, advertising, popular culture, and romantic literature. Twitchell has written widely on advertising and material culture in America. His books include Adcult USA: The Triumph of Advertising in American Culture *(1996),* For Shame: The Loss of Common Decency in American Culture *(1997),* Lead Us into Temptation: The Triumph of American Materialism *(1999), and* Living It Up: Our Love Affair with Luxury *(2001). The following essay is a chapter in Twitchell's book* Twenty Ads That Shook the World: The Century's Most Groundbreaking Advertising and How It Changed Us All *(2000). Here he discusses the development of the ad campaign that introduced "Miss Clairol Hair Color Bath" to America in the 1950s. He takes us behind the scenes to better appreciate the verbal and visual strategies of Shirley Polykoff's original Miss Clairol ad campaign.*

WRITING TO DISCOVER: *Imagine that you have been given the assignment to write an advertisement for one of the following products: paper napkins, skim milk, laundry detergent, staples, or pizza. Explain how you would market your product. What "claims" could you make for your product to help distinguish it from similar products?*

Two types of products are difficult to advertise: the very common and the very radical. Common products, called "parity products," need contrived distinctions to set them apart. You announce them as "New and Improved, Bigger and Better." But singular products need the illusion of acceptability. They have to appear as if they were *not* new and big, but old and small.

So, in the 1950s, new objects like television sets were designed to look like furniture so that they would look "at home" in your living room. Meanwhile, accepted objects like automobiles were growing massive tail fins to make them seem bigger and better, new and improved.

Although hair coloring is now very common (about half of all American women between the ages of thirteen and seventy color their hair, and about one in eight American males between thirteen and seventy does the same), such was certainly not the case generations ago. The only women who regularly dyed their hair were actresses like Jean Harlow, and "fast women," most especially prostitutes. The only man who dyed his hair was Gorgeous George, the professional wrestler. He was also the only man to use perfume.

In the twentieth century, prostitutes have had a central role in developing cosmetics. For them, sexiness is an occupational necessity, and hence anything that makes them look young, flushed, and fertile is quickly assimilated. Creating a full-lipped, big-eyed, and rosy-cheeked image is the basis of the lipstick, eye shadow, mascara, and rouge industries. While fashion may come *down* from the couturiers, face paint comes *up* from the street. Yesterday's painted woman is today's fashion plate.

In the 1950s, just as Betty Friedan was sitting down to write *The Feminine Mystique,* there were three things a lady should not do. She should not smoke in public, she should not wear long pants (unless under an overcoat), and she should not color her hair. Better she should pull out each gray strand by its root than risk association with those who bleached or, worse, dyed their hair.

This was the cultural context into which Lawrence M. Gelb, a chemical broker and enthusiastic entrepreneur, presented his product to Foote, Cone & Belding. Gelb had purchased the rights to a French hair-coloring process called Clairol. The process was unique in that unlike other available hair-coloring products, which coated the hair, Clairol actually penetrated the hair shaft, producing softer, more natural tones. Moreover, it contained a foamy shampoo base and mild oils that cleaned and conditioned the hair.

When the product was first introduced during World War II, the application process took five different steps and lasted a few hours. The users were urban and wealthy. In 1950, after seven years of research and development, Gelb once again took the beauty industry by storm. He introduced the new Miss Clairol Hair Color Bath, a single-step hair-coloring process.

This product, unlike any hair color previously available, lightened, darkened, or changed a woman's natural hair color by coloring and shampooing hair in one simple step that took only twenty minutes. Color results were more natural than anything you could find at the corner beauty parlor. It was hard to believe. Miss Clairol was so technologically advanced that demonstrations had to be done onstage at the International Beauty Show, using buckets of water, to prove to the industry that it was not a hoax. This breakthrough was almost too revolutionary to sell.

In fact, within six months of Miss Clairol's introduction, the number of women who visited the salon for permanent hair-coloring services increased by more than five hundred percent! The women still didn't think they could do it themselves. And *Good Housekeeping* magazine rejected hair-color advertising because they too didn't believe the product would work. The magazine waited for three years before finally reversing its decision, accepting the ads, and awarding Miss Clairol's new product the "Good Housekeeping Seal of Approval."

FC&B passed the "Yes you *can* do it at home" assignment to Shirley   10
Polykoff, a zesty and genial first-generation American in her late twenties. She was, as she herself was the first to admit, a little unsophisticated, but her colleagues thought she understood how women would respond to abrupt change. Polykoff understood emotion, all right, and she also knew that you could be outrageous if you did it in the right context. You can be very naughty if you are first perceived as being nice. Or, in her words, "Think it out square, say it with flair." And it is just this reconciliation of opposites that informs her most famous ad.

She knew this almost from the start. On July 9, 1955, Polykoff wrote to the head art director that she had three campaigns for Miss Clairol Hair Color Bath. The first shows the same model in each ad, but with slightly different hair color. The second exhorts "Tear up those baby pictures! You're a redhead now," and plays on the American desire to refashion the self by rewriting history. These two ideas were, as she says, "knock-downs" en route to what she really wanted. In her autobiography, appropriately titled *Does She . . . Or Doesn't She?: And How She Did It,* Polykoff explains the third execution, the one that will work:

> #3. Now here's the one I really want. If I can get it sold to the client. Listen to this: "*Does she . . . or doesn't she?*" (No. I'm not kidding. Didn't you ever hear of the arresting question?) Followed by: "*Only her mother knows for sure!*" or "*So natural, only her mother knows for sure!*"
>
> I may not do the mother part, though as far as I'm concerned mother is the ultimate authority. However, if Clairol goes retail, they may have a problem of offending beauty salons, where they are presently doing all of their business. So I may change the word "mother" to "hairdresser." This could be awfully good business — turning the hairdresser into a color expert. Besides, it reinforces the claim of naturalness, and not so incidentally, glamorizes the salon.
>
> The psychology is obvious. I know from myself. If anyone admires my hair, I'd rather die than admit I dye. And since I feel so strongly that the average woman is me, this great stress on naturalness is important.[1]

While her headline is naughty, the picture is nice and natural. Exactly what "Does She . . . Or Doesn't She" do? To men the answer was clearly sexual, but to women it certainly was not. The male editors of *Life*

---

1. Shirley Polykoff, *Does She . . . Or Doesn't She?: And How She Did It* (Garden City, N.Y.: Doubleday, 1975), 28–29.

magazine balked about running this headline until they did a survey and found out women were not filling in the ellipsis the way they were.

Women, as Polykoff knew, were finding different meaning because they were actually looking at the model and her child. For them the picture was not presexual but postsexual, not inviting male attention but expressing satisfaction with the result. Miss Clairol is a mother, not a love interest.

If that is so, then the product must be misnamed: it should be *Mrs.* Clairol. Remember, this was the mid-1950s, when illegitimacy was a powerful taboo. Out-of-wedlock children were still called bastards, not love children. This ad was far more dangerous than anything Benetton or Calvin Klein has ever imagined.

The naughty/nice conundrum was further intensified *and* diffused   15
by some of the ads featuring a wedding ring on the model's left hand. Although FC&B experimented with models purporting to be secretaries, schoolteachers, and the like, the motif of mother and child was always constant.

So what was the answer to what she does or doesn't do? To women, what she did had to do with visiting the hairdresser. Of course, men couldn't understand. This was the world before unisex hair care. Men still went to barber shops. This was the same pre-feminist generation in which the solitary headline "Modess . . . because" worked magic selling female sanitary products. The ellipsis masked a knowing implication that excluded men. That was part of its attraction. Women know, men don't. This you-just-don't-get-it motif was to become a central marketing strategy as the women's movement was aided *and* exploited by Madison Avenue nichemeisters.

Polykoff had to be ambiguous for another reason. As she notes in her memo, Clairol did not want to be obvious about what they were doing to their primary customer — the beauty shop. Remember that the initial product entailed five different steps performed by the hairdresser, and lasted hours. Many women were still using hairdressers for something they could now do by themselves. It did not take a detective to see that the company was trying to run around the beauty shop and sell to the end-user. So the ad again has it both ways. The hairdresser is invoked as the expert — only he knows *for sure* — but the process of coloring your hair can be done without his expensive assistance.

FOCUSING ON CONTENT

1. According to Twitchell, what kinds of products are difficult to advertise? Explain what causes the difficulty in each instance.

2. In what sense could Miss Clairol Hair Color Bath be considered a "dangerous" product? What does Twitchell mean when he says that this product "was almost too revolutionary to sell" (8)?

3. Twitchell says that Shirley Polykoff, the woman assigned to develop the ad campaign for Miss Clairol, "knew that you could be outrageous if you did it in the right context" (10). What is outrageous about her "Does she . . . or doesn't she?" campaign? In what sense is the context she created "right"?

4. Much of the power of the "Does she . . . or doesn't she?" campaign resides in its intended ambiguity, in the different ways in which men and women fill in the ellipses. How did Polykoff use ambiguity to appease Clairol's primary customers, beauty shops?

FOCUSING ON WRITING

1. In paragraphs 3–5, Twitchell describes the cultural context into which Miss Clairol Hair Color Bath was introduced. Why is it important for Twitchell to establish this cultural context before he explains the thinking behind the verbal and visual strategies of Clairol's ad campaign?

2. Why do you think Twitchell paraphrases Polykoff's description of her first two ideas for ad campaigns for Miss Clairol Hair Color Bath but quotes directly from her autobiography the explanation of the third execution? As a writer, what insights into the use of direct quotations does this example give you?

3. How does Twitchell use the example of the Miss Clairol ad campaign to illustrate the difficulties involved in advertising a "radical or dangerous" product? Explain.

LANGUAGE IN ACTION

Consider the Clairol "Does she . . . or doesn't she?" print ad from the 1960s on page 460. Is it what you expected after reading Twitchell's analysis of it? How do you react to the relationship between the ad's verbal message and the visual image?

Now check out Clairol's Web site at www.clairol.com. How is Clairol hair-coloring being marketed today? In what ways has Clairol's message changed from Polykoff's original "Does she . . . or doesn't she?" campaign? In what ways, if any, has it stayed the same?

WRITING SUGGESTIONS

1. Each year we hear consumer warnings about products that have been deemed "dangerous" by consumer watchdog groups. These groups identify products such as car seats and toys for children and diet pills that can cause bodily harm or even death. Once alerted, it's easy for us to see the danger in such products. But Twitchell explains how such commonplace products as televisions and hair coloring were once considered "dangerous" in a way other than causing bodily harm. What contemporary products can you think of that could be considered "radical" and need special attention when marketing them? Write a paper in which you explore how the advertisements for the product(s) you choose created "the illusion of acceptability" for the product. Use examples from actual advertisements to support your claims.

2. Design an ad campaign for a new commonplace product — for example, pencils, toothpicks, paper clips, potato chips, candy — of your own choosing. Start by giving your product a name. Then, as Twitchell suggests, brainstorm "contrived distinctions" that set your product apart from the competition. You may find it helpful to review your response to the journal prompt for this selection before you start. Using the ideas that you generate, write a proposal for an ad campaign complete with verbal and visual components.

Case Study:
Marketing Diet and Health

Any night you sit down to watch television, you can almost predict the commercials that you'll see for snack foods, soft drinks, nutritional supplements, conveniently packaged diet meals, weight loss products, beer, and fast food chains. Radio, newspapers, and magazines contain the same message. Americans want their food, and they want it now! Convenience is the name of the game. Gone are the days when a family sat down together for the evening meal. Americans are becoming a society of grazers, eating their meals on the run. But Americans pay a price. Remember the advertisements for medications treating heartburn, constipation, acid-reflux disease, and intestinal gas? How can a so-called health-conscious society like ours be raising a generation of children for whom obesity is the number one problem? When does a health problem like obesity cease to be an individual's problem and become one that the nation attacks head-on?

The articles in this Case Study educate us about what happens when health, diet, and advertising interface. In "Claims Crazy: Which Can You Believe?" nutritionist Bonnie Liebman examines the various types of claims that food manufactures put in their advertisements and on their labels. She exposes unreliable, unregulated "structure/function claims" that utilize the wily euphemism and tells how to differentiate them from "solid health claims" which are both regulated and based on scientific evidence. In the last decade, manufacturers have seized on the word *natural* and literally plastered it all over their products. The connotations of *natural* — like its partners *fresh* and *organic* and *wholesome* — let consumers think they are buying something that will be good for them. Not necessarily so, says Sarah Federman in "What's Natural about Our Natural Products?" We know that it sounds good, but because the word is unregulated, it is never really clear what *natural* means when attached to any given product. In "Let Them Eat Fat," social commentator Greg Critser stumbles on a connection between fast food and an explosion in the number of new cases of diabetes among Hispanics while researching America's staggering problem with obesity. He reports on how America's fast food giants like Krispy Kreme and McDonald's unfairly target America's poor with their advertising. The Case Study concludes with a portfolio of advertisements. These ads for Stonyfield Organic Yogurt, butter, vitamin supplements, and sugar encourage you to apply the ideas and concepts that you learned elsewhere in the Case Study or the chapter as a whole.

WRITING TO DISCOVER: *Take a moment to reflect on your experiences with food. How would you describe your daily diet and your* *eating habits? Do you try to eat a nutritionally balanced diet, or are you a junk food junkie? Where do you usually eat? Do you regularly take time out to have sit-down meals with others, or do you tend to eat on the run? What food advertisements do you find particularly appealing? Do you see any connections between your own patterns with food and the claims or appeals advertisers make to you and your peers? Explain.*

Claims Crazy: Which Can You Believe?

BONNIE LIEBMAN

After receiving a master's degree in nutritional sciences from Cornell University in 1977, Bonnie Liebman became Director of Nutrition at the Center for Science in the Public Interest, a Washington, D.C.-based nonprofit consumer advocacy organization. CSPI advocates honest food labeling and advertising, safer and more nutritious foods, and pro-health alcohol policies. Liebman's work at CSPI has focused on the links between diet and heart disease, cancer, stroke, osteoporosis, and other health-related issues, such as vitamin supplements, food labeling, and advertising. She has testified at hearings held by Congressional committees and federal agencies, and her articles regularly appear in Ladies Circle, Essence, *and* Pharmaceutical Executive. *She is coauthor of* Salt: The Brand Name Guide to Sodium Content *(1983). In the following article, which first appeared in the June 2003 issue of CSPI's* Nutrition Action Healthletter, *Liebman examines the crazy world of food advertising and instructs her readers how to differentiate the three main types of product claims.*

It's a brave new world. Walk down the aisles of any supermarket these days and you'll see claims that were never there before. Cereals that will help you "lose more weight!" Fruit drinks with "energy-releasing B-vitamins!" Raisins with antioxidants that "can slow the effects of aging."

It's been more than a decade since Congress passed a law that over-hauled food labels and required companies to get the Food and Drug Administration's approval before making claims that mention a disease. But food companies, emboldened by the success of the supplement in-dustry, have discovered a back door into the claims business.

And that leaves consumers on their own, trying to separate the good from the bad.

Here's a quiz for the astute shopper: Which (one or more) of these claims can appear on a food or supplement label without approval from the Food and Drug Administration?

(a) improves memory
(b) relieves stress
(c) suppresses appetite
(d) helps reduce difficulty in falling asleep
(e) supports the immune system

The answers: a, b, c, and e. They're called "structure/function claims," because they describe how a food or supplement affects the body's structure (say, the skeleton) or its function (for example, diges-tion). And manufacturers can slap one on virtually any food or supple-ment with or without evidence to back it up.   5

"The law says that structure/function claims can't be misleading, but the FDA has never said how much evidence a company needs to substan-tiate a claim," says Bruce Silverglade, director of legal affairs for the Cen-ter for Science in the Public Interest, publisher of *Nutrition Action Healthletter*.

Is one good study enough? What if that study is contradicted by a dozen others? "With no rules ensuring uniformity in structure/function claims, the resulting free-for-all could end up confusing consumers and encouraging them to buy unhealthy foods," says Representative Henry Waxman. The California Democrat is one of the strongest advocates of honest food labeling in Congress.

The FDA has no rules, in part because, until recently, structure/function claims only showed up on supplements.

No Approval Needed

In 1994, under strong industry pressure, Congress passed the Dietary Supplement Health and Education Act. The law gives supplement-makers free rein to make structure/function claims, as long as the companies:

- notify the FDA within 30 days after using a new claim, and
- print the following disclaimer on the label:

> These statements have not been evaluated by the Food and Drug Administration. This product is not intended to diagnose, treat, cure, or prevent any disease.

"Not evaluated" is right. "The FDA doesn't even look at the evidence behind structure/function claims," says Silverglade. "It just makes sure that the supplement doesn't make a disease claim — one that's approved only for drugs." 10

According to the law, a disease claim promises to "diagnose, cure, mitigate, treat, or prevent disease." If a supplement makes a disease claim, then legally it becomes a drug. "Drugs must be pre-approved for safety and effectiveness, so that would make the supplement illegal," explains Silverglade.

But the distinction between a structure/function claim and a disease claim can be subtle. For example, "helps restore sexual vigor, potency, and performance" is a disease claim, says the FDA. In contrast, "arouses sexual desire" is a structure/function claim. (see "A Fine Line").

A Fine Line

Which claims need FDA approval and which don't? When does a claim cross the line between offering to "affect the structure or function of the body" and promising to "prevent, treat, cure, mitigate, or diagnose" a disease? It's not easy to tell.

In January 2000, the FDA tried to answer that question, at least for claims on supplements. Here are some examples of claims that fall into each category.

No Prior Approval Needed (Structure/Function Claim)	Approval Needed (Disease Claim)
Helps maintain normal cholesterol levels	Lowers cholesterol
Maintains healthy lung function	Maintains healthy lung function in smokers
Provides relief of occasional constipation	Provides relief of chronic constipation
Suppresses appetite to aid weight loss	Suppresses appetite to treat obesity

(continued)

Supports the immune system

Relief of occasional heart-
    burn or acid indigestion
For relief of occasional
    sleeplessness
Arouses sexual desire

Supports the body's antiviral
    capabilities
Relief of persistent heartburn or
    acid indigestion
Helps reduce difficulty in falling
    asleep
Helps restore sexual vigor,
    potency, and performance

Other structure/function claims that need no prior approval

- Improves memory
- Improves strength
- Promotes digestion
- Boosts stamina
- For common
  symptoms of PMS

- Helps you relax
- Helps enhance
  muscle tone or size
- Relieves stress
- Helps promote
  urinary tract health
- Maintains intestinal
  flora

- For hair loss
  associated with
  aging
- Prevents wrinkles
- For relief of
  muscle pain after
  exercise
- To treat or
  prevent nocturnal
  leg muscle cramps
- For hot flashes

Got that?

"Studies show that consumers can't distinguish between disease claims and structure/function claims," says Silverglade.

And if shoppers can't, why should food companies bother with health claims when they can say just about anything they want by using structure/function claims?   15

Textbook Talk

"For years, the law has allowed structure/function claims on foods," explains Silverglade. "But companies rarely made them, probably because they didn't have much appeal."

The classic example was a statement like "calcium builds strong bones." "Structure/function claims were supposed to be something you might read in a textbook," says Silverglade.

Instead, the industry was fired up about health claims — that a food could, "as part of an overall diet," help reduce the risk of heart disease, cancer, or osteoporosis. In 1990, Congress passed a law permitting health claims, but with clear limits.

"The FDA had to approve the claim, and the food couldn't be too high in harmful nutrients like saturated fat or sodium or too low in vitamins and minerals," says Silverglade. "And the FDA could only approve the claim if it was backed by 'significant scientific agreement.'" In other words, the claim had to be supported by strong and consistent evidence.

Since 1990, the FDA has approved 14 health claims (see "The 'A' List"). Apparently, that hasn't been enough for the food industry.   20

The "A" List: Approved Health Claims

Here are the 14 (slightly edited) health claims that the FDA has approved. Some are more popular than others.

- Diets rich in **whole grain foods** and other plant foods and low in total fat, saturated fat, and cholesterol may help reduce the risk of **heart disease** and certain **cancers**.
- Diets containing foods that are good sources of **potassium** and low in **sodium** may reduce the risk of **high blood pressure** and **stroke**.
- A diet low in **total fat** may reduce the risk of some **cancers**.
- Three grams of soluble fiber from [**oatmeal**] daily in a diet low in saturated fat and cholesterol may reduce the risk of **heart disease.** This [cereal] has [two] grams per serving.
- While many factors affect **heart disease,** diets low in **saturated fat** and **cholesterol** may reduce the risk of this disease.
- Diets low in **sodium** may reduce the risk of **high blood pressure**.
- Low fat diets rich in **fiber**-containing **grains, fruits,** and **vegetables** may reduce the risk of some types of **cancer**.
- Diets low in saturated fat and cholesterol that include 25 grams of **soy protein** per day may reduce the risk of **heart disease.** One serving of this product provides at least [6.25 g] of soy protein.
- Healthful diets with adequate **folate** may reduce a woman's risk of having a child with a **brain or spinal cord defect.**
- Two or three servings per day with meals, providing 3.4 grams of **plant stanol esters** daily, added to a diet low in saturated fat and cholesterol may reduce the risk of **heart disease.** [Benecol Spread] contains [1.7 g] stanol esters per serving.
- Diets low in saturated fat and cholesterol and rich in **fruits, vegetables,** and **grains** that contain some types of fiber, particularly **soluble fiber,** may reduce the risk of **heart disease.**

(continued)

- Does not promote **tooth decay**.
- Low fat diets rich in **fruits** and **vegetables** containing **vitamin A, vitamin C,** and **fiber** may reduce the risk of some types of **cancer**.
- Regular exercise and a healthy diet with enough **calcium** help teens and young adult white and Asian women maintain good bone health and may reduce their high risk of **osteoporosis** later in life.

NOTE: Each food that makes a health claim must meet specific criteria. For example, foods with the soy claim must contain at least 6.25 grams of soy protein per serving and be low in saturated fat and cholesterol. "Does not promote tooth decay" can only appear on sugar-free foods that contain maltitol, xylitol, or other sugar alcohols. Foods that make health claims must also meet general criteria. They can't be high in fat, saturated fat, cholesterol, or sodium and must have some naturally occurring nutrients.

Tower of Babel

The Grocery Manufacturers of America, like other industry groups, has been hot under the collar over health claims for years.

The FDA approves claims "only where there is overwhelming science to support a diet/disease relationship, thus preventing the public from learning about new scientific developments until they have matured into hard science," a GMA spokesperson told Congress in May 2001. "As a result, the FDA has approved only a handful of disease/health claims. . . ."

Not to worry, GMA. Last December [2002], the FDA created a new kind of health claim. The agency announced that it would allow health claims for foods based on preliminary evidence as long as the label qualified it with a disclaimer like "this evidence is not conclusive."

These preliminary health claims haven't shown up on many foods yet. But even when they do, most companies will no doubt stick with anything-goes structure/function claims.

Why shouldn't they? Even preliminary health claims require approval and are prohibited on unhealthy or empty-calorie foods. What's more, structure/function claims have gotten jazzier. Goodbye, textbook. Hello, Madison Avenue.

"The supplement industry made a mint with structure/function claims," observes Silverglade. "Why should the food industry bother with health claims when they've got a free ride with structure/function claims?

Food companies don't even have to notify the FDA or print a disclaimer, like supplement companies do."

Structure/function claims are starting to hit the marketplace . . . and no one's watching. So far, many are showing up on decent foods, like fruit juice and fruit (see "The Bottom Line"). But it's only a matter of time before they start to pop up in the cookie, chip, and soft-drink aisles.

Says Waxman: "The growth of structure/function claims for foods threatens to return us to the days when the Secretary of Health and Human Services called the food marketplace a 'Tower of Babel' for the consumer."

The Bottom Line

Here's how to tell one claim from another:

- **Solid Health Claims.** These reliable claims — based on solid evidence — name a disease like cancer, stroke, or heart disease; usually refer to a "diet" that's low (or high) in some nutrient; and can't appear on unhealthy or empty-calorie foods.
- **Preliminary Health Claims.** These unreliable claims are based on incomplete, shaky evidence. They have a disclaimer that ranges from the cautious ("the FDA has determined that this evidence is limited and not conclusive") to the silly ("the FDA concludes that there is little scientific evidence supporting this claim"). They can't appear on unhealthy or empty-calorie foods.
- **Structure/Function Claims.** These unreliable claims require no approval — in practice, that may mean no evidence. Instead of diseases, look for words like "maintains," "supports," and "enhances" and euphemisms (like "optimizes bone health"). They can appear on any food.

EXAMINING THE ISSUE CRITICALLY

1. What is a "structure/function claim"? What does Liebman see as the problem of such claims for consumers? Why do many food companies favor using structure/function claims?

2. According to the Food and Drug Administration, when does a supplement become a drug?

3. Currently, the food industry can use two types of health claims — "solid health claims" and "preliminary health claims." What is the essential difference

between the two? Why, according to Liebman, is the food industry likely to use structure/function claims on its products more than health claims?

4. Now that you understand the different types of claims that manufacturers can make, do you think that food companies are deliberately trying to deceive consumers, or simply trying to sell their products in a highly competitive marketplace? Do you think that some claims put customers at real risk? Explain.

What's Natural about Our Natural Products?

SARAH FEDERMAN

A freelance writer, Sarah Federman was born in New York City in 1976. She graduated from the University of Pennsylvania in 1998, where she majored in Intellectual History. A strong interest in alternative medicine led her to work at the Institute for Health and Healing at California Pacific Medical Center in San Francisco. In 2003 she returned to New York where she works in media advertising.

Federman wrote the following essay expressly for Language Awareness. *She first became curious about the word* natural *as an undergraduate when she defended its use as a meaningful word on food labels in a debate with one of her professors. Since that time, however, Federman has had a change of heart. As she reports in her essay, the meaning of* natural *is elusive and extremely difficult to pin down.*

Whether you're picking up Nature's Energy Supplements, Natrol, Nature's Way, Naturade, Nature's Gate, or Nature's Herbs in the vitamin aisle, attending a lecture on "Natural Sleep Aids," or diving into a bowl of Quaker 100% Natural Granola, you cannot escape the hype. Variations of the words "nature" and "natural" are used for product naming: to distinguish alternative medicine practitioners from their western counterparts and as slogans or names for everything from toothpaste to blue jeans. In a recent issue of *Delicious* magazine, for example, these words were used 85 times in the first 40 pages, with advertisements using them 8 times! Now pet owners can even skim through a copy of *Natural Dog* or *Natural Cat* while waiting at the vet.

Nowhere is the buzzword "natural" more prevalent than at the local grocery store where Fantastic Soups, Enrico's Pizza Sauce, Health Valley Cereals, and Celestial Seasonings tea, among others, brag unabashedly about the "naturalness" of their products. I often find myself seduced by the lure of the "natural" label on goods and services. I throw Tom's Natural Toothpaste, Pop-Secret Natural Flavored Popcorn, and Grape-Nuts Natural Wheat and Barley Cereal into my shopping cart with the utmost confidence that these natural varieties prove far superior to their "unnatural" or "less natural" counterparts. Recently, I took a closer look at the labels of my revered products only to discover the widespread abuse of the word "natural." The word "natural" has become more a marketing ploy than a way to communicate meaningful information about a product.

But this is not news. More than a decade ago the Consumers Union first sounded the alarm about "natural." The report alerted consumers to the fact that their beloved Quaker 100% Natural Cereal contained 24 percent sugar, not to mention the nine grams of fat which, according to the March 1999 *Nutrition Action Healthletter,* is the same as a small McDonald's hamburger. But despite the best efforts of the Union, nothing has changed. In fact, things have gotten worse, *especially* in the cereal aisle where 22 varieties, including Froot Loops, proclaim their commitment to "natural" ingredients. Berry Berry Kix, a brightly colored kids' cereal, promises "natural Fruit Flavors." Sure there is some grape juice, right after the sugar, partially hydrogenated oils, and corn syrup, and some strawberry juice, right after the dicalcium and trisodium phosphates. That's it for the fruits, the rest is corn meal and starch.

The Consumer Union's report also pointed out products using "natural" as an "indeterminate modifier," rather than as an adjective to convey some meaningful information about the product. In other words, placing the word "natural" in a slogan or product description without having it refer to anything in particular. For example, most major U.S. supermarkets sell Kraft's Natural Shredded Non-Fat Cheese, Natural Reduced Fat Swiss, and Natural Cheese Cubes. But don't dare to ask the question, What does that mean? Kraft has done nothing special with the cheese itself; "natural" in this case presumably relates to the shredding, reducing, and cubing process. What is natural cubing?

To me, a "natural" product or service suggests any or all of the following: a healthy alternative, an environmentally friendly product, vegetarian, and or produced without synthetic chemicals. Friends and family have also taken natural to mean wholesome, pure, low-fat, healthy, organic, and, simply, better. The meanings given in one popular dictionary, however, prove less specific: 1) determined by nature, 2) of or relating to nature, 3) having normal or usual character, 4) grown without human care, 5) not artificial, 6) present in or produced by nature. Interestingly, these definitions make no value judgments. There is nothing in the dictionary meaning to suggest, for instance, that a natural banana (one grown in the wild) is healthier than one raised by banana farmers. This positive spin we add ourselves.

Unlike using "low-fat," "organic," and "vegetarian," food manufacturers can use "natural" any way they choose. The Nutritional Labeling and Education Act of 1990 (ULEA) restricted the use of the following terms on food labels: low fat, low sodium, low cholesterol, low calorie, lean, extra lean, reduced, good source, less, fewer, light, and more. A calorie-free product, for example, must have fewer than 5 calories per serving, while a cholesterol-free product must have 2 milligrams or less of cholesterol per serving. *Mother Earth News* reports that products labeled "organic" must align themselves with one of the 40 sets of organic standards, most often the California Organic Foods Act of 1990. This leaves "natural" as one of the few unregulated words.

Health-food companies and mainstream producers use the word to create an aura around the product. Actually, they use the word and "we" create the aura, allowing them to get away with higher prices or simply to take up more shelf space at the supermarket. For example, every month thousands of bags of Lays "Naturally Baked" Potato Chips travel through desert and farmland to enable us to "Ohh, ahh" and purchase these natural wonders. When first seeing this name, I had visions of organic farms and rugged, healthy farmers cultivating a much-loved product. Unfortunately, a closer look at the label served to shatter rather than support my countryside fantasy. While the ingredients reveal less fat per serving than the standard chip (1.5 grams versus 9 grams), I found nothing that explained the meaning of "naturally baked." Do you think this means they leave the chips out in the sun to crispen up? Probably not, so why does this natural process cost more per ounce (5.5 ounces for $1.99 versus 7.5 ounces) when it uses less fat?

Motts and Delmonte use "natural" to promote a new line without knocking their standard product. Motts applesauce has three products on the shelf of my local San Francisco market — "Apple Sauce," "Natural Apple Sauce," and "Chunky Apple Sauce." A comparison of the labels reveals that the "natural" version has no corn syrup added. Now, if they just wrote "no corn syrup added" on the label, we consumers would immediately become aware that there is, indeed, sweetener added to their standard version. Delmonte Fruit Cocktail has a two-product line-up with "Fruit Naturals" right next to "Fruit Cocktail." The natural variety costs 6 cents more and actually has *fewer* ingredients, presumably requiring less manufacturing. The natural version has no sugar and preservatives; the standard version has added corn syrup and sugar.

Fantastic, maker of dried soups and instant mixes, uses "natural" to connote something about the food and the type of person who may buy it. Under the heading Instant Black Beans, Fantastic writes "All Natural. Vegetarian." A vegetarian product, we know, means without meat. But what does "all natural" mean? Adding this phrase right before Vegetarian suggested to me that this product should appeal to vegetarians and self-proclaimed naturals. Mildly health-conscious people surely would prefer to ally themselves with natural rather than unnatural foods. Whether or not this product serves as a healthy alternative to other brands is irrelevant because the point is that Fantastic could sell you artery-clogging lard and still use the word.

Next to vitamins, bottled beverages probably use the word more than any other product. Every Snapple bottle promises an "all natural" treat, although the most natural iced tea is quite simply brewed tea with ice. In Snapple's case, you end up paying more for tasty sugar water, but with Hansen's Natural Soda you are outright deceived. Hansen's soda has exactly the same ingredients as Sprite and 7-Up minus the sodium citrate. Blue Sky Natural Soda has fructose sweetener, caramel color, and something called tartaric acid. Doesn't Blue Sky Natural Soda sound refreshing? Too bad your intestines can't distinguish it from Coca-Cola.

At least we have natural bottled water as an alternative. Or do we? The Natural Resources Defense Council, a national environmental group, found dangerous amounts of arsenic in Crystal Geyser's "Natural" Spring water. A four-year study revealed that one-third of the 103 bottled waters tested contained contaminants beyond safe federal limits. Odwalla "Natural" Spring Water, another popular beverage company, especially among health-food lovers, had high bacteria counts in a number of bottles. Hey, bacteria are natural so what's the problem? The problem is that natural or not, some bacteria make us sick. So it seems you cannot win with beverages. "Natural" serves as a meaningless label, a deceptive marketing tool, or means "contains natural critters and natural toxins that may make you sick." Best to just purchase a "Pur" (pronounced "pure") water filter; just don't ask what they mean by pure.

Some products come closer to meeting my expectations. The Hain Food Group, a "natural-food producer" whose projected 1999 annual sales are $300 million, manufactures soup called "Healthy Naturals." Although the split peas are not certified organic, Hain uses no preservatives or MSG. The ingredients are listed as water, split green peas, carrots, celery, onion powder, and spices. This product lives up to my notion of natural. But even Hain veers from their presumed commitment to health food. The 14 product "Hain Kidz" line, introduced early in 1999, includes marshmallow crisp cereal and snack bars, gummybear-like candy, and animal cookies. It appears that as major brands (Krafts, Motts, Quaker) increasingly tout their new-found "naturalness," health-food companies such as Hain have started going toward more "unnatural" products.

So as the line between specialty health-food company and standard food producer becomes more elusive, I begin to wonder why the extra cost? Why do plain peas and carrots cost *more* than highly refined and processed soups? And how did we get to a point where we need a special label to tell us that the product is what it says it is? Before I infuse one more dollar into this industry, I will assuredly read the list of ingredients more carefully and do some research at www.naturalinvestor.com.

EXAMINING THE ISSUE CRITICALLY

1. According to Federman, what is the literal meaning of the word *natural*? What connotations do consumers bring to the word? (Glossary: *Connotation/Denotation*)

2. What restrictions does the Nutritional Labeling and Education Act of 1990 place on what manufacturers can say on food labels? How is the word *organic* regulated? What restrictions, if any, are imposed on the use of the term *natural*?

3. What does Federman point to as the two main reasons that companies use the word *natural*? What does she mean when she says companies "use the word and 'we' create the aura" (7)?

4. Why do you think Federman talks about Kraft's Natural Shredded Non-Fat Cheese and Lays "Naturally Baked" Potato Chips? Name some other products whose labels use the word *natural* or *naturally* in an unclear or ambiguous manner.

5. Why do you suppose manufacturers charge more for their "natural" products when, in fact, these products may cost less to produce?

Let Them Eat Fat

GREG CRITSER

The author of National Geographic California *(2000), Greg Critser writes regularly for* USA Today *and the* Los Angeles Times *on issues of nutrition, health, and medicine. His writing on obesity earned him a James Beard nomination for best feature writing in 1999. An authority on the subject of food politics, Critser has been interviewed on PBS and other media. His most recent book on the subject of obesity is* Fat Land: How Americans Became the Fattest People in the World *(2003). This book had its beginnings in the following cover story for* Harper's Magazine *in March 2000. Embarrassed by a passing motorist who shouted, "Watch it, fatso," Critser went on a diet and lost forty pounds. In the process he discovered that in America, weight is a class issue — fat and poor often go together. In exposing the heavy truths about American obesity, Critser gives our bloated nation a wake-up call. Not only does he outline the extent of the problem, he explains how we have been seduced by the language of fast food advertising.*

Not long ago, a group of doctors, nurses, and medical technicians wheeled a young man into the intensive care unit of Los Angeles County–USC Medical Center, hooked him to a ganglia of life-support systems — pulse and respiration monitors, a breathing apparatus, and an IV line — then stood back and collectively stared. I was there visiting an ailing relative, and I stared, too.

Here, in the ghastly white light of modern American medicine, writhed a real-life epidemiological specter: a 500-pound twenty-two-year-old. The man, whom I'll call Carl, was propped up at a 45-degree angle, the better to be fed air through a tube, and lay there nude, save for a small patch of blood-spotted gauze stuck to his lower abdomen, where surgeons had just labored to save his life. His eyes darted about in abject fear. "Second time in three months," his mother blurted out to me as she stood watching in horror. "He had two stomach staplings, and they both came apart. Oh my God, my boy. . ." Her boy was suffocating in his own fat.

I was struck not just by the spectacle but by the truth of the mother's comment. This was a boy — one buried in years of bad health, relative poverty, a sedentary lifestyle, and a high-fat diet, to be sure, but a boy nonetheless. Yet how surprised should I have been? That obesity, particularly among the young and the poor, is spinning out of control is hardly a secret. It is, in fact, something that most Americans can agree upon. Along with depression, heart disease, and cancer, obesity is yet another chew in our daily rumination about health and fitness, morbidity and mortality. Still, even in dot-com America, where statistics fly like arrows, the numbers are astonishing. Consider:

- Today, one-fifth of all Americans are obese, meaning that they have a body mass index, or BMI, of more than 30. (BMI is a universally recognized cross-measure of weight for height and stature.) The epidemiological figures on chronic corpulence are so unequivocal that even the normally reticent dean of American obesity studies, the University of Colorado's James O. Hill, says that if obesity is left unchecked almost all Americans will be overweight within a few generations. "Becoming obese," he told the *Arizona Republic*, "is a normal response to the American environment."

- Children are most at risk. At least 25 percent of all Americans now under age nineteen are overweight or obese. In 1998, Dr. David Satcher, the new U.S. surgeon general, was moved to declare childhood obesity to be epidemic. "Today," he told a group of federal bureaucrats and policymakers, "we see a nation of young people seriously at risk of starting out obese and dooming themselves to the difficult task of overcoming a tough illness."

- Even among the most careful researchers these days, "epidemic" is the term of choice when it comes to talk of fat, particularly fat children. As William Dietz, the director of nutrition at the Centers for Disease Control, said last year, "This is an epidemic in the U.S. the likes of which we have not had before in chronic disease." The cost to the general public health budget by 2020 will run into the hundreds of billions, making HIV look, economically, like a bad case of the flu.

Yet standing that day in the intensive care unit, among the beepers and buzzers and pumps, epidemic was the last thing on my mind. Instead I felt heartbreak, revulsion, fear, sadness — and then curiosity: Where did this boy come from? Who and what had made him? How is it that we Americans, perhaps the most health-conscious of any people in the history of the world, and certainly the richest, have come to preside over the deadly fattening of our youth?

The beginning of an answer came one day last fall, in the same week   5
that the Spanish language newspaper *La Opinion* ran a story headlined "Diabetes epidemia en latinos," when I attended the opening of the newest Krispy Kreme doughnut store in Los Angeles. It was, as they say in marketing circles, a "resonant" event, replete with around-the-block lines, celebrity news anchors, and stem cops directing traffic. The store, located in the heart of the San Fernando Valley's burgeoning Latino population, pulsed with excitement. In one corner stood the new store's manager, a young Anglo fellow, accompanied by a Krispy Kreme publicity director. Why had Krispy Kreme decided to locate here? I asked.

"See," the manager said, brushing a crumb of choco-glaze from his fingers, "the idea is simple — accessible but not convenient. The idea is to make the store accessible — easy to get into and out of from the street — but just a tad away from the — eh, mainstream so as to make sure that the customers are presold and very intent before they get here," he said, betraying no doubts about the company's marketing formula. "We want them intent to get at least a dozen before they even think of coming in."

But why this slightly non-mainstream place?

"Because it's obvious . . . "He gestured to the stout Mayan donas queuing around the building. "We're looking for all the bigger families." Bigger in size? "Yeah." His eyes rolled, like little glazed crullers.

"Bigger in size."

Of course, fast-food and national restaurant chains like Krispy Kreme   10 that serve it have long been the object of criticism by nutritionists and dietitians. Despite the attention, however, fast-food companies, most of them publicly owned and sprinkled into the stock portfolios of many striving Americans (including mine and perhaps yours), have grown more aggressive in their targeting of poor inner-city communities. One of every four hamburgers sold by the good folks at McDonald's, for example, is now purchased by inner-city consumers who, disproportionately, are young black men.

In fact, it was the poor, and their increasing need for cheap meals consumed outside the home, that fueled the development of what may well be the most important fast-food innovation of the past twenty years, the sales gimmick known as "supersizing." At my local McDonald's, located in a lower-middle-income area of Pasadena, California, the supersize bacchanal goes into high gear at about five P.M., when the various urban caballeros, drywalleros, and jardineros get off work and head for a quick bite. Mixed in is a sizable element of young black kids traveling between school and home, their economic status apparent by the fact that they've walked instead of driven. Customers are cheerfully encouraged to "supersize your meal!" by signs saying, "If we don't recommend a supersize, the supersize is free!" For an extra seventy-nine cents, a kid ordering a cheeseburger, small fries, and a small Coke will get said cheeseburger plus a supersize Coke (42 fluid ounces versus 16, with free refills) and a supersize order of french fries (more than double the weight of a regular order). Suffice it to say that consumption of said meals is fast and, in almost every instance I observed, very complete.

But what, metabolically speaking, has taken place? The total caloric content of the meal has been jacked up from 680 calories to more than 1,340 calories. According to the very generous U.S. dietary guidelines, 1,340 calories represent more than half of a teenager's recommended daily caloric consumption, and the added calories themselves are protein-poor but fat- and carbohydrate-rich. Completing this jumbo dietetic horror is the fact that the easy availability of such huge meals arrives in the same years in which physical activity among teenage boys and girls drops by about half.

Now consider the endocrine warfare that follows. The constant bombing of the pancreas by such a huge hit of sugars and fats can eventually wear out the organ's insulin-producing "islets," leading to diabetes and its inevitable dirge of woes: kidney, eye, and nerve damage; increased risk of heart disease; even stroke. The resulting sugar-induced hyperglycemia in many of the obese wreaks its own havoc in the form of glucose toxicity, further debilitating nerve endings and arterial walls. For the obese and soon to be obese, it is no overstatement to say that after supersized teen years the pancreas may never be the same. Some 16 million Americans suffer from Type 2 diabetes, a third of them unaware of their condition. Today's giggly teen burp may well be tomorrow's aching neuropathic limb.

Diabetes, by the way, is just the beginning of what's possible. If childhood obesity truly is "an epidemic in the U.S. the likes of which we have not had before in chronic disease," then places like McDonald's and Winchell's Donut stores, with their endless racks of glazed and creamy goodies, are the San Francisco bathhouses of said epidemic, the places where the high-risk population indulges in high-risk behavior. Although open around the clock, the Winchell's near my house doesn't get rolling until seven in the morning, the Spanish-language talk shows frothing in the background while an ambulance light whirls atop the Coke dispenser. Inside, Mami placates Miguelito with a giant apple fritter. Papi tells a joke and pours ounce upon ounce of sugar and cream into his 20-ounce coffee. Viewed through the lens of obesity, as I am inclined to do, the scene is not so feliz. The obesity rate for Mexican-American children is shocking. Between the ages of five and eleven, the rate for girls is 27 percent; for boys, 23 percent. By fourth grade the rate for girls peaks at 32 percent, while boys top out at 43 percent. Not surprisingly, obesity-related disorders are everywhere on display at Winchell's, right before my eyes — including fat kids who limp, which can be a symptom of Blount's disease (a deformity of the tibia) or a sign of slipped capital femoral epiphysis (an orthopedic abnormality brought about by weight-induced dislocation of the femur bone). Both conditions are progressive, often requiring surgery.

The chubby boy nodding in the corner, waiting for his Papi to finish his cafe, is likely suffering from some form of sleep apnea; a recent study of forty-one children with severe obesity revealed that a third had the condition and that another third presented with clinically abnormal sleep patterns. Another recent study indicated that "obese children with obstructive sleep apnea demonstrate clinically significant decrements in learning and memory function." And the lovely but very chubby little girl tending to her schoolbooks? Chances are she will begin puberty before the age of ten, launching her into a lifetime of endocrine bizarreness that not only will be costly to treat but will be emotionally devastating as well. Research also suggests that weight gain can lead to the development of pseudotumor cerebri, a brain tumor most common in females. A recent review of 57 patients with the tumor revealed that 90 percent were obese. This little girl's chances of developing other neurological illnesses are profound as well. And she may already have gallstones: obesity accounts for up to 33 percent of all gallstones observed in children. She is ten times more likely than her non-obese peers to develop high blood pressure, and she is increasingly likely to contract Type 2 diabetes, obesity being that disease's number-one risk factor.

Of course, if she is really lucky, that little girl could just be having a choco-sprinkles doughnut on her way to school.

What about poor rural whites? Studying children in an elementary school in a low-income town in eastern Kentucky, the anthropologist Deborah Crooks was astonished to find stunting and obesity not just present but prevalent. Among her subjects, 13 percent of girls exhibited notable stunting; 33 percent of all kids were significantly overweight; and 13 percent of the children were obese — 21 percent of boys and 9 percent of girls. A sensitive, elegant writer, Crooks drew from her work three important conclusions: One, that poor kids in the United States often face the same evolutionary nutritional pressures as those in newly industrializing nations, where traditional diets are replaced by high-fat diets and where labor-saving technology reduces physical activity. Second, Crooks found that "height and weight are cumulative measures of growth . . . reflecting a sum total of environmental experience over time." Last, and perhaps most important, Crooks concluded that while stunting can be partially explained by individual household conditions — income, illness, education, and marital status — obesity "may be more of a community-related phenomenon." Here the economic infrastructure-safe playgrounds, access to high-quality, low-cost food, and transportation to play areas — was the key determinant of physical-activity levels.

Awareness of these national patterns of destruction, of course, is a key reason why Eli Lilly & Co., the $75 billion pharmaceutical company, is now building the largest factory dedicated to the production of a single drug in industry history. That drug is insulin. Lilly's sales of insulin products totaled $357 million in the third quarter of 1999, a 24 percent increase over the previous third quarter. Almost every leading pharmaceutical conglomerate has like-minded ventures under way, with special emphasis on pill-form treatments for non-insulin-dependent forms of the disease. Pharmaceutical companies that are not seeking to capture some portion of the burgeoning market are bordering on fiduciary mismanagement. Said James Kappel of Eli Lilly, "You've got to be in diabetes."

Wandering home from my outing, the wondrous smells of frying foods wafting in the air, I wondered why, given affluent America's outright fetishism about diet and health, those whose business it is to care — the media, the academy, public-health workers, and the government — do almost nothing. The answer, I suggest, is that in almost every public-health arena, the need to address obesity as a class issue — one that transcends the inevitable divisiveness of race and gender — has been blunted by bad logic, vested interests, academic cant, and ideological chauvinism.

Consider a story last year in the *New York Times* detailing the rise in delivery-room mortality among young African American mothers. The increases were attributed to a number of factors — diabetes, hypertension, drug and alcohol abuse — but the primary factor of obesity, which can foster both diabetes and hypertension, was mentioned only in passing. Moreover, efforts to understand and publicize the socioeconomic factors of the deaths have been thwarted. When Dr. Janet Mitchell, a New York obstetrician charged with reviewing several recent maternal mortality studies, insisted that socioeconomics were the issue in understanding the "racial gap" in maternal mortality, she was unable to get government funding for the work. "We need to back away from the medical causes," she told the *Times*, clearly exasperated, "and begin to take a much more ethnographic, anthropological approach to this tragic outcome." 20

In another example, a 1995 University of Arizona study reported that young black girls, who are more inclined toward obesity than white girls, were also far less likely to hold "bad body images" about themselves. The slew of news articles and TV reports that followed were nothing short of jubilant, proclaiming the "good news." As one commentator I watched late one evening announced, "Here is one group of girls who couldn't care less about looking like Kate Moss!" Yet no one mentioned the long-term effects of unchecked weight gain. Apparently, when it comes to poor black girls the media would rather that they risk diabetes than try to look like models.

"That's the big conundrum, as they always say," Richard MacKenzie, a physician who treats overweight and obese girls in downtown L.A., told me recently. "No one wants to overemphasize the problems of being fat to these girls, for fear of creating body-image problems that might lead to anorexia and bulimia." Speaking anecdotally, he said that "the problem is that for every one affluent white anorexic you create by 'overemphasizing' obesity, you foster ten obese poor girls by downplaying the severity of the issue." Judith Stem, a professor of nutrition and internal medicine at UC Davis, is more blunt. "The number of kids with eating disorders is positively dwarfed by the number with obesity. It sidesteps the whole class issue. We've got to stop that and get on with the real problem."

Moreover, such sidestepping denies poor minority girls a principal, if sometimes unpleasant, psychological incentive to lose weight: that of social stigma. Only recently has the academy come to grapple with this. Writing in a recent issue of the *International Journal of Obesity*, the scholar Susan Averett looked at the hard numbers: 44 percent of African American women weigh more than 120 percent of their recommended body weight yet are less likely than whites to perceive themselves as overweight.[1] Anglo women, poor and otherwise, registered higher anxiety about fatness and experienced far fewer cases of chronic obesity. "Social stigma may serve to control obesity among white women," Averett reluctantly concluded. "If so, physical and emotional effects of greater pressure to be thin must be weighed against reduced health risks associated with overweight and obesity." In other words, maybe a few more black Kate Mosses might not be such a bad thing.

While the so-called fat acceptance movement, a very vocal minority of super-obese female activists, has certainly played a role in the tendency to deny the need to promote healthy thinness, the real culprits have been those with true cultural power, those in the academy and the publishing industry who have the ability to shape public opinion. Behind much of their reluctance to face facts is the lingering influence of the 1978 bestseller, *Fat Is a Feminist Issue*, in which Susie Orbach presented a nuanced, passionate look at female compulsive eating and its roots in patriarchal culture. But although Orbach's observations were keen, her conclusions were often wishful, narcissistic, and sometimes just wrong. "Fat is a social disease, and fat is a feminist issue," Orbach wrote. "Fat is not about self-control or lack of will power. . . . It is a response to the inequality of the sexes."[2]

Perhaps so, if one is a feminist, and if one is struggling with an eating disorder, and if one is, for the most part, affluent, well-educated, and politically aware. But obesity itself is preeminently an issue of class, not of ethnicity, and certainly not of gender. True, the disease may be refracted though its concentrations in various demographic subgroupings — in Native Americans, in Latinos, in African Americans, and even in some Pacific Island Americans, but in study after study, the key adjective is poor: poor African Americans, poor Latinos, poor whites, poor women, poor children, poor Latino children, etc. From the definitive *Handbook of Obesity:* "In heterogeneous and affluent societies like the United States, there is a strong inverse correlation of social class and obesity, particularly

---

1. Certainly culture plays a role in the behavior of any subpopulation. Among black women, for example, obesity rates persist despite increases in income. A recent study by the National Heart, Lung, and Blood Institute concludes that obesity in black girls may be "a reflection of a differential social development in our society, wherein a certain lag period may need to elapse between an era when food availability is a concern to an era of affluence with no such concern." Other observers might assert that black women find affirmation for being heavy from black men, or believe themselves to be "naturally" heavier. Such assertions do not change mortality statistics.

2. At the edges of the culture, the inheritors of Susie Orbach's politics have created Web sites called FaT GIRL and Largesse: The Network for Size Esteem, which claim that "dieting kills" and instruct how to induce vomiting in diet centers as protest.

for females." From *Annals of Epidemiology*: "In white girls . . . both TV viewing and obesity were strongly inversely associated with household income as well as with parental education."

Yet class seems to be the last thing on the minds of some of our better social thinkers. Instead, the tendency of many in the academy is to fetishize or "postmodernize" the problem. Cornell University professor Richard Klein, for example, proposed in his 1996 book, *Eat Fat*, "Try this for six weeks: Eat fat." (Klein's mother did and almost died from sleep apnea, causing Klein to reverse himself in his epilogue, advising readers: "Eat rice.") The identity politics of fat, incidentally, can cut the other way. To the French, the childhood diet has long been understood as a serious medical issue directly affecting the future of the nation. The concern grew directly from late-nineteenth-century health issues in French cities and the countryside, where tuberculosis had winnowed the nation's birth rate below that of the other European powers. To deal with the problem, a new science known as puericulture emerged to educate young mothers about basic health and nutrition practices. Long before Americans and the British roused themselves from the torpor of Victorian chub, the French undertook research into proper dietary and weight controls for the entire birth-to-adolescence growth period. By the early 1900s, with birth rates (and birth weights) picking up, the puericulture movement turned its attention to childhood obesity. Feeding times were to be strictly maintained; random snacks were unhealthy for the child, regardless of how "natural" it felt for a mother to indulge her young. Kids were weighed once a week. All meals were to be supervised by an adult. As a result, portion control — perhaps the one thing that modern obesity experts can agree upon as a reasonable way to prevent the condition — very early became institutionalized in modern France. The message that too much food is bad still resounds in French child rearing, and as a result France has a largely lean populace.

What about the so-called Obesity Establishment, that web of researchers, clinicians, academics, and government health officials charged with finding ways to prevent the disease? Although there are many committed individuals in this group, one wonders just how independently minded they are. Among the sponsors for the 1997 annual conference of the North American Association for the Study of Obesity, the premier medical think tank on the subject, were the following: the Coca-Cola Company, Hershey Foods, Kraft Foods, and, never to be left out, Slim Fast Foods. Another sponsor was Knoll Pharmaceuticals, maker of the new diet drug Meridia. Of course, in a society where until recently tobacco companies sponsored fitness pageants and Olympic games, sponsorship hardly denotes corruption in the most traditional sense. One would be hard-pressed to prove any kind of censorship, but such underwriting effectively defines the parameters of public discussion. Everybody winks or blinks at the proper moment, then goes on his or her way.

Once upon a time, however, the United States possessed visionary leadership in the realm of childhood fitness. Founded in 1956, the President's Council on Youth Fitness successfully laid down broad-based fitness goals for all youth and established a series of awards for those who excelled in the effort. The council spoke about obesity with a forthrightness that would be political suicide today, with such pointed slogans as "There's no such thing as stylishly stout" and "Hey kid, if you see yourself in this picture, you need help."

By the late 1980s and early 1990s, however, new trends converged to undercut the council's powers of moral and cultural suasion. The ascendancy of cultural relativism led to a growing reluctance to be blunt about fatness, and, aided and abetted by the fashion industry's focus on baggy, hip-hop-style clothes, it became possible to be "stylishly stout." Fatness, as celebrated on rap videos, was now equated with wealth and power, with identity and agency, not with clogging the heart or being unable to reach one's toes. But fat inner-city black kids and the suburban kids copying them are even more disabled by their obesity. The only people who benefit from kids being "fat" are the ones running and owning the clothing, media, food, and drug companies. In upscale corporate America, meanwhile, being fat is taboo, a surefire career-killer. If you can't control your own contours, goes the logic, how can you control a budget or a staff? Look at the glossy business and money magazines with their cooing profiles of the latest genius entrepreneurs: to the man, and the occasional woman, no one, I mean no one, is fat.

Related to the coolification of homeboyish fat — perhaps forcing its new status — is the simple fact that it's hard for poor children to find opportunities to exercise. Despite our obsession with professional sports, many of today's disadvantaged youth have fewer opportunities than ever to simply shoot baskets or kick a soccer ball. Various measures to limit state spending and taxing, among them California's debilitating Proposition 13, have gutted school-based physical-education classes. Currently, only one state, Illinois, requires daily physical education for all grades K-12, and only 19 percent of high school students nationwide are active for twenty minutes a day, five days a week, in physical education. Add to this the fact that, among the poor, television, the workingman's babysitter, is now viewed at least thirty-two hours a week. Participation in sports has always required an investment, but with the children of the affluent tucked away either in private schools or green suburbias, buying basketballs for the poor is not on the public agenda.

Human nature and its lazy inclinations aside, what do America's affluent get out of keeping the poor so fat? The reasons, I'd suggest, are many. An unreconstructed Marxist might invoke simple class warfare, exploitation fought through stock ownership in giant fast-food firms. The affluent know that the stuff will kill them but need someone (else) to eat it so as to keep growing that retirement portfolio. A practitioner of vulgar social psychology might argue for "our" need for the "identifiable outsider." An economist would say that in a society as overly competitive as our own, the affluent have found a way to slow down the striving poor from inevitable nipping at their heels. A French semiotician might even say that with the poor the affluent have erected their own walking and talking "empire of signs." This last notion is perhaps not so far-fetched. For what do the fat, darker, exploited poor, with their unbridled primal appetites, have to offer us but a chance for we diet- and shape-conscious folk to live vicariously? Call it boundary envy. Or, rather, boundary-free envy. And yet, by living outside their boundaries, the poor live within ours; fat people do not threaten our way of life; their angers entombed in flesh, they are slowed, they are softened, they are fed.

Meanwhile, in the City of Fat Angels, we lounge through a slow-motion epidemic. Mami buys another apple fritter. Papi slams his second sugar and cream. Another young Carl supersizes and double supersizes, then supersizes again. Waistlines surge. Any minute now, the belt will run out of holes.

EXAMINING THE ISSUE CRITICALLY

1. How did you feel when you read about Carl, the five-hundred-pound twenty-two-year-old man? What did you want to know after hearing about his case? What questions did Critser have after witnessing Carl come into the intensive care unit?

2. Critser claims that "'epidemic' is the term of choice when it comes to talk of fat, particularly fat children" (3). What evidence does he present to support the claim that obesity is indeed an epidemic in America?

3. Critser gives a detailed account of his discussion of marketing strategies with the manager of the new Los Angeles Krispy Kreme doughnut shop. What connection does this store opening have with the headline "Diabetes epi demia en latinos" in the Spanish language newspaper? How is this connection related to Critser's thesis about obesity? Explain.

4. Why do you think the "supersizing" advertising campaign has been so successful for McDonald's? What do customers think they are getting when they "supersize" a meal? Why does Critser consider a supersized meal a "jumbo dietetic horror" (12)?

5. What fault does Critser find with Susie Orbach's argument that "Fat is a social disease, and fat is a feminist issue" (24)? How do you react to such Web site names as "FaT GIRL," "Largesse," and the "Network for Size Esteem"?

6. What do you think it will take for America to win its obesity problem? What incentives are needed to encourage change?

Marketing Food:
A Portfolio of Advertisements

The following print advertisements present a variety of food products, supplements, and services, each appealing to a particular audience. With specific customers in mind, advertising copywriters carefully weigh the language of each ad and choose images that best complement the

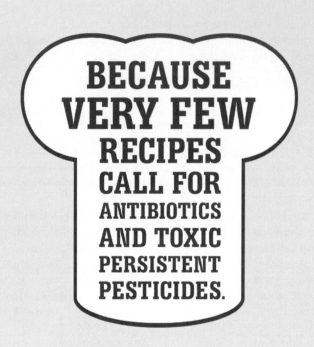

product and the text. As you analyze each of the following ads, look for solid marketing claims as well as deceiving ones and for obvious uses of weasel words. Identify the audience that you believe the advertiser has in mind and note the language and visual appeals made to this audience.

BUTTER
NOW MORE THAN EVER THE NATURAL CHOICE.

Today, life is full of choices. Maybe too many. And perhaps one of the hardest choices of all is deciding on the kinds of foods you want your family to eat.

That's why it's so reassuring to know that when it comes to table-spreads, now, more than ever, butter is the natural choice.

Butter is the only spread that's pure, natural and made from fresh, wholesome milk. There is just no substitute for butter.

Nothing else tastes like it. Looks like it. Smells like it. Or bakes like it. Because butter is the only spread that's 100% pure, natural dairy.

Of course, a lot of other spreads try to convince you that there is a substitute for butter. Some spreads claim they taste just like butter. Others claim you'll find it hard to believe they're not butter.

But if you're looking for a spread that's natural and delicious, choose the one millions choose every day. The one you and your family can feel good about. Now, more than ever, the natural choice.

For more information call: 1-800-852-1542.

THERE'S NO REAL SUBSTITUTE FOR
BUTTER

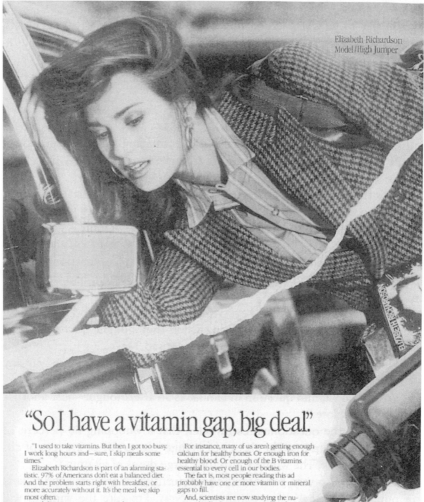

Elizabeth Richardson
Model / High Jumper

"So I have a vitamin gap, big deal."

"I used to take vitamins. But then I got too busy. I work long hours and—sure, I skip meals sometimes."

Elizabeth Richardson is part of an alarming statistic. 97% of Americans don't eat a balanced diet. And the problem starts right with breakfast, or more accurately without it. It's the meal we skip most often.

And dieters are even more at risk.

Cutting out meals, even whole categories of food.

But even eating three meals a day is no guarantee your body is getting all the vitamins and minerals it needs.

Problems like physical stress and illness rob you of vitamins and minerals. So do smoking and drinking. And, birth control pills, pregnancy and lactation also increase nutritional needs.

For instance, many of us aren't getting enough calcium for healthy bones. Or enough iron for healthy blood. Or enough of the B vitamins essential to every cell in our bodies.

The fact is, most people reading this ad probably have one or more vitamin or mineral gaps to fill.

And, scientists are now studying the nutritional role of vitamins, minerals and other nutrients in helping to protect against diseases such as cancer, heart disease and osteoporosis.

So why live at risk? Fill the gap. Take vitamin and mineral supplements every day. Is it a big deal?

You bet your life it is.

Council For Responsible Nutrition. An association of the nutritional supplement industry.

WHICH WOULD YOU RATHER PUT ON YOUR KIDS' CEREAL?

The decision is in your hands. But before you make it, here are some things to think about...

SUGAR IS SAFE.
People have been eating sugar for more than 2000 years. It is a safe food ingredient that can easily and guiltlessly be included, in moderation, as part of an overall healthy diet and lifestyle.

SUGAR IS 100% NATURAL.
Sugar is pure and natural. It is not made from nor does it contain any mysterious, hard-to-pronounce ingredients. It is separated from sugar cane and sugar beets–not made in a laboratory, no man-made chemicals that require warning labels.

SUGAR HAS ONLY 15 CALORIES PER TEASPOON.
Sugar has 15 calories per teaspoon and it's a smart way to add flavor and functionality to foods.

SUGAR HAS ONLY 4 GRAMS OF CARBOHYDRATES PER TEASPOON.
For those watching their carbohydrate intake, sugar fits perfectly into a healthy diet with only 4 grams of carbohydrates in a teaspoon.

SUGAR TASTES BEST.
Sugar is the gold-standard of sweeteners. In taste tests, sugar is preferred 3 to 1 over artificial sweeteners.

Now that you know the facts...relax! If you want your kids to have a sweetener that's 100% safe, pure and natural, give them real sugar!

100% NATURAL SUGAR.

THERE IS NO SUBSTITUTE.

THE SUGAR ASSOCIATION, INC. 1101 15th St., NW, Suite 600, Washington, DC 20005. (202) 785-1122   WWW.SUGAR.ORG

Splenda, Equal, and Sweet'N Low are trademarks of their respective owners.

MAKING CONNECTIONS:
MARKETING DIET AND HEALTH

The following questions are offered to help you start to make meaningful connections among the three articles and visual portfolio in this Case Study. These questions can be used for class discussion, or you can answer any one of the questions by writing an essay. If you choose the essay option, be sure to make specific references to at least two of the Case Study articles.

1. Analyze the ads in the preceding Case Study portfolio, paying particular attention to the types of claims being made in each one. Does your analysis support Liebman's conclusion that structure/function claims dominate because they are not regulated? Present your findings in a brief essay.

2. Some in advertising believe that advertising performs a useful service to consumers and that most consumers know enough not to be taken in by half-truths and exaggerations. Do you agree? How do you think Liebman, Federman, and Critser would respond to such a statement? What benefits, if any, do you think people receive either directly or indirectly from food advertising? Does food advertising arm consumers with information that in turn leads to informed buying decisions? Or is advertising harmful? Using the advertisements in the preceding Case Study portfolio as well as others that you have seen, write an essay in which you clearly articulate and support your position on this issue.

3. Using Hugh Rank's "Intensify/Downplay" schema (pp. 437–38), analyze the advertisements of three or four fast food restaurants in your area. What food product is being sold in each ad? What kinds of information about the nutritional value of the product are presented? Who is the audience for the ad? Is the ad's appeal mainly logical or emotional? What is the relationship, if any, between the text of the ad and the visuals? How do you think Liebman, Federman, and Critser would respond to the ads you analyzed? Write up your analysis in an essay.

4. In the wake of all the media attention given to America's obesity problem and lawsuits claiming that fast food restaurants are negligent about warning their customers about potential health problems associated with their products, what have America's fast food chains done to improve their tarnished image and to attract customers? Have any of them made an effort to change the ingredients in their current food products? Have any of them introduced new, more healthy product lines? If so, what claims are being made for these modified and new products? Using what you learned about advertising claims from Liebman, about the word *natural* from Federman, and about portion size from Critser, analyze the responses to public scrutiny made by a fast food chain like Wendy's, Kentucky Fried Chicken, Dunkin' Donuts, Burger King, Krispy Kreme, Subway, or a chain of your choosing.

5. For you, what are the connotations of the words *natural, fresh,* and *organic*? Do you believe that these words are inherently deceptive? What do you think you are buying when you purchase a product with one or more of these words on its label? Should these words be regulated in advertisements for

food products? Federman, for example, claims that "'natural' has become more of a marketing ploy than a way to communicate meaningful information about a product" (2). How are these words and words like them used in the four print ads included in the Case Study portfolio? Write an essay either for or against regulation, using examples from the four ads to support your position.

8

AMERICA WIRED

Social critics, news analysts, political scientists, volunteers, religious and community leaders across America have voiced concern over what appears to be a general decline in how much we value the actual concept of community. They worry about our failure or unwillingness to gather in meaningful and beneficial community-spirited groups and causes. In short, our "social capital," as one authority labeled our community and our desire to build and sustain it, appears to be declining. No thoughtful citizen who looks upon such a trend can help but wonder what this means. Are we seeing a loss of community or is the very idea of community undergoing a transformation?

Community is not only the coming together of people with similar interests and goals in a particular geographic location — the hospital auxiliary, the Little League, the neighborhood fundraiser, the school board — it is also the communication that takes place amongst those participants as they share their thoughts, beliefs, and aspirations. Central to communication within groups, whether based on geography, a commonality of interest, or a combination of the two, is language itself and the emerging technologies we use to transmit it. In recent years, e-mail, chat groups, bulletin boards, listservs, and Web-based synchronous communication such as AOL's Instant Messenger, have been added to our use of print media and the telephone as a way of keeping us informed and grouped together. So, while there is less of an interest in gathering physically in community groups, there is a great deal of community-building going on through e-communications. We set up meetings and share agendas, proposals, and the minutes of meetings that we attend or those we cannot be physically present for, but community is being built nonetheless. We are very much a member of a community when we use the city's listserv as a way of finding a specialty grocery store, a reliable auto mechanic, or a dentist available on weekends. These communications make us a part of something, even if it's not a group where handshaking and face-to-face encounters occur. Of course, there is a certain degree of depersonalization that results in using technology to accomplish what we used to do in a more personal manner, and that loss of personal contact has changed the manner in which we use our language, too.

The essays we have gathered here in one way or another speak to the issue of the loss of "social capital" and the way our language and communications are changing because we are increasingly becoming a "wired society." We begin "America Wired" with Robert D. Putnam and Lewis M. Feldstein's "Craigslist.org: Is Virtual Community Real?" wherein the authors discuss the concept of social capital and look at the potentially bright possibilities for bringing people together through a community listserv operating in San Francisco. The noted columnist William Safire then looks into "blogs," a shortened term for Web logs, as a way for people to share their personal lives through online diaries. In "Text Messaging: Take Note," Jennie Bristow looks at text messaging and answers the question of whether this new form of communication will affect the way we speak and write, leading her to argue for the continued teaching of grammar. Vanessa Bauza addresses the use of Spanglish, the melding of Spanish and English, as it is taking place in e-mails and on the Web and what representative members of the huge Spanish community in Miami think about it. Peter Mandaville's article, "Digital Islam: Changing the Boundaries of Religious Knowledge," looks at the way community is being built in Islamic countries as well as in Islamic cyber communities around the world. He is concerned with the interpretation of texts, religious teachings and practices, and the evolution of Islamic learning as a function of e-communications. Finally, Frederick L. McKissack argues that there is a "disparity between the techno-rich and the techno-poor" in America and that, because African Americans have not been given equal access to computers and computer skills, there is an information gap and a loss of real earning power in the African American community. In all these articles, we see the ways in which community, communication, and language intersect, interact, cross-fertilize, and evolve. Our social capital is changing in character, diminishing in certain ways, but also being reconstructed in others. Language is playing a key role as an impetus for a whole new definition of community and communication.

Craigslist.org: Is Virtual Community Real?

ROBERT D. PUTNAM AND LEWIS M. FELDSTEIN

In a review of Robert D. Putnam's groundbreaking book, Bowling Alone: The Collapse and Revival of American Community *(2000), Alan Ehrenhalt of the* Wall Street Journal *writes, "Bowling Alone is a minutely documented catalog of social disengagement of virtually every kind: political apathy, retreat from church attendance, eroding union membership, decline of bridge clubs and dinner parties, volunteering, and blood donation." Robert D. Putnam is a Professor of Public Policy at Harvard University and has had a distinguished career as an expert in the history and dynamics of our civic institutions. He is also the founder of the well-known Saguaro Seminar: Civic Engagement in America, a think tank that seeks to develop ideas for improving our nation's civic connectedness, or what he refers to as "social capital." Despite what he described as a thirty-year decline in civic involvement in our country, Putnam saw some reasons to be hopeful. In his latest book,* Better Together: Restoring the American Community *(2003), Putnam and his coauthor Lewis M. Feldstein, the president of the New Hampshire Charitable Foundation, have published a sampling of some of those hopeful signs from around the country.*

In the following selection, taken from Better Together, *Putnam and Feldstein raise the question of whether e-communications have the potential to bring people, ideas, and services together meaningfully. Craigslist.com is a powerful San Francisco-based virtual community, and, although things are changing very fast on the Web, it is one place where the authors believe it might be possible to get "some useful insights and perspective" on how social capital is being created in cyberspace.*

WRITING TO DISCOVER: *Think about your involvement in communities, whether they are local, regional, or national. Examples of the kinds of communities that you might focus on are religious groups, fraternities or sororities, support groups, sports groups, listservs, computer groups, online course groups, chat rooms, study groups, service organizations, and musical groups. Make a list of the groups to which you belong and reflect on your various memberships. Does the length of the list surprise you? Are you in more or fewer community groups than you imagined? Would you describe yourself as a joiner, a loner, or somewhere in between?*

Ever since the World Wide Web caught the public imagination and began to grow in the 1990s we have been hearing about the promise of online community. Some of the discussion has focused on the idea of electronic communities of interest — groups of people who may live thousands of miles apart coming together on the Web because of their common involvement in a particular subject or issue. (Support groups for victims of rare diseases and their families illustrate this sort of Net-based community.) Proponents of these communities have argued that ties of mutual interest mean more than the accident of physical proximity. Many such groups exist; whether they are communities in any but the very loosest sense of that word and whether they create new social capital, as we understand the term, are open questions.

Internet-based connections can be broadly divided into those that link you to people you already know and may have met face-to-face (such as e-mail) and those that link you to people whom you don't know and who may even be anonymous (such as chat rooms). (Of course, some uses of the Internet, such as listservs for common-interest groups, may involve a mixture of these two types.) Much of the hype about "virtual community" has revolved around the latter form of impersonal, even anonymous connection, but in terms of actual usage thus far, the former, more personal type of connection is far more common. For example, the authoritative UCLA annual survey of Internet usage found that the average user spends nearly twenty times more hours e-mailing than in chat rooms. As of 2002, "62.5 percent of all Americans send e-mail or instant messages."[1]

E-ties to people you don't know are, by definition, purely virtual, but e-ties to people whom you also know offline constitute a kind of alloy that combines the advantages of both computer-based and face-to-face connections. E-mail, instant messaging, and similar techniques join the ease, reach, and immediacy of electronic communication with the trust, sensitivity, and durability of relationships based on repeated face-to-face communication. Like the telephone, these forms of electronic communication can strengthen, broaden, and deepen existing personal ties. For example, e-mail (combined with the relative ease of tracking long-lost acquaintances through the Web's astonishing powers of information retrieval) can make it dramatically easier to renew personal ties with former schoolmates or distant family members. The UCLA survey in 2002 found that more than half of all users say that the Internet has increased the number of people with whom they stay in contact.[2] Similarly, in many parts of the world Internet entrepreneurs are seeking ways to use technology to foster greater communication within a single neighborhood. Such use of electronic communication as a supplement (not an alternative) to face-to-face communication may ultimately prove to be the most important effect of the Internet on social connectedness.

On the other hand, use of electronic means to communicate with people we already know offline, however much it permeates our lives, is not likely to produce entirely new forms of community. The more revolutionary potential of Internet technology is the possibility of creating connections among people who don't (or at least didn't) know each other offline. So in exploring the potential of the Internet for social-capital success stories, we looked especially hard for cases that seemed to promise the creation of new social ties among people who did not initially know one another.

We are in no position to judge authoritatively how much real com-   5
munity building and social-capital building happen on the Web. Although we looked hard for candidates for a case study of online social capital, our investigations usually turned up less solid evidence of new social capital than we had hoped. Some apparently promising sites were in decline; some turned out to be commercial ventures with a veneer of community vocabulary; most offered no clear evidence of members' building the relationships of trust and reciprocity that we understand to be central to social capital.

Obviously we cannot generalize about the vast and changing content of the World Wide Web, and we make no claim to a definitive survey. But we judged craigslist, which we examine here, the most interesting candidate for a social-capital case among the sites that came to our attention. It stands out in terms of longevity, growth, and the persistent commitment of its founder and users to the idea of a noncommercial electronic community meeting place owned and shaped by the people who post messages there. Craigslist began in San Francisco, and its San Francisco site, by far the most active of more than a dozen craigslist sites, is the one we examine. Studying craigslist will not answer all the important questions about social capital and cyberspace, but it can provide some useful insights and perspective.

WWW.CRAIGSLIST.ORG

Visit the San Francisco craigslist and you find a site that most closely resembles an electronic version of a newspaper's classified ads, with listings of jobs and housing, services, activities, items wanted and for sale, and personals. There are also discussion forums on topics including the arts, computers, parenting, pets, politics, and recreation. Compared with most Web sites, it is shockingly plain. There are no banner ads, no eye-catching colors, no animations — no graphics of any kind, in fact. What you see is a plain gray background and columns of text: lists of subcategories under the basic headings of "jobs," "housing," "personals," "community," etc. Click on a subcategory ("admin/office/cust serv," for instance, one of two dozen items under "jobs") and you find a list of jobs organized by the date they were posted (seventeen new listings on September 5, 2002, in this one area). Most of the job postings are similar to what you would find in the newspaper, though more detailed, since longer items cost no more to post than short ones. Many listings of houses and apartments for rent are similar — fairly detailed, but not much different from rental listings elsewhere. So what is going on here? What gives craigslist a possible claim to community and social-capital creation?

FROM ONE DOZEN USERS
TO 1.6 MILLION

Craigslist started small. In 1995, Craig Newmark worked for Charles Schwab, "evangelizing the Net inside the company," he says, talking to management about the role the Internet could play in the investment brokerage business. "I saw a lot of people helping each other out on the Net," he adds. "I figured I could do that, too."[3] Initially he sent e-mail messages to a list of about a dozen friends, telling them about technology events and arts events that he thought might interest them. The list of re-cipients grew as his friends forwarded the messages to their friends, and the kinds and amount of information increased as well. Within the year, Newmark replaced the e-mail list with a Web site. Job and housing leads became the core content; new categories and discussion forums were added as participation expanded, growing out of the interests of the peo-ple who used the site.

As of the spring of 2003, craigslist ranked among the 200 top Web sites in the world in terms of activity — actually 187 and climbing — with about 2.8 million unique visitors a month at its sites in nearly two dozen cities. The majority of activity occurs on the San Francisco site. But Newmark says the participation in the New York City site "took off" in 2001, and if its current growth rate continues, he expects it to equal or surpass the San Francisco site's sometime in 2004. All postings except job offers are free; those cost the posting organization seventy-five dollars for each listing. Because of their volume, the job listings generate enough revenue to support a staff of fourteen full-time employees.

The high level of activity on the San Francisco site may be one factor arguing in favor of craigslist as community or, at the very least, as deeply embedded in community. Craigslist has a presence in San Francisco. It has become a feature of the city's social landscape, something many peo-ple (especially but not exclusively those in their twenties and early thir-ties) use and discuss, something people who live there know about, part of the culture they share. The experience of one new user, Katherine Rose, shows how widely it is known and how closely it is identified with San Francisco. When Rose graduated from an East Coast university in the spring of 2002, she and some school friends decided to move to San Francisco. None of them had jobs lined up, but they trusted they would find work when they got there. Having grown up in the Boston area, Rose wanted the experience of living somewhere else.

10

She remembers, "As soon as I told people, 'I'm moving to San Francisco. I have to find an apartment,' they said, 'Have you looked on craigslist?' My mother's college roommate, who lives in Oakland, also suggested craigslist."

Once in San Francisco (she and her roommates rented a Russian Hill apartment they located through the site), Rose found that "everyone here says, 'Look at craigslist' for jobs, for furniture, for whatever you need." Many Web sites that are familiar to Internet enthusiasts seem to be invisible or unknown to the culture at large. In San Francisco, craigslist is an exception.

Then there is the fact that even in requests for housing or postings of rooms for rent, many people reveal much more about themselves on the site than we usually expect in such transactions, sharing the kinds of information we exchange when we are building a social connection with a new acquaintance. This excerpt is fairly typical:

> I am an adventurous, outdoorsy and athletic person when I am not hunkered down at my desk during the prime hours of the work day. CD's in rotation right now: Radiohead, The White Stripes, Beatles, Stones, and Coldplay. I am not a raging party guy but enjoy nights out on the weekends and good wine buzz from time to time.

as is this one:

> I am a 21 yr old student (biology major)/bartender/assistant private investigator. I take school very seriously. I enjoy going out on the weekends, or some week nights if all my homework is in place, and I usually stay out till pretty late (2–3AM). I am a pretty clean person, some would consider me anal, but I don't push it upon others to clean as vigorously as I do. I just like cleaning (weird, I know).

and this:

> We like intellectuals, hippies, poets, musicians, writers, auto mechanics, gardeners, techies, yogis, and many other types of persons as well. If you are rich and beautiful, that helps, but it is not necessary. If you are "normal," don't even bother. We like persons who can pay rent on time. We like eating healthy and organic. We like persons who have radical ideas, but who are also willing to clean the bathroom.

Personals are often many paragraphs long. Some are mini-autobiographies or short stories about failed relationships or little essays about what makes life good or horrible or the writer's hopes for the future. Craig Newmark has commented:

> Because we're not charging by the word, people can say as much as they want. And in their postings, people reveal something of themselves — and others feel a sense of connection. One woman told me that she reads our lists just for the personal stories. It's a window into what's going on around her, and it provides a sense of connection and intimacy with others. That's the common theme: What's going on around us?[4]

Newmark believes that the physical proximity of the people who visit   15
craigslist, the fact that they all know and experience the same metropolitan area, is crucial to the sense of community it generates. Although
technology commentators have often emphasized the globe-spanning
potential of the World Wide Web, Newmark insists that the localness of
the craigslist sites is what keeps them alive and growing and what makes
it possible for people to feel a community connection online. Studies of
e-mail use conducted by Barry Wellman and his colleagues at the University of Toronto support the idea of local focus rather than global reach.
Their research found that a significant majority of e-mail traffic passes between people who live within thirty miles of one another.

Periodically there are craigslist parties, announced in open invitations
to anyone who visits the site to get together at a restaurant or bar for a
few hours on a particular night. But only a tiny proportion of craigslist
users ever attend these gatherings, and Newmark does not believe that
actually meeting in a group is essential to feeling part of a craigslist community. He says:

> The idea that these are people in your neighborhood is what matters,
> that these are people you might know or see around town, or at least
> have a sense of the same local considerations. The idea that people
> *might* be around is more important than actual face-to-face contact.

Most of the postings are locally rooted by references to the events,
locations, and vocabulary of the area. Because of that, and also because
most postings are tied to specific needs (for housing, jobs, companion-
ship, help in a crisis), these electronic messages feel much more grounded
in the daily life of the city and more social than, say, the entries you find
on "blog" sites. (These are sites where "bloggers" — authors of Web
logs — post running commentaries about their smallest experiences in
often excruciating detail, frequently without any sense of where they are
or who might be interested in what they have to say.) On craigslist, some
messages, posted where a million people might read them, have a startling immediacy and localness:

> Looking for a lunch partner today. I'm at Market and 4th and could use
> some good food and conversation at about 1:00.

and:

> Anyone up for sushi tonight?

and:

> I'll be washing clothes shortly at 25th and Clement. Would anyone like
> to join me for a game of backgammon while the clothes spin?

On the community bulletin boards, along with people looking for
ride-sharing arrangements, musicians hoping to join bands, people seeking and offering child care, and others making similar requests that you
might also find in the classifieds of many newspapers, you come across

people asking for advice and support on intimate matters that we usually think of as shared only among close friends:

> I feel so ignorant for asking this question, but I was wondering how early you can tell if you are pregnant? My husband and I just got married three weeks ago and I feel like I am — symptoms like that time of the month, only more severe — very moody, have to pee all the time, dizzy — and I have this weird bloaty sort of feeling in my belly. I am just wondering if I am wishful thinking or if I could really tell this quickly?

and:

> All this week when I tried calling my son I have been told he is not available or asleep. Last night when I called I was told by his grandfather not to call his house anymore. This has me really distraught and I am leaning on this community for some help advice & support.

In the discussion forums, the almost-real-time conversations made up of e-mail questions, response, and comments sometimes have the character of conversation among friends who meet in a café or who have lunch together in the cafeteria at work and talk about the latest movie or some news item that has captured public attention. So, in the "parenting" forum, half a dozen participants talk about whether or not they lost their single friends after they had children. In the same forum, another group goes back and forth about what to think of the news of a baby killed by a bear in a state park: Were the parents negligent in leaving the baby outside in a carriage? Did they deserve sympathy or censure? Another thread of discussion deals with the question of whether women can have a full-time job and raise children without becoming totally exhausted, discouraged, or crazed.

These discussions are *like* conversations with friends in the local café,   20
but of course they are different, too, and different in ways that are important to community and social capital. Written messages lack the physical expressions and gestures that are such an important part of face-to-face conversation, clarifying and deepening the meanings of the words while adding their own unspoken meaning and providing an instantaneous response to what is being said. That combination of spoken language and body language helps us understand the tone and substance of what is being communicated and also helps us judge whether we should trust the person we are speaking to, and to what degree. In face-to-face conversation, we also get signals we use to judge *our* contributions: whether we are puzzling people or making them angry, boring them or fascinating them. The rich attributes of face-to-face conversation are one key reason why members of Valley Interfaith and other IAF groups go door-to-door in their communities to talk with people directly. (The other most important reason is that the investment of time and energy in showing up at people's homes demonstrates commitment and respect.)

Lacking all of the elements of conversation except the words, the exchanges of messages in the craigslist discussion forums are more fragile than "real" conversations. Without tone and gesture as guides to meaning, readers can easily misunderstand the intent of the writers. Without the (usually) moderating influence of facing the person you are speaking to, it becomes too easy to become extreme or abusive (hence the prevalence of "flaming" in e-mail exchanges), and some of the discussion boards in fact include messages that are much harsher than you would find in most face-to-face conversations. Finally, people can leave the online discussion in an instant, maybe joining in for only a few seconds to drop a bombshell into the conversation or disappearing as soon as they get bored or read something they do not like. If part of building the trusting relationships that define social capital is sticking with the conversation, hearing one another's stories, and working toward some mutual respect and understanding, then the disembodied and volatile world of online discussion is a flawed medium for creating social capital.

TRYING TO UNDERSTAND WEB COMMUNITY

To argue that the million-plus people who visit the San Francisco craigslist site every month form a "community" would, we believe, reduce that word almost to meaninglessness. The people who use craigslist simply to find a job or an apartment or those who visit the site for fifteen minutes for the voyeuristic pleasure of reading other people's personal ads can hardly be called members of a craigslist community. As our discussion of online conversation suggests, even some more actively engaged users who participate in forums about parenting or technology or politics connect with one another only in a limited and tenuous way.

Experience in the Blacksburg, Virginia, electronic community network suggests that "when you overlay an electronic community directly on top of a physical community, that creates a very powerful social pressure to be civil. If you're going to yell at somebody on the 'Net, or flame them out, you may run into them at the grocery store, and they may turn out to be your neighbor."[5] Alloys of face-to-face and e-based ties can sustain social capital.

By contrast, building trust and goodwill is not easy in the largely anonymous, easy-in, easy-out, surf-by world of pure cyberspace. Craig himself clearly understands how delicate are the norms of civility, reciprocity, and trustworthiness — the social capital — that undergird his site's success. "We're trying to figure out how to run the site as a commons, yet avoid the tragedy of the commons," Craig tells reporters. "We still have a ways to go. There's always going to be something." And "the culture of trust we've built is a really big deal. We have to re-earn that every day."[6]

But there are indications even beyond the intimacy and trust of the   25
postings we have quoted that many craigslist users *feel* connected to a
community and see their participation in the site as part of their identity.
Like members of other groups, they share a specialized vocabulary that
separates insiders from outsiders: not only "CL" (for craigslist), but
"420," (marijuana), "MC" (missed connection), and "flags" (objections
to postings) as well as standard ways of advertising for roommates who
will not cause a lot of fuss ("no drama"). Newmark says that one indication that craigslist was becoming more than just a bulletin board was that,
much to his surprise, he started getting fan mail. Past fifty, balding, soft-
spoken, he describes himself as having been one of those nerdy kids in
school who wore taped-together glasses and a plastic pocket protector —
an unlikely candidate for adulation. But craigslist habitués look up to
him as the founder and protector of "their" site, as a central and admired
personality in their community. Newmark has been invited to a number
of weddings of couples who found each other through craigslist
personals.

Which brings up an important point: However much craigslist may
be a community itself, it unquestionably functions as a tool to create
community by bringing people together, by helping runners, soccer players, readers, theater lovers, wine enthusiasts, Asian Americans, rock
climbers, sports fans, and European expatriates find one another. Many
hundreds of groups, clubs, and teams have been formed or populated
through craigslist.

Newmark says that the WELL, an early online community, was one
of the inspirations for craigslist. Created in 1985, the WELL was exhibit
A in Howard Rheingold's argument in *The Virtual Community* that electronic meeting places can be genuine communities.[7] At the time Rheingold wrote about the WELL (an acronym for "Whole Earth 'Lectronic
Link"), it had a lot in common with what we see today on craigslist. Localness mattered. The WELL was also based in San Francisco, and its
members lived mostly in that area. Many regularly got together at "real"
gatherings as well as online: at picnics and parenting groups, and at a variety of social get-togethers of people who first found one another in cyberspace. More than Newmark does with regard to craigslist, Rheingold
credited these get-togethers with making the community a real one. He
commented, "The WELL felt like an authentic community to me from
the start because it was grounded in my everyday physical world," and he
mentioned the weddings, outings, and parties he had attended.[8] The
WELL had a similar range of topics and forums growing out of the interests of users (though not the housing and job lists that are a central part
of craigslist). "WELLites" had their own vocabulary ("IRL," meaning
"in real life," and "Thanks to everyone for your generous WELLbeams,
good wishes, prayers . . . ").[9] Most of all, the WELL, like craigslist, had
strikingly intimate, trusting exchanges as people posted messages about

relationships and medical problems, their work and their aspirations. Rheingold's strongest evidence for the WELL as a community was the exchanges he quoted.

Once considered *the* outstanding example of an online community, the WELL has seen its presence and reputation fade. Now a commercial discussion site owned by Salon Media, it has lost its localness and much of its community sense. Even aside from the important question of financing, craigslist may thrive where the WELL failed in part because of the centrality of job and housing listings on craigslist. The job listings are certainly the least personal category on the site, and housing less personal than many of the others. But these are the categories that most attract new people to craigslist, that create a mass of potential community members. Also, our observations of other social-capital-creating groups show mainly people coming together for purposes other than creating new social ties — for political action or economic advantage, for instance. Having an important aim other than simply being together or meeting new people — finding a job or a place to live — may provide a useful foundation for robust social capital.

Newmark himself attributes the WELL's decline in part to a membership mechanism that was not as free and open as he believes it could have been and in part to inattention to real human needs in other cities. "Their membership model didn't seem to be right," he says. The founders of the WELL identified free access as a goal but admitted that they could not survive without charging a fee. Certainly the current, commercial version of the WELL, with its sign-up and monthly fee required before a newcomer can join the conversation or even eavesdrop to discover whether the conversation is worth joining, does not feel like a welcoming community. The idea of paying to meet people is unsettling.

Craigslist, on the other hand, is as free and open as possible. Anyone   30 can read all the postings and discussion threads simply by clicking on them — no need to pay, sign in, or provide any information about yourself. Posting a listing is almost as easy (with the exception of the fee-based job listings). Posters do have to give their e-mail address so that they can be sent a "self-publishing kit," but otherwise they are entirely free to create a message of any length, indicate the category it belongs in, and see it quickly posted on the site. The whole process happens without staff intervention.

This openness and ease of use must certainly contribute to the amount of traffic the site gets, but it raises another question about community. Since communities generally define themselves by both what they are and what they are not, by the norms that represent common community behavior, how can a Web site that is open to everyone, and has more than a million people at least "passing through" every month, be a community? How can it establish and maintain community norms?

Remarkably, for the most part, craigslist seems to do exactly that. Newmark says, "Norms were originally based on the idea that people should give each other a break. People have built a culture of trust on the site, managing the amount of abuse." They manage it through the mechanism of "flagging." Every posting on the site (except in the discussion forums) includes a "flag for review" feature that allows any reader to indicate that he or she thinks a particular posting should be removed: because the item is miscategorized, is "spam" (Internet junk mail), is an example of ticket scalping or other unapproved commercial scheme, or is unacceptably abusive. Until recently, craigslist staff reviewed postings that received a certain number of flags and decided whether or not to remove them. Now the process has been automated. As soon as a posting receives a set number of flags for the same reason, the site's software automatically removes it and returns it to the poster.

The system is not foolproof. Newmark says that he knows it can be abused, but generally it is not. It in fact seems to function reasonably well as an automated, community-managed system for defining and maintaining community norms of acceptable and unacceptable behavior. Disagreements exist, including objections to the removal of items that are offensive to some and not to others, but those electronic discussions sound very much like the discussions that go on in any community as it defines and refines its values. Such user-controlled social machinery is not common on the Web, but William A. Galston, in "(How) Does the Internet Affect Community? Some Speculation in Search of Evidence," suggests that collective definition of norms is a feature of many Internet groups: "Internet groups rely to an unusual degree on norms that evolve through iteration over time and are enforced through moral suasion and group disapproval of conspicuous violators . . . the medium is capable of promoting a kind of socialization and moral learning through mutual adjustment."[10]

The amount of user influence on the content of craigslist means that users have as much or more power than staff to shape the sites in various cities. Newmark says, "The sites will evolve, sometimes in unexpected ways. Over time, I'm hoping people who live in these places will set the tone." So far, the clearest differences are between sites like those of San Francisco and New York City, which have a lot of traffic, and those of Boston, Denver, Seattle, and other cities, which have much less. The first thing you notice when you look at those smaller sites is that there are dramatically fewer categories and postings. But you can also find differences between San Francisco and New York that reflect the characteristic preoccupations of people in each city. So, for instance, San Francisco has a computer forum and a "transport" forum, where you find discussions about how to keep salt air from rusting cars and comparisons of Honda and Toyota hybrid cars. The New York craigslist forum has nothing about cars (not surprisingly) or even computers, but it has a "nightlife" forum, where people ask for recommendations for dance clubs and bars, and an "eateries & cuisine" forum, where people respond to questions

like "Are there any good bakeries in the Gramercy Park area?" and
"Where should I take my parents to dinner when they visit?" You could
almost certainly guess which city the participants live in by dipping into
their discussions. The user control over norms and content that is gradually differentiating these sites from one another argues in favor of there
being at least a core of genuine community at craigslist.

Newmark is deeply committed to maintaining craigslist's character   35
and sense of user ownership. It is no surprise that a site that is among the
top few hundred sites on the Web in terms of traffic would attract commercial interests. In 1999, Newmark turned down an offer for the site
that would have made him a wealthy man. The buyout offers continue.
Recently, he says, "I got a call from some investors who wanted to buy it,
but when they heard we were publicly committed to no banner ads, they
gave up." Commercialization would unquestionably change the character
of the site, destroying the sense of user ownership and control and, probably, the sense of community.

With the qualifications that we have expressed here, we think that
craigslist has elements of community to a surprising degree and that its
community nature has a great deal to do with elements that we see in
other forms of community: localness, member participation in defining
the norms of the group, aims and purposes beyond that of simply being
together. This example does not imply a future in which masses of people
will migrate from local, traditional communities to communities of interest in cyberspace — quite the contrary — but it does suggest a role for
the Internet in the mix of ways that people come to know, trust, and connect with one another. Newmark himself is relatively unconcerned about
whether what happens on craigslist meets any particular definition of
community or social capital:

> People started telling me that they felt connected in some kind of com-
> munity sense. I used to be doctrinaire about definitions and I didn't feel
> it was a community site, but I eventually said, if people feel connected,
> it must be a community.

Notes

1. UCLA Internet report, "Surveying the Digital Future: Year Three" (Los Angeles:
   UCLA Center for Communication Policy, January 2003), pp. 19, 54.
       Of course, another important use of the Internet for most people is information
   processing and retrieval. That, too, is having powerful effects on our lives — this
   book, for example, could hardly have been completed without our ability to retrieve
   information from the Web easily. However, information processing and retrieval in itself does not build social capital, so we disregard that function here.
2. Ibid., p. 55.
3. Unless otherwise noted, quotations from Craig Newmark are from a phone interview
   with Cohen, August 29, 2002.

4. Craig Newmark, interview with Katharine Mieszkowski, *Net Company*, Winter 2000, p. 26.

5. Andrew Cohill and Andrea Kavanaugh, *Community Networks: Lessons from Blacksburg, Virginia* (Norwood, Mass.: Artech House, 2000).

6. Bill Werde, "A Web Site as 18-Ring Circus of Supply and Demand," *New York Times*, January 23, 2003; Anita Hamilton, "Find It on Craig's List," *Time*, March 3, 2003.

7. Howard Rheingold, *The Virtual Community: Homesteading on the Electronic Frontier* (Reading, Mass.: Addison-Wesley, 1993).

8. Ibid., p. 2.

9. Ibid., pp. 2, 32.

10. William A. Galston, "(How) Does the Internet Affect Community? Some Speculation in Search of Evidence," in Elaine Ciulla Kamarck and Joseph S. Nye Jr., eds., *democracy.com? Governance in a Networked World* (Hollis, N.H.: Hollis Publishing, 1999), p. 53.

FOCUSING ON CONTENT

1. Putnam and Feldstein say that Internet-based connections can be divided into roughly two types. What are those types? Why is the division they make helpful in understanding social capital in cyberspace? For example, which type is more helpful in building social capital?

2. What may be one factor arguing for craigslist as community? What does Newmark believes may be some others?

3. Explain why Newmark believes that longer personal ads may be a factor in community development. What makes longer ads possible on craigslist?

4. Why are the entries on craigslist considered more social than "blogs"?

5. Why did the WELL fail to live up to the potential that craigslist has achieved? How is ethical behavior controlled on craigslist? Does that ethical oversight reveal that a genuine community exists among the users of craigslist?

FOCUSING ON WRITING

1. How helpful are the authors in providing definitions? (Glossary: *Definitions*)

2. Describe the authors' use of examples in building a case for craigslist as a community builder. (Glossary: *Examples*)

3. How would you characterize the authors' attitude toward craigslist? (Glossary: *Attitude*) Negative? Positive? Neutral? Skeptical? What about the authors' tone? (Glossary: *Tone*) Cool? Encouraging? Distant? Accessible?

4. Why is it important for Putnam and Feldstein to rely on Newmark for information and to quote him directly? (Glossary: *Evidence*)

5. With what kinds of statements do the authors use to make it clear that they don't want to make promises for sites such as craigslist as to the future of community building in cyberspace? Why are they careful not to oversell the idea?

LANGUAGE IN ACTION

Visit the craigslist site (www.craigslist.org) and make an assessment about the nature of the information contained there, both its content and style of presentation. What comments can you make about the site with respect to the building of social capital? Do you experience community there?

WRITING SUGGESTIONS

1. Based on your reading of Putnam and Feldstein's discussion of craigslist, argue that it is or is not a virtual community. Of course, it will be necessary to define what you mean by community before going on to argue your position. What else beyond what Putnam and Feldstein present as evidence might you bring to the discussion? In the writing of your argument, you might want to consult with professors whose expertise is in this area of language and technology as well as interview friends who are interested in e-communications.

2. Write an essay in which you establish your own definition of community. Your work should consider such resource material as dictionary and encyclopedia definitions and more contextual reference attempts at definitions in the reading you have done in your college coursework, especially in literature courses, where authors often attempt less direct, more contextual definitions of community by way of creating settings for their characters. How has language, in particular, played a role in shaping the definition of community, whether real or virtual?

Picturing Language

This graphic was used to accompany an article in *Wired* magazine on "the blogging revolution." Do you agree that blogs have transformed the ways in which we use technology to transmit our inner feelings? How does this graphic represent a possible revolution? What is the effect of using different forms of the word *blog*, as this graphic artist has done? What is the effect of organizing these words into a spiral that culminates in the formation of the figure's head? What does this say about the role that blogs have assumed in communication, language, and culture?

Blog

WILLIAM SAFIRE

There is perhaps no more well-known authority on the English language than William Safire. His popular "On Language" column for the New York Times *addresses usage, the history of words and phrases, as well as new words that are coming into the language. Safire has written both novels and nonfiction books that include a dictionary, a history, and political commentary. His most recent book is a collection of his "On Language" columns entitled* No Uncertain Terms *(2003). As a former political insider and speech writer, Safire takes pleasure in writing political commentaries that skewer the opponents of his former boss Richard Nixon for not applying the same standards to White House administrators who came after Nixon. He won the 1978 Pulitzer Prize for his commentaries on one such insider, Bert Lance, in the Carter administration. After attending Syracuse University for several years, Safire dropped out, but was invited back some years later to receive an honorary degree and to serve as a trustee of the university.*

In the following selection, which first appeared in the July 28, 2002, issue of the New York Times, *Safire zeroes in on the word* blog *and deems it "a useful addition to the lexicon."*

WRITING TO DISCOVER: *Reflect on some of the new words that you have heard lately related to computers, software, or surfing the Web. How useful are the words? How many of those words do you think will still be in use over the next few years?*

In an upbeat Independence Day column in the *Wall Street Journal*, Peggy Noonan, the incurable optimist, wrote about all "the lights that didn't fail" America — from cops and firemen to peach-growing farmers and cancer-curing scientists, from local churches to TV comedians, to *blogging*.

Blogging? She explained the word as "the 24/7 opinion sites that offer free speech at its straightest, truest, wildest, most uncensored, most thoughtful, most strange. Thousands of independent information entrepreneurs are informing, arguing, adding information."

Blog is a shortening of *Web log*. It is a Web site belonging to some average but opinionated Joe or Josie who keeps what used to be called a "commonplace book" — a collection of clippings, musings, and other things like journal entries that strike one's fancy or titillate one's curiosity. What makes this online daybook different from the commonplace book is that this form of personal noodling or diary-writing is on the Internet, with links that take the reader around the world in pursuit of more about a topic.

To set one up (which I have not done because I don't want anyone to know what I think), you log on to a free service like blogger.com or xanga.com, fill out a form, and let it create a Web site for you. Then you follow the instructions about how to post your thoughts, photos, and clippings, making you an instant publisher. You then persuade or coerce your friends, family, or colleagues to log on to you and write in their own loving or snide comments.

"Will the *blogs* kill old media?" asked *Newsweek*, an old-media publi-   5
cation, perhaps a little worried about this disintermediation leading to an invasion of alien ad-snatchers. My answer is no; gossips like an old-fashioned party line, but most information seekers and opinion junkies will go for reliable old media in zingy new digital clothes. Be that as it may (a phrase to avoid the voguism *that said*), the noun *blog* is a useful addition to the lexicon.

Forget its earliest sense, perhaps related to *grog*, reported in 1982 in the *Toronto Globe and Mail* as "a lethal fanzine punch concocted more or less at random out of any available alcoholic beverages." The first use I can find of the root of *blog* in its current sense was the 1999 "Robot Wisdom Weblog," created by Jorn Barger of Chicago.

Then followed *bloggers*, for those who perform the act of *blogging* and — to encompass the burgeoning world of Web logs — *blogistan* as well as the coinage of William Quick on the *blog* he calls *The Daily Pundit*, the *blogosphere*. Sure to come: the *blogiverse*.

FOCUSING ON CONTENT

1. What is a *blog*? When and how did the word originate? Did *blog* mean the same thing in 1982 as it means today? Explain.

2. When was the current meaning of the word established?

3. How does Safire answer those at *Newsweek* who want to know what effect blogs will have on print media?

4. Have you heard of *blogistan*, *blogosphere*, or *blogiverse*, a word Safire playfully thinks may exist one day?

5. What might the development of blogging say about our sense of language and community? Might blogging be a way of building community? Explain.

FOCUSING ON WRITING

1. Safire engages in some irony when he explains why he hasn't set up a blog. Why is his comment ironic? (Glossary: *Irony*)

2. What is a "commonplace book"? Of what use is it?

3. What is Safire's attitude and tone regarding blogging? (Glossary: *Attitude* and *Tone*) Does he think it's a good thing or a bad thing, or does he appear

to have no attitude at all toward blogs and bloggers? Is his tone serious, playful, cynical, or some combination between those extremes?

LANGUAGE IN ACTION

Visit a blog — Safire suggests www.blogger.com or www.xanga.com, or you can peruse www.livejournal.com or www.diaryland.com — and spend 10–15 minutes becoming familiar with the site and the kinds of writing that bloggers have done. Make a list of the characteristics of the site that you visit so that you contribute what you saw and read on the site to a classroom discussion about blog sites and blog writing. What, if anything, differentiates bloggers' style from that of other kinds of familiar writing styles?

WRITING SUGGESTIONS

1. If you have a blog of your own, write a paper characterizing what your goals are for the site. Is your site focused on any topics or group of topics, or is it a diary format in which you write about what you have experienced since you last wrote or what new directions your thinking and reflections have been taking you?

2. Much of what we have been asking students to consider writing about in our Writing to Discover journal prompts is very often similar to what students choose to write about in their blogs. You may want, therefore, to set up your own blog on an official blogging Web site (if you do not already have a blog) and in it offer reactions to the articles you are reading for class assignments. Perhaps there are others in your class who would like to do the same so that you and your classmates can become each other's audience. Blogging sites such as www.livejournal.com even offer a "Friends" option that lets you link your online journal to a classmate's.

Text Messaging: Take Note

JENNIE BRISTOW

Jennie Bristow is the editor in charge of commissioning articles for
spiked, *a British online publication.* spiked *describes itself as "an online publication with the modest ambition of making history as well as
reporting it.* spiked *stands for liberty, enlightenment, experimenta-
tion, and excellence. Its priorities are content, content, and content.
(Although the design is not bad either.) Based in London but talking
to the world,* spiked *is entirely independent. It is designed and built by
volunteers, financed by supporters and sponsors, and written for by
unpaid contributors." A writer herself, Bristow focuses on the politics
of everyday life and is frequently in demand as both a writer and a
speaker across the United Kingdom. She is the author of* May I Do?
Marriage and Commitment in Singleton Society, *published in 2002.*

In the following article, which first appeared in spiked *on January 29, 2001, Bristow uses the topic of text messaging to reflect on
the need to teach grammar in an age that seems disinterested in the
subject.*

WRITING TO DISCOVER: *Are you a text messenger? Do you have
friends who are? What do you think of text messaging? Will it
change the way we write, in your opinion? What about e-mails that
you write? Do you send them with errors or are you careful to edit
before sending them? Has using e-mail changed the way you write
or regard correctness in writing?*

If you're going to write a column about text messaging, I know it's
the done thing to use the lingo (as in the best-selling guidebook
WAN2TLK: ltl bk of txt msgs). Sorry.

I am not one of the world's great text messagers. Until last week, I
had a mobile phone that was so big, basic, and ancient that people started
asking "Is that a WAP phone?" (Answer: no, it's a crap phone.) I am also,
I suppose, too grammatically old-fashioned for my age. I like words; I
like sentences; I like punctuation. Even as a teenager, I had misgivings
about the Me 4 U graffiti, and suffered a nerd-like compulsion to correct
it on school toilet walls.

But I cannot get into this idea, promoted by Dr. Ken Lodge of the
University of East Anglia, that text messaging is destroying literacy. Dr.
Lodge claims that, by abbreviating the English language to the extreme
and by substituting numbers for letters, we can lose sight of what it
means to read and write properly.[1]

---

1. Reported in *The Guardian*, 22 January 2001.

"I think it's a weird way to communicate," said Dr. Lodge. "Inevitably it'll affect the way people talk to each other." He points out that "there are already problems with university students with their inability to write English. The more people use it, the less they'll be aware of different styles of communicating."

There is a temptation here to point out that if Dr. Lodge's grasp   5
of grammar is anything to go by, students may be better off without it
(although maybe the issue is the way the reporter has paraphrased his
comments — which could support Dr. Lodge's argument). In either case,
the question is: what are we really talking about here? Is the technology
the problem — or something else?

That young people don't know no grammar is fairly obvious. My education in English grammar stopped with nouns (being words), verbs (doing words) and adjectives (describing words). What grammar I did learn came through modern languages; and that only happened because frustrated French language assistants could not believe our ignorance. Even now, I can tell you what the pluperfect of a French verb is, but defining the pluperfect tense *itself*? Forget it.

But the grammar issue is about education. Teachers have not taught it — with the consequence, as many commentators have remarked, that when young teachers are forced to teach grammar through the UK National Literacy Scheme, they don't even know what they are supposed to be teaching. Even if grammar is high on today's government's list of educational priorities, it is suffering from having been educationally unfashionable. Nothing to do with mobile phones.

In any case, text messaging has very little to do with grammar. If young people write a bad letter, you can tell they are grammatically deficient. Text messaging, by contrast, is just note writing. If I leave a note for my husband reading "GONE 2 SAINSBRY J," I do not expect him to criticize the lack of paragraph breaks (or anything else — after all, who's cooking?). It might not be poetry — but it gets the point across.

Brendan, my colleague on *spiked*, is trained as a proofreader. The result? He sends terrible text messages: all proper words, in sentences with full stops, which take you forever (4eva?) to read. Just as I have bought a slinky new mobile phone, which might encourage me to get into text messaging, my colleague Helene (the original IT girl — she's had the same model for months) tells me that the phone turns your text messages into proper words. Regardless of how succinctly and numerically I write, everybody receiving my messages will think I am doing a Brendan. Damn.

I do have to confess to a formality-fetish with e-mail. I thought my pen-   10
chant for using a proper form of address, and always including a sign-off,
made me infinitely superior to the people who reply to my carefully crafted
e-mails with statements like "OK." But then somebody told me about a colleague of his, who maintains that anybody who writes e-mails as though they were letters obviously has too much time on his hands. Fair enough.

There is a problem with people's use of text messaging and e-mail — but this is about sloppiness, not grammar. E-mail might be more like memo-writing than letter-writing; but while it is good to be succinct, whatever you write has to be comprehensible. People who write an unpunctuated stream of consciousness with no capital letters excEpt for those in tHE WRong places and words spelt worngly should as far as im concerned be lined up against a wall and given a damn good talking to by their least favorite ex-schoolteacher.

E-mail is supposed to ease communication — not make the recipient spend hours with a dictionary, wondering "What the hell is this supposed to say?" Be informal, if you like; be efficient, certainly. But if any of this is going to benefit us, in work or socially, other people need to understand what we are saying. Otherwise we'll all be climbing the walls of a modern-day Tower of Babel.

FOCUSING ON CONTENT

1. What is Bristow's thesis in this article? (Glossary: *Thesis*)

2. Bristow says that there may be one of two problems with Dr. Lodge's statement about university students' ability to write English. What are the two problems?

3. Comment on Bristow's first sentence in paragraph 6.

4. Why does Bristow think that the issue of grammar is a misguided one with respect to text messaging? What is the real problem?

5. What is the difference between e-mail writing and text messaging as far as correctness is concerned, according to Bristow?

FOCUSING ON WRITING

1. Where in her article does Bristow write incorrectly? Why?

2. Why is Bristow upset with the new phones that convert text messaging into proper words?

3. What characterizes text messaging? How is it different from correct English?

4. Why do you think it has been "educationally unfashionable" (7) to teach grammar?

LANGUAGE IN ACTION

Text messaging is created by rewriting words in shorthand. What relationship, if any, do you see between text messaging and what is being demonstrated in the following prose passage?

Aoccdrnig to a rscheearch at Cmabrigde Uinervtisy, it deosn't mttaer in waht oredr the ltteers in a wrod are, the olny iprmoatnt tihng is taht the frist and lsat ltteer be at the rghit pclae. The rset can be a ttoal mses and you can sitll raed it wouthit porbelm. Tihs is bcuseae the huamn mnid deos not raed ervey lteter by istlef, but the wrod as a wlohe. Amzanig huh?

WRITING SUGGESTIONS

1. Some argue that the more technological our communications become, the less we actually communicate. Is there any truth to this idea, in your view? Is there something wrong, or has there always been room to improve our ability to communicate with one another? Is technology too easy a target as the source of the problem? Write an essay arguing your position. Before proceeding, however, think about what might be meant by "room to improve our ability to communicate."

2. Schoolteachers complain that youngsters use text messaging across the classroom and while sitting next to each other on the school bus rather than engage in face-to-face exchanges. On a larger scale, e-mail may be diminishing the desire of people to gather for conversation and discussion by making it easier to ask questions and make comments while in the relative isolation of their homes and dorm rooms. Certainly, if distance is a factor, e-mail is a wonderful way to stay in touch. But the question is: Are we becoming increasingly disconnected while we become increasingly connected? To put the question in terms that would be familiar to Putnam and Feldstein, has communication technology been a factor in reducing our social capital? Or, has technology been instrumental in increasing social capital. After carefully weighing both sides of the issue, write an essay in which you express your views on the effects of technology on our ability to communicate.

Internet Spanglish

VANESSA BAUZA

Vanessa Bauza is a reporter for the South Florida Sun-Sentinel *and regularly writes reports on people and events from Havana, Cuba. In the following article, which first appeared in the* Sun-Sentinel *on May 27, 1998, Bauza reports on the increasing use of Spanglish on the Internet. Spanglish is an evolving dialect, a mixture of Spanish and English words or inventive forms of words, that defies strict definition. It is sneered upon by many older and more conservative speakers of Spanish who take it upon themselves to "protect" the integrity of their language from such corrupting influences, but it's useful to younger speakers as a solution to the obscurity of English technospeak or when there are no Spanish translations available for technical terms. We know that its variety is tied to the regions where it is spoken, so that the Spanglish of Miami is not the Spanglish of New York or Los Angeles. The Internet has propelled the use of Spanglish further into both Spanish and Anglo cultures, but only time will tell with what results.*

WRITING TO DISCOVER: *What is your reaction when you hear someone who is speaking a language other than English suddenly drop in an English word or phrase? Are you surprised? Do you wonder why English is used? What about when you hear someone speaking English who suddenly drops in words from another language? Why do suppose people mix languages in this way? Do you do it?*

Javier Sotomayor speaks in either English or Spanish — not the controversial concoction called Spanglish.

But, like thousands of other Latinos, he peppers a daily slew of e-mail messages with Spanglish phrases like *estoy surfeando el Internet* (I'm surfing the Internet) and *emaileame* (e-mail me).

"I only use Spanglish for technical terms," said Sotomayor, who moved to Miami from Puerto Rico seven years ago. "I feel embarrassed with older people who are new to technology, and I've been criticized by a few."

From South Beach to Palm Beach, Spanglish — already a standard in homes, on radio shows and I-95 billboards — has conquered cyberspace.

According to the Miami-based marketing firm, Strategy Research, one-third of South Florida's Latinos have personal computers, the highest proportion in the country's Latino communities. They are no strangers to the Cyber Spanglish debates popping up in chatrooms and Web sites.

Some say using English words with Spanish conjugations leads to the corruption of the Spanish language.

For others, it's a natural evolution rising from the lack of Spanish translations for English technospeak.

All agree that Cyber Spanglish is as pervasive on the Net as cortaditos and Cuban sandwiches are on local menus.

Like chameleons straddling two cultures, many Latinos here tailor their language to their audience.

Amelia Iglesias, who was born and raised in Peru, said she avoids   10
Spanglish when speaking but uses it often on the Internet, which she considers a more relaxed form of communication. She feels Spanglish is lazy.

"I have a problem with people who carry on a conversation in Spanish and use a word they have created," said Iglesias, of Miami. "That's when the language starts to deteriorate."

Mauricio Paniagua, of Delray Beach, agrees.

"Every language should be spoken correctly," said the Bolivian native. "It's like Americans are taking more and more of Latin culture when we use their terms."

Spanish translations for technological terms can be awkward. "Dar un tapecito" seems a mouthful, while "click" is quick and efficient.

"I don't blame people for using Spanglish because there aren't   15
enough translations," said Professor Alfred Gomez, a computer science professor at Broward Community College.

Like others, Gomez would like to see an approved list of translations, so Latinos from Buenos Aires to Boca Raton can share a common computer vocabulary.

Last year, MCI released a Spanish and English Technoguía that defines nearly 1,000 computer terms.

Also, a CyberSpanglish Web site has 650 English, Spanish, and Spanglish technical terms. Yolanda Rivas, a Ph.D. candidate at the University of Texas at Austin, founded the site in 1995 with 100 words and has received hundreds of contributions since then.

Some feel Rivas is promoting a bastardized version of the language. One Spanish Web site refers to her as a Peruvian who has lived in Texas too long.

"But that's the way we talk," Rivas counters. "One of the beauties of   20
our culture is that we are very flexible."

Since founding the site, Rivas has noticed more Latinos using Spanish translations like *ratón* and *enlace* rather than opting for the English "mouse" and "link." Transliterations like *escaner* for "scanner" are appearing in dictionaries.

"Users will become more comfortable using Spanish words as they become more comfortable with the technology," Rivas said from Austin. "With a little time, we'll stop saying 'cookies' and start saying *galletas.*"

As U.S. Latinos gain more political and commercial clout, so will the Spanish language, predicted University of Miami professor of bilingual communications Sandra Fradd.

"Spanish is very vulnerable to the intrusions of English," Fradd said. "But we're about to see a resurgence in purism in Spanish because the economic value of (speaking) Spanish is going up."

According to *Hispanic Business Magazine*, Miami in 1997 was second   25
only to Los Angeles in its number of Hispanic-owned companies: 136,204. Fort Lauderdale came in 12th with 23,211 Hispanic-owned companies.

The future of Spanglish on the Internet is as wide open as the technology itself. But some, like Bill Teck, editor of the Miami-based Spanglish magazine *Generation ñ*, refuse to take it too seriously.

"It's proof of the completeness of a culture when it has its particular dialect that only those people in the culture understand," Teck said. "People enjoy the humor. It gives language a little more flavor, a little more spice."

FOCUSING ON CONTENT

1. What is Bauza's thesis, and where does she offer the best statement of it? (Glossary: *Thesis*)

2. What are some of the arguments for and against the use of Spanglish, according to Bauza?

3. Why does Javier Sotomayor use Spanglish for technical terms only, and not for general conversation?

4. What relationship does Bauza see between the resurgence of purism in Spanish and the increased power in politics and business in the Spanish community in Miami?

5. In paragraph 5, Bauza cites Strategy Research as saying that "one-third of South Florida's Latinos have personal computers, the highest proportion in the country's Latino communities." What role does being wired play in the building of social capital amongst the area's Latino population?

FOCUSING ON WRITING

1. Bauza's paragraphs frequently contain only one or two sentences because her article appeared in the *Sun-Sentinel* where such short paragraphs are necessary for ease of reading the narrow columns of the newspaper. Do those short paragraphs make it easier or more difficult for you to read? Explain.

2. Bauza quotes a number of people in her article who explain how they use or refrain from using Spanglish. How do those sources help her in the writing of her article? (Glossary: *Evidence*)

3. Does Bauza offer her own opinion on the advisability of using Spanglish? Why or why not? (Glossary: *Attitude*)

4. Bauza uses a number of words and expressions to illustrate what she means by Spanglish. In your opinion, does she offer enough examples, too many, or just the right number to aid your understanding? (Glossary: *Examples*) Explain.

LANGUAGE IN ACTION

Comment in class on these examples of cyber Spanglish from an article by Liz Doup in the January 19, 2003 issue of the South Florida *Sun-Sentinel*:

Save a file and you make el backup.
Don't forget to baquear your work.
When your computer locks up it's time to resetear.
Take el maus to clickear on icons.
Talk to people and you chateas online.
You deleteas a file.

WRITING SUGGESTIONS

1. As Bauza has already hinted at, changes in culture are often represented in the language that the members of that culture use in everyday life. What changes have occurred in the life of the Latinos in Miami? If you are from a community that has a large Latino population, write an essay in which you attempt to draw parallels between the social changes that have been taking place over the past ten to twenty years in your community and the changes that are occurring in the language that is spoken in the homes, on the streets, and in the businesses of the community.

2. In his recent book *Spanglish: The Making of a New American Language* (2003), Amherst College professor Ilan Stavans, a Mexican-born linguist, analyzes the dynamics of Spanglish and then offers an impressive dictionary of Spanglish that takes up 188 pages of his 274-page critical study. Obtain a copy of the book from your college library and write a report on what it has to offer. After you have read the book, you might want to begin preparing to write by reading various reviews of the book that you find in your library as well as on the Internet. As a result of reading the articles in this chapter of *Language Awareness*, you may want to focus your review on the degree to which social capital is an issue for Stavans.

Digital Islam: Changing the Boundaries of Religious Knowledge

PETER MANDAVILLE

Peter Mandaville is an assistant professor of government and politics at George Mason University in Fairfax, Virginia, and was previously a lecturer in international relations at the University of Kent in Canterbury, England. Born and raised in the Middle East, he is a graduate of Blair Academy in New Jersey, St. Andrews University in Scotland, and the University of Kent. Mandaville's scholarly interests are the area of transnational connections between Islamic movements, as well as intellectual developments in the Muslim community in the West. He is the author of several books, among them Transnational Muslim Politics: Reimagining the Umma *(2001), and coeditor of* The Zen of International Relations: International Relations Theory from East to West *(2001). He is presently at work on a new book,* Political Islam, Global Politics: The International Relations of the Muslim World, *which is to be published in 2005.*

In the following article, which first appeared in ISIM *Newsletter* [International Institute for the Study of Islam in the Modern World], *No. 2, 1999, Mandaville explores the effects of IT (Information Technology) on the sociology of religious information that is spreading throughout the Muslim community around the world.*

WRITING TO DISCOVER: *Religion is among the many subject areas in which the Internet, chat rooms, and e-mail build "social capital" by connecting people who have similar interests. Are you or anyone you know connected through e-communications with others who share the same religious or spiritual views? Reflect on the kinds of information that might be communicated through such connections. Also, think about the accuracy and authority of the information being shared. Do you see any potential problems?*

The book, pamphlet, and newsletter were taken up with urgency by Muslims in the nineteenth century in order to counter the threat posed to the Islamic world by European imperialism. The *'ulama*[1] were initially at the forefront of this revolution, using a newly expanded and more widely distributed literature base to create a much broader constituency for their teachings. An inevitable side effect of this phenomenon, however, was the demise of their stranglehold over the production and

---

1. *'ulama*: religious scholars; the traditional interpreters and transmitters of religious knowledge

dissemination of religious knowledge. Muslims found it increasingly easy to bypass formally-trained religious scholars in the search for authentic Islam and for new ways of thinking about their religion. The texts were in principle now available to anyone who could read them; and to read is, of course, to interpret. These media opened up new spaces of religious contestation where traditional sources of authority could be challenged by the wider public. As literacy rates began to climb almost exponentially in the twentieth century, this effect was amplified even further. The move to print technology hence meant not only a new method for transmitting texts, but also a new idiom of selecting, writing, and presenting works to cater to a new kind of reader.[1]

Contemporary Muslims have been speculating about the utility of electronic information technology in the organization of religious knowledge for some time now. Abdul Kadir Barkatulla, director of London's Islamic Computing Center, explains that he first became attracted to computer-mediated data storage in his capacity as a scholar of *hadith*,[2] a field which involves the archiving and retrieval of thousands upon thousands of textual references. The CD–ROM has provided an invaluable medium for his work. The entire Qur'an (including both text and recitation) along with several collections of *hadith, tafsir*,[3] and *fiqh*[4] can easily fit on a single disc. Barkatulla sees this development as having the greatest relevance for those Muslims who live in circumstances where access to religious scholars is limited, such as in the West. For him, such CD–ROM selections offer a useful alternative. "It doesn't change the individual's relationship with his religion," he says, "but rather it provides knowledge supplements and clarifies the sources of information such that Muslims can verify the things they hear for themselves." Barkatulla sees IT as a useful tool for systematizing religious knowledge, but — crucially — only pre-existing juridical opinions. In his terms, IT is only for working with knowledge that has already been "cooked," and not for generating new judgments. There are, however, those who disagree with him. Sa'ad al-Faqih, for example, leader of the London-based "Movement for Islamic Reform in Arabia" and another keen advocate of information technology, believes that the average Muslim can now revolutionize Islam with just a basic understanding of Islamic methodology and a CD–ROM. In his view, the technology goes a long way to bridging the "knowledge gap" between an *'alim*[5] and a lay Muslim by placing all of the relevant texts at the fingertips of the latter. "I am not an *'alim*," he says, "but with these

---

2. *hadith*: a narrated report about the Prophet Muhammad detailing a particular moral/behavioral tradition established during his lifetime

3. *tafsir*: critical or explanatory literature relating to the Muslim holy book, the Qur'an

4. *fiqh*: religious jurisprudence

5. *'alim*: singular form of *'ulama*

tools I can put together something very close to what they would produce when asked for a *fatwa*."[6]

That is certainly not to say, however, that the *'ulama* have been entirely marginalized. In fact, some religious scholars have become quite enthusiastic about computer technology themselves. "Traditional centers of Islamic learning (such as al-Azhar in Cairo and Qom in Iran) did not respond to the opportunities offered by IT for about ten years," Barkatulla observes, "but now they are forced to." He alludes to something like a "race to digitize Islam" among leading centers of religious learning around the world. Because the modern religious universities have developed comprehensive information systems, the more conservative, traditional institutions are now forced to respond in kind in order to keep up with the times. At the Center for Islamic Jurisprudence in Qom, Iran, several thousand texts, both Sunni and Shi'i,[7] have been converted to electronic form. While Sunni institutions tend to ignore Shi'i texts, the Shi'i centers are digitizing large numbers of Sunni texts in order to produce databases which appeal to the Muslim mainstream, and hence capture a larger share of the market for digital Islam.

Neither has the rise of electronic "print Islam" eradicated the saliency of the oral tradition. Electronic media are as adept with sound as they are with the written word. Certainly we have heard much about the role of audio cassettes in Iran's Islamic revolution, where recordings of Khomeini's sermons were smuggled over from his Neauphle-le-Chateau headquarters near Paris and, much to the Shah's dismay, widely distributed in Iran. The Friday sermon, or *khutba*, is today recorded at many mosques throughout the Muslim world and the distribution of these recordings along with addresses by prominent ideologues consciously emulating the rhetoric of influential modern Muslim thinkers such as Sayyid Qutb, Ali Shariati, and Abu'l Ali Mawdudi, serves to politicize Islam before an audience of unprecedented proportions. Recordings of sermons by dissident Saudi *'ulama*, such as Safer al-Hawali and Salman al-'Awda, also circulate widely both in and outside the Kingdom, and this marks the first time that material openly critical of the Saudi regime has been heard by relatively large sections of that country's population. The Web site of a London-based Saudi opposition group has also made Salman al-'Awda's sermons available over the Internet using the latest audio streaming technology.[(2)] "Now that media technology is increasingly able to deal with other symbolic mode," notes the anthropologist Ulf Hannerz, "we may wonder whether imagined communities are increasingly moving beyond words."[(3)]

It is perhaps on the Internet, however, that some of the most interesting things are happening. Can we meaningfully speak today about the

5

---

6. *fatwa*: the legal opinion of a religious scholar

7. Sunni & Shi'i: the two main factions of Islam whose original split relates to the question of political succession following the death of the Prophet Muhammad

emergence of new forms of Islamic virtual community? To begin with, we need to make sure that we have a more nuanced understanding of those Muslim identities which use the Internet. We cannot start talking about new forms of diasporic Muslim community simply because many users of the Internet happen to be Muslims. Noting that in many instances Muslim uses of the Internet seem to represent little more than the migration of existing messages and ideas into a new context, Jon Anderson rightfully warns that "new talk has to be distinguished from new people talking about old topics in new settings."[4] Yet we also have to acknowledge the possibility that the hybrid discursive spaces of the Muslim Internet can give rise, even inadvertently, to new formulations and critical perspectives on Islam and the status of religious knowledge. As regards notions of political community in Islam, there is also the Internet's impact on "center-periphery" relations in the Muslim world to be examined. A country such as Malaysia, usually considered to be on the margins of Islam both in terms of geography and religious influence, has invested heavily in information and networking technologies. As a result, when searching on the Internet for descriptions of programs which offer formal religious training, one is far more likely to encounter the comprehensive course outlines provided by the International Islamic University of Malaysia than to stumble across the venerable Institutions of Cairo, Medina, or Mashhad.

It is usually amongst the diasporic Muslims of the Western world that we find the Internet being appropriated for political purposes. The American media has recently been full of scare-mongering about "radical fundamentalists" who use the United States as a fundraising base for their overseas operations. Reports often cite the Internet as a primary tool for the dissemination of propaganda by Islamic militants. A more sober examination of the situation, however, reveals that very few of the Muslim groups who have a presence on the Internet are involved in this sort of activity. Moreover, there are also those who argue that the Internet has actually had a moderating effect on Islamist discourse. Sa'ad al-Faqih, for example, believes that Internet chat rooms and discussion forums devoted to the debate of Islam and politics serve to encourage greater tolerance. He believes that in these new arenas one sees a greater convergence in the center of the Islamist political spectrum and a weakening of its extremes.

Thus, for the overwhelming majority of Muslims who seek Islam online, the Internet is a forum for the conduct of politics *within* their religion. In the absence of sanctioned information from recognized institutions, Muslims are increasingly taking religion into their own hands. Through various popular newsgroups and e-mail discussion lists, Muslims can solicit information about what "Islam" says about any particular problem. Not only that, notes al-Faqih, "but someone will be given information about what Islam says about such and such and then others will write in to correct or comment on this opinion/interpretation." Instead of having to go down to the mosque in order to elicit the advice of the local *mullah*,[8] Muslims can also now receive supposedly "authoritative" religious pronouncements via the various e-mail *fatwa* services which have sprung up in recent months. The Sheikhs of al-Azhar are totally absent, but the enterprising young *mullah* who sets himself up with a colorful Web site in Alabama suddenly becomes a high-profile representative of Islam for a particular constituency.[5] Due to the largely anonymous nature of the Internet, one can also never be sure whether the "authoritative" advice received via these services is coming from a classically-trained religious scholar or an electrical engineer moonlighting as an amateur *'alim*.

More than anything else, the Internet and other information technologies provide spaces where diasporic Muslims can go in order to find others "like them." It is in this sense that we can speak of the Internet as allowing Muslims to create a new form of imagined community, or an imagined *umma*.[9] The Muslim spaces of the Internet hence offer a reassuring set of symbols and a terminology which attempt to reproduce and recontextualize familiar settings and terms of discourse in locations far remote from those in which they were originally embedded. As has become apparent, the encounter between Islam and the transnational technologies of communication is as multifaceted as the religion itself. The rise of IT has led to considerable intermingling and dialogue between disparate interpretations of what it means to be "Islamic" and the politics of authenticity which inevitably ensue from this also serve to further fragment traditional sources of authority, such that the locus of "real" Islam and the identity of those who are permitted to speak on its behalf become ambiguous. This, in many ways, is an Islam with a distinctly modern, or perhaps even post-modern ring to it. The vocabulary here is eclectic, combining soundbites of religious knowledge into novel fusions well suited to complex, transnational contexts. Most importantly, the changing connotations of authority and authenticity in digital Islam appear to be contributing to the critical reimagination of the boundaries of Muslim politics.

Notes

1. Geoffrey Roper (1995), "Faris al-Shidyaq and the Transition from Scribal to Print Culture in the Middle East," in: George N. Atiyeh (ed.), *The Book in the Islamic World: The Written Word and Communication in the Middle East*, Albany: SUNY Press, 1995, p. 210.
2. See www.miraserve.com/.
3. Ulf Hannerz (1996), *Transnational Connections: Culture, People, Places*, London: Routledge, p. 21.
4. Jon Anderson (1996), "Islam & the Globalization of Politics." Paper presented to the Council on Foreign Relations Muslim Politics Study Group, New York City, June 25, 1996, p. 1.

8. *mullah*: a preacher or prayer leader
9. *umma*: the global community of Muslims (cf. Christendom)

5. Some of these sites are registering several thousand hits per day. Their users are often "nomadic," spending several days or weeks in one discussion forum before moving on to populate another site.

FOCUSING ON CONTENT

1. What is Mandaville's thesis? (Glossary: *Thesis*) In general, what does he see as the benefits and the drawbacks of e-communications as far as Muslims' religious knowledge is concerned?

2. Who is Abdul Kadir Barkatulla, and why is he an important source of information and opinion for Mandaville?

3. What is meant by the term "digital Islam"? What role has sound reproduction played in the world of "digital Islam"?

4. In Mandaville's view, has the Internet been instrumental in the spreading of fundamentalist Islamic propaganda and for fundraising for "overseas operations"? Explain.

5. Does Mandaville believe a "virtual Islam community" has been created? Why or why not?

FOCUSING ON WRITING

1. Mandaville speaks of a diasporic Islamic community. What is a "diaspora"? Why is the term an appropriate one for him to use?

2. Mandaville presents his ideas and information in a highly organized manner. Briefly summarize the topics he covers in each of his paragraphs. (Glossary: *Organization*)

3. The issue of definition is important, particularly as Mandaville concludes his discussion of the changing shape of Islamic religious knowledge. What are the key terms that he thinks need to be defined and perhaps redefined? (Glossary: *Definition*)

4. Mandaville uses a number of Islamic terms in his article. Why do you suppose he uses these terms? What effect does his use of them have on you as a reader?

LANGUAGE IN ACTION

Read the following excerpt from the mission statement of the Center for the Study of Muslim Networks at Duke University www.duke.edu/web/muslimnets/csmn_about.html:

We presume that the information revolution emerges out of technological developments and organizational patterns long in place throughout the world. What is different is speed, scope, and directness of communication. The Internet emphasizes communicative process over administrative structure, interaction over fixity, and it thus provides a lens through which community formation in the past may be analyzed and the present may be theorized, but its impact needs to be differentiated, and assessed from several perspectives.

Telepresence is a new form of association, and as such, it compels a reconsideration of the meaning of community: What is community when participants do not share place but can communicate as if they did? If shared place is not a necessary condition, is the notion of community as embodied contact a romantic projection of an idealized past? Sociologists since the 19th century have been worrying about the impact of technology on community, as though it possessed a solid, immutable core. But a century later, communities survive if in less solid but no less real forms.

The challenge for Muslim cybernauts is the same as for other communitarian netizens: how to define place and community in new ways that do not oppose virtual and real but rather see them as complementary? Can social networking in the space of flows of the Information Superhighway provide an alternate context within which to build communities as small as a kinship group, or as large as a nation?

In your own words, how do you interpret the Center's Mission Statement? Having read Mandaville's "Digital Islam," how would you assess the ability of technology to bring the virtual and the real together in the future? Or, are the two already melding? Has technology forced a new definition of community on Muslims? Is place necessary for building a community?

WRITING SUGGESTIONS

1. Using Mandaville's article as a model, write a report on the effects of IT (Information Technology) on your religious beliefs or on a religion which interests you. What are the major Internet links available for information on major events and local happenings, for authoritative views on dogma and practices, and for building community within the religion? If possible, speculate on how IT is changing the face of the religion, the language used in order to describe that religion, and its adherents' beliefs and practices.

2. Many people are not practitioners of any organized religion or sectarian group but are nonetheless spiritual beings with individualized views, practices, and beliefs. If you visit Google and use its subject directory, "Society and Religion," you will be offered a number of links and sub-links to religious and quasi-religious groups that have an online presence. Browse some of these links and write a report on the diversity you find in these sites, and, by delving deeper into some of the sites that especially interest you, address how e-communications has been bringing people of similar spiritual interests together. Would the groups you research be able to have the same presence without the aid of e-communications? Would they have the same national or transnational capabilities for building social capital? What provisions are made, if any, for overcoming barriers in language?

Cyberghetto: Blacks Are Falling Through the Net

FREDERICK L. MCKISSACK

Frederick L. McKissack and his wife, Pat, have collaborated on more than fifty books, mostly for young readers, focusing on African American topics. He provides the background research, while his wife does most of the writing. Several of their books have won awards over the years, including Christmas in the Big House, Christmas in the Quarters *(1994), which won the Coretta Scott King and the* Boston Globe Horn Book *awards. More recently, they have authored the book* Rebels Against Slavery: Americans Slave Revolts *(1999). This writing team lives outside of St. Louis, Missouri.*

In the following selection, first published in the June 1998 issue of The Progressive, *McKissack argues that minorities are being left out of current technological advancements spearheaded by the Internet. Without access to the business opportunities and information that are at the fingertips of those who are online, McKissack contends, the financial gap between the wealthy and the poor in our society can only widen.*

WRITING TO DISCOVER: *How much time did you spend on computers during your grade school years (kindergarten through eighth grade)? Do you think it was too much, not enough, or about enough time? What effect do you think increased computer time would have had? How have your computer skills — or lack thereof — shaped your later education and your career goals?*

I left journalism last year and started working for an Internet development firm because I was scared. While many of my crypto-Luddite friends ("I find e-mail so impersonal") have decided that the Web is the work of the devil and is being monitored by the NSA, CIA, FBI, and the IRS, I began to have horrible dreams that 16-year-old punks were going to take over publishing in the next century because they knew how to write good computer code. I'd have to answer to some kid with two earrings who'll make fun of me because I have one earring and didn't study computer science in my spare time.

You laugh, but one of the best Web developers in the country is a teenager who has written a very sound book on Web design and programming. He's still in his prime learning years, and he's got a staff.

What should worry me more is that I am one of the few African Americans in this country who has a computer at home, uses one at work, and can use a lot of different kinds of software on multiple platforms.

According to those in the know, I'm going to remain part of that very small group for quite some time.

The journal *Science* published a study . . . which found that, in households with annual incomes below $40,000, whites were six times more likely than blacks to have used the World Wide Web in the last week. Low-income white households were twice as likely to have a home computer as low-income black homes. Even as computers become more central to our society, minorities are falling through the Net.

The situation is actually considerably worse than the editors of *Sci-*   5 *ence* made it seem. Some eighteen percent of African American households don't even have phones, as Philip Bereano, a professor of technical communications at the University of Washington, pointed out in a letter to the *New York Times.* Since the researchers who published their study in *Science* relied on a telephone survey to gather their data, Bereano explains, the study was skewed — it only included people who had at least caught up to the twentieth century.

About thirty percent of American homes have computers, with the bulk of those users being predominantly white, upper-middle-class households. Minorities are much worse off: Only about fifteen percent have a terminal at home.

The gulf between technological haves and have-nots is the difference between living the good life and surviving in what some technologists and social critics term a "cyberghetto." Professor Michio Kaku, a professor of theoretical physics at City University of New York, wrote in his book *Visions: How Science Will Revolutionize the Twenty-first Century*, of the emergence of "information ghettos."

"The fact is, each time society made an abrupt leap to a new level of production, there were losers and winners," Kaku wrote. "It may well be that the computer revolution will exacerbate the existing fault lines of society."

The term "cyberghetto" suggests that minorities have barely passable equipment to participate in tech culture. But most minorities aren't even doing that well.

Before everybody goes "duh," just think what this means down the   10 line. Government officials are using the Web more often to disseminate information. Political parties are holding major online events. And companies are using the Web for making job announcements and collecting resumes. Classes, especially continuing-education classes, are being offered more and more on the Web. In politics, commerce, and education, the Web is leaving minorities behind.

The disparity between the techno-rich and techno-poor comes to a head with this statistic: A person who is able to use a computer at work earns fifteen percent more than someone in the same position who lacks computer skills.

"The equitable distribution of technology has always been the real moral issue about computers," Jon Katz, who writes the "Rants and Raves" column for *Wired* online, wrote in a recent e-mail. "The poor can't afford them. Thus they will be shut out of the booming hi-tech job market and forced to do the culture's menial jobs."

This technological gap, not Internet pornography, should be the public's main concern with the Web.

"Politicians and journalists have suggested frightening parents into limiting children's access to the Internet, but the fact is they have profoundly screwed the poor, who need access to this technology if they are to compete and prosper," Katz said. "I think the culture avoids the complex and expensive issues by focusing on the silly ones. In twenty-five years, when the underclass wakes up to discover it is doing all the muscle jobs while everybody else is in neat, clean offices with high-paying jobs, they'll go berserk. We don't want to spend the money to avoid this problem, so we worry about Johnny going to the *Playboy* Web site. It's sick."

In his 1996 State of the Union address, President Clinton challenged   15
Congress to hook up schools to the Internet.

"We are working with the telecommunications industry, educators, and parents to connect . . . every classroom and every library in the entire United States by the year 2000," Clinton said. "I ask Congress to support this educational technology initiative so that we can make sure the national partnership succeeds."

The national average is approximately ten students for every one computer in the public schools. According to a study by the consulting firm McKinsey & Co., the President's plan — a ratio of one computer to every five students — would cost approximately $11 billion per year over the next ten years.

Some government and business leaders, worried about a technologically illiterate work force in the twenty-first century, recognize the need for increased spending. "AT&T and the Commerce Department have suggested wiring up schools at a 4:1 ratio for $6 or $7 billion," says Katz.

But according to the U.S. Department of Education, only 1.3 percent of elementary and secondary education expenditures are allocated to technology. That figure would have to be increased to 3.9 percent. Given the tightness of urban school district budgets, a tripling of expenditures seems unlikely.

Then there's the question of whether computers in the schools are   20
even desirable. Writer Todd Oppenheimer, in a July 1997 article for *Atlantic Monthly* entitled "The Computer Delusion," argued that there is no hard evidence that computers in the classroom enhance learning. In fact, he took the opposite tack: that computers are partially responsible for the decline of education.

Proponents of computers in the classroom struck back. "On the issue of whether or not technology can benefit education, the good news is that it is not — nor should be — an all-or-nothing proposition," writes Wendy Richard Bollentin, editor of *OnTheInternet* magazine, in an essay for *Educom Review*.

There is an unreal quality about this debate, though, since computer literacy is an indispensable part of the education process for many affluent, white schoolchildren.

Consumers are seeing a decline in prices for home computers. Several PC manufacturers have already introduced sub-$1,000 systems, and there is talk of $600 systems appearing on the market by the fall. Oracle has spent a great deal of money on Network Computers, cheap hardware where software and files are located on large networks. The price is in the sub-$300 range. And, of course, there is WebTV, which allows you to browse on a regular home television set with special hardware.

Despite the trend to more "affordable" computers, a Markle Foundation-Bellcore Labs study shows that this may not be enough to help minorities merge onto the Information Superhighway. There is "evidence of a digital divide," the study said, with "Internet users being generally wealthier and more highly educated, and blacks and Hispanics disproportionately unaware of the Internet."

So, what now?   25

"For every black family to become empowered, they need to have computers," journalist Tony Brown told the *Detroit News*. "There is no way the black community is going to catch up with white society under the current system. But with a computer, you can take any person from poverty to the middle class."

This is the general line for enlightened blacks and community leaders. But having a computer won't bridge the racial and economic divide. Even if there is a 1:1 ratio of students to computers in urban schools, will students' interest be piqued when they don't have access to computers at home? One out of every forty-nine computer-science professors in the United States is black. Will this inhibit black students from learning how to use them? And even if every black student had a computer at home and at school, would that obliterate all racial obstacles to success?

Empowerment is not just a question of being able to find your way around the Web. But depriving minorities of access to the technology won't help matters any. We need to make sure the glass ceiling isn't replaced by a silicon ceiling.

FOCUSING ON CONTENT

1. What does the term *cyberghetto* mean? Why is it potentially misleading?

2. How has Internet pornography served as a diversion from what Jon Katz, as quoted by McKissack, views as the main problem regarding the Web?

3. Summarize McKissack's answer to his own question, "So, what now?" (25). What solution, if any, does he offer to the problem of the "cyberghetto"?

FOCUSING ON WRITING

1. Before he begins to make his argument, McKissack refers to the future power of "16-year-old punks" (1) and the current teenage Web developer. Why does he begin in this way? (Glossary: *Beginnings and Endings*) How does the information subsequently strengthen McKissack's argument?

2. What is McKissack's thesis? (Glossary: *Thesis*) Why is he particularly qualified to argue his point?

3. What evidence does McKissack provide to show that the dropping of prices for computers and specialized Web accessing devices does not translate into increased Internet use by minorities? (Glossary: *Evidence*)

LANGUAGE IN ACTION

Frederick L. McKissack's article focuses on the "digital divide" separating whites and blacks. Most people expect that the gap between the two groups will narrow, and an online article, "African-Americans Using Wealth of Web Information," www.clickz.com/stats/big_picture/demographics/article.php/ 493751, published on October 24, 2000, already began to report on the way that African Americans were "catching up" in their Internet usage. The statistics on the increased number of blacks using computers (3.5 million more blacks used the Internet in the twelve months preceding the issuing of the report) also revealed some interesting differences between the way blacks and whites used the Internet. According to statistics from the Pew Internet & American Life Project, African Americans are:

*   69 percent more likely to have listened to music on the Web
*   45 percent more likely to have played a game on the Web
*   38 percent more likely to have downloaded music from the Web
*   38 percent more likely to have sought information about jobs on the Web
*   20 percent more likely to have conducted school research or gotten job training on the Web

What conclusions, if any, can you draw from these statistics? How might McKissack react to them? What questions do you have about the statistics?

WRITING SUGGESTIONS

1. McKissack argues that minorities have far less access to computers and to the Internet than affluent whites do, but he presents no explicit remedy for the situation. If readers accept his argument that there is an information gap,

what should be done about it? Does the answer lie in the schools, with government subsidies, in private education efforts, or in other means? Write an argument paper in which you present one possible way to start to bridge the gap and argue its merits versus the status quo and other possible solutions.

2. Write an essay in which you argue against. McKissack's thesis that we are creating a cyberghetto and that there is, in fact, no so-called information gap in our society. As part of your preparation for writing you may want to read "The Myth of an Emerging Information Underclass" by Gary T. Dempsey, which appeared in *The Freeman* in April 1998.

9

CULTURAL DIVERSITY

According to the latest edition of the U.S. Department of Homeland Security, *Yearbook of Immigration Statistics, 2002*, the number of immigrants who entered the United States between the years 1820 and 2002 was 68,217,481. In 2002 alone, the year for which we have the most recent data, 1,063,732 immigrants entered the United States. These figures should serve to explain why cultural diversity or multiculturalism is a subject of intense interest for all of us. In another sense, we hardly need such hard evidence of the fact that we are a nation of great cultural interaction. The Haitian cab driver in Boston, the Nigerian sales associate in a Washington department store, the Vietnamese clothes designer in Los Angeles, the Latina actress in Atlanta, the Bosnian auto technician in Memphis, the Sri Lankan computer scientist in Seattle, the South African professor of literature in Detroit, as well as the hundreds of thousands of other people who have come to America for a new life are bringing these statistics to life before our eyes.

In examining the subject of diversity in this section of *Language Awareness*, we have focused on issues involving the nexus of language and culture. Language is both a magnetic center of solidarity and a point of access for immigrants. Their cultural memories are embodied in their native language, and their developing experience with English gives them a way of feeling a part of their new culture.

In "English Belongs to Everybody," Robert MacNeil champions the remarkable resilience and flexibility of the English language to accommodate change while at the same time being a source of great joy. Edite Cunha, a Portuguese immigrant, narrates her story of arriving in America and the frustrations of becoming her family's translator and how she came to resent that role. In a remarkable document, the illiterate preacher and abolitionist Sojourner Truth shows great flourish and rhetorical skill in a speech asking for the rights of African Americans and women. Judith Ortiz Cofer, of Puerto Rican heritage, speaks of adapting rather than assimilating when it comes to her relationship with American language and culture. For her, assimilating means the loss of her native culture while adaptation is the "ongoing great American experiment" that is being played out now with uncertain but exciting results. In a well-crafted and poignant essay, the late Audre Lorde tells of her family's silence when they came face-to-face with the bitterness of racism. Barbara Kingsolver tells us what she learned from her attempts to bridge the cultural gulf between her culture and Japan's. Finally, Harlan Lane, a distinguished psychologist, examines the rich language and culture of deafness and explains why we in the hearing world should not view deaf culture though our own lens. In his article he offers a profound lesson as well as a cautionary note on assuming that all populations desire the same form of communication.

CASE STUDY: UNDERSTANDING AFFIRMATIVE ACTION

On June 23, 2003, in a 5–4 decision, the United States Supreme Court ruled that race can be taken into consideration in admissions policies at our nation's colleges and universities. The Court, however, also warned that race cannot be an overriding factor in the selection of college students because such policies could lead to unconstitutional practices. While the debate appears to be stilled for the moment, the practice of Affirmative Action is still very much on the minds of a great many Americans. Some fear that there will be an erosion of support for Affirmative Action, while others worry that such policies have gone too far and are unconstitutional. In the spirit of continuing the debate beyond the Supreme Court's ruling, we have included four articles in this Case Study which examine Affirmative Action. We begin with a pair of essays that lay out the basic facts in the debate: one by Lee C. Bollinger, the president of Columbia University, that puts forth the case for Affirmative Action, and the other by African American journalist Armstrong Williams that provides an alternative view. Perry Bacon Jr. in "How Much Diversity Do You Want from Me?" shows "tepid" support for Affirmative Action, asking if, while joining the leadership class envisioned as a goal of Affirmative Action, he can offer the unique experiences of his "whole life rather than an assumed experience based solely on the color of [his] skin." Finally, the widely read African American journalist William Raspberry wonders if the debate over Affirmative Action is a diversion from the serious work that black parents need to consider with respect to their children's education.

English Belongs to Everybody

ROBERT MACNEIL

Born in Montreal, Canada, Robert MacNeil is probably best known as the former coanchor of the Public Broadcasting Service's MacNeil/Lehrer NewsHour, *which was broadcast from 1975 to 1995 and which continues to this day under Jim Lehrer's tutelage. During MacNeil's long career in broadcasting and journalism, he covered many major events in American history, including the John F. Kennedy assassination, the 1968 Democratic National Convention, and the 1973 Senate Watergate hearings. MacNeil's publications include* The People Machine: The Influence of Television on American Politics *(1968), which examines the frailties of television news organizations;* The Right Place at the Right Time *(1982), which recounts his experiences as a journalist;* Wordstruck *(1989), an autobiography; and* The Story of English *(1986), which he originally created as a PBS series on the history and development of the English language. In 1998 he published* Breaking News, *a fictional attack on the media's handling of an Oval Office sex scandal, and in 2003, he published a memoir entitled* Looking for My Country: Finding Myself in America.

In the following essay from Wordstruck, *MacNeil asserts that the supposed demise of English today is actually healthy change. As much as it may disturb grammarians, the ability of English to change keeps it strong and dynamic. English still remains as vital as the many people who speak it.*

WRITING TO DISCOVER: *Do you change the way you use language in different situations? If you are like most people, you probably do. Write about how your use of language changes and why. How is your spoken English different from your written English?*

This is a time of widespread anxiety about the language. Some Americans fear that English will be engulfed or diluted by Spanish and want to make it the official language. There is anxiety about a crisis of illiteracy, or a crisis of semiliteracy among high school, even college, graduates.

Anxiety, however, may have a perverse side effect: experts who wish to "save" the language may only discourage pleasure in it. Some are good-humored and tolerant of change, others intolerant and snobbish. Language reinforces feelings of social superiority or inferiority; it creates insiders and outsiders; it is a prop to vanity or a source of anxiety, and on both emotions the language snobs play. Yet the changes and the errors that irritate them are no different in kind from those which have shaped our language for centuries. As Hugh Kenner wrote of certain British critics in *The Sinking Island*, "They took note of language only when it annoyed them." Such people are killjoys: they turn others away from an interest in the language, inhibit their use of it, and turn pleasure off.

Change is inevitable in a living language and is responsible for much of the vitality of English; it has prospered and grown because it was able to accept and absorb change.

As people evolve and do new things, their language will evolve too. They will find ways to describe the new things and their changed perspective will give them new ways of talking about the old things. For example, electric light switches created a brilliant metaphor for the oldest of human experiences, being *turned on* or *turned off*. To language conservatives those expressions still have a slangy, low ring to them; to others they are vivid, fresh-minted currency, very spendable, very "with-it."

That tolerance for change represents not only the dynamism of the   5
English-speaking peoples since the Elizabethans, but their deeply rooted ideas of freedom as well. This was the idea of the Danish scholar Otto Jespersen, one of the great authorities on English. Writing in 1905, Jespersen said in his *Growth and Structure of the English Language:*

> The French language is like the stiff French garden of Louis XIV, while the English is like an English park, which is laid out seemingly without any definite plan, and in which you are allowed to walk everywhere according to your fancy without having to fear a stern keeper enforcing rigorous regulations. The English language would not have been what it is if the English had not been for centuries great respecters of the liberties of each individual and if everybody had not been free to strike out new paths for himself.

I like that idea and do not think it just coincidence. Consider that the same cultural soil, the Celtic-Roman-Saxon-Danish-Norman amalgam, which produced the English language also nourished the great principles of freedom and rights of man in the modern world. The first shoots sprang up in England and they grew stronger in America. Churchill called them "the joint inheritance of the English-speaking world." At the very core of those principles are popular consent and resistance to arbitrary authority; both are fundamental characteristics of our language. The English-speaking peoples have defeated all efforts to build fences around their language, to defer to an academy on what was permissible English and what was not. They'll decide for themselves, thanks just the same.

Nothing better expresses resistance to arbitrary authority than the persistence of what grammarians have denounced for centuries as "errors." In the common speech of English-speaking peoples — Americans, Englishmen, Canadians, Australians, New Zealanders, and others — these usages persist, despite rising literacy and wider education. We hear them every day:

Double negative: "I don't want none of that."

Double comparative: "Don't make that any more heavier!"

Wrong verb: "Will you learn me to read?"

These "errors" have been with us for at least four hundred years, because you can find each of them in Shakespeare.

Double negative: in *Hamlet*, the King says:

Nor what he spake, though it lack'd form a little,
Was not like madness.

Double comparative: In *Othello*, the Duke says:

Yet opinion . . . throws a more safer voice on you.

Wrong verb: In *Othello*, Desdemona says:

My life and education both do learn me how to respect you.

I find it very interesting that these forms will not go away and lie down. They were vigorous and acceptable in Shakespeare's time; they are far more vigorous today, although not acceptable as standard English. Regarded as error by grammarians, they are nevertheless in daily use all over the world by a hundred times the number of people who lived in Shakespeare's England.

It fascinates me that *axe,* meaning "ask," so common in black Ameri- 10
can English, is standard in Chaucer in all forms — *axe, axen, axed:* "and *axed* him if Troilus were there." Was that transmitted across six hundred years or simply reinvented?

English grew without a formal grammar. After the enormous creativity of Shakespeare and the other Elizabethans, seventeenth- and eighteenth-century critics thought the language was a mess, like an overgrown garden. They weeded it by imposing grammatical rules derived from tidier languages, chiefly Latin, whose precision and predictability they trusted. For three centuries, with some slippage here and there, their rules have held. Educators taught them and written English conformed. Today, English-language newspapers, magazines, and books everywhere broadly agree that correct English obeys these rules. Yet the wild varieties continue to threaten the garden of cultivated English and, by their numbers, actually dominate everyday usage.

Nonstandard English formerly knew its place in the social order. Characters in fiction were allowed to speak it occasionally. Hemingway believed that American literature really did not begin until Mark Twain, who outraged critics by reproducing the vernacular of characters like Huck Finn. Newspapers still clean up the grammar when they quote the ungrammatical, including politicians. The printed word, like Victorian morality, has often constituted a conspiracy of respectability.

People who spoke grammatically could be excused the illusion that their writ held sway, perhaps the way the Normans thought that French had conquered the language of the vanquished Anglo-Saxons. A generation ago, people who considered themselves educated and well-spoken might have had only glancing contact with nonstandard English, usually in a well-understood class, regional, or rural context.

It fascinates me how differently we all speak in different circumstances. We have levels of formality, as in our clothing. There are very formal occasions, often requiring written English: the job application or the letter to the editor — the dark-suit, serious-tie language, with everything pressed and the lint brushed off. There is our less formal out-in-the-world language — a more comfortable suit, but still respectable. There is language for close friends in the evenings, on weekends — blue-jeans-and-sweatshirt language, when it's good to get the tie off. There is family language, even more relaxed, full of grammatical short cuts, family slang, echoes of old jokes that have become intimate shorthand — the language of pajamas and uncombed hair. Finally, there is the language with no clothes on; the talk of couples — murmurs, sighs, grunts — language at its least self-conscious, open, vulnerable, and primitive.

Broadcasting has democratized the publication of language, often at its 15 most informal, even undressed. Now the ears of the educated cannot escape the language of the masses. It surrounds them on the news, weather, sports, commercials, and the ever-proliferating talk and call-in shows.

This wider dissemination of popular speech may easily give purists the idea that the language is suddenly going to hell in this generation, and may explain the new paranoia about it.

It might also be argued that more Americans hear more correct, even beautiful, English on television than was ever heard before. Through television more models of good usage reach more American homes than was ever possible in other times. Television gives them lots of colloquial English, too, some awful, some creative, but that is not new.

Hidden in this is a simple fact: our language is not the special private property of the language police, or grammarians, or teachers, or even great writers. The genius of English is that is has always been the tongue of the common people, literate or not.

English belongs to everybody: the funny turn of phrase that pops into the mind of a farmer telling a story; or the traveling salesman's dirty joke; or the teenager saying, "Gag me with a spoon"; or the pop lyric — all contribute, are all as valid as the tortured image of the academic, or the line the poet sweats over for a week.

Through our collective language sense, some may be thought beauti- 20 ful and some ugly, some may live and some may die; but it is all English and it belongs to everyone — to those of us who wish to be careful with it and those who don't care.

FOCUSING ON CONTENT

1. Who does MacNeil describe as "killjoys" (2)? Why does MacNeil believe their influence is destructive to the vitality of the English language?

2. Why does MacNeil claim that various examples of "improper" English are not likely to go away soon? Whose work does he cite to reinforce his conclusion? (Glossary: *Examples*)

3. When was standardization imposed on the English language? Why was it thought necessary to do so?

4. React to MacNeil's statement that English "has always been the tongue of the common people" (18). What does he mean? What does the statement imply to you?

5. What does MacNeil say is the real reason behind the recent perception that American English is undergoing a sudden turn for the worse? What role do television and other forms of mass media play in the modern evolution of the language?

6. What do you think MacNeil would have to say about immigrants' willingness to learn English?

FOCUSING ON WRITING

1. In paragraph 2, MacNeil says the current anxiety about language may lead to a "perverse side effect." What is this side effect? Why does MacNeil describe it as perverse? What other words could he have used to describe it? What impact would the use of a word other than *perverse* have on the overall tone of the essay? (Glossary: *Tone*)

2. In paragraph 4, MacNeil uses the terms *turned on* and *turned off* as examples of how modern influences can contribute to new language metaphors. He characterizes these expressions as being very "with-it." What does he mean? Why do you think he uses one slang term to describe other such terms? Do you find this an effective part of his argument? Why or why not?

3. What simile does Otto Jespersen use in the passage quoted by MacNeil? (Glossary: *Figures of Speech*) Do you find it an effective image? MacNeil adopts the simile and uses it later in the essay. Is it an appropriate simile for MacNeil's argument? Why or why not?

4. What terms does MacNeil use to describe those who favor a rigid grammar and a correct, unchanging use of English? How does he describe the way they react to the current use of the language? What point is he making?

LANGUAGE IN ACTION

English is a dynamic language, but even MacNeil would probably concede that "pushing the envelope" of acceptable speech can be overdone, as the following selection demonstrates. This excerpt is taken from the

Web page "Jargon, Weasel Words, and Gobbledygook" by G. Jay Christensen. (You may also want to check Christensen's Web site at www.csun.edu/~vcecn006/public1.htm.) How careful do you think you should be in using the English language? Should there be a balance between dynamic change and consistent, coherent structure and diction? Discuss your answers with your class.

PARAGRAPHS OF BUZZWORDS BUZZ LOUDLY

Dr. Michael Wunsch from Northern Arizona University offered some delightful parodies about how buzzwords are taking over our language. With his permission I quote some of the paragraphs he gave at a recent business communication conference.

> Now that we have talked the talk and viably interfaced in a politically correct, huge attempt to jump start, kick start, downsize, rightsize, bash, or showcase something, may I have, my fellow Americans, some of your cutting-edge, walk-the-walk, super input that will hopefully debut and impact somebody's bottom line as we speak while we are on a mission to dig deeper and then move up to the next level, and beyond that, to take care of business on the information superhighway and earn bragging rights?

> I knew that you would turn this perceived worst-case scenario around and echo somebody by responding with "Exactly!" Let's be honest, a person doesn't have to be a rocket scientist or heart surgeon to know the big news that you are a happy camper who is cool and great, you know, despite your cautious optimism. No question, you are a warm-and-fuzzy, world-class, wave-of-the-future, state-of-the-art, high-tech, totally awesome, less-than-slow-lane, more-than-happy, user-friendly, outrageously key dude who can and will give much, much more. (In an ad, the point at which the copywriter ran out of hype!) The huge upside is that you are arguably neither a wimp nor a sucker. In my mind, I'm proactively fed up with hanging around; therefore, my agenda is that I am reactively out of here, under condition of anonymity, in an effort to put it all together to bring everybody up to speed. Let's rumble on a big-time roll at a huge 110 percent effort to make things happen at crunch time by advocating zero tolerance! There you go! Have a nice day!

As Bill Maher is fond of saying on *Politically Incorrect,* the previous information has been "satirized" for your protection. Are you convinced to be careful how you use the English language?

WRITING SUGGESTIONS

1. MacNeil contends that television makes all forms of English accessible to everyone. It does broadcast "bad" English, but it also brings a lot of correct, elegant English into viewers' homes. Think about the language usage on the television shows you watch and the radio stations you listen to. How do they

handle slang, dialogue, and other word usage? For example, the show *Sein-feld* was very aggressive in coining clever phrases and word associations, and *NYPD Blue* and *The Sopranos* sometimes use vocabulary that many consider profane. Also, how does your favorite form of music use language? Are the lyrics poetic or direct? Do they include a lot of slang? Write an essay in which you examine the influence television and radio have had on your own language. Do you and your peers incorporate expressions from these sources into your own speech?

2. MacNeil uses *gag me with a spoon*, the familiar phrase from Sun-Belt Speak, as an example of a contribution to the English language. Think about other recent contributions to the language that you have heard — and perhaps even used yourself. Write an essay in which you argue for or against Mac-Neil's contention that such new phrases or uses of the language contribute to English as a whole. What advantages or features do they offer? What dangers do they pose to the integrity of the language? As a writer, how do you regard such changes?

Talking in the New Land

EDITE CUNHA

A native of Portugal, Edite Cunha moved with her family to Peabody, Massachusetts, when she was seven years old. In 1991 Cunha graduated from Smith College, where she was an Ada Comstock scholar. Later, she went on to earn an M.F.A. degree in literature and creative writing at Warren Wilson College, and she now has her own business. Despite this success, her experiences in the United States were not always easy ones. Shortly after moving to Massachusetts, Cunha's first and middle names were changed by her elementary school teacher. Although her teacher may have viewed this as a helpful gesture, which would allow Cunha to fit into a new culture, the name change left the young girl feeling deprived of her personal identity. It also added to her difficulties in learning a new language.

Because of the challenges of a bilingual world, Cunha became her family's translator; being her father's "voice" was a responsibility she dreaded. As a consequence of her unusual childhood chore, Cunha learned far more about the conflict between cultures — and conflict in general — than she wanted to at an early age. In the following essay, which first appeared in the New England Monthly *in August 1990, Cunha recounts some of her early experiences in America.*

WRITING TO DISCOVER: *Imagine that you moved to a new country and had to adopt new first and middle names when you reached your destination. Write about what you would lose if you lost your name. What might you gain? How strongly do you identify with your name? Why?*

Before I started school in America I was Edite. Maria Edite dos Anjos Cunha. Maria, in honor of the Virgin Mary. In Portugal it was customary to use Maria as a religious and legal prefix to every girl's name. Virtually every girl was so named. It had something to do with the apparition of the Virgin to three shepherd children at Fatima. In naming their daughters Maria, my people were expressing their love and reverence for their Lady of Fatima.

Edite came from my godmother, Dona Edite Baetas Ruivo. The parish priest argued that I could not be named Edite because in Portugal the name was not considered Christian. But Dona Edite defended my right to bear her name. No one had argued with her family when they had christened her Edite. Her family had power and wealth. The priest considered privileges endangered by his stand, and I became Maria Edite.

The dos Anjos was for my mother's side of the family. Like her mother before her, she had been named Mario dos Anjos. And Cunha was for my father's side. Carlos dos Santos Cunha, son of Abilio dos Santos Cunha, the tailor from Saíl.

I loved my name. "Maria Edite dos Anjos Cunha," I'd recite at the least provocation. It was melodious and beautiful. And through it I knew exactly who I was.

At the age of seven I was taken from our little house in Sobreira, São Martinho da Cortiça, Portugal, and brought to Peabody, Massachusetts. We moved into the house of Senhor João, who was our sponsor in the big land. I was in America for about a week when someone took me to school one morning and handed me over to the teacher, Mrs. Donahue. 5

Mrs. Donahue spoke Portuguese, a wondrous thing for a woman with a funny, unpronounceable name.

"Como é que te chamas?" she asked as she led me to a desk by big windows.

"Maria Edite dos Anjos Cunha," I recited, all the while scanning Mrs. Donahue for clues. How could a woman with such a name speak my language?

In fact, Mrs. Donahue was Portuguese. She was a Silva. But she had married an Irishman and changed her name. She changed my name, too, on the first day of school.

"Your name will be Mary Edith Cunha," she declared. "In America you only need two or three names. Mary Edith is a lovely name. And it will be easier to pronounce." 10

My name was Edite. Maria Edite. Maria Edite dos Anjos Cunha. I had no trouble pronouncing it.

"Mary Edith, Edithhh, Mary Edithhh," Mrs. Donahue exaggerated it. She wrinkled up her nose and raised her upper lip to show me the proper positioning of the tongue for the *th* sound. She looked hideous. There was a big pain in my head. I wanted to scream out my name. But you could never argue with a teacher.

At home I cried and cried. *Mãe* and *Pai* wanted to know about the day. I couldn't pronounce the new name for them. Senhor João's red face wrinkled in laughter.

Day after day Mrs. Donahue made me practice pronouncing that name that wasn't mine. Mary Edithhhh. Mary Edithhh. Mary Edithhh. But weeks later I still wouldn't respond when she called it out in class. Mrs. Donahue became cross when I didn't answer. Later my other teachers shortened it to Mary. And I never knew quite who I was. . . .

Mrs. Donahue was a small woman, not much bigger than my seven-year-old self. Her graying hair was cut into a neat, curly bob. There was a smile that she wore almost every day. Not broad. Barely perceptible. But it was there, in her eyes, and at the corners of her mouth. She often wore 15 gray suits with jackets neatly fitted about the waist. On her feet she wore matching black leather shoes, tightly laced. Matching, but not identical. One of them had an extra-thick sole, because like all of her pupils, Mrs. Donahue had an oddity. We, the children, were odd because we were of different colors and sizes, and did not speak the accepted tongue. Mrs. Donahue was odd because she had legs of different lengths.

I grew to love Mrs. Donahue. She danced with us. She was the only teacher in all of Carroll School who thought it was important to dance. Every day after recess she took us all to the big open space at the back of the room. We stood in a circle and joined hands. Mrs. Donahue would blow a quivering note from the little round pitch pipe she kept in her pocket, and we became a twirling, singing wheel. Mrs. Donahue hobbled on her short leg and sang in a high trembly voice, "Here we go, loop-de-loop." We took three steps, then a pause. Her last "loop" was always very high. It seemed to squeak above our heads, bouncing on the ceiling. "Here we go, loop-de-lie." Three more steps, another pause, and on we whirled. "Here we go, loop-de-loop." Pause. "All on a Saturday night." To anyone looking in from the corridor we were surely an irregular sight, a circle of children of odd sizes and colors singing and twirling with our tiny hobbling teacher.

I'd been in Room Three with Mrs. Donahue for over a year when she decided that I could join the children in the regular elementary classes at Thomas Carroll School. I embraced the news with some ambivalence. By then the oddity of Mrs. Donahue's classroom had draped itself over me like a warm safe cloak. Now I was to join the second-grade class of Miss Laitinen. In preparation, Mrs. Donahue began a phase of relentless drilling. She talked to me about what I could expect in second grade. Miss Laitinen's class was well on its way with cursive writing, so we practiced that every day. We intensified our efforts with multiplication. And we practiced pronouncing the new teacher's name.

"Lay-te-nun." Mrs. Donahue spewed the *t* out with excessive force to demonstrate its importance. I had a tendency to forget it.

"Lay-nun."

"Mary Edith, don't be lazy. Use that tongue. It's Lay-te" — she bared her teeth for the *t* part — "nun."   20

One morning with no warning, Mrs. Donahue walked me to the end of the hall and knocked on the door to Room Six. Miss Laitinen opened the door. She looked severe, carrying a long rubber-tipped pointer which she held horizontally before her with both hands. Miss Laitinen was a big, masculine woman. Her light, course hair was straight and cut short. She wore dark cardigans and very long, pleated plaid kilts that looked big enough to cover my bed.

"This is Mary Edith," Mrs. Donahue said. Meanwhile I looked at their shoes. Miss Laitinen wore flat, brown leather shoes that laced up and squeaked on the wooden floor when she walked. They matched each other perfectly, but they were twice as big as Mrs. Donahue's.

"Mary Edith, say hello to Miss Laitinen." Mrs. Donahue stressed the
t — a last-minute reminder.

"Hello, Miss Lay-te-nun," I said, leaning my head back to see her
face. Miss Laitinen was tall. Mrs. Donahue's head came just to her chest.
They both nodded approvingly before I was led to my seat.

Peabody, Massachusetts. "The Leather City." It is stamped on the   25
city seal, along with the image of a tanned animal hide. And Peabody, an
industrial city of less than fifty thousand people, has the smokestacks to
prove it. They rise up all over town from sprawling, dilapidated factories.
Ugly, leaning, wooden buildings that often stretch over a city block.
Strauss Tanning Co. A. C. Lawrence Leather Co. Gnecco & Grilk Tanning Corp. In the early sixties, the tanneries were in full swing. The jobs
were arduous and health-threatening, but it was the best-paying work
around for unskilled laborers who spoke no English. The huge, firetrap
factories were filled with men and women from Greece, Portugal, Ireland, and Poland.

In one of these factories, João Nunes, who lived on the floor above
us, fed animal skins into a ravenous metal monster all day, every day. The
pace was fast. One day the monster got his right arm and wouldn't let go.
When the machine was turned off João had a little bit of arm left below
his elbow. His daughter Teresa and I were friends. She didn't come out
of her house for many days. When she returned to school, she was very
quiet and cried a lot.

"Rosa Veludo's been hurt." News of such tragedies spread through the
community fast and often. People would tell what they had seen, or what
they had heard from those who had seen. *"She was taken to the hospital by
ambulance. Someone wrapped her fingers in a paper bag. The doctors may be
able to sew them back on."*

A few days after our arrival in the United States, my father went to
work at the Gnecco & Grilk leather tannery, on the corner of Howley
and Walnut streets. Senhor João had worked there for many years. He
helped *Pai* get the job. Gnecco & Grilk was a long, rambling, four-story
factory that stretched from the corner halfway down the street to the railroad tracks. The roof was flat and slouched in the middle like the back of
an old workhorse. There were hundreds of windows. The ones on the
ground were covered with a thick wire mesh.

Pai worked there for many months. He was stationed on the ground
floor, where workers often had to stand ankle-deep in water laden with
chemicals. One day he had a disagreement with his foreman. He left his
machine and went home vowing never to return. . . .

Pai and I stood on a sidewalk in Salem facing a clear glass doorway.   30
The words on the door were big. DIVISION OF EMPLOYMENT SECURITY.
There was a growing coldness deep inside me. At Thomas Carroll

School, Miss Laitinen was probably standing at the side blackboard, writing perfect alphabet letters on straight chalk lines. My seat was empty. I was on a sidewalk with *Pai* trying to understand a baffling string of words. DIVISION had something to do with math, which I didn't particularly like. EMPLOYMENT I had never seen or heard before. SECURITY I knew. But not at that moment.

Pai reached for the door. It swung open into a little square of tiled floor. We stepped in to be confronted by the highest, steepest staircase I had ever seen. At the top, we emerged into a huge, fluorescently lit room. It was too bright and open after the dim, narrow stairs. *Pai* took off his hat. We stood together in a vast empty space. The light, polished tiles reflected the fluorescent glow. There were no windows.

Far across the room, a row of metal desks lined the wall. Each had a green vinyl-covered chair beside it. Off to our left, facing the empty space before us, was a very high green metal desk. It was easily twice as high as a normal-size desk. Its odd size and placement in the middle of the room gave it the appearance of a kind of altar that divided the room in half. There were many people working at desks or walking about, but the room was so big that it still seemed empty.

The head and shoulders of a white-haired woman appeared to rest on the big desk like a sculptured bust. She sat very still. Above her head the word CLAIMS dangled from two pieces of chain attached to the ceiling. As I watched the woman she beckoned to us. *Pai* and I walked over toward her.

The desk was so high that *Pai's* shoulders barely cleared the top. Even when I stood on tiptoe I couldn't see over it. I had to stretch and lean my head way back to see the woman's round face. I thought that she must have very long legs to need a desk that high. The coldness in me grew. My neck hurt.

"My father can't speak English. He has no work and we need money."   35

She reached for some papers from a wire basket. One of her fingers was encased in a piece of orange rubber.

"Come around over here so I can see you." She motioned to the side of the desk. I went reluctantly. Rounding the desk I saw with relief that she was a small woman perched on a stool so high it seemed she would need a ladder to get up there.

"How old are you?" She leaned down toward me.

"Eight."

"My, aren't you a brave girl. Only eight years old and helping daddy   40
like that. And what lovely earrings you have."

She liked my earrings. I went a little closer to let her touch them. Maybe she would give us money.

"What language does your father speak?" She was straightening up, reaching for a pencil.

"Portuguese."

"What is she saying?" Pai wanted to know.

"*Wait,*" I told him. The lady hadn't yet said anything about money.   45
"Why isn't your father working?"
"His factory burned down."
"*What is she saying?*" *Pai* repeated.
"*She wants to know why you aren't working.*"
"*Tell her the factory burned down.*"   50
"*I know. I did.*" The lady was looking at me. I hoped she wouldn't ask me what my father had just said.
"What's your father's name?"
"Carlos S. Cunha. C-u-n-h-a." No one could ever spell *Cunha*. *Pai* nodded at the woman when he heard his name.
"Where do you live?"
"Thirty-three Tracey Street, Peabody, Massachusetts." *Pai* nodded   55
again when he heard the address.
"When was your father born?"
"*Quando é que tu naçestes?*"
"When was the last day your father worked?"
"*Qual foi o último dia que trabalhastes?*"
"What was the name of the factory?"   60
"*Qual éra o nome de fábrica?*"
"How long did he work there?"
"*Quanto tempo trabalhastes lá?*"
"What is his Social Security number?"
I looked at her blankly, not knowing what to say. What was a Social   65
Security number?
"*What did she say?*" *Pai* prompted me out of silence.
"*I don't know. She wants a kind of number.*" I was feeling very tired and worried. But *Pai* took a small card from his wallet and gave it to the lady. She copied something from it onto her papers and returned it to him. I felt a great sense of relief. She wrote silently for a while as we stood and waited. Then she handed some paper to *Pai* and looked at me.
"Tell your father that he must have these forms filled out by his employer before he can receive unemployment benefits."
I stared at her. What was she saying? Employer? Unemployment benefits? I was afraid she was saying we couldn't have any money. Maybe not, though. Maybe we could have money if I could understand her words.
"*What did she say? Can we have some money?*"   70
"*I don't know. I can't understand her words.*"
"*Ask her again if we can have money,*" *Pai* insisted. "*Tell her we have to pay the rent.*"
"We need money for the rent," I told the lady, trying to hold back tears.
"You can't have money today. You must take these forms to your father's employer and bring them back completed next week. Then your father must sign another form which we will keep here to process his

claim. When he comes back in two weeks there may be a check for him."
The cold in me was so big now, I was trying not to shiver.

"Do you understand?" The lady was looking at me.   75

I wanted to say, "No, I don't," but I was afraid we would never get
money and *Pai* would be angry.

"Tell your father to take the papers to his boss and come back next
week."

Boss. I could understand boss.

*"She said you have to take these papers to your 'bossa' and come back
next week."*

"We can't have money today?"   80

"No. She said maybe we can have money in two weeks."

"Did you tell her we have to pay the rent?"

"Yes, but she said we can't have money yet."

The lady was saying good-bye and beckoning the next person from
the line that had formed behind us.

I was relieved to move on, but I think *Pai* wanted to stay and argue   85
with her. I knew that if he could speak English, he would have. I knew
that he thought it was my fault we couldn't have money. And I myself
wasn't so sure that wasn't true.

That night I sat at the kitchen table with a fat pencil and a piece of
paper. In my second-grade scrawl I wrote: Dear Miss Laitinen, Mary
Edith was sick.

I gave the paper to *Pai* and told him to sign his name.

"What does it say?"

"It says that I was sick today. I need to give it to my teacher."

"You weren't sick today."   90

"Ya, but it would take too many words to tell her the truth."

Pai signed the paper. The next morning in school, Miss Laitinen
read it and said that she hoped I was feeling better.

When I was nine, *Pai* went to an auction and bought a big house on
Tremont Street. We moved in the spring. The yard at the side of the
house dipped downward in a gentle slope that was covered with a dense
row of tall lilac bushes. I soon discovered that I could crawl in among the
twisted trunks to hide from my brothers in the fragrant shade. It was
paradise. . . .

I was mostly wild and joyful on Tremont Street. But there was a
shadow that fell across my days now and again.

"Ó Ediiiite." *Pai* would call me without the least bit of warning, to   95
be his voice. He expected me to drop whatever I was doing to attend
him. Of late, I'd had to struggle on the telephone with the voice of a
woman who wanted some old dishes. The dishes, along with lots of old
furniture and junk, had been in the house when we moved in. They were

in the cellar, stacked in cardboard boxes and covered with dust. The woman called many times wanting to speak with *Pai*.

"My father can't speak English," I would say. "He says to tell you that the dishes are in our house and they belong to us." But she did not seem to understand. Every few days she would call.

"*Ó Ediiiite.*" *Pai's* voice echoed through the empty rooms. Hearing it brought on a chill. It had that tone. As always, my first impulse was to pretend I had not heard, but there was no escape. I couldn't disappear into thin air as I wished to do at such calls. We were up in the third-floor apartment of our new house. *Pai* was working in the kitchen. Carlos and I had made a cavern of old cushions and were sitting together deep in its bowels when he called. It was so dark and comfortable there I decided not to answer until the third call, though that risked *Pai's* wrath.

"*Ó Ediiite.*" Yes, that tone was certainly there. *Pai* was calling me to do something only I could do. Something that always awakened a cold beast deep in my gut. He wanted me to be his bridge. What was it now? Did he have to talk to someone at City Hall again? Or was it the insurance company? They were always using words I couldn't understand: liability, and premium, and dividend. It made me frustrated and scared.

"You wait. My dotta come." *Pai* was talking to someone. Who could it be? That was some relief. At least I didn't have to call someone on the phone. It was always harder to understand when I couldn't see people's mouths.

"*Ó Ediiiiite.*" I hated Carlos. *Pai* never called his name like that. He   100
never had to do anything but play.

"*Que éééé?*"

"*Come over here and talk to this lady.*"

Reluctantly I crawled out from the soft darkness and walked through the empty rooms toward the kitchen. Through the kitchen door I could see a slim lady dressed in brown standing at the top of the stairs in the windowed porch. She had on very skinny high-heeled shoes and a brown purse to match. As soon as *Pai* saw me he said to the lady, "Dis my dotta." To me he said, "*See what she wants.*"

The lady had dark hair that was very smooth and puffed away from her head. The ends of it flipped up in a way that I liked.

"Hello. I'm the lady who called about the dishes."   105

I stared at her without a word. My stomach lurched.

"*What did she say?*" *Pai* wanted to know.

"*She says she's the lady who wants the dishes.*"

Pai's face hardened some.

"*Tell her she's wasting her time. We're not giving them to her. Didn't*   110
you already tell her that on the telephone?"

I nodded, standing helplessly between them.

"*Well, tell her again.*" *Pai* was getting angry. I wanted to disappear.

"My father says he can't give you the dishes," I said to the lady. She clutched her purse and leaned a little forward.

"Yes, you told me that on the phone. But I wanted to come in person and speak with your father because it's very important to me that — "

"My father can't speak English," I interrupted her. Why didn't she   115
just go away? She was still standing in the doorway with her back to the stairwell. I wanted to push her down.

"Yes, I understand that. But I wanted to see him." She looked at *Pai*, who was standing in the doorway to the kitchen holding his hammer. The kitchen was up one step from the porch. *Pai* was a small man, but he looked kind of scary staring down at us like that.

"What is she saying?"

"She says she wanted to talk to you about getting her dishes."

"Tell her the dishes are ours. They were in the house. We bought the house and everything in it. Tell her the lawyer said so."

The brown lady was looking at me expectantly.   120

"My father says the dishes are ours because we bought the house and the lawyer said everything in the house is ours now."

"Yes, I know that, but I was away when the house was being sold. I didn't know . . . "

"Eeii." There were footsteps on the stairs behind her. It was *Mãe* coming up from the second floor to find out what was going on. The lady moved away from the door to let *Mãe* in.

"Dis my wife," *Pai* said to the lady. The lady said hello to *Mãe*, who smiled and nodded her head. She looked at me, then at *Pai* in a questioning way.

"It's the lady who wants our dishes," *Pai* explained.   125

"Ó." *Mãe* looked at her again and smiled, but I could tell she was a little worried.

We stood there in kind of a funny circle; the lady looked at each of us in turn and took a deep breath.

"I didn't know," she continued, "that the dishes were in the house. I was away. They are very important to me. They belonged to my grandmother. I'd really like to get them back." She spoke this while looking back and forth between *Mãe* and *Pai*. Then she looked down at me, leaning forward again. "Will you please tell your parents, please?"

The cold beast inside me had begun to rise up toward my throat as the lady spoke. I knew that soon it would try to choke out my words. I spoke in a hurry to get them out.

"She said she didn't know the dishes were in the house she was away they   130
were her grandmother's dishes she wants them back." I felt a deep sadness at the thought of the lady returning home to find her grandmother's dishes sold.

"We don't need all those dishes. Let's give them to her," Mãe said in her calm way. I felt relieved. We could give the lady the dishes and she would go away. But *Pai* got angry.

"I already said what I had to say. The dishes are ours. That is all."

"Pai, she said she didn't know. They were her grandmother's dishes. She needs to have them." I was speaking wildly and loud now. The lady looked at me questioningly, but I didn't want to speak to her again.

"She's only saying that to trick us. If she wanted those dishes she should have taken them out before the house was sold. Tell her we are not fools. Tell her to forget it. She can go away. Tell her not to call or come here again."

"What is he saying?" The lady was looking at me again.   135

I ignored her. I felt sorry for *Pai* for always feeling that people were trying to trick him. I wanted him to trust people. I wanted the lady to have her grandmother's dishes. I closed my eyes and willed myself away.

"Tell her what I said!" Pai yelled.

"Pai, just give her the dishes! They were her grandmother's dishes!" My voice cracked as I yelled back at him. Tears were rising.

I hated *Pai* for being so stubborn. I hated the lady for not taking the dishes before the house was sold. I hated myself for having learned to speak English.

FOCUSING ON CONTENT

1. Explain the importance of Cunha's given name. How does she describe it? In what way does it give her identity?

2. Why is it important for Cunha to describe Mrs. Donahue? What ironic information do we get from that description? (Glossary: *Irony*)

3. Why does Mrs. Donahue change Cunha's name? Do you think Mrs. Donahue's own ethnic heritage is part of her motivation? Why or why not?

4. Why does Cunha say she hated her brother?

FOCUSING ON WRITING

1. Cunha refers to a "coldness" (34) or "cold" (74) or "the cold beast" (129) that comes over her. What does she mean by these references to coldness? What brings about the feeling?

2. Why does Cunha re-create the scene in which she and her father visit the Division of Employment Security in such detail? How does the scene help her achieve her purpose in writing the essay? (Glossary: *Purpose*)

3. Cunha ends her essay with the sentence "I hated myself for having learned to speak English." Why does she say this? Do you find the ending effective? Why or why not? (Glossary: *Beginnings and Endings*)

4. Cunha does not explicitly describe her relationship with the members of her family, but she provides many clues. What impressions does the essay give you regarding Cunha's relationship with her brothers, her mother, and her father? Use passages from the essay to support your answer. Would it have been better for her to be more explicit? Why or why not?

LANGUAGE IN ACTION

The following passage is from Mari Tomasi's *Like Lesser Gods* (1949), an immigration novel about Italian stone carvers living in Vermont. In this excerpt, the protagonist Mr. Tiff is met at the train station by Petra, his friend's daughter, and Tiff later explains how he came to acquire his name. Read the passage in light of Cunha's comments about the significance of her name and the change that was made to it. Is Mr. Tiff's situation similar to Edite Cunha's? Why or why not?

"Look," she bargained. "I'll teach you English after I do my lessons every night, if you teach me to read Italian. I'll — gee, I don't even know your name — "

"I have a name, and to spare," he assured her gravely. "*Maestro* Michele Pio Vittorio Giuseppe Tiffone."

"Gee — "

He counted them off on his fingers. "Michele for the great Archangel — this one." He indicated the silver San' Michele figurine on the dresser. "Pio for the pope who reigned when I was born and whom you may some day call *Santo Pio;* Vittorio, who is king and whose birthday is November 11 — the same as mine; and Giuseppe for my father, who humbled his name into obscurity by tacking it at the end."

Tiffone. She frowned. *Maestro* Michele Pio. . . . A happy thought smoothed the wrinkles from her brow. "I'll call you Mister Tiff. I'm glad, glad I saw you first — I mean at the station."

WRITING SUGGESTIONS

1. Write an essay in which you discuss what your name means to you. You might consider addressing some of the following questions: Who named you? How did that person or persons decide on your name? Does your surname carry any ethnic identification? How do you like your name? What does your name mean? How do others respond to your name? Do you have any nicknames? How do people react to your nickname?

2. Write an essay in which you put yourself in Cunha's shoes as the only speaker of a new language in your family. How would your reactions and those of your family differ from those of Cunha and her family? What difficulties would you have if you had to translate everything for your parents? How do you think the job of "translator" would affect your relationships with the rest

of your family? How would it feel to have your parents dependent on you for communication?

3. It is not always possible to know a person's cultural background from a surname. Edite Cunha was surprised to learn that Mrs. Donahue was, in fact, Portuguese. A woman who marries a man from a cultural background different from her own and takes her husband's name may be surprised to find that she is regarded differently because of her surname. Either find someone for whom this is true and interview her about her change of name, or search through newspaper and magazine databases for articles about women who have married into a different culture. Did the women find that they had a new identity? Were they regarded differently? What revealing stories, if any, can they tell? Write an essay discussing what you learned from your research that you think might be interesting for your readers.

And Ain't I a Woman?

SOJOURNER TRUTH

Sojourner Truth was born a slave named Isabella in Ulster County, New York, in 1797. Freed by the New York State Emancipation Act of 1827, she went to New York City and underwent a profound religious transformation. She worked as a domestic servant and, in her active evangelism, tried to reform prostitutes. Adopting the name Sojourner Truth in 1843, she became a traveling preacher and abolitionist.

Although she remained illiterate, Truth's compelling presence gripped her audience as she spoke eloquently about emancipation and women's rights. Truth dictated her memoirs to Olive Gilbert and they were published as The Narative of Sojourner Truth: A Northern Slave *(1850). After the Civil War, she worked to provide education and employment for emancipated slaves until her death in 1883.*

WRITING TO DISCOVER: *How do you respond to someone giving a speech? What speaking styles do you respond to the most, the ones that captivate you as a listener? What language requirements need to be in place in order for you to be moved by others' words? Try your hand at writing something you will deliver as a speech to the class.*

Well, children, where there is so much racket there must be something out of kilter. I think that 'twixt the Negroes of the South and the women at the North, all talking about rights, the white men will be in a fix pretty soon. But what's all this here talking about?

That man over there says that women need to be helped into carriages, and lifted over ditches, and to have the best place everywhere. Nobody ever helps me into carriages, or over mud puddles, or gives me any best place! And ain't I a woman? Look at me! Look at my arm. I have plowed and planted, and gathered into barns, and no man could head me! And ain't I a woman? I could work as much and eat as much as a man — when I could get it — and bear the lash as well! And ain't I a woman? I have borne thirteen children, and seen them most all sold off to slavery, and when I cried out with my mother's grief, none but Jesus heard me! And ain't I a woman?

Then they talk about this thing in the head; what's this they call it? [Intellect, someone whispers.] That's it, honey. What's that got to do with women's rights or Negro's rights? If my cup won't hold but a pint, and yours holds a quart, wouldn't you be mean not to let me have my little half-measure full?

Then that little man in black there, he says women can't have as much rights as men, 'cause Christ wasn't a woman! Where did your Christ come from? Where did your Christ come from? From God and a woman! Man had nothing to do with him.

If the first woman God ever made was strong enough to turn the 5 world upside down all alone, these women together ought to be able to turn it back, and get it right side up again! And now they is asking to do it, the men better let them.

Obliged to you for hearing me, and now old Sojourner ain't got nothing more to say.

FOCUSING ON CONTENT

1. What does Truth mean when she says, "Where there is so much racket there must be something out of kilter" (1)? Why does Truth believe that white men are going to find themselves in a "fix" (1)?

2. What does Truth put forth as her "credentials" as a woman?

3. How does Truth counter the argument that "women can't have as much rights as men, 'cause Christ wasn't a woman" (4)?

FOCUSING ON WRITING

1. What is Truth's purpose in this essay? (Glossary: *Purpose*) Why is it important for her to define what a woman is for her audience?

2. How does Truth use the comments of "that man over there" (2) and "that little man in black" (4) to help her establish her definition of woman?

3. What is the effect of Truth's repetition of the question "And ain't I a woman?" four times? What other questions does she ask? Why do you suppose Truth doesn't provide answers to questions in paragraph 3, but does for the question in paragraph 4?

4. How would you characterize Truth's tone in this speech? What phrases in the speech suggest that tone to you? (Glossary: *Tone*)

LANGUAGE IN ACTION

Carefully read the following letter to the editor of the *New York Times*. In it Nancy Stevens, president of a small Manhattan advertising agency, argues against using the word *guys* to address women. How do you think Truth would react to the use of the word *guys* to refer to women? Do you find such usage objectionable?

WOMEN AREN'T GUYS

A young woman, a lawyer, strides into a conference room. Already in attendance, at what looks to be the start of a high-level meeting, are four smartly dressed women in their 20's and 30's. The arriving woman plunks her briefcase down at the head of the polished table and announces, "O.K., guys, let's get started."

On "Kate and Allie," a television show about two women living together with Kate's daughter and Allie's daughter and son, the dialogue often runs to such phrases as, "Hey, you guys, who wants pizza?" All of the people addressed are female, except for Chip, the young son. "Come on, you guys, quit fighting," pleads one of the daughters when there is a tiff between the two women.

Just when we were starting to be aware of the degree to which language affects people's perceptions of women and substitute "people working" for "men working" and "humankind" for "mankind," this "guy" thing happened. Just when people have started becoming aware that a 40-year-old woman shouldn't be called a girl, this "guy" thing has crept in.

Use of "guy" to mean "person" is so insidious that I'll bet most women don't notice they are being called "guys," or, if they do, find it somehow flattering to be one of them.

Sometimes, I find the courage to pipe up when a bunch of us are assembled and are called "guys" by someone of either gender. "We're not guys," I say. Then everyone looks at me funny.

One day, arriving at a business meeting where there were five women and one man, I couldn't resist. "Hello, ladies," I said. Everyone laughed embarrassedly for the blushing man until I added, "and gent." Big sigh of relief. Wouldn't want to call a guy a "gal" now, would we?

Why is it not embarrassing for a woman to be called "guy"? We know why. It's the same logic that says women look sexy and cute in a man's shirt, but did you ever try your silk blouse on your husband and send him to the deli? It's the same mentality that holds that anything male is worthy (and to be aspired toward) and anything female is trivial.

We all sit around responding, without blinking, "black with one sugar, please," when anyone asks, "How do you guys like your coffee?"

What's all that murmuring I hear?

"Come on, lighten up."

"Be a good guy."

"Nobody means anything by it."

Nonsense.

WRITING SUGGESTIONS

1. Truth spoke out against the injustice she saw around her. In arguing for the rights of women, she found it helpful to define *woman* in order to make her point. What social cause do you find most compelling today? Human rights? AIDS awareness? Domestic abuse? Alcoholism? Gay marriage? Racism? Select

an issue about which you have strong feelings. Now carefully identify all key terms that you must define before arguing your position. Write an essay in which you use definition to make your point convincingly.

2. Truth's speech holds out hope for the future. She envisioned a future in which women join together to take charge and "turn [the world] back, and get it right side up again" (5). What she envisioned has, to some extent, come to pass. Write an essay in which you speculate about how Truth would react to the world as we know it. What do you think would please her? What would disappoint her? What do you think she would want to change about our society? Explain your reasoning.

And May He Be Bilingual

JUDITH ORTIZ COFER

Author and educator Judith Ortiz Cofer was born in Hormigueros, Puerto Rico, in 1952, but her family immigrated to the United States in 1954, settling first in Paterson, New Jersey, and later in Augusta, Georgia. She earned her B.A. at Augusta College in 1974 and her M.A. from Florida Atlantic University in 1977. Currently, she is Franklin Professor of English and Creative Writing at the University of Georgia. She has published a novel and collections of poetry, essays, and short fiction, including Terms of Survival *(1987),* Reaching for the Mainland *(1987),* The Line of the Sun *(1989),* Silent Dancing: A Partial Remembrance of a Puerto Rican Childhood *(1990),* The Latin Deli *(1993),* An Island Like You: Stories of the Barrio *(1995), and* Call me Maria *(2004). Much of Cofer's writing focuses on Hispanic issues and the culture clashes that occur between the Anglo and Hispanic communities.*

In the following autobiographical essay, which first appeared in Woman in Front of the Sun: On Becoming a Writer *(2000), Cofer explores the "coalescing of languages and cultures" in a culturally diverse country like America. Cofer's straightforward, almost conversational, tone engages readers at once and draws them into her reflections about teaching and writing in her second language.*

WRITING TO DISCOVER: *In this essay, Cofer talks about the importance of literature in expressing human experience — no matter what language or culture from which it originates. Write a one-page essay on a story or poem you have read from another culture that has had an effect on you.*

LATIN WOMEN PRAY

Latin women pray
In incense sweet churches
They pray in Spanish
To an Anglo God
With a Jewish heritage.
And this Great White Father
Imperturbable
In his marble pedestal
Looks down upon
His brown daughters
Votive candles shining like lust
In his all seeing eyes
Unmoved

By their persistent prayers.
Yet year after year
Before his image they kneel
Margarita, Josefina, Maria, and Isabel
All fervently hoping
That if not omnipotent
At least He be bilingual.

In this early poem I express the sense of powerlessness I felt as a non-native speaker of English in the United States. Nonnative. Nonpartici-pant in the mainstream culture. *Non*, as in no, not, nothing. This little poem is about the non-ness of the nonspeakers of the ruling language making a pilgrimage to the only One who can help, hopeful in their faith that someone is listening, yet still suspicious that even He doesn't under-stand their language. I grew up in the tight little world of the Puerto Rican community in Paterson, New Jersey, and later moved to Augusta, Georgia, where my "native" universe shrank even further to a tiny group of us who were brought to the Deep South through the military channels our fathers had chosen out of economic necessity. I wrote this ironic poem years ago, out of a need to explore the loneliness, the almost hope-lessness, I had felt and observed in the other nonnative speakers, many my own relatives, who would never master the English language well enough to be able to connect with the native speakers in as significant ways as I did.

Having come to age within the boundaries of language exiles, and making only brief forays out into the vast and often frightening landscape called *the mainstream*, it's easy for the newcomer to become ethnocen-tric. That's what Little Italy, Little Korea, Little Havana, Chinatown, and barrios are, centers of ethnic concerns. After all, it's a natural human re-sponse to believe that there is safety only within the walls around the cir-cle of others who look like us, speak like us, behave like us: it is the animal kingdom's basic rule of survival — if whatever is coming toward you does not look like you or your kin, either fight or fly.

It is this primal fear of the unfamiliar that I have conquered through education, travel, and my art. I am an English teacher by profession and a writer by vocation. I have written several books of prose and poetry based mainly on my experiences in growing up Latina in the United States. Until a few years ago, when multiculturalism became part of the Ameri-can political agenda, no one seemed to notice my work; suddenly I find myself a Puerto Rican/American (Latina)/Woman writer. Not only am I supposed to share my particular vision of American life, but I am also supposed to be a role model for a new generation of Latino students who expect me to teach them how to get a piece of the proverbial English lan-guage pie. I actually enjoy both of these public roles, in moderation. I love teaching literature. Not my own work, but the work of my literary ancestors in English and American literature — my field, that is, the main source of my models as a writer. I also like going into my classrooms at the University of Georgia, where my English classes at this point are still composed mainly of white American students, with a sprinkling of African American and Asian American, and only occasionally a Latino, and sharing my bicultural, bilingual views with them. It is a fresh audience. I am not always speaking to converts.

I teach American literature as an outsider in love with the Word — whatever language it is written in. They, at least some of them, come to understand that my main criterion when I teach is excellence and that I will talk to them about so-called minority writers whom I admire in the same terms as I will the old standards they know they are supposed to honor and study. I show them why they should admire them, not blindly, but with a critical eye. I speak English with my Spanish accent to these native speakers. I tell them about my passion for the genius of humankind, demonstrated through literature: the power of language to affect, to enrich, or to diminish and destroy lives, its potential to empower someone like me, someone like them. The fact that English is my second language does not seem to matter beyond the first few lectures, when the students sometimes look askance at one another, perhaps wondering whether they have walked into the wrong classroom and at any moment this obviously "Spanish" professor will ask them to start conjugating regular and irregular verbs. They can't possibly know this about me: in my classes, everyone is safe from Spanish grammar recitation. Because almost all of my formal education has been in English, I avoid all possible risk of falling into a discussion of the uses of the conditional or of the merits of the subjunctive tense in the Spanish language: Hey, I just *do* Spanish, I don't explain it.

Likewise, when I *do* use my Spanish and allude to my Puerto Rican heritage, it comes from deep inside me where my imagination and memory reside, and I do it through my writing. My poetry, my stories, and my essays concern themselves with the coalescing of languages and cultures into a vision that has meaning first of all for me; then, if I am served well by my craft and the transformation occurs, it will also have meaning for others as art.

My life as a child and teenager was one of constant dislocation. My father was in the U.S. Navy, and we moved back to Puerto Rico during his long tours of duty abroad. On the Island, my brother and I attended a Catholic school run by American nuns. Then it was back to Paterson, New Jersey, to try to catch up, and sometimes we did, academically, but socially it was a different story altogether. We were the perennial new kids on the block. Yet when I write about these gypsy days, I construct a continuity that allows me to see my life as equal to any other, with its share of chaos, with its own system of order. This is what I have learned from writing as a minority person in America that I can teach my students: Literature is the human search for meaning. It is as simple and as profound as that. And we are all, if we are thinking people, involved in the process. It is both a privilege and a burden.

Although as a child I often felt resentful of my rootlessness, deprived of a stable home, lasting friendships, the security of one house, one country, I now realize that these same circumstances taught me some skills that I use today to adapt in a constantly changing world, a place where you can remain in one spot for years and still wake up every day to strangeness wrought by technology and politics. We can stand still and find ourselves in a different nation created overnight by decisions we did not participate in making. I submit that we are all becoming more like the immigrant and can learn from her experiences as a stranger in a strange land. I know I am a survivor in language. I learned early that possessing the secret of words was to be my passport into mainstream life. Notice I did not say "assimilation" into mainstream life. This is a word that has come to mean the acceptance of loss of native culture. Although I know for a fact that to survive everyone "assimilates" what they need out of many different cultures, especially in America, I prefer to use the term "adapt" instead. Just as I acquired the skills to adapt to American life, I have now come to terms with a high-tech world. It is not that different. I learned English to communicate, but now I know computer language. I have been greedy in my grasping and hoarding of words. I own enough stock in English to feel secure in almost any situation where my language skills have to serve me; and I have claimed my rich Puerto Rican culture to give scope and depth to my personal search for meaning.

As I travel around this country I am constantly surprised by the diversity of its peoples and cultures. It is like a huge, colorful puzzle. And the beauty is in its complexity. Yet there are some things that transcend the obvious differences: great literature, great ideas, and great idealists, for example. I find Don Quixote[1] plays almost universal; after all, who among us does not have an Impossible Dream? Shakespeare's wisdom is planetary in its appeal; Ghandi's[2] and King's[3] message is basic to the survival of our civilization, and most people know it; and other voices that are like a human racial memory speak in a language that can almost always be translated into meaning.

And genius doesn't come in only one package. The Bard[4] happened to be a white gentleman from England, but what about our timid Emily

---

1. *Don Quixote:* the title character in a widely translated and adapted Spanish novel by Miguel de Cervantes (1547–1616) about a quest motivated by the "impossible dream." [Eds.]

2. *Mahatma Gandhi* (1869–1948): leader of the nonviolent Indian nationalist movement against British rule. [Eds.]

3. *Dr. Martin Luther King Jr.* (1929–1968): civil rights leader and Nobel Peace Prize recipient. [Eds.]

4. *The Bard:* William Shakespeare. [Eds.]

Dickinson? Would we call on her in our class, that mousy little girl in the back of the room squinting at the chalkboard and blushing at everything? We almost lost her art to neglect. Thank God poetry is stronger than time and prejudices.

This is where my idealism as a teacher kicks in: I ask myself, who is to   10
say that at this very moment there isn't a Native American teenager gazing dreamily at the desert outside her window as she works on today's assignment, seeing the universe in a grain of sand,[5] preparing herself to share her unique vision with the world. It may all depend on the next words she hears, which may come out of my mouth, or yours. And what about the African American boy in a rural high school in Georgia who showed me he could rhyme for as long as I let him talk. His teachers had not been able to get him to respond to literature. Now they listened in respectful silence while he composed an ode to his girl and his car extemporaneously, in a form so tight and so right (contagious too) that when we discuss the exalted Alexander Pope's oeuvre, we call it heroic couplets. But he was intimidated by the manner in which Pope and his worthy comrades in the canon had been presented to him and his classmates, as gods from Mt. Olympus, inimitable and incomprehensible to mere mortals like himself. He was in turn surprised to see, when it was finally brought to his attention, that Alexander Pope and he shared a good ear.

What I'm trying to say is that the phenomenon we call culture in a society is organic, not manufactured. It grows where we plant it. Culture is our garden, and we may neglect it, trample on it, or we may choose to cultivate it. In America we are dealing with varieties we have imported, grafted, cross-pollinated. I can only hope the experts who say that the land is replenished in this way are right. It is the ongoing American experiment, and it has to take root in the classroom first. If it doesn't succeed, then we will be back to praying and hoping that at least He be bilingual.

FOCUSING ON CONTENT

1. When she was young, how did Cofer feel as a nonnative speaker of English living in the United States? What did she observe in other nonnative speakers? How is her poem "Latin Women Pray" related to these experiences? What is ironic about the poem? (Glossary: *Irony*)

2. According to Cofer, why do non-English-speaking immigrants to the United States find mainstream culture frightening? How did Cofer conquer her own fear of the mainstream?

3. How did the rise of multiculturalism in the United States affect Cofer as a teacher and a writer?

---

5. Cofer is referring to a line from a poem by English poet, artist, and visionary mystic William Blake (1757–1827). [Eds.]

FOCUSING ON WRITING

1. According to Cofer, what is the power of language? And how is language related to culture? How would you describe Cofer's diction in this essay? (Glossary: *Diction*)

2. What do you think Cofer means when she says, "This is what I have learned from writing as a minority person in America that I can teach my students: Literature is the human search for meaning" (6)? In what ways can most writing be called a "human search for meaning"? Explain.

3. What does Cofer believe all Americans can learn from the immigrant experience? What do you think she means when she says, "I know I am a survivor in language" (7)?

4. In paragraph 7, Cofer states that she prefers to use the word *adapt* instead of *assimilate*. What, for her, are the differences between these two words? Do you agree with her position? Why or why not? What does Cofer see as the promise of America's ongoing experiment with multiculturalism?

5. How would you describe Cofer's tone in this essay? (Glossary: *Tone*)

LANGUAGE IN ACTION

Spanglish is the result of the impulse to bridge two languages and cultures: Spanish and English. The following excerpt is from "It's the Talk of Nueva New York: The Hybrid Called Spanglish," by Lizette Alvarez, which first appeared in the *New York Times* on March 25, 1997. Study both examples of Spanglish and Alvarez's translations of them, and then write about your own reactions to Spanglish.

TALKING THE TALK

Of the two basic forms of Spanglish, borrowing — saying English words "Spanish style" and spelling them accordingly — is more common among first-generation speakers; later generations tend to switch back and forth. Here are examples of the hybrid language — often spoken with a sense of humor — that has vaulted from streets to talk shows to the pages of magazines like *Latina* and *generation ñ*.

bacuncliner: vacuum cleaner
biper: beeper, pager
boyla: boiler
chileando: chilling out
choping: shopping
fafu: fast food
jangear: hang out

joldoperos: muggers, holdup artists
liqueo: leak
maicrogüey: microwave oven
pulóver: T-shirt
roofo: roof
sangüiche: sandwich
tensén: 10-cent store, like Kmart or Woolworth's

Spanglish	Translation
EL Oye, me estoy frisando y el estin está broken — close the door. ¿Vamos a lonchar, or what? I need to eat before I go to my new job as a chiroquero.	**HE** Hey, I'm freezing and the steam [or heat] is broken — close the door. Are we going to have lunch or what? I need to eat before I go to my new job as a Sheet-rocker.
ELLA ¿Quieres que te cocine some rice en la jitachi, or should I just get you some confley con leche? By the way, you embarkated me el otro día. ¿What did you do, pick up some fafu en vez de ir al restaurante where I was waiting? Eres tan chipero.	**SHE** Do you want me to cook you some rice in the Hitachi [catchall term for all steam cookers], or should I just get you some cornflakes [ditto for any kind of cereal] with milk? By the way, you stood me up the other day. What did you do, pick up some fast food instead of going to the restaurant where I was waiting? You're so cheap.

WRITING SUGGESTIONS

1. Put yourself in Cofer's place and imagine you were to emigrate somewhere where another language is spoken. How hard would you work to learn the predominate language of your chosen country? What advantages would there be in learning that language? How would you feel if the country had a law that forced you to learn its language as quickly as possible? Write an essay in which you explore the advantages of being multilingual.

2. Using your response to the Writing to Discover journal prompt for this selection as a starting point, write an essay in which you discuss cultural diversity at your college or university. How would you characterize your school? Are the faculty and student body culturally diverse? What still needs to be done? Is the administration at your school actively trying to promote cultural diversity? What have been the benefits of diversity for you and other students both in and out of the classroom? You may find it helpful to talk with several faculty members and with other students about their views on campus diversity before you start to write.

The Fourth of July

Audre Lorde

Audre Lorde (1934–1992) was a professor of English at Hunter College in New York City. Born in New York, she studied at Hunter and at Columbia University. Her published works include several volumes of poetry, such as Undersong: Chosen Poems Old and New *(1982), which was revised in 1992; essay collections like* Sister Outsider *(1984) and* Burst of Light *(1988); and an autobiography,* Zami: A New Spelling of My Name *(1982). Her book of poems* The Arithmetics of Distance *appeared posthumously in 1993. The following selection from* Zami *eloquently communicates the tragedy of racism. Take special note of Lorde's tone as you read, particularly the way it intensifies as the essay continues and how it culminates in the anger of the final paragraph.*

Writing to Discover: *Think about the Fourth of July or some other national holiday like Memorial Day or Thanksgiving. Perhaps you celebrate Cinco de Mayo or Bastille Day. What are your memories of celebrating that holiday? What meaning does the holiday have for you?*

The first time I went to Washington, D.C., was on the edge of the summer when I was supposed to stop being a child. At least that's what they said to us all at graduation from the eighth grade. My sister Phyllis graduated at the same time from high school. I don't know what she was supposed to stop being. But as graduation presents for us both, the whole family took a Fourth of July trip to Washington, D.C., the fabled and famous capital of our country.

It was the first time I'd ever been on a railroad train during the day. When I was little, and we used to go to the Connecticut shore, we always went at night on the milk train, because it was cheaper.

Preparations were in the air around our house before school was even over. We packed for a week. There were two very large suitcases that my father carried, and a box filled with food. In fact, my first trip to Washington was a mobile feast; I started eating as soon as we were comfortably ensconced in our seats, and did not stop until somewhere after Philadelphia. I remember it was Philadelphia because I was disappointed not to have passed by the Liberty Bell.

My mother had roasted two chickens and cut them up into dainty bite-size pieces. She packed slices of brown bread and butter and green pepper and carrot sticks. There were little violently yellow iced cakes with scalloped edges called "marigolds," that came from Cushman's Bakery. There was a spice bun and rock-cakes from Newton's, the West Indian bakery across Lenox Avenue from St. Mark's School, and iced tea in a wrapped mayonnaise jar. There were sweet pickles for us and dill pickles for my father, and peaches with the fuzz still on them, individually wrapped to keep them from bruising. And, for neatness, there were piles of napkins and a little tin box with a washcloth dampened with rosewater and glycerine for wiping sticky mouths.

I wanted to eat in the dining car because I had read all about them,   5
but my mother reminded me for the umpteenth time that dining car food always cost too much money and besides, you never could tell whose hands had been playing all over that food, nor where those same hands had been just before. My mother never mentioned that black people were not allowed into railroad dining cars headed south in 1947. As usual, whatever my mother did not like and could not change, she ignored. Perhaps it would go away, deprived of her attention.

I learned later that Phyllis's high school senior class trip had been to Washington, but the nuns had given her back her deposit in private, explaining to her that the class, all of whom were white, except Phyllis, would be staying in a hotel where Phyllis "would not be happy," meaning, Daddy explained to her, also in private, that they did not rent rooms to Negroes. "We will take you to Washington, ourselves," my father had avowed, "and not just for an overnight in some measly fleabag hotel."

American racism was a new and crushing reality that my parents had to deal with every day of their lives once they came to this country. They handled it as a private woe. My mother and father believed that they could best protect their children from the realities of race in America and the fact of American racism by never giving them name, much less discussing their nature. We were told we must never trust white people, but *why* was never explained, nor the nature of their ill will. Like so many other vital pieces of information in my childhood, I was supposed to know without being told. It always seemed like a very strange injunction coming from my mother, who looked so much like one of those people we were never supposed to trust. But something always warned me not to ask my mother why she wasn't white, and why Auntie Lillah and Auntie Etta weren't, even though they were all that same problematic color so different from my father and me, even from my sisters, who were somewhere in-between.

In Washington, D.C., we had one large room with two double beds and an extra cot for me. It was a back-street hotel that belonged to a friend of my father's who was in real estate, and I spent the whole next day after Mass squinting up at the Lincoln Memorial where Marian Anderson had sung after the D.A.R. refused to allow her to sing in their auditorium because she was black. Or because she was "Colored," my father said as he told us the story. Except that what he probably said was "Negro," because for his times, my father was quite progressive.

I was squinting because I was in that silent agony that characterized all of my childhood summers, from the time school let out in June to the end of July, brought about by my dilated and vulnerable eyes exposed to the summer brightness.

I viewed Julys through an agonizing corolla of dazzling whiteness 10 and I always hated the Fourth of July, even before I came to realize the travesty such a celebration was for black people in this country.

My parents did not approve of sunglasses, nor of their expense.

I spent the afternoon squinting up at monuments to freedom and past presidencies and democracy, and wondering why the light and heat were both so much stronger in Washington, D.C., than back home in New York City. Even the pavement on the streets was a shade lighter in color than back home.

Late that Washington afternoon my family and I walked back down Pennsylvania Avenue. We were a proper caravan, mother bright and father brown, the three of us girls step-standards in-between. Moved by our historical surroundings and the heat of early evening, my father decreed yet another treat. He had a great sense of history, a flair for the quietly dramatic and the sense of specialness of an occasion and a trip.

"Shall we stop and have a little something to cool off, Lin?"

Two blocks away from our hotel, the family stopped for a dish of 15 vanilla ice cream at a Breyer's ice cream and soda fountain. Indoors, the soda fountain was dim and fan-cooled, deliciously relieving to my scorched eyes.

Corded and crisp and pinafored, the five of us seated ourselves one by one at the counter. There was I between my mother and father, and my two sisters on the other side of my mother. We settled ourselves along the white mottled marble counter, and when the waitress spoke at first no one understood what she was saying, and so the five of us just sat there.

The waitress moved along the line of us closer to my father and spoke again. "I said I kin give you to take out, but you can't eat here. Sorry." Then she dropped her eyes looking very embarrassed, and suddenly we heard what it was she was saying all at the same time, loud and clear.

Straight-backed and indignant, one by one, my family and I got down from the counter stools and turned around and marched out of the store, quiet and outraged, as if we had never been black before. No one would answer my emphatic questions with anything other than a guilty silence. "But we hadn't done anything!" This wasn't right or fair! Hadn't I written poems about Bataan and freedom and democracy for all?

My parents wouldn't speak of this injustice, not because they had contributed to it, but because they felt they should have anticipated it and avoided it. This made me even angrier. My fury was not going to be acknowledged by a like fury. Even my two sisters copied my parents' pretense that nothing unusual and anti-American had occurred. I was left to write my angry letter to the president of the United States all by myself, although my father did promise I could type it out on the office typewriter next week, after I showed it to him in my copybook diary.

The waitress was white, and the counter was white, and the ice cream I   20
never ate in Washington, D.C., that summer I left childhood was white, and the white heat and the white pavement and the white stone monuments of my first Washington summer made me sick to my stomach for the whole rest of that trip and it wasn't much of a graduation present after all.

FOCUSING ON CONTENT

1. Why do you think Lorde's family dealt with racism by ignoring it? How is Lorde different?

2. Why did Lorde dislike the Fourth of July as a child? Why does she dislike it as an adult? Lorde takes great care in describing the food her family took on the train with them to Washington. What is Lorde's purpose in describing the food? (Glossary: *Purpose*)

3. What is the role of silence in Lorde's family? How does it enable or impede the racism they experience?

FOCUSING ON WRITING

1. Lorde's essay is not long or exaggerated, but it is a very effective indictment of a country that in 1947 held up the ideal of equality but reinforced institutions that argued against it. Identify some of the words Lorde uses to communicate her outrage when she writes of the racism that she and her family faced. How does her choice of words contribute to her message?

2. What is the tone of Lorde's essay? (Glossary: *Tone*) Identify passages to support your answer.

3. Do you see any irony in Lorde's title? (Glossary: *Irony*) In what way? Do you think it is an appropriate title for her essay?

LANGUAGE IN ACTION

Read the following poem by Maria Mazziotti Gillan, which depicts how non-English speakers were treated in previous generations. Discuss the reasons for Gillan's anger. Is her anger Audre Lorde's? If so, in what ways? How have they both dealt with their memories of incidents that have caused them emotional pain?

PUBLIC SCHOOL NO. 18: PATERSON, NEW JERSEY

Miss Wilson's eyes, opaque
as blue glass, fix on me:
"We must speak English.
We're in America now."
I want to say, "I am American,"
but the evidence is stacked against me.

My mother scrubs my scalp raw, wraps
my shining hair in white rags
to make it curl; Miss Wilson
drags me to the window, checks my hair
for lice. My face wants to hide.

At home, my words smooth in my mouth,
I chatter and am proud. In school,
I am silent; I grope for the right English
words, fear the Italian word will sprout
from my mouth like a rose.

I fear the progression of teachers
in their sprigged dresses,
their Anglo-Saxon faces.

Without words, they tell me
to be ashamed.
I am.
I deny that booted country
even from myself,
want to be still
and untouchable
as these women
who teach me to hate myself.

Years later, in a white
Kansas City house,
the psychology professor tells me
I remind him of the Mafia leader
on the cover of *Time* magazine.
My anger spits
venomous from my mouth:

I am proud of my mother,
dressed all in black,
proud of my father
with his broken tongue,
proud of the laughter
and noise of our house.

Remember me, ladies,
the silent one?
I have found my voice

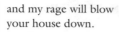

and my rage will blow
your house down.

WRITING SUGGESTIONS

1. When read with the ideals of the American Revolution and the Constitution in mind, Lorde's essay is strongly ironic. What does the Fourth of July mean to you? Why? How do your feelings relate to the stated ideals of our fore-bears? Choose your words carefully, and use specific personal experiences to support your general statements.

2. Imagine that you are Lorde in 1947. Write a letter to President Harry Tru-man in which you protest the reception you received in the nation's capital on the Fourth of July. Do not overstate your case. Show the president in what ways you and your family were treated unfairly rather than merely stat-ing that you were discriminated against, and carefully choose words that will help President Truman see the irony of your experience.

Going to Japan

BARBARA KINGSOLVER

The popular and prolific author Barbara Kingsolver was born in 1955 in eastern Kentucky. A born storyteller, Kingsolver has also kept a journal since she was a child and dreamed she might one day become a published writer. After graduating from DePauw University in Indiana, where she majored in biology, Kingsolver lived in Greece and France, taking a variety of jobs to support herself. She returned to the United States and received her M.S. in biology and ecology at the University of Arizona, where she also enrolled in a writing course with author Francine Prose. Soon after, she took a job as a science writer and gradually developed into a features writer for newspapers and scientific journals. Kingsolver has published poetry, essays, and an oral history along with her novels, which include The Bean Trees *(1988),* Animal Dreams *(1990),* Pigs in Heaven *(1993), and* Prodigal Summer *(2002).*

In "Going to Japan," taken from her collection of essays Small Wonder *(2002), Kingsolver tells us what it was like to be a foreign traveler in Japan as she confronted a very different language and culture and what she learned from the experience.*

WRITING TO DISCOVER: *Reflect on your encounters with different cultures, whether through travel abroad or in the ethnic neighborhoods where you grew up or now attend college. What impressions did you have when you were at the point where two cultures, the one you are a part of and the one you visited, came into contact? What did you learn from your experiences?*

My great-aunt Zelda went to Japan and took an abacus, a bathysphere, a conundrum, a diatribe, an eggplant. That was a game we used to play. All you had to do was remember everything in alphabetical order. Right up to Aunt Zelda.

Then I grew up and was actually invited to go to Japan, not with the fantastic Aunt Zelda but as myself. As such, I had no idea what to take. I knew what I planned to be doing: researching a story about the memorial at Hiroshima; visiting friends; trying not to get lost in a place where I couldn't even read the street signs. Times being what they were — *any* times — I intended to do my very best to respect cultural differences, avoid sensitive topics I might not comprehend, and, in short, be anything but an Ugly American. When I travel, I like to try to blend in. I've generally found it helps to be prepared. So I asked around, and was warned to expect a surprisingly modern place.

My great-aunt Zelda went to Japan and took Appliances, Battery packs, Cellular technology. . . . That seemed to be the idea.

And so it came to pass that I arrived in Kyoto an utter foreigner, unprepared. It's true that there are electric streetcars there, and space-age gas stations with uniformed attendants who rush to help you from all directions at once. There are also golden pagodas on shimmering lakes, and Shinto shrines in the forests. There are bamboo groves and nightingales. And finally there are more invisible guidelines for politeness than I could fathom. When I stepped on a streetcar, a full head taller than all the other passengers, I became an awkward giant. I took up too much space. I blended in like Igor would blend in with the corps de ballet in *Swan Lake*. I bumped into people. I crossed my arms when I listened, which turns out to be, in Japanese body language, the sign for indicating brazenly that one is bored.

But I wasn't! I was struggling through my days and nights in the grip   5
of boredom's opposite — i.e., panic. I didn't know how to eat noodle soup with chopsticks, and I did it most picturesquely *wrong*. I didn't know how to order, so I politely deferred to my hosts and more than once was served a cuisine with heads, including eyeballs. I managed to wrestle these creatures to my lips with chopsticks, but it was already too late by the time I got message that *one does not spit out anything*.

I undertook this trip in high summer, when it is surprisingly humid and warm in southern Japan. I never imagined that in such sweltering heat women would be expected to wear stockings, but every woman in Kyoto wore nylon stockings. Coeds in shorts *on the tennis court* wore nylon stockings. I had packed only skirts and sandals; people averted their eyes.

When I went to Japan I took my Altitude, my Bare-naked legs, my Callous foreign ways. I was mortified.

My hosts explained to me that the Japanese language does not accommodate insults, only infinite degrees of apology. I quickly memorized an urgent one, "*Sumimasen*," and another for especially extreme cases, "*Moshi wake gozaimasen*." This translates approximately to mean, "If you please, my transgression is so inexcusable that I wish I were dead."

I needed these words. When I touched the outside surface of a palace wall, curious to know what it was made of, I set off screeching alarms and a police car came scooting up the lawn's discreet gravel path. "*Moshi wake gozaimasen*, Officer! Wish I were dead!" And in the public bath, try as I might, I couldn't get the hang of showering with a hand-held nozzle while sitting fourteen inches from a stranger. I sprayed my elderly neighbor with cold water. In the face.

"*Moshi wake gozaimasen*," I declared, with feeling.   10

She merely stared, dismayed by the foreign menace.

I visited a Japanese friend, and in her small, perfect house I spewed out my misery. "Everything I do is wrong!" I wailed like a child. "I'm a blight on your country."

"Oh, no," she said calmly. "To forgive, for us, is the highest satisfaction. To forgive a foreigner, ah! Even better." She smiled. "You have probably made many people happy here."

To stomp about the world ignoring cultural differences is arrogant, to be sure, but perhaps there is another kind of arrogance in the presumption that we may ever really build a faultless bridge from one shore to another, or even know where the mist has ceded to landfall. When I finally arrived at Ground Zero in Hiroshima, I stood speechless. What I found there was a vast and exquisitely silent monument to forgiveness. I was moved beyond words, even beyond tears, to think of all that can be lost or gained in the gulf between any act of will and its consequence. In the course of every failure of understanding, we have so much to learn.

I remembered my Japanese friend's insistence on forgiveness as the   15
highest satisfaction, and I understood it really for the first time: What a rich wisdom it would be, and how much more bountiful a harvest, to gain pleasure not from achieving personal perfection but from understanding the inevitability of imperfection and pardoning those who also fall short of it.

I have walked among men and made mistakes without number. When I went to Japan I took my Abject goodwill, my Baleful excuses, my Cringing remorse. I couldn't remember everything, could not even recite the proper alphabet. So I gave myself away instead, evidently as a kind of public service. I prepared to return home feeling empty-handed.

At the Osaka Airport I sat in my plane on the runway, waiting to leave for terra cognita, as the aircraft's steel walls were buffeted by the sleet and winds of a typhoon. We waited for an hour, then longer, with no official word from the cockpit, and then suddenly our flight was canceled. Air traffic control in Tokyo had been struck by lightning; no flights possible until the following day.

"We are so sorry," the pilot told us. "You will be taken to a hotel, fed, and brought back here for your flight tomorrow."

As we passengers rose slowly and disembarked, we were met by an airline official who had been posted in the exit port for the sole purpose of saying to each and every one of us, "Terrible, terrible. *Sumimasen.*" Other travelers nodded indifferently, but not me. I took the startled gentleman by the hands and practically kissed him.

"You have no idea," I told him, "how thoroughly I forgive you."   20

FOCUSING ON CONTENT

1. What is Kingsolver's purpose in this essay? (Glossary: *Purpose*)
2. What cultural mistakes does she make while traveling in Japan?
3. What reversal of expectations does Kingsolver come to understand when talking to her friend about cultural miscues and how much she worried about them? (Glossary: *Irony*)
4. Kingsolver went to Japan to research a story about the memorial at Hiroshima where one of the two atomic bombs was dropped that ended

World War II in the Pacific theater. What did Kingsolver learn about the memorial in the course of her contacts with Japanese culture?

FOCUSING ON WRITING

1. Kingsolver repeatedly refers to the alphabetic game "My Great Aunt Zelda." What function(s) do her references serve? (Glossary: *Coherence* and *Organization*)

2. In paragraph 14, Kingsolver writes of a possible arrogance beyond transgressing cultural customs. What is the metaphor she uses to explain her idea, and how does the metaphor work? (Glossary: *Figurative Language*)

3. Discuss the effectiveness of Kingsolver's conclusion. (Glossary: *Beginnings and Endings*)

4. Kingsolver might have titled her essay "Forgiveness." What would have been gained or lost with the new title?

LANGUAGE IN ACTION

If you are interested in learning more about the differences between American lifestyles and Japanese lifestyles, visit the Japan-Guide.com Web site:

www.japan-guide.com/forum/advreadisplay.html?0+10031

The site covers just about every aspect of Japanese life, including food, comparative dating observations, living arrangements, language training, cultural differences, and living arrangements. Also included is a forum where users can post and reply to questions and comments.

WRITING SUGGESTIONS

1. Return to your journal and review what you wrote. If you think that your recounting of the experience(s) that you had in interacting with a culture different than your own has the potential to be developed into a larger piece of writing, brainstorm for more ideas, information, and examples that would make your observations come alive for your readers. Keep in mind that in crafting your remembrances into a formal essay, you need to develop a thesis, an assertion which all your ideas and illustrative examples should support.

2. We are a society made up of people from many cultures but are viewed elsewhere as being a single culture with an ethnocentric outlook. Ethnocentrism is the idea that one's culture is the superior culture and that the worldview from any other culture is therefore inaccurate. Write an essay in which you explore the paradoxical idea of our being thought to be an ethnocentric society while at the same time multicultural in our makeup.

3. Conduct some research regarding different cultures' rules for body language and compare them with what those same gestures mean in American culture. Experiment with altering your own body gestures to conform to a culture that is not your own. Record your experiences.

Representations of Deaf People: The Infirmity and Cultural Models

Harlan Lane

A University Distinguished Professor at Northeastern University in Boston, Harlan Lane is a psychologist who specializes in speech, language, deafness, and deaf culture. He received both his B.A. and M.A. degrees from Columbia University in 1958 and his Ph.D. from Harvard University in 1960. He earned a second doctorate from the Université de Paris, Sorbonne, in 1973. He has been a lecturer at the Harvard Medical School, has been the recipient of many grants, has published numerous articles and books, and has appeared before Congress and on television. His most recent books are The Mask of Benevolence: Disabling the Deaf Community *(1992),* A Journey into the Deaf-World *(1996),* The Signs of Language Revisited *(2000), and* Make Every Minute Count *(2000).*

In the following essay, taken from The Mask of Benevolence, *Lane explores how we tend to think about cultures, and deaf culture specifically, and commit what he calls the "extrapolative error." He writes that those in one culture erroneously regard other cultures for what they lack relative to their own instead of what they actually are. In other words, those who hear tend to look at the deaf and ask, "What would it be like if I were deaf?" instead of asking what makes up deaf language and culture in order to understand it on its own terms. Lane hopes the day will come when we can move beyond the "extrapolative error" and the cross-cultural misunderstanding it creates.*

WRITING TO DISCOVER: *What is culture? What does it mean to be a part of a culture? Are cultures only racial or ethnic in character? What is meant by a business or corporate culture?*

A DIFFERENT CENTER

On June 27, 1990, the United States Food and Drug Administration approved a proposal by the Cochlear Corporation to market a "bionic ear" for surgical insertion in deaf children over the age of two. More properly called a cochlear prosthesis, this device converts sound waves into electrical currents that are delivered to a wire implanted in the child's inner ear. With the headline "New Hope for Deaf Children: Implant Gives Them Hearing and Speech," *American Health* enthused: "Results promise to be even more dramatic for very young children [than they have been for adults]. The implants will actually allow them to speak."[1] The modern miracle of biotechnology, you say, as do the media, and yet the National Association of the Deaf has called the FDA approval "unsound scientifically, procedurally, and ethically."[2] Audiologists and otologists — those who measure hearing and those who treat it medically, experts who "have only the best interests of deaf children at heart" — proclaim a dramatic advance; yet the American deaf community, whose members could not love deaf children more, proclaim a dangerous setback to their interests.

Cochlear implantation is a surgical procedure, lasting about three and a half hours under general anesthesia, and it requires hospitalization for two to four days. A broad crescent-shaped incision is made behind the operated ear, and the skin flap is elevated. A piece of temporalis muscle is removed. A depression is drilled in the skull and reamed to make a seat for the internal electrical coil of the cochlear implant. A section of the mastoid bone is removed to expose the middle ear cavity. Further drilling exposes the membrane of the round window on the inner ear. Observing the procedure under a microscope, the surgeon pierces the membrane. A wire about twenty-five millimeters long is pushed through the opening. Sometimes the way is blocked by abnormal bone growth in the inner ear; the surgeon will generally drill through this but may have to settle in the end for only partial insertion of the wire. The wire seeks its own path as it moves around and up the coiled inner ear, shaped like a snail and called the cochlea, from the Latin for "snail." The exquisitely detailed microstructure of the inner ear is often ripped apart as the electrode weaves its way, crushing cells and perforating membranes; if there was any residual hearing in the ear, it is almost certainly destroyed. The auditory nerve itself is unlikely to be damaged, however, and the implant stimulates the auditory nerve directly. The internal coil is then sutured into place. Finally, the skin is sewn back over the coil.

Not long after the FDA gave the green light to surgeons to implant the Cochlear Corporation prosthesis in children, the manufacturer announced a promotional meeting in Boston and I attended. Two sets of satisfied parents and their implanted children were flown in for the occasion and seated center stage. "Barry," nine, had become deaf when he was six and a half; "June" was four and a half and born deaf. Both children had been using their implants for about a year, and both attended special programs for deaf children housed in ordinary public schools. Barry could understand much of what his teachers said, but June required a sign language interpreter. Both children spent several hours every day practicing listening and speaking, under their mothers' tutelage or that of therapists.

During the presentation, researchers from the Cochlear Corporation reported on their investigations with several hundred implanted children, and then the members of an implant team spoke in turn: first the surgeon, then an audiologist and a speech therapist, and finally a special educator. While the scholars held forth and the parents beside them listened attentively, I noticed the two children, half-screened from the audience behind their parents' backs, signing furiously to each other across the stage.

Will the typical deaf child, who was born deaf, like June, or who became so early in life, be able to understand ordinary conversation after undergoing the surgery and a lot of training? Probably not. Will he or she be able to speak intelligibly? Probably not. Will he learn English better than he would have without the implant? Probably not, but we do not know. Will he be able to succeed in an ordinary school with hearing children? Probably not. Will he then generally rely on vision rather than hearing? Yes.

Although the implanted deaf child will not move easily in the hearing world, it is unlikely that he will move easily in the deaf community either, unlikely that he will learn American Sign Language (ASL) fluently and make his own the fundamental values of that community. So there is a real danger that he will grow up without any substantive communication, spoken or signed. He may develop problems of personal identity, of emotional adjustment, even of mental health — this has not been studied. You may well ask: If the benefits are so small and the psychological and social risks so great, why did the FDA approve general marketing of the device and why do surgeons implant it?

Why indeed? Why would such heroic medicine be practiced on young deaf children? For this to be justified, the plight of the deaf child must be seen as truly desperate. But surely, you say, the plight of the deaf child *is* desperate. The child is unable to communicate with his mother and father — nine out of ten deaf children have hearing parents. He will receive a "special" education — in fact an especially unsuccessful education that commonly leads to underemployment. He will take a deaf spouse and be shut off from the world of his hearing parents and the mainstream of American society.

Most people who were born deaf or became so early in life, like the child we are discussing, and who grew up deaf as part of the deaf community have a different point of view. They see themselves as fundamentally visual people, with their own visual language, social organization, history, and mores — in short, with their own way of being, their own language and culture. Scholarly research since the 1970s in such fields as linguistics, anthropology, sociology, and history supports them in this claim. Yes, the deaf child faces many obstacles in life, but the lack of communication at home, inferior education in school, discrimination in employment, are obstacles placed in his way by hearing people who, if only they came to know the deaf community, could readily remove them.

In their book on American deaf culture, deaf authors Carol Padden and Tom Humphries say that hearing professionals who work with deaf people have a different "center" than their clients, which they illustrate with this observation: From a hearing point of view, it is better to be hard of hearing than deaf; someone who is "a little hard of hearing" is much less deaf than someone who is "very hard of hearing." Deaf people see things the other way around. When they sign that an acquaintance is A-LITTLE HARD-OF-HEARING,[1] they mean that the person has some of the ways of hearing people but basically is quite deaf. When they sign that someone is VERY HARD-OF-HEARING, they mean that the person is very much like hearing people, scarcely like deaf people at all. The same opposing points of view of the hearing benefactor and the deaf beneficiary are revealed in this observation: Members of the deaf community commonly condemn a deaf acquaintance who is ORAL — that is, who does not fully acknowledge that he is deaf. They say disparagingly that that person ALWAYS-PLANS actions for every situation, in order to pass acceptably in a hearing world. Hearing experts, however, do not understand why some deaf people condemn others who are oral and trying to pass; they use terms like "afflicted" for the first group, deaf people who do not speak, and applaud the efforts of those who try to.[3]

Two cultures, two points of view, two different "centers."   10

HEARING REPRESENTATIONS OF DEAF PEOPLE

What are deaf people like? There are at least three approaches to answering the question. You may, first, reflect on the social identity of deaf people; they belong to a category, and the category has attributes that are part of our popular culture, as a result of the treatment of deaf people in literature and in the media. Second, you may make an extrapolative leap and try to imagine what your world would be like if you were deaf. Most hearing people, if they are led to think about deaf people, soon make this extrapolative leap, for they have little else to guide them; they have not read about deaf language and culture, and extrapolation must stand in for real knowledge. If it happens that you know someone who is deaf, a third way of apprehending deafness is open; it takes on the characteristics of that particular deaf person, as in: "John understands me when I talk to him directly; therefore, deaf people can lip-read."

All of these approaches commonly lead hearing people to the same point of departure in their representations of deaf people: Deafness is a bad thing. In hearing society, deafness is stigmatized.

The sociologist Erving Goffman distinguishes three kinds of stigma: physical, characterological, and tribal.[4] "There is only one complete, unblushing male in America," he explains. "[He is] a young, married, white, urban northern heterosexual Protestant father of college education, fully

---

1. English glosses for the signs in American Sign Language (ASL) are conventionally written in capital letters. Hyphens connect glosses that are one word in ASL. It is important to note that glosses omit most of the grammar of ASL. They are *not* translations.

employed, of good complexion, weight, and height, and a recent record in sports." Any deviation is likely to entail a stigma, and we tend to impute many stigmas when we find a single one. All three categories of stigma are ascribed to deaf people. Physically they are judged defective; this is commonly taken to give rise to undesirable character traits, such as concreteness of thought and impulsive behavior. Hearing people may also view deaf people as clannish — even, indeed, an undesirable world apart, social deviants like those Goffman lists: prostitutes, drug addicts, delinquents, criminals, jazz musicians, bohemians, gypsies, carnival workers, hoboes, winos, show people, full-time gamblers, beach dwellers, gays, and the urban unrepentant poor. But even if the American deaf community were known for what it is, a linguistic and cultural minority with a rich and unique heritage, it would still be subject to a tribal stigma, as is, for example, the Hispanic-American community.

Stigma is relational. In the deaf community, to be called ORAL, we have seen, is unacceptable. ORAL means you have made the wrong life choices, you have uncritically embraced alien values that place a premium on speech. Hearing people fail to see what is wrong with deaf people's being ORAL; articulateness is prized in American society; gesturing is not.[5]

In the hearing stereotype, deafness is the lack of something, not the presence of anything. Silence is emptiness. The deaf community, say Padden and Humphries, recognizes that "silent" "is part of a way of viewing deaf people that is pervasive in hearing society; they accept it and use it as an easy way for others to recognize them." Thus the magazine published by the National Association of the Deaf (NAD) was long called *The Silent Worker*. But for hearing people, "silent" represents the dark side of deaf people. They must not have the orientation and security in their environment that we have; of course, they can't appreciate music, we tell ourselves; nor can they engage in conversation, hear announcements, use the telephone. The deaf person moves about, it seems to us, encapsulated; there's a barrier between us. Hence the deaf person is isolated. Ivan Turgenev's character Gerasim, for example, was "shut off by his affliction from the society of men," as was Carson McCullers's deaf protagonist in *The Heart Is a Lonely Hunter*.[6]

In the parlance of hearing people, ordinary deaf people can't really communicate; for them to attempt it is to engage in a *dialogue des sourds* — a deaf dialogue, meaning mutual incomprehension. Hearing people are called deaf, by metaphorical extension, when they refuse to listen, especially to moral advice. If great flourishes in English are associated with a refined mind, simple, awkward speech and gesticulation are associated with a simple mind. Because language and intellect are so linked in our representations of people (we are surprised to hear a towering intellect expressed — unless by deliberate intent — in a Southern drawl or in ungrammatical sentences), deafness seems a defect of intellect. The

15

"dumb" or "deaf and dumb" appears to refer not only to muteness but to weakness of mind. Joanne Greenberg's deaf couple in *In This Sign*[7] are ignorant even about childbearing. Paradoxically, in a reaction formation, deafness may also seem ennobling: the very simplicity of mind, the childlikeness, bespeaks a pure soul, one free of the artifices of civilization. Dickens's Sophy seems to have descended from heaven; Maupassant's Gargan is speechless, an ignorant shepherd, but strong, upright, pure in his misery.[8]

In fact, we imagine two kinds of deafness. The more usual kind is linked in our minds with blue-collar jobs or even poverty. Eudora Welty's deaf couple in "The Key" are poor, naive, "afflicted," and childlike. A deaf person may sell cards inscribed with the finger alphabet; or work in the manual trades, say as a printer. But then there is the exceptional deaf person who can speak and lip-read — who is just like you and me, except for some slight difference. (What a relief!) This person does not sell cards or labor with his hands; he is not poor or even middle-class in our imagination, but distinguished, elegant. Henry Kisor, book editor at the Chicago *Sun-Times*, confirmed this comfortable image of the deaf person in his 1990 autobiography, *What's That Pig Outdoors*.[9] (The title was chosen to illustrate the perils of lip-reading.)

Our society is sufficiently rich and enlightened that we are prepared to sympathize with marginal people who endorse our norms but, for reasons beyond their control, cannot live up to them. The deaf actress Marlee Matlin won the admiration of many hearing people when she chose to speak aloud on national television, rather than through an interpreter, on receiving the Oscar for her role as a culturally deaf person in the film *Children of a Lesser God*. By the same act she incurred criticism from some members of the American deaf community. For them, in those few halting words she negated the principles of the story she had so brilliantly enacted; she chose symbolically not to accept the award as a member of the deaf community; and she seemed to endorse the view that any amount of English is better for deaf people than the most eloquent American Sign Language.

Late-deafened people who make an effort to speak English and lip-read, to overcome the hurdles of their handicap, are much less discomfiting to hearing people than the members of the deaf community, with their distinctly different ways and language. What is unforgivable is that members of the deaf community insist they are fine — for example, two-thirds of deaf adults interviewed in a 1988 survey thought their social life was better than hearing people's[10] — when in fact we can give them a thousand reasons why they can't be. Goffman points out that the stigmatized are expected to keep a bargain: "they should not test the limits of the acceptance shown them, nor make it the basis for still further demands."[11] Thus, the person who is disabled (in our eyes) is expected to *be* disabled; to accept his role as such as to conform, *grosso modo*, to our representation of him. In return we will class him not among the bad (prostitutes, drug addicts, delinquents) but among the sick. The sick and the infirm have a claim on our tolerance and, even more, on our "reasonable accommodation," our compassion, our help.

But we've got it all wrong. Come with me to the annual convention of the Massachusetts State Association of the Deaf, for example. Friends, frequently former schoolmates, embrace at the joy of seeing each other after long separation. There's a lot of catching up to do, and throughout the hotel there are groups of deaf people conversing intently in ASL. At the same time, there are workshops in various meeting rooms to explore issues of common concern, such as the political, social, and athletic program for the year; the governance of the association; outreach to hearing parents; wise personal investing; new technology of interest to deaf people; and deaf awareness — including the roles of various deaf organizations in community service like teaching ASL or counseling unemployed deaf people. At dinner, there will be a banquet speaker — the last time I attended, it was the deaf president of Gallaudet University, the world's premier institution of higher learning in the liberal arts for deaf students. Speakers commonly urge on the audience some course of organized social action — protests at the statehouse in behalf of funding for interpreters; activism in the schools in favor of ASL; letters to the networks to promote captioning — action to enhance the lives of deaf children and adults.

The pageant to choose Miss Deaf Massachusetts has been part of the annual convention in some years. Young women sponsored by various Massachusetts high schools (or high school programs) for deaf students are judged by a committee of deaf community notables for their knowledge of state and national deaf history, for their presentation of their background and career goals, and for the sheer delight of looking at them. The winner becomes a contestant in the national competition held during the convention of the National Association of the Deaf. It has been my pleasure to come to know Miss Deaf New Jersey of some years ago, now a colleague at my university, and Miss Deaf America of 1989, both extraordinarily keen and beautiful young women. When I left the packed auditorium where the 1989 winner was being selected, a deaf student leader hailed me and asked what I thought of the pageant. I told her I liked parts of it but felt a little uneasy at seeing young women displayed like so many pounds of beef on the hoof. "You've a lot to learn about deaf culture," she replied. "I think it's just fine!"

In the course of the state convention there may be events that the deaf clubs in towns and cities across the nation also feature traditionally: a theatrical performance, a raffle, games, a dance, a sporting match. The state convention ends with numerous awards in recognition of service to the deaf community. The master of ceremonies (the last one I recall was B. J. Wood, who directs the state Commission for the Deaf and Hard of

Hearing) recounts the many achievements of each recipient, who is given a plaque and asked to say a few words — they're usually about how he (or she) could not have done it (organized a successful tournament, put on a show, conducted a fund-raiser, run the summer camp for deaf children, published the community newspaper) without the help of A, B, and C. The recognition of service and the warm congratulations all around continue for hours, until friends bid each other a reluctant good night.

So the members of the American deaf community are not characteristically isolated, or uncommunicative, or unintelligent, or childlike, or needy, or any of these things we imagine them to be. Why, then, do we think they are? This mistake arises from an extrapolative leap, an egocentric error. To imagine what deafness is like, I imagine my world without sound — a terrifying prospect, and one that conforms quite well with the stereotype we project onto members of the deaf community. I would be isolated, disoriented, uncommunicative, and unreceptive to communication. My ties to other people would be ruptured. I remember my parents censuring me with silence; it was bearable for four hours, and then I implored their forgiveness. I recall the "silent treatment" of offenders in the Army. The Tunisian novelist Albert Memmi, author of several sociological studies of oppression, observes in his book on dependency: "The person who refuses to communicate severs the psychological ties that connect him to the other person. In so doing he isolates the other person and can drive him to despair."[12] A world without sound would be a world without meaning.[13] What could be more fundamental to my sense of myself than my sensory milieu — unless it be my spoken language.

What motivates the extrapolative error in disinterested laymen is existential dread. There but for the grace of God go I. "Contact with someone afflicted with a disease is regarded as a mysterious malevolency," writes critic and author Susan Sontag.[14] Some of my hearing friends say they are uneasy around deaf people for a different reason, because they don't know how to communicate with them; but then I ask them if they give blind people a wide berth and look away from physically handicapped people, and they acknowledge that they do.[15] Each meeting with a person we perceive as handicapped is an invitation to make the extrapolation — and to experience dread. They are deserving of our sympathy because we are deserving of our sympathy. Nineteenth-century authors catered to such sentiments by idealizing their deaf characters. The American poet Lydia Sigourney sang of "the silent ecstasy refined" displayed by a pupil at the first school for deaf children in America, and Alfred de Musset's beautiful deaf Camille "had admirable purity and freshness."[16]

Mothers in one central African nation report that on discovering that their child was deaf, their first thought was to verify that their ancestors had been properly buried.[17] Mothers in many societies consider the cause of their child's deafness to be spirit aggression.[18] We are fragile

25

and dependent beings, they seem to imply, and deafness can be retribution for a moral failing. So, too, American mothers experience inexplicable guilt on discovering that they have a deaf child. There is a persistent belief, Sontag notes, that illness reveals, and is a punishment for, moral laxity. It is somehow reassuring when contracting a disease like AIDS is the result of doing something "wrong"; that hemophiliacs contract it through no act of their own arouses our rage at an immoral universe. It would be better if there were a reason for contracting deafness, something we could do, or refrain from doing, to avoid it. Such a reason might also justify our holding deaf people at arm's length, even justify our treating them badly. But there generally isn't one; so deafness or some other physical handicap may happen to us, as it were, whimsically, and that is dreadful.

The hearing person's extrapolation to what deafness must be like — a world without sound, without facile communication — is not entirely without a counterpart in the real world, for each year thousands of people lose substantial hearing because of illness, trauma, or old age. A few may take steps to enter the deaf community, to learn ASL, make friends in that community, join deaf organizations, attend a deaf club, and so on; most do not.

Growing up deaf, as have most users of ASL, is quite another matter. To evaluate that world of the deaf community, extrapolation from the hearing world is of no use at all. Is it better to be deaf or is it better to be hearing? Anthropologist Richard Shweder asks, "Is it better to have three gods and one wife or one god and three wives?"[19] Of course, the question makes no sense except in relation to a cultural "frame." To know what it is to be a member of the deaf community is to imagine how you would think, feel, and react if you had grown up deaf, if manual language had been your main means of communication, if your eyes were the portals of your mind, if most of your friends were deaf, if you had learned that there were children who couldn't sign only after you had known dozens who could, if the people you admired were deaf, if you had struggled daily for as long as you can remember with the ignorance and uncommunicativeness of hearing people, if . . . if, in a word, you *were* deaf.

The extrapolative error is an error twice over: True representations of the members of another culture cannot be had without a change in frame of reference, which requires, at least, understanding and empathy.[20] It is naive to imagine otherwise, and it is self-defeating. There will be no successful relations between hearing and deaf people, no successful education of deaf children, until the extrapolative error is set aside.

Notes

1. G. Weiss (1990). New hope for deaf children: Implant gives them hearing and speech. *American Health, 9,* 17.

2. National Association of the Deaf, Cochlear Implant Task Force. Cochlear implants in children: A position paper of the National Association of the Deaf. February 2, 1991. Reprint: *The National Association of the Deaf Broadcaster, 13,* March 1991, p. 1.

3. C. Padden and T. Humphries (1988). *Deaf in America: Voices from a Culture.* Cambridge, MA: Harvard University Press. "THINK-HEARING is . . . just as insulting as ORAL but can be used to label any Deaf person, even those who are not ORAL . . . HEARING is not just a category of people who hear; it is a category of those who are the opposite of what Deaf people are; e.g., students at schools for Deaf children sometimes call their football opponents HEARING even when the team is from another school for Deaf children" T. Humphries (1990). An introduction to the culture of deaf people in the United States: Content notes and reference materials for teachers. *Sign Language Studies, 72,* 209–40, p. 222.

4. E. Goffman (1963). *Stigma: Notes on the Management of Spoiled Identity.* Englewood Cliffs, NJ: Prentice-Hall.

5. C. Padden and T. Humphries (1988). *Deaf in America: Voices from a Culture.* Cambridge, MA: Harvard University Press.

6. C. McCullers (1967). *The Heart Is a Lonely Hunter.* Boston: Houghton Mifflin. Also see I. Turgenev, *Mumu.* Reprinted in T. Batson and E. Bergman (1985). *Angels and Outcasts: An Anthology of Deaf Characters in Literature,* 3rd ed. Washington, DC: Gallaudet University Press, p. 86.

7. J. Greenberg (1970). *In This Sign.* New York: Holt, Rinehart & Winston.

8. Charles Dickens's *Dr. Marigold* and Guy de Maupassant's *The Deaf-Mute* are reprinted in *Angels and Outcasts: An Anthology of Deaf Characters in Literature,* 3rd ed. Washington, DC: Gallaudet University Press.

9. H. Kisor (1990). *What's That Pig Outdoors?* New York: Hill and Wang.

10. J. G. Kyle and G. Pullen (1988). Cultures in contact: Deaf and hearing people. *Disability, Handicap and Society, 3,* 49-61, p. 56.

11. E. Goffman (1963). *Stigma: Notes on the Management of Spoiled Identity.* Englewood Cliffs, NJ: Prentice-Hall, p. 121.

12. A. Memmi (1984). *Dependence.* Boston: Beacon Press, p. 108.

13. C. Padden and T. Humphries (1988). *Deaf in America: Voices from a Culture.* Cambridge, MA: Harvard University Press.

14. S. Sontag (1989). *Illness as Metaphor and AIDS and Its Metaphors.* New York: Anchor.

15. Undergraduates studying education were asked, "How do you feel when you meet someone who is disabled?" The strongest reaction encountered was unease and uncertainty as to how to behave, and therefore embarrassment. The next most common response was: It is not different from meeting anyone else when you get used to the situation. In third place by frequency came emotions such as pity, guilt, and "thank goodness it's not me." Students were disinclined to share a house with someone disabled, but living next door they found acceptable. From L. Barton, ed. (1988). *The Politics of Special Educational Needs.* Philadelphia: Falmer Press, p. 138.

16. L. H. Sigourney (1866). *Letters of Life.* New York: Appleton, pp. 222-33. Also see A. de Musset, *Pierre et Camille,* reprinted in T. Batson and E. Bergman (1985). *Angels and Outcasts: An Anthology of Deaf Characters in Literature,* 3rd ed. Washington, DC: Gallaudet University Press.

17. A. Naniwe (1991). *L'enfant sourd et la société burundaise.* Ph.D. dissertation, University of Brussels.

18. Cf. G. P. Murdock (1980). *Theories of Illness.* Pittsburgh: University of Pittsburgh Press.

19. R. Shweder (1984). Anthropology's romantic rebellion against the enlightenment. In R. Shweder and R. A. LeVine, eds., *Culture Theory* (pp. 27–66). New York: Cambridge University Press, p. 55.

20. Z. Vendler (1984). Understanding people. In R. Shweder and R. A. LeVine, eds., *Culture Theory* (pp. 200–13). New York: Cambridge University Press, p. 209. Also see C. Geertz (1984). "From the native's point of view." On the nature of anthropological understanding. In R. Shweder and R. A. LeVine, eds., *Culture Theory* (pp. 123–36). New York: Cambridge University Press, p. 135.

FOCUSING ON CONTENT

1. Briefly explain what is involved in cochlear implant surgery. How effective is a cochlear implant for a deaf child over the age of two?

2. Why has the National Association for the Deaf called the United States Food and Drug Administration's approval of the procedure "'unsound scientifically, procedurally, and ethically'"? (1)

3. Why have the members of the American deaf community proclaimed the cochlear implants a "dangerous setback to their interests"? (1)

4. Cochlear implants are not recommended by Lane. What do such operations represent for him in terms of cultural misunderstanding?

5. What is the "existential dread" that characterizes the hearing culture when it comes to contemplating deaf culture (24)? Give some examples of what Lane means by the term.

FOCUSING ON WRITING

1. What is Lane's purpose in this essay? (Glossary: *Purpose*)

2. Why do you think Lane gives such a detailed description of cochlear implant surgical procedure? (Glossary: *Description*) If you had a child who was deaf, would you have the procedure performed on your child? Why or why not?

3. Explain how hearing and deaf communities operate from a different "center," according to deaf authors Carol Padden and Tom Humphries. How do the two groups view a person who is "ORAL — that is, does not fully acknowledge that he is deaf"? (9) (Glossary: *Comparison and Contrast*)

4. Why does Lane include an account of his attendance at the Massachusetts State Association for the Deaf annual convention in his essay? What purpose does it serve his argument?

5. How effective is Lane's last paragraph in concluding his essay? (Glossary: *Beginnings and Endings*) What does he accomplish in that last paragraph?

LANGUAGE IN ACTION

As a classroom exercise in understanding the world of the hearing-impaired, try carrying on the business of a typical class for twenty minutes or so without using spoken language. How did the members of your class improvise communication? What problems did you encounter? How did you solve the problems? Be prepared to give examples from your experience to illustrate how you gave and received messages without using spoken language. What did you learn from the experience?

WRITING SUGGESTIONS

1. Write an essay in which you attempt to define culture using what you wrote in your Writing to Discover journal prompt as well as what you have learned in reading Harlan Lane's essay. Naturally, after reading Lane's essay, you will want to consider the reasons why we have difficulty understanding other cultures. Lane asks the question: "Is it better to be deaf or is it better to be hearing?" In offering a way of thinking about that question, Lane quotes anthropologist Richard Shweder: "'Is it better to have three gods and one wife or three wives and one god'"? Lane writes: "Of course, the question makes no sense except in relation to a cultural 'frame'" (27).

2. Write an essay in which you recount the experiences you have had with people who are deaf or disabled in some way. How have you related to those people? Is Lane correct in his statement: "In hearing society, deafness is stigmatized" (12)? Does Erving Goffman's classification of stigmas and Harlan Lane's "extrapolation error" help to explain your own responses to people with disabilities, or have your experiences taught you something else?

3. Write an essay on the role of language in understanding the various cultures of people with disabilities. What role has language played, for example, in Lane's analysis of the misunderstanding that exists between the hearing culture and the deaf culture?

CASE STUDY:
Understanding Affirmative Action

The issues surrounding the debate over whether admission officers at our nation's colleges and universities should continue to use criteria that take into account an applicant's race are important to everyone, but they are especially important for students and higher education policymakers. The Supreme Court has ruled in favor of taking race into account in some measure, but supporters and critics alike wonder if Affirmative Action is helping minority students, or if it simply distracts from discovering real solutions to ensure that minority students succeed. The essays in this Case Study by Lee C. Bollinger, Armstrong Williams, Perry Bacon Jr., and William Raspberry provide essential information about the reasons for Affirmative Action, its difficulties, and theories on the kind of work that remains for students, their parents, and educators. As the Supreme Court ruling further implies, the issue of Affirmative Action may come before the court again in the future, and the ruling may be reversed if the Court thinks that the advantage of giving special consideration to minorities has ceased to be for the greater good. Whatever our personal opinions on Affirmative Action, we need to stay abreast of developments and changing policies as we seek ways to ease the burdens of those seeking their rightful place in our pluralistic society.

WRITING TO DISCOVER: *What have you heard about Affirmative Action? Have you followed the Supreme Court's ruling on Affirmative Action? Do you think that students applying to law school, for example, should be given special consideration because of their race? If not, how should we attempt to correct the injustices of slavery that have created two unequal societies in this country?*

WE DON'T HIRE BLACKS.
WE DON'T HIRE WOMEN.
WE DON'T HIRE HISPANICS.
WE DON'T HIRE ASIANS.
WE DON'T HIRE JEWS.
WE DON'T HIRE DISABLED.
WE DON'T HIRE WHITES.

We hire people.

People with drive and ambition. People who love their work. People who want to help our company grow.

We're Federal Express. And we believe it's our commitment to hiring the best person for the job—regardless of race or religion, age, sex or handicap—that has allowed us to become the number one air express company in the world.

Others agree. *Working Mother* and *Black Enterprise* magazines both placed us

twice in their rankings of great companies to work for. And our employees, over a third of whom belong to minority groups, continue to rate their job satisfaction at Very Good or Excellent.

But we want you to judge for yourself. The next time you see someone wearing our uniform, ask them how they feel about Federal Express.

A word of warning. They may be prejudiced.

An Equal Opportunity Employer. M/F/H/V.

Federal Express Corporation, P.O. Box 727-AA, Memphis, TN 38194-9310.

Picturing Language

This is an employment advertisement for the FedEx Corporation, championing their open hiring policy. What do you think was the intended effect of the seven statements in large, bold letters? Were they meant to shock? Surprise? Or simply to grab your attention? What statement does this advertisement make concerning FedEx's policy on Affirmative Action? Why do you suppose a company would choose to place an ad such as this in a major magazine? Reread the last sentence of the advertisement. How does this statement, which would normally be considered negative, work in favor of FedEx?

Diversity Is Essential . . .

LEE C. BOLLINGER

Lee C. Bollinger is the president of Columbia University and a member of its law school faculty. He has had a distinguished career in higher education. A native of Santa Rosa, California, and a graduate of the University of Oregon and Columbia Law School, Bollinger clerked for Chief Justice Warren Burger of the United States Supreme Court. In 1973 he joined the faculty of the University of Michigan Law School and then became president of Dartmouth College. In 1994 he was named president of the University of Michigan. Bollinger's major scholarly interest has been free speech and First Amendment rights. Among his many publications are The Tolerant Society: Freedom of Speech and Extremist Speech in America *(1986),* Images of a Free Press *(1991), and* Eternally Vigilant: Free Speech in the Modern Era *(2001). The following article appeared in the January 27, 2003, issue of* Newsweek *as part of a larger feature on Affirmative Action in public higher education and the Supreme Court case against it. In this argument, Bollinger explains why he's in favor of Affirmative Action for minorities.*

When I became president of the University of Michigan in 1997, Affirmative Action in higher education was under siege from the right. Buoyed by a successful lawsuit against the University of Texas Law School's admissions policy and by ballot initiatives such as California's Proposition 209, which outlawed race as a factor in college admissions, the opponents set their sights on affirmative-action programs at colleges across the country.

The rumor that Michigan would be the target in this campaign turned out to be correct. I believed strongly that we had no choice but to mount the best legal defense ever for diversity in higher education and take special efforts to explain this complex issue, in simple and direct language, to the American public. There are many misperceptions about how race and ethnicity are considered in college admissions. Competitive colleges and universities are always looking for a mix of students with different experiences and backgrounds — academic, geographic, international, socioeconomic, athletic, public-service oriented, and, yes, racial and ethnic.

It is true in sorting the initial rush of applications, large universities will give "points" for various factors in the selection process in order to ensure fairness as various officers review applicants. Opponents of Michigan's undergraduate system complain that an applicant is assigned more points for being black, Hispanic, or Native American than for having a perfect SAT score. This is true, but it trivializes the real issue: whether, in principle, race and ethnicity are appropriate considerations. The simple fact about the Michigan undergraduate policy is that it gives overwhelming weight to traditional academic factors — some 110 out of a total of 150 points. After that, there are some 40 points left for other factors, of which 20 can be allocated for race or socioeconomic status.

Race has been a defining element of the American experience. The historic *Brown v. Board of Education*[1] decision is almost fifty years old, yet metropolitan Detroit is more segregated now than it was in 1960. The majority of students who each year arrive on a campus like Michigan's graduated from virtually all-white or all-black high schools. The campus is their first experience living in an integrated environment.

This is vital. Diversity is not merely a desirable addition to a well-   5
rounded education. It is as essential as the study of the Middle Ages, of international politics, and of Shakespeare. For our students to better understand the diverse country and world they inhabit, they must be immersed in a campus culture that allows them to study with, argue with, and become friends with students who may be different from them. It broadens the mind, and the intellect — essential goals of education.

Reasonable people can disagree about Affirmative Action. But it is important that we do not lose the sense of history, the compassion, and the largeness of vision that defined the best of the civil-rights era, which has given rise to so much of what is good about America today.

EXAMINING THE ISSUE CRITICALLY

1. Bollinger says that Affirmative Action was "under siege from the right" (1) when he became president of the University of Michigan. What does he mean by "under siege"? To what or whom is he referring to when he says "the right"?

2. Bollinger says there are "many misperceptions" (2) regarding Affirmative Action efforts by colleges and universities. What does he say those misperceptions are? Does he explain the case for Affirmative Action in "simple and direct language" (2)? Explain.

3. Bollinger declares diversity to be as "essential" as the study of the Middle Ages, international politics, and Shakespeare. Is the comparison a fair one?

4. If the *Brown v. Board of Education* ruling has left Detroit more segregated than it was in 1960, what does Bollinger see as the benefits of Affirmative Action in higher education?

5. Does a diverse campus population necessarily lead to an integration of the students? What is the situation on your campus? Is there an integration of students?

---

1. Unanimous 1954 Supreme Court decision disbanding segregated education.

... But Not at This Cost

ARMSTRONG WILLIAMS

Armstrong Williams is one of the "most widely recognized conserva-
tive voices in America," according to the Washington Post. *A com-*
mentator, radio talk show host, and columnist, Williams is also
CEO of Graham Williams Group, an international public rela-
tions firm. As a provocative standard bearer for the ideals of the
right, Williams has written for such publications as USA Today,
the Washington Post, *the* Los Angeles Times, *the* Washington
Times, *and* Reader's Digest. *Williams also writes a nationally syn-*
dicated newspaper column that is carried by seventy-five newspapers
across the country, in addition to hosting a daily nationally syndi-
cated television show, The Right Side with Armstrong Williams.
His best-selling Beyond Blame *(1995) is a book of advice for a mis-*
guided young man. A native of Marion, South Carolina, and a
1981 graduate of South Carolina State College, Williams currently
lives in Washington, D.C. The following essay is the con side of the
Affirmative Action debate and appeared alongside the preceding
selection written by Lee C. Bollinger in the January 27, 2003, issue
of Newsweek.

Back in 1977, when I was a senior in high school, I received scholarship offers to attend prestigious colleges. The schools wanted me in part
because of my good academic record — but also because Affirmative Action mandates required them to encourage more black students to enroll.
My father wouldn't let me take any of the enticements. His reasoning was
straightforward: scholarship money should go to the economically deprived. And since he could pay for my schooling, he would. In the end, I
chose a historically black college — South Carolina State.

What I think my father meant, but was perhaps too stern to say, was
that one should always rely on hard work and personal achievements to
carry the day — every day. Sadly, this rousing point seems lost on the
admissions board at the University of Michigan, which wrongly and
unapologetically discriminates on the basis of skin color. The university
ranks applicants on a scale that awards points for SAT score, high-school
grades and race. For example, a perfect SAT score is worth twelve points.
Being black gets you twenty points. Is there anyone who can look at
those two numbers and think they are fair?

Supporters maintain that the quota system is essential to creating a diverse student body. And, indeed, there is some validity to this sort of thinking. A shared history of slavery and discrimination has ingrained racial
hierarchies into our national identity, divisions that need to be erased.

There is, however, a very real danger that we are merely reinforcing the idea that minorities are first and foremost victims. Because of this victim status, the logic goes, they are owed special treatment. But that isn't progress, it's inertia.

If the goal of Affirmative Action is to create a more equitable society, it should be need-based. Instead, Affirmative Action is defined by its tendency to reduce people to fixed categories: at many universities, it seems, admissions officers look less at who you are than *what* you are. As a result, Affirmative Action programs rarely help the least among us. Instead, they often benefit the children of middle- and upper-class black Americans who have been conditioned to feel they are owed something.

This is alarming. We have finally, after far too long, reached a point   5
where black Americans have pushed into the mainstream — and not just in entertainment and sports. From politics to corporate finance, blacks succeed. Yet many of us still feel entitled to special benefits — in school, in jobs, in government contracts.

It is time to stop. We must reach a point where we expect to rise or fall on our own merits. We just can't continue to base opportunities on race while the needs of the poor fall by the wayside. As a child growing up on a farm, I was taught that personal responsibility was the lever that moved the world. That is why it pains me to see my peers rest their heads upon the warm pillow of victim status.

EXAMINING THE ISSUE CRITICALLY

1. What is Williams's chief argument against Affirmative Action? Does he believe that there is no need to redress the social inequities created in the past?

2. How do you respond to the fact that at the University of Michigan, a perfect SAT score is awarded twelve points while being a minority is awarded twenty points towards admission? Is such a rating system fair, in your view?

3. What does Williams mean when he says college admissions officers "look less at who you are than *what* you are" (4).

4. What is the "warm pillow of victim status" that Williams refers to in his last paragraph? Is he simply a person who is successful and thinks others have to struggle because it is good for them to do so? Explain.

How Much Diversity Do You Want from Me?

PERRY BACON JR.

Perry Bacon Jr. is a general assignment reporter in the Washington, D.C., bureau for Time *covering politics, international affairs, and education. The Louisville, Kentucky, native came to the magazine in October 2002, after graduating from Yale University, where he earned a B.A. with distinction in political science and worked as a reporter and editor for the* Yale Daily News. *He also had internships at the* (Louisville) Courier-Journal, National Journal, *and the* Washington Post. *In commenting about his essay, Bacon wrote the following:*

"This piece was one of the easiest and at the same time one of the hardest I've ever written. I've thought long and hard about Affirmative Action for years, both because it's an issue that has profound political, social, and moral implications, and because I have had such a personal connection to the issue, as someone who has probably benefited from it. And when I heard the Court's opinion, I immediately knew where I thought it was inadequate and was able to write on that easily. What was difficult was to find a way to incorporate my life experiences without making it too personal and not analytical, but at the same time, giving enough personal details so readers would understand my personal perspective on the issue. I'm neither an opinion writer nor someone who writes personal narratives frequently, so this was a unique, challenging task. I wanted to communicate with readers that it wasn't that I fiercely objected to being representative for black people, but that I thought this had profound implications, many of which were negative and that the Supreme Court could have found a much better way to address the issue."

Bacon's essay appeared in Time *on July 7, 2003.*

I'm from Louisville, Ky., attended Yale University, and work as a *Time* journalist. Since I haven't met any other person who shares these three characteristics, I suppose I add some diversity to most discussions I'm a part of. But at most colleges and workplaces in America, something else about me would make me add much more diversity. I'm black. And as Justice Sandra Day O'Connor wrote in a landmark Supreme Court opinion last week, borrowing language from a lower court, once a few people like me are sitting in a classroom, "discussion is livelier, more spirited, and simply more enlightening and interesting." In her defense of Affirmative Action, O'Connor argued that our presence "helps to break down racial stereotypes and 'enables [students] to better understand persons of different races.'" And since nearly every major employer in America has a diversity policy, I will be expected to share what O'Connor calls the "unique experience of being a racial minority" with my coworkers as well.

O'Connor says other traits bring diversity too. But let's be honest here. Growing up on a farm in Arizona might help broaden a résumé, but checking "black" has the effect of leapfrogging me over many comparable applicants gunning for a prestigious school or job. Although I'm sure my race improved my odds of being admitted to Yale and hired at *Time*, I don't carry around the "stigma" that Justice Clarence Thomas claims all blacks do because of Affirmative Action, wondering if they received a benefit based on merit or race. For me, the question has never been "Do I belong?" but rather "Since I'm here in part to contribute diversity, how do I do that?" O'Connor's diversity rationale doesn't just pressure colleges to admit more minority students. It gives me and other underrepresented minority students an added burden: delivering diversity. It creates expectations that I have a uniquely black viewpoint to contribute and that part of my responsibility as a student or worker is to do that.

At Yale, I often felt obligated to present these diverse views. On the campus paper there, I edited feature stories and had little desire to influence other sections of the paper. But when some minority students complained about the lack of diversity in our coverage and on our staff, I felt dutybound to press other editors to cover minorities more and explore ways to recruit more black students. When students debated whether Yale should have a day off for Martin Luther King Jr. Day, I saw this as a largely symbolic issue that I wasn't passionately interested in. But eventually I found myself questioning how anyone could not agree that we should have this day off, in part because I felt that as one of the few blacks around I should be speaking up.

As a full-time journalist, I feel these same pressures. Since I'm more interested in politics than in racial issues, am I fulfilling my sociojournalistic mission? I suppose I could bring a black perspective by talking to more minority sources or by closely examining how Bush administration policies affect minorities. But isn't this something a white reporter could do too? Similarly, if you're white and discussing racial profiling in a class, isn't it part of your role as a student to think about how you would feel about this issue if you were black? This is a core problem with O'Connor's diversity rationale. It suggests that only a black person can articulate what it means to be black and that others shouldn't bother to try. Further, O'Connor suggests that simply by attending a law school with a "critical mass" of blacks, Hispanics, and Native Americans, you come away understanding the perspectives of minorities. But the fact is, a Michigan Law School student would learn a lot more about the "unique experience" of blacks in America if he spent a day at an inner-city school in Detroit than he would in a torts class with me. In fact, a white person who grew up poor has an equally or perhaps more diverse perspective, and yet my blackness counts so much more in Affirmative Action.

Maybe O'Connor really believes in this diversity notion. But here's 5
what I suspect she and other Affirmative-Action proponents really think:
nearly twenty-seven percent of the population is black or Hispanic, but
few of these minorities are in the upper ranks of most fields, in part because of past discrimination or current inequalities. And they think that
the leadership class of our society should look like the rest of it. It's a
laudable goal, and it's why I remain at least a tepid supporter of Affirmative Action. But let's stop using this notion of diversity to sidestep the
real issue. Colleges don't want more minority students so we can all hold
hands and sing *It's a Small World*. Why can't we just say what the real
goal is: the creation of a multiethnic élite. I think young minorities can
help form that élite. But I want to join that élite and be expected to deliver the "unique experience" of my whole life rather than an assumed experience based solely on the color of my skin.

EXAMINING THE ISSUE CRITICALLY

1. What is Bacon's problem with Justice Sandra Day O'Connor's argument in
   favor of Affirmative Action? What kind of pressure do her statements put on
   minorities in colleges and in the employment world, according to Bacon?
   Reread and consider Bacon's last two sentences in formulating your answer.

2. What does Bacon think is wrong with Justice O'Connor's statement that
   "simply by attending a law school with a 'critical mass' of blacks, Hispanics,
   and Native Americans, you come away understanding the perspectives of minorities" (4)?

3. Bacon, as did Armstrong Williams, makes the point that being poor may be a
   bigger obstacle to progressing within our society than being a minority. Do
   you agree with that perspective? Isn't being poor often a consequence of
   being denied access to good paying jobs because of prejudice and one's minority status?

4. In your experiences in the classroom, are minorities unduly, perhaps even
   unfairly, expected to speak for the minority experience? Have you been put
   in such a position?

There's More to Affirmative Action

WILLIAM RASPBERRY

William Raspberry was born in the small community of Okolona, Mississippi, in 1935. He says of his community, "We had two of everything there, one for whites and one for blacks." After graduating in 1960 from Indiana Central College with a degree in history, Raspberry went to work at the Washington Post *in 1962 after two years of military service. As one of the most influential journalists of his time, Raspberry has won numerous journalism awards and been honored with fifteen honorary degrees. He won the Pulitzer Prize for Distinguished Commentary in 1994. As a* Washington Post *op-ed commentator since 1971, Raspberry has given his views on such subjects as crime, justice, drug abuse, terrorism, Affirmative Action, prisons, and education. Raspberry has a tremendous following across the country through the syndication of columns, and readers enjoy his positive approach to social problems. He says, "I don't enjoy celebrating problems. I talk about problems with a view to inching towards solutions."*

In "There's More to Affirmative Action," one of his Washington Post *columns, Raspberry welcomes the Supreme Court's 2003 ruling on Affirmative Action but also points to another kind of affirmative action that needs to take place if the number of minority students enrolled in our country's colleges and universities is to increase.*

In the angst-tinged aftermath of last week's Supreme Court Affirmative Action rulings, we would do well to separate two important questions.

The first — whether there is racial disparity — is easy, and the clear answer is yes. In almost every aspect of American life — employment, housing, wealth, as well as graduate and undergraduate college admissions — blacks lag behind whites.

The other question is: Why?

The answer isn't as easy as Affirmative Action advocates (and I include myself in the category) sometimes make it out to be. We usually begin with the assumption that the deck is stacked against minorities and without some intervening mechanism, white-run institutions will revert to their "natural" preference for whites.

The assumption is validated over and over — by every careful test of 5 applicants for jobs or apartments and by our ordinary experience. That is why it makes sense to us that — at least for a time — a subtle thumb on the scale might serve the interest of justice. We need a mechanism to keep people from reverting to form.

But the case of undergraduate admissions seems different. Here, we have screeners who want minorities admitted. The whole court case was whether admissions officers at the University of Michigan went too far to see to it that minorities — blacks especially — were admitted.

How reasonable can it be to conclude that, because the court has made it more difficult for them to do what they clearly would like to do, they will now revert to form and discriminate against black applicants?

Yet most of us expect that, as a result of the court's ruling, there will be a decline in minority admissions at the University of Michigan and, by extension, at other highly competitive public universities subject to last week's ruling.

And the question is: Why? Why, if admissions officers want black kids in and have demonstrated their willingness to do anything legal to get them in, do we expect their numbers to decline? Since it can't be racism on the part of the screeners, what can it be?

Our usual answer is that it has to do with earlier denial of opportu- 10
nity — less adequate elementary and secondary education in poor neighborhoods, relative economic and political powerlessness, and, finally, the lasting psychic injuries of slavery and Jim Crow. Our children deserve a break today because they have inherited through us the debilitations of white bigotry.

We used to think the problem was economics. But when the University of Texas tried to use poverty as a proxy for race (after a federal circuit court ruling outlawed the university's Affirmative Action plan), it found that the chief result was that more poor white kids were being admitted.

Moreover, black affluence doesn't seem to make the difference we always imagined it would. Harvard University's Ronald Ferguson has surveyed 34,000 middle- and high-school youngsters in fifteen affluent and racially mixed communities around the nation and he has found a consistent achievement gap: whites averaging B-plus, blacks C-plus.

As the professor told Michael Winerip of the *New York Times*, economic differences could account for no more than half the gap. What might account for the rest?

Twenty-two percent of the black households surveyed had no computer, compared to just three percent of whites. Forty percent of black households owned 100 or more books; eighty percent of the white families did. Fifty-three percent of the black children live in homes from which at least one parent is absent, but only fifteen percent of white kids.

There's more — a good deal more. And yet at the end, Ferguson, 15
who is black, does what figure skaters used to call the "compulsories." "Politically," Winerip wrote, "he believes the damage from two centuries of slavery plus legalized segregation will not be undone in a generation, not even in suburbia. On a personal level, he has studied the data for ways to narrow the gap."

The work of Ferguson and the University of California's John Ogbu, whose study of the black achievement gap in affluent Shaker Heights, Ohio, brought him to similar conclusions, suggests to me that the fight over undergraduate Affirmative Action is a diversion. There are serious problems facing black children, and, at the risk of seeming to blame the victims, there are serious things black parents can do about them.

EXAMINING THE ISSUE CRITICALLY

1. Raspberry says, "most of us expect that, as a result of the court's ruling, there will a decline in minority admissions at the University of Michigan and, by extension, at other highly competitive public universities subject to last week's ruling" (8). Why does he (and others) believe this will happen?

2. Why does Raspberry think that the "fight over undergraduate Affirmative Action is a diversion" (16)? On what does he base his opinion?

3. What is the performance gap, and why is it so important? Is economics a factor in the performance gap, according to Raspberry's research? Why or why not?

4. Raspberry says he's not blaming the victims for the performance gap. Do you agree or disagree? Why?

5. In your view, will the problems Affirmative Action aims to remedy likely be solved by the court's ruling? If you disagree, does that mean that Affirmative Action should not be supported?

MAKING CONNECTIONS:

UNDERSTANDING AFFIRMATIVE ACTION

The following questions are offered to help you start to make meaningful connections among the four articles in this Case Study. These questions can be used for discussion, or you can answer any one of the questions in writing an essay. If you choose the essay option, be sure to make specific references to at least two of the Case Study articles.

You may feel the need for more data, ideas, and points of view as you begin writing about this topic; therefore, we encourage you to visit The Affirmative Action and Diversity Project: A Web Page for Research at the University of California, Santa Barbara, where over 1,250,000 visitors have found useful resources to help them in their work: aad.english.ucsb.edu/.

1. Write an essay on the history of Affirmative Action in the United States. Where did the idea of Affirmative Action begin? What role has federal legislation played in the development or hindrance of Affirmative Action? What have been the major legal cases involved in the establishment of Affirmative Action in this country? Try to use information and ideas from the authors of the articles in the Case Study wherever possible.

2. Write a letter to the editor of a newspaper or magazine that has run a story on Affirmative Action. Your letter can praise the coverage offered by the publication, correct information in the article, expand on a topic, argue with the evidence presented, or present a unique perspective on the topic. Much of the concern of the recent U.S. Supreme Court ruling on Affirmative Action grows out of college and university concerns with admissions decisions, so your perspective as a college student would be appropriate and is likely to be well received by editors. Keep the letter brief, cite the article you are writing about by title and date, be logical, present valid evidence for your point of view, and assume an appropriate tone, one that is free of anger or sarcasm. Feel free to offer quotations from the writings of Bollinger, Williams, Bacon, and Raspberry that are included in the Case Study.

3. Look to the ideas and information provided by the authors of the articles in the Case Study to supplement your own position on Affirmative Action. For example, Williams and Raspberry make the point that Affirmative Action has a lot to do with economics and the circumstances of students who come from low income backgrounds. Write an essay focusing chiefly on the economic issues of Affirmative Action.

4. Proponents of Affirmative Action point to the need to have a critical mass of minority students in college classes for those classes to be representative of points of view that would not be present otherwise. "But," Bacon says, "a Michigan Law School student would learn a lot more about the 'unique experience' of blacks in America if he spent a day at an inner-city school in Detroit than he would in a torts class with me. In fact, a white person who grew up poor has an equally or perhaps more diverse perspective, and yet my blackness counts so much more in Affirmative Action" (4). Williams also

thinks that the issue is about money. He would rather see scholarship money go to poor families who would otherwise not be able to attend college than to middle- and upper-class minorities because of the color of their skin. Write an essay in which you discuss the economic side of the Affirmative Action debate.

5. Many African American college students express resentment at being called upon in their classes to give the minority viewpoint on just about every topic addressed by college instructors. Many, including Bacon, say they are tired of having to "diversify" their courses because they are in attendance first and foremost to learn, just like the rest of the students. Write an essay about your experiences in the classroom and outside of classes within the context of what you have read in the Case Study. Is Bacon's assessment of the added burden that minority students face in the classroom a fair one based on your experiences?

6. Read the recent ruling on Affirmative Action rendered by the United States Supreme Court at www.bamn.com/literature/lit-um-case.asp. Contained in that ruling is the implication by Justice Sandra Day O'Connor that the affirmative action ruling the court handed down may one day have to be reexamined in the light of the progress that minorities will likely have made in entering the mainstream of American life. The further implication is that the ruling might be overturned at that time. Write an essay expressing your viewpoint on the possible overturning of the Supreme Court's ruling supporting Affirmative Action at some point in the future.

10

NAMES AND IDENTITY

Naming is one of the most important things humans do. Naming gives us a measure of power over people, plants and animals, ideas, and material objects. To name is to differentiate, to compare and contrast, to recognize, to value, to validate. Names can be colorful, descriptive, magical, prosaic, poetic, uplifting, familiar and warm, formal and rigid, ambiguous and razor edged. Names can remind us of where we've been and where we'd like to go.

Names can also be annoying or worse. Think how much improved your life could have been if your schoolmates had stopped calling you that hurtful nickname or taunting you because your behavior or dress was not quite up to their standards. Think on a larger scale of how prejudice is often carried in the names we give people who are different from us in skin color, culture, lifestyle, dress, and language. Nicknames and terms of abuse are often used to dehumanize people who, once deprived of their dignity, become the prey of those who would harm them.

Our goal in this chapter is to introduce you to the complexity of the naming process, to present authors and essays that delve into some interesting aspects of the naming process. Bonnie Wach, in "What's in a Name?" discusses unusual personal names and what the research indicates about whether they make people stand out in a positive or negative way. Linguists S. I. Hayakawa and Alan R. Hayakawa, in "Giving Things Names," examine the relationship between names, words, and thoughts, and how the words we use to classify people, objects, and concepts affect the way we regard them.

In "Changing My Name after Sixty Years," Tom Rosenberg offers an interesting essay on what motivated him to return to his original surname and Jewish heritage after his parents took on a new name when they fled Nazi Germany prior to the beginning of World War II. Next, we include Louise Erdrich's "The Names of Women" and learn how women in her Native American culture got their names and how those names help to recapture for Erdrich the roles those women played in her culture. With Natalie Goldberg's "Be Specific," we hear from a popular writing teacher on why it is so important to give things their "actual" names in order to understand our world and write effectively about it. Finally, in J. C. Herz's "A Name So Smooth, the Product Glides In," we read how new products are given names and why so much careful thought is applied to the name of a new product. So, when we ask "What's in a Name?" as Bonnie Wach does and Shakespeare did so famously four centuries earlier, we can now offer some answers to this most intriguing of questions.

What's in a Name?

BONNIE WACH

Bonnie Wach is a San Francisco-based writer who was an editor for various city magazines before making a career of freelance writing. Her articles have appeared in SFWeekly, Health, Travel & Leisure, *and the* New York Times, *among other magazines and newspapers. In 1998 she published* San Francisco As You Like It: 20 Tailor-Made Tours for Culture Vultures, Shopaholics, Non-Bohemians, Fitness Freaks, Savvy Natives, and Everyone Else, *a guide book to the city.*

In the following article, originally published in Health *magazine in September 1992, Wach explores the impact names can have on people. As anyone who has faced teasing about an unusual name can attest, children bear the consequences of the names their parents choose. "To be sure," writes Wach, "in the search for uncommon names, some parents have gone off the deep end. The living, breathing results are kids named Fuzzy, Whisper, Pitbull, Demon, Nausea, and Mischief, to name just a few recent examples." As Wach notes, however, at least one researcher believes that an unusual name may be beneficial because it increases a person's recognition factor. Whether such names are harmful or helpful, parents should act thoughtfully when naming a child. Our names, after all, are inseparable from our identities.*

WRITING TO DISCOVER: *Reflect on your first name, your last name, or your name taken in its entirety. Jot down answers to some of these questions: Do you regard your name as common or uncommon? Why? Aside from the fact that it is your name, does it have any special significance? In other words, were you named after someone or something? Does your name reveal your heritage? What overtones does your name carry for you? What overtones do you think it carries for others?*

A person with a bad name is already half-hanged, an old proverb goes. But in modern times, we reserve the right to buck convention — and the fates be damned. Not that we don't believe in the power of names. The problem is that when it comes time to name our offspring, we discover that bucking convention isn't so easy.

Take, for instance, the plight of Ty and Dione Affleck in Seattle, whose efforts to pick the right monikers for their two children became a major project:

"We looked through lists of Old English or Gaelic names to tie in with Affleck, and then scanned lists of the most popular names and nixed anything above seventieth place," Dione says. The couple — she's a physical therapist, he's a doctor — considered McKenzie, Paige, Ethan, Calvin, Blake, Keith, and Kevin, but feared they were becoming over-used. Finally, a few years ago, after poring over the book *10,000 Baby Names,* they settled on Chelsea for their daughter and, more recently, Ryan for their son. Unfortunately, they soon found they were hardly alone.

"Little did we know. Here we were trying so desperately to be indi-vidual and unique, and now we already know dozens of Chelseas and Ryans," says Dione. To top it off, now there's a Chelsea in the White House.

So it goes. For girls, such "unusual" names as Ashley, Amanda, Samantha, and Jessica have all been in the top ten since 1988. Brittany, with a push from TV's "thirtysomething," hit number one in 1989 and stayed there. Common baby boomer names like Susan and Linda didn't even make the top 50 last year. Boys' names tend to be a bit more stable: Census figures show that Michael, Christopher, Matthew, David, and An-drew have held their top spots for more than a decade. But Ethan, Nicholas, and Tyler have jumped in popularity.

What's so awful about having a common name? Edwin (don't call him Eddie) Lawson, a psychology professor emeritus at State University of New York in Fredonia, puts it this way: "Imagine that you've got a special outfit and you wear it out to dinner. You won't like it if another woman is wearing the same outfit."

And so the quest for one-of-a-kind "outfits" takes some inventive turns. For the most part, the days when hip parents named their children Moon Unit and Nirvana are gone. In their place, geographical names such as Paris, Madison, and Dakota have become chic (actresses Melanie Griffith and Melissa Gilbert-Brinkman both have children named Dakota), as have ones that sound like they belong to someone's grand-parents, like Nell and Gus.

Many parents are suddenly rediscovering — or simply inventing — their roots, according to Cleveland Kent Evans, a psychology professor at Bellevue College in Nebraska who's spent years tracking name trends. Upper-middle-class Jewish couples have started looking to their ancestral heritage for nineteenth century immigrant names like Max or Hannah. Working-class African American parents fashion ethnic-sounding names with the prefixes La and Sha or with suffixes such as isha, onda, ita, or ika, as in LaToya and Shandrika. And educated, upper-middle-class couples of various ethnic backgrounds have taken to bestowing gender-neutral family names, such as Jordan and Taylor, on their daughters.

"People are trying harder and harder to be more original," says Leonard Ashley, an onomastician (that's someone who studies names) at Brooklyn College. "But they shouldn't try to be too original. When peo-ple give their daughter a name like Tempest, it's like making her wear a spangled rhinestone dress to the supermarket. It's not for everyday wear."

To be sure, in the search for uncommon names, some parents have 10
gone off the deep end. The living, breathing results are kids named Fuzzy, Whisper, Pitbull, Demon, Nausea, and Mischief, to name just a few recent examples.

Some say there's a danger such names could become self-fulfilling prophesies. After all, in the seventies, a New York psychologist looked into the subject and found 180 examples of people whose names seemed to lead them down a particular career path, including Bacon Chow the nutritionist, Lionel Tiger the animal behavior researcher, and Cardinal Sin, the archbishop. Does it follow that the girl whose parents dubbed her Fayle (pronounced *fail*) is destined to flop?

"A name like that can handicap and scar you for life," says Albert Mehrabian, a UCLA psychology professor who isn't fond of being called Al. "I think children have enough pressure on them without the additional disadvantage of an unpleasant name."

Mehrabian cites studies like the one in which researchers asked teachers to grade identical essays titled "What I Did Last Sunday." The ones signed by a "David" or "Lisa" consistently got better grades than those by an "Elmer" or "Bertha." In another study, researchers asked college students at Tulane University to pick a beauty queen from six photos of women who had previously been judged equally attractive. The photos marked Jennifer, Kathy, and Christine consistently beat out the ones labeled Gertrude, Harriet, and Ethel.

"A bad name affects how a person is perceived by friends, coworkers, and total strangers. It's like forcing someone to walk around all their life with blue-colored hair," Mehrabian says.

But what exactly is a "bad" name? To find out, Mehrabian surveyed 15
2,000 people, asking them to judge a slew of first names. "I told people, 'You're about to meet somebody for the first time and you know only their name and their sex. Tell me what that person is going to be like.'" The respondents rated each name in terms of success, morality, health, warmth, cheerfulness, and masculinity or femininity.

The survey results, published in *The Name Game,* "a comprehensive guide to first names," confirm what we already know: Some names carry definite stereotypes. Bunny and DiDi, for example, scored high on femininity but bombed on success and morality. Brunhilde was a loser in all categories. For boys, John, Rick, Chad, and Buck all had high success and masculinity scores. Melvin, on the other hand, scored zero in the health category, which includes characteristics like popularity, athleticism, good looks, confidence, and assertiveness.

So what about Mel Gibson?

"This is a statistical relationship," Mehrabian says. "Not everyone with a bad name will be unsuccessful."

Nicknames didn't fare well in Mehrabian's survey, either. Robert did better in all categories than Bob. Jacqueline scored the highest among girls' names under success, but Jackie did only about half as well. Mehrabian says that people with nicknames are often not taken seriously. (Don't tell Johnny Carson or Tip O'Neill.)

"Names aren't as important as people think," Evans says. "If you just   20 have a name to react to, you're bound to come up with a prejudiced judgment. But when you add a real person to the name, it's not that much of an influence." He points out that surveys singling out supposedly undesirable names say nothing about how those names actually influence a person's self-image.

In fact, researchers have tried for decades to link unusual or less desirable names to everything from psychological maladjustment to criminal misdeeds. For the most part, they've come up empty-handed. One 1948 study, for example, set out to test the then-current opinion that there was a greater likelihood of success in marriage if a man "selects a girl with a common name." Of 414 women at a black college, those with uncommon names such as Florenda, Janafea, Honthalena, and Aluesta were found to be no more neurotic — and thus less marriageable — than women with names like Mary, Helen, Susie, Ethel, and Daisy.

More recent research suggests that if unusual names have *any* effect on social or psychological development, it may very well be a positive one: A 1980 study of Wesleyan University students found that women with unusual names actually scored higher in "sociability" and "social presence" on psychological tests than women with more common names.

Nevertheless, Mehrabian's heard enough sad stories — from a man named Jack Daniels to a woman called Latrina — to be convinced that, for some people at least, an unusual name spells trouble. "Parents can be very egocentric when it comes to naming their children. They pick names that make an intellectual statement, like Alpha or Beta, or ones, like Ima Hogg and Ura Hogg, that they think are kind of funny. It's not funny for the child."

His advice to expectant parents: Think before you dub. "Remember, you're tagging your child with something that will become a permanent part of his or her identity," he says.

FOCUSING ON CONTENT

1. Wach begins her article with the proverb "A person with a bad name is already half-hanged." What point is Wach making about onomastics? (Glossary: *Onomastics*) How does her use of this proverb influence your reading of the rest of the article?

2. According to Wach, what were the trends in children's names during the 1990s? How do her observations compare to what you have observed about your own age group? How have names changed since you were born?

3. Mel Gibson is obviously not handicapped by his "bad" name. Explain why, based on the conclusions that Albert Mehrabian and Cleveland Evans draw from their studies. What other people have succeeded in spite of what you might consider "bad" names?

FOCUSING ON WRITING

1. Look through Wach's essay for examples of questions that she asks the reader. For what purpose(s) does Wach use those questions? (Glossary: *Purpose*) Do you ever use questions in your own essays? Explain.

2. It is clear from her essay that Wach has interviewed people with regard to the power of names. How has she used quotations from her interviews to develop her essay? (Glossary: *Examples*)

3. Describe Wach's style in this essay. Study Wach's particular use of words, sentence construction, and transitions to help you do your assessment. (Glossary: *Diction, Style,* and *Transitions*) Is her style appropriate for her audience and subject matter? (Glossary: *Audience*) Explain.

LANGUAGE IN ACTION

Explain the relationship you see, if any, between Wach's essay and the following report by Lois B. Morris, which is taken from the March 1999 issue of *Allure*.

NAMING NAMES

Some parents believe that old-fashioned names for their daughters sound beautiful. But according to a new study, women with these names are at a disadvantage when it comes to first impressions. In several studies, psychologist Andrew N. Christopher of the University of Florida in Gainesville asked a total of three hundred and sixteen men and women to describe their reactions to female names from three categories — those that were popular earlier in the century (such as Betty, Alice, Gloria, and Phyllis); contemporary favorites (including Jennifer, Theresa, and Michelle); and familiar but uncommon names (Holly, Jill, and Vanessa). Christopher found that men who evaluated identical personal ads from women with a variety of names invariably rejected the Ediths, Eleanors, and other "oldies." In another test, both men and women who evaluated identical résumés of female job applicants gave the lowest potential employment ratings to those with old-fashioned monikers. Such names evoke unfavorable and probably unconscious biases against old people, says Christopher, and that can affect first impressions when other information is limited.

WRITING SUGGESTIONS

1. A major part of learning in any field involves becoming familiar with the names for ideas and things that characterize the subject. For example,

photographers need to know the meaning of wide angle, 35 mm, single-lens reflex, frame, focal length, shutter speed, ASA, exposure, large format, F-stop, contact sheet, fixer, red eye, and so forth. Choose a subject you are familiar with, such as your major, a hobby, or a sport, and write an essay in which you discuss the terms that are most important to that subject. Be sure to include information about how you learned the critical terms, what can go wrong it you don't know them, and what you are unable to do if you are unfamiliar with them.

2. Do a study of the names of the people in your dormitory or in one of your social groups. Analyze those names in light of Wach's essay. In your opinion, are any of the names unusual? Why? Do they sound strange? Do they represent a culture different from your own? Do they remind you of another word that you find humorous? Which of the names are rather common sounding? Write an essay in which you discuss your findings. Make sure that you don't simply describe the names you found. Instead, build a context for your essay and provide a thesis for your comments. (Glossary: *Thesis*)

3. The names of cities, towns, rivers, and mountains provide clues to settlement and migration patterns and reflect local history as well. After examining a map of your state or region, select six place names and write a report in which you discuss the origin of each name and what it tells of local history. To begin this research, look in your library or on the Internet for any comprehensive books or articles about the place names in your area. If none exists, inquire in the municipal offices or libraries of the places you have chosen to study.

Giving Things Names

S. I. HAYAKAWA AND ALAN R. HAYAKAWA

S. I. Hayakawa (1906–1992), a former senator from California and honorary chair of the English-only movement, wrote the influential semantics text Language in Thought and Action *in 1941. With the help of his son Alan, he brought out the fifth edition of the book in 1991. Born in Vancouver, Canada, to Japanese parents, Hayakawa attended the University of Manitoba, McGill University, and the University of Wisconsin before beginning a career as a professor of English. He later became president of San Francisco State University. Hayakawa's other language books include* Our Language and Our World *(1959) and* Symbol, Status, and Personality *(1963).*

Alan Hayakawa was born in Chicago on July 16, 1946, and received a B.A. in mathematics from Reed College in 1970. He began his writing career as a reporter for the Oregonian *in Portland, Oregon, in 1975, and he moved to Washington, D.C., in 1987 as the* Oregonian's *Washington correspondent. He is now the manager of the InsideLine, a telephone news and information service, at the* Patriot-News *in Harrisburg, Pennsylvania. In addition to coauthoring the fifth edition of* Language in Thought and Action, *Hayakawa has coauthored* The Blair Handbook *(2003), now in its fourth edition, and the* College Writer's Reference *(2002), now in its third edition.*

In the following selection, taken from Language in Thought and Action, *the Hayakawas reveal the power that words can have over thoughts. The terms we use to classify things — whether people, objects, or concepts — can and do affect our reactions to them. As the Hayakawas make clear, words can be powerful tools for prejudice and stereotyping.*

WRITING TO DISCOVER: *We like to use words to classify things and, in particular, other people. Think about your classmates. You have probably classified people you do not know well — "He's a nerd," "She's a preppie," "He's a jock," and so on. Write about why you think such labeling is so common. What are its advantages? What problems do you think labeling can create?*

The figure on page 612 shows eight objects, let us say animals, four large and four small, a different four with round heads and another four with square heads, and still another four with curly tails and another four with straight tails. These animals, let us say, are scampering about your village, but since at first they are of no importance to you, you ignore them. You do not even give them a name.

One day, however, you discover that the little ones eat up your grain, while the big ones do not. A differentiation sets itself up, and, abstracting the common characteristics of A, B, C, D, you decide to call these *gogo;* E, F, G, and H you decide to call *gigi.* You chase away the *gogo,* but leave the *gigi* alone. Your neighbor, however, has had a different experience; he finds that those with square heads bite, while those with round heads do not. Abstracting the common characteristics of B, D, F, and H, he calls them *daba,* and A, C, E, and G, he calls *dobo.* Still another neighbor discovers, on the other hand, that those with curly tails kill snakes, while those with straight tails do not. He differentiates them, abstracting still another set of common characteristics: A, B, E, and F are *busa,* while C, D, G, and H are *busana.*

Now imagine that the three of you are together when E runs by. You say, "There goes the *gigi*"; your first neighbor says, "There goes the *dobo*"; your other neighbor says, "There goes the *busa.*" Here, immediately, a great controversy arises. What is it *really,* a *gigi,* a *dobo,* or a *busa?* What is the *right name?* You are quarreling violently when along comes a fourth person from another village who calls it a *muglock,* an edible animal, as opposed to *uglock,* an inedible animal — which doesn't help matters a bit.

Of course, the question, "What is it *really?*" "What is its *right name?*" is a nonsense question. By a nonsense question is meant one that is not capable of being answered. Things can have "right names" only if there is a necessary connection between symbols and things symbolized, and we have seen that there is not. That is to say, in the light of your interest in protecting your grain, it may be necessary for you to distinguish the animal E as *gigi;* your neighbor, who doesn't like to be bitten, finds it practical to distinguish it as a *dobo;* your other neighbor, who likes to see snakes killed, distinguishes it as a *busa.* What we call things and where we draw the line between one class of things and another depend upon the interests we have and the purposes of the classification. For example, animals are classified in one way by the meat industry, in a different way by the leather industry, in another different way by the fur industry, and in a still different way by the biologist. None of these classifications is any more final than any of the others; each of them is useful for its purpose.

This holds, of course, regarding everything we perceive. A table "is" a table to us, because we can understand its relationship to our conduct and interests; we eat at it, work on it, lay things on it. But to a person living in a culture where no tables are used, it may be a very strong stool, a small platform, or a meaningless structure. If our culture and upbringing were different, that is to say, our world would not look the same to us.

Many of us, for example, cannot distinguish between pickerel, pike, salmon, smelt, perch, crappie, halibut, and mackerel; we say that they are "just fish, and I don't like fish." To a seafood connoisseur, however, these distinctions are real, since they mean the difference to him between one kind of a good meal, a very different kind of good meal, or a poor meal. To a zoologist, who has other and more general ends in view, even finer distinctions assume great importance. When we hear the statement, then, "This fish is a specimen of pompano, *Trachinotus carolinus*," we accept this as being "true," even if we don't care, not because that is its "right name," but because that is how it is *classified* in the most complete and most general system of classification that people scientifically interested in fish have evolved.

When we name something, then, we are classifying. *The individual object or event we are naming, of course, has no name and belongs to no class until we put it in one.* To illustrate again, suppose that we were to give the extensional meaning of the word "Korean." We would have to point to all "Koreans" living at a particular moment and say, "The word 'Korean' denotes at the present moment these persons: $A_1, A_2, A_3, \ldots A_n$." Now, let us say, a child, whom we shall designate as Z, is born among these "Koreans." *The extensional meaning of the word "Korean," determined prior to the existence of Z, does not include Z.* Z is a new individual belonging to no classification, since all classifications were made without taking Z into account. Why, then, is Z also a "Korean"? *Because we say so.* And, saying so — fixing the classification — we have determined to a considerable extent future attitudes toward Z. For example, Z will always have certain rights in Korea; in other nations he will be regarded as an "alien" and will be subject to laws applicable to "aliens."

In matters of "race" and "nationality," the way in which classifications work is especially apparent. For example, I am by birth a "Canadian," by "race" a "Japanese," and am now an "American." Although I was legally admitted to the United States on a Canadian passport as a "non-quota immigrant," I was unable to apply for American citizenship until after 1952. Until 1965, American immigration law used classifications based on "nationality" and on "race." A Canadian entering the United States as a permanent resident had no trouble getting in, unless he happened to be of Oriental extraction, in which case his "nationality" became irrelevant and he was classified by "race." If the quota for his "race" — for example, Japanese — was filled (and it often was), and if he could not get himself classified as a non-quota immigrant, he was not

able to get in at all. (Since 1965, race and national origin have been replaced with an emphasis on "family reunification" as the basis for American immigration law, and race is no longer explicitly mentioned.) Are all
these classifications "real"? Of course they are, *and the effect that each of
them has upon what he may or may not do constitutes their "reality."*

I have spent my entire life, except for short visits abroad, in Canada
and the United States. I speak Japanese haltingly, with a child's vocabulary and an American accent; I do not read or write it. Nevertheless, because classifications seem to have a kind of hypnotic power over some
people, I am occasionally credited with (or accused of) having an "Oriental mind." Since Buddha, Confucius, General Tojo, Mao Tse-tung, Pan-
dit Nehru, Rajiv Gandhi, and the proprietor of the Golden Pheasant
Chop Suey House all have "Oriental minds," it is difficult to know
whether to feel complimented or insulted.

When is a person "black"? By the definition once widely accepted in   10
the United States, any person with even a small amount of "Negro
blood" — that is, whose parents or ancestors were classified as "Negroes" — is "black." *It would be exactly as justifiable to say that any person
with even a small amount of "white blood" is "white."* Why say one rather
than the other? Because the former system of classification *suits the convenience of those making the classification.* (The classification of blacks and
other minorities in this country has often suited the convenience of
whites.) Classification is not a matter of identifying "essences." It is simply a reflection of social convenience or necessity — and different necessi-
ties are always producing different classifications.

There are few complexities about classifications at the level of dogs
and cats, knives and forks, cigarettes and candy, but when it comes to
classifications at high levels of abstraction, for example, those describing
conduct, social institutions, philosophical and moral problems, serious
difficulties occur. When one person kills another, is it an act of murder,
an act of temporary insanity, an act of homicide, an accident, or an act of
heroism? As soon as the process of classification is completed, our attitudes and our conduct are, to a considerable degree, determined. We
hang the murderer, we treat the insane, we absolve the victim of circum-
stance, we pin a medal on the hero.

THE BLOCKED MIND

We need not concern ourselves here with the injustices done to
"Jews," "Roman Catholics," "Republicans," "redheads," "chorus girls,"
"sailors," "Southerners," "Yankees," and so on, by snap judgments or, as
it is better to call them, fixed reactions. "Snap judgments" suggest that
such errors can be avoided by thinking more slowly; this, of course, is not
the case, for some people think very slowly with no better results. What

we are concerned with is the way in which we block the development of our own minds by automatic reactions.

In the grip of such reactions some people may say, "A Jew's a Jew. There's no getting around that" — confusing the denoted, extensional Jew with the fictitious "Jew" inside their heads. Such persons, the reader will have observed, can usually be made to admit, on being reminded of certain "Jews" whom they admire — perhaps Albert Einstein, Sandy Koufax, Jascha Heifetz, Benny Goodman, Woody Allen, Henry Kissinger, or Kitty Dukakis — that "there are exceptions, of course." They have been compelled by experience, that is to say, to take cognizance of at least a few of the multitude of Jews who do not fit their preconceptions. At this point, however, they continue triumphantly, "But exceptions only prove the rule?"[1] — which is another way of saying, "Facts don't count."

People who "think" in this way may identify some of their best friends as "Jewish"; but to explain this they may say, "I don't think of them as Jews at all. They're just friends." In other words, the fictitious "Jew" inside their heads remains unchanged *in spite of their experience.*

People like this may be said to be impervious to new information. They continue to vote Republican or Democratic, no matter what the Republicans or Democrats do. They continue to object to socialists, no matter what the socialists propose. They continue to regard mothers as sacred, no matter who the mother. A woman who had been given up on both by physicians and psychiatrists as hopelessly insane was being considered by a committee whose task it was to decide whether or not she should be committed to an asylum. One member of the committee doggedly refused to vote for commitment. "Gentlemen," he said in tones of deepest reverence, "you must remember that this woman is, after all, a mother." Similarly, some people continue to hate Protestants or Catholics, no matter which Protestant or Catholic. Ignoring characteristics left out in the process of classification, they overlook — when the term Republican is applied to the party of Abraham Lincoln, the party of Warren Harding, the party of Richard Nixon, and the party of Ronald Reagan — the rather important differences among them.

COW₁ IS NOT COW₂

How do we prevent ourselves from getting into such intellectual blind alleys, or, finding we are in one, how do we get out again? One way is to remember that practically all statements in ordinary conversation,

---

1. This extraordinarily fatuous saying originally meant, "The exception tests the rule" — *Exception probat regulum.* This older meaning of the word "prove" survives in such an expression as "automobile proving ground."

debate, and public controversy taking the form "Republicans are Republicans," "Business is business," "Boys will be boys," "Women drivers are women drivers," and so on, are *not true*. Let us put one of these blanket statements back into a context in life.

> "I don't think we should go through with this deal, Bill. Is it altogether fair to the railroad company?"
> "Aw, forget it! *Business is business,* after all."

Such an assertion, although it looks like a "simple statement of fact," is not simple and is not a statement of fact. The first "business" *denotes* the transaction under discussion; the second "business" invokes the *connotations* of the word. The sentence is a *directive,* saying, "Let us treat this transaction with complete disregard for considerations other than profit, as the word 'business' suggests." Similarly, when a father tries to excuse the mischief done by his sons, he says, "Boys will be boys"; in other words, "Let us regard the actions of my sons with that indulgent amusement customarily extended toward those whom we call 'boys,'" though the angry neighbor will say, of course, "Boys, my eye! They're little hoodlums; that's what they are!" Such assertions are not informative statements but directives, directing us to classify the object or event under discussion in given ways, in order that we may feel or act as suggested by the terms of the classification.

There is a simple technique for preventing such directives from having their harmful effect on our thinking. It is the suggestion made by Korzybski that we add "index numbers" to our terms, thus: Englishman$_1$, Englishman$_2$ . . . ; cow$_1$, cow$_2$, cow$_3$ . . . ; communist$_1$, communist$_2$, communist$_3$. The terms of the classification tell us what the individuals in that class have in common; *the index numbers remind us of the characteristics left out.* A rule can then be formulated as a general guide in all our thinking and reading: police officer$_1$ *is not* police officer$_2$; mother-in-law$_1$ *is not* mother-in-law$_2$, and so on. This rule, if remembered, prevents us from confusing levels of abstraction and forces us to consider the facts on those occasions when we might otherwise find ourselves leaping to conclusions which we may later have cause to regret.

"TRUTH"

Many semantic problems are, ultimately, problems of classification and nomenclature. Take, for example, the extensive debate over abortion. To opponents of legalized abortion, the unborn entity within a woman's womb is a "baby." Because abortion foes *want* to end abortion, they insist that the "baby" *is* a human being with its own legal rights and that therefore "*abortion is murder.*" They call themselves "pro-life" to emphasize their position. Those who *want* individual women to be able to choose whether or not to end a pregnancy call that same unborn entity a "fetus" and insist that a "fetus" *is not* a viable human being capable of living on its own, and claim that a woman has a "right" to make such a choice. Partisans of either side have accused the other of "perverting the meanings of words" and of "not being able to understand plain English."

The decision finally rests not upon appeals to past authority, but   20
upon *what society wants*. In the case *Roe v. Wade*, the Supreme Court found that a "right" — specifically, a right to privacy — permits women to make a private, medical decision before a certain stage of pregnancy. If society again wants doctors prosecuted for performing abortions, as they often were before 1973, it will obtain a new decision from Congress or the Supreme Court that abortion "is" murder or that the unborn entity "is" a human being. Either way, society will ultimately get the decision it collectively wants, even if it must wait until the present members of the Supreme Court are dead and an entirely new court is appointed. When the desired decision is handed down, people will say, "Truth has triumphed." *Society, in short, regards as "true" those systems of classification that produce the desired results.*

The scientific test of "truth," like the social test, is strictly practical, except for the fact that the "desired results" are more severely limited. The results desired by society may be irrational, superstitious, selfish, or humane, but the results desired by scientists are only that our systems of classification produce predictable results. Classifications, as amply indicated already, determine our attitudes and behavior toward the object or event classified. When lightning was classified as "evidence of divine wrath," no courses of action other than prayer were suggested to prevent one's being struck by lightning. But after Benjamin Franklin classified it as "electricity," a measure of control over it was achieved by the invention of the lightning rod. Certain physical disorders were formerly classified as "demonic possession," and this suggested that we "drive the demons out" by whatever spells or incantations we could think of. The results were uncertain. But when those disorders were classified as "bacillus infections," courses of action were suggested that led to more predictable results. Science seeks only the *most generally useful* systems of classification; these it regards for the time being, until more useful classifications are invented, as "true."

FOCUSING ON CONTENT

1. According to the authors, "What we call things and where we draw the line between one class of things and another depend upon the interests we have and the purposes of the classification" (4). They cite the different methods of animal classification by the meat, leather, and fur industries as one example

of what they mean. Choose a popular song, motion picture, or book, and list four or five terms that could be used to classify it. Who would be likely to use each of these terms, and why?

2. The Hayakawas remind us that the United States once defined "any person with even a small amount of 'Negro blood' . . . as 'black'" (10). Why do you think this system of classification suited the convenience of American whites? What were some of the implications of this system for those individuals so classified?

3. What do the authors mean by "the blocked mind" (12–15)? Provide some examples that are not mentioned in the essay.

4. According to the Hayakawas, is there any such thing as a "true" system of classification? Can language convey "truth"? How does the idea of ethnocentricity enter into your answer? (Glossary: *Ethnocentricity*) Explain.

FOCUSING ON WRITING

1. How do the Hayakawas make their fairly abstract subject matter clear to the reader? For example, do they use induction, deduction, or both to develop their explanation of the relationship between naming and classifying? (Glossary: *Deduction* and *Induction*)

2. What is the relationship that you as a writer see between concreteness and abstraction in writing? (Glossary: *Concrete/Abstract*) Why is the ability to move up and down the ladder of abstraction an essential writing skill? Are there any guidelines that tell writers when to be concrete or abstract in their writing? Explain.

3. Discuss the authors' use of examples as evidence. Are their examples concrete, abstract, or both? Why are examples so important in this particular selection? (Glossary: *Evidence* and *Examples*)

LANGUAGE IN ACTION

The accompanying drawing is a basic exercise in classification. By determining the features that the figures have in common, establish the general class to which they all belong. Next, establish subclasses by determining the distinctive features that distinguish one subclass from another. Then place each figure in an appropriate subclass within your classification system. You may wish to compare your classification system to those developed by other members of your class and to discuss any differences that exist. Finally, discuss this exercise in light of the Hayakawas' comments regarding the dynamics and importance of classification.

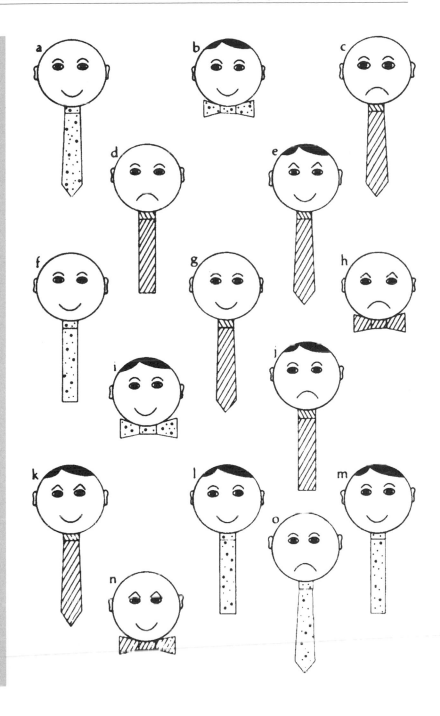

WRITING SUGGESTIONS

1. Write an essay in which you discuss Korzybski's idea of using index numbers (18) to avoid confusion and misunderstanding. Although the Hayakawas give a number of examples that show how such indexing can be helpful, try to come up with your own examples for your paper. If possible, explain how not understanding the indexing principle has created problems for you.

2. Review what you have learned from reading the Hayakawas' essay. Then explain in an essay how naming things is not merely attaching labels to them but an action that reflects and affects our fundamental thought processes.

Changing My Name after Sixty Years

TOM ROSENBERG

*Tom Rosenberg was born in Berlin, Germany, but in 1938 his fam-
ily fled Nazi persecution, settling in New York City when Rosenberg was six years old. In an attempt to downplay their Jewish
heritage, the Rosenbergs changed their surname to Ross upon arriving in the United States. As Tom Ross, Rosenberg grew up in New
York, graduated from the University of Pittsburgh, then joined the
Marines and served in the Korean War. He moved to the West
Coast upon returning to the United States and served as a political
consultant for nearly thirty years, spearheading environmental and
outdoor recreation initiatives. He recently published his first novel,*
Phantom on His Wheels *(2000), which draws upon his interests in
journalism, environmentalism, and politics.*

*The following essay, which appeared in the July 17, 2000, issue
of* Newsweek, *shows how Rosenberg spent most of his life denying his
heritage and explains why he has chosen to embrace it now.*

WRITING TO DISCOVER: *Surnames mean a lot in our culture;
whether or not we like it, they tell others something about our ethnicity, our heritage, and our possible cultural influences. Not long ago,
having a surname that was readily identifiable as "foreign" could
be a liability. For the most part, attitudes about names have
changed for the better. What do you think of your surname? Have
you ever felt hindered or discriminated against because of it? If you
could change it, would you? Why or why not?*

My parents left Nazi Germany in 1938, when I was six and my
mother was pregnant with my sister. They arrived in America with a lot of
baggage — guilt over deserting loved ones, anger over losing their home
and business, and a lifelong fear of anti-Semitism.

Shortly thereafter, whether out of fear, a desire to assimilate, or a
combination of both, they changed our family name from Rosenberg to
Ross. My parents were different from the immigrants who landed on Ellis
Island and had their names changed by an immigration bureaucrat. My
mother and father voluntarily gave up their identity and a measure of
pride for an Anglicized name.

Growing up a German-Jewish kid in the Bronx in the 1940s, a time
when Americans were dying in a war fought in part to save Jews from the
hated Nazis, was difficult. Even my new name failed to protect me from
bigotry; the neighborhood bullies knew a "sheenie" when they saw one.

The bullying only intensified the shame I felt about my family's religious and ethnic background. I spent much of my youth denying my

roots and vying for my peers' acceptance as "Tom Ross." Today I look
back and wonder what kind of life I might have led if my parents had
kept our family name.

In the '50s, I doubt Tom Rosenberg would have been accepted as a   5
pledge by Theta Chi, a predominantly Christian fraternity at my college.
He probably would have pledged a Jewish fraternity or had the self-confidence and conviction to ignore the Greek system altogether. Tom Rosenberg might have married a Jewish woman, stayed in the East, and
maintained closer ties to his Jewish family.

As it was, I moved west to San Francisco. Only after I married and
became a father did I begin to acknowledge my Jewish heritage.

My first wife, a liberal Methodist, insisted that I stop running from
Judaism. For years we attended both a Unitarian church and a Jewish
temple. Her open-minded attitude set the tone in our household and was
passed on to our three kids. As a family, we celebrated Christmas and
went to temple on the High Holidays. But even though my wife and I
were careful to teach our kids tolerance, their exposure to either religion
was minimal. Most weekends, we took the kids on ski trips, rationalizing
that the majesty of the Sierra was enough of a spiritual experience.

So last year, when I decided to tell my children that I was legally
changing my name back to Rosenberg, I wondered how they would
react. We were in a restaurant celebrating the publication of my first
novel. After they toasted my tenacity for staying with fiction for some
thirty years, I made my announcement: "I want to be remembered by the
name I was born with."

I explained that the kind of discrimination and stereotyping still evident today had made me rethink the years I'd spent denying my family's
history, years that I'd been ashamed to talk about with them. The present
political climate — the initiatives attacking social services for immigrants,
bilingual education, Affirmative Action — made me want to shout "I'm
an immigrant!" My children were silent for a moment before they smiled,
leaned over, and hugged me.

The memories of my years of denial continued to dog me as I told   10
friends and family that I planned to change my name. The rabbi at the
Reform temple that I belong to with my second wife suggested I go a
step further. "Have you thought of taking a Hebrew first name?" he
asked.

He must have seen the shocked look on my face. I wondered, is he
suggesting I become more religious, more Jewish?" "What's involved?" I
asked hesitatingly.

The rabbi explained that the ceremony would be simple and private,
just for family and friends. I would make a few remarks about why I had
selected my name, and then he would say a blessing.

It took me a moment to grasp the significance of what the rabbi
was proposing. He saw my name change as a chance to do more than

reclaim a piece of my family's history; it was an opportunity to renew my commitment to Jewish ideals. I realized it was also a way to give my kids the sense of pride in their heritage that they had missed out on as children.

A few months later I stood at the pulpit in front of an open, lighted ark, flanked by my wife and the rabbi. Before me stood my children, holding their children. I had scribbled a few notes for my talk, but felt too emotional to use them. I held on to the lectern for support and winged it.

"Every time I step into a temple, I'm reminded that Judaism has   15 survived for 4,000 years. It's survived because it's a positive religion. My parents, your grandparents, changed their name out of fear. I'm changing it back out of pride. I chose the name Tikvah because it means hope."

FOCUSING ON CONTENT

1. Why did Rosenberg's parents change their surname soon after arriving in the United States?

2. What advantages did Rosenberg enjoy as Tom Ross? How might his life have been different if he had grown up as a Rosenberg?

3. When and why did Rosenberg stop denying his Jewish heritage? When and why did he decide to change his name?

4. What is the significance of Rosenberg's not only changing his last name but also taking a Hebrew first name? Why does he do it?

FOCUSING ON WRITING

1. Rosenberg's title, along with his name, grab the reader's attention. What are some of the questions that his title raises? How effectively does he answer them?

2. Trace the causal chain that begins with the primary cause of Rosenberg's parents changing their name to Ross. What are the effects on their lives and on the life of their son?

3. Rosenberg uses a mostly chronological organization for his essay. (Glossary: *Organization*) Why is this organization effective? How does he foreshadow his conclusion?

LANGUAGE IN ACTION

Comment on the importance of one's name as revealed in the following Ann Landers column.

REFUSAL TO USE NAME IS THE ULTIMATE INSULT

DEAR ANN LANDERS: Boy, when you're wrong, you're really wrong. Apparently, you have never been the victim of a hostile, nasty, passive-aggressive person who refuses to address you by name. Well, I have.

My husband's mother has never called me by my name in the 21 years I've been married to her son. Nor has she ever said "please" or "thank you," unless someone else is within hearing distance. My husband's children by his first wife are the same way. The people they care about are always referred to by name, but the rest of us are not called anything.

If you still think this is a "psychological glitch," as you said in a recent column, try speaking to someone across the room without addressing that person by name. To be nameless and talked at is the ultimate put-down, and I wish you had said so. — "Hey You" in Florida

DEAR FLORIDA: Sorry I let you down. Your mother-in-law's refusal to call you by name is, I am sure, rooted in hostility. Many years ago, Dr. Will Menninger said, "The sweetest sound in any language is the sound of your own name." It can also be a valuable sales tool. My former husband, one of the world's best salesmen, said if you want to make a sale, get the customer's name, use it when you make your pitch, and he will be half sold. His own record as a salesman proved him right.

What is the meaning of Dr. Will Menniger's statement: "The sweetest sound in any language is the sound of your own name"?

WRITING SUGGESTIONS

1. Write a personal essay, using your name, heritage, religion, or some form of inner identification as the primary cause. What effects has it had on your life? How has it enhanced your life? What adverse effects, if any, has it had on you? Without it, how might you be a different person?

2. Choose a grandparent from either your maternal or paternal lineage. Write a narrative history of his or her life. What challenges did he or she face? How did ethnic and cultural heritage affect the way he or she lived? What has this grandparent passed along to you that you are proud of and wish to pass along to your children? What would you just as soon forget?

The Names of Women

Louise Erdrich

*Born in Minnesota in 1954 to Ralph and Rita Erdrich, who both
worked for the Bureau of Indian Affairs, Louise Erdrich grew up
in North Dakota and belongs to the Turtle Mountain band of
Chippewa Native Americans. She received her B.A. from Dartmouth College and M.A. from Johns Hopkins University. Author of
numerous poems, novels, and short stories, Erdrich won the National Book Critics Circle Award in 1984 for her novel* Love Medicine. *Her other novels include* The Beet Queen *(1986),* Tracks
(1988), The Bingo Palace *(1994),* The Antelope Wife *(1998),
and, with her late husband Michael Dorris,* The Crown of Columbus *(1991). She has also written two collections of poetry,* Jacklight
(1984) and Baptism of Desire *(1990).*

"The Names of Women," originally published in Erdrich's book
The Blue Jays *(1995), is about both personal discovery and an entire culture that has been swept away over time. The essay reveals
parts of Erdrich's own heritage, and it gives readers a glimpse at
some of what was lost when Native American cultures were diluted
and then died out.*

WRITING TO DISCOVER: *If you had a descriptive name, as do
many Native Americans, what would you like it to be? Why? Write
about your hypothetical name. Would there be any advantages or
disadvantages in having a descriptive name?*

Ikwe is the word for woman in the language of the Anishinabe, my
mother's people, whose descendants, mixed with and married to French
trappers and farmers, are the Michifs of the Turtle Mountain reservation in
North Dakota. Every Anishinabe *Ikwe*, every mixed-blood descendent like
me, who can trace her way back a generation or two, is the daughter of a
mystery. The history of the woodland Anishinabe — decimated by disease,
fighting Plains Indian tribes to the west and squeezed by European settlers
to the east — is much like most other Native American stories, a confusion
of loss, a tale of absences, of a culture that was blown apart and changed so
radically in such a short time that only the names survive.

And yet, those names.

The names of the first women whose existence is recorded on the
rolls of the Turtle Mountain Reservation, in 1892, reveal as much as
we can ever recapture of their personalities, complex natures, and relationships. These names tell stories, or half stories, if only we listen closely.

There once were women named *Standing Strong, Fish Bones, Different Thunder*. There once was a girl called *Yellow Straps*. Imagine what it

was like to pick berries with *Sky Coming Down,* to walk through a storm with *Lightning Proof.* Surely, she was struck and lived, but what about the person next to her? People always avoided *Steps Over Truth,* when they wanted a straight answer, and *I Hear,* when they wanted to keep a secret. *Glittering* put coal on her face and watched for enemies at night. The woman named *Standing Across* could see things moving far across the lake. The old ladies gossiped about *Playing Around,* but no one dared say anything to her face. *Ice* was good at gambling. *Shining One Side* loved to sit and talk to *Opposite the Sky.* They both knew *Sounding Feather, Exhausted Wind,* and *Green Cloud,* daughter of *Seeing Iron. Center of the Sky* was a widow. *Rabbit, Prairie Chicken,* and *Daylight* were all little girls. *She Tramp* could make great distance in a day of walking. *Cross Lightning* had a powerful smile. When *Setting Wind* and *Gentle Woman Standing* sang together the whole tribe listened. *Stop the Day* got her name when at her shout the afternoon went still. *Log* was strong, *Cloud Touching Bottom* weak and consumptive. *Mirage* married *Wind.* Everyone loved *Musical Cloud,* but children hid from *Dressed in Stone. Lying Down Grass* had such a gentle voice and touch, but no one dared to cross *She Black of Heart.*

We can imagine something of these women from their names. 5 Anishinabe historian Basil Johnston notes that "such was the mystique and force of a name that it was considered presumptuous and unbecoming, even vain, for a person to utter his own name. It was the custom for a third person, if present, to utter the name of the person to be identified. Seldom, if ever, did either husband or wife speak the name of the other in public."

Shortly after the first tribal roll, the practice of renaming became an ecclesiastical exercise, and, as a result, most women in the next two generations bear the names of saints particularly beloved by the French. *She Knows the Bear* became Marie. *Sloping Cloud* was christened Jeanne. *Taking Care of the Day* and *Yellow Day Woman* turned into Catherines. Identities are altogether lost. The daughters of my own ancestors, *Kwayzancheewin — Acts Like a Boy* and *Striped Earth Woman —* go unrecorded, and no hint or reflection of their individual natures comes to light through the scattershot records of those times, although they must have been genetically tough in order to survive: there were epidemics of typhoid, flu, measles, and other diseases that winnowed the tribe each winter. They had to have grown up sensible, hard-working, undeviating in their attention to their tasks. They had to have been lucky. And if very lucky, they acquired carts.

It is no small thing that both of my great-grandmothers were known as women with carts.

The first was Elise Eliza McCloud, the great-granddaughter of *Striped Earth Woman.* The buggy she owned was somewhat grander than a cart. In her photograph, Elise Eliza gazes straight ahead, intent, elevated in her pride. Perhaps she and her daughter Justine, both wearing reshaped felt fedoras, were on their way to the train that would take them from Rugby, North Dakota, to Grand Forks, and back again. Back and forth across the upper tier of the plains, they peddled their hand-worked tourist items — dangling moccasin brooches and little beaded hats, or, in the summer, the wild berries, plums, and nuts that they had gathered from the wooded hills. Of Elise Eliza's industry there remains in the family only an intricately beaded pair of buffalo horns and a piece of real furniture, a "highboy," an object once regarded with some awe, a prize she won for selling the most merchandise from a manufacturer's catalogue.

The owner of the other cart, Virginia Grandbois, died when I was nine years old: she was a fearsome and fascinating presence, an old woman seated like an icon behind the door of my grandparents' house. Forty years before I was born, she was photographed on her way to fetch drinking water at the reservation well. In the picture she is seated high, the reins in her fingers connected to a couple of shaggy fetlocked draft ponies. The barrel she will fill stands behind her. She wears a man's sweater and an expression of vast self-pleasure. She might have been saying *Kaygoh*, a warning, to calm the horses. She might have been speaking to whomever it was who held the camera, still a novel luxury.

Virginia Grandbois was known to smell of flowers. In spite of the potato picking, water hauling, field and housework, she found the time and will to dust her face with pale powder, in order to look more French. She was the great-great-granddaughter of the daughter of the principal leader of the *A-waus-e*, the Bullhead clan, a woman whose real name was never recorded but who, on marrying a Frenchman, was "recreated" as Madame Cadotte. It was Madame Cadotte who acted as a liaison between her Ojibway relatives and her husband so that, even when French influence waned in the region, Jean-Baptiste Cadotte stayed on as the only trader of importance, the last governor of the fort at Sault St. Marie.

By the time I knew Virginia Grandbois, however, her mind had darkened, and her body deepened, shrunk, turned to bones and leather. She did not live in the present or in any known time at all. Periodically, she would awaken from dim and unknown dreams to find herself seated behind the door in her daughter's house. She then cried out for her cart and her horses. When they did not materialize, Virginia Grandbois rose with great energy and purpose. Then she walked towards her house, taking the straightest line.

That house, long sold and gone, lay over one hundred miles due east and still Virginia Grandbois charged ahead, no matter what lay in her path — fences, sloughs, woods, the yards of other families. She wanted home, to get home, to be home. She wanted her own place back, the place she had made, not her daughter's, not anyone else's. Hers. There

10

was no substitute, no kindness, no reality that would change her mind. She had to be tied to the chair, and the chair to the wall, and still there was no reasoning with Virginia Grandbois. Her entire life, her hard-won personality, boiled down in the end to one stubborn, fixed, desperate idea.

I started with the same idea — this urge to get home, even if I must walk straight across the world. Only, for me, the urge to walk is the urge to write. Like my great-grandmother's house, there is no home for me to get to. A mixed-blood, raised in the Sugarbeet Capital, educated on the Eastern seaboard, married in a tiny New England village, living now on a ridge directly across from the Swan Range in the Rocky Mountains, my home is a collection of homes, of wells in which the quiet of experience shales away into sweet bedrock.

Elise Eliza pieced the quilt my mother slept under, a patchwork of shirts, pants, other worn-out scraps, bordered with small rinsed and pressed Bull Durham sacks. As if in another time and place, although it is only the dim barrel of a four-year-old's memory, I see myself lying wrapped under smoky quilts and dank green army blankets in the house in which my mother was born. In the fragrance of tobacco, some smoked in home-rolled cigarettes, some offered to the Manitous whose presence still was honored, I dream myself home. Beneath the rafters, shadowed with bunches of plants and torn calendars, in the nest of a sagging bed, I listen to mice rustle and the scratch of an owl's claws as it paces the shingles.

Elise Eliza's daughter-in-law, my grandmother Mary LeFavor, kept that house of hand-hewed and stacked beams, mudded between. She managed to shore it up and keep it standing by stuffing every new crack with disposable diapers. Having used and reused cloth to diaper her own children, my grandmother washed and hung to dry the paper and plastic diapers that her granddaughters bought for her great-grandchildren. When their plastic-paper shredded, she gathered them carefully together and one day, on a summer visit, I woke early to find her tamping the rolled stuff carefully into the cracked walls of that old house. 15

It is autumn in the Plains, and in the little sloughs ducks land, and mudhens, whose flesh always tastes greasy and charred. Snow is coming soon, and after its first fall there will be a short, false warmth that brings out the sweet-sour odor of highbush cranberries. As a descendant of the women who skinned buffalo and tanned and smoked the hides, of women who pounded berries with the dried meat to make winter food, who made tea from willow bark and rosehips, who gathered snakeroot, I am affected by the change of seasons. Here is a time when plants consolidate their tonic and drop seed, when animals store energy and grow thick fur. As for me, I start keeping longer hours, writing more, working harder, though I am obviously not a creature of a traditional Anishinabe culture. I was not raised speaking the old language, or adhering to the cycle of religious ceremonies that govern the Anishinabe spiritual relationship to the land and the moral order within human configurations. As the wedding of many backgrounds, I am free to do what simply feels right.

My mother knits, sews, cans, dries food and preserves it. She knows how to gather tea, berries, snare rabbits, milk cows, and churn butter. She can grow squash and melons from seeds she gathered the fall before. She is, as were the women who came before me, a repository of all of the homey virtues, and I am the first in a long line who has not saved the autumn's harvest in birch bark *makuks* and skin bags and in a cellar dry and cold with dust. I am the first who scratches the ground for pleasure, not survival, and grows flowers instead of potatoes. I record rather than practice the arts that filled the hands and days of my mother and her mother, and all the mothers going back into the shadows, when women wore names that told us who they were.

FOCUSING ON CONTENT

1. Erdrich begins her essay with the Anishinabe word for woman, *Ikwe*. Why is this word important? What does Erdrich accomplish by introducing it at the beginning of her essay?

2. The quotation from Basil Johnston in paragraph 5 mentions the "mystique and force" of Anishinabe names. Why did the names have such mystique? What happened to the Anishinabe culture when the French made naming an ecclesiastical exercise?

3. Summarize Erdrich's descriptions of her great-grandmothers in one or two sentences. Why do you think Erdrich describes them at length? How do their stories represent what happened to the Anishinabe culture as a whole?

4. In paragraph 4, why do you think Erdrich makes associations with so many Anishinabe names? What does this list tell you about the culture that was lost? Provide some alternative associations for ten of the names. How do you think your ethnocentricity, your immersion in a particular culture, influences the way you interpret names? (Glossary: *Ethnocentricity*)

FOCUSING ON WRITING

1. What does Erdrich mean when she writes in paragraph 13, "I started with the same idea — this urge to get home, even if I must walk straight across the world. Only, for me, the urge to walk is the urge to write"? How is writing like walking? Do you think Erdrich "gets home" in this essay? What in her style leads you to your answer? (Glossary: *Style*)

2. Erdrich's paragraphs are well developed. Although most are of average length or a bit longer, she includes several paragraphs (2, 3, and 7) that are shorter than normal. What is the function of each of those paragraphs?

3. In paragraph 16, Erdrich begins the last section of her essay with the following description: "It is autumn in the Plains, and in the little sloughs ducks land, and mudhens, whose flesh always tastes greasy and charred. Snow is coming soon, and after its first fall there will be a short, false warmth that brings out the sweet-sour odor of highbrush cranberries." Why do you think Erdrich includes this description of place? How does it tie in with her heritage?

LANGUAGE IN ACTION

Show business people often change their names to further their careers. Here are the professional names and the original names of a number of celebrities. Discuss with your classmates the significance of the names and the reasons they might have been changed.

Professional Names	*Original Names*
Tony Curtis	Bernard Schwartz
Mick Jagger	Michael Philip
Simone Signoret	Simone Kaminker
Roy Rogers	Leonard Sly
Raquel Welch	Raquel Tejada
James Garner	James Bumgarner
Bob Dylan	Robert Zimmerman
Doris Day	Doris von Kappelhoff
Fred Astaire	Frederick Austerlitz
John Wayne	Marion Michael Morrison
Cyd Charisse	Tula Finklea
Anne Bancroft	Annemaria Italiano
Michael Caine	Maurice J. Micklewhite
Jack Benny	Benjamin Kubelsky
Connie Francis	Concetta Franconero
Ringo Starr	Richard Starkey
Hugh O'Brian	Hugh J. Krampe

WRITING SUGGESTIONS

1. In an essay entitled "Going Home," write with the same general purpose that Louise Erdrich has written "The Names of Women," not about names necessarily but about the way writing can create a home or a number of homes. Before you write, think about the implications of Erdrich's metaphor and consider the various kinds of writing experiences that constitute going home. How does the creative process of writing provide not only

a sense of power and control but also a sense of the familiarity and comfort of home?

2. As a general subject area for further research and writing, Native American languages are varied and interesting. With the renaissance of interest in Native American studies, especially over the past few decades, there is a vast quantity of information from which to draw. Choose an area of Native American languages that interests you and, using library and Internet research, write an essay explaining your findings to other students who may not know about that area. Following are some possible general subjects: the migration patterns of early North American native peoples and the influence of those patterns on language, genetic research tracing the movement of tribes, the use of carbon-dating techniques to verify the age of antiquities, languages that existed but are now extinct, the various strategies being used to save native languages, and the grammatical structure of a particular native language.

Picturing Language

In your own words, what point does Scott McCloud make in his cartoon strip "Show and Tell"? At what point does the cartoon shift from "showing" to "telling"? As a cartoonist, McCloud is continually exploring the relationship

between images and words. What's lost for McCloud when children in our society are encouraged to "grow out" of their dependence on pictures? As writers, how can we use words to create mental pictures in the absence of physical objects?

Be Specific

NATALIE GOLDBERG

Author Natalie Goldberg has made her specialty writing about writing. Her first and best-known work, Writing Down the Bones: Freeing the Writer Within, *was published in 1986. Goldberg's advice to would-be writers is, on the one hand, practical and pithy; on the other, it is almost mystical in its call to know and appreciate the world. "Be Specific," the excerpt that appears below, is representative of the book as a whole. Amid widespread acclaim for the book, one critic commented, "Goldberg teaches us not only how to write better, but how to live better."* Writing Down the Bones *was followed by three more successful books about writing:* Wild Mind: Living the Writer's Life *(1990),* Living Color: A Writer Paints Her World *(1996), and* Thunder and Lightning: Cracking Open the Writer's Craft *(2000). Altogether, more than half a million copies of these books are now in print. Goldberg has also written fiction; her first novel,* Banana Rose, *was published in 1994.*

Notice the way in which Goldberg demonstrates her advice to be specific in the following selection.

WRITING TO DISCOVER: *Suppose someone says to you, "I walked in the woods." What do you envision? Write down what you see in your mind's eye. Now suppose someone says, "I walked in the Redwood Forest." Again, write what you see. What's different about your two descriptions, and why?*

Be specific. Don't say "fruit." Tell what kind of fruit — "It is a pomegranate." Give things the dignity of their names. Just as with human beings, it is rude to say, "Hey, girl, get in line." That "girl" has a name. (As a matter of fact, if she's at least twenty years old, she's a woman, not a "girl" at all.) Things, too, have names. It is much better to say "the geranium in the window" than "the flower in the window." "Geranium" — that one word gives us a much more specific picture. It penetrates more deeply into the beingness of that flower. It immediately gives us the scene by the window — red petals, green circular leaves, all straining toward sunlight.

About ten years ago I decided I had to learn the names of plants and flowers in my environment. I bought a book on them and walked down the tree-lined streets of Boulder, examining leaf, bark, and seed, trying to match them up with their descriptions and names in the book. Maple, elm, oak, locust. I usually tried to cheat by asking people working in their yards the names of the flowers and trees growing there. I was amazed how few people had any idea of the names of the live beings inhabiting their little plot of land.

When we know the name of something, it brings us closer to the ground. It takes the blur out of our mind; it connects us to the earth. If I walk down the street and see "dogwood," "forsythia," I feel more friendly toward the environment. I am noticing what is around me and can name it. It makes me more awake.

If you read the poems of William Carlos Williams, you will see how specific he is about plants, trees, flowers — chicory, daisy, locust, poplar, quince, primrose, black-eyed Susan, lilacs — each has its own integrity. Williams says, "Write what's in front of your nose." It's good for us to know what is in front of our noses. Not just "daisy," but how the flower is in the season we are looking at it — "The dayseye hugging the earth/in August . . . brownedged,/green and pointed scales/armor his yellow." Continue to hone your awareness: to the name, to the month, to the day, and finally to the moment.

Williams also says: "No idea, but in things." Study what is "in front of   5
your nose." By saying "geranium" instead of "flower," you are penetrating more deeply into the present and being there. The closer we can get to what's in front of our nose, the more it can teach us everything. "To see the World in a Grain of Sand, and a heaven in a Wild Flower . . ."

In writing groups and classes too, it is good to quickly learn the names of all the other group members. It helps to ground you in the group and make you more attentive to each other's work.

Learn the names of everything: birds, cheese, tractors, cars, buildings. A writer is all at once everything — an architect, French cook, farmer — and at the same time, a writer is none of these things.

FOCUSING ON CONTENT

1. In paragraphs 3, 5, and 6, Goldberg cites a number of advantages to be gained by knowing the names of things. Review these advantages. What are they? Do they ring true?

2. Goldberg says that to name an object gives it dignity and integrity. What does she mean in each case?

3. Throughout the essay, Goldberg instructs readers to be specific and to be aware of the world around them. Of what besides names is the reader advised to be aware? Why?

FOCUSING ON WRITING

1. How does Goldberg "specifically" follow the advice she gives writers in this essay?

2. Goldberg makes several lists of the names of things. What purpose do these lists serve? How does she use these specifics to exemplify her point?

3. What specific audience is Goldberg addressing in this essay? (Glossary: *Audience*) How do you know?

LANGUAGE IN ACTION

John Updike wrote the following poem about "some Frenchmen" who lent their names to our vocabulary. After reading the poem, consult your desk dictionary or another reference work to learn more about the actual contributions of these men. Summarize the inventions of each man, and comment on Updike's effectiveness in capturing the nature of each invention in poetry.

SOME FRENCHMEN

Monsieur Etienne de Silhouette
   Was slim and uniformly black;
His profile was superb, and yet
   He vanished when he turned his back.

Humane and gaunt, precise and tall
   Was Docteur J. I. Guillotin;
He had one tooth, diagonal
   And loose, which, when it fell, spelled *fin*.

André Marie Ampère, a spark,
   Would visit other people's homes
And gobble volts until the dark
   Was lit by his resisting ohms.

Another type, Daguerre (Louis),
   In silver salts would soak his head,
Expose himself to light, and be
   Developed just in time for bed.

WRITING SUGGESTIONS

1. "No idea, but in things," says William Carlos Williams. Read a collection of his short poems and a good critical study of his poetry. Write an essay in which you analyze Williams's statement by exploring how it is illustrated in his poems.

2. In the final paragraph, the three occupations that Goldberg names are probably familiar to you, but many of the practices and products connected to them may not be familiar at all. With several classmates, brainstorm an expanded list of occupations. Choose one that interests you and learn about the activities and functions served by a person in that profession. You might consider using the Internet to help you with brainstorming and research. Following are several helpful Web sites. Write a report to share what you

have learned about the various jobs and the need to be specific in describing them.

Job Descriptions

www.umsystem.edu/hrs/comp/contents.htm

Maintained by the University of Missouri, this site provides an extensive listing of job titles and descriptions.

JobGenie

www.stepfour.com/jobs

JobGenie features an alphabetical index of job titles and descriptions that are certified by the U.S. Department of Labor.

A Name So Smooth, the Product Glides In

J. C. HERZ

*Born in 1971, "vid kid" J. C. Herz has established herself as the pre-
eminent chronicler of the world of video games, the six-billion-
dollar electronics-entertainment industry. A clever and inventive
writer, Herz explores the dark nether regions of the Internet and the
mysteries of online discussions with cyberpunks and hackers. She also
analyzes such cultural phenomena as* Myst, Super Mario, Pac-
Man, Frogger, *and* Doom. *Her very popular books are* Surfing on
the Internet *(1995) and* Joystick Nation *(1997), and she's now
working on a PBS special on computer games.*

*The following selection was originally published in the "Games
Theory" column of the* New York Times *on November 26, 1998.
Herz explores the creation of the name* Nuon *for a powerful new
computer microchip being developed by VM Labs.*

WRITING TO DISCOVER: *Have you ever thought about where
the names of new products like the Saturn Ion automobile, X-Box
video game system, or iPod MP3 music recorder come from? What
are some of your favorite product names? Why do you like them?
What do you think might be a cool name for a new video game
system?*

Nuon. Say it a few times. Roll it around on your tongue. Nnnnnnn.
Nnnnnnuon. Nuuuu-on. Ooooooh.

Hmmmm . . .

How does that feel? Does it feel cutting edge? Does it feel futuristic?
Does it feel authentic? Would you drive it? Would you buy running tights
made out of it? Would you order it in a bar? Would you use it to charge a
major purchase? Would you take it for a migraine? Would you play video
games with it?

If you answered yes to the last question, you've justified a five-figure
fee paid to Lexicon, a professional naming agency, by VM Labs, a technology company whose microchip, the newly christened Nuon, will be
powering DVD players and set-top boxes in 1999.

The idea behind Nuon is to piggyback a video game platform   5
on top of a digital video system so people who might never buy a
Nintendo 64 or Playstation will suddenly find themselves in possession
of a video game machine. And once they own it, why not buy a game
or two, just for kicks? The Nuon audience (Nuonites?) are not hardcore gamers. But then, neither are the hundreds of thousands of people
who made Deer Hunter the best-selling computer game in North
America.

But if a rose is a rose is a rose, a consumer electronics device by any other name does not smell as sweet. There are, in the patois of marketing, "branding considerations."

For instance, the name of this new product needs to be short because it has to fit inside a stamp-size space, along with a logo, on the front of a smallish device. "We needed something under five letters to make a good graphic impact on the front of the panel," said Greg Labrec, VM Labs' vice president for marketing, describing the name game as a high-stakes corporate crossword puzzle. "Under five letters, describes our chip and the operating system and the architecture as a whole. Something that somebody would want to have in a high-tech device."

"We had a bunch of combinations like Intervision, which combined interactive and vision, and Active DVD, which sort of gave a sense of active as opposed to passive DVD. On our own, we hit about four hundred different names over the course of a year and a half. Actually, there were at least double that — I disqualified a lot of them. Like, there was one that everybody really, really liked, Actavid. And after I said it sounded like an aspirin, no one could get that out of their mind. As soon as I said that, it was like, boom, off the list."

After eighteen months of beer-fueled brainstorming marathons, the team determined that it could not shuffle the English language skillfully enough to produce the magic moniker, the golden open-sesame word whose very sound would persuade consumers to part with hundreds of dollars.

Clearly, this was a job for professionals. Namely, the squad of linguists at Lexicon, who named Intel's Pentium chip, Oldsmobile's Alero sports coupe, Vibrance shampoo, Slates dress slacks, Embassy Suite Hotels, an osteoporosis drug called Evista, and a sassy clear malt beverage for the younger set. Yes — Zima.

"The process is very simple," said David Placek, Lexicon's chief executive, whose vocal timbre and speech rhythms bear a strong resemblance to Dana Carvey's caricature of George Bush. "You make up some word. Let's say we take a word like zoka. Z-o-k-a, zoka. Now we'll just change one letter in there. We'll change zoka to vaka to loka, and m and n. And we'll show four or five names, all from that similar zoka structure. And we'll tell someone: 'Think about pain relief. Think that you have a headache right now. Now, you can take any one of these for that aspirin. Pick it, whether it's zoka, voka, whatever, pick it.' And then you probe why. What is it? Is it faster? Is it harder?"

"Then we take those same names, and we go to another group of people and say: 'Think about a sports car. I'm going to give you one of these sports cars. Which one are you going to take?' And you probe again as to why. And if you do that with enough people in enough languages, you can begin to identify certain phonetic properties. For example, I can tell you that 'z' is one of the fastest sounds in the alphabet. So if speed would have been the only important thing, we might have ended up with zunos or something like that. I can tell you that the sound of p and b, as in Powerbook, another brand we created, those are very dependable sound properties. So if you're out there with a lightweight portable, one of the underlying requirements will be dependability, reliability. If it drops, will it work again? So those sound properties go to work for you.

"In the case of Nuon, the word starts with an n and it ends with an n," Placek continued.

"That's called consonant harmony. It has a quick start and a quick stop to it. Nuon. And that, we felt, gave it precision. So we started working with that n in front and the n on the back. And we wanted to open it up. O is one of the fullest sounds, so we started experimenting with that. And we took a look at that 'nu' for newness there, which is quite appropriate and convenient, and we took that 'on,' as in interactive, as in playing a game, and we put them together. And interestingly enough, there's a very tiny elementary particle called a muon. And then there's neon, which is this bright gas. And then you also have things like proton and neutron. So we felt that it would deliver performance."

In that respect, Nuon is a phonetic sibling to Xeon, Intel's high-performance workstation chip, which Lexicon also named. "You have a *faster* thing there," Placek explained, emphasizing the linguistic nuance. "You have the x there, pronounced like z, so it's fast. It's got a lot of *power* there. That was about power versus — you can see how Nuon was more interactive, a little subtler, a little more approachable."

And indeed it is. If Nuon were a car, it would be a small, egg-shaped, electric one, a mid-twenty-first-century version of the Dodge Neon, whose name includes an exuberant squeal (eeeeee!!!!) between the friendly edges of beveled n's. It's fun to say. Nnnnnn. Oooooooh. Noodle. It's toothsome. Sounds consumable. It's new!

I'm sold, and Orwell was dead wrong. The language isn't being crushed under the weight of oppression. It is experiencing an algal bloom of new vocabulary. Synthetic words. Words with no history — and no historical baggage. Words that are globally palatable, bred as they are in the petri dish of international market research. Words that make new things, especially technology and pharmaceuticals, seem tasty.

Words that are about pleasure (Viagra), health (Slimfast) and entertainment (Web TV). Words that have no meaning outside the commercial sphere.

Our language, like our food supply, has become a triumph of genetic engineering and synthetic additives. Pehaps a video game machine is the epitome of this process, this shift to a virtual economy and a virtual language. Because video games are a product whose material existence is vestigial: ones and zeroes stored on a disk, for now, until that goes away and they become streams of code on a network: pure experience, purely spatial and kinesthetic and imaginary, and beyond language.

FOCUSING ON CONTENT

1. Herz indicates that the creation of a new name is built on subtle expressions and nuanced impressions. Give some examples of where these characteristics are evident in her description of the naming process as practiced by professionals in the naming business.

2. What is the "idea behind Nuon" (5) as a product? What is Nuon supposed to allow designers and engineers in the electronics industry to do?

3. Herz says that there are certain "'branding considerations'" (6) that need to be taken into account when developing a new name in the consumer electronics business. What are those considerations, as far as Nuon is concerned?

4. In paragraph 7 Herz says that Greg Labrec of VM Labs referred to the search for a name for the new product as a "high-stakes corporate crossword puzzle." In what ways is this true?

5. What process do the linguists at Lexicon use in finding a name for a new product (11)?

FOCUSING ON WRITING

1. In paragraph 6 Herz makes an allusion to lines in Shakespeare's play *Romeo and Juliet* wherein he writes that a rose is a rose and would smell as sweet even if it were called by another name. How does Herz use the allusion, and what does she mean by it? (Glossary: *Allusion*)

2. Comment on Herz's opening paragraph and her last paragraph. How appropriate are they in setting up what she has to say about Nuon? (Glossary: *Beginnings and Endings*)

3. Describe Herz's attitude and tone in this essay. (Glossary: *Attitude* and *Tone*) Does she have respect for the naming process, think it's a bit foolish, or somewhere in between? Does she approach her subject with a formal tone, in a chatty manner, or somewhere in between? Do you think her attitude and tone are appropriate for her topic and audience? (Glossary: *Audience*) Explain.

4. Herz's diction is vibrant and lends a bite to her writing. (Glossary: *Diction*) Use your desk dictionary to determine the meaning of the following words and expressions as Herz uses them in this essay: *patois* (6), *architecture* (7), *moniker* (9), *open-sesame* (9), *timbre* (11), *phonetic* (15), *approachable* (15), *beveled* (16), *algal* (17), *palatable* (17), *kinesthetic* (19).

LANGUAGE IN ACTION

A "sniglet" is a made-up word that refers to a person, place, thing, idea, or an action. A sniglet is a word that doesn't appear in the dictionary but should. For example:

Lactomangulation: Manhandling the "open here" spout on a milk container and rendering it so unusable that one has to revert to the "illegal" side of the container.

Elbonics: The actions of two people maneuvering for one armrest in a movie theater or airplane.

Search the Web for *sniglets* and bring six examples and their definitions to class for discussion. What sniglets can you make up?

WRITING SUGGESTIONS

1. Many product names are chosen for their connotative or suggestive value. (Glossary: *Connotation/Denotation*) For example, the name *Tide* for the detergent suggests the power of ocean tides and the rhythmic surge of cleansing waters; the name *Pride* for the wax suggests how the user will feel after using the product. And the name *Taurus* for the car suggests the strength and durability of a bull. Taking into account what you've learned from Herz's essay, write an essay about how the connotations of brand names enhance the appeal of various products. Base your essay on the brand names in one of the following categories: cosmetics, deodorants, candy, paint, car batteries, motorcycles, fast food sandwiches, greeting cards, disposable diapers, video games, or cat food.

2. Linguist Alleen Pace Nilsen writes, "In what comes close to the kinds of language play that we're accustomed to from poets and punsters, we see how name makers choose combinations of letters that suggest or hint at more than a company can actually promise." In Herz's essay, we see how wordsmiths worked to give VM Labs' latest microchip, the Nuon, a name that implied precision and performance. Write an essay in which you take one of the following positions:

   a. The clever names of products lead most people to expect more of products than they can deliver.

   b. You are not at all deceived by the clever name of products, and you don't think most consumers are.

   c. We are all subconsciously deceived by product names that hint at more than a company can actually promise.

APPENDIX: WRITING A RESEARCH PAPER

The research paper is an important part of a college education and for good reason. In writing such a paper, you acquire a number of indispensable research skills that you can adapt to other college assignments and to situations after graduation.

The real value of writing a research paper, however, goes beyond acquiring basic skills; it is a unique hands-on learning experience. The purpose of a research paper is not to present a collection of quotations that show you can report what others have said about your topic. Rather, your goal is to analyze, evaluate, and synthesize the materials you research — and thereby learn how to do so with any topic. You learn how to view the results of research from your own perspective and arrive at an informed opinion of a topic.

Writing a researched essay is not very different from the other writing you will be doing in your college writing course. You will find yourself drawing heavily on what you have learned in "On Writing Well" (pp. 14–33). First you determine what you want to write about. Then you decide on a purpose, consider your audience, develop a thesis, collect your evidence, write a first draft, revise and edit, and prepare a final copy. What differentiates the researched paper from other kinds of papers is your use of outside sources and how you acknowledge them.

In this chapter you will learn how to choose a research topic; how to pose a worthwhile research question; how to locate and use print and Internet sources; how to evaluate these sources; how to take useful notes; how to summarize, paraphrase, and quote your sources; how to integrate your notes into your paper; how to acknowledge your sources; and how to avoid plagiarism. You will also find extensive guidelines for documenting your essay in MLA (Modern Language Association) style. MLA guidelines are widely accepted by English and foreign-language scholars and teachers, and we encourage their use. Before you begin work on your research paper, your instructor will let you know which style you should follow.

Your library research will involve working with print as well as electronic sources. In both cases, however, the process is essentially the same: Your aim is to select the most appropriate sources for your research from the many that are available on your topic.

CHOOSING A RESEARCH TOPIC AND POSING A WORTHWHILE QUESTION

The first step in the research process — selecting a suitable topic — may be the most important task in the entire project. A clearly focused topic makes researching and writing the paper manageable and the likelihood of finding sound — even exciting — results possible.

Sometimes your instructor will assign a topic or give you a list of topics from which to choose. Be sure that you understand what your instructor is asking for and that the topic you select from the list really interests you. But what happens when you are given the freedom to choose your own topic and nothing comes to mind immediately? Relax. Spend a day or two brainstorming ideas and observing what interests you about the language issues explored in *Language Awareness*. You can start by reviewing the table of contents. Take time to jot down the titles of particular articles or language issues. You can use the Internet and enter a few topic candidates into a search engine and see what results look tantilizing.

Once you have compiled your list of possible language-related research subjects, you will find that one or two of them interest you most. Concentrate your efforts on these. There are some categories of subjects, however, that are best to avoid because they may lead to conclusions that are highly subjective on the one hand or too technical on the other. For example, avoid subjects so recent or so obscure that very little has been published about them anywhere — even on the Internet. Also avoid subjects based almost exclusively on your own experiences, subjects that are highly speculative, and subjects that are too technical for your general audience.

Choosing a Topic

Having settled on a general subject, you now need to limit that subject to a manageable topic. It cannot be emphasized enough that your topic should feel right from the start. Do not select a topic because you think is will be easy to write about — too often, seemingly easy topics are the most difficult to write about because you can't find any room to take a stand or voice your position. Also, do not select a topic because it happens to be popular. Rather, choose a topic that genuinely interests you, one perhaps that you already have an opinion about and want to test. Your topic, in addition, should be manageable, given your time and resources. Finally, if you have any doubts about your topic, consult with your instructor about its suitability for the assignment.

One effective way of focusing on a topic is to make a list of as many specific questions about your subject that come to mind. At the start of his research project, Jake Jamieson, the student who wrote the sample research paper that begins on page 674, chose the *English-only movement* as his subject and compiled the following list of possible *research questions*.

> What social, cultural, or economic conditions in the United States brought about the formation of the English-only movement?
>
> Why has there been no call to make English the "official" language of the United States before the 1990s?
>
> How do non-English-speaking Americans feel about the prospect of being forced to adopt English?
>
> In what ways does the English-only debate illustrate the relationship between language and power?
>
> Do immigrants really need to learn English to assimilate fully into American society?
>
> Do other countries have official languages? Why or why not?
>
> Should immigrants be pushed toward learning English or encouraged to retain their native tongues?
>
> What harm, if any, could result from the passage of English-only legislation?
>
> Is the English-only controversy a political issue, a social issue, an economic issue, or some combination of the three?

Choosing a Research Question

Although each of the above questions narrows the general subject area, suggesting a more manageable research project, some of the questions are more focused than others. For example, the question "Why has there been no call to make English the 'official' language of the United States before the 1990s?" is more focused than "Do other countries have official languages? Why or why not?" Some questions (such as "In what ways does the English-only debate illustrate the relationship between language and power?") are more grounded — less speculative than "Do immigrants really need to learn English to assimilate fully into American society?" And "Is the English-only controversy a political issue, a social issue, an economic issue, or some combination of the three?" is certainly one of the more challenging questions. Your goal is to generate a research question that is *focused, grounded,* and *challenging*.

Simply phrasing your topic as a question may give you a starting point; that is, if you think in terms of answering your research question, you have ownership and a sense of direction for your work from the outset. A one- or two-sentence answer to your research question often provides you with a tentative or preliminary thesis statement.

Jamieson reviewed his list of possible research questions and found that he kept returning to the one about whether immigrants should be pushed to learn English or encouraged to retain their native language. At this point Jamieson was ready to head to the library.

USING PRINT SOURCES

In most cases you should use print sources (books, newspapers, journals, periodicals, encyclopedias, pamphlets, brochures, and government publications) as your primary tools for research. Print sources, unlike many Internet sources, are often reviewed by experts in the field before they are published, are generally overseen by a reputable publishing company or organization, and are examined by editors and fact checkers for accuracy and reliability. Unless you are instructed otherwise, you should try to use print sources in your research.

To find print sources, search through your library's reference works, computer catalog, periodical indexes, and other databases to generate a preliminary listing of books, magazine and newspaper articles, public documents and reports, and other sources that may be helpful in exploring your topic. At this early stage, it is better to err on the side of listing too many sources. Then, later on, you will not have to relocate sources you discarded too hastily.

Preview Print Sources

Although you want to be thorough in your research, you will soon realize that you do not have enough time to read every source you encounter. Rather, you must preview your sources to decide what you will read, what you will skim, and what you will simply eliminate.

QUESTIONS FOR PREVIEWING PRINT SOURCES

1. Is the book or article directly related to your research topic?
2. Is the book or article obviously outdated (for example, a source on language-related brain research that is from the 1970s)?
3. Have you checked tables of contents and indexes in books to locate material that may be important and relevant to your topic?
4. If an article appears to be what you are looking for, have you read the abstract (a summary of the main points of the article, which appears in some journals) or the opening and concluding paragraphs?
5. Is it necessary to quickly read the entire article to be sure that it is relevant?

Develop a Working Bibliography

It is important to develop a working bibliography of the books, articles, and other materials that you think are relevant to your topic. Compiling such a bibliography lets you know at a glance which works you have consulted and the shape your research is taking. A working bibliography also guides you to other materials you may wish to consider. Naturally, you will want to capture early on all the information you need for each work so that you do not have to return to the library at a later time to retrieve publication data for your final bibliography or list of works cited. Accuracy and completeness are, of course, essential at this final stage of the research.

For books, record the following information:

- All authors; any editors or translators
- Title and subtitle
- Edition (if not the first)
- Publication data: city, publishing company, and date
- Call number

For periodical articles, record the following information:

- All authors
- Title and subtitle
- Title of journal, magazine, or newspaper
- Volume and issue numbers
- Date and page numbers

Using correct bibliographic form ensures that your entries are complete, reduces the chance of introducing careless errors, and saves time when you are ready to prepare your final list of works cited. You will find MLA style guidelines for the List of Works Cited on pages 664–70.

Evaluate Print Sources

Before beginning to take notes, you should read your sources and evaluate them for their relevance and reliability in helping you explore your topic. Examine your sources for the writer's main ideas. Pay particular attention to abstracts or introductions, tables of contents, section headings, and indexes. Also, look for information about the authors themselves — information that will help you determine their authority and perspective on the issues.

QUESTIONS FOR EVALUATING PRINT SOURCES

1. Is your source focused on your particular research topic?
2. Is your source too abstract, too general, or too technical for your needs?
3. Does your source build on current thinking and existing research in the field?
4. Does your source promote a particular view, or is it meant to provide balanced coverage of the topic? What biases, if any, does your source exhibit?
5. Is the author of your source an authority on the topic? Do other writers mention the author of your source in their work?

USING INTERNET SOURCES

You will find that Internet sources can be informative and valuable additions to your research. The Internet is especially useful in providing recent data, stories, and reports. For example, you might find a just-published article from a university study or a news story in your local newspaper's online archives. Generally, however, Internet sources should be used along with print sources and not as a replacement for them. Whereas print sources are generally published under the guidance of a publisher or an organization, practically anyone with access to a computer and a modem can put text and pictures onto the Internet; there is often no governing body that checks for content or accuracy. The Internet offers a vast number of useful and carefully maintained resources, but it also contains many bogus facts and much unreliable information. It is your responsibility to evaluate whether or not a given Internet source should be trusted.

Your Internet research will probably produce many more sources than you can reasonably use. By carefully previewing Web sites and other Internet sources, developing a working bibliography of potentially useful ones, and evaluating them for their reliability, you will ensure that you are making the best use of Internet sources in researching your topic.

If you do not know how to access the Internet, or if you need more instruction on conducting Internet searches, you should consult the material on conducting directory and keyword searches on pages 650–55 or go to your on-campus computer center for more information. You can also access the links to Internet information offered by Bedford/St. Martin's at www.bedfordstmartins.com/hacker/resdoc.

Preview Internet Sources

The key to successful Internet research is being able to identify those sites that will help you the most. Answering the following questions will help you weed out sources that hold no promise.

QUESTIONS FOR PREVIEWING INTERNET SOURCES

1. Scan the Web site. Do the contents and links appear to be related to your research topic?
2. Can you identify the author of the site? Are the author's credentials available, and are they appropriate to the content of the site?
3. Has the site been updated within the last six months? It is not always necessary to use updated information, especially if your topic is not a current one and the information about it is fairly stable. Information about the most recent update is usually provided at the bottom of the homepage of the Web site.

If you answer "no" to any of these questions, you should consider eliminating the source from further consideration.

Develop a Working Bibliography

Just as for print sources, you must maintain accurate records for the Internet sources you use. Here is what you need for each source:

- All authors or sponsoring agents
- Title and subtitle of the document
- Title of complete work (if applicable)
- Document date (or date "last modified")
- Date you accessed the site
- Publishing data for print version (if available)
- Address of the site, uniform resource locator (URL), or network path

Evaluate Internet Sources

Because the quality of sources on the Internet varies tremendously, it is important to evaluate the information you find there. Answering the following questions will help you evaluate the sites you have included in your working bibliography.

QUESTIONS FOR EVALUATING WEB SITES

1. *What type of Web site is it?*

   Who sponsors the site? A corporation? An individual? The URL indicates the sponsor of the site. Some common domain names are:

.com	Business/Commercial
.edu	Educational institution
.gov	Government sponsored
.mil	Military
.net	Various types of networks
.org	Nonprofit organization

2. *Who is the authority or author?*

   What individual or company is responsible for the site?

   Can you verify if the site is official, actually sanctioned by an organization or company?

   What are the author's or company's qualifications for writing on this subject?

   Is there a way to verify the legitimacy of this individual or company? Are there links to a homepage or résumé?

3. *What is the site's purpose and audience?*

   What appears to be the author's or sponsor's purpose or motivation?

   Who is the intended audience?

4. *Is the site objective?*

> Are advertising, opinion, and factual information clearly distinguished?

> What biases, if any, can you detect?

5. *How accurate is the site?*

> Is important information documented through links so that it can be verified or corroborated by other sources?

> Is the text well written and free of careless errors in spelling and grammar?

6. *Is the coverage thorough and current?*

> Is there any indication that the site is still under construction?

> For sources with print equivalents, is the Web version more or less extensive than the print version?

> How detailed is the site's treatment of its subject matter?

> Is there any indication of the currency of the information (the date of the last update or a statement regarding frequency of updates)?

7. *Is the site easy to use?*

> Is the design and navigation of the site user-friendly?

> Do all links work, and do they take you to relevant information?

> Can you return to the homepage easily?

> Are the graphics helpful, or are they simply window dressing?

INTERNET RESEARCH: SUBJECT DIRECTORIES AND KEYWORD SEARCHES

Using Subject Directories to Refine Your Research Topic

Subject directories make it easy to browse various subjects and topics, a big help if you are undecided about your exact research question, or if you want to see if there is enough material on the Web to supplement your research work with print sources. Often the most efficient approach to Web research is to start with the subject directories provided by most search engines. Once you choose a subject area in the directory, you can narrow the subject directories and eventually arrive at a list of sites closely related to your topic.

Suppose you want to research journalists and the language of reporting in America, and you are using the search engine Google (www.google.com). Following is the Web Directory screen where you would start your search. Your first task is to choose, from the sixteen categories of topics listed, the subject category most likely to contain information about journalists and their language. Remember that just as you browse through tables of contents and indexes of books on a subject to uncover three or four sources that will be most useful to you, more than one general subject category in a Web directory may seem appropriate.

The most common question students have at this stage is, *How can I tell if I'm looking in the right place?* If more than one subject category sounds plausible, you will have to look at each of their subdirectories, using logic and the process of elimination to determine which one is likely to produce the best listings for your topic. In most cases, it doesn't take long — usually just one or two clicks — to figure out whether you are searching in the right subject area. If you click on a subject category and none of the topics listed in its subdirectories seems to pertain remotely to your research topic, try a different subject area. Given the general subject "the language of journalists," the most logical category is "News." Click on this subject category and you will see a screen that lists twenty-three more subject categories, including one, "Media," for which there are 1,951 Web sites listed. Chances are good that some of those sites will address your subject.

When you click on "Media," you bring up a screen listing categories of sites related to media.

Because you are interested in journalists, the "Journalism" category, which lists 1,601 Web sites, is a natural starting point. Click on this link to find a number of subdirectory categories, including one for "Issues," a promising heading that could lead to hot topics or debates in the world of journalism. Click on "Issues," and you arrive at a screen that lists a number of interesting and controversial issues in journalism.

Click on "Bias and Balance" and you arrive at a screen that lists potentially valuable Web sites that provide good overviews of media bias in reporting.

Using Keyword Searches to Find Specific Information

When you type in a keyword in the "Search" box on a search engine's homepage, the search engine looks for Web sites that match your term. One problem with keyword searches is that they can produce tens of thousands of matches, making it difficult to locate sites of immediate value. For that reason, make your keywords specific, and make sure that you are spelling them correctly. It is a good idea to consult help screens or advanced search instructions before initiating a keyword search. Once you start a search, you may want to narrow or broaden it depending on the number of hits, or matches, you get.

Refining Keyword Searches on the Web

While some variation in command terms and characters exists among electronic databases and popular search engines, the following functions are almost universally accepted. If you have a particular question about refining your keyword search, seek assistance by clicking on "Help" or "Advanced Search."

(continued)

> • Use quotation marks or parentheses to indicate that you are searching for words in exact sequence — e.g., "whooping cough"; (Supreme Court).
> • Use AND or a plus sign (+) between words to narrow your search by specifying that all words need to appear in a document — e.g., tobacco AND cancer; Shakespeare + sonnet.
> • Use NOT or a minus sign (−) between words to narrow your search by eliminating unwanted words — e.g., monopoly NOT game; cowboys − Dallas.
> • Use an asterisk (*) to indicate that you will accept variations of a term — e.g., "food label*."

When using a keyword search, you need to be careful about selecting the keywords that will yield the best results. If your word or words are too general, your results can be at best unwieldy and at worst not usable at all. During her initial search for her paper on bilingual education, student Erin O'Neill typed in "bilingual education." To her surprise, this produced approximately 321,000 hits.

After thinking about how to narrow her search, O'Neill decided to type in "bilingual education" + Spanish. This search yielded a far more manageable 158 hits.

Among these hits, she located Web sites that presented arguments both for and against bilingual education in largely Hispanic areas. These sites provided a perfect starting point for O'Neill. Equipped with a basic understanding of the pro and con positions, she was prepared to research additional studies of bilingual education and develop her own position on the issue.

TAKING NOTES

As you gather and sort your source materials, you'll want to record the information that you consider most pertinent to your topic. As you read, take notes. You're looking for ideas, facts, opinions, statistics, examples, and other evidence that you think will be useful in writing your paper. As you work through books and articles, look for recurring themes and notice where writers are in agreement and where they differ. Try to remember that the effectiveness of your paper is largely determined by the quality — not necessarily the quantity — of your notes. You will want to analyze, evaluate, and synthesize the information you collect to use it for your own purpose.

Now for some practical advice on taking notes: First, be systematic in your note-taking. As a rule, write one note on a card and include the author's full name, the complete title of the source, and a page number indicating the origin of the note. Use cards of uniform size, preferably 4 × 6-inch cards because they are large enough to accommodate even a long note on a single card and yet small enough to be easily handled and conveniently carried. Following this system will also help you when you get to the planning and writing stage because you will be able to sequence your notes according to the plan you have envisioned for your paper. Furthermore, should you decide to alter your organizational plan, you can easily reorder your cards to reflect your revisions. You can, of course, do note-taking on your computer as well, which makes it easy for you to reorder your notes. An added advantage of the computer is that the Copy and Paste features let you move notes and their citations directly into your essay.

Second, try not to take too many notes. One good way to control your note-taking is to ask yourself, "How exactly does this material help prove or disprove my thesis?" Try to envision where in your paper you could use the information. If it does not seem relevant to your thesis, don't bother to take a note. Once you decide to take a note, you must decide whether to summarize, paraphrase, or quote directly. The approach you take should be determined by the content of the passage and the way you plan to use it in your paper.

Summary

When you *summarize* material from one of your sources, you capture in condensed form the essential idea of a passage, article, or entire chapter. Summaries are particularly useful when you are working with lengthy, detailed arguments or long passages of narrative or descriptive background information in which the details are not germane to the overall thrust of your paper. You simply want to capture the essence of the passage because you are confident that your readers will readily understand the point being made or do not need to be convinced about its validity. Because you are distilling information, a summary is always shorter than the original; often a chapter or more can be reduced to a paragraph, or several paragraphs to a sentence or two. Remember, in writing a summary you should use your own words.

Consider the following paragraphs in which Gordon Allport discusses the prejudicial power of the labels humans use to describe one another.

> Some labels, such as "blind man," are exceedingly salient and powerful. They tend to prevent alternative classification, or even cross-classification. Ethnic labels are often of this type, particularly if they refer to some highly visible feature, e.g., Negro, Oriental. They resemble the labels that point to some outstanding incapacity — *feeble-minded, cripple, blind man.* Let us call such symbols "labels of primary potency." These symbols act like shrieking sirens, deafening us to all finer discriminations that we might otherwise perceive. Even though the blindness of one man and the darkness of pigmentation of another may be defining attributes for some purposes, they are irrelevant and "noisy" for others.

Most people are unaware of this basic law of language — that every label applied to a given person refers properly only to one aspect of his nature. You may correctly say that a certain man is *human, a philanthropist, a Chinese, a physician, an athlete*. A given person may be all of these; but the chances are that *Chinese* stands out in your mind as the symbol of primary potency. Yet neither this nor any other classificatory label can refer to the whole of a man's nature. (Only his proper name can do so.)

—GORDON ALLPORT, *"The Language of Prejudice,"* P. 218

A student wishing to capture the gist of Allport's point without repeating his detailed explanation wrote the following summary·

SUMMARY NOTE

Labels of primacy potency
Allport warns about the dangers of using labels — especially ethnic labels — because of their power to distort our perceptions of other human beings.

Allport, 218

Paraphrase

When you *paraphrase* material from a source, you restate the information in your own words instead of quoting directly. Unlike a summary, which gives a brief overview of the essential information in the original, a paraphrase seeks to maintain the same level of detail as the original to aid readers in understanding or believing the information presented. A paraphrase presents the original information in approximately the same number of words, but in your own wording. To put it another way, your paraphrase should closely parallel the presentation of ideas in the original, but it should not use the same words or sentence structure as the original. Even though you are using your own words in a paraphrase, it's important to remember that you are borrowing ideas and therefore must acknowledge the source of these ideas with a citation.

How would you paraphrase the following passage from "Selection, Slanting, and Charged Language" by Newman P. and Genevieve B. Birk, which appears on pages 351–59 of this text?

When we put our knowledge into words, a second process of selection, the process of slanting, takes place. Just as there is something, a rather mysterious principle of selection, which chooses for us what we will notice, and what will then become our knowledge, there is also a principle which operates, with or without our awareness, to select certain facts and feelings from our store of knowledge, and to choose the words and the emphasis that we shall use to communicate our meaning.

The following note illustrates how a student paraphrased the passage:

PARAPHRASE NOTE

> Every time we communicate information and ideas, we engage in a secondary process known as slanting. An even earlier selection process, that of acquiring knowledge, remains something of a mystery because who can say why we notice what we do and why it becomes a part of what we know. Slanting, a conscious or subconscious process, further selects the facts and emotions we convey; it finds not only the words we use but also the way we emphasize them when we communicate.
>
> Newman P. Birk, Genevieve B. Birk, "Selection, Slanting and Charged Language," 352–53

It is important to note how carefully the student captures the essence of the Birks' ideas in her own words as well as her own sentence structure.

In most cases it is better to summarize or paraphrase material — which by definition means using your own words — instead of quoting verbatim (word for word). Capturing an idea in your own words ensures that you have thought about and understood what your source is saying. (Note that for passages from essays in *Language Awareness*, page numbers refer to this text.)

Direct Quotation

To quote a source directly, copy the exact words of your source, putting all quoted material in quotation marks. When you take a quotation note, check the passage carefully for accuracy, including punctuation and capitalization. Be selective about what you choose to quote; reserve direct quotation for important ideas stated memorably, for especially clear explanations by authorities, and for arguments by proponents of a particular position in their own words.

Consider, for example, the following passage from William Zinsser's "Simplicity," on page 98 included in this text, emphasizing the importance — and current rarity — of clear, concise writing:

QUOTATION NOTE

> "Clutter is the disease of American writing. We are a society strangling in unnecessary words, circular constructions, pompous frills, and meaningless jargon."
>
> William Zinsser, "Simplicity," 98

On occasion you'll find a useful passage with some memorable wording in it. Avoid the temptation to quote the whole passage; instead, try combining summary or paraphrase with direct quotation.

Consider the following paragraph from Martin Luther King Jr.'s "I Have a Dream" speech, which appears on pages 244–47 of this text.

> Five score years ago, a great American, in whose symbolic shadow we stand today, signed the Emancipation Proclamation. This momentous decree came as a great beacon light of hope to millions of Negro slaves who had been seared in the flames of withering injustice. It came as a joyous daybreak to end the long night of their captivity. But one hundred years later, the Negro still is not free. One hundred years later, the life of the Negro is still sadly crippled by the manacles of segregation and the chains of discrimination. One hundred years later, the Negro lives on a lonely island of poverty in the midst of a vast ocean of material prosperity. One hundred years later, the Negro is still anguished in the corners of American society and finds himself in exile in his own land. And so we have come here today to dramatize a shameful condition.

Notice how the student in taking the following note was careful to put quotation marks around all the words that were borrowed directly.

QUOTATION AND SUMMARY NOTE

> According to MLK, the promise of the Emancipation Proclamation has not been fulfilled. "One hundred years later, the Negro is still anguished in the corners of American society and finds himself in exile in his own land."
>
> Martin Luther King Jr., "I Have a Dream," 244

Notes from Internet Sources

Working from the computer screen or from a printout, you can take notes just as you would from print sources. You will need to decide whether to summarize, paraphrase, or quote directly the information you wish to borrow. The medium of the Internet has an added advantage. An easy and accurate technique for capturing passages of text from the Internet is to copy the material into a separate computer file on your hard drive or diskette. In Netscape, for example, you can use your mouse to highlight the portion of the text you want to save and then use the Copy and Paste features to add it to your file of research notes. You can also use the same commands to capture the bibliographic information you will need later.

INTEGRATING BORROWED MATERIAL INTO YOUR TEXT

Being familiar with the material in your notes will help you decide how to integrate it into your drafts. Though it is not necessary to use all of your notes, nor to use them all at once in your first draft, you do need to know which ones support your thesis, extend your ideas, offer better wording of your ideas, and reveal the opinions of noted authorities. Occasionally you will want to use notes that include ideas contrary to your own so that you can rebut them in your own argument. Once you have analyzed all of your notes, you may even alter your thesis slightly in light of the information and ideas you have found.

Whenever you want to use borrowed material, be it a summary, paraphrase, or quotation, it's best to introduce the material with a *signal phrase* — a phrase that alerts the reader that borrowed information is to follow. A signal phrase usually consists of the author's name and a verb. Well-chosen signal phrases help you integrate quotations, paraphrases, and summaries into the flow of your paper. Besides, signal phrases let your reader know who is speaking and, in the case of summaries and paraphrases, exactly where your ideas end and someone else's begin. Never confuse your reader with a quotation that appears suddenly without introduction. Unannounced quotations leave your reader wondering how the quoted material relates to the point you are trying to make. Look at the following example. The quotation is from Rita Dove's essay "Loose Ends," which appears on pages 98–99 of her 1995 book *The Poet's World*.

UNANNOUNCED QUOTATION

Television, it could be argued, presents life in tidy, almost predictable 30- and 60-minute packages. As any episode of Friends or West Wing or Law and Order demonstrates, life on television, though exciting, is relatively easy to follow. Humor, simultaneous action, and special effects cannot overshadow the fact that each show has a beginning, a middle, and an end. "Life [. . .] is ragged. Loose ends are the rule" (Dove 99). For many Americans, television provides an escape from their monotonous day-to-day lives.

In the following rewrite, the student writer has integrated the quotation into the text not only by means of a signal phrase, but in a number of other ways as well. By giving the name of the writer being quoted, referring to that writer's credentials, and noting that the writer is arguing for a difference she sees between television life and real life, the student provides more context so that the reader can better understand how the quotation fits into the discussion.

INTEGRATED QUOTATION

Television, it could be argued, presents life in tidy, almost predictable 30- and 60-minute packages. As any episode of Friends or West Wing or Law and Order demonstrates, life on television, though exciting, is relatively easy to follow. Humor, simultaneous action, and special effects do not overshadow the fact that each show has a beginning, a middle, and an end. In contrast, real "life," argues Pulitzer Prize–winning poet and university professor Rita Dove, "is ragged. Loose ends are the rule" (99). For many Americans, television provides an escape from their monotonous day-to-day lives.

How well you integrate a quote, paraphrase, or summary into your paper depends partly on varying your signal phrases and, in particular, choosing a verb for the signal phrase that accurately conveys the tone and intent of the writer you are citing. If a writer is arguing, use the verb *argues* (or *asserts, claims,* or *contends*); if a writer is contesting a particular position or fact, use the verb *contests* (or *denies, disputes, refutes,* or *rejects*). In using verbs that are specific to the situation in your paper, you bring your readers into the intellectual debate and avoid the monotony of such all purpose verbs as *says* or *writes.* Following are just a few examples of how you can vary signal phrases to add precision to your paper:

Malcolm X confesses that . . .
To summarize Deborah Tannen's observations, . . .
Louise Erdrich, popular fiction writer, emphasizes . . .
George Orwell rejects the widely held belief that . . .

Other verbs that you should keep in mind when constructing signal phrases include the following:

acknowledges	declares	points out
adds	endorses	reasons
admits	grants	reports
believes	implies	responds
compares	insists	suggests
confirms		

DOCUMENTING SOURCES

Whenever you summarize, paraphrase, or quote a person's thoughts and ideas, and when you use facts or statistics that are not commonly known or believed, you must properly acknowledge the source of your information. If you do not properly acknowledge ideas and information created by someone else, you are guilty of *plagiarism*, of using someone else's material but making it look as if it were your own. You must document the source of your information whenever you do the following:

- quote a source word-for-word
- refer to information and ideas from another source that you present in your own words as either a paraphrase or a summary
- cite statistics, tables, charts, or graphs

You do not need to document these types of information:

- your own observations, experiences, and ideas
- factual information available in a number of reference works (known as "common knowledge")
- proverbs, sayings, and familiar quotations

A reference to the source of your borrowed information is called a *citation*. There are many systems for making citations, and your citations must consistently follow one of these systems. As noted earlier, the documentation style recommended by the Modern Language Association (MLA) is commonly used in English and the humanities and is the style used throughout this book. Another common system is the American Psychological Association (APA) style, which is generally used in the social sciences. Your instructor will usually tell you which style to use. For more information on documentation styles, consult the appropriate manual or handbook. For MLA style, consult the *MLA Handbook for Writers of Research Papers*, 6th ed. (New York: MLA, 2003). You may also check MLA guidelines on the Internet at www.mla.org.

There are two components of documentation: *in-text citations* are placed in the body of your paper; the *list of works cited* provides complete publication data for your in-text citations and is placed at the end of your paper. Both are necessary for complete documentation.

In-Text Citations

In-text citations, also known as parenthetical citations, give the reader citation information immediately, at the point at which it is most meaningful. Rather than having to turn to a footnote or an endnote, the reader sees the citation as a part of the writer's text.

Most in-text citations consist of only the author's last name and a page reference. Usually the author's name is given in an introductory or signal phrase at the beginning of the borrowed material and the page reference is given in parentheses at the end. If the author's name is not given at the beginning, put it in parentheses along with the page reference. The parenthetical reference signals the end of the borrowed material and directs your readers to the list of works cited should they want to pursue a particular source. Treat electronic sources as you do print sources, keeping in mind that some electronic sources use paragraph numbers instead of page numbers. Consider the following examples of in-text citations.

IN-TEXT CITATION (MLA STYLE)

Every day Americans are bombarded with an assortment of advertising for everything from cars, clothing, and vacations to cosmetics, foods, and over-the-counter medicines. Unless people know how

Citation with author's name in the signal phrase

advertising language works, they are at the mercy of Madison Avenue. Advertisers, as William Lutz asserts, manipulate us with weasel words, words that "appear to say one thing when in fact they say the opposite, or nothing at all" (443). For example, when we hear the word *helps* as in "helps relieve pain," we think "relieves

Citation with author's name in parentheses

pain." Not necessarily true. And to make matters worse, a consumer advocate says, "these unreliable claims require no approval — in practice, that may mean no evidence" (Liebman 469).

The preceding in-text citations should appear as follows in the list of works cited at the end of the essay.

LIST OF WORKS CITED ENTRIES (MLA STYLE)

Liebman, Bonnie. "Crazy Claims: Which Can You Believe?" *Language Awareness.* Ed. Paul Eschholz, Alfred Rosa, and Virginia Clark. 9th ed. Boston: Bedford/St. Martin's, 2004. 463–69.

Lutz, William. "Weasel Words." Language Awareness. Ed. Paul
　　　Eschholz, Alfred Rosa, and Virginia Clark. 9th ed. Boston:
　　　Bedford/St. Martin's, 2004. 442–52.

List of Works Cited

In this section you will find general MLA guidelines for creating a
works cited list followed by sample entries that cover the citation situations you will encounter most often. Make sure that you follow the formats as they appear on the following pages.

GENERAL GUIDELINES

- Begin the list on a new page following the last page of text.
- Organize the list alphabetically by author's last name. If the entry has
  no author name, alphabetize the first major word of the title.
- Double-space within and between entries.
- Begin each entry at the left margin. If the entry is longer than one line,
  indent the second and subsequent lines five spaces or one-half inch.
- Do not number entries.

Books

BOOKS BY ONE AUTHOR

List the author's last name first, followed by a comma and first name.
Underline the title. Follow with the city of publication and a shortened
version of publisher's name — for example, *Houghton* for *Houghton Mifflin*, or *Cambridge UP* for *Cambridge University Press*. End with the date
of publication.

Pinker, Steven. The Language Instinct: How the Mind Creates
　　　Language. New York: Morrow, 1994.

BOOKS BY TWO OR THREE AUTHORS

List the first author (following order on title page) in the same way as
for a single-author book; list subsequent authors first name first in the
order they appear on the title page.

Jones, Charisse, and Kumea Shorter–Gooden. Shifting: The Double
　　　Lives of Black Women in America. New York: HarperCollins,
　　　2003.

BOOKS BY FOUR OR MORE AUTHORS

List the first author in the same way as for a single-author book, followed by a comma and the abbreviation *et al.* ("and others").

Chomsky, Noam, et al. Acts of Aggression. New York: Seven
Stories, 1999.

TWO OR MORE BOOKS BY THE SAME AUTHOR

List two or more books by the same author in alphabetical order by
title. List the first book by the author's name. After the first book, in
place of the author's name substitute three unspaced hyphens followed
by a period.

Lederer, Richard. Anguished English. Charleston: Wyrick, 1987.

--- Crazy English: New York: Pocket Books, 1990.

REVISED EDITION

Aitchison, Jean. Language Change: Process or Decay? 2nd ed.
Cambridge: Cambridge UP, 1991.

EDITED BOOK

Douglass, Frederick. Narrative of the Life of Frederick Douglass,
an American Slave, Written by Himself. Ed. Benjamin
Quarles. Cambridge: Belknap, 1960.

TRANSLATION

Dumas, Alexandre. The Knight of Maison Rouge. Trans. Julie
Rose. New York: Modern Library, 2003.

CORPORATE AUTHOR

The Carnegie Foundation for the Advancement of Teaching.
Campus Life: In Search of Community. Princeton: Princeton
UP, 1990.

MULTIVOLUME WORK

Cassidy, Frederic G., and J. H. Hall, eds. Dictionary of American
Regional English. 3 vols. Cambridge: Harvard UP, 1985.

ANTHOLOGY

Rosa, Alfred, and Paul Eschholz, eds. Language: Readings in
Culture and Language. 6th ed. New York: St. Martin's, 1998.

WORK IN AN ANTHOLOGY

Giovanni, Nikki. "Campus Racism 101." Subjects/Strategies. Ed.
Paul Eschholz and Alfred Rosa. 9th ed. Boston: Bedford/
St. Martin's 2002. 298-301.

SECTION OR CHAPTER IN A BOOK

Lamott, Anne. "Shitty First Drafts." Bird by Bird: Some Instructions on Writing and Life. New York: Pantheon, 1994. 21–27.

Periodicals

ARTICLE IN A JOURNAL WITH CONTINUOUS PAGINATION THROUGHOUT AN ANNUAL VOLUME

Some journals paginate issues continuously, by volume; that is, the page numbers in one issue pick up where the previous issue left off. For these journals, follow the volume number by the date of publication in parentheses.

Gazzaniga, Michael S. "Right Hemisphere Language Following Brain Bisection: A Twenty-Year Perspective." American Psychologist 38 (1983): 528–49.

ARTICLE IN A JOURNAL WITH SEPARATE PAGINATION IN EACH ISSUE

Some journals paginate by issue; each issue begins with page 1. For these journals, follow the volume number with a period and the issue number. Then give the date of publication in parentheses.

Douglas, Ann. "The Failure of the New York Intellectuals."Raritan 17.4 (1998): 1–23.

ARTICLE IN A WEEKLY OR BIWEEKLY MAGAZINE

Keizer, Garret. "Sound and Fury: The Politics of Noise in a Loud Society." Harper's Magazine Mar. 2001: 39–48.

ARTICLE IN A NEWSPAPER

If an article in a newspaper or magazine appears discontinuously — that is, if it starts on one page and skips one or more pages before continuing — include only the first page followed by a plus sign.

Wade, Nicholas. "A Prolific Genghis Khan, It Seems, Helped People the World." New York Times 11 Feb. 2003, late ed.: D3+.

EDITORIAL OR LETTER TO THE EDITOR

Rose, Lowell C. "Public Education's Trojan Horse?" Editorial. Phi Delta Kappan 85.1 (2003): 2.

McEwan, Barbara. Letter. Nature Conservancy 52.4 (2002): 6.

Electronic Sources

The following guidelines and models for citing information retrieved from the Internet and other electronic sources have been
adapted from the most recent advice of the MLA, as detailed in the
MLA Handbook for Writers of Research Papers 6th ed. (2003) and from
the "MLA Style" section on the MLA's Web site www.mla.org. When
listing an electronic source in your list of works cited, include the following elements, if they are available and relevant, in the reference. All elements should be followed by a period with the exception of the date the
site is accessed.

- **Author.**   Write the name of the author, editor, compiler, or translator of the source with the last name first, followed by a comma and
  the first name. If appropriate, follow the name with an abbreviation
  such as *ed.* If no author is given, begin with the title.
- **Title.**   Write the title of the poem, short story, article, essay, or similar short work within a scholarly project, database, or periodical in
  quotation marks. If the source is a posting to a discussion list or
  forum, take the title from the subject line and put it in quotation
  marks, followed by *Online posting*. If you are citing an entire online
  book, the title should be underlined.
- **Editor/translator.**   Add the name of the editor, compiler, or translator of the text if it is relevant and not cited earlier, preceded by the
  appropriate abbreviation, such as *Ed.*
- **Print publication information.**   Give the publication information
  of any print version of the source that the site provides.
- **Electronic publication information.**   Give the title of the scholarly project, database, periodical, or professional or personal site
  (underlined) or, for a professional or personal site with no title, give
  a general description, such as *home page.* Follow the title with the
  name of the editor of the scholarly project or database (if available);
  a version, volume, or any other identifying number of the source
  (if not part of the title); the date of the electronic publication or
  the latest update or posting; the name of the discussion list or
  forum; the number range or total number of pages, paragraphs, or
  other sections, if they are numbered; and finally the name of the institution or organization sponsoring or associated with the Web site,
  if any.
- **Access information.**   The final elements to add are the date when
  you accessed the source and the electronic address, or URL, of the
  source (in angle brackets).

MLA style requires that you break URLs extending over more than
one line only after a slash. Do *not* add spaces, hyphens, or any other
punctuation to indicate the break.

ONLINE BOOK OR PART OF BOOK

Hawthorne, Nathaniel. Twice-Told Tales. Ed. George Parsons Lath-
    rop. Boston: Houghton, 1883. 1 Mar. 2003
    <http://209.11.144.65/eldritchpress/nh/ttt.html>.

Woolf, Virginia. "Kew Gardens." Monday or Tuesday. New York:
    Harcourt, 1921. Bartleby.com: Great Books Online. 28 Feb.
    2004 <http://www.bartleby.com/85/>.

WORK IN A SCHOLARLY PROJECT OR DATABASE

Electrifying the Renaissance: Hypertext, Literature, and the World
    Wide Web. Mar. 1997. U of California, Santa Barbara. 20
    Apr. 2001
    <http://humanitas.ucsb.edu/depts/english/english/
    coursework/rar>.

WORK FROM ONLINE SUBSCRIPTION SERVICE SUCH AS INFOTRAC

McEachern, William Ross. "Teaching and Learning in Bilingual
    Countries: The Examples of Belgium and Canada." Education
    123 (2002): 103. Expanded Academic ASAP Plus. InfoTrac.
    U of Vermont Lib., Burlington. 15 Aug. 2003.

Sanders, Joshunda. "Think Race Doesn't Matter? Listen to Em-
    inem." San Francisco Chronicle 20 July 2003. Lexis-Nexis.
    U of Vermont Lib., Burlington. 14 Nov. 2003.

ARTICLE IN AN ONLINE SCHOLARLY JOURNAL

Rist, Thomas. "Religion, Politics, Revenge: The Dead in Renais-
    sance Drama." Early Modern Literary Studies 9.1 (2003):
    4.1-20. 28 Feb. 2004 <http://www.shu.ac.uk/emls/
    09-1 ristdead.html>.

ARTICLE IN AN ONLINE MAGAZINE

Lamott, Anne. "Because I'm the Mother." Salon.com 4 July 2003.
    10 Sept. 2003 <http://www.salon.com/mwt/col/lamott/
    2003/07/04/church/index.html>.

ARTICLE IN AN ONLINE NEWSPAPER

Morley, Jefferson. "In Schwarzenegger, Online Pundits See Ameri-
    can Delusions, Opportunities." Washington Post 9 Oct. 2003.
    2 Dec. 2003 <http://www.washingtonpost.com/wp-dyn/
    articles/A3065-2003Oct9.html>.

ARTICLE IN AN ONLINE REFERENCE WORK

"Vietnam War." Encyclopedia.com. 2003. The Concise Columbia
      Electronic Encyclopedia. 6th ed. 29 Sept. 2003
      <http://www.encyclopedia.com/html/v/vietnamwl.asp>.

CD-ROM

Shakespeare, William. Macbeth. Ed. A. R. Branmuller. CD-ROM.
      New York: Voyager, 1994.

"Proactive." The Oxford English Dictionary. 2nd ed. CD-ROM.
      Oxford: Oxford UP, 1992.

ELECTRONIC MAIL

Bristow, Amanda. "Re: Gender and Language Issues."
      E-mail to the author. 12 May 2003.

POSTING TO A DISCUSSION LIST

Preston, Dennis R. "Re: Basketball Terms." Online posting. 8 Nov.
      1997. American Dialect Society. 1 Mar. 2001
      <http://www2.et.byu.edu/~lilliek/ads/indes.htm>.

PROFESSIONAL ONLINE SITE

National Organization for Women. 10 Oct. 2003. National
      Organization for Women. 12 Oct. 2003
      <http://www.now.org>.

PERSONAL ONLINE SITE

Rosa, Alfred. English 104: Language Awareness. 22 Mar. 2003.
      9 Nov. 2003 <http://www.uvm.edu/~arosa/1041a.htm>.

Other Sources

TELEVISION OR RADIO PROGRAM

The American Experience: Chicago 1968. Writ. Chana Gazit. Narr.
      W. S. Merwin. PBS. WNET, New York, 13 Nov. 1997.

MOVIE, VIDEOTAPE, RECORD, OR SLIDE PROGRAM

The X Files. Dir. Rob Bowman. Perf. David Duchovny, Gillian
      Anderson, Martin Landau, Blythe Danner, and Armin
      Mueller-Stahl. Twentieth Century Fox, 1998.

An Oral Historian's Work. With Edward D. Ives. Videocassette.
      Northeast Archives of Folklore and Oral History, 1987.

PERSONAL INTERVIEW

Losambe, Lokangaka. Personal interview. 16 Jan. 2004.

PUBLIC PRESENTATION OR CLASS LECTURE

Hayford, Helen. "Robert Frost and the Language of New England."
    Class lecture. English 160: Regional Literature. Johnson
    State Coll., Johnson, VT. 20 Feb. 2003.

CARTOON

Smaller, Barbara. Cartoon. New Yorker 31 Mar. 2003: 50.

MAP OR CHART

Maine Map and Guide. Map. Yarmouth: Delorme, 2003.

ADVERTISEMENT

Verizon Wireless. Advertisement. Newsweek 6 Oct. 2003: 40.

TAKING STEPS TO AVOID PLAGIARISM

The importance of honesty and accuracy in doing library research cannot be stressed enough. Any material borrowed word for word must be placed within quotation marks and be properly cited: any idea, explanation, or argument you have paraphrased or summarized must be documented, and it must be clear where the paraphrased material begins and ends. In short, to use someone else's ideas, whether in their original or altered form, without proper acknowledgment, is to be guilty of plagiarism. The Council of Writing Program Administrators offers the following helpful definition of plagiarism in academic settings for administrators, faculty, and students: "In an instructional setting, plagiarism occurs when a writer deliberately uses someone else's language, ideas, or other (not common-knowledge) material without acknowledging its source." And accusations of plagiarism can be substantiated even if plagiarism is accidental. A little attention and effort at the note-taking stage can help to eliminate the possibility of inadvertent plagiarism. Check all direct quotations against the wording of the original, and double-check your paraphrases to be sure that you have not used the writer's wording or sentence structure. It is easy to forget to put quotation marks around material taken verbatim, or to use the same sentence structure and most of the same words — substituting a synonym here and there — and record it as a paraphrase. In working closely with the ideas and words of others, intellectual honesty demands that we distinguish between what we borrow — acknowledging it in a citation — and what is our own.

While writing your paper, be careful whenever you incorporate one of your notes into your paper. Make sure that you put quotation marks around material taken verbatim, and double-check your text against your note card — or, better yet, against the original if you have it — to make sure that your quotation is accurate. When paraphrasing or summarizing, make sure you have not inadvertently borrowed key words or sentence structures from the original.

Using Quotation Marks for Language Borrowed Directly

When you use another person's exact words or sentences, you must enclose the borrowed language in quotation marks. Without quotation marks, you give your reader the impression that the wording is your own. Even if you cite the source, you are guilty of plagiarism if you fail to use quotation marks. The following example demonstrates both plagiarism and a correct citation for a direct quotation.

ORIGINAL SOURCE

In the last decade, Standards departments have become more tolerant of sex and foul language, but they have cracked down on violence and become more insistent about the politically correct presentation of minorities. Lately, however, they seem to be swinging wildly back and forth between allowing everything and allowing nothing.

–TAD FRIEND, *"You Can't Say That: The Networks Play Word Games,"*
P. 374

PLAGIARISM

In the last decade, Standards departments have become more tolerant of sex and foul language, but, according to social commentator Tad Friend, they have cracked down on violence and become more insistent about the politically correct presentation of minorities. Lately, however, they seem to be swinging wildly back and forth between allowing everything and allowing nothing.

CORRECT CITATION OF BORROWED WORDS IN QUOTATION MARKS

"In the last decade, Standards departments have become more tolerant of sex and foul language, but," according to social commentator Tad Friend, "they have cracked down on violence and become more insistent about the politically correct presentation of minorities. Lately, however, they seem to be swinging wildly back and forth between allowing everything and allowing nothing" (374).

Using Your Own Words

When summarizing or paraphrasing a source, you must use your own language. Pay particular attention to word choice and word order, especially if you are paraphrasing. Remember, it is not enough simply to use a synonym here or there and think you have paraphrased the source; you *must* restate the idea(s) from the original in your own words, using your own style and sentence structure. In the following example, notice how plagiarism can occur when care is not taken in the wording or sentence structure of a paraphrase. Notice that in the acceptable paraphrase, the student writer uses her own language and sentence structure.

ORIGINAL SOURCE

Punctuation, one is taught, has a point: to keep up law and order. Punctuation marks are the road signs placed along the highway of our communications — to control speeds, provide directions, and prevent head-on collisions. A period has the unblinking finality of a red light; the comma is a flashing yellow light that asks us only to slow down; and the semicolon is a stop sign that tells us to ease gradually to a halt, before gradually starting up again.
                    —PICO IYER, "*In Praise of the Humble Comma*," p. 112

UNACCEPTABLY CLOSE WORDING

According to Iyer, the point of punctuation is to keep a sense of order. Like road signs, punctuation marks are placed in our written communications. We use these punctuation marks to control pace, give direction, and prevent serious accidents. For example, a period can be compared to the finality of a red traffic light. The comma, on the other hand, functions like a flashing yellow light, cautioning to slow down or pause. And the semicolon acts as a stop sign, telling us to come to rest before proceeding (112).

UNACCEPTABLY CLOSE SENTENCE STRUCTURE

Iyer believes that punctuation, we learn in school, has a purpose: to give meaning and structure to our writing. Marks of punctuation can be likened to traffic signs along the roads we all travel — signs that dictate speed, give directions, and prevent accidents. For example, a period, like a red traffic light, brings readers to a total stop; the comma, like a flashing yellow light, tells readers to move ahead slowly with caution; and the semicolon, like a stop sign, tells readers to come to a complete stop before moving ahead (112).

ACCEPTABLE PARAPHRASE

Iyer believes that punctuation is meaningful, that it provides order to our writing. People can more easily understand the meaning conveyed by marks of punctuation by thinking of them in terms of road signs that help readers navigate the streets and highways of our writing. A period, for example, has the force of a red light; it signals the reader to stop and wait. The comma, like a flashing yellow, tells readers to proceed slowly with caution. And the semicolon, like a stop sign, directs readers to come to a complete stop before moving on (112).

Preventing Plagiarism

Questions to Ask about Direct Quotations

- Do quotation marks clearly indicate the language that I borrowed verbatim?
- Is the language of the quotation accurate, with no missing or misquoted words or phrases?
- Do the brackets or ellipsis marks clearly indicate any changes or omissions I have introduced?
- Does a signal phrase naming the author introduce each quotation? Does the verb in the signal phrase help establish a context for each quotation?
- Does a parenthetical page citation follow each quotation?

Questions to Ask about Summaries and Paraphrases

- Is each summary and paraphrase written in my own words and style?
- Does each summary and paraphrase accurately represent the opinion, position, or reasoning of the original writer?
- Does each summary and paraphrase start with a signal phrase so that readers know where my borrowed material begins?
- Does each summary and paraphrase conclude with a parenthetical page citation?

Questions to Ask about Facts and Statistics

- Do I use a signal phrase or some other marker to introduce each fact or statistic that is not common knowledge so that readers know where the borrowed material begins?
- Is each fact or statistic that is not common knowledge clearly documented with a parenthetical page citation?

Finally, as you proofread your final draft, check your citations one last time. If at any time while you are taking notes or writing your paper you have a question about plagiarism, consult your instructor for clarification and guidance before proceeding.

WRITING FROM RESEARCH:
AN ANNOTATED STUDENT ESSAY

Each semester in our "Language Awareness" course at the University of Vermont, we ask students to write papers in which they take a position on a language issue. One student, Jake Jamieson, decided to write on the English-only movement, and what follows is his essay. To help you get more out of Jake's essay, we have provided Jake's comments about his writing process and our annotations pointing out the composition strategies he used.

Why did I choose this topic? I chose this topic on which to do my paper because it is an aspect of speech that I had not previously explored, and my interest was piqued when I heard Professor Rosa speak of it during class. I have done research before on aspects of free speech and people who are attempting to restrict it, but I had never really looked into this issue. After doing some reading on the subject, I realized that it absolutely intrigued me, from the prospect of banning languages other than English right down to the question of funding for bilingualism. It is hard for me to believe that this type of legislation can be construed as helpful and inclusive, when it is merely showcasing ignorance and fear of what is different. It is an outright lie to say that this kind of legislation is intended to include immigrants. In actuality, all it is doing is driving a wedge between immigrants and "mainstream" society, forcing the immigrants to choose between their heritage and their newfound home.

The English-Only Movement: Can America
Proscribe Language with a Clean Conscience?
Jake Jamieson

Melting pot debate announced
A common conception among many people in this country is that the United States is a giant cultural "melting pot." For these people, the melting pot is a place where people from other places come together and bathe in the warm waters of assimilation. For many others, however, the melting pot analogy doesn't work. They see the melting pot as a giant cauldron into which immigrants are placed; here their cultures, values, and backgrounds are boiled away in the scalding waters of discrimination.

Asks question to be answered in paper
One major point of contention in this debate is language: Should immigrants be pushed toward learning English or encouraged to retain their native tongues?

I chose the melting pot analogy in this paragraph because I liked the way in which I was able to turn its normal, comfortable meaning on its head. The connotation was changed from something that was acceptable and even desirable to something that was frightening and even oppressive, which is how I see the melting pot.

Those who argue that the melting pot analogy is valid believe that people who come to America do so willingly and should be expected to become a part of its culture instead of hanging on to their past. For them, the expectation that people who come to this country celebrate this country's holidays, dress as we do, embrace our values, and most importantly speak our language is not unreasonable. They believe that assimilation offers the only way for everyone in this country to live together in harmony and the only way to dissipate the tensions that inevitably arise when cultures clash. A major problem with this argument, however, is that no one seems to be able to agree on what exactly constitutes "our way" of doing things.

I definitely chose a side in this paragraph, but I tried to do so fairly subtly. Even though I was trying to be persuasive in this paper, I did not just come out and say "English-only legislation is stupid." Instead, what I did was describe the opinion to which I am opposed, and then pulled the rug out from under it a bit by stating that there was no objective way to decide what "our way" of living is.

Defines English as the official language

Not everyone in America is of the same religious persuasion or has the exact same set of values, and different people affect vastly different styles of dress. There are so many sets of variables that it would be hard to defend the argument that there is only one culture in the United States. What seems to be the most widespread constant in our country is that much of the population speaks English, and a major movement is being staged in favor of making English the official language. Making English America's official language would, according to William F. Buckley, involve making it the only language in which government business can be conducted on any level, from federal dealings right down to the local level (71). Many reasons are given to support the notion that making English the official language is a good idea and that it is exactly what this country needs, especially in the face of growing multilingualism. Indeed, one Los Angeles school recently documented sixty different languages spoken in the homes of its students (National Education Association, par. 4).

Use of in-test MLA citation format which includes introductory signal phrase and parenthetical page number

There were many reasons given for supporting official English, and I state some of them in the next paragraph. It was hard to choose only a few of these reasons. I paged through my research notes and the articles I had and noted those that made me raise an eyebrow or throw up my hands in frustration. These, I decided, were the examples I would use.

Introduces
English-only
position

Supporters of English-only contend that all government communication must be in English. Because communication is absolutely necessary for a democracy to survive, they believe that the only way to insure the existence of our nation is to make sure a common language exists. Making English official would insure that all government business from ballots to official forms to judicial hearings would have to be conducted in English. According to former senator and presidential candidate Bob Dole, "Promoting English as our national language is not an act of hostility but a welcoming act of inclusion." He goes on to state that while immigrants are encouraged to continue speaking their native languages, "thousands of children [are] failing to learn the language, English, that is the ticket to the 'American Dream.'" (qtd. in Donegan 52).

I found Mr. Dole's comment in an article I read during my research. It seemed to exemplify the exact opinion that I was railing against. His name recognition helps to emphasize the pervasiveness of such thinking.

Introduces
anti-English-
only position

For those who do not subscribe to this way of thinking, however, this type of legislation is anything but the "welcoming act of inclusion" that it is described to be. For them, anyone attempting to regulate language is treading dangerously close to the First Amendment and must have a hidden agenda of some type. Why, it is asked, make a language official when it is already firmly entrenched and widely used in this country and, according to the United States General Accounting Office statistics, 99.96 percent of all federal documents are already in English without legislation to mandate it (Underwood, par. 2)? According to author James Crawford, the answer is quite plain: discrimination. He states that "it is certainly more respectable to discriminate by language than by race." He points out that "most people are not sensitive to language discrimination in this nation, so it is easy to argue that you're doing someone a favor by making them speak English" (qtd. in Donegan 51). English-only legislation has been described as bigoted, anti-immigrant, mean-spirited, and steeped in nativism by those who oppose it, and some go so far as to say that this type of legislation will not foster better communication as is the claim, but will instead encourage a "fear of being subsumed by a growing 'foreignness' in our midst" (Underwood, "At Issue," 65).

The main reason that I waited before introducing the viewpoint with which I obviously agree is simple: I'm bloodthirsty. I like to set up the opposition, examine it for a moment, and then cut it off at the knees. I have found that this technique has worked for me in many situations in which I was trying to write subjectively or persuasively. I then explain the opinion I endorse, discuss it, and then bring in facts that support it much more strongly and try to win over the reader. I have found it to be a more effective technique than coming on strong with my own opinion from the outset.

Uses example to question English-only position that speaking Spanish in the home is abusive

For example, when a judge in Texas ruled that a mother was abusing her five-year-old girl by speaking to her only in Spanish, an uproar ensued. This ruling was accompanied by the statement that by talking to her in a language other than English, she was "abusing that child and . . . relegating her to the position of house maid." This statement was condemned by the National Association for Bilingual Education (NABE) for "labeling the Spanish language as abuse." The judge, Samuel C. Kiser, subsequently apologized to the housekeepers of the nation, adding that he held them "in the highest esteem," but stood firm on his ruling (qtd. in Donegan 51). One might notice that he went out of his way to apologize to the housekeepers he might have offended but saw no need to apologize to the hundreds of thousands of Spanish speakers whose language had just been belittled in a nationally publicized case.

Every time I mentioned this case to someone, they would roll their eyes and groan. Even people who do not agree with my stand on this topic agree with the fact that this judge was out of line.

Argues against the English-only idea of multilingualism as irrational

This tendency of official-English proponents to put down other languages is one that shows up again and again, even though it is maintained that they have nothing against other languages or the people who speak them. If there is no malice toward other languages, why is the use of any language other than English tantamount to lunacy according to an almost constant barrage of literature and editorial opinions? In an article about the "New Year's Resolutions" of various conservative organizations, a group called U.S. English, Inc. stated that the U.S. government was not doing its job of convincing immigrants that they "must learn English to succeed in this country." Instead, according to this publication, "in a bewildering display of irrationality, the U.S. government makes it possible to vote, file a tax return, get married, obtain a driver's license, and become a U.S. citizen in many languages" (Moore 46).

As I stated earlier, I chose my examples based on the reactions they bring up in myself and the people I share them with. This quote by U.S. English actually made my stomach churn because the connotation is that those who speak other languages are undeserving of such things as being able to vote or get a driver's license, or even stay in this country.

Asks rhetorical questions

Now, according to this mindset, not only is speaking any language other than English abusive, but it is also irrational and bewildering. What is this world coming to when people want to speak and make transactions in their native language? Why do they refuse to change and become more like us? Why can immigrants not see that speaking English is right and anything else is wrong? These and many other questions are implied by official-English proponents as they discuss the issue.

I have always enjoyed using these kinds of rhetorical questions, and I was excited when I got a chance to sneak them into this paper, lampooning the air of superiority and unwillingness to accept differences that seem to fill the English-only viewpoint.

Points to growing popularity of English-only position

Conservative attorney David Price wrote that official-English legislation is a good idea because many English-speaking Americans prefer "out of pride and convenience to speak their native language on the job" (13). Not only does this statement imply that the pride and convenience of non-English-speaking Americans is unimportant, but that their native tongues are not as important as English. The scariest prospect of all is that this opinion is quickly gaining popularity all around the country.

In this paragraph, I wanted to show the only convenience on the minds of English-only proponents was their own and that of people like them. The fact that this opinion can be couched in terms that make it seem like a favor is being done for non-English speakers blows my mind.

Presents status report of English-only legislation

As of early 1996, six official-English bills and one amendment to the Constitution have been proposed in the House and Senate. There are twenty-two states, including Alabama, California, and Arizona, that have made English their official language, and more are debating it every day (Donegan 52). An especially disturbing fact about this debate is that official-English laws always seem to be linked to other anti-immigrant legislation, such as proposals to "limit immigration and restrict government benefits to immigrants" ("English-Only Law Faces Test" 1).

As I was writing this paper, it seemed that this topic showed up everywhere I turned. It came up in many of my classes. There were endless stories about it on the evening news. I have found that the best way to research for something like this is not just to pore over books and articles, but also watch the news and have discussions with people, and see what can be found out about it in other ways. This paragraph was the only place that I used facts and figures to state exactly what was happening around the country instead of just speaking of the entire issue on more general terms. I actually wish that I had spent more time with this information because I think that it might have made this part of the paper more convincing.

Concludes that English-only legislation is not in our best interest

Although official-English proponents maintain that their bid for language legislation is in the best interest of immigrants, the facts tend to show otherwise. A decision has to be made in this country about what kind of message we will send to the rest of the world. Do we plan to allow everyone in this country the freedom of speech that we profess to cherish, or will we decide to reserve it only for those who speak the same language as we do? Will we hold firm to our belief that everyone is deserving of life, liberty, and the pursuit of happiness in this country? Or will we show the world that we believe in these things only when they pertain to ourselves and people like us?

This may seem self-evident, but I have always felt that the two most important things about a paper are the opening and closing paragraphs. The other stuff in the middle is important as well, of course, but I think that the opening paragraph is necessary to draw readers in, and the closing paragraph is needed to give the reader a sense of closure. I like my closing paragraph, and I hope that it brought my closing point across effectively.

Works Cited

Follows MLA citation guidelines

Buckley, William F. "Se Hable Ingles: English as the Official American Language." National Review 9 Oct. 1995: 70–71.

Donegan, Craig. "Debate over Bilingualism: Should English Be the Nation's Official Language?" CQ Researcher 19 Jan. 1996: 51–71.

"English-Only Law Faces Test." Burlington Free Press 26 Mar. 1996: 1.

Moore, Stephen, et al. "New Year's Resolutions." National Review 29 Jan. 1996: 46–48.

Mujica, Mauro, E. "At Issue: Should English Be the Official Language of the United States?" CQ Researcher 19 Jan. 1996: 65.

National Education Association. "NEA Statement on the Debate over English Only." Teacher's College, U of Nebraska, Lincoln. 27 Sept. 1999 <http://www.tc.unl.edu/enemeth/biling/engonly.html>.

Price, David. "English-Only Rules: EEOC Has Gone Too Far." USA Today 28 Mar. 1996, final ed.: A13.

Underwood, Robert A. "At Issue: Should English Be the Official Language ofthe United States? CQ Researcher 19 Jan. 1996: 65."

---. "English-Only Legislation." U.S. House of Representatives, Washington, D.C., 28 Nov. 1995. 26 Sept. 1999 <http://www.house.gov/underwood/speeches/english.htm>.

GLOSSARY OF RHETORICAL AND LINGUISTIC TERMS

Abstract   See *Concrete/Abstract*.

Accent   Characteristics of pronunciation that reflect regional or social identity.

Acronym   A word made from the initial letters (in some cases, the first few letters) of a phrase or organization; for example, NATO (North Atlantic Treaty Organization) and scuba (self-contained underwater breathing apparatus).

Allusion   A passing reference to a familiar person, place, or thing drawn from history, the Bible, mythology, or literature. An allusion is an economical way for a writer to capture the essence of an idea, atmosphere, emotion, or historical era, as in "The scandal was his Watergate," "He saw himself as a modern Job," or "Everyone there held those truths to be self-evident."

American Sign Language (ASL, Ameslan)   A system of communication used by deaf people in the United States, consisting of hand symbols that vary in the shape of the hands, the direction of their movement, and their position in relation to the body. It is different from finger spelling, in which words are signed in the order in which they are uttered, thus preserving English structure and syntax.

Analogy   A special form of comparison in which the writer explains something complex or unfamiliar by comparing it to something familiar: "A transmission line is simply a pipeline for electricity. In the case of a water pipeline, more water will flow through the pipe as water pressure increases. The same is true of a transmission line for electricity." When a subject is unobservable or abstract, or when readers may have trouble understanding it, analogy is particularly useful.

Argument   A strategy for developing an essay. To argue is to attempt to convince a reader to agree with a point of view, to make a given decision, or to pursue a particular course of action. Logical argument is based on reasonable explanations and appeals to the reader's intelligence. See also *Persuasion, Logical Fallacies, Deduction,* and *Induction*.

Attitude   A writer's opinion of a subject, which may be very positive, very negative, or somewhere between these two extremes. See also *Tone*.

Audience   The intended readership for a piece of writing. For example, the readers of a national weekly newsmagazine come from all walks of life and have diverse opinions, attitudes, and educational experiences. In contrast, the readership for an organic chemistry journal may be comprised of people with similar scientific interests and educational backgrounds. The essays in this book are intended for general readers, intelligent people who may lack specific information about the subjects being discussed.

Beginnings and Endings   A *beginning* is the sentence, group of sentences, or section that introduces an essay. Good beginnings usually identify the thesis or main idea, attempt to interest the reader, and establish a tone. Some effective ways to begin essays include (1) telling an anecdote that illustrates the thesis, (2) providing a controversial statement or opinion that engages the reader's interest, (3) presenting startling statistics or facts, (4) defining a term that is central to the discussion that follows, (5) asking thought-provoking questions, (6) providing a quotation that illustrates the thesis, (7) referring to a current event that helps to establish the thesis, or (8) showing the significance of the subject or stressing its importance to the reader.

An *ending* is the sentence or group of sentences that brings an essay to closure. Good endings are well planned; they are the natural outgrowths of the essays themselves and give readers a sense of finality or completion. Some of the techniques mentioned above for beginnings may be effective for endings as well.

Biased Language   Language that is used by a dominant group within a culture to maintain its supposed superior position and to disempower others. See also *Racist Language* and *Sexist Language*.

Bidialectalism   The use of two dialects of the same language.

Bilingual Education   Teaching in a child's primary language, which may or may not be the language of the dominant population.

Black English   A vernacular variety of English used by some black people; it may be divided into Standard Black English and Black English Vernacular (BEV). See also *Ebonics*.

Brainstorming   A discovery technique in which writers list everything they know about a topic, freely associating one idea with another. When writers brainstorm, they also make lists of questions about aspects of the topic for which they need information. See also *Clustering* and *Freewriting*.

Cause and Effect Analysis   A strategy for developing an essay. Cause and effect analysis answers the question *why*. It explains the reasons for an occurrence or the consequences of an action. Whenever a question asks *why*, answering it will require discovering a *cause* or series of causes for a particular *effect*; whenever a question asks *what if*, its answer will point out the effect or effects that can result from a particular cause.

Classification   See *Division and Classification*.

Cliché   An expression that has become ineffective through overuse, such as *quick as a flash, dry as dust, jump for joy*, and *slow as molasses*. Writers normally avoid such trite expressions and seek instead to express themselves in fresh and forceful language. See also *Figures of Speech*.

Clustering   A discovery technique in which a writer puts a topic or keyword in a circle at the center of a blank page and then generates main ideas about that topic, circling each idea and connecting it with a line to the topic in the center. Writers often repeat the process in order to add specific examples and details to each main idea. This technique allows writers to generate material and sort it into meaningful clusters at the same time. See also *Brainstorming* and *Freewriting*.

Coherence   A quality of good writing that results when all of the sentences, paragraphs, and longer divisions of an essay are naturally connected. Coherent writing is achieved through (1) a logical sequence of ideas (arranged in chronological order, spatial order, order of importance, or some other appropriate order), (2) the thoughtful repetition of keywords and ideas, (3) a pace suitable for your topic and your reader, and (4) the use of transitional words and expressions. Coherence should not be confused with unity. See also *Unity* and *Transitions*.

Colloquial Expressions Informal expressions that are typical of a particular language. In English, phrases such as *come up with, be at loose ends,* or *get with the program* are colloquial expressions. Such expressions are acceptable in formal writing only if they are used for a specific purpose.

Comparison and Contrast A strategy for developing an essay. In comparison and contrast, the writer points out the similarities and differences between two or more subjects in the same class or category. The function of any comparison and contrast is to clarify — to reach some conclusion about the items being compared and contrasted. An effective comparison and contrast does not dwell on obvious similarities or differences; instead, it tells readers something significant that they may not already know.

Conclusions See *Beginnings and Endings*.

Concrete/Abstract A *concrete word* names a specific object, person, place, or action that can be directly perceived by the senses: *car, bread, building, book, John F. Kennedy, Chicago,* or *hiking*. An *abstract word*, in contrast, refers to general qualities, conditions, ideas, actions, or relationships that cannot be directly perceived by the senses: *bravery, dedication, excellence, anxiety, friendship, thinking,* or *hatred*.

Although writers must use both concrete and abstract language, good writers avoid using too many abstract words. Instead, they rely on concrete words to define and illustrate abstractions. Because concrete words appeal to the senses, they are easily comprehended by a reader.

Connotation/Denotation Both terms refer to the meanings of words. *Denotation* is the dictionary meaning of a word, its literal meaning. *Connotation*, on the other hand, is a word's implied or suggested meaning. For example, the denotation of *lamb* is a "a young sheep." The connotations of lamb are numerous: *gentle, docile, weak, peaceful, blessed, sacrificial, blood, spring, frisky, pure, innocent,* and so on. Good writers are sensitive to both the denotations and the connotations of words and use these meanings to advantage in their writing.

Deduction The process of reasoning that moves from stated premises to a conclusion that follows necessarily. This form of reasoning moves from the general to the specific. See also *Induction* and *Syllogism*.

Definition A strategy for developing an essay. A definition, which states the meaning of a word, may be either brief or extended; it may be part of an essay or an entire essay itself.

Denotation See *Connotation/Denotation*.

Description A strategy for developing an essay. Description tells how a person, place, or thing is perceived by the five senses. Objective description reports these sensory qualities factually, whereas subjective description gives the writer's interpretation of them.

Descriptivism A school of linguistic analysis that seeks to describe linguistic facts as they are. See also *Prescriptivism*.

Dialect   A variety of language, usually regional or social, that is set off from other varieties of the same language by differences in pronunciation, vocabulary, and grammar.

Diction   A writer's choice and use of words. Good diction is precise and appropriate — the words mean exactly what the writer intends, and the words are well suited to the writer's subject, intended audience, and purpose. The word-conscious writer knows, for example, that there are differences among *aged, old,* and *elderly; blue, navy,* and *azure;* and *disturbed, angry,* and *irritated.* Furthermore, this writer knows when to use each word. See also *Connotation/Denotation.*

Direct Quotation   A writer's use of the exact words of a source. Direct quotations, which are put in quotation marks, are normally reserved for important ideas stated memorably, for especially clear explanations by authorities, and for proponents' arguments conveyed in their own words. See also *Paraphrase, Summary,* and *Plagiarism.*

Division and Classification   A strategy for developing an essay. *Division* involves breaking down a single large unit into smaller subunits, or separating a group of items into discrete categories. *Classification,* on the other hand, involves arranging or sorting people, places, or things into categories according to their differing characteristics, thus making them more manageable for the writer and more understandable for the reader. Division, then, takes apart, while classification groups together. Although the two processes can operate separately, most often they work hand in hand.

Doublespeak   According to doublespeak expert William Lutz, "Doublespeak is a blanket term for language which pretends to communicate but doesn't, language which makes the bad seem good, the negative appear positive, the unpleasant attractive, or at least tolerable. It is language which avoids, shifts, or denies responsibility."

Ebonics   A term coined in 1973 for African American Vernacular English (AAVE). Public debate centers on whether it is a dialect of English or a separate language with its own grammatical rules and rhythms. See also *Black English.*

Endings   See *Beginnings and Endings.*

English-Only Movement   The ongoing attempts, which began in the Senate in 1986, to declare English the official language of the United States. Although these attempts have failed thus far at the federal level, a number of states have passed various forms of English-only legislation.

Essay   A relatively short piece of nonfiction in which the writer attempts to make one or more closely related points. A good essay is purposeful, informative, and well organized.

Ethnocentricity   The belief that one's culture (including language) is at the center of things and that other cultures (and languages) are inferior.

Euphemism   A pleasing, vague, or indirect word or phrase that is substituted for one that is considered harsh or offensive. For example, *pacify* is a euphemism for *bomb, pavement deficiency* for *pothole, downsize* or *release from employment* for *fire.*

Evidence   The data on which a judgment or argument is based or by which proof or probability is established. Evidence usually takes the form of statistics, facts, names, examples or illustrations, and opinions of authorities.

Examples   Ways of illustrating, developing, or clarifying an idea. Examples enable writers to show and not simply to tell readers what they mean. The terms *example* and *illustration* are sometimes used interchangeably. An example may be anything from a statistic to a story; it may be stated in a few words or go on for several pages. An example should always be *relevant* to the idea or generalization it is meant to illustrate. An example should also be *representative*. In other words, it should be typical of what the writer is trying to show.

Exemplification   A strategy for developing an essay. In exemplification, the writer uses examples — facts, opinions, anecdotes, or statistics — to make ideas more vivid and understandable. Exemplification is used in all types of essays. See also *Examples*.

Fallacy   See *Logical Fallacies*.

Figures of Speech   Brief, imaginative comparisons that highlight the similarities between things that are basically dissimilar. They make writing vivid and interesting and therefore more memorable. Following are the most common figures of speech:

Simile: An implicit comparison introduced by *like* or *as*. "The fighter's hands were like stone."

Metaphor: An implied comparison that uses one thing as the equivalent of another. "All the world's a stage."

Onomatopoeia: The use of words whose sound suggests the meaning, as in *buzz, hiss,* and *meow.*

Personification: A special kind of simile or metaphor in which human traits are assigned to an inanimate object. "The engine coughed and then stopped."

Freewriting   A discovery technique that involves writing for a brief uninterrupted period of time — ten or fifteen minutes — on anything that comes to mind. Writers use freewriting to discover new topics, new strategies, and other new ideas. See also *Brainstorming* and *Clustering*.

Gobbledygook   The use of technical or unfamiliar words that confuse rather than clarify an issue for an audience.

Grammar   The system of a language including its parts and the methods for combining them.

Idiom   A word or phrase that is used habitually with a particular meaning in a language. The meaning of an idiom is not always readily apparent to nonnative speakers of that language. For example, *catch cold, hold a job, make up your mind,* and *give them a hand* are all idioms in English.

Illustration   See *Examples*.

Indo-European Languages   A group of languages descended from a supposed common ancestor and now widely spoken in Europe, North and South America, Australia, New Zealand, and parts of India.

Induction   A process of reasoning whereby a conclusion about all members of a class is reached by examining only a few members of the class. This form of reasoning moves from a set of specific examples to a general statement or principle. As long as the evidence is accurate, pertinent, complete, and sufficient to represent the assertion, the conclusion of the inductive argument can be regarded as valid; if, however, readers can spot inaccuracies in the evidence or point to contrary evidence, they have good reason to doubt the assertion as it stands. Inductive reasoning is the most common of argumentative structures. See also *Deduction.*

Introductions See *Beginnings and Endings.*

Irony The use of words to suggest something different from their literal meaning. A writer can use irony to establish a special relationship with the reader and to add an extra dimension or twist to the meaning.

Jargon See *Technical Language.*

Language Words, their pronunciation, and the conventional and systematic methods for combining them as used and understood by a community.

Lexicography The art of dictionary-making.

Linguistic Relativity Hypothesis The belief that the structure of a language shapes the way speakers of that language view reality. Also known as the Sapir-Whorf Hypothesis after Edward Sapir and Benjamin Lee Whorf.

Logical Fallacies Errors in reasoning that render an argument invalid. Some of the more common logical fallacies are listed here:

Oversimplification: The tendency to provide simple solutions to complex problems. "The reason we have inflation today is that OPEC has unreasonably raised the price of oil."

Non sequitur ("It does not follow"): An inference or conclusion that does not follow from established premises or evidence. "It was the best movie I saw this year, and it should get an Academy Award."

Post hoc, ergo propter hoc ("After this, therefore because of this"): Confusing chance or coincidence with causation. Because one event comes after another one, it does not necessarily mean that the first event caused the second. "I won't say I caught cold at the hockey game, but I certainly didn't have it before I went there."

Begging the question: Assuming in a premise that which needs to be proven. "If American autoworkers built a better product, foreign auto sales would not be so high."

False analogy: Making a misleading analogy between logically unconnected ideas. "He was a brilliant basketball player; therefore, there's no question in my mind that he will be a fine coach."

Either/or thinking: The tendency to see an issue as having only two sides. "Used car salesmen are either honest or crooked."

Logical Reasoning See *Deduction* and *Induction.*

Metaphor See *Figures of Speech.*

Narration A strategy for developing an essay. To narrate is to tell a story, to tell what happened. Although narration is most often used in fiction, it is also important in nonfiction, either by itself or in conjunction with other strategies. A good narrative essay has four essential features. The first is *context:* The writer makes clear when the action happened, where it happened, and to whom. The second is *point of view:* The writer establishes and maintains a consistent relationship to the action, either as a participant or as a reporter simply looking on. The third is *selection of detail:* The writer carefully chooses what to include, focusing on those actions and details that are most important to the story while merely mentioning or actually eliminating others. The fourth is *organization:* The writer organizes the events of the narrative into an appropriate sequence, often a strict chronology with a clear beginning, middle, and end.

Objective/Subjective   *Objective writing* is factual and impersonal, whereas *subjective writing*, sometimes called impressionistic, relies heavily on personal interpretation.

Onomastics   The study of the meaning and origins of proper names of persons and places.

Onomatopoeia   See *Figures of Speech*.

Organization   In writing, the thoughtful arrangement and presentation of one's points or ideas. Narration is often organized chronologically, whereas other kinds of essays may be organized point by point or from most familiar to least familiar. Argument may be organized from least important to most important. There is no single correct pattern of organization for a given piece of writing, but good writers are careful to discover an order of presentation suitable for their subject, audience, and purpose.

Paradox   A seemingly contradictory statement that may nonetheless be true. For example, *we little know what we have until we lose it* is a paradoxical statement.

Paragraph   A series of closely related sentences and the single most important unit of thought in an essay. The sentences in a paragraph adequately develop its central idea, which is usually stated in a topic sentence. A well-written paragraph has several distinguishing characteristics: a clearly stated or implied topic sentence, adequate development, unity, coherence, and an appropriate organizational pattern.

Paraphrase   A restatement of the information a writer is borrowing. A paraphrase closely parallels the presentation of the ideas in the original, but it does not use the same words or sentence structure. See also *Direct Quotation*, *Summary*, and *Plagiarism*.

Personification   See *Figures of Speech*.

Persuasion   An attempt to convince readers to agree with a point of view, to make a given decision, or to pursue a particular course of action. See also *Argument*, *Induction*, and *Deduction*.

Phonetics   The study of speech sounds.

Phonology   The study of sounds systems in languages.

Plagiarism   The use of someone else's ideas in their original form or in an altered form without proper documentation. Writers avoid plagiarism by (1) putting direct quotations within quotation marks and properly citing them and (2) documenting any idea, explanation, or argument that is borrowed and presented in a summary or paraphrase, making it clear where the borrowed material begins and ends. See also *Direct Quotation*, *Paraphrase*, and *Summary*.

Point of View   The grammatical person of the speaker in an essay. For example, a first-person point of view uses the pronoun *I* and is commonly found in autobiography and the personal essay; a third-person point of view uses the pronouns *he*, *she*, or *it* and is commonly found in objective writing.

Prescriptivism   A grammar that seeks to explain linguistic facts as they should be. See also *Descriptivism*.

Process Analysis   A strategy for developing an essay. Process analysis answers the question *how* and explains how something works or gives step-by-step directions for doing something.

Propaganda   Ideas, facts, or rumors purposely spread to further one's cause or to damage the cause of an opponent.

Purpose   What a writer wants to accomplish in a particular piece — his or her reason for writing. The three general purposes of writing are *to express* thoughts and feelings and lessons learned from life experiences, *to inform* readers about something about the world around them, or *to persuade* readers to accept some belief or take some action.

Racist Language   A form of biased language that makes distinctions on the basis of race and deliberately or subconsciously suggests that one race is superior to all others.

Rhetorical Questions   Questions that are asked but require no answer from the reader. "When will nuclear proliferation end?" is such a question. Writers use rhetorical questions to introduce topics they plan to discuss or to emphasize important points.

Sapir-Whorf Hypothesis   See *Linguistic Relativity Hypothesis.*

Semantics   The study of meanings in a language.

Sexist Language   A form of biased language that makes distinctions on the basis of sex and shows preference for one sex over the other.

Signal Phrase   A phrase alerting the reader that borrowed information is to follow. A signal phrase usually consists of the author's name and a verb (for example, "Keesbury argues") and helps to integrate direct quotations, paraphrases, and summaries into the flow of a paper.

Simile   See *Figures of Speech.*

Slang   The unconventional, very informal language of particular subgroups in a culture. Slang words such as *zonk, split, rap, cop,* and *stoned* are acceptable in formal writing only if they are used for a specific purpose. A writer might use slang, for example, to re-create authentic dialogue in a story.

Specific/General   *General words* name groups or classes of objects, qualities, or actions. *Specific words,* on the other hand, name individual objects, qualities, or actions within a class or group. To some extent the terms *general* and *specific* are relative. For example, *dessert* is a class of things. *Pie,* however, is more specific than *dessert* but more general than *pecan pie* or *chocolate cream pie.* Good writing judiciously balances the general with the specific. Writing with too many general words is likely to be dull and lifeless because general words do not create vivid responses in the reader's mind. On the other hand, writing that relies exclusively on specific words may lack focus and direction, which more general statements provide.

Standard English   A variety of English that is used by the government and the media and that is taught in the schools. It is often best expressed in written form.

Style   The individual manner in which a writer expresses his or her ideas. Style is created by the author's particular selection of words, construction of sentences, and arrangement of ideas.

Subjective   See *Objective/Subjective.*

Summary   A condensed form of the essential idea of a passage, article, or entire chapter. A summary is always shorter than the original. See also *Paraphrase, Direct Quotation,* and *Plagiarism.*

Syllogism   An argument that utilizes deductive reasoning and consists of a major premise, a minor premise, and a conclusion. For example,

All trees that lose leaves are deciduous. (major premise)
Maple trees lose their leaves. (minor premise)
Therefore, maple trees are deciduous. (conclusion)
See also *Deduction.*

Symbol   A person, place, or thing that represents something beyond itself. For example, the eagle is a symbol of America, and the bear is a symbol of Russia.

Syntax   The way words are arranged to form phrases, clauses, and sentences. Syntax also refers to the grammatical relationships among the words themselves.

Taboo Language   Language that is avoided in a given society. Almost all societies have language taboos.

Technical Language   The special vocabulary of a trade or profession. Writers who use technical language do so with an awareness of their audiences. If the audience is a group of peers, technical language may be used freely. If the audience is a more general one, technical language should be used sparingly and carefully so as not to sacrifice clarity. Technical language that is used only to impress, hide the truth, or cover insecurities is termed *jargon* and is not condoned. See also *Diction.*

Thesis   A statement of the main idea of an essay, the point the essay is trying to make. A thesis may sometimes be implied rather than stated directly.

Tone   The manner in which a writer relates to an audience, the "tone of voice" used to address readers. Tone may be described as friendly, serious, distant, angry, cheerful, bitter, cynical, enthusiastic, morbid, resentful, warm, playful, and so forth. A particular tone results from a writer's diction, sentence structure, purpose, and attitude toward the subject. See also *Attitude.*

Topic Sentence   The sentence that states the central idea of a paragraph and thus limits and controls the subject of the paragraph. Although the topic sentence normally appears at the beginning of the paragraph, it may appear at any other point, particularly if the writer is trying to create a special effect. See also *Paragraph.*

Transitions   Words or phrases that link the sentences, paragraphs, and larger units of an essay in order to achieve coherence. Transitional devices include parallelism, pronoun references, conjunctions, and the repetition of key ideas, as well as the many transitional expressions such as *moreover, on the other hand, in addition, in contrast,* and *therefore.* See also *Coherence.*

Unity   A quality that is achieved in an essay when all the words, sentences, and paragraphs contribute to its thesis. The elements of a unified essay do not distract the reader. Instead, they all harmoniously support a single idea or purpose.

Usage   The way in which words and phrases are actually used in a language community. See also *Descriptivism* and *Prescriptivism.*

Rhetorical Contents

The essays in *Language Awareness* are arranged in Chapters 1–10 according to their subjects. The following alternate table of contents, which is certainly not exhaustive, classifies the essays according to the rhetorical strategies they exemplify.

NARRATION

PROCESS ANALYSIS

(*continued from page iv*)

Gordon Allport, "The Language of Prejudice." From *The Nature of Prejudice* by Gordon Allport. Copyright © 1979, 1985, 1954 by Addison-Wesley Publishing Company, Inc. Reprinted by permission of Perseus Books Publishers, a member of Perseus Books, LLC.

Eugene R. August, "Real Men Don't: Anti-Male Bias in English." From *The University of Dayton Review* 18 (Winter/Spring, 1986–87). Copyright © 1987 by the University of Dayton Review. Reprinted by permission of the publisher.

Perry Bacon Jr., "How Much Diversity Do You Want from Me?" From *Time*. Copyright © 2003. Reprinted by permission of the publisher.

Vanessa Bauza, "Internet Spanglish." Originally titled "Hispanics on Internet Fuel Growth of Spanglish." From *South Florida Sun-Sentinel*, Fort Lauderdale, Fl., May 26, 1998, p. 1A. Copyright © 1998. Reprinted by permission.

Newman P. Birk and Genevieve B. Birk, "Selection, Slanting, and Charged Language." From *Understanding and Using English*. Copyright © 1972 by Allyn & Bacon. Reprinted/adapted by permission of the publisher.

Lee C. Bollinger, "Diversity Is Essential . . ." From *Newsweek*. Copyright © 2003. Reprinted by permission of the publisher.

Jennie Bristow, "Text Messaging: Take Note." From *www.spiked-online.com*. Copyright © 2001. Reprinted by permission.

Ethan Bronner, "Big Brother Is Listening." From *The New York Times*, April 4, 1999. Copyright © 1999 by the New York Times Company. Reprinted by permission of the publisher.

Bill Bryson, "The Hard Sell: Advertising in America." From *Made in America: An Informal History of the English Language in the United States* by Bill Bryson. Copyright © 1994 by Bill Bryson. William Morrow & Company, Inc. Reprinted by permission of HarperCollins.

G. Jay Christensen, "Paragraphs of Buzzwords Buzz Loudly." Reprinted with permission of Michael Wunsch.

Nathan Cobb, "Gender Wars in Cyberspace." From *The Boston Globe*. Copyright © 1995 by the *Boston Globe*. Reprinted by permission of the *Boston Globe* via the Copyright Clearance Center.

Judith Ortiz Cofer, "And May He Be Bilingual." From *Woman in Front of the Sun: On Becoming a Writer*. Copyright © 2000 by Judith Ortiz Cofer. Reprinted by permission of the University of Georgia Press.

Greg Critser, "Let Them Eat Fat." From *Harper's Magazine*, March 2000. Copyright © 2000 by Greg Critser. Reprinted by permission of Harper's Magazine.

Donna Woolfolk Cross, "Propaganda: How Not to Be Bamboozled." From *Speaking of Words: A Language Reader*. Copyright © 1997. Reprinted with the permission of the author.

Edite Cunha, "Talking in the New Land." From *The New England Monthly*, August 1990. Copyright © 1990. Reprinted by permission of the author.

Annie Dillard, "Living Like Weasels." From *Teaching a Stone to Talk*. Copyright © 1982 by HarperCollins, Inc. Reprinted by permission of the publisher.

Steven Doloff, "Racism and the Risks of Ethnic Humor." From *Free Inquiry*, winter 1998/99. Copyright © 1999. Reprinted by permission of the publisher.

Louise Erdrich, "The Names of Women." From *Four Souls* by Louise Erdrich. Copyright © 2004 by Louise Erdrich. Reprinted by permission of the author.

Bergen Evans, Excerpt from *The Word-a-Day Vocabulary Builder*. Copyright © 1963 by Bergen Evans. Reprinted by permission of Random House, Inc.

Sarah Federman, "What's Natural about Our Natural Products?" Copyright © 2000 by Sarah Federman. Reprinted by permission.

Aisha K. Finch, "If Hip-Hop Ruled the World." From *Essence*, March 1998, Volume 28, Issue 11, p. 58. Copyright © 1998 by Aisha K. Finch. Reprinted by permission of the publisher.

Linda Flower, "Writing for an Audience." From *Problem-Solving Strategies for Writing*, 4th ed., by Linda Flower. Copyright © 1993 by Harcourt, Inc. Reprinted by permission of Thomson Learning.

Tad Friend, "You Can't Say That." First appeared in *The New Yorker*, November 19, 2001. Copyright © 2001 by the author. Reprinted by permission of International Creative Management, Inc.

Juliet Gabriel, "Make Me Sound Like I Don't Suck." From *Salon.com*. Copyright © 2003. Reprinted by permission of *Salon.com*.

Henry Louis Gates Jr., "'What's in a Name?' Some Meanings of Blackness." From *Dissent* Vol. 36, No. 4 (Fall 1989), p. 487. Copyright © 1989 by Henry Louis Gates, Jr. Reprinted with permission of the publisher.

Ted Gest, "Indictment & Trial of Media's Crime Coverage." From the *Journal of the Institute of Justice and International Studies*, Number 2. Copyright © 2003. Reprinted by permission of the author.

Natalie Goldberg, "Be Specific." From *Writing Down the Bones: Freeing the Writer Within*. Copyright © 1986 by Shambhala Publications. Reprinted by permission of the publisher.

Maxine Hairston, "What Happens When People Write?" From *Successful Writing*, 3rd ed., by Maxine C. Hairston. Copyright © 1992, 1986, 1981 by Maxine C. Hairston. Reprinted by permission of W. W. Norton & Company, Inc.

S. I. Hayakawa, "Bilingualism in America: English Should Be the Official Language." From *USA Today*, July 1989. Copyright © 1989 by S. I. Hayakawa. Reprinted with permission of Alan R. Hayakawa.

S. I. Hayakawa and Alan R. Hayakawa, "Words with Built-in Judgments," and "Giving Things Names." From *Language in Thought and Action*, 5th ed., by S. I. Hayakawa and Alan R. Hayakawa. Copyright © 1990 by Harcourt, Inc. Reprinted with the permission of Thomson Learning.

Susan C. Herring, "Gender and Democracy in Computer-Mediated Communication." From *Computerization and Controversy*, 2nd ed., edited by Rob Kling, pp. 476–89. Copyright © 1996 by Academic Press. Reprinted by permission of Elsevier Ltd.

J. C. Herz, "A Name So Smooth, the Product Glides In." From *The New York Times*. Copyright © 1998 by the New York Times. Reprinted by permission.

Walter Isaacson, "How They Chose These Words." From *Time*, July 7, 2003, pp. 76–77. Reprinted by permission.

Martha Irvine, "'Queer' Evolution: Word Goes Mainstream," From *The Burlington Free Press*, November 10, 2003. Copyright © 2003. Reprinted by permission of The Associated Press.

Pico Iyer, "In Praise of the Humble Comma." From *Time*, July 13, 1988, p. 80. Reprinted by permission.

Joanmarie Kalter, "Exposing Media Myths: TV Doesn't Affect You as Much as You Think." From *TV Guide* May 1987. Copyright © 1987 by Joanmarie Kalter. Reprinted by permission of the author.

Martin Luther King Jr., "I Have a Dream." Copyright © 1963 by Martin Luther King Jr., copyright renewed 1991 by Coretta Scott King. Reprinted by arrangement with The Heirs to the Estate of Martin Luther King Jr., c/o Writer's House, Inc., as agent for the proprietor.

Robert D. King, "Should English Be the Law?" As appeared in *The Atlantic Monthly*. Copyright © 1997 by Robert D. King. Reprinted by permission of the author.

Barbara Kingsolver, "Going to Japan," and "Life Is Precious, or It's Not." From *Small Wonder*. Copyright © 2002. Reprinted by permission of HarperCollins.

Nedra Newkirk Lamar, "Does a Finger Fing?" From *The Christian Sciencee Monitor*. Copyright © 1970. Reprinted by permission of the publisher.

Anne Lamott, "Shitty First Drafts." From *Bird by Bird*. Copyright © 1994 by Anne Lamott. Originally published by Pantheon Books: New York, 1994. Reprinted with permission of the publisher.

Ann Landers, "The Ultimate Insult." Copyright by Ann Landers.

Harlan Lane, "Representations of Deaf People." Reproduced from *The Mask of Benevolence: Disabling the Deaf Community* with permission of Dawn Sign Press. Copyright © 1992, 1999.

Susanne K. Langer, "Language and Thought." From *Ms. Magazine*. Reprinted by permission of *Ms. Magazine*.

Charles R. Larson, "Its Academic, or Is It?" From *Newsweek*, November 6, 1995. All rights reserved. Reprinted by permission.

Richard Lederer, "Verbs with Verve." Reprinted with permission of Pocket Books, a Division of Simon & Schuster, Inc., from *The Play of Words* by Richard Lederer. Copyright © 1990 by Richard Lederer.

John Leo, "Who Said PC Is Passé?" From *U.S. News & World Report*, May 12, 1997. Copyright © 1997 by U.S. News & World Report. Reprinted by permission of the publisher.

Greg Lewis, "An Open Letter to Diversity's Victims." From *The Washington Dispatch*, Aug. 12, 2003. Copyright © 2003 by Greg Lewis. Reprinted by permission of the author.

Bonnie Liebman, "Claims Crazy: Which Can You Believe?" From *The Nutrition Action Health Letter*, a publication of the Center for Science in the Public Interest. June 2003, Volume 30, no. 5. Copyright © 2003. Reprinted by permission of the publisher.

Audre Lorde, "The Fourth of July." From *Zami*. Copyright © 1982 by Audre Lorde. The Crossing Press, Freedom, CA. Reprinted by permission of the publisher. "The Transformation of Silence into Language and Action." From *Sister Outsider* by Audre Lorde. Copyright © 1984 by The Crossing Press. Reprinted by permission.

William Lutz, "Weasel Words." From *Doublespeak: From Revenue Enhancement to Terminal Living*. Copyright © 1980. Reprinted with the permission of the author. "The World of Doublespeak." From *The State of Language*. Copyright © 1989 William Lutz. Reprinted with permission of the author.

Elizabeth Lyon, "Honoring the Lost Writers of 9-11-01." Copyright © 2001. Reprinted by permission of the author.

Frederick L. McKissack, "Cyberghetto: Blacks are Falling Through the Net." From *Progressive* June 1998, pp. 20–22. Copyright © 1998. Reprinted by permission of the publisher.

Robert MacNeil, "English Belongs to Everybody." From *Wordstruck* by Robert MacNeil. Copyright © 1989 by Neely Productions, Ltd. Used by permission of Viking Penguin, a division of Penguin Putnam (USA) Group, Inc.

Peter Mandaville, "Digital Islam: Changing the Boundaries of Religious Knowledge." From *International Institute for Asian Studies Newsletter*. Copyright © 1999 by Peter Mandaville. Reprinted by permission of the author.

Myriam Marquez, "Why and When We Speak Spanish in Public." From *The Orlando Sentinel*, June 28, 1999. Copyright © 1999 by The Orlando Sentinel. Reprinted by permission.

Scott McCloud, pages 138–39 from Chapter 6, "Show and Tell," from *Understanding Comics* by Scott McCloud. Copyright © 1993, 1994 by Scott McCloud. Reprinted by permission of HarperCollins Publishers Inc.

Barbara Mellix, "From Outside, In." Originally appeared in *The Georgia Review* Volume XLI, Number 2 (Summer 1987), pp. 258–67. Copyright © 1987 by The University of Georgia/© 1987 by Barbara Mellix. Reprinted by permission of Barbara Mellix and *The Georgia Review*.

Lois Morris, "Naming Names." Copyright by Lois B. Morris. Reprinted by permission of the author.

Cullen Murphy, "The E Word." From *The Atlantic Monthly*, September 1996. Copyright © 1996 by Cullen Murphy. Reprinted with permission of the author and The Atlantic Monthly.

Donald M. Murray, "The Maker's Eye: Revising Your Own Manuscripts." From *The Writer*, by Donald Murray. Copyright © 1973 by Donald Murray. Reprinted by permission of the author.

INDEX OF AUTHORS AND TITLES